ISSN 0276-816X

something ABOUT THE AUTHOR®

Facts and Pictures about Authors and Illustrators of Books for Young People

volume 124

GALE GROUP

★

THOMSON LEARNING™

Detroit • New York • San Diego • San Francisco
Boston • New Haven, Conn. • Waterville, Maine
London • Munich

Library of Congress Catalog Card Number 72-27107

ISBN 0-7876-4712-8
ISSN 0276-816X

Printed in the United States of America

10 9 8 7 6 5 4 3 2 1

Contents

Authors in Forthcoming Volumes

Below are some of the authors and illustrators that will be featured in upcoming volumes of *SATA*. These include new entries on the swiftly rising stars of the field, as well as completely revised and updated entries (indicated with *) on some of the most notable and best-loved creators of books for children.

*Jose Aruego: Author and illustrator Aruego has built a body of work noted for its inventiveness and enduring appeal. Born in the Philippines but a resident of New York City since the mid-1950s, Aruego combines humor and sensitivity in the pen-and-ink drawings of funny animals that have become his hallmark. Many of Aruego's most popular books are collaborations with his former wife, illustrator Ariane Dewey, including the 2000 title *Mouse in Love.*

*Quentin Blake: Three-time winner of the Hans Christian Andersen Award for illustration, the "Nobel" of such prizes, British author-illustrator Blake is regarded by many critics as a master artist whose line drawings and watercolors are touched with genius. Considered an especially inventive and adaptable illustrator, he has created a highly recognizable style that ranges from the childlike to the highly sophisticated. In 2000 Blake provided the artwork for William Steig's *Wizzil.*

Ian Falconer: Falconer's award-winning premier children's book, *Olivia,* has been widely hailed as an important debut for both author-artist and his creation, a memorable child heroine who has garnered comparisons to Kay Thompson's Eloise and Kevin Henkes's Lilly. Coupled with Falconer's laconic text and his bold, black-and-white-and-red illustrations, Olivia's spirit quickly captured the hearts of reviewers and readers. A sequel, *Olivia Saves the Circus,* in which the fearless pig gets the chance to play the role of every performer in the circus, was published in 2001.

Marie-Louise Fitzpatrick: Irish author and illustrator Fitzpatrick received a special merit award from the Reading Association of Ireland for her 1998 work *The Long March,* about the impoverished Choctaw nation's efforts to relieve the suffering of Ireland's famine victims in 1847. Fitzpatrick released *Lizzy and Skunk,* a self-illustrated picture book, in 2000.

*Jamila Gavin: Gavin brings her understanding of the special concerns of children with a multicultural heritage to her stories and novels for young readers. Born in India of an Indian father and a British mother, Gavin has focused on her Indian heritage in such books as *Three Indian Princesses: The Stories of Savitri, Damayanti, and Sita,* as well as in her highly praised epic trilogy that begins with the 1992 novel *The Wheel of Surya.* She was awarded the Whitbread Children's Book Award in 2001 for *Coram Boy.*

Elissa Haden Guest: Guest is the author of picture books for children and novels for young adults. Her 2000 work *Lisa and Walter,* which follows the adventures of two young friends, received the PEN Center USA West Literary Award, among other honors.

*Lee Bennett Hopkins: Hopkins is a prolific anthologist of poetry for young readers. His collections encompass a variety of topics, including animals, holidays, the seasons, and the works of noted poets like Walt Whitman and Carl Sandburg. Hopkins has also penned his own works, including autobiographies, classroom materials, poetry, picture books, and novels for young adults. In 2001, he published a compilation titled *Hoofbeats, Claws, and Rippled Fins: Creature Poems.*

Luis J. Rodriguez: Rodriguez is the author of *Always Running: La Vida Loca, Gang Days in L.A.,* which recounts his childhood and adolescence in East Los Angeles. Rodriguez has also written books of poetry and children's books in addition to this partly fictionalized memoir, and he has contributed articles to national publications such as the *Los Angeles Times* and *U.S. News and World Reports,* chronicling the Mexican-American experience and speaking out articulately for social justice and equity in the country.

*Colin Thiele: A poet, novelist, biographer, and playwright, the prolific Australian author Thiele has written a number of award-winning books for young people, including *Storm Boy, Jodie's Journey,* and *The Fire in the Stone.* Thiele has become an active force in all areas of children's publishing, from textbooks to plays to poetry anthologies to picture books to young adult novels.

Arvella Whitmore: Whitmore has written three novels for young adults, each an unusual coming-of-age story in which a young person finds within him or herself the courage to face down adversity. *Trapped between the Lash and the Gun,* a 1999 work, received a Best Book for Young Adults citation from the American Library Association.

Introduction

Something about the Author (*SATA*) is an ongoing reference series that examines the lives and works of authors and illustrators of books for children. *SATA* includes not only well-known writers and artists but also less prominent individuals whose works are just coming to be recognized. This series is often the only readily available information source on emerging authors and illustrators. You'll find *SATA* informative and entertaining, whether you are a student, a librarian, an English teacher, a parent, or simply an adult who enjoys children's literature.

What's Inside SATA

SATA provides detailed information about authors and illustrators who span the full time range of children's literature, from early figures like John Newbery and L. Frank Baum to contemporary figures like Judy Blume and Richard Peck. Authors in the series represent primarily English-speaking countries, particularly the United States, Canada, and the United Kingdom. Also included, however, are authors from around the world whose works are available in English translation. The writings represented in *SATA* include those created intentionally for children and young adults as well as those written for a general audience and known to interest younger readers. These writings cover the entire spectrum of children's literature, including picture books, humor, folk and fairy tales, animal stories, mystery and adventure, science fiction and fantasy, historical fiction, poetry and nonsense verse, drama, biography, and nonfiction.

Obituaries are also included in *SATA* and are intended not only as death notices but also as concise overviews of people's lives and work. Additionally, each edition features newly revised and updated entries for a selection of *SATA* listees who remain of interest to today's readers and who have been active enough to require extensive revisions of their earlier biographies.

New Autobiography Feature

Beginning with Volume 103, *SATA* features three or more specially commissioned autobiographical essays in each volume. These unique essays, averaging about ten thousand words in length and illustrated with an abundance of personal photos, present an entertaining and informative first-person perspective on the lives and careers of prominent authors and illustrators profiled in *SATA*.

Two Convenient Indexes

In response to suggestions from librarians, *SATA* indexes no longer appear in every volume but are included in alternate (odd-numbered) volumes of the series, beginning with Volume 57.

SATA continues to include two indexes that cumulate with each alternate volume: the Illustrations Index, arranged by the name of the illustrator, gives the number of the volume and page where the illustrator's work appears in the current volume as well as all preceding volumes in the series; the Author Index gives the number of the volume in which a person's biographical sketch, autobiographical essay, or obituary appears in the current volume as well as all preceding volumes in the series.

These indexes also include references to authors and illustrators who appear in Gale's *Yesterday's Authors of Books for Children, Children's Literature Review,* and *Something about the Author Autobiography Series.*

Easy-to-Use Entry Format

Whether you're already familiar with the *SATA* series or just getting acquainted, you will want to be aware of the kind of information that an entry provides. In every *SATA* entry the editors attempt to give as complete a picture of the person's life and work as possible. A typical entry in *SATA* includes the following clearly labeled information sections:

- *PERSONAL:* date and place of birth and death, parents' names and occupations, name of spouse, date of marriage, names of children, educational institutions attended, degrees received, religious and political affiliations, hobbies and other interests.

- *ADDRESSES:* complete home, office, electronic mail, and agent addresses, whenever available.

- *CAREER:* name of employer, position, and dates for each career post; art exhibitions; military service; memberships and offices held in professional and civic organizations.

- *AWARDS, HONORS:* literary and professional awards received.

- *WRITINGS:* title-by-title chronological bibliography of books written and/or illustrated, listed by genre when known; lists of other notable publications, such as plays, screenplays, and periodical contributions.

- *ADAPTATIONS:* a list of films, television programs, plays, CD-ROMs, recordings, and other media presentations that have been adapted from the author's work.

- *WORK IN PROGRESS:* description of projects in progress.

- *SIDELIGHTS:* a biographical portrait of the author or illustrator's development, either directly from the biographee—and often written specifically for the *SATA* entry—or gathered from diaries, letters, interviews, or other published sources.

- *BIOGRAPHICAL AND CRITICAL SOURCES:* cites sources quoted in "Sidelights" along with references for further reading.

- *EXTENSIVE ILLUSTRATIONS:* photographs, movie stills, book illustrations, and other interesting visual materials supplement the text.

How a SATA Entry Is Compiled

A *SATA* entry progresses through a series of steps. If the biographee is living, the *SATA* editors try to secure information directly from him or her through a questionnaire. From the information that the biographee supplies, the editors prepare an entry, filling in any essential missing details with research and/or telephone interviews. If possible, the author or illustrator is sent a copy of the entry to check for accuracy and completeness.

If the biographee is deceased or cannot be reached by questionnaire, the *SATA* editors examine a wide variety of published sources to gather information for an entry. Biographical and bibliographic sources are consulted, as are book reviews, feature articles, published interviews, and material sometimes obtained from the biographee's family, publishers, agent, or other associates.

Entries that have not been verified by the biographees or their representatives are marked with an asterisk (*).

Contact the Editor

We encourage our readers to examine the entire *SATA* series. Please write and tell us if we can make *SATA* even more helpful to you. Give your comments and suggestions to the editor:

BY MAIL: Editor, *Something about the Author,* The Gale Group, 27500 Drake Rd., Farmington Hills, MI 48331-3535.

BY TELEPHONE: (800) 877-GALE

BY FAX: (248) 699-8054

Something about the Author Product Advisory Board

The editors of *Something about the Author* are dedicated to maintaining a high standard of excellence by publishing comprehensive, accurate, and highly readable entries on a wide array of writers for children and young adults. In addition to the quality of the content, the editors take pride in the graphic design of the series, which is intended to be orderly yet inviting, allowing readers to utilize the pages of *SATA* easily and with efficiency. Despite the longevity of the *SATA* print series, and the success of its format, we are mindful that the vitality of a literary reference product is dependent on its ability to serve its users over time. As literature, and attitudes about literature, constantly evolve, so do the reference needs of students, teachers, scholars, journalists, researchers, and book club members. To be certain that we continue to keep pace with the expectations of our customers, the editors of *SATA* listen carefully to their comments regarding the value, utility, and quality of the series. Librarians, who have firsthand knowledge of the needs of library users, are a valuable resource for us. The *Something about the Author* Product Advisory Board, made up of school, public, and academic librarians, is a forum to promote focused feedback about *SATA* on a regular basis. The five-member advisory board includes the following individuals, whom the editors wish to thank for sharing their expertise:

- **Eva M. Davis,** Teen Services Librarian, Plymouth District Library, Plymouth, Michigan

- **Joan B. Eisenberg,** Lower School Librarian, Milton Academy, Milton, Massachusetts

- **Francisca Goldsmith,** Teen Services Librarian, Berkeley Public Library, Berkeley, California

- **Monica F. Irlbacher,** Young Adult Librarian, Middletown Thrall Library, Middletown, New York

- **Caryn Sipos,** Librarian--Young Adult Services, King County Library System, Washington

Acknowledgments

Grateful acknowledgment is made to the following publishers, authors, and artists whose works appear in this volume.

AL-KHALILI, JIM. A cover of *Black Holes, Wormholes, and Time Machines,* by Jim Al-Khalili. Institute of Physics Publishing, 1999. © IOP Publishing Ltd 1999. Reproduced by permission of the publisher and the author.

ALLEN, JUDY (CHRISTINA). Humphries, Tudor, illustrator. From a cover of *Eagle,* by Judy Allen. Candlewick Press, 1994. Illustrations copyright © 1994 by Tudor Humphries. Reproduced by permission./ Allen, Judy, photograph. Reproduced by permission./ Humphries, Tudor, illustrator. From an illustration in *Are You a Ladybug?* by Judy Allen. Kingfisher, 2000. Copyright © Kingfisher Publications Plc 2000. Reproduced by permission.

AMMON, RICHARD. Farnsworth, Bill, illustrator. From a jacket of *Conestoga Wagons,* by Richard Ammon. Holiday House, Inc., 2000. Reproduced by permission of Holiday House, Inc./ Ammon, Richard, photograph by Elizabeth Ammon. Reproduced by permission of Richard Ammon.

ATWATER-RHODES, AMELIA. Dinyer, Eric, illustrator. From a cover of *In the Forests of the Night,* by Amelia Atwater-Rhodes. Dell Laurel Leaf, 1999. Reproduced by permission of Eric Dinyer./ Nielsen, Cliff, illustrator. From a jacket of *Demon in My View,* by Amelia Atwater-Rhodes. Delacorte, 2000. Jacket illustration © 2000 by Cliff Nielsen. Reproduced by permission of Shannon Associates.

BACHE, ELLYN. Stitzer, Barbara, photographer. From a cover of *The Activist's Daughter,* by Ellyn Bache. Spinster's Ink, 1997. © 1997 by Ellyn Bache. Reproduced by permission.

BEIL, KAREN MAGNUSON. Meisel, Paul, illustrator. From an illustration in *A Cake All for Me!,* by Karen Magnuson Beil. Holiday House, Inc., 1998. Illustrations copyright © 1998 by Paul Meisel. Reproduced by permission of Holiday House, Inc.

BERCAW, EDNA COE. Bercaw, Edna Coe, photograph. Reproduced by permission.

BERGER, MELVIN. All photographs reproduced by permission of the author.

BIRD, CARMEL. Bird, Carmel, photograph. Reproduced by permission.

BLAIR, MARGARET WHITMAN. West, Harry A., illustrator. From a cover of *Brothers at War,* by Margaret Whitman Blair. White Mane Publishing Company, Inc, 1997. Cover Design © Harry A. West, 1997. Reproduced by permission.

BRENNER, BARBARA (JOHNES). Degen, Bruce, illustrator. From an illustration in *Lion and Lamb Step Out,* by Barbara Brenner and William H. Hooks. Bantam Little Rooster Books, 1990. Illustrations copyright © 1990 by Bruce Degen and Byron Preiss Visual Publications, Inc. All rights reserved. Reproduced by permission of Bantam Books, a division of Random House,Inc./ Schwartz, Carol, illustrator. From a cover of *Where's That Insect?* by Barbara Brenner and Bernice Chardiet. Cartwheel Books, 1993. Illustrations copyright © 1993 by Carol Schwartz. Reproduced by permission of Scholastic, Inc./ Otani, June, illustrator. From a cover of *Chibi: A True Story from Japan,* by Barbara Brenner and Julia Takaya. Clarion Books, 1996. Illustrations copyright © 1996 by June Otani. Reproduced by permission of Houghton Mifflin Company./ Dunrea, Olivier, illustrator. From a jacket of *The Boy Who Loved To Draw: Benjamin West,* by Barbara Brenner. Houghton Mifflin Company, 1999. Jacket art © 1999 by Olivier Dunrea. Reproduced by permission of Houghton Mifflin Company./ Brenner, Barbara, photograph by Fred Brenner. Reproduced by permission of Barbara Brenner.

BRILL, MARLENE TARG. Cover photograph from *Let Women Vote!* by Marlene Targ Brill. The Millbrook Press, Inc., 1996. Copyright © 1996 by Marlene Targ Brill. Reproduced by permission./ Brill, Marlene Targ, photograph by Richard Brill. Reproduced by permission of Marlene Targ Brill.

BROEKSTRA, LORETTE. Broekstra, Lorette, photograph. Reproduced by permission.

CANN, HELEN. Cann, Helen, illustrator. From an illustration in *Mother and Daughter Tales,* retold by Josephine Evetts-Secker. Abbeville Kids, 1996. Illustrations copyright © 1996 by Helen Cann. Reproduced by permission. of Barefoot Books, Ltd.

CARTER, CAROL S(HADIS). Carter, Carol S., photographer. From a photograph in *Seeing Things My Way,* by Alden R. Carter. Albert Whitman & Company, 1998. Photographs copyright © 1998 by Carol S. Carter. Reproduced by permission.

SOMETHING ABOUT THE AUTHOR

AL-KHALILI, Jim 1962-

Personal

Born September 20, 1962, in Baghdad, Iraq; son of Sadik (an engineer) and Jean Kathleen (a homemaker; maiden name, Wheatcroft) Al-Khalili; married Julie Helen Frampton (an accounts clerk), September 27, 1986; children: David Robert, Kate Helen. *Education:* University of Surrey, B.Sc. (with honors), 1986, Ph.D., 1989. *Politics:* Liberal. *Religion:* None. *Hobbies and other interests:* Soccer, philosophy, parenthood.

Addresses

Home—48 Bramshott Rd., Portsmouth, Hampshire PO4 8AN, England. *Office*—Department of Physics, University of Surrey, Guildford GU2 7XH, England. *E-mail*—j.al-khalili@surrey.ac.uk.

Career

University of London, London, England, research assistant, 1989-91; University of Surrey, Guildford, England, lecturer, 1991-94, advanced research fellow, 1994-99, lecturer in physics, 1999—. Member of European Public Awareness of Nuclear Physics Committee. Public speaker; guest on television and radio programs, including *Leading Edge* and *Tomorrow's World.* Wimborne Infant School, vice-chairperson of board of governors. *Member:* Institute of Physics (fellow; honorary secretary of Nuclear Physics Group, 1996—), British Association.

Awards, Honors

Public Awareness of Physics Award, Institute of Physics, 2000.

Writings

(Author and illustrator) *Black Holes, Wormholes, and Time Machines,* Institute of Physics (Philadelphia, PA), 1999.

Contributor of more than forty articles to scientific journals.

Work in Progress

Quantum Magic: The Strangest Truth (tentative title); *Nucleus: A Trip into the Heart of Matter,* with Raymond Macintosh; translating *A Stroll through the Thoughts of Niels Bohr,* a biography written in Danish; a chapter on quantum mechanics, to be included in *Collins Encyclopaedia of the Universe,* for HarperCollins; research on theoretical nuclear physics, particularly "the study of certain types of exotic atomic nuclei containing neutron halos."

Sidelights

Him Al-Khalili told *SATA:* "I am a theoretical nuclear physicist and full-time lecturer in the Department of Physics at the University of Surrey. Apart from my teaching and research commitments I have devoted a considerable amount of energy to issues concerning the public understanding of science. In 1998, I was the

BLACK HOLES WORMHOLES & TIME MACHINES

It's successful, it's humorous and it's up to date.
New Scientist

JIM AL-KHALILI

IoP

Theoretical physicist Jim Al-Khalili explains Albert Einstein's theory of relativity and explores the related possibility of time travel.

'schools and colleges lecturer' for the Institute of Physics. This involved touring the country giving a popular physics lecture to fourteen- to eighteen-year-old students. This resulted in a commission from the publishing arm of the Institute to write the lecture as a popular science book. The result was *Black Holes, Wormholes, and Time Machines.* Since then I have written several magazine and Web articles and have lectured at venues such as the Royal Institution and the Science Museum.

"In the last couple of years I have given radio and television interviews on topics ranging from the meaning of human free will to the science behind *Star Wars.* I have been a guest on *Leading Edge* on Radio 4 and *Tomorrow's World* on BBC1-TV. I took part in a couple of documentaries that were screened last year on BBC2-TV. One was a *Horizon* production as part of a theme evening on the nature of time. It featured, along with me, the mathematician Sir Roger Penrose. I am particularly proud of my first venture as a television presenter when, as part of another BBC2-TV theme evening—this time all about *Dr. Who*—I presented a five-minute slot on

how the TARDIS might work as a time machine. It was a light-hearted attempt to explain, in lay terms, what physical theories would need to be correct if such a contraption *were* possible.

"My first book, *Black Holes,* involved explaining some of the mind-blowing ideas that follow from Einstein's theories of relativity. But my longer-term ambition has always been to write a similar book (similar in style and level) on an even stranger, and yet more relevant, theory of modern physics: quantum mechanics. After all, that is the area of physics in which I am an expert and where my research interests lie. With the success of *Black Holes* I am both confident and excited about the prospect of uncovering, at the level of the complete lay reader, the many weird and wonderful mysteries of the quantum world. In three-quarters of a century since its discovery, very few authors have succeeded in this, certainly not in the past decade when so many new experimental discoveries have been made.

"Apart from my proposed new book, to which I have given the working title *Quantum Magic: The Strangest Truth,* I am already involved in writing (jointly) two other popular science books. The first is called *Nucleus: A Trip to the Heart of Matter,* a full-color, glossy book aimed at teenagers. The second book, *A Stroll through the Thoughts of Niels Bohr,* is a biographical and philosophical book on the life and works of the Danish physicist. It was written originally in Danish, and I am now collaborating with its author to produce an extended English version."

Biographical and Critical Sources

PERIODICALS

Booklist, October 15, 1999, Gilbert Taylor, review of *Black Holes, Wormholes, and Time Machines,* p. 401.*

*   *   *

ALAN, Robert
See SILVERSTEIN, Robert Alan

*   *   *

ALLEN, Judy (Christina) 1941-

Personal

Born July 8, 1941, in Old Sarum, Salisbury, Wiltshire, England; daughter of John Turner (a British Army officer) and Janet Marion (a playwright; maiden name, Beall) Allen. *Hobbies and other interests:* Walking, reading, spending time with friends.

Addresses

Agent—Pat White, Rogers, Coleridge & White, 20 Powis Mews, London W11 1JN, England.

Career

Freelance editor and writer, 1972—; full-time writer since the early 1980s. Has worked variously in the offices of two theaters, as a temporary secretary, in a literary agency, and in publishing. *Member:* Society of Authors, Friends of the Earth, Greenpeace.

Awards, Honors

Best Specialist Guidebook Award, London Tourist Board, 1984, for *London Arts Guide;* Christopher Award, 1987, for television adaptation of *December Flower;* Whitbread Award (children's section), and Carnegie Medal Commendation, Library Association (England), both 1988, and Earthworm Award, Friends of the Earth, 1989, all for *Awaiting Developments;* Sir Peter Kent Conservation Book Prize commendation, 1993, for *Seal;* Nevada Young Readers Award nomination, and Washington Children's Choice Award nomination, 1994, both for *Tiger.*

Writings

FOR YOUNG ADULTS

The Spring on the Mountain, J. Cape, 1973, revised edition, Hodder Children's (London, England), 2000.

The Stones of the Moon, J. Cape, 1975, revised edition, Hodder Children's (London, England), 2000.

The Lord of the Dance, Hamish Hamilton (London, England), 1976, Dutton (New York, NY), 1977, revised edition, Hodder Children's (London, England), 2001.

Song for Solo and Persistent Chorus, Hamish Hamilton (London, England), 1977.

The Dream Thing, Hamish Hamilton (London, England), 1978.

Barriers (novelization of William Corlett's television series of the same name), Hamish Hamilton (London, England), 1981.

Something Rare and Special, Julia MacRae (London, England), 1985.

Travelling Hopefully, Julia MacRae (London, England), 1987.

Awaiting Developments, Julia MacRae (London, England), 1988.

Between the Moon and the Rock, Julia MacRae (London, England), 1992.

Amsterdam Quest, Red Fox (London, England), 1996.

Highland Quest, Red Fox (London, England), 1996.

Paris Quest, Julia MacRae (London, England), 1996.

Spanish Quest, Red Fox (London, England), 1996.

Sydney Quest, Red Fox (London, England), 1996.

New York Quest, Red Fox (London, England), 1996.

(Editor) *Anthology for the Earth* (nonfiction), Walker (London, England), 1997, Candlewick Press (Cambridge, MA), 1998.

FOR CHILDREN; FICTION

The Dim Thin Ducks, Julia MacRae (London, England), 1990.

The Great Pig Spring, Julia MacRae (London, England), 1990.

Judy Allen

The Cheap Sheep Shock, Julia MacRae (London, England), 1991.

The Long-Loan Llama, Julia MacRae (London, England), 1991.

Elephant, illustrated by Tudor Humphries, Walker (London, England), 1992, Candlewick Press (Cambridge, MA), 1993.

Panda, illustrated by Tudor Humphries, Walker (London, England), 1992, Candlewick Press (Cambridge, MA), 1993.

Tiger, illustrated by Tudor Humphries, Walker (London, England), 1992, Candlewick Press (Cambridge, MA), 1992.

Whale, illustrated by Tudor Humphries, Walker (London, England), 1992, Candlewick Press (Cambridge, MA), 1993.

Seal, illustrated by Tudor Humphries, Walker (London, England), 1993, Candlewick Press (Cambridge, MA), 1994.

Eagle, illustrated by Tudor Humphries, Candlewick Press (Cambridge, MA), 1994.

Auntie Billie's Greatest Invention, illustrated by Chris Mould, Walker (London, England), 1997.

The Most Brilliant Trick Ever, illustrated by Scoular Anderson, Walker (London, England), 1997.

Seven Weird Days at Number 31, illustrated by Derek Brazell, Walker (London, England), 1998.

The Great Pig Sprint, Walker (London, England), 1998.

Five Weird Days at Aunt Carly's, illustrated by Derek Brazell, Walker (London, England), 1999.

Challenge to Efrafa, Red Fox (London, England), 1999.

Escape to the Hills, Red Fox (London, England), 1999.

Rabbits in Danger, Red Fox (London, England), 1999.

The Raid, Red Fox (London, England), 1999.

Friend and Foe, Red Fox (London, England), 2000.

The Hidden World, Red Fox (London, England), 2000.

The Spring on the Mountain, Hodder Children's (London, England), 2000.

The Burning, Hodder Children's (London, England), 2000.

Are You a Ladybug?, illustrated by Tudor Humphries, Kingfisher (London, England), 2000.

Are You a Butterfly?, illustrated by Tudor Humphries, Kingfisher (New York, NY), 2000.

Are You a Spider?, illustrated by Tudor Humphries, Kingfisher (New York, NY), 2000.

Are You a Snail?, illustrated by Tudor Humphries, Kingfisher (New York, NY), 2000.

Are You a Bee?, illustrated by Tudor Humphries, Kingfisher (New York, NY), 2001.

Are You a Dragonfly?, illustrated by Tudor Humphries, Kingfisher (New York, NY), 2001.

Also author of the dramatization of Frances Hodgson Burnett's *The Secret Garden* for BBC-Radio 5, rebroadcast on Radio 4, and available on BBC Enterprises Audio-Cassette; the dramatization of Phillipa Pearce's *Tom's Midnight Garden* for BBC-Radio 4 and available on BBC Enterprises Audio-Cassette; and the dramatization of Rumer Godden's *The River* for BBC-Radio 4 and available on BBC Enterprises Audio-Cassette.

FOR CHILDREN; NONFICTION

How to Amuse Yourself on a Journey, Studio Vista, 1974.

(With Sharon Finmark) *How to Recycle Your Rubbish,* Studio Vista, 1975.

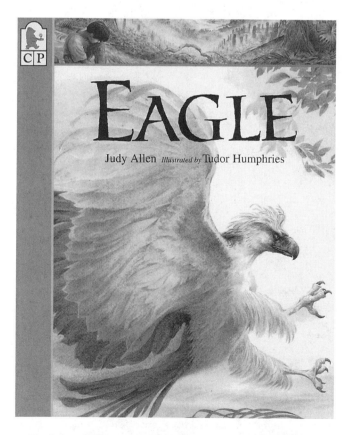

During a field trip into a jungle in the Philippines, Miguel learns about eagles from his teacher and from his own encounter with the bird. (Cover illustration by Tudor Humphries.)

Step-by-Step Models, Marshall Cavendish, 1977.

Exciting Things to Do with Nature Materials, illustrated by Barbara Firth, Lippincott, 1977, published as *Exciting Things to Do with Nature,* Cavendish (England), 1977.

Stamps and Stamp Collecting, Usborne, 1981.

Chips, Computers and Robots, Usborne, 1982.

Lasers and Holograms, Pepper Press, 1983.

Electronic Wizardry, Picadilly Press, 1984.

Tricks of the Light, Picadilly Press, 1985.

Wildlife in the Country, Julia MacRae (London, England), 1992.

Wildlife in the Town, Julia MacRae (London, England), 1992.

What Is a Wall, After All?, illustrated by Allen Baron, Candlewick Press (Cambridge, MA), 1993.

The Last Green Book on Earth? (young adult), Julia MacRae (London, England), 1994.

Frogs and Toads, Oxford University Press (Oxford, England), 2000.

The Blue Death, Hodder Children's (London, England), 2001.

FOR ADULTS

Survival (play), produced by BBC-Radio 4, 1973.

(With Jeanne Griffiths) *The Book of the Dragon* (nonfiction), Orbis, 1977.

Squatters Rights (play), produced by BBC-Radio 4, 1979.

Tourist London (travel guide), Nicholson, 1981.

December Flower (novel), Duckworth, 1982.

The Sailors Return (play), produced by BBC-Radio 4, 1983.

In London (travel guide), Nicholson, 1983.

Unicorn Calling (play), produced by BBC-Radio 4, 1984.

London Arts Guide, Nicholson, 1984.

The Diary of Minnie Gorrie (abridged from family diary of 1876), BBC-Radio, 1985.

Picking on Men (quotations), Ballantine, 1985.

(With Dyan Sheldon) *Picking on Men Again* (quotations), Arrow, 1986.

Holiday Guide to Devon, Nicholson, 1986.

The Guide to London by Bus and Tube, Nicholson, 1987.

Nicholson's London Pub Guide, Nicholson, 1987.

London Arts and Cultural Guide, Nicholson, 1988.

Royal London Guide, Nicholson, 1988.

(With Jane Carroll) *London Docklands Street Atlas and Guide,* Nicholson, 1988.

Bag and Baggage (novel), The Women's Press, 1988.

Adaptations

December Flower was filmed for television by Granada TV, 1985, and shown on PBS-TV in the United States, as well as broadcast on BBC-Radio 4; *Bag and Baggage* was broadcast in five episodes on BBC-Radio 4 Woman's Hour.

Sidelights

Judy Allen's picture books for children and novels for young adults interweave elements of the supernatural and a concern for the environment with realistic characters and situations. Her writing has been praised for its humor, its lack of sentimentality, and for the depth of its insights into human psychology. In 1988, her young adult novel *Awaiting Developments* was commended for Great Britain's highest award for children's writers, the Carnegie Medal.

Allen's picture books for young children highlight her concern for the environment and for endangered species. In *Tiger,* set in a Chinese village, young Lee is the only one who is not thrilled when a hunter comes to track a tiger that has been spotted near the village. Though they know it is illegal, the villagers hope to eat some tiger meat to give them bravery and to sell the animal's valuable pelt; Lee would rather have the animal left alone. Diane Nunn wrote in *School Library Journal,* "The eloquent text skillfully maintains excitement and tension while subtly providing information about tiger habitat and behavior." Several other reviewers praised the inclusion of a fact sheet at the end of the book listing efforts to save this endangered species. *Bulletin of the Center for Children's Books* reviewer Betsy Hearne concluded, "A high-powered picture book, this offers listeners the triple attraction of animal tale, Asian backdrop, and nature lesson."

Allen used a similar format for *Whale,* which tells of Anya and her parents, who witness the rescue of a whale and her newborn calf by a number of ghostly, injured whales who disappear mysteriously after the calf recovers. While several critics faulted the author's reliance on magic to save the whales, Carolyn Phelan of *Booklist* found that "Allen's delicate, precise use of language" makes for an "unusual and effective" tale. Other books in Allen's series cover endangered species from various continents, including Asia's *Panda,* Africa's *Elephant,* the Philippines's *Eagle,* and Europe's *Seal.*

Similarly, *Exciting Things to Do with Nature Materials* was praised for its attention to environmental concerns while inspiring children to play with nature. The book is "beautifully organized, nicely written and brightly illustrated," according to Ellen Rodman in a *New York Times Book Review* article. Allen has also brought her talents to other nonfiction subjects. *Times Educational Supplement* contributor John Laski praised Allen's *Chips, Computers and Robots* as a "lively popularizing book," introducing technology to young children. And 1993's *What Is a Wall, After All?* was commended for its "lighthearted but searching and intelligent exploration of the concept and lore of walls," according to a *Kirkus Reviews* critic. Cartoon characters and rhyming text lead the reader through a chronological survey of the variety and parts of walls, resulting in a book that Janice Del Negro described in *Booklist* as "unusual, informative, and fun."

In 2000 Allen, along with illustrator Tudor Humphries, issued a series of animal books for young readers as part of the "Backyard Books" series. *Are You a Snail?, Are You a Butterfly?,* and *Are You a Ladybug?* are all books that introduce young children to animals they are likely to encounter in their homes or backyards. The text in each book, which includes questions and answers, is accompanied by bright illustrations that work together to

From a series that introduces young readers to animals they are likely to encounter in their backyard, Allen's picture book teaches preschoolers about the life cycles of the ladybug. (From Are You a Ladybug?, *illustrated by Tudor Humphries.)*

point out similarities and differences between children and the featured animals in these books. Reviewing *Are You a Snail?* and *Are You a Ladybug?* for *Booklist,* Carolyn Phelan characterized them as "well-conceived animal books for children." She similarly felt that *Are You a Butterfly?* and *Are You a Spider?,* the next two books in the series, were "two fine additions" to an "informative and enjoyable" collection of nature books for young readers.

In addition to writing children's nonfiction, Allen has also written several works of fiction for children. Among these is *Seven Weird Days at Number 31,* a horror book that "offers a rare opportunity to get spooked by some good old-fashioned ghosts," said E. Baynton-Clarke in *School Librarian.* In this book, after Mike and his parents move into their new home at Number 31, they begin to notice strange things, including clocks chiming, clothes flying, and doors slamming shut on their own. The house is, it appears, haunted, and Mike has to deal with it. In Allen's *Auntie Billie's Greatest Invention,* another children's story, Dan and Ally are visiting their aunt and uncle. Their inventor aunt has created a spray that can send things back in time—unfortunately she has used it on herself and sprayed herself out of existence. The kids figure out how the spray works and eventually bring their aunt back. David Churchill, writing in the *School Librarian,* called this "a very enjoyable book."

The bulk of Allen's work has been in the genre of fiction for young adults. Her first work in this vein, *The Spring on the Mountain,* concerns the magical revelations of a trip up a local mountain taken by three bored, vacationing youths. Similarly, *The Stones of the Moon* centers on an ancient stone circle once used to conjure up rain in times of drought that has been activated by the vibration of new machines at a nearby textile mill. *The Lord of the Dance,* another young adult novel, also mixes supernatural elements with a realistic backdrop. In this work, a boy is introduced to the symbolic forces that rule life—male and female, positive and negative, intellectual and emotional—under the guidance of Magnus, which prepares him to return to the real world as a more active participant. *The Spring on the Mountain* and *The Stones of the Moon* were both "gently updated," Allen told *SATA,* and have been republished in 2000. *The Lord of the Dance,* on the other hand, has been "largely rewritten," said Allen, and republished in 2001.

Allen's *Song for Solo and Persistent Chorus* is a realistic story about a group of young friends sharing a flat together as they enter adulthood. In *The Dream Thing* Allen turned to a psychological fantasy in which a young girl believes that a group of gypsies camping on nearby public land has placed a curse on her, causing her to have nightmares. Her struggle with her own illegitimacy, her dead gypsy father, and the teasing she is subjected to at school give rise to an anger the girl releases on all those around her, until she is told a few truths by the grandmother of the gypsies. In a *Times Literary Supplement* review, Cecilia Gordon praised Allen's "lively and interesting characters," while Margery Fisher recommended the work in *Growing Point* for the "unity of technique and passion which distinguishes it from the mass of problem stories directed at adolescent readers."

Allen's *Something Rare and Special* was also warmly received by Fisher, who wrote in another *Growing Point* review that this book "explores, candidly and perceptively, a sensitive area in the relations of a mother and her teenage daughter." In this young adult novel, Lyn and her mother must move from the city to the country after Lyn's father leaves them. Lyn finds the isolation of the seaside dull until she meets Bill, an avid birdwatcher whose interest in her mother causes a strain in their relationship. Stephanie Nettell, writing in the *Times Literary Supplement,* found the novel "delicately handled" with "funny, touching and very believable dialogue." *Travelling Hopefully,* Allen's next young adult work, also centers on the relationship between an adolescent girl and her adult female caretaker. In this novel, Maggie, a freelance journalist, takes her niece Clare along on a holiday when the girl's mother goes to the hospital.

Allen continued realistic characterizations in her *Awaiting Developments.* In this book, Joanna—known as Jo—lives a quiet life with her parents and younger brother, Sam, until the announcement that a nearby house and park will be demolished and replaced by a row of apartment houses. Inspired by her visiting cousin Kathleen's stories of an adventurous nineteenth-century ancestor, Jo decides to rally her neighbors' support to fight the development. Fisher remarked in *Growing Point* that "balance, moderation, and a shrewd practical eye on urban life are as notable in the book as the firm

detail and the emotional warmth." A *Junior Bookshelf* reviewer concluded that this "richly humorous and understanding story" is "definitely not a book to be left to the kids. All the family can enjoy this one, and in doing so may recognize something of their own condition." Likewise, *Between the Moon and the Rock,* Allen's 1992 young adult novel, handles the controversial issue of cults and their special attraction to vulnerable teenagers "with great authority as well as humanity," according to another *Junior Bookshelf* article.

Allen has continued her extensive list of young adult fiction publications with a series of adventure and mystery stories, including *Paris Quest* and *Amsterdam Quest.* In these first-person narratives, Jo and her friend Ruth relate their adventures while working at Jo's parents' travel agency. *Paris Quest* tells the tale of their attempts to deliver a camera to an elusive client, while in the second story, the two girls serve as couriers for a family hunting for antiques in Amsterdam. Helen Allen, writing in *School Librarian,* was especially appreciative of the "wit, humour and style of the writing" in both works, calling them "outstanding books" for twelve- to sixteen-year-olds.

In 1998 Allen edited her first nonfiction title for young adults, *Anthology for the Earth.* In this collection, she brings together works from various cultures and authors, including Aldo Leopold, Ian Frazier, Kayapo Indian chief Paulino Paiakan, and even Thomas Hardy, all of whom speak in defense of the natural world. A *Publishers Weekly* reviewer related that Allen began collecting these pieces in her early teens, bringing together a wide variety of works, both fiction and nonfiction, to create a "complex yet harmonious blend of artistry that offers new insight into the natural world." Included in the collection are over forty poems, essays, and fiction pieces, all helping to "remind the reader of the fragility of our world," noted Jamie S. Hansen in *Voice of Youth Advocates.* Hansen was also appreciative of the brief biography Allen included for each author featured in the anthology and felt that the collection would compel readers to find other works by the authors included.

Biographical and Critical Sources

PERIODICALS

Booklist, July, 1993, Carolyn Phelan, review of *Whale;* September 1, 1993, Janice Del Negro, review of *What Is a Wall, After All?;* May 15, 2000, Carolyn Phelan, review of *Are You a Snail?* and *Are You a Ladybug?,* p. 1745; October 15, 2000, Carolyn Phelan, reviews of *Are You a Butterfly?* and *Are You a Spider?,* p. 441.

Bulletin of the Center for Children's Books, November, 1992, Betsy Hearne, review of *Tiger.*

Growing Point, September, 1978, Margery Fisher, review of *The Dream Thing,* p. 3390; May, 1986, Margery Fisher, review of *Something Rare and Special,* pp. 4623-4624; November, 1988, Margery Fisher, review of *Awaiting Developments,* p. 5053-5054.

Junior Bookshelf, April, 1989, review of *Awaiting Developments,* p. 78; December, 1992, review of *Between the Moon and the Rock,* p. 250.
Kirkus Reviews, July 15, 1993, review of *What Is a Wall, After All?;* September 15, 1994, review of *Eagle,* p. 1263.
Magpies, March, 1995, review of *Whale,* p. 34; September, 1998, review of *Elephant,* p. 44.
New York Times Book Review, November 13, 1977, Ellen Rodman, review of *Exciting Things to Do with Nature Materials,* p. 58.
Publishers Weekly, March 23, 1998, review of *Anthology for the Earth,* p. 100.
School Librarian, May, 1996, Helen Allen, review of *Paris Quest* and *Amsterdam Quest,* p. 71; summer, 1998, David Churchill, review of *Auntie Billie's Greatest Invention,* p. 76; summer, 1999, E. Baynton-Clarke, review of *Seven Weird Days at Number 31,* p. 78.
School Library Journal, December, 1992, Diane Nunn, review of *Tiger;* February, 1994, Susan Scheps, review of *Panda,* p. 76.
Times Educational Supplement, September 30, 1983, John Laski, "Men and Machines," p. 26.
Times Literary Supplement, October 28, 1977, Cecilia Gordon, review of *Song for Solo and Persistent;* July 7, 1978, Cecilia Gordon, review of *The Dream Thing,* p. 765; June 9, 1989, Stephanie Nettell, review of *Something Rare and Special,* p. 648.
Voice of Youth Advocates, February, 1999, Jamie S. Hansen, review of *Anthology for the Earth,* p. 449.

*   *   *

AMMON, Richard 1942-

Personal

Born August 22, 1942, in Ephrata, PA; son of Richard Ammon, Sr. and Fern Leisey Ammon; married Jeannie (a middle school librarian), June 27, 1970; children: Cari Roberts, Elizabeth. *Education:* The Pennsylvania State University, B.S., 1964, D. Ed., 1972, Temple University, M.Ed., 1967. *Politics:* Democrat. *Religion:* Lutheran. *Hobbies and other interests:* Fly fishing, playing euphonium.

Addresses

Home—905 Ebenezer Rd., Middletown, PA, 17057-2908. *Office*—W351 Olmsted Bldg., 777 West Harrisburg Pike, Middletown, PA 17057-4898.

Career

Pennsylvania State University at Harrisburg, associate professor of education, 1972—. *Member:* National Council of Teachers of English, International Reading Association.

Awards, Honors

Golden Light Award, Photographic Book of the Year, 1993, for *Trains at Work.*

Writings

The Kids' Book of Chocolate, Atheneum Books for Young Readers (New York, NY), 1987.
Growing up Amish, Atheneum Books for Young Readers (New York, NY), 1989.
(Editor, with Michael O. Tunnell) *The Story of Ourselves: Teaching History through Children's Literature,* Heinemann (Portsmouth, NH), 1993.
(Photographs by Darrell Peterson and Ammon) *Trains at Work,* Atheneum Books for Young Readers (New York, NY), 1993.
(Illustrated by Pamela Patrick) *An Amish Christmas,* Atheneum Books for Young Readers (New York, NY), 1996.
(Illustrated by Pamela Patrick) *An Amish Wedding,* Atheneum Books for Young Readers (New York, NY), 1998.
(Illustrated by Bill Farnsworth) *Conestoga Wagons,* Atheneum Books for Young Readers (New York, NY), 2000.
(Illustrated by Pamela Patrick) *An Amish Year,* Atheneum Books for Young Readers (New York, NY), 2000.
(Illustrated by Pamela Patrick) *Amish Horses,* Atheneum Books for Young Readers (New York, NY), 2001.

Richard Ammon

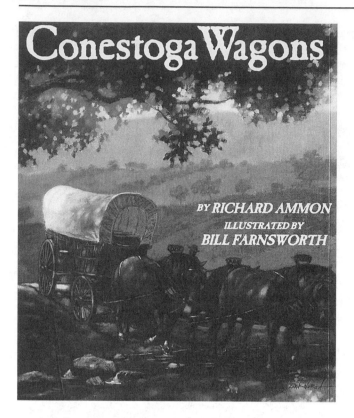

The construction and uses of the pioneer wagon are coupled with stories about the arduous journeys of the early settlers in Ammon's Conestoga Wagons. *(Cover illustration by Bill Farnsworth.)*

Work in Progress

George Washington at Valley Forge, Holiday House, 2002.

Sidelights

Richard Ammon told *SATA:* "As an undergraduate at Penn State I played euphonium and trumpet in both the marching and concert Blue Band. Over the years I've continued playing in a brass ensemble and town band. The self-discipline of practicing every day just to keep the chops in shape is not unlike the self-discipline necessary to write. Playing my own horn helps clean out the cobwebs in my brain, enabling me to get something reasonable down on paper. While I write I usually listen to baroque brass music, such as Bach, Gabrelli, Albinon, or jazz, including Marsalis, Monk, Ellington, and others.

"While in college I enrolled in a course in which the professor taught me to teach reading with children's books. After graduation, I taught a number of years in elementary schools. Following graduate school in 1972, I began full-time teaching at Penn State Harrisburg, where I've been ever since. As an instructor of children's literature, I naturally read a lot of books. After I finished reading one book, I thought, 'How hard can that be?' Over fifteen rejections later, I realized just how difficult it is to write a children's book.

"One evening I was leaving Hersheypark Arena with my youngest daughter, who had been taking ice skating lessons, when we sniffed the smell of chocolate wafting from the nearby plant. I thought that chocolate might be a good topic for a children's book. So, I did my research, wrote a manuscript, and sent it off. Over a period of about four years, I received one rejection after another. Finally, Atheneum sent me a contract for my first book, *The Kids' Book of Chocolate.* What a wonderful day that was! Later that day, I received a traffic ticket for making a left-hand turn, but I didn't mind. I had my first contract.

"When my editor returned my manuscript, I noticed that she had liberally marked it with comments and corrections. She concluded her note of instructions with 'Have fun!' Ugh! I thought, this is a lot of work. But she was right. Over the years I have come to enjoy the process of rewriting." In this first book, Ammon walks his readers through the history of chocolate, including information about the Aztecs' use of chocolate and its eventual spread to the rest of the world. He also describes the creation and manufacture of chocolate, as well as including some recipes, chocolate-related jokes, and a bibliography. Reviewing this work for *Horn Book,* Elizabeth S. Watson noted that "the author's research is evident in both text and illustration." Watson went on to praise Ammon's effort as being "readable and instructive." Similarly, Ilene Cooper of *Booklist* called this book "an appealing introduction to a mouth-watering subject."

Ammon continued: "Following *The Kids' Book of Chocolate* I began writing *Growing Up Amish,* which is about the Amish who are neighbors to our property in up-state Pennsylvania. Being good neighbors helps in getting inside the rather closed community of Older Order Amish. But I'm also lucky to have the same last name as the founder of the Amish religion—Jakob Amman (which he also spelled as Ammon). Many Amish want to know whether I am related to Jakob. The truth is that no one knows since no one knows what happened to him. But most historians believe that neither he nor any of his descendants came to America after they left Switzerland for the area between France and Germany divided by the Rhine River. Ironically, my father traced his mother's family back to the daughter of Hans Reist, the Swiss Brethren (Mennonite) leader from whom Ammon broke."

In a summary of *Growing Up Amish* for the *Washington Post Book World,* Jim Naughton characterized the work as "admirable" and "thoughtful," calling it a "thorough introduction to Amish culture." Once again, Ammon's text is accompanied by photographs, maps and illustrations, prompting *Horn Book* reviewer Mary M. Burns to laud the author for providing a "warm, interesting view of the durable Amish culture." Ammon returned to Amish culture again in *An Amish Christmas,* a book that tells of the holiday customs of Amish farm families. A critic for *Publishers Weekly* called Ammon's work "enlightening and refreshing," especially noting the author's use of Pennsylvania Dutch in his text. Similarly, *An Amish Wedding* once again takes Ammon's readers into the Amish culture, this time detailing the events surrounding the preparation and celebration of an Amish wedding. Lauren Peterson, reviewing this work for *Booklist*, recommended it as a "wonderful" introduction to Amish culture.

Ammon related, "Everything I write is something close to me. I simply look for ideas right around me. Chocolate plants—Hershey, Wilbur, and Godiva—are nearby. I took all the photographs of *Trains at Work* locally. The Amish are our neighbors, and I do not live far from Lancaster County where I grew up and where there are museums with Conestoga wagons. In addition, one of the world's foremost authorities on Conestoga wagons lives near Lancaster. Ironically, this expert, Arthur Reist, is the brother of my high school English teacher! So *Conestoga Wagons* was there, practically under my nose, waiting to be written. Valley Forge, my latest project, is an hour-and-a-half down the turnpike.

"Everything, except historical references, I have experienced—from watching women carefully take walnuts from their shells inside the Godiva plant (*The Kids' Book of Chocolate*); to climbing around railroad cars and engines (*Trains at Work*); to spending time with the Amish at Christmas, weddings, making hay, and going to horse sales; to touching every part of a Conestoga wagon; and to walking the grounds at Valley Forge."

Ammon concluded: "For the Amish books I was lucky enough for the publisher to assign Pamela Patrick as the illustrator. Because she lives just outside of Baltimore, Pam has been able to go on-site with me to Amish farms and homes. She has sketched inside an Amish school during the Christmas program, in horse barns, their homes, and in blacksmith shops."

Biographical and Critical Sources

PERIODICALS

Booklist, February 15, 1988, Ilene Cooper, review of *The Kids' Book of Chocolate*, p. 997; November 1, 1993, Christie Sylvester, review of *Trains at Work*, p. 524; September 1, 1996, Stephanie Zvirin, review of *An Amish Christmas*, p. 135; October 1, 1998, Lauren Peterson, review of *An Amish Wedding*, p. 342; January 1, 2000, Carolyn Phelan, review of *An Amish Year*, p. 908.

Bulletin of the Center for Children's Books, March 1988, Betsy Hearne, review of *The Kids' Book of Chocolate*, p. 129; July 1989, Roger Sutton, review of *Growing Up Amish*, pp. 268-269.

Horn Book, May, 1988, Elizabeth S. Watson, review of *The Kids' Book of Chocolate*, p. 369; September, 1989, Mary M. Burns, review of *Growing Up Amish*, p. 634.

Kirkus Reviews, December 15, 1999, review of *An Amish Year*, p. 1954.

Publishers Weekly, September 30, 1996, review of *An Amish Christmas*, p. 91; January 24, 2000, review of *An Amish Year*, p. 313.

School Library Journal, December, 1993, Eldon Younce, review of *Trains at Work*, p. 99; December, 1998,

Susan Knell, review of *An Amish Wedding*, p. 98; September, 2000, Anne Chapman, review of *Conestoga Wagons*, p. 213.

Washington Post Book World, July 9, 1989, Jim Naughton, review of *Growing Up Amish*, p. 10.

*   *   *

ANGELETTI, Roberta 1964-

Personal

Born May 14, 1964, in Civitavecchia, Italy; daughter of Roberto (a physician) and Anna (a teacher; maiden name, Pasqualucci) Angeletti; married Luigi Belli (a ceramic artist), 1997; children: Filippo, Giulio. *Education:* Academy of Fine Arts. *Religion:* Roman Catholic.

Addresses

Home—Via di San Martino 39, 01016 Tarquinia (VT), Italy.

Career

Secondary school teacher. *Exhibitions:* Angeletti's illustrations have been displayed at exhibitions in Bologna, Venice, Padova, Genoa, Turin, Treviso, and other Italian cities, and in Tokyo, Paris, Nairobi, and Addis Ababa.

Writings

ILLUSTRATOR

G. B. Basile, *La Pulce*, Villarica Editora (Belo Horizonte, Brazil), 1996.

Lewis Carroll, *Alice nel paese delle meraviglie* (title means "Alice in Wonderland"), Villarica Editora (Belo Horizonte, Brazil), 1996.

G. Boccaccio, *Chichibio cuoco dal Decamerone*, Villarica Editora (Belo Horizonte, Brazil), 1997.

Collodi, *Pinocchio*, Villarica Editora (Belo Horizonte, Brazil), 1997.

Brothers Grimm's Fairy Tales, Grimm Press (Taipei, Taiwan), 1997.

Beaumarchais, *The Barber of Sevilla*, Grimm Press (Taipei, Taiwan), 1999.

Justine entre au CP, Belin Editions (Parigi, Italy), 2000.

Justine part en vacances (title means "Justine Goes on Vacation"), Belin Editions (Parigi, Italy), 2000.

Gli acquarielli (title means "The Small Waterfall"), Edizioni Colors (Genoa, Italy), 2000.

La figlia del mago della pietra bianca, (title means "The Wizard's Daughter's White Stone"), Edizioni Falzea (Reggio Calabria, Italy), 2000.

Stefano Bordiglioni, *La chiave magica*, EL (S. Dorligio della Valle, Italy), 2001.

Angeletti has also illustrated other works for the publisher Einaudi Edizioni (Milan, Italy).

"JOURNEY THROUGH TIME" SERIES; SELF-ILLUSTRATED

Nefertari principessa d'Egitto, Instituto geografico De Agostini (Novara, Italy), 1998, translation published as *Nefertari, Princess of Egypt,* Oxford University Press (New York, NY), 1998.

Vulca l'etrusco, Instituto geografico De Agostini (Novara, Italy), 1998, translation published as *Vulca the Etruscan,* Oxford University Press (New York, NY), 1998.

L' uomo primitivo, Instituto geografico De Agostini (Novara, Italy), 1999, translation published as *The Cave Painter of Lascaux,* Oxford University Press (New York, NY), 2000.

Il Minotauro, mostro di Cnosso, Instituto geografico De Agostini (Novara, Italy), 1999, translation published as *The Minotaur of Knossos,* Oxford University Press (New York, NY), 2000.

Work in Progress

A collection of children's fiction for an Italian publisher; illustrations for *La Ballata del Soldato prima scapolo poi sposato,* written by Mara Picinich and Sergio Bozzi, for Falzea Edizioni.

Sidelights

Roberta Angeletti is the illustrator of more than a dozen books for children, including retellings in Italian of such classic stories as Pinocchio and Alice in Wonderland. Of her works, the "Journey Through Time" series is the most widely disseminated, being published simultaneously in Italian, French, and English. Both written and illustrated by Angeletti, the premise of these stories, geared to children aged two to five years, is that the main character travels back in time to visit a famous ancient historical site. In *Nefertari, Princess of Egypt,* the setting is along the Nile, in *The Minotaur of Knossos,* the story is set in the island of Crete, and so on. The illustrations in colored pencil are cartoon-like and "vigorous and colorful," according to Clive Barnes in a review of *Vulca the Etruscan* and *Nefertari, Princess of Egypt* for *Books for Keeps.* The stories play a secondary role to the illustrations, whose purpose is to introduce young readers to ancient civilizations. Brief nonfiction explanations follow each fictional text. While finding weaknesses in the stories, many reviewers nonetheless praised Angeletti's illustrations. Reviewing *The Cave Painter of Lascaux* in *School Library Journal,* Wendy Lukehart described Angeletti's cave art as "a respectable imitation of the real thing," going on to say that "the cartoon characters and perspectives are dynamic."

Angeletti told *SATA:* "I took to illustrating after a variety of experiences focusing on young people, both as a teacher and as an organizer of a drama workshop for which I also wrote scripts. Underlying my work is commitment, study, research, and creativity, as well as love and respect for children. Every day I experience the importance of books and of creative play with my own children. A book is a living object, a source of pleasure that is also tactile, manipulative. Children love making books because they can pour their needs and experiences into them. Pictures can be drawn, colored, cut out, and pasted on. The end result is something that can be browsed through, smelled, recounted, read and re-read, lost and found again, something to cuddle and gain knowledge from, a garden of funny-sounding words, of images calling to mind other images that may be captured on paper."

Biographical and Critical Sources

PERIODICALS

Archeo, November, 1998, Stefano Mammini, "Per i più Piccoli," p. 113.

Booklist, January 1, 2000, review of *The Minotaur of Knossos,* p. 922.

Books for Keeps, January, 1999, Clive Barnes, review of *Vulca the Etruscan,* p. 22

Horn Book Guide, spring, 2000, Erica L. Stahler, review of *Vulca the Etruscan,* p. 26.

Impressions, September, 1998, p. 19.

Publishers Weekly, January 3, 2000, review of *The Cave Painter of Lascaux,* p. 78.

School Library Journal, September, 1999, Cynthia M. Sturgis, review of *Nefertari, Princess of Egypt,* p. 174; February, 2000, Cheri Estes, review of *The Minotaur of Knossos,* p. 91; March, 2000, Wendy Lukehart, review of *The Cave Painter of Lascaux,* p. 178.

* * *

ATWATER-RHODES, Amelia 1984-

Personal

Born April 16, 1984, in Silver Spring, MD; daughter of William (a public-policy consultant in econometrics) and Susan (a school vice principal).

Addresses

Home—Concord, MA. *Agent*—c/o Kathleen Dunn, Random House, 201 East 50th St., New York, NY 10022.

Career

Author.

Awards, Honors

Quick Picks for Reluctant Young Readers citation, American Library Association, 2001, for *Demon in My View.*

Writings

In the Forests of the Night, Delacorte (New York, NY), 1999.

Demon in My View, Delacorte (New York, NY), 2000.

Work in Progress

Further novels in her vampire, witches, and shape shifters cycle.

Sidelights

Young adult author Amelia Atwater-Rhodes has proved herself a publishing phenomenon. At age fifteen, she found herself a literary celebrity after the publication of her vampire novel *In the Forests of the Night* in 1999. A resident of Concord, Massachusetts, she shares literary fame with a host of big names from the American literary canon who were also once residents in that town, including Henry David Thoreau, Ralph Waldo Emerson, Nathaniel Hawthorne, and Louisa May Alcott, yet she shares a similarity only with Alcott. Alcott also penned a novel as a teenager, but had to wait for adult fame to get her first book published. No such hardships attach to Atwater-Rhodes, who penned her first novel at age thirteen and then landed a publishing contract for it on her fourteenth birthday. Other early writers come to mind: Anne Frank, who began writing her diaries at thirteen, and S. E. Hinton, who wrote *The Outsiders* at sixteen.

The novelty of Atwater-Rhodes's youth attracted a great deal of media attention. Reviewers gave her debut book guarded praise, complimenting, in particular, its darkly atmospheric prose style. With publication of her second novel, *Demon in My View,* at age sixteen, however, the Atwater-Rhodes phenomenon appeared to have turned into a one-person publishing industry: two further books were quickly contracted and, with her shelves full of twenty-five more completed novels of witchcraft and vampirism and another couple of dozen percolating inside her computer, it seems the youthful novelist runs no risk of being discounted as a one-trick pony. But notoriety, if not fame, has not gone to the teenager's head. "Her mother still makes her do the dishes," commented Susan Carpenter in the *Los Angeles Times,* writing about a plethora of teen writers making it in publishing.

Atwater-Rhodes was born in Silver Spring, Maryland, on April 16, 1984. Her family subsequently moved to Concord, Massachusetts, where she attended Peabody Middle School and Concord Carlisle High School. Her mother, Susan, serves as a vice principal at Acton-Boxborough High School, while her father, William, is an econometrician employed as a public-policy consultant. While both parents acknowledged being horror fiction fans, loving in particular the novels of Anne Rice, Atwater-Rhodes particularly credits her mother with whetting her appetite for the genre. "My mother was a great influence on me, disturbing my mind," she told *USA Today* writer Katy Kelly. "She pretty much raised me on Stephen King and Dracula and aliens. She'd say, 'Just keep in mind: it's fiction. You're not supposed to take an ax to your neighbor. You're not to bite your friend.'"

The urge to create seized Atwater-Rhodes early. As a writer for *People Weekly* noted, at age three she was making up elaborate stories about a stuffed animal of hers named Meow Stripe, who ruled the upside-down world of Catland. The drawings she made to accompany

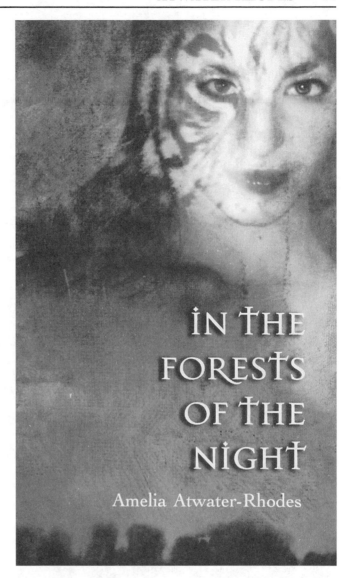

At age thirteen, Amelia Atwater-Rhodes created her tale of Risika, a vampire who must journey three hundred years into the past to confront her archenemy, Aubrey. (Cover illustration by Eric Dinyer.)

her stories were odd enough to prompt one of her teachers into thinking she had a learning disability. From there, she became interested in fantasy and futuristic science fiction before turning to vampires. When she was in the second grade, Atwater-Rhodes crafted a sci-fi novel, subsequently lost when she forgot her password. By age nine, she had discovered Christopher Pike's *The Last Vampire,* a book that served as an inspiration for her own efforts. Atwater-Rhodes explained to *SATA,* "It served as an inspiration by pointing out that vampires do not have to fit into stereotypes." As she told William Plummer and Tom Duffy of *People Weekly,* "I really liked the way [Pike] portrayed the character's voice."

Atwater-Rhodes began writing in earnest after completing the fifth grade in 1995. She found time after school, in the middle of the night, or whenever inspiration struck. Sometimes she would write sixty pages at a sitting, and while composing her published first novel, she balanced a tiger Beanie Baby on her head and took inspiration from the singer Alanis Morisette's *Jagged Little Pill* album, listening to several tracks over and over. Begun in her middle-school cafeteria, she completed *In the Forests of the Night,* the story of a 300-year-old vampire named Risika who was once a teenager in colonial Concord, in 1997. This human persona, Rachel Weatere, was born in 1684, but after centuries as an Undead, Risika has become adjusted to her status, and as Holly Koelling noted in a *Booklist* review, she "has grown distant from the mortal world. Humans are prey, needed solely for nourishment." Risika sleeps by day and goes hunting in New York City by night, seeking fresh blood. But one night, returning home, she discovers a black rose on her pillow just as she did centuries before, on the eve of her own changeover from human to vampire. She knows this is a sign, a challenge, from her archenemy, the powerful vampire Aubrey, who

In her second novel, Atwater-Rhodes relates the story of a teenage writer of horror fiction who feels somewhat of a misfit at school, then suddenly finds herself the object of a battle between vampires and witches. (Cover illustration by Cliff Nielsen.)

long ago helped arrange her transformation and who she believes murdered her human brother. Risika goes into action, deciding to confront her old enemy.

With completion of the novel, Atwater-Rhodes began looking for a literary agent. When her eighth grade class went to tour their future high school before moving in the next year as freshmen, Atwater-Rhodes met Tom Hart, an English teacher who was representing the humanities department. Recognizing Atwater-Rhodes from his own son's class a few years before, Hart asked the budding author how she was doing. A friend started bragging that Atwater-Rhodes wrote songs, poetry, and books, and was even trying to get a book published. Hart, having taught Atwater-Rhodes's sister Rachel a few year earlier and remembering what a good writer she was, offered to read Atwater-Rhodes's book and give her suggestions to where she should send it. After reading it, he signed on as her agent and sent the novel to Delacorte Press, a division of Random House. While celebrating her fourteenth birthday, Atwater-Rhodes received a phone call from Hart telling her that Delacorte had accepted the novel for publication. "Amy almost fell out of her chair," her mother told Plummer and Duffy for *People Weekly.* "She had huge eyes like she was in a cartoon." But a contract was only the beginning of a long and complicated revision process that took this debut novel through a dozen drafts before publication. "Once I got over the initial 'I hate my editor'," Atwater-Rhodes told Matt Peiken of the *Houston Chronicle,* "most of the editing process made sense." The young novelist also relied on her built-in support group, her group of friends who looked for mistakes in consistency and characterization.

Reviews of *In the Forests of the Night* were generally favorable, with some reservations. A reviewer for *Publishers Weekly* praised Atwater-Rhodes for being "skillful at building atmosphere, insightful in creating characters and imaginative in varying and expanding upon vampire lore," although the same writer also found evidence of "easy, adolescent cynicism." *Booklist*'s Koelling criticized the novel's story as "derivative" and "meandering," but went on to comment that Atwater-Rhodes's "use of language is surprisingly mature and polished for a thirteen-year-old writer." Koelling concluded, "Both the book's subject and the age of the author will ensure its popularity, especially with middle-schoolers, and it may encourage other young writers to pursue the craft." Kendra Nan Skellen, reviewing the novel in *School Library Journal,* felt that *In the Forests of the Night* "is well written and very descriptive, and has in-depth character development.... This first novel by an author with great ability and promise is sure to be popular."

Speaking with Atwater-Rhodes in a *New Yorker* interview, Melanie Thernstrom summed up the critical response to the rather startling first novel from a very young writer: "Amelia has an uncanny understanding of the kind of narrative that makes for a successful potboiler: she's skilled at creating characters the reader easily and instantly bonds with, and she's resourceful when it comes to putting them in jeopardy.... No one in the world of young-adult publishing has managed to come up with an analogy to Amelia: other early-teenage writers simply don't write coherent multiple-character, time-weaving, metafictional novels."

But Atwater-Rhodes was too busy working on her novels to bother reading reviews. "Horror keeps my interest," she said in a *Seventeen* interview. "I want to know what's happening to the characters. It's not like when you read a romance and know the main characters will eventually get together." "I read anything and everything," Atwater-Rhodes told *SATA,* "sci-fi horror just happens to be my most common interest." Thus Atwater-Rhodes stuck to her favorite topic for her second novel, *Demon in My View.* Like her first, it draws upon an elaborate genealogy of vampires and related supernatural beings that Atwater-Rhodes had created as background for her characters. By 2001, she told *SATA* that she has completed some twenty-five and a half novels and has forty-three uncompleted stories in her computer. As Thernstrom noted, "It will require a dizzying number of books to straighten ... out" the histories of her elaborate character genealogy, some 260 and growing. "Unless Amelia manages to achieve the immortality of her characters, her imagination has already extended beyond her own life span."

Demon in My View is a companion to the first novel, this time focusing on Jessica, a high school student who had a walk-on part in the previous novel. Jessica Ashley Allodola, who writes under the pen name of Ash Night, has just published her first novel, a vampire tale titled *Tiger, Tiger.* At school she is an outsider, something of a misfit, but when writing she goes into a dreamlike state, describing a world of vampires and witches with vivid and detailed accuracy. Jessica marvels at the way her fertile imagination works; what she doesn't realize is that these doings are, in fact, real. The characters she has spread across the pages of her book take great umbrage at Jessica's cheek. As a reviewer for *Publishers Weekly* put it, the vampires "aren't too happy that she's spilled their secrets and wittingly alerted vampire-hunting witches to the location of their undead village, New Mayhem." To reek vengeance, Aubrey, the nemesis of *In the Forests of the Night,* appears at Jessica's high school disguised as a new student, Alex. But Aubrey, attracted to Jessica's aura, is torn between a desire for revenge and the wish to turn her into a vampire like himself. Jessica, too, finds herself attracted to Aubrey. Meanwhile, the plot thickens with the arrival of another student, actually a witch of the Smoke Line, Caryn, who has arrived to protect Jessica from the vampires.

"The clash between the witches and the vampires and the truth of Jessica's birth take the plot down many twisting and suspenseful paths," according to Jane Halsall, writing in *School Library Journal.* Though Halsall felt there were "too many subplots and minor characters," the reviewer also thought that the book "comes alive when it focuses on the relationship between Jessica and Alex/Aubrey," two characters who are "finely drawn and believable." A reviewer for *Publishers Weekly* commented that "fantastic fights will keep readers turning pages quickly." This same writer concluded: "Atwater-Rhodes exercises impressive control over the complex lineages she has imagined, and she comes up with creative solutions to advance her story. Readers will drain this book in one big gulp."

However, not all reviewers were ready with praise for her second novel. Ellen Creager of the *Detroit Free Press* wrote that Atwater-Rhodes's second novel "is nowhere near as polished as the first" with its "compelling plot" and "immediacy." Creager felt that *Demon in My View* "is a bit too close to [the television series] 'Buffy the Vampire Slayer' for comfort" and also "a bit sloppy around the edges as it barrels along." Halsall, writing in *School Library Journal,* noted that the second novel "is not as tightly plotted or generally as well written as ... [the] first."

But whether the critics agree or not, Atwater-Rhodes's books have already found intense popularity with young readers. Whereas young adult books normally sell only in four-digit editions, *In the Forests of the Night* went back to press repeatedly, resulting in over 50,000 copies in print only a few months after publication. Such popularity has its residual effects. For an adolescent who once banded with other young girls for protection in middle school, Atwater-Rhodes has become a center of attention. However, she explained to *SATA,* "I haven't gotten much attention from my peers since the initial flurry.... The phenomena has mostly died away."

For Atwater-Rhodes, there is life after writing. She told Thernstrom that she could not imagine being a full-time writer because, as she put it, "I need to get away from it." In the same article, Atwater-Rhodes's mother noted that her daughter had other interests in addition to writing: "Amy's a doer, a collector, a person with a million interests.... She sews, she fences, is deep into the Internet, animals, ecology. I guess I would be surprised if in twenty years all she's doing is writing." As for the author's father, he has more immediate plans: "What I'm concerned about is that she does her homework," he told Thernstrom.

Atwater-Rhodes has plans to attend college even as she continues her writing career. In her interview with Vaughan of *Teen People,* she offered a clear-eyed assessment of her creative strengths at age fourteen: "As a teen, I bring a different perspective to writing. I can offer immediate emotions, experiences and insight that adult writers often have to reach back and find in order to write about them." And as she told Peiken, she is also getting used to celebrity. "At first, it was a little weird and unnerving to think lots of people would be reading my book, but now I like having fans." Her advice to other would-be writers? "Write when you feel like writing is my usual phrase," Atwater-Rhodes told *SATA.* "Write because you love to write. Write for yourself and no one else."

Biographical and Critical Sources

PERIODICALS

Booklist, June 1, 1999, Holly Koelling, review of *In the Forests of the Night,* p. 1812.

Book Report, November-December, 1999, p. 65.

Detroit Free Press, July 16, 2000, Ellen Creager, "15-year-old Is on a Roll with Her Second Novel," p. 5E.

Entertainment Weekly, March 26, 1999, p. 80.

Houston Chronicle, July 29, 1999, Matt Peiken, "Characters Speak to Author," p. 6.

Literary Cavalcade, October, 1999, p. 37.

Los Angeles Times, July 30, 2000, Susan Carpenter, "Teen Author's Novel Approach," p. E2.

New Yorker, October 18-25, 1999, Melanie Thernstrom, "The Craft," pp. 136, 138, 140-142.

People Weekly, August 9, 1999, William Plummer and Tom Duffy, "Author Rising," pp. 103-104.

Publishers Weekly, May 24, 1999, review of *In the Forests of the Night,* p. 80; April 24, 2000, review of *Demon in My View,* p. 92.

School Library Journal, July, 1999, Kendra Nan Skellen, review of *In the Forests of the Night,* p. 92; May 1, 2000, Jane Halsall, review of *Demon in My View,* p. 166.

Seventeen, June, 1999, Curtis Sittenfeld, "Freshman Debut."

Teen People, February, 1999, Kellie Vaughan, interview with Amelia Atwater-Rhodes.

USA Today, May 6, 1999, Katy Kelly, "A Writer Grave beyond Her Years," p. 1D.

B

BACHE, Ellyn
(Ellen Matthews; E. M. J. Benjamin, a joint pseudonym with husband, Terry Bache)

Personal

Surname rhymes with "h"; born in Washington, DC; daughter of Herman and Clara Olefsky; married Terry Bache, 1969; children: Beth, Matt, James, Ben. *Education:* University of North Carolina at Chapel Hill, B.A., 1964; University of Maryland at College Park, M.A., 1967. *Religion:* Jewish.

Addresses

Agent—c/o Author Mail, Banks Channel Books, P.O. Box 4446, Wilmington, NC 28403. *E-mail*—erbache@ aol.com; emjbenjamin@hotmail.com.

Career

Freelance writer and journalist. *Raleigh News and Observer,* book reviewer, 1995—; *Greenville News,* contributing writer. *Member:* Authors Guild.

Awards, Honors

Winner in Readers and Writers Series competition, 1987; winner of O. Henry Festival competition, 1989, for "Star"; winner of North Carolina Fiction Syndicate competition, 1989, for "Garden Pests"; Willa Cather Fiction Prize, 1992, for *The Value of Kindness;* finalist for Book of the Year Award in the young adult category, *Foreword Magazine,* 1999, for *Takedown.*

Writings

NOVELS

Safe Passage, Crown (New York, NY), 1988.
Festival in Fire Season, August House (Little Rock, AR), 1992.

The Activist's Daughter, Spinster's Ink (Duluth, MN), 1997.

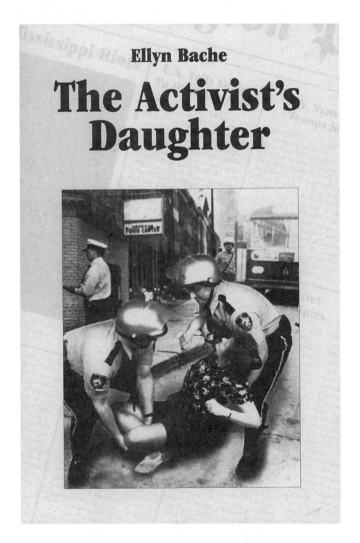

Set in the turbulent 1960s, Ellyn Bache's novel follows seventeen-year-old Beryl, the daughter of a civil rights activist, who must answer questions about her own beliefs. (Cover photo by Barbara Stitzer.)

(Under pseudonym E. M. J. Benjamin) *Takedown,* Banks Channel Books (Wilmington, NC), 1999.
Holiday Miracles: A Christmas/Hanukkah Story, Banks Channel Books (Wilmington, NC), 2001.

OTHER

(Under pseudonym Ellen Matthews) *Culture Clash* (nonfiction), Intercultural (Chicago, IL), 1982, revised edition (under name Ellyn Bache), 1989.
The Value of Kindness (stories), Helicon Nine (Kansas City, MO), 1993.
(With others, and editor) *What Locals Know about Wilmington and Its Beaches,* Banks Channel Books (Wilmington, NC), 1993.

Work represented in anthologies, including *O. Henry Festival Stories,* 1989. Contributor of stories, articles, and reviews to magazines, including *McCall's, Ascent, Southern Humanities Review, Seventeen, YM,* and *Virginia Country,* and newspapers. Editor of *Antietam Review,* 1983-85; books editor of *Encore,* 1986-89.

Adaptations

The novel *Safe Passage* was adapted as a film by Deena Goldstone, directed by Robert Allan Ackerman, and released by New Line Cinema in 1995.

Work in Progress

Ladies Who Don't, "a murder mystery about five 'older' ladies who helped start a woman's shelter twenty years earlier."

Sidelights

Novelist Ellyn Bache began her literary career as a freelance journalist for the *Washington Post* and *Washington Star,* working from home while her four children were young. She formerly edited the *Antietam Review* and in 1982 published her first book, *Culture Clash,* a journal about Vietnamese refugees in American. Subsequently she has focused on writing fiction, making her debut as a short-story writer with a story in *McCall's* magazine.

When her youngest child was in first grade, Bache wrote her first novel, *Safe Passage.* The book follows the story of a family torn apart as they wait for news about the possible death of one son. Percival, a serviceman stationed in Lebanon, is feared dead after terrorists bomb a U.S. Marine barrack in Beirut, an actual incident that took place in 1983. *Safe Passage* was later adapted for the 1995 film of the same name, starring Susan Sarandon and Sam Shepherd.

Her second novel, *Festival in Fire Season,* takes place in coastal North Carolina, during the 1980s, and revolves around the lives of a county commissioner, his teenage stepdaughter Cassie, and several others at her high school. "It's important to me that my novels be 'about' something," Bache once stated. "*Festival in Fire* season is on the surface about a wildfire that threatens a Southern coastal town during its azalea festival, but it's also about race relations." The novel caught reviewers' attention. In *Kirkus Reviews,* a critic remarked, "Bache's ability to evoke a particular time and place is remarkable." A *Publishers Weekly* critic and *Booklist* contributor Mary Romano Marks, each writing in separate reviews, both described the book as "compelling."

Bache visited another decade with her novel *The Activist's Daughter,* which takes place during the 1960s, and tells the story of Beryl, whose mother is an activist and absentee mother. Beryl attends the University of North Carolina at Chapel Hill and becomes involved in a number of activities, though she tries to steer clear of the activism that has marred her relationship with her mother. Some of the issues Bache takes up in this novel include racism, sexism, and bias against the handicapped. "While I want the underlying themes to be serious," Bache once said, "it's also important to me that the work itself be funny, entertaining, suspenseful, not ponderous." According to reviewers, Bache succeeded on several accounts. "Bache capably reflects the complexities of this volatile period," creating a "solid and absorbing third novel," declared a *Publishers Weekly* contributor. "Those studying the '60s and those of us who actually were there will take interest in this novel," predicted Ann Bouricius in *Voice of Youth Advocates.*

In 1999, Bache published the teen novel *Takedown,* written with her husband under the pen name, E. M. J. Benjamin, about a high school senior who thinks the big challenge of his year will be the wrestling championship, until he begins having seizures. The diagnosis of epilepsy throws everything he values into doubt—his wrestling career, driving privileges, relationships with friends, and even his college scholarship—until, during the course of one grueling wrestling season, he learns that a "takedown" in life can be handled with the same grace as a takedown on the wrestling mats. Termed "an exciting read with a positive lesson" by a reviewer for *Today's Librarian,* a "fast-paced novel with emotional depth" by a *Greensboro News & Record* critic, and "highly" recommended in a *Kliatt* review for "middle school readers, especially reluctant readers, because it moves rapidly and has a simple, easy-to-follow plot," the book became a *Forward Magazine* Book of the Year Award finalist.

Bache's 2001 novel, *Holiday Miracles: A Christmas/Hanukkah Story,* is the first book of its type—mainstream fiction about an interfaith family celebrating both holidays when their son gets sick and doesn't recover, calling into question many of the religious choices they've made.

In addition to her novels, Bache has published a collection of sixteen short stories, titled *The Value of Kindness,* a "large-hearted collection" dealing with the lives of strong women, according to a *Kirkus Reviews* critic. Among these stories are "Pigeons," about an elderly woman who ends up in court when her neighbors demand she not feed the pigeons at her home. In the title story, a middle-aged woman deals with menopause and her disappointment at the sexually irresponsible behavior of her teenage son. For this collection, Bache won the Willa Cather Fiction Prize.

Bache told *SATA:* "I think of myself as a mainstream fiction writer who deals with women's issues—raising children in *Safe Passage;* the second-class status of women college students in the sixties in *The Activist's Daughter;* and the challenges women over age fifty face in my current work in progress."

Biographical and Critical Sources

PERIODICALS

Bloomsbury Review, May-June, 1994, Patricia Dubrava Keuning, review of *The Value of Kindness,* pp. 11-12.

Booklist, February 1, 1992, Mary Romano Marks, review of *Festival in Fire Season,* p. 1016.

Greensboro News & Record, October 17, 1999, review of *Takedown.*

Kirkus Reviews, June 1, 1988, review of *Safe Passage,* p. 776; December 15, 1991, review of *Festival in Fire Season,* p. 1547; June 15, 1993, review of *The Value of Kindness,* p. 736; March 1, 1997, review of *The Activist's Daughter,* p. 316.

Kliatt, November, 2000, review of *Takedown,* p. 11.

New York Times Book Review, January 22, 1989, Martha Southgate, review of *Safe Passage,* p. 22.

Publishers Weekly, January 1, 1992, review of *Festival in Fire Season,* p. 46; July 5, 1993, review of *The Value of Kindness,* p. 67; April 7, 1997, review of *The Activist's Daughter,* p. 76.

Today's Librarian, January, 2000, review of *Takedown.*

Voice of Youth Advocates, December, 1997, Ann Bouricius, review of *The Activist's Daughter,* p. 313.

Washington Post Book World, August 21, 1988, Melissa Greene, review of *Safe Passage,* p. 6.

ON-LINE

Ellyn Bache Web site, http://www.ellynbache.com (August 1, 2001).

*   *   *

BEIL, Karen Magnuson 1950-

Personal

Born February 15, 1950, in Boston, MA; daughter of Victor (a pattern maker for aeronautics) and Dorothy (Hall) Magnuson; married James A. Beil (a forester), February 24, 1973; children: Kimberly Erika, Kirsten Annika. *Education:* Attended Upsala College, 1967-68; Syracuse University, B.A. (cum laude), 1971. *Politics:* Independent. *Religion:* "Independent." *Hobbies and other interests:* Reading, traveling, walking, dancing, swimming, building and flying kites, listening to music, taking photographs (especially of people).

Addresses

Home—3048 New Williamsburg Dr., Schenectady, NY 12303.

Career

Freelance writer and editor. City News Bureau of Chicago, Chicago, IL, reporter, 1971-72; New York State Department of Environmental Conservation, Albany, NY, research editor, 1973-75, assistant editor, 1975-76, editor, 1976-78, associate director of information services for *The Conservationist* and *New York State Environmental Notice Bulletin,* 1978-81. Worked as a lifeguard, face painter, scientific translator, and magazine writer. *Member:* Children's Literary Connection (cofounder, vice president, treasurer, and member of the executive board of directors), Society of Children's Book Writers and Illustrators, National Audubon Society, Cape Cod Museum of Natural History.

Awards, Honors

Fire in Their Eyes: Wildfires and the People Who Fight Them was named a top 20 nonfiction book by the National Council of Teachers of English, 2000, a Quick Picks selection for reluctant readers, American Library Association, 2000, to the Maine Students Book Award list, 2000-2001, a nonfiction honor book, *Voice of Youth Advocates*, and a Young Adults Top Forty book, Pennsylvania School Librarians Association.

Writings

Grandma According to Me, illustrated by Ted Rand, Doubleday (New York, NY), 1992.

A Cake All for Me!, illustrated by Paul Meisel, Holiday House (New York, NY), 1998.

Fire in Their Eyes: Wildfires and the People Who Fight Them, Harcourt Brace (San Diego, CA), 1999.

Contributor to periodicals, including *National Geographic World, Ranger Rick, Lady Bug,* and *Storyworks.*

Work in Progress

Moove Over!, "a counting book about a rude cow in an overcrowded trolley," for Holiday House; retelling of a Norwegian folktale, and a historical novel set in the 1930s.

Sidelights

Karen Magnuson Beil told *SATA:* "I grew up in the hills of Connecticut, the only child in a family of story-loving, creative people. My mother was a children's librarian and bird carver (shore birds, not turkeys). My father, ready with a poem, joke, or story for every occasion, brought history to life with stories of his sailing days during the Depression. My aunts were children's book illustrators. Books were essential, like food, in my family.

"When I was five, I loved stories and books—their language, their rhythm, their energy. My mother read my favorites over and over. But when I was six, Dick, Jane, and their lifeless pets, Spot and Fluff, taught me that reading was dull. I learned to hate to read. Lucky for me,

Seven, eight, chop and grate.

1 CUP

SOW BRAND

CHOCOLATE CHIPS

Using counting rhymes, Karen Magnuson Beil composed the tale of a pig who bakes a delicious cake and then must decide if he will share it. (From A Cake All for Me!, *illustrated by Paul Meisel.)*

mother was tenacious. Unlucky for her and probably embarrassing too (she was the librarian in my elementary school), I preferred to do most anything but read. By the time I was nine, she was waging a quiet war, sneaking the latest books into my room, inviting authors to our school: Elizabeth George Speare, Oliver Butterworth, and even her old childhood friend Virginia Haviland, folktale collector and children's librarian for the Library of Congress. She was invincible. I didn't stand a chance.

"After school one day my mother asked me to shelve some library books while she went to a meeting. I picked up a biography of Jane Addams, illustrated in black silhouettes. I read the first page and couldn't put it down. This 'Jane' saved people. She never said dumb stuff like 'Look Dick, look. See Spot run.' After I'd read all the biographies in my mother's library, I moved on to historical fiction, nature stories, adventure, and all the rest.

"From then on my favorite trips of summer were our excursions to buy library books at the H. R. Huntting bookbindery in Chicopee, Massachusetts. There, my mother's friend Ben Silberman always let me choose

two books to take home—gifts from him to his only school-age customer.

"I am convinced that, just like love, there is a book for every person. It only takes one book to spark a whole lifetime of reading. I believe this deeply. When I visit schools, I tell kids who hate to read to keep looking for their book.

"After graduating from college, I searched Chicago for a job. I failed miserably at dreaming up a mattress commercial (it put the boss to sleep). I tried editing a college math textbook (let's just say, math was the only course I managed not to pass in college—I was too busy reading). I finally landed a job as a news reporter. My first assignment: a five-alarm fire. Gosh, I was a country kid. What's 'five-alarm?' Very spicy chili? What a terrific job that turned out to be. I learned to meet fast deadlines and to interview people—cops, robbers, con artists, judges—to ask the tough questions (and to read upside down).

"When our first daughter turned two, I left my day job as an editor to learn how to make play-dough. While I was practicing my defensive maneuvers to duck flying food, my daughter was learning how easy it was to delay bedtime by sweet-talking me into reading books. And I fell in love all over again with the rhythms and art and beautiful language of children's books.

"I already had a stack of rejected manuscripts before my mother asked me to write a book about wrinkles. *Grandma According to Me* was written for her. Her friends had been talking about their grandkids. One told her grandmother her skin 'didn't fit her face any more.' Another was worried that her grandmother's face had 'cracked.' Try as I might, I couldn't turn an explanation of wrinkles into an exciting book. So I took it from a different angle. How do people see themselves? How does a granddaughter see her grandmother? Is it different from the grandmother's view of herself? As I thought about my mother's relationship with my daughters, the book seemed to write itself. It was a personal tribute to my mother and a celebration of the special relationship between grandmothers and granddaughters. I love that teachers use it to teach point-of-view. I'm delighted how many people have given this book to their mothers and grandmothers. Best of all was the first grader who 'loved it because it made (him) feel.'

"I loved working on *Fire in Their Eyes.* It was an adventure right from the start. The idea grabbed me over dinner one night as I listened to my husband and friends talk about fighting forest fires in California. Their stories had everything—adventure, danger, nature, and heroes who were both men and women. I could hardly wait to get home to start making notes. I wanted to write a book that would keep kids on the edges of their seats, just as I'd been. To do this, I needed first-hand experience. So I worked two seasons on a prescribed burn crew. I interviewed firefighters across the country. I photographed new smoke jumpers at a tough training camp in Montana. Ten years later, the research and interviews were done. Then the hardest part became deciding which stories to leave out so there'd be room for photos in the sixty-four-page book.

"*A Cake All For Me,* about a hungry pig who bakes a cake all for himself, came from playing with words one morning. A little book about numbers sat on my desk, handmade by my aunt, Bette Darwin (illustrator of Beverly Cleary's book, *Socks*). The old rhyme 'One, two, buckle my shoe' showed up in my doodles. It always left me so unsatisfied as a child because it never made sense. 'A big fat hen? Dig and delve? Maids a-courting?' Huh? What? I decided this was my chance to make some sense of it.

"Back then my office was in a closet in my kitchen. The kitchen was the place where my daughters got their early starts experimenting in math and science. So I had my setting. And I was hungry, really hungry. So I had my character: me. (The kitchen, by the way, is not a good place to work unless you're a chef.) But when my editor asked later what kind of animal the character was, I had to confess I hadn't thought about it. She wanted an animal. So, who would eat a whole cake? Had to be a PIG! Next Piggy had to have a recipe. My younger

daughter and her friends spent the rest of the summer as taste-testers. They were tough critics. Pineapple? No! Coconut? Yuck. Walnuts, lemon, chopped peanuts? No, no, no! Spinach jello? (Just kidding.) Chocolate chips? Yes! It was unanimous. After that, the book was a piece of cake."

Beil is a freelance editor and writer and the author of children's books. Illustrated by Ted Rand, Beil's *Grandma According to Me* portrays how a preschooler views her grandmother. The little girl finds her grandmother beautiful, as the elderly woman has a "comfortable" figure and "story lines," not wrinkles. "The childlike text contains several striking images," wrote Joy Fleishhacker in the *School Library Journal,* adding that the book conveys a "warmhearted mood." *Booklist* contributor Christie Sylvester observed that *Grandma According to Me* is "lovingly told from the child's point of view."

School Library Journal contributor Pamela K. Bomboy called Beil's *A Cake All for Me!* "a tasty treat." It features a pig who initially bakes a cake for himself, but later decides to share his treat with visiting friends. Beil uses counting rhymes to tell readers how to make the cake: "One, two, get out the moo./Three, four, open and pour." Illustrator Paul Meisel's pictures depict the happy chef sifting and mixing ingredients and performing other baking-related tasks. A *Publishers Weekly* reviewer commented that the book contains "high spirits and simple pleasures." For hungry readers, *A Cake All for Me!* includes recipes for a cake and frosting.

Beil wrote *Fire in Their Eyes: Wildfires and the People Who Fight Them* for slightly older children. The author has written extensively about environmental conservation and includes her own photographs in the book. The photographs depict the work of firefighters, including smoke jumpers—people who parachute from airplanes to fight forest fires. Photographs include a tree exploding in flames and a man repairing his parachute. Beil profiles firefighters and describes their training, methods, and tools. *Booklist* contributor Randy Meyer wrote that Beil evokes "the drama, excitement, and danger of their job."

Beil commented to *SATA:* "Why do I write for children? How could I not? Children are the best of audiences. They are perceptive, and full of important questions. I want to write books that turn kids into readers, the kind of books I would have loved as a child—books that make a reader laugh and cry, explore new ideas, try on somebody else's life or time. I want to write books that make a difference.

"When I write, I realize I'm part of an ancient circle of readers and storytellers inventing and passing stories along, like the squeeze of a hand. Sitting beside me is my mother who invited me in when she opened my very first book and took me to this place where words make magic."

Biographical and Critical Sources

BOOKS

Beil, Karen Magnuson, *A Cake All for Me!*, illustrated by Paul Meisel, Holiday House, 1998.
Beil, Karen Magnuson, *Grandma According to Me*, illustrated by Ted Rand, Doubleday, 1992.

PERIODICALS

Booklist, December 1, 1992, p. 674; May 1, 1999.
Children's Book Review Service, December, 1992, p. 37.
Children's Book Watch, November, 1992, p. 4.
Conservationist, September-October, 1988, p. 52.
Horn Book Magazine, spring, 1993, p. 21.
Publishers Weekly, August 17, 1998, p. 71.
School Library Journal, February, 1993, p. 68; September, 1998, p. 164.

* * *

BENJAMIN, E. M. J.
See BACHE, Ellyn

* * *

BERCAW, Edna Coe 1961-

Personal

Born April 19, 1961, in Cambridge, MA; daughter of Kenneth Coe (a lawyer) and Mary Ryan (a genetic scientist); married Joseph A. Bercaw III (a business owner), February, 1987; children: Joseph A. IV, Luke A., Jennifer L. *Education:* Syracuse University, B.A., 1984. *Religion:* Presbyterian.

Addresses

Office—3220 Route 22 W., Branchburg, NJ 08876. *E-mail*—ecbercaw@aol.com.

Career

Writer. Hunterdon County Park System, writing instructor; Eagle Fence and Supply, Inc., marketing director. *Member:* Society of Children's Book Writers and Illustrators, Warren Writers Group.

Writings

Halmoni's Day, illustrated by Robert Hunt, Dial Books for Young Readers (New York, NY), 2000.

Sidelights

Edna Coe Bercaw told *SATA:* "Growing up as a second-generation Korean-American, I never learned to speak

Edna Coe Bercaw

Korean and only visited Korea twice as a young child. Hence, I knew very little about my own Korean heritage. When I married my husband, a non-Korean, and we had children, I realized that the only way they could ever learn about their 'Korean half' was through exposure to the traditions and customs I myself had never learned.

"Today my children enjoy a wonderful bond with their own *halmoni* (Korean word for grandmother), my mother, and together we are exploring and experiencing what it means to be a Korean-American, past, present, and future."

Biographical and Critical Sources

PERIODICALS

Booklist, November 1, 2000, Linda Perkins, review of *Halmoni's Day*, p. 545.
School Library Journal, August, 2000, Marian Drabkin, review of *Halmoni's Day*, p. 144.

* * *

Autobiography Feature

Melvin Berger

1927-

"Mr. Berger," the high-school guidance counselor said to my father, "we've got the results of Melvin's vocational guidance tests. He shows two areas of strength—science and music. We would guess that he would do well in either career."

She then turned to me. "What are your feelings? What would you like to study in college?"

My main love and interest at the time was playing the viola (an instrument like the violin, but a little bigger and with a deeper tone), so it was easy for me to answer, "I'd like to be a musician."

"That's fine," she said. "But my advice to you is to get a degree in science first, then go out and try to get a job in an orchestra. If you find one, that's fine. If not, you'll always have your science training to fall back on."

The suggestion struck me as very sensible. So while continuing to study and play the viola, I enrolled at the City College of New York, working for a degree in electrical engineering. From then on, until today, science and music, with the important addition of writing, have dominated my working life.

I was born on August 23, 1927, in Brooklyn, New York. Both my parents had emigrated from Russia to this country. My mother, Esther Hochman, arrived in New York from Minsk in the year 1897, at the age of ten. My father, Ben Berger, who grew up in a town near Odessa, came to the United States three years later, when he was twenty years old.

The third youngest of eight children, my mother had four sisters and three brothers. Her father and oldest sister had settled in America first, followed later by my grandmother and the rest of the children. The family settled on the Lower East Side of New York City, a center of Russian-Jewish immigrant life around the turn of the century. She advanced far enough in school to become a bookkeeper.

My father's family, which was much smaller, included only a younger brother and sister. His brother, Louis, gave him the money for his passage to America. Louis had actually found it on the street of their town. He wanted my father to leave Russia because he was about to be drafted into the Czar's army.

There was no one waiting on the dock to welcome my father to New York. My grandfather had emigrated earlier, but he was living in Providence, Rhode Island, at the time.

Very soon after he came to this country, my father had the misfortune to slip on the ice and break his arm. Alone, and without money to live on, he had to stay in the hospital until his arm healed.

Although mother had been a bookkeeper before she and my father married, on August 24, 1926, she did not work outside the home while I was growing up. Mostly she looked after me, an only child, and helped Dad run his small upholstery business. The three of us lived in an apartment above the small shop in Brooklyn. While doing his errands, my father would sometimes let me ride next to

Melvin Berger

"My mother, Esther Hochman (left), with her brother Sam and sister Dora a few years after her arrival in America."

overnight, his shop had been burglarized. Every single plate—his whole year's work—was gone. As though that was not enough of a tragedy, the exact same thing happened the following year!

In those Depression times, money was very scarce. To put bread on the table, my parents rented out one of the rooms in our three-room apartment. For several years, our family slept in one room. On weekends we either had company or visited one of my mother's brothers or sisters—Harry, Sam, Dora, Henrietta, Lena, Fanny, or Julius, or my father's brother Louis or sister Rose. Everyone usually sat around talking, eating, and laughing during those parties. While the adults socialized, I would fall asleep, usually on my mother's lap.

My neighborhood friends and classmates at the elementary school I attended also came from poor homes. But to my mind, we had less money than any of them. At a summer recreational program, an acting group was going to perform the Gilbert and Sullivan operetta, *Pirates of Penzance*. Admission was one nickel. Most of my friends were going and I wanted very much to be there, too. But I didn't feel it was right to ask for the five cents. Later, when I told my mother about missing the show, she was very upset.

Not long after starting school, I acquired a violin. My older cousin, Matty, who played already, gave me the small-sized instrument that he had outgrown. According to family lore, I pretended to play this violin, which had no strings, using a yardstick for the bow. Around second grade, my mother found a government-sponsored music school that gave free music lessons. After one month of studies my teacher put me on the stage to play "Lightly Row" in a school concert. Everyone agreed I was going to be a famous violinist one day.

A lot of the cultural interest I developed came from my cousin, Vivienne Hochman, who nurtured me during most of my growing-up years. Vivienne brought me wonderful leather pants from Switzerland and a beautiful school bag from England. She gave me stamps for my collection, took me to concerts and Broadway shows, introduced me to eating in restaurants, bought me books, and invited me to spend my summers at her sleep-away camp.

My years at Cunningham Junior High School went by very fast. A special program, called Rapid Advance, allowed me to complete two years of schooling in one year. Since I had also skipped a term in elementary school, I then entered Lincoln High School a year and a half ahead of my age.

Always an avid reader, I now decided to go through every book in the local library. Starting at the beginning of the fiction section, I methodically plowed through book after book. But after a few weeks I gave up this hopeless task and began to read only what I really enjoyed.

It was in high school that I first tried my hand at writing. I wrote a short story about a student (not very different from me) who was bored in school and always annoyed the teacher. The hero grew up and became a teacher himself. To his great dismay, though, he had a pupil who tormented him just as he had tormented his teacher. So proud was I of the story that I decided to publish it myself. I had once bought a copy of Edgar Allen Poe's *Tales* on sale for twenty-five cents. At that rate, I figured out, publishing a small edition of my short story would cost

him in his delivery truck, which he called a "Tin Lizzie." The smell of gasoline in the garage where he parked the "Tin Lizzie" is still a fondly recalled memory.

When I was four years old, my dad gave up his upholstery business and we moved to an apartment in Brighton Beach, also in Brooklyn, but very close to the ocean. By this time his brother Louis had come to America and become a furrier. He offered my father a chance to work for him. The job was to sew together small pieces and scraps of Persian lamb skins into big squares called "plates." The plates were then used to make collars and add decorative touches to coats. After a while, my father opened a similar business of his own.

For a whole year, starting in the spring, my father would sew together the fur plates. A few of them would be sold during the year. But most of them would be stored in a warehouse. The following spring he would take the whole year's work out of storage and sell the plates to buyers.

One spring evening, my father came home from work. He looked tired and worn, but entered without a word to either my mother or me. Walking to his favorite seat near the window he opened up the newspaper and started to read. Then suddenly, he put down the paper and began to cry.

In a choked voice he told us how, a few days earlier, he had received all the plates back from the warehouse. But very little. It was left to Uncle Herman, a practical man who was a printer by trade, to convince me how little I understood the publishing business.

*

On December 7, 1941, the Japanese bombed the American naval base at Pearl Harbor, drawing America into World War II. But that fateful day is seared in my memory for another reason. That is when we learned that my mother had cancer. Despite surgery and radiation treatment, the disease spread very rapidly. She died on July 5, 1943.

At about the same time, my father developed a terrible allergy to fur. He had difficulty breathing whenever he was near the skins, and the parts of his arms that actually touched the fur became red and painfully inflamed. In despair, he went back to his old upholstery work. But instead of renting a shop, he only took on small jobs that he could do in the customer's houses. Getting work meant leaving cards in mailboxes and then going door-to-door giving estimates. To do the job, he had to drag his tools and materials around, working on the heavy pieces of furniture in small, crowded apartments. The pay was a pittance.

My father and I lived a sad life without my mother. I graduated high school in January 1944 and entered City College as an electrical engineering student. But I was moving through life in a daze. The school work was extremely difficult. To add to the pressure, I was taking viola lessons and was playing three afternoons a week in a training orchestra for young musicians. The other two afternoons, I worked in my Uncle Lou's fur shop, soaking and stretching the Persian lamb paws before they were sewn together into plates. Between studying for school, practicing the viola, working and spending at least three hours a day on the subway, I was always exhausted. Any time I sat down I fell asleep. I even developed the ability to doze standing up in the subway!

By the start of 1945, I was close to the breaking point. I found it increasingly difficult to keep up the pace. The only activity that I really enjoyed was playing the viola. In May I heard about an opening for a violist in the New Orleans Philharmonic. After taking the audition, I was offered the job. Although it would not start until the following October, I dropped out of college, just weeks before the end of the semester. Needing a change of scenery and time to recuperate, I took a bus to Woodstock, New York, an artists' and musicians' colony in the Catskill Mountains just north of New York City. On my arrival I went to bed and slept for some forty-eight hours before venturing out of my room.

I loved being in New Orleans, devoting myself to the viola, and for the first time having a little money in my pocket. After a season in New Orleans, at $42.50 a week, I moved to the more prestigious orchestra in Columbus, Ohio, where I earned $60 a week. Finally I got a position in the outstanding Pittsburgh Symphony paying $85 a week. The salaries, although very low by today's standards, were considered high at that time—and seemed absolutely munificent to me.

Playing in orchestras was a splendid experience! Not only did I hear and play great music, see new parts of the country, meet interesting people, sleep in hotels, eat in fine restaurants, but I earned a good living at the same time.

Yet, after three years, I felt something was missing. I began to regret the lack of a college education. There were too many things that I wanted to know about music and other subjects. I started to look for a way to return to college.

The Eastman School of Music of the University of Rochester in Rochester, New York, came to my rescue. Howard Hanson, director of the school, awarded me a full scholarship. And the Rochester Philharmonic, which rehearsed in the school's Eastman Theater, offered me a position in the viola section. Thus, I was able to carry a full program, while supporting myself by playing in the orchestra. In fact, from time to time I was able to send a few dollars home to help out my father. With the credits I had previously earned at City College, I received a bachelor's degree in three years.

Equipped with a college diploma, I returned to New York City and found a double position as Lecturer in the Music Department of City College and Fellow in the Music Department of Teacher's College of Columbia University. The latter appointment also enabled me to get a master's degree in Music Education, although I had no intention at that time of ever teaching music.

"A 'walk' on the boardwalk in Coney Island with my parents when I was six months old."

Sometimes, as we all know, fate works in mysterious ways. While still teaching at City College I helped to found the Nassau School of Music at Hicksville, Long Island, a suburb of New York City. When asked to teach music in the nearby Plainview Public Schools a few mornings a week, I thought it an ideal way to fill in the time when there was little to do at the music school. It seemed like a good idea for a year or two. By the following year, though, the Plainview job was offered to me full-time. It was a hard decision to make. But since I was already based on Long Island, I decided to leave City College and go into school music.

My duties at Plainview were mostly in the high school, teaching the string instruments and conducting the orchestra. Afternoons and on Saturdays, I taught at the music school. In between I performed as a freelance musician in New York City and on Long Island. To make matters a little more complicated, I "officially" lived with my father at home in Brooklyn, even though I also had a small apartment in the music-school building. While it was now in a car instead of on the subways, I still commuted several hours a day.

Melvin at age four with his parents before moving to Brighton Beach.

Life continued in this hectic way until the summer of 1957 when I was playing in the Symphony of the Air at the Empire State Music Festival in Ellenville, New York. One afternoon as I was sitting on the porch of the Arrowhead Lodge, the hotel at which I was staying, I saw a most attractive young woman arrive at the hotel for the July 4 weekend. Striking up a conversation, I discovered she was Gilda Shulman from the Bronx, up to attend the Music Festival. Throughout the season, we spent a lot of time together. When the Festival was over and I returned home, I added another stop—Gilda's home in the Bronx—to my Plainview-Hicksville-Brooklyn commute. In the middle of September, Gilda and I decided to get married.

Our wedding took place on December 22, 1957. The date was chosen because both of us were teaching and that was the beginning of our Christmas vacation. Although I foolishly cut short our honeymoon in upstate New York in order to play a concert in New York City, we made up for it by spending over two months in Europe the following summer. Just before leaving for Europe we bought our first house, a small one in Levittown, Long Island, a suburb of New York City. A little over a year later, we started our family with Eleanor, born January 29, 1959. Nancy arrived twenty months after that, on September 25, 1960.

*

Some months before Nancy was born, an unexpected meeting turned my life around, although I was hardly aware anything momentous was happening at the time. My cousin, Vivienne Hochman, introduced me to her friend, Julius Schwartz, science editor for the children's book division of the well-known publisher, McGraw-Hill. At the end of a very stimulating conversation about the relationship between science and music, Julius told me that there was a great demand for good children's books. In 1957 the Russians had launched *Sputnik,* the first step in the exploration of space. This made the Americans realize how badly they were falling behind in science and science education. To help us catch up, he said, schools and libraries needed books on science topics for young people.

Julius asked me to write a book that would explain to children the science of making music with instruments and recordings. Although the idea of writing children's books had never before occurred to me, I didn't even hesitate. The prospect of writing on two of my favorite subjects was irresistible. I immediately agreed to prepare an outline and description of the book, which I titled *Science and Music.*

Right from the start, Gilda worked with me—reading, suggesting, editing, typing, and helping in any number of ways. In fact, she often reminds me that I brought the proofs of *Science and Music* to her in the hospital right after Nancy's birth, saying that since she had nothing else to do she might as well proofread the manuscript!

Science and Music (1961) was very successful. It went into six printings and the editors at McGraw-Hill asked for another book. I suggested various topics. The one that caught their interest was a book on the effect of science, politics, and philosophy on contemporary music. But the more we discussed the concept the more it changed. Eventually it evolved into a book on the major scientific achievements of recent times and their effects on everyone's lives.

Conducting the high school orchestra at Plainview, Long Island, after college.

Entitled *Triumphs of Modern Science* (1964), the book sold many copies, mostly to libraries and schools. Most notable, perhaps, was the book's large number of foreign publications. It appeared in over twenty different translations, including Spanish, French, Portuguese, Vietnamese, and Hindi. One interesting version, printed in Japan, was to be used to teach English to Japanese students. In actual fact, *Triumphs of Modern Science* became the most-translated book published by McGraw-Hill.

Like a crusader, I hoped *Triumphs of Modern Science* would alert people to the amazing advances in all branches of science. The new research findings were clearly much too important to be left to the scientists alone. My goal was, and still is, to bring a knowledge and understanding of the latest scientific discoveries to young people in a readable and interesting way.

Having always closely followed news reports on science topics, I now kept up with the latest findings in nuclear energy, medicine, computers, space exploration, pollution, and the environment, with a view to working up these ideas into books for young people. In addition to being concerned about the latest advances in science, I also wanted to provide readers with a clear grasp of basic scientific principles. My chance to write a number of very fundamental science books also came about through a casual meeting with an editor.

Since 1961 we had been spending our summers on Cape Cod in Massachusetts, enjoying the beautiful scenery, swimming, and meeting some very interesting people who vacationed there. Through a friend who was also on the Cape, I met Margaret Farrington Bartlett, the editor of Coward-McCann's "Science Is What and Why" series of science books for very young children.

Margaret and I talked about a book that would explain atoms to six- to ten-year-olds, *without* ever talking down to them. We agreed to include some of the latest discoveries about atoms. The book was to be forty-eight pages long with many illustrations, so that the typewritten manuscript could be no more than four or five pages.

Any ideas that I had about how easy it would be to write a four-page book were quickly dispelled. There was so much to say and so little space in which to say it. Every word was essential to telling the story. It is possible that *Atoms* (1968) went through more revisions than any of my other books.

Margaret had a unique way of editing. Basically, she went through the manuscript with a fine-tooth comb. At every word or concept that bothered her, she inserted a large, bright red question mark. Rarely was she specific. She preferred to let me rethink the problem and find a new solution. Most often the changes necessitated a reworking of the entire text. But each revision brought us closer and closer together. When she was finally pleased, I felt extremely satisfied as well.

Atoms taught me a great deal about writing for very young readers. Among the things I discovered, for example, is that the writer and the illustrator rarely meet before the book is published. The only drawings that I was shown in advance for *Atoms* were those that I had to check for scientific accuracy. Otherwise, the artist worked from the text independently. It seemed odd to have no idea of the finished product until I saw the printed books.

"Gilda and I drinking the first toast at our wedding, December 22, 1957."

*

In 1963, Gilda and I thought it would be wonderful to take a sabbatical from teaching and live for a year in England. I signed up to study for an advanced degree at London University. And for living accommodations we were able to exchange houses with an English family. In August 1964, we moved with Eleanor and Nancy, now aged five and three, along with thirteen fully loaded suitcases, to Great Bookham, a suburb south of London.

We had not even unpacked when a messenger brought us a telegram with the shocking news that my father had died on August 15, 1964. Although he had suffered a severe stroke the year before and been hospitalized, he seemed to be in stable condition when we sailed for England. The pain of learning that he had died, with us so far away, was nearly unbearable. Since it was impossible for all of us to return, I rushed by myself to the airport for the difficult flight home.

After this dreadful start, the rest of our year in Great Bookham was really quite wonderful. Gilda taught part-time in an English elementary school, enriching the children's regular classroom work by answering their many questions about life in America. Both girls attended school. Ellie was in the English equivalent of first grade at the Eastwick School; Nancy was at the Spinney Hill Nursery School. And I commuted to London each morning, taking courses for an advanced degree at London University, as well as practicing for a recital and two solo recordings with the English Chamber Orchestra.

In England I began my life-long fascination with old scientific instruments. Often bored while Gilda browsed in the English antique shops, I was one day unexpectedly attracted by an exquisite old brass microscope. Stunned by its beauty and amazed to think that researchers had used it for about two hundred years, I bought it. From then on I took a new interest in "antiquing." Now it is I who drags

Gilda to musty shops, hoping to find microscopes, telescopes, scales, balances, medical kits, or other paraphernalia of years gone by. Among my collectibles are some extremely interesting and valuable "scopes," but my favorite piece is still a very old Chinese balance that was once used for weighing out opium!

While I did some literary research in England, most of my writing was for the thesis that was required by my studies at London University. A motoring trip through England, however, proved to be the inspiration for a whole series of children's books that I was to write some years later.

I had long known about Jodrell Bank, the largest movable radio telescope in the world, which was located in the Midland region of England. One day, when we were in the vicinity, we were able to arrange a visit to the world-famous observatory. As we approached the huge, white, gleaming dishlike antenna, we were startled to see it suddenly looming up over the calm, peaceful cow pasture. In a nearby laboratory, we met the scientists who worked there. They graciously shared with us some of their findings made possible by this astounding new tool of science.

The glimpse we had of Jodrell Bank was so intriguing that we thought of visiting other scientific sites in England such as the famous Greenwich Observatory and the Cavendish Laboratory at Cambridge University. From these trips came the idea of writing a series of books that would teach youngsters about modern science by taking them behind-the-scenes to a number of well-known laboratories.

Before returning to the United States, we spent a few weeks in France at the end of August 1965. Hardly had we settled back into our own home when I got a call from Edna Barth, my former editor at McGraw-Hill. Now working for another publisher, T. Y. Crowell, she invited me to write for her. The topic we agreed on was a collective biography of outstanding nineteenth- and twentieth-century biologists, focusing on their most important discoveries and their impact on our lives.

Entitled *Famous Men of Modern Biology* (1968), this was my first book to be based on actual contact with contemporary scientists. Of the fourteen important biologists that were discussed, I exchanged letters with the four who were still living. I learned many details of their lives and their research. Later, they were kind enough to check the individual chapters for factual accuracy.

Advances in the science of measurement were the subject of my next book. I chose the topic because there were few up-to-date books on this vital subject and the changeover to the metric system seemed imminent. Also, I was intrigued at the prospect of getting a close look at the National Bureau of Standards. During the several days I spent at their labs just outside of Washington, D.C., I met some of the leading figures in the science of measurement and saw the actual weights and rods used to set the official standards of ounce, pound, inch, and yard for the United States. The book, which I called *For Good Measure,* was published in 1969.

By 1970, Edna Barth had become editor-in-chief at still another publishing house, Lothrop, Lee and Shepard. She again invited me to write for her. Knowing of my continuing interest in music, she and I came up with the idea of a biography of the contemporary composer Igor Stravinsky. I had already started researching Stravinsky's life when Edna learned that another publisher was preparing a similar book. After discussing whether to continue the project, drop it, or change its basic focus, we chose to expand the biography to cover fourteen outstanding composers, and named it *Masters of Modern Music* (1970).

Meanwhile, I continued to visit laboratories in the United States and to think about a series of books describing what I saw. Most young people's science books were concerned with the results of scientific research. I wanted to write about the process and methods of science by taking a close, firsthand look at the actual laboratory experiments. The proposal that I prepared for the "Scientists at Work" series described two books, *South Pole Station* and *National Weather Service.* I submitted the proposals to John Day publishers because I knew that they had put out a number of excellent science books. They were indeed interested, and undertook to put out a whole series of "Scientists at Work" books over the years. In time, though, John Day was taken over by another publisher, T. Y. Crowell, and most of the books were put out by Crowell.

Since the scientific base located at the South Pole is administered by the Navy and the National Science Foundation from their offices in Washington, D.C., I did most of my research in the capital. Seeing my great interest, a Navy officer actually invited me to visit the South Pole station for a short stay. The idea was intriguing. But

unfortunately, all flights to the South Pole occur during their summer, which is our winter, and I could not leave school for that period.

During the months I worked on the book, the public was very interested in the South Pole. Accounts of the life and the research at the Pole appeared frequently in newspapers and magazines. Yet, by the time the book was published, nobody seemed at all concerned about this fantastic outpost at one of the last frontiers on earth. As a result, this book never sold very well.

The research for *National Weather Service* (1971), the second title in the series, also began in Washington, at the National Meteorological Center. Weather reports flowed in here from all over America and the world. The walls were lined with weather maps and charts showing the conditions in every remote corner of the globe. The scientists kept very busy updating the maps and charts, preparing the forecasts and sending them out to pilots, ship captains, farmers, and others who depend on up-to-the-minute weather reports.

To get a full picture of the weather service, I was advised to visit three different types of weather stations: a big city station, an airport station, and a small-sized, average station.

Fortunately I live close to the very large New York City station at Rockefeller Center and to an airport station at New York's LaGuardia Airport. At LaGuardia an official drove me around the field, pointing out the various pieces

"While Gilda takes notes, I photograph a scientist for a book in the 'Scientists at Work' series."

of weather equipment. We actually drove across the runways used by the planes. Each time, though, the driver had to radio the control tower to ask permission. A few times we had to stop and wait—at what felt like a hairbreadth distance from a plane landing or taking off.

The typical average-sized station I went to see is located at Albany, New York. I arranged to spend a full twelve hours, from 10:00 a.m. to 10:00 p.m., at the station to observe meteorologists at work around the clock. Since this book was to be illustrated by photographs, I packed my brand-new Miranda camera and several rolls of film. All day long, I scribbled notes and took pictures of the different meteorologists at work—releasing a weather balloon, receiving and reading the weather maps, preparing the forecasts, sending out reports to local radio and television stations, and so on.

When I returned home that evening I was tired, but also very pleased that I had received such a good idea of what goes on in an average-sized weather station. Early the next morning I brought the films, containing over one hundred pictures, to a custom photo lab for developing and printing. I planned to select about twenty or thirty shots to use in the book. Somewhat later I got a phone call from the lab with the awful message, "All of your film is ruined. It looks like your camera's meter was not working." Hearing the despair in my voice, the lab technician went on to explain that he could salvage some key pictures by printing them in a special way.

Still one more hurdle had to be overcome. Just before publication the government changed the agency's name from Weather Bureau to National Weather Service. Thousands of full-color covers had already been printed and the manuscript was being set into type with the old name. To throw out the covers and change the type would cost a lot of money. But otherwise, the book would be out of date right from the start.

Fortunately, the publisher agreed to print new covers and change the name throughout the manuscript. Although the book came out a little late, reviewers praised it for being very timely and the first with the agency's new name.

Enzymes in Action was also published in 1971. In a way, my experiences with this book were similar to those connected with *South Pole Station.* Enzymes were big news at the time I was writing the book, and people wanted to know what they are and how they work. Several big soap manufacturers advertised that enzymes boosted their products' ability to destroy dirt. The word was on everyone's lips as a "miracle cleaner." By the time the book came out, however, the excitement was over. Enzymes had not proven as effective as had been expected. While the book sold moderately well, it was hardly the smash success that the publisher and I hoped it would be.

*

Hard as it may be to believe, computers were scarcely known in the early 1970s. Few people knew what computers were, how they worked, and what they could do. Still carrying on my mission to inform young readers about the important advances of modern science, I undertook a really challenging assignment—to explain computers to six- to ten-year-old readers of the Coward-McCann "Science Is What and Why" series. Simply entitled *Computers,* the book was selected as an outstanding trade book of 1972

by both the Children's Book Council and the National Science Teachers Association.

That same year also saw the publication of my first book in a series on the various musical instruments for Lothrop, Lee and Shepard. These books were designed to meet the interests of youngsters who were just starting the study of an instrument. Having introduced many students to the instruments of the orchestra in my teaching, I was familiar with their questions and had a ready audience for testing my ideas. Over the next six years, I completed four such books—*The Violin Book* (1972), *The Flute Book* (1973), *The Clarinet and Saxophone Book* (1975), and *The Trumpet Book* (1978).

Coincidentally, our daughter Nancy was studying the violin at the time and Ellie was playing the flute. Since I was illustrating each book with photographs, I quite naturally used the girls as subjects to illustrate some of the points made in the text. Not long after *The Violin Book* was released, Nancy got an excited call from a girl in Jamestown, New York, whom she had met during the summer. The girl had received a copy of *The Violin Book* for her birthday and was surprised to come across the picture of Nancy. Our twelve-year-old daughter, on the other hand, having grown up with publishing, was rather blasé about the entire incident.

Ellie benefited a great deal more from my work on *The Flute Book.* As part of the research, I toured the William S. Haynes flute factory in Boston, Massachusetts. With camera in hand, I followed every step of the flute-making process, starting with the rough metal tubes through to the final adjustments. As a result I had a good chance to see the exacting standards to which each instrument was held. Since Ellie was a serious student, we decided to buy her a silver Haynes flute, a fine, professional-level instrument that she still cherishes.

To brighten the tone of my books and incidentally to shed some light on the topics, I often include humorous stories and anecdotes. Over the years I have been collecting and inventing jokes for this purpose. It seemed very natural, therefore, to assemble a number of these tidbits in a book others could enjoy. I titled it *The Funny Side of Science* (1973). My friend, J. B. Handelsman, an artist

The Berger family celebrating Nancy's graduation from law school, May 1985.

whose work frequently appears in *The New Yorker* magazine, supplied a number of original cartoons.

Three new "Scientists at Work" books—*Animal Hospital, Oceanography Lab,* and *Pollution Lab*—came out during 1973. Visiting the labs, watching the scientists doing their research, and getting to know them as human beings continued to be great fun. Not only did I get caught up with the scientists' triumphs, successes and achievements, but also with their problems, failures, and struggles. Their difficulties became my own. In fact, in my recurring fantasy, I was able to find solutions to problems that were stumping them!

One time, while I was researching *Oceanography Lab* at the Woods Hole Oceanographic Institution on Cape Cod, Massachusetts, I came close to getting more involved with the work than usual. A research ship was leaving for a three-month tour of the Indian Ocean—and there was room for one more, if I wanted to go. Unfortunately it was about two weeks before the start of the school year and it wasn't possible to leave on such short notice.

The many science books that were published in the early 1960s, right after *Sputnik,* covered most of the basic subject areas of science. They became the backbone of the science book collections in school and public libraries. By the early 1970s, though, many of these books were out of date. There was a real need for fundamental science books that would include the latest findings.

In 1973 I began a series for T. Y. Crowell that grew to four titles over the next ten years: *The New Water Book* (1973), *The New Air Book* (1974), *The New Food Book* (1978), and *The New Earth Book* (1980). *The New Food Book* was different from the others in the series, since it was written as a collaboration with Gilda. Always well informed about food and nutrition, she made a major contribution in researching and writing the book. It therefore seemed only fair to acknowledge her participation by listing our two names as joint authors.

Around 1974, the U.S. Department of Health, Education, and Welfare was stressing career education in the school. Teachers and librarians were looking for materials that would inform young people about the opportunities in the various careers. Edna Barth, at Lothrop, Lee and Shepard, asked me to write two books in a career series they were publishing, *Jobs in Fine Arts and Humanities* and *Jobs That Save the Environment* (1974).

Perhaps the most personally gratifying book of my writing career was *Cancer Lab* (1975), another publication in the "Scientists at Work" series. As with the others, I focused the book on a leading research center, in this instance, the National Cancer Institute (NCI), just outside of Washington, D.C. And as was also usual, I got to know some of the researchers and staff members quite well. William S. Gray, Chief of the Education Branch, had been particularly helpful in introducing me to the various researchers and in having each section of the manuscript checked for accuracy by an expert. Knowing of his great expertise and high position at the Institute, I invited him to write the Foreword.

Days and weeks went by, but Bill did not mail out the promised material. Nor did he reply to my notes or telephone calls. As the deadline for delivery of the manuscript approached, I made one last attempt to reach him on the telephone.

Gilda and Melvin Berger are coauthors of most of the books they write.

This time Bill explained the reason for the long delay. Some years ago, he had been a very successful writer on a national news magazine. Although still a very young man, he learned that he had a fatal form of cancer. The doctors who were treating him offered little hope. That is when he came to the NCI. The doctors there gave him some newly developed treatments that literally saved his life.

Bill was an excellent writer, but powerful memories of his illness evoked by my book were blocking his ability to put his story into words. He promised, however, to keep trying to write the Foreword.

On a Sunday morning, the day before the book was due, Bill called me long distance. He dictated the entire two-page introduction over the phone. In a very moving way, it told the story of his battle against cancer and encouraged the book's readers to work to conquer this dread disease.

Cancer Lab proved to be one of the most meaningful books to me personally. I was deeply touched by the powerful emotional effect it had on Bill. The brilliant scientists I observed doing research at the NCI gave me high hopes that we were on the way toward the conquest of cancer. And through all this time I was constantly reminded of my mother's untimely, cancer-caused death.

The three other books that came out in 1975 were quite different, one from the other, yet each one advanced a series I was writing. *Consumer Protection Lab* was the latest "Scientists at Work" book. Another volume in Coward-McCann's easy-to-read "Science Is What and Why" series was *Time after Time.* And *The Clarinet and Saxophone Book* was added to the Lothrop, Lee and Shepard series of musical instrument books.

By the end of 1975 I had written just under thirty books. Seemingly on a wide variety of subjects, the books fell into three basic categories. The main group dealt with the important topics of science, presented as clearly and accurately as possible, and in terms young people could easily understand. The second category had to do with the process of science, how and why modern researchers work as they do, and what they hope to achieve. And finally, the last group included the books on music, each one exploring some aspect of this wonderful art.

With Kate Waters (left), the editor of the Scholastic "Question and Answer" series.

In 1976 I added three more books to the various series I was writing. *Medical Center Lab* and *Police Lab* were for "Scientists at Work." *Fitting In: Animals and Their Habitats,* for the young "Science Is What and Why" series, was the first book on which both Gilda's and my name appeared as collaborators.

Until this point all of my writing had been for large, major publishing houses. Now a call came from Sidney Phillips, president of S. G. Phillips, a small company, for a book on folk music. Although I hesitated, he convinced me that his books got the same distribution as larger houses, but with more care and attention in editing, design, production, and marketing. Just as he said, *The Story of Folk Music* (1976) proved to be a best-seller. It also was named an outstanding book by the National Council for the Social Studies and the Children's Book Council.

A new challenge came from Franklin Watts around the same time. It was an offer to edit a series of books modeled on the "Scientists at Work" idea. The concept was to give readers close-up views of work in various occupations, so that they might become familiar with a variety of career and job opportunities. My editor at Franklin Watts, Wendy Barish (who had been at Crowell), suggested that I write some of the books myself; engage other authors to do the rest, and do the preliminary editing on all of the manuscripts.

Over the next two years we produced six books in the "Industry at Work" series. Unfortunately, librarians and teachers did not quite know how to use these books and they did not sell very well. The series was stopped after the six books were published.

The amazing accomplishments of the American space program spurred my interest in astronomy—a concern that continues to the present day. Fortunately, the publisher G. P. Putnam shares this fascination. In 1977 they published *Quasars, Pulsars, and Black Holes in Space,* the first of a "triple-header" series of astronomy books. This one was followed by *Planets, Stars, and Galaxies* (1978), *Comets, Meteoroids, and Asteroids* (1981), *Space Shots, Shuttles, and Satellites* (1983) and *Star Gazing, Comet Watching, and Sky Mapping* (1985). The books in this series have

been particularly well received, having won awards from the Child Study Association, the Library of Congress, the National Science Teachers Association, and the Children's Book Council.

*

Throughout history the quest to understand the natural world has gone hand in glove with a curiosity about supernatural phenomena, such as ghosts, extrasensory perception (ESP), and unidentified flying objects (UFOs). Two personal encounters with the supernatural sparked my interest in the occult. The first occurred on Cape Cod, Massachusetts, where we spent our summers during the 1960s. At an art gallery one Sunday afternoon, I was approached by a stranger who introduced himself as a painter whose works were being exhibited.

"You grew up in Brooklyn, New York, didn't you?" he asked.

"That's right," I answered, trying hard to remember him from my youth. "Did you?"

"No," he said, and then went on. "You lived around Eleventh Street, didn't you?"

"Yes, but how did you know?" I answered, still struggling to recall his face.

"And you attended Public School 225."

"Yes, I did," I stammered, amazed that he could know so much about me when I did not know him at all.

"Your birthday is in August," he continued. "August 23 to be exact."

Now I was entirely confused. Only my closest friends and relations knew my birthday. When I insisted that he tell me how he happened to have this information he explained that he had a special ability to receive mental messages from certain people. From the moment I entered the room, he claimed, messages began to fly from me to him.

He kept on providing information. "Your father was an upholsterer. You own two cars; they are both black. One is an American product; the other is German—a Mercedes, I think."

I nodded my head in assent as I tried to figure out how this outsider could know so much about me. It was hard to believe that he was receiving messages from me. But it was even more difficult to explain it any other way.

My second brush with the supernatural came some years later when we were spending our summers at the Chautauqua Institution in upstate New York. One day we drove over to Lilydale, a nationally known spiritualist center that was located nearby. Passing through the gates of Lilydale was like taking a trip back in time and space. In the Victorian houses of this community lived spiritualists who did everything from read palms to communicate with the dead. They claimed to be able to see into the past and forecast the future. While no one succeeded in bringing me a message from loved ones who had "passed over," I was impressed by many others who claimed to have heard from spirits.

All this aroused my curiosity, and I decided to learn more about supernatural phenomena. I read widely and had long discussions with many people, from astrologers to psychics to witches. My studies also included interviews with scientists who do research on the occult. And I also looked into material on illusion and trickery written by professional magicians. From my research I learned that much that is called supernatural is really either coincidence, fraud, or human error. But I also came across many supernatural happenings that I could not explain in logical, scientific terms. I wrote up my findings in *The Supernatural: From ESP to UFOs* (1977). In the book I try to provide the facts and information as objectively as I can, allowing the readers to draw their own conclusions. Since the book came out, I am often asked whether or not I believe in the supernatural. It is a question that I go to great lengths to avoid answering.

The research for *FBI* (1977) was as different as could be from that on the supernatural. For a couple of days I visited the FBI Headquarters in Washington, D.C., spending time in each of the divisions, from the crime lab to the National Crime Information Center. Then, as with the National Weather Service, I was advised to go to a typical FBI office.

I chose the FBI office in Buffalo, New York. Two special agents took me out with them as they sought witnesses and suspects in a particular bank robbery case. I listened, sometimes uneasily, as they stopped, questioned, and spoke with people on the street and in their homes. At day's end, I accompanied them to the firing range where they practice their marksmanship.

"Four wonderful grandsons: (from left) Matthew, Jacob, Maxwell, and Benjamin."

They handed me a gun and let me take a few shots at the target. They said I did very well for a beginner, but I hope never to fire a gun again.

*

For my entire adult life, I had juggled three basic activities: writing books, playing viola, and teaching music. The writing, which had begun as an enjoyable sideline, was now occupying an increasing amount of time and represented a growing part of my income. I began to think of giving up teaching and devoting all of my time to writing and playing.

The problem was largely financial. Our two daughters were in college and our chief source of support had always come from my teaching job. Writing books and playing classical music are both notoriously low-paying occupations. Time after time, Gilda and I went over the figures to see how we could make ends meet if I gave up my teaching job. We asked each other "What if?" questions. "What if there is a bad depression, and no one buys books?" "What if libraries stop buying young people's science books?" "What if we get sick and cannot write?"

Gradually, however, I built up my confidence and resolve. I felt that we could probably succeed even under the worst scenario. Finally, in June 1979, after more than twenty-six years of teaching, I resigned from the public school system.

The summer that followed my last days of teaching did not feel different in any way. We rented our house, and went up to Chautauqua, as usual. But when we returned at the end of August the full impact of what I had done hit me.

Any thoughts that I would be working less hard now that I wasn't teaching were soon put to rest. True, I didn't have to drive a half hour to school every day. Now I just walked downstairs to the writing studio in the basement to go to work. But while I had left school at three o'clock, finished for the day, now I'd work on the books morning, noon, and night. And as my own boss I was tougher on myself than the principal had ever been at school.

In part, these long hours were due to anxiety about making a living and the pressure to deliver manuscripts on time. But an even more important reason was that I really loved what I was doing, and I enjoyed all the time I spent working on the books.

For me, writing does not involve sitting at my desk all day long. Every book starts with a period of research, preferably from prime sources. Sometimes this means taking trips to scientific labs, offices, conferences, or other places. Here I meet with the people I will be writing about and have actual hands-on experiences, where possible. Other times it entails visits to special libraries for hard-to-obtain materials. Almost always it requires checking out stacks of books from nearby public or college libraries. There is also correspondence with people who live in places I can't visit. In my letters I usually ask them questions and request specific reports or publications.

During the research period I immerse myself in the subject—talking, observing, reading. I collect information until I reach a point when I feel I could write the entire book without even looking at my notes. It is then that I start putting the book together.

The first step is usually to prepare an outline, a framework that organizes the material in an orderly, logical

Celebrating Gilda's birthday with the whole Melvin-Gilda Berger clan on the beach at East Hampton.

fashion. Often, this is the most difficult step of all. Then I start the actual writing. I always prepare the first draft in longhand. The manuscript then goes through a number of typed versions. My goal is to clarify the concepts, make the writing interesting and engaging, and see that the different ideas flow along in a clear, well-ordered way. Some manuscripts I revise as many as a half-dozen times before I am satisfied.

The task of revising the manuscript has been made much easier by the word processor that I got in 1983. I can change or move anything from a single word to a whole paragraph by just pressing a few keys! A whole book can be automatically typed out by this amazing machine in less than a half hour. It takes longer than that for me to walk to the post office and mail it off to the publisher!

The Photo Dictionary of Football, which was published in 1980, caused me more problems and headaches than any other book. The original concept was to follow the adventures of one high-school football player through a whole season. I was going to write the text and take the photos. The very first day I was on the field with my camera I got knocked over trying to take a particularly exciting shot. I realized that I was not skilled enough with the camera for this type of assignment. Fortunately, I was able to hire Mel Finkelstein, a leading sports photographer from the *New York Daily News,* to take the action pictures.

Then, during the second game of the season, the hero of the book broke his leg. The doctor said he could not play for the rest of the year! This was a really tough situation, I had a contract to fulfill, and Mel Finkelstein had already taken dozens of pictures.

The solution that my editor and I hit on was to use a selection of the action photos to illustrate dictionary-like definitions of the terms, players, and plays of football. With the photos I already had, plus some more that I collected from various college and professional football teams, I was able to compile a complete dictionary of football. So attractive and successful was this book that the editor decided to do a similar book, *The Photo Dictionary of the Orchestra* (1981). Here I was able to handle both the text *and* the photos.

A number of subsequent publications were heavily illustrated with photographs, some original, some borrowed from other sources. Among these were *Robots in Fact and Fiction* and *Mad Scientists in Fact and Fiction* (both 1980), as well as *Disastrous Floods and Tidal Waves* and *Disastrous Volcanoes* (both 1981).

One book has a way of leading to another. While working on the football dictionary, I became familiar with the fascinating world of sports medicine. This new area of medicine, the prevention and treatment of injuries to athletes, inspired *Sports Medicine* (1982), which won an award from the Children's Book Council and the National

Science Teachers Association. The research took me into a number of leading sports-medicine centers in New York, Boston, and Philadelphia. I met the doctors and other professionals who treat everyone from the players on the New York Jets and Philadelphia 76ers to amateur joggers, tennis players, skiers, and school athletes.

Unfortunately, I required some medical assistance of my own at a sports-medicine clinic that I visited in Massachusetts. The doctor suggested that I view a video-tape of a special kind of knee operation that he performed before discussing the surgery with me. Forgetting for the moment that I become very queasy at the sight of blood, I watched the screen intently. Presently I felt myself growing light-headed and faint. After being revived by water and receiving some expert attention, I was able to go ahead with the interview.

A chance meeting with brain researcher Tom Carew led to the next book in the "Scientists at Work" series, *Exploring the Mind and Brain* (1983). While speaking to him I learned about his exciting field of study. Tom had discovered actual changes that occur in nerve cells during learning. Working with a big glob of a snail called *Aplysia,* he had found a chemical difference in these animals after they learned a simple type of behavior. I felt privileged to be present at this major scientific breakthrough. *Exploring the Mind and Brain* also covers nine other areas of brain research, ranging from a study on whether mental illness runs in families to tracing the specific action of various drugs in the brain.

From considering the scientific study of the brain I became interested in ways in which people control the brains and minds of others. In an age rife with drugs, cults, and therapies of all kinds, I was amazed to find the growing number of ways to change and direct other people's thoughts. *Mind Control* (1985) was a report on my voyage of discovery into this fascinating subject.

Two of the books I wrote around this time were additions to Crowell's delightful series for very young children, "Let's Read and Find Out." They are *Why I Cough, Sneeze, Shiver, Hiccup, and Yawn* and *Germs Make Me Sick!* (1983 and 1985).

*

Writers rarely have the chance to observe firsthand the spontaneous response of a child to a book they have written. One of the most heartwarming moments of my career came unexpectedly while on a holiday trip through upstate New York in August 1985. We had stopped in a bookstore in Corning, New York, to buy a gift for a friend. Having wandered into the children's section, however, I saw a young girl sitting cross-legged in a corner, complete-ly absorbed in *Germs Make Me Sick!*

Lately publishers have expressed a need for reference books on many different subjects for young readers. I was asked to write four such books. They were divided between Franklin Watts, who issued *Energy* and *Sports* (1983), and Julian Messner, who published *Computer Talk* and *Space Talk* (1984 and 1985).

Gilda and I have long enjoyed reading and collecting accounts of the strangest and most notorious crimes. When we mentioned this hobby to our editor at Messner she thought that many young people would be intrigued by these stories. So we retold the very best in two books, *Bizarre Murders* and *Bizarre Crimes* (1983 and 1984).

Around 1983 the interest in computers reached an all-time high. Everyone seemed to be involved with computer games and home computers. Since I had been writing about computers since 1972, I was asked to do several new books on this amazing tool of the twentieth century.

For Franklin Watts I wrote the basic texts, *Data Processing* and *Word Processing* (1983 and 1984). I also served as the consulting editor for their whole series of books on computer-related topics. The computer book I did for Crowell, on the other hand, presented a basic introduc-tion to computers in the form of questions and answers. It had the obvious title *Computers: A Question and Answer Book* (1985).

While almost all of my writing was on science for young readers, I continued my deep interest in music. From this came my idea to write an adult book that would help listeners understand and enjoy chamber music.

In 1985, Dodd, Mead published *Guide to Chamber Music.* Some years after publication, Dodd, Mead went out of business, but I was lucky enough to find another publisher, Anchor Books, which issued the book in 1995. A few years later, lightning struck again and Anchor dropped the book from their list. This time a third publisher, Dover Books, took it over, releasing an updated edition in July 2001.

Based on the success of *Guide to Chamber Music,* Anchor Books asked me to write books covering other parts of the classical music repertoire. The result was *Guide to Sonatas* (1991), *Guide to Choral Masterpieces* (1993), and *The Anchor Guide to Orchestral Masterpieces* (1995).

Late in the 1980s my personal life and writing career took a major turn. Since my daughters were both grown and on their own—Ellie in publishing and Nancy, an elder lawyer—Gilda and I decided to sell our Great Neck house in the suburbs of New York City. We purchased a lovely house across the street from Gardiner's Bay in East Hampton and a small apartment in New York City. At the same time, I began writing for Scholastic, almost exclusive-ly.

My first project for Scholastic was a series of four "Simple Science" books—*Simple Science Says: Take One Balloon* (1988), *Simple Science Says: Take One Mirror* (1989), *Simple Science Says: Take One Magnifying Glass* (1989), and *Simple Science Says: Take One Compass* (1990). Each book explores science using the object itself, which was packaged within the book.

For many years I have been collecting and making up science jokes that I use in my books. This led to a whole book of science humor, *101 Wacky Science Jokes* (1989). Over the following years I completed five more—*101 President Jokes* (1990), *101 Wacky State Jokes* (1991), *101 Wacky Camping Jokes* (1992), *101 Spooky Halloween Jokes* (1993), and *101 Nutty Nature Jokes* (1994). Truth be known, I always include more than 101 jokes. I just can't bear to cut any, because they all make me chuckle!

The most recent series of books for Scholastic, a collaboration between Gilda and me, includes eighteen books of the Scholastic "Question and Answer" series. The first one, *Did Dinosaurs Live in Your Backyard? Questions and Answers About Dinosaurs,* came out in 1998. We followed it with seventeen other books in the question/answer format.

When I was approached about writing science readers for first and second graders, I found the idea intriguing and a real challenge. I couldn't resist. The result was four books in Scholastic's "Hello Readers" series—*Chomp! A Book About Sharks* (1999), *Growl! A Book About Bears* (1999), *Buzz! A Book About Insects* (1999), *Dive! A Book of Deep-Sea Creatures* (2000). After these four, Gilda and I teamed up to write *Screech! A Book About Bats* (2000), *BRRR! A Book About Polar Animals* (2000), and *Splash! A Book About Whales and Dolphins* (2001).

Two recent books—the *Scholastic Science Dictionary* (2000) and *Mummies of the Pharaohs: Exploring the Valley of the Kings* (2001)—were very difficult to write, requiring a tremendous amount of research and many, many drafts. But in the end both volumes filled me with pride, especially for the striking art in the *Dictionary* and the outstanding art and photographs in *Mummies*.

I am now at an age when many of my friends have retired. But I find myself very reluctant to stop writing as long as I can and as long as publishers are interested in publishing what I write. Hardly a day passes when I don't have some thoughts of new book ideas and writing projects that I would like to pursue.

Writings

FOR CHILDREN; NONFICTION

Atoms, illustrated by Arthur Schaffert, Coward (New York, NY), 1968.

Gravity, illustrated by Arthur Schaffert, Coward (New York, NY), 1969.

Storms, illustrated by Joseph Cellini, Coward (New York, NY), 1970.

Stars, illustrated by Marilyn Miller, Coward (New York, NY), 1971.

Computers (part of "Science Is What and Why" series), illustrated by Arthur Schaffert, Coward (New York, NY), 1972.

Time after Time (part of "Science Is What and Why" series), illustrated by Richard Cuffari, Coward (New York, NY), 1975.

Energy from the Sun, illustrated by Giulio Maestro, Crowell (New York, NY), 1976.

(With wife, Gilda Berger) *Fitting In: Animals in Their Habitats* (part of "Science Is What and Why" series), illustrated by James Arnosky, Coward (New York, NY), 1976.

Jigsaw Continents, illustrated by Bob Totten, Coward (New York, NY), 1978.

Energy, illustrated by Anne Canevari Green, F. Watts (New York, NY), 1983.

Sports, illustrated by A. C. Green, F. Watts (New York, NY), 1983.

Why I Cough, Sneeze, Shiver, Hiccup, and Yawn, illustrated by Holly Keller, Crowell (New York, NY), 1983.

Computer Talk, photographs by Geri Greinke, Messner (New York, NY), 1984.

Space Talk, Messner (New York, NY), 1984.

Germs Make Me Sick!, illustrated by Marilyn Hafner, Crowell (New York, NY), 1985.

Switch On, Switch Off, HarperCollins (New York, NY), 1989.

Where Did Your Family Come From?, Ideals (Nashville, TN), 1993.

How's the Weather?, Ideals (Nashville, TN), 1993.

Round and Round the Money Goes: What Money Is and How We Use It, Ideals (Nashville, TN), 1993.

Telephones, Televisions, and Toilets, Ideals (Nashville, TN), 1993.

Where Are the Stars During the Day?, Ideals (Nashville, TN), 1993.

The Whole World In Your Hands, Ideals (Nashville, TN), 1993.

Where Does the Mail Go?, Ideals (Nashville, TN), 1994,

Life in the Rain Forest, Ideals (Nashville, TN), 1994.

Oil Spill, HarperCollins, 1994.

What Do Animals Do in the Winter?, Ideals (Nashville, TN), 1995.

Water, Water, Everywhere, Ideals (Nashville, TN), 1995.

Why Did the Dinosaurs Disappear?, Ideals (Nashville, TN), 1995.

How Do Airplanes Fly?, Ideals (Nashville, TN), 1996.

Look Out for Turtles, HarperCollins, 1996.

Chirping Crickets, HarperCollins, 1998.

The Scholastic Science Dictionary, Scholastic (New York, NY), 2000.

Mummies of the Pharaohs: Exploring the Valley of the Kings, Scholastic (New York, NY), 2001.

"SIMPLE SCIENCE" SERIES

Simple Science Says: Take One Balloon, Scholastic (New York, NY), 1988.

Simple Science Says: Take One Mirror, Scholastic (New York, NY), 1989.

Simple Science Says: Take One Magnifying Glass, Scholastic (New York, NY), 1989.

Simple Science Says: Take One Compass, Scholastic (New York, NY), 1990.

"JOKES" SERIES

101 Wacky Science Jokes, Scholastic (New York, NY), 1989.

101 President Jokes, Scholastic (New York, NY), 1990.

101 Wacky State Jokes, Scholastic (New York, NY), 1991.

101 Wacky Camping Jokes, Scholastic (New York, NY), 1992.

101 Spooky Halloween Jokes, Scholastic (New York, NY), 1993.

101 Nutty Nature Jokes, Scholastic (New York, NY), 1994.

"QUESTION AND ANSWER" SERIES

Did Dinosaurs Live in Your Backyard? Questions and Answers about Dinosaurs, Scholastic (New York, NY), 1998.

Do Whales Have Belly Buttons? Questions and Answers About Whales and Dolphins, Scholastic (New York, NY), 1999.

Do Stars Have Points? Questions and Answers About Stars and Planets, Scholastic (New York, NY), 1999.

Can It Rain Cats and Dogs? Questions and Answers About the Weather, Scholastic (New York, NY), 1999.

How Do Flies Walk Upside Down? Questions and Answers About Insects Scholastic (New York, NY), 1999.

Why Don't Haircuts Hurt? Questions and Answers About the Human Body, Scholastic (New York, NY), 1999.

Do Tarantulas Have Teeth? Questions and Answers About Poisonous Creatures, Scholastic (New York, NY), 1999.

Why Do Volcanoes Blow Their Tops? Questions and Answers About Volcanoes and Earthquakes, Scholastic (New York, NY), 1999.

Do Tornadoes Really Twist? Questions and Answers About Tornadoes and Hurricanes, Scholastic (New York, NY), 2000.

Do All Spiders Spin Webs? Questions and Answers About Spiders, Scholastic (New York, NY), 2000.

What Makes an Ocean Wave? Questions and Answers About Oceans and Ocean Life, Scholastic (New York, NY), 2000.

Can You Hear a Shout in Space? Questions and Answers About Space Exploration, Scholastic (New York, NY), 2000.

What Do Sharks Eat for Dinner? Questions and Answers About Sharks, Scholastic (New York, NY), 2000.

Do Penguins Get Frostbite? Questions and Answers About Polar Animals, Scholastic (New York, NY), 2000.

Why Do Wolves Howl? Questions and Answers About Wolves, Scholastic (New York, NY), 2001.

Does It Always Rain in the Rain Forest? Questions and Answers About Tropical Rain Forests, Scholastic (New York, NY), 2001.

"HELLO READERS" SERIES

Chomp! A Book about Sharks, Scholastic (New York, NY), 1999.

Growl! A Book about Bears, Scholastic (New York, NY), 1999.

Buzz! A Book about Insects, Scholastic (New York, NY), 1999.

Dive! A Book about Deep-Sea Creatures, Scholastic (New York, NY), 2000.

(With Gilda Berger) *Screech! A Book about Bats,* Scholastic (New York, NY), 2000.

(With Gilda Berger) *BRRR! A Book about Polar Animals,* Scholastic (New York, NY), 2000.

(With Gilda Berger) *Splash! A Book about Whales and Dolphins,* Scholastic (New York, NY), 2001.

FOR YOUNG ADULTS; NONFICTION

(With Frank Clark) *Science and Music,* illustrated by Gustav Schrotter, McGraw (New York, NY), 1961.

(With Frank Clark) *Music in Perspective,* Sam Fox Music Publishers (New York, NY), 1962.

Choral Music in Perspective, Sam Fox Music Publishers (New York, NY), 1964.

Triumphs of Modern Science, illustrated by John Kaufmann, McGraw (New York, NY), 1964.

Famous Men of Modern Biology, Crowell (New York, NY), 1968.

For Good Measure, illustrated by Adolph E. Brotman, McGraw (New York, NY), 1969.

Masters of Modern Music, Lothrop (New York, NY), 1970.

Tools of Modern Biology, illustrated by Robert Smith, Crowell (New York, NY), 1970.

Enzymes in Action, Crowell (New York, NY), 1971.

National Weather Service, John Day (New York, NY), 1971.

South Pole Station, John Day (New York, NY), 1971.

The Violin Book, Lothrop (New York, NY), 1972.

Animal Hospital (part of "Scientists at Work" series), John Day (New York, NY), 1973.

Careers in Environmental Control, Lothrop (New York, NY), 1973.

The Flute Book, Lothrop (New York, NY), 1973.

The Funny Side of Science, illustrated by J. B. Handelsman, Crowell (New York, NY), 1973.

(With consultants Leo Eisel and Carl Tausig) *Jobs That Save Our Environment,* Lothrop (New York, NY), 1973.

The New Water Book, illustrated by Leonard Kessler, Crowell (New York, NY), 1973.

Oceanography Lab (part of "Scientists at Work" series), John Day (New York, NY), 1973.

Those Amazing Computers!, John Day (New York, NY), 1973.

Pollution Lab (part of "Scientists at Work" series), John Day (New York, NY), 1973.

(With consultants Arthur Kerr and Carl Tausig) *Jobs in Fine Arts and Humanities,* Lothrop (New York, NY), 1974.

The New Air Book, illustrated by Giulio Maestro, Crowell (New York, NY), 1974.

Cancer Lab (part of "Scientists at Work" series), John Day (New York, NY), 1975.

The Clarinet and Saxophone Book, Lothrop (New York, NY), 1975.

Consumer Protection Lab (part of "Scientists at Work" series), Lothrop (New York, NY), 1975.

Medical Center Lab (part of "Scientists at Work" series), John Day (New York, NY), 1976.

Police Lab (part of "Scientists at Work" series), John Day (New York, NY), 1976.

The Story of Folk Music, S. G. Phillips (New York, NY), 1976.

Automobile Factory, F. Watts (New York, NY), 1977.

FBI, F. Watts (New York, NY), 1977.

Food Processing, F. Watts (New York, NY), 1977.

Quasars, Pulsars, and Black Holes in Space, Putnam (New York, NY), 1977.

The Supernatural: From ESP to UFOs, John Day (New York, NY), 1977.

Bionics, F. Watts (New York, NY), 1978.

Building Construction, F. Watts (New York, NY), 1978.

Disease Detectives, Crowell (New York, NY), 1978.

(With Gilda Berger) *The New Food Book,* illustrated by Byron Barton, Crowell (New York, NY), 1978.

Planets, Stars, and Galaxies, Putnam (New York, NY), 1978.

Printing Plant, F. Watts (New York, NY), 1978.

The Trumpet Book, Lothrop (New York, NY), 1978.

The World of Dance, S. G. Phillips (New York, NY), 1978.

The Stereo Hi-Fi Handbook, illustrated with diagrams by Lloyd Birmingham, Lothrop (New York, NY), 1979.

Mad Scientists in Fact and Fiction, F. Watts (New York, NY), 1980.

The New Earth Book: Our Changing Planet, illustrated by George DeGrazio, Crowell (New York, NY), 1980.

The Photo Dictionary of Football, photographs by Mel Finkelstein, Methuen (New York, NY), 1980.

Putting on a Show, F. Watts (New York, NY), 1980.

Robots in Fact and Fiction, F. Watts (New York, NY), 1980.

Comets, Meteors, and Asteroids, Putnam (New York, NY), 1981.

Computers in Your Life, Crowell (New York, NY), 1981.

Disastrous Floods and Tidal Waves, F. Watts (New York, NY), 1981.

Disastrous Volcanoes, F. Watts (New York, NY), 1981.

The Photo Dictionary of the Orchestra, photographs by Berger, Methuen (New York, NY), 1981.

Censorship, F. Watts (New York, NY), 1982.

Sports Medicine, Crowell (New York, NY), 1982.

(With Gilda Berger) *The Whole World of Hands,* illustrated by True Kelley, Houghton (Boston, MA), 1982.

Bright Stars, Red Giants, and White Dwarfs, Putnam (New York, NY), 1983.

Data Processing, F. Watts (New York, NY), 1983.

Exploring the Mind and Brain (part of "Scientists at Work" series), Crowell (New York, NY), 1983.

Space Shots, Shuttles, and Satellites, Putnam (New York, NY), 1983.

(With Gilda Berger) *Bizarre Murders,* Messner (New York, NY), 1983.

Word Processing, F. Watts (New York, NY), 1984.

(With Gilda Berger) *Bizarre Crimes,* illustrated by Cheryl Chalmers, Messner (New York, NY), 1984.

Computers: A Question and Answer Book, Crowell (New York, NY), 1985.

Mind Control, Crowell (New York, NY), 1985.

Star Gazing, Comet Watching, and Sky Mapping, Putnam (New York, NY), 1985.

Atoms, Molecules, and Quarks, Putnam (New York, NY), 1986.

The Whole Book of Hazardous Substances, Enslow (Hillside, NJ), 1986.

FOR ADULTS; NONFICTION

Guide to Chamber Music, Dodd (New York, NY), 1985.

Guide to Sonatas, Anchor (New York, NY), 1991.

Guide to Choral Masterpieces, Anchor (New York, NY), 1993.

The Anchor Guide to Orchestral Masterpieces, Anchor (New York, NY), 1995.

OTHER

Also fifty-two Big Books for very young children with minimal texts by Melvin Berger and teaching guides for teachers provided by Gilda Berger, published by Newbridge, New York, including *From Peanuts to Peanut Butter,* 1992.

BERNARD, Bruce 1928-2000

OBITUARY NOTICE—See index for SATA sketch: Born March 21, 1928, in London, England; died March 29, 2000, in London, England. Artist, editor, author. Bernard was a visual arts editor who collected exceptional photography and imagery. He wrote, edited, and gathered artwork for several of his own books, including his *Photodiscovery: Masterworks of Photography, 1840-1940* from 1980, the 1987 *Queen of Heaven: A Selection of Paintings of the Virgin Mary from the Twelfth to the Eighteenth Centuries. Van Gogh,* his 1992 offering, was aimed at a younger audience, and included biographical information on the artist, as well as images of his paintings, tools, and preliminary sketches. Bernard also served as picture editor of London's *Sunday Times Magazine* from 1972 to 1980.

OBITUARIES AND OTHER SOURCES:

PERIODICALS

Daily Telegraph (London), March 31, 2000, p. 39.
Times (London), April 1, 2000.

BIRD, Carmel 1940-

Personal

Born August 8, 1940, in Launceton, Tasmania, Australia; daughter of William (an optician) and Lavra (a homemaker) Power; children: Camilla. *Education:* University of Tasmania, B.A., Diploma of Education, M.A., 1960; Diplome de Langue, Paris; Licentiate of the London College of Music. *Politics:* "Left." *Religion:* Catholic.

Addresses

Office—Balwyn College, Australia 3103. *Agent*—Fran Bryson, P.O. Box 226, Flinders Lane Post Office, Melbourne, Australia 8009. *E-mail*—carmel@carmel-bird.com.

Career

Author. Secondary school teacher, 1961-80. Lecturer and instructor at numerous institutions, including

Holmesglen College, 1987, Sydney University, 1989, Deakin University, 1990, Preston Institute, 1992, Victoria University, 1993, 1994, Council of Adult Education, 1995, and Victoria College of the Arts, 1996; writer-in-residence at various institutions, including Methodist Ladies College, 1989, 1990, 1992.

Awards, Honors

Australia Council Grants, 1988, 1989, 1993, 1994, 1997, and 1998.

Writings

Cherry Ripe (novel), 1985.
Dear Writer (nonfiction), 1988.
The Bluebird Café (novel), New Directions (New York, NY), 1990.
Not Now Jack—I'm Writing a Novel (nonfiction), Picador (Sydney, Australia), 1994.
The White Garden, University of Queensland Press (St. Lucia, Australia), 1995.
Crisis (novel), Vintage (Milsons Point, Australia), 1996.
Red Shoes (novel and CD-ROM), 1998.

SHORT STORIES

Births, Deaths, and Marriages, 1983.
The Woodpecker Toy Fact, 1987, published in the United States and United Kingdom as *Woodpecker Point, and Other Stories,* New Directions (New York, NY), 1987.
The Common Rat, McPhee Gribble (South Yarra, Australia), 1993.
Automatic Teller (stories and essays), [Milsons Point, Australia], 1996.

EDITOR

The Stolen Children—Their Stories, 1998.
Relations: Australian Short Stories, Houghton Mifflin (Wantirna South, Australia), 1991.
Red Shoes, Vintage (Milsons Point, Australia), 1996.
Daughters and Fathers (short stories), University of Queensland Press (St. Lucia, Australia), 1997.

Founding coeditor of *Syllable* and *Fine Line,* fiction editor of *Voices,* 1995, and former fiction editor of *New Post.*

Work in Progress

Cape Grimm, a sequel to *Red Shoes; The Cassowary's Quiz,* a children's picture book; *Matilda Allover Downunder,* a children's picture book and CD-ROM.

Sidelights

"Because I always reckoned I was going to be a novelist, my parents gave me a typewriter for my seventeenth birthday," Carmel Bird wrote on her Web site, commenting about her career. Bird related that she taught herself to type and began writing a novel on her typewriter. She eventually published her first short story in the *Australian Women's Weekly,* and moved on to publish several novels and nonfiction works. She said of

Carmel Bird

her first acceptance letter that "when I read the letter from the editor I felt faint. I felt shaky. I wept.... You can sit in the garden in the sun tapping away and dreaming that your story will be published, and as long as the dream remains a kind of warm hallucination, it and you are safe. But get a big magazine saying that they want to turn that particular dream into reality, and dark panic and a spinning terror can take hold of your heart." Bird agreed to the publication of her short story, thus beginning her career as a writer and editor.

Over the years, Bird has issued several novels and short story collections of her own work, as well as edited short story anthologies. *Woodpecker Point, and Other Stories* was her first collection to be published in the United States. *New Statesman & Society* reviewer Lucasta Miller called the stories in this collection "beautifully crafted" and the writing reminiscent of Katherine Mansfield. Robert Carver noted in the London *Observer* the deceptive simplicity of Bird's stories, calling *Woodpecker Point* a "disquieting enigmatic collection."

In addition to short stories, Bird has also published several novels, including *The Bluebird Café.* Set in Tasmania, it features Nancy Best, a successful businesswoman who has resurrected a defunct mining town as an amusement park—the focus of the complex is the Bluebird Café. As the novel unfolds, various mysteries of the now extinct town, as well as the eccentric characters who are part of the park, are brought to life.

Peggy Kaganoff, writing in *Publishers Weekly,* lauded Bird for creating a "realm full of unexplained wonders, tenacious love, and tragedies for which there is no prevention and only limited recovery." Characterizing *The Bluebird Café* as a book that "simply refuses to be categorized," Irving Malin noted in the *Review of Contemporary Fiction* that Bird presents "an intricately structured novel."

Biographical and Critical Sources

PERIODICALS

Canadian Literature, winter, 1990, p. 182.
New Statesman & Society, April 20, 1990, Jenny Turner, "Apocalypse Then," p. 37; July 13, 1990, Lucasta Miller, "Thoroughly Modern Fiction," pp. 42-44.
Observer (London), August, 1990, Robert Carver, "Irish Taties, Aussie Pizzas," p. 52.
Publishers Weekly, March 15, 1991, Penny Kaganoff, review of *The Bluebird Café,* p. 55.
Review of Contemporary Fiction, fall, 1991, Irving Malin, review of *The Bluebird Café,* pp. 276-277.
Studies in Short Fiction, spring, 1993, Marty Ennes-Marvin, review of *Australian Short Stories,* p. 198.
Times Literary Supplement, November 27, 1987, Howard Jacobson, "Measuring Up to the Age and Place," p. 1307.
Women's Review of Books, July, 1991, Christina Thompson, "Lost in the Bush," p. 17.

ON-LINE

Carmel Bird's Web site, http://www.carmelbird.com/ (October 27, 2000).

*   *   *

BLAIR, Margaret Whitman 1951-

Personal

Born April 25, 1951, in Chicago, IL; daughter of Morton R. (an engineer) and Frances (a certified public accountant; maiden name, Pornes) Whitman; married Robert M. Blair (an economist), July 30, 1978; children: Matthew, David. *Education:* American University, B.A., 1973, M.A., 1979. *Politics:* Independent. *Religion:* Jewish.

Addresses

Home—Rockville, MD. *Agent*—c/o White Mane Publishing Co., P.O. Box 152, Shippensburg, PA 17257. *E-mail*—Blairfamily@erols.com.

Career

U.S. Peace Corps, Washington, DC, volunteer English teacher in Thailand, 1975-77; League of Women Voters, Washington, DC, worked in international relations at national office, 1977-78; *Business International,* Washington, DC, reporter and editor, 1980-82; Bureau of National Affairs, Washington, DC, reporter and editor, 1982-84; American-Israeli Public Affairs Committee, Washington, DC, senior trade specialist, 1984-85. Also

worked as an English teacher in Japan. Smithsonian Associates, lecturer on writing historical fiction; Writers Center, Bethesda, MD, teacher. *Member:* National Press Club (chairperson of Spring Writers' Conference, 2000-01), Washington Independent Writers (member of board of directors).

Awards, Honors

National Press Club Award for best series in a newsletter.

Writings

Brothers at War (novel), White Mane Publishing (Shippensburg, PA), 1997.
House of Spies: Danger in Civil War Washington (novel), White Mane Publishing (Shippensburg, PA), 1999.

Contributor to newsletters.

Two antagonistic brothers are transported back to the Civil War era and find themselves on opposite sides of the battle in Margaret Whitman Blair's time-travel novel. (Cover illustration by Harry A. West.)

Work in Progress

Every Inch a King, an adult historical novel set during the Civil War.

Sidelights

Margaret Whitman Blair told *SATA:* "I always have so many thoughts and feelings to express that I would drive the people around me crazy if I did not write on a regular basis. I've been keeping a journal since fifth grade. I write in it when I have something important to say, rather than making a daily entry. Often I record my dreams just as I wake up if I can remember them.

"I particularly like writing—and reading—historical novels. I find the past more interesting and romantic than contemporary times.

"When I was young, I longed to travel and live in far-off, exotic lands. I did that, thanks to a job teaching English in Japan, being a Peace Corps volunteer in Thailand, working on a kibbutz in Israel, and backpacking through Europe. Now I still like to travel, but best of all is to journey through my imagination to distant periods of history. I'm glad I traveled so much while I was young and healthy, with no family responsibilities. I think it made me a more open person, appreciative of the differences as well as the common ground among all peoples of the world.

"I am very disciplined when I am in the process of writing a novel, with a self-imposed requirement that I write four or five pages five days a week. I maintain a log in which I write down exactly what I accomplished each day—the date, what I did, and how I felt about it. It's an excellent record when I'm trying to remember the things I've done, and it keeps me on target and motivated.

"Since writing is a solitary activity, I make it a point to be active in local writers' groups and attend other authors' book signings. I am a big believer in supporting other writers, and they in turn will nourish you. Only another writer can understand the difficulties you are experiencing during the creative process as well as during the later marketing phase."

Biographical and Critical Sources

PERIODICALS

Booklist, August, 1997, Kay Weisman, review of *Brothers at War,* p. 1900.

* * *

BRADSTREET, T. J.
See THESMAN, Jean

BRENNER, Barbara (Johnes) 1925-

Personal

Born June 26, 1925, in Brooklyn, NY; daughter of Robert Lawrence (a real estate broker) and Marguerite (Furboter) Johnes; married Fred Brenner (an illustrator), March 16, 1947; children: Mark, Carl. *Education:* Attended Seton Hall College (now Seton Hall University), 1942-43, Rutgers University, 1944-46, New York University, 1953-54, and New School for Social Research, 1960-62. *Politics:* Independent. *Hobbies and other interests:* Gardening, swimming, traveling, bird watching.

Addresses

Home—Box 1826, Hemlock Farms, Hawley, PA 18428.

Career

Prudential Insurance Co., copywriter, 1942-46; freelance artist's agent, 1946-52; freelance writer, 1957—; writer-consultant and eventual senior editor in Publications Division, Bank Street College of Education, 1962-90. Parson's School of Design, instructor, 1980-81. County chairperson, Committee for a Sane Nuclear Policy, 1960-61. *Member:* Authors Guild, Authors League of America, PEN, Royal Society for the Arts, National Audubon Society, Society of Children's Book Writers and Illustrators.

Awards, Honors

New York Herald Tribune Children's Spring Book Festival honor book award, 1961, for *Barto Takes the Subway; Washington Post Book World* Spring Book Festival honor book award, and *New York Times* best children's book list, both 1970, and American Library Association (ALA) notable book citation, all for *A*

Barbara Brenner

Snake-Lover's Diary; Outstanding Science Trade Book for Children Award, National Science Teachers Association and Children's Book Council, 1974, for *Baltimore Orioles,* 1975, for *Lizard Tails and Cactus Spines,* 1977, for *On the Frontier with Mr. Audubon,* 1979, for *Beware! These Animals Are Poison,* and 1980, for *Have You Heard of a Kangaroo Bird?: Fascinating Facts about Unusual Birds;* American Library Association notable book citation, 1978, for *Wagon Wheels;* Best of the Best Award, *School Library Journal,* 1982, for *On the Frontier with Mr. Audubon;* named outstanding Pennsylvania Author, 1986; Edgar Allan Poe award nomination, Mystery Writers of America, 1988, for *The Falcon Sting;* ALA notable book citation, 2000, for *Voices: Poetry and Art from around the World.*

Writings

FOR CHILDREN

Somebody's Slippers, Somebody's Shoes, W. R. Scott, 1957.

Barto Takes the Subway, Knopf (New York, NY), 1961.

A Bird in the Family, W. R. Scott, 1962.

Unlikely best friends Lion and Lamb, featured in Brenner's books for early independent readers, share three stories of a hike, a circus, and a lesson in reconciliation. (From *Lion and Lamb Step Out, written by Brenner and William H. Hooks and illustrated by Bruce Degen.*)

Amy's Doll, Knopf (New York, NY), 1963.

The Five Pennies, illustrated by Erik Blegvad, Knopf (New York, NY), 1963.

Careers and Opportunities in Fashion (young adult), Dutton (New York, NY), 1964.

Our Class Presents Ostrich Feathers: A Play in Two Acts (first produced off-Broadway, 1965), illustrated by Vera B. Williams, Parents' Magazine Press (New York, NY), 1978.

Beef Stew, illustrated by John E. Johnson, Knopf (New York, NY), 1965, reprinted with illustrations by Catherine Siracusa, 1990.

The Flying Patchwork Quilt, illustrated by husband, Fred Brenner, Knopf (New York, NY), 1965.

Mr. Tall and Mr. Small, illustrated by Tomi Ungerer, W. R. Scott, 1966, reprinted with illustrations by Mile Shenon, Holt, 1994.

Nicky's Sister, illustrated by John E. Johnson, Knopf (New York, NY), 1966.

Summer of the Houseboat, illustrated by Fred Brenner, Knopf (New York, NY), 1968.

Faces, illustrated with photographs by George Ancona, Dutton (New York, NY), 1970.

A Snake-Lover's Diary, W. R. Scott, 1970.

A Year in the Life of Rosie Bernard, illustrated by Joan Sandin, Harper (New York, NY), 1971, revised edition, Avon (New York, NY), 1983.

Is It Bigger Than a Sparrow?: A Box for Young Bird Watchers, Knopf (New York, NY), 1972.

(Reteller) *Walt Disney's "Three Little Pigs,"* Random House, 1972.

Bodies, illustrated with photographs by George Ancona, Dutton (New York, NY), 1973.

If You Were an Ant, Harper (New York, NY), 1973.

(Adaptor) *Walt Disney's "The Penguin That Hated the Cold,"* Random House, 1973.

Hemi: A Mule, Harper (New York, NY), 1973.

Baltimore Orioles, illustrated by J. Winslow Higginbottom, Harper (New York, NY), 1974.

Cunningham's Rooster, illustrated by Anne Rockwell, Parents' Magazine Press (New York, NY), 1975.

Lizard Tails and Cactus Spines, illustrated with photographs by Merrit S. Keasey III, Harper (New York, NY), 1975.

Little One Inch, illustrated by Fred Brenner, Coward, 1977.

On the Frontier with Mr. Audubon, Coward, 1977.

We're Off to See the Lizard, illustrated by Shelley Dietreichs, Raintree (Milwaukee, WI), 1977.

Wagon Wheels, illustrated by Don Bolognese, Harper (New York, NY), 1978.

Beware! These Animals Are Poison, illustrated by Jim Spanfeller, Coward, 1979.

(With May Garelick) *The Tremendous Tree Book,* illustrated by Fred Brenner, Four Winds Press (New York, NY), 1979.

Have You Ever Heard of a Kangaroo Bird?: Fascinating Facts about Unusual Birds, illustrated by Irene Brady, Coward, 1980.

The Prince and the Pink Blanket, illustrated by Nola Langner, Four Winds Press (New York, NY), 1980.

A Killing Season, Four Winds Press (New York, NY), 1981.

Mystery of the Plumed Serpent, illustrated by Blanche Sims, Knopf (New York, NY), 1981.

Mystery of the Disappearing Dogs, Knopf (New York, NY), 1982.

A Dog I Know, illustrated by Fred Brenner, Harper (New York, NY), 1983.

The Gorilla Signs Love, Lothrop (New York, NY), 1984.

The Snow Parade, Crown (New York, NY), 1984.

Saving the President: What If Lincoln Had Lived?, illustrated by Steve Madsen, Simon & Schuster (New York, NY), 1987.

The Falcon Sting, Bradbury (Scarsdale, NY), 1988.

(With May Garelick) *Two Orphan Cubs,* Walker (New York, NY), 1989.

(With William H. Hooks) *Lion and Lamb,* Bantam (New York, NY), 1989.

Annie's Pet, Bantam (New York, NY), 1989.

The Color Wizard, illustrated by Leo and Diane Dillon, Bantam (New York, NY), 1989.

(With William H. Hooks) *Lion and Lamb Step Out,* Bantam (New York, NY), 1990.

Moon Boy, Bantam (New York, NY), 1990.

The Magic Box, Bantam (New York, NY), 1990.

Good News, Bantam (New York, NY), 1991.

If You Were There in 1492, Atheneum (New York, NY), 1991.

(With William H. Hooks) *Ups and Downs with Lion and Lamb,* illustrated by Bruce Degen, Bantam (New York, NY), 1991.

(With William H. Hooks and Joanne Oppenheim) *No Way, Slippery Slick!,* illustrated by Joan Auclair, Harper (New York, NY), 1991.

(With William H. Hooks and Joanne Oppenheim) *How Do You Make a Bubble?,* illustrated by Doug Cushman, Bantam (New York, NY), 1992.

Rosa and Marco and the Three Wishes, Bradbury (Scarsdale, NY), 1992.

Beavers Beware, Bantam (New York, NY), 1992.

Too Many Mice, illustrated by John Emil Cymerman, Bantam (New York, NY), 1992.

Noah and the Flood, illustrated by Annie Mitra, Bantam (New York, NY), 1992.

Group Soup, Viking (New York, NY), 1992.

Dinosaurium, illustrated by Donna Bragenitz, Bantam (New York, NY), 1993.

Planetarium, illustrated by Ron Miller, Bantam (New York, NY), 1993.

If You Were There in 1776, Atheneum (New York, NY), 1994.

(Editor) *The Earth Is Painted Green* (poetry anthology), illustrated by S. D. Schindler, Scholastic (New York, NY), 1994.

The United Nations Fiftieth Anniversary Book, Atheneum (New York, NY), 1995.

(With Bernice Chardiet) *Where's That Cat?,* illustrated by Schwartz, Scholastic (New York, NY), 1995.

(With Julia Takaya) *Chibi: A True Story from Japan,* illustrated by June Otani, Clarion (Boston, MA), 1996.

The Plant That Kept on Growing, illustrated by Melissa Sweet, Bantam (New York, NY), 1996.

Thinking about Ants, illustrated by Schwartz, Mondo, 1997.

Lucky Dog, Scholastic (New York, NY), 1997.

Brenner leads young readers in an inventive game of hide-and-seek, during which they learn about insects by searching for them in their natural surroundings. (Cover illustration by Carol Schwartz.)

The Boy Who Loved to Draw: Benjamin West, illustrated by Olivier Dunrea, Houghton Mifflin, 1999.

(Compiler) *Voices: Poetry and Art from around the World,* National Geographic, 2000.

If You Lived in Williamsburg in Colonial Days, Scholastic (New York, NY), 2000.

"HIDE AND SEEK SCIENCE BOOK" SERIES; WITH BERNICE CHARDIET; ILLUSTRATED BY CAROL SCHWARTZ

Where's That Reptile?, Scholastic (New York, NY), 1993.

Where's That Insect?, Scholastic (New York, NY), 1993.

Where's That Fish?, Scholastic (New York, NY), 1994.

Where's That Bat?, Scholastic (New York, NY), 1999.

Where's That Spider?, Scholastic (New York, NY), 1999.

OTHER

(Editor) Edward Turner and Clive Turner, *Frogs and Toads,* Raintree, 1976.

(Editor) Ralph Whitlock, *Spiders,* Raintree, 1976.

Love and Discipline (adult), Ballantine (New York, NY), 1983.

(With Mari Endreweit) *Bank Street's Family Guide to Home Computers* (adult), Ballantine (New York, NY), 1984.

(With Joanne Oppenheim and Betty Boeghold) *Raising a Confident Child: The Bank Street Year-by-Year Guide,* (adult), Pantheon (New York, NY), 1984.

(With Joanne Oppenheim and Betty Boeghold) *Choosing Books for Kids: Choosing the Right Book for the Right Kid at the Right Time* (adult), Ballantine (New York, NY), 1986.

The Preschool Handbook: Making the Most of Your Child's Education, Pantheon (New York, NY), 1990.

Contributor of articles to periodicals, including *Cricket, Good Housekeeping, Newsweek,* and *Sierra Club.* Editor of "Talkabout Program" for Adult Resource Books.

Adaptations

Wagon Wheels and *The Tremendous Tree Book* were adapted for the Public Broadcasting Service's *Reading Rainbow* television series.

Sidelights

The author of over eighty books for young readers, Barbara Brenner is best known for her handling of nature and ecological matters. In award-winning titles such as *On the Frontier with Mr. Audubon, A Snake-Lover's Diary,* and *Lizard Tales and Cactus Spines,*

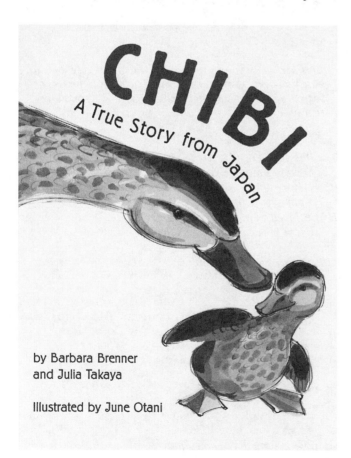

Using Japanese vocabulary, Brenner and cowriter Julia Takaya describe contemporary Tokyo in their tale of a family of spotbill ducklings. (Cover illustration by June Otani.)

Brenner combines crisp attention to detail with age-appropriate language in her fiction and nonfiction entries. Her picture books for young readers span the gamut from the adventures of a lion and lamb to the story of the biblical Flood, and her nonfiction titles include topics from dinosaurs to the history of the United Nations.

Born in Brooklyn, New York, Brenner was raised largely by her maternal grandparents after the death of her mother when Brenner was only a year old. Her father would travel from Brooklyn to upstate New York on the weekends to see his daughter and would read her favorite books to her: *Winnie the Pooh* and *When We Were Very Young* by A. A. Milne, *The Tale of Peter Rabbit,* and *Pinocchio.* These books stayed with her through childhood, forming the backdrop of her literary heritage. With the advent of the Great Depression, Brenner moved back to Brooklyn in a large extended family under one roof.

Another major move came at age eight with the remarriage of her father and removal to a new home in New Jersey, away from the extended family she had known since she was a small child. "I think that what got me through that next year was my books," Brenner wrote in *Something about the Author Autobiography Series* (SAAS). "By this time I was an excellent reader. I proceeded to bury myself in my reading. I escaped from having to deal with all the new things in my life by stepping into the world of *Hans Brinker, Little Women,* and *Blackie's Children's Annual.*" Soon there was a baby brother in her new family, and Brenner became the spoiling and bossing older sister. Mainly a good student at school, Brenner had trouble only with math. In junior high school she became interested in writing, an interest that deepened in high school, with Brenner writing the book and lyrics for the annual Senior Show.

Upon graduation from high school, Brenner took a job with the Prudential Life Insurance Company, eventually working for the in-house magazine. At the end of the Second World War she met an illustrator, Fred Brenner, who had just returned from the United States Air Force. It took the couple only two weeks to determine they were right for each other and to decide to get married. For the next several years, Brenner worked as an artist's agent both for her husband and other illustrators. During all these years, Brenner continued her education, taking courses at Seton Hall College, Rutgers University, New York University, and Manhattan's New School for Social Research.

After five years of marriage, Brenner had the first of two children, and once their son Mark was old enough to go to nursery school, Brenner began writing again. Reading children's books to her son had encouraged her to try her own hand at such tales. In the event, writing children's books was not as easy as she thought it would be, but finally her first book, *Somebody's Slippers, Somebody's Shoes* was published in 1957, the same year her second son was born. Her second title, *Barto Takes the Subway,* earned the Children's Spring Book Festival honor award

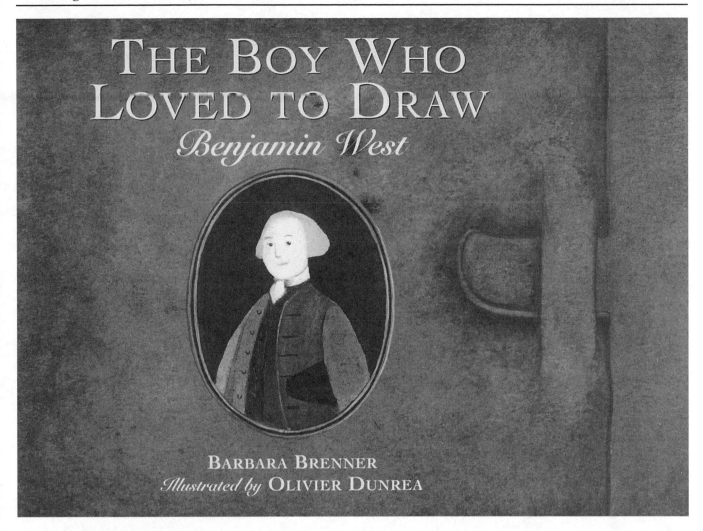

Brenner's juvenile biography depicts the life of the colonial who became the first American artist to gain worldwide fame. (Cover illustration by Olivier Dunrea.)

from the *New York Herald Tribune,* and Brenner was on her way to a career writing children's books. During the 1960s Brenner joined the staff of the Bank Street College of Education as a writer-consultant, later becoming a senior editor. That job, she explained in *SAAS,* "enabled me to get another perspective on children, parents, and on children's learning, as well as on some of the new forms of communication available to kids."

Some of Brenner's early books were illustrated by her artist husband. *The Tremendous Tree Book,* for example, coauthored with May Garelick, featured his "striking paper cutouts," according to a reviewer for *Horn Book,* who also called the text an "imaginative blending of art and science." By this time, Brenner had set her course on nature and environmental themes primarily.

One of her most popular early books on nature deals with the life of the great ornithologist John James Audubon, *On the Frontier with Mr. Audubon.* Paul Showers noted in the *New York Times Book Review* that with this book Brenner "again demonstrates her gift for invention and respect for facts. This is a combination of fiction and fact that works so well it might almost be the

thing it imitates." Showers went on to explain that the book is "written in the polite but colloquial language of the frontier sketching in Audubon's biographical background and recording events of the journey as they might have been observed by a serious, very perceptive thirteen-year-old."

Another title that holds particularly fond memories for Brenner is her 1965 work *The Flying Patchwork Quilt.* The idea for this lighthearted tale—about a little girl named Ellen who learns to fly on a magic quilt—"took shape when my son Carl went through what is referred to in our house as a 'flying stage,'" she remarked in *SAAS.* "During this time he tried constantly and unsuccessfully to become airborne. Since this was the second time I had encountered this phase (my older boy, too, had a flying stage), I decided there must be something fairly typical in it." The quilt "is modeled after an old patchwork quilt that I bought several years ago," she continued. "The children have always been fond of it, and for that reason I thought it would be interesting to use it as the focal point of a fantasy."

A move to Pennsylvania brought Brenner closer to nature, as she spent time in the woods of the northeastern part of the state studying bears. Two books grew out of the experience, her first young adult title, *A Killing Season,* and another collaboration with her long-time friend May Garelick, *Two Orphan Cubs.* The latter is "an informative, beautifully-designed book about black bears for young children," according to Arlene Bernstein in an *Appraisal: Science Books for Young People* review.

Brenner's other nonfiction works deal with both historical as well as environmental matters. Brenner researched and penned a work for the five hundredth anniversary of Columbus's voyage to the Americas. *If You Were There in 1492* was a "sometimes awkward time-slice that nevertheless contains a lot of information," according to Betsy Hearne in *Bulletin of the Center for Children's Books.* "Brenner conveys a remarkable amount of material at a snappy pace," wrote Mary Harris Veeder in a *Tribune Books* review of the same title.

Another anniversary celebration prompted the writing of *The United Nations Fiftieth Anniversary Book,* a work that "recounts the formation of the organization and is packed with up-to-date detail about its ongoing role in promoting better lives for all people, especially children," according to *School Library Journal* contributor Joan Soulliere. She also concluded that Brenner's book "provides a strong introduction to multicultural appreciation and global responsibility." A reviewer for *Voice of Youth Advocates* called the same book a "cogent explication of the humanitarian accomplishments of the UN around the world."

Nature topics are brought up in many other nonfiction books from Brenner. Working with Bernice Chardiet, she has produced many titles in the "Hide and Seek Science Book" series. A writer for *Kirkus Reviews* mentioned that *Where's That Insect?* is an "attractive and effective introduction to insect identification," while their *Where's the Cat?* "is a good browsing item for beginning readers," according to Rosanne Cerny in *School Library Journal.* Brenner's *Dinosaurium* and *Planetarium* are "impressive books," wrote Cathryn A. Camper in *School Library Journal.* Camper likened the two titles to "museums squeezed between book covers," so thorough are they in detailed information and illustrations. In *Thinking about Ants,* Brenner presents eleven different varieties of picnic-spoilers in "an easy narrative," written in "short, occasionally rhyming sentences or phrases," as John Peters described the work in *Booklist.* "Text and large, clear pictures combine to make this an unusually promising candidate for a read-aloud science book," Peters claimed.

Equally prolific in fiction picture books and easy readers as in nonfiction, Brenner has also continued her focus on nature in stories and tales for young readers. *Good News* features a Canada goose who honks the good news that she is sitting on four eggs, but each time news of the event travels to a new pond, the number and size of the eggs increases. "The cumulative text should appeal to young readers," predicted Sharron McElmeel in a *School Library Journal* review of the picture book. Collaborating with William H. Hooks, Brenner has also produced several tales about the friendship between Lion and Lamb, a rather unlikely duo. In a review of the third title in the series, *Ups and Downs with Lion and Lamb,* *Booklist*'s Ilene Cooper observed, "Gentle humor and dollops of adventure will snare new readers."

More nature tales are served up in *Beavers Beware!,* in which a young girl is intrigued by the lodge that beavers have built on her family's dock. *Booklist*'s Kay Weisman noted that although Brenner chose a fictional presentation, "she provides a great deal of factual information, making this an appealing title for nature enthusiasts as well as beginning readers." A mouse and giraffe argue over the relative merits of size in *Mr. Tall and Mr. Small,* a "story hour winner," according to Elizabeth Bush reviewing the 1994 reprint in *Bulletin of the Center for Children's Books.* In *Chibi: A True Story from Japan,* Brenner relates the actual story of a mother duck who chose to build her nest in the pool in front of a Tokyo office building. Maria B. Salvadore, writing in *Horn Book,* observed that the telling was "in a crisp, straightforward style."

In *The Boy Who Loved to Draw: Benjamin West,* Brenner turned once again to history to tell the story of the painter called the "father of American art." Born in 1738, West was the tenth child in his family. Largely self-taught, he learned of color from the Native Americans, of paintbrushes from a traveler. Soon young Benjamin was sent to Philadelphia to study with a real artist. Brenner summarizes his subsequent successful career as a portrait painter and friend of Benjamin Franklin, as well as his life in exile in England. "This is a fine introduction to artists and the Colonial period," wrote Kathleen Staerkel in *School Library Journal.* Mary M. Burns, writing in *Horn Book,* called *The Boy Who Loved to Draw* "a handsome interpretation, faithful to its subject, lively to read." *Booklist*'s Carolyn Phelan thought the book was a "fascinating look at art in colonial times, and a likable portrait of the artist as a young boy."

The multi-talented Brenner has also edited books of poetry, including *Voices: Poetry and Art from around the World* and *The Earth Is Painted Green,* but whether editing or writing about animals in the wild and events in history, Brenner has shown, according to critics, that she understands what children enjoy: a way with words that breathes life into cold facts. "I consider writing books for children a very difficult and challenging art form," Brenner once said. "Amateur or professional, you're still faced with that blank page and the need to put your thoughts in order."

Biographical and Critical Sources

BOOKS

Something about the Author Autobiography Series, Volume 14, Gale (Detroit, MI), 1991.

PERIODICALS

Appraisal: Science Books for Young People, winter, 1990, Arlene Bernstein, review of *Two Orphan Cubs,* pp. 15-16.

Booklist, June 1, 1991, Ilene Cooper, review of *Ups and Downs with Lion and Lamb,* p. 1883; April 1, 1992, Kay Weisman, review of *Beavers Beware!,* p. 1459; June 1, 1992, p. 1766; August, 1993, p. 2064; January 15, 1994, p. 923; February 15, 1996, p. 1023; June 1, 1997, John Peters, review of *Thinking about Ants,* p. 1708; September 15, 1999, Carolyn Phelan, review of *The Boy Who Loved to Draw: Benjamin West,* p. 262; December 1, 2000, p. 701.

Bulletin of the Center for Children's Books, October, 1991, Betsy Hearne, review of *If You Were There in 1492,* pp. 27-29; April, 1992, p. 200; November, 1994, Elizabeth Bush, review of *Mr. Tall and Mr. Small,* p. 81.

Horn Book, January-February, 1993, review of *The Tremendous Tree Book,* p. 105; July-August, 1996, Maria B. Salvadore, review of *Chibi: A True Story from Japan,* p. 476; September-October, 1999, Mary M. Burns, review of *The Boy Who Loved to Draw: Benjamin West,* p. 622.

Kirkus Reviews, June 15, 1991, p. 796; May 15, 1993, review of *Where's That Insect?,* p. 656; February, 15, 1994, p. 223.

New York Times Book Review, March 27, 1977, Paul Showers, review of *On the Frontier with Mr. Audubon;* November 10, 1991, p. 56.

Publishers Weekly, February 17, 1992, p. 63; April 13, 1992, p. 59; March 22, 1993, p. 81; December 20, 1993, p. 72; March 27, 1995, p. 86; March 29, 1999, p. 106; November 20, 2000, p. 70.

School Library Journal, December, 1991, Sharron McElmeel, review of *Good News,* pp. 78, 80; March, 1992, p. 208; April, 1992, p. 89; August, 1992, p. 133; December, 1992, p. 95; August, 1993, Cathryn A. Camper, review of *Dinosaurium* and *Planetarium,* p. 169; January, 1994, pp. 103-104; January, 1995, p. 81; April, 1995, Rosanne Cerny, review of *Where's That Cat?,* p. 122; July, 1995, Joan Soulliere, review of *The United Nations Fiftieth Anniversary Book,* pp. 83-84; October, 1999, Kathleen Staerkel, *The Boy Who Loved to Draw: Benjamin West,* p. 134.

Tribune Books (Chicago), October 6, 1991, Mary Harris Veeder, review of *If You Were There in 1492,* p. 4.

Voice of Youth Advocates, August, 1996, review of *The United Nations Fiftieth Anniversary Book,* p. 149.

—*Sketch by J. Sydney Jones*

*   *   *

BRILL, Marlene Targ 1945-

Personal

Born September 27, 1945, in Chicago, IL; daughter of Irving (a pharmacist) and Genevieve (a homemaker; maiden name, Worshill) Targ; married Richard Brill (a consultant in marketing and public relations), February 4, 1973; children: Alison. *Education:* University of

Marlene Targ Brill

Illinois, B.S., 1967; Roosevelt University, M.A., 1973; Loyola University, Administrative Certificate, 1978.

Addresses

Home—Wilmette, IL. *Office*—Marlene Targ Brill Communications, 314 Lawndale, Wilmette, IL 60091.

Career

Worked as a curriculum specialist, media coordinator, and special education classroom teacher, 1967-80; Marlene Targ Brill (MTB) Communications, Wilmette, IL, children's book author, speaker about writing, and writer/editor for businesses and textbook and health care publishers, 1980—. Consultant and advocate for special education. *Member:* Authors Guild, Society of Children's Book Writers and Illustrators, Society of Midland Authors.

Awards, Honors

Chicago Women in Publishing merit award, 1988, for *Hide-and-Seek Safety;* School of Librarians International Top Ten Social Studies Choice, 1993, for *Allen Jay and the Underground Railroad;* Honor Book, Society of

Midland Authors, 1997, for *Women for Peace,* and 1998, for *Diary of a Drummer Boy;* Children's Choice Award, International Reading Association and Children's Book Council, 1998, for *Tooth Tales from around the World.*

Writings

FOR CHILDREN

(With Kathi Checker) *Unique Listening/Mainstreaming Stories,* Instructional Dynamics, 1980.

John Adams: Second President of the United States, Children's Press (Chicago, IL), 1986.

I Can Be a Lawyer, Children's Press (Chicago, IL), 1987.

James Buchanan: Fifteenth President of the United States, Children's Press (Chicago, IL), 1988.

Hide-and-Seek Safety, World Book (Chicago, IL), 1988.

Rainy Days and Rainbows, World Book (Chicago, IL), 1989.

Why Do We Have To?, World Book (Chicago, IL), 1990.

Allen Jay and the Underground Railroad (fiction), illustrated by Janice Lee Porter, Carolrhoda Books (Minneapolis, MN), 1993.

Trail of Tears: The Cherokee Journey Home, Millbrook Press (Brookfield, CT), 1995.

Building the Capital City, Children's Press (New York, NY), 1996.

Extraordinary Young People, Children's Press (New York, NY), 1996.

Journey for Peace: The Story of Rigoberta Menchú, illustrated by Rubén De Anda, Dutton (New York, NY), 1996.

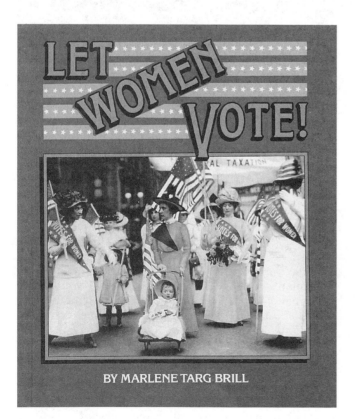

Brill's title from the "Spotlight on American History" series examines the struggle to pass the Nineteenth Amendment, which gave women the right to vote.

Let Women Vote!, Millbrook Press (Brookfield, CT), 1996.

Women for Peace, Franklin Watts (New York, NY), 1997.

Diary of a Drummer Boy (fiction), illustrated by Michael Garland, Millbrook Press (Brookfield, CT), 1998.

Tooth Tales from around the World, illustrated by Katya Krenina, Charlesbridge (Watertown, MA), 1998.

Margaret Knight: Girl Inventor (fiction), Millbrook Press (Brookfield, CT), 2000.

Tourette Syndrome, Millbrook Press (Brookfield, CT), 2002.

Georgia O'Keefe and the Horse, Barron's (Hauppauge, NY), 2002.

"ENCHANTMENT OF THE WORLD" SERIES

Libya, Children's Press (Chicago, IL), 1987.

Algeria, Children's Press (Chicago, IL), 1990.

Mongolia, Children's Press (Chicago, IL), 1992.

(With Harry R. Targ) *Guatemala,* Children's Press (Chicago, IL), 1993.

Guyana, Children's Press (Chicago, IL), 1994.

(With Harry R. Targ) *Honduras,* Children's Press (Chicago, IL), 1995.

RETELLER; "CHILDREN'S BIBLE STORIES" SERIES

Daniel in the Lion's Den, illustrated by Thomas Gianni, Publications International (Lincolnwood, IL), 1992.

David and Goliath, illustrated by Thomas Gianni, Publications International (Lincolnwood, IL), 1992.

Noah's Ark, illustrated by Thomas Gianni, Publications International (Lincolnwood, IL), 1992.

Joseph's Coat of Many Colors, illustrated by Gary Torrisi, Publications International (Lincolnwood, IL), 1992.

Jonah and the Whale, illustrated by Gary Torrisi, Publications International (Lincolnwood, IL), 1992.

"CELEBRATE THE STATES" SERIES

Illinois, Benchmark Books (New York, NY), 1997.

Indiana, Benchmark Books (New York, NY), 1997.

Michigan, Benchmark Books (New York, NY), 1998.

"SPORT SUCCESS" SERIES

Winning Women in Ice Hockey, Barron's (Hauppauge, NY), 1999.

Winning Women in Soccer, Barron's (Hauppauge, NY), 1999.

Winning Women in Baseball and Softball, Barron's (Hauppauge, NY), 2000.

Winning Women in Basketball, Barron's (Hauppauge, NY), 2000.

FOR ADULTS

Washington D.C. Travel Guide, World Book (Chicago, IL), 1982.

Infertility and You, Budlong Press (Chicago, IL), 1984.

Keys to Parenting a Child with Down Syndrome, Barron's Educational Series (Hauppauge, NY), 1993.

Keys to Parenting the Child with Autism, Barron's Educational Series (Hauppauge, NY), 1993, 2nd edition, 2001.

American Medical Association Essential Guide to Asthma, Pocket Books (New York, NY), 1998.

OTHER

Project Aware (slide-tape production), Illinois Association for Retarded Citizens, 1980.

Contributor to *The President's World,* World Book, 1982, and *Scholastic Book of American Indians,* Scholastic, 1997. Author of "The Important You" column for *Career World,* 1981.

Work in Progress

The Picture Girl; Wild Dog; Birds in the Hills.

Sidelights

Marlene Targ Brill is a prolific writer of children's books that aim to enrich young people's lives and enhance their learning experience. Although she has written several books with a geographic theme, Brill concentrates on historical topics and tales of achievers from all walks of life. The list of her titles reveals a wide range of topics—from *John Adams* to *Libya,* from *Let Women Vote!* to *Winning Women in Soccer.* A special education teacher and educational consultant, Brill has also written extensively on the needs of children with disabilities. She views her dual careers—writer and teacher—as complementary.

Brill's books include *Allen Jay and the Underground Railroad,* a 1993 fictional diary based on the true story of a Quaker boy in Ohio in the 1840s. Jay and his family are human links in the fabled Underground Railroad, helping slaves reach the "free" northern states. "The story is told with dramatic simplicity," declared *Booklist*'s Hazel Rochman. Brill wrote about a less rewarding journey in another of her books published in the mid-1990s, *Trail of Tears: The Cherokee Journey Home.* The largest Native American nation was forced to vacate its ancestral lands in the southeast United States after gold was discovered there. A federal order stipulated their removal in 1838. Thousands of Cherokee made their arduous journey on foot and by wagon to what is now Oklahoma, and many died along the way. George Gleason, writing in *School Library Journal,* called it "a handsome volume that is a fine addition to literature on the subject."

Brill continued to focus on the lives of achievers in *Extraordinary Young People,* which appeared in 1996. In this book, she profiles fifty individuals, all of whom encountered hardship or difficulties at an early age, but persevered to accomplish their goals. Genghis Khan, for instance, fought battles when he was still a child; Joan of Arc was just sixteen when she achieved military glory in fifteenth-century France, and soccer star Pelé grew up in desperate poverty in Brazil. Other achievers in *Extraordinary Young People* include dancer Maria Tallchief, golf champion Tiger Woods, Broadway star Savion Glover, and Ryan White, an AIDS-afflicted youth who fought for the right to attend school. "Coverage is brief but highly informative and lively," remarked *School Library Journal* critic Jerry D. Flack, who also termed it "an entertaining and inspiring book."

The women's suffrage movement in United States history was Brill's subject in another 1996 book, *Let Women Vote!* She recounts the origins of the movement, which grew in part out of the abolitionist cause, in which many committed women worked to call attention to the injustice of slavery. Brill also profiles early feminist leaders, such as Elizabeth Cady Stanton and Susan B. Anthony, and introduces the important events of the women's struggle, such as the Seneca Falls Woman's Rights Convention and the rise of the National Women's Party. It was World War I, however, which finally resolved the seven-decade-long battle with a constitutional amendment. Brill's book draws upon many quotes from primary sources, and an epilogue recounts victories—and setbacks—since that historic national election of 1920. *School Library Journal* reviewer Judith L. Miller called it "a spirited account" with "energetic writing" and "a well-organized text."

In her 1996 biography, *Journey for Peace: The Story of Rigoberta Menchú,* Brill gives young readers a glimpse of the life of an impoverished Guatemalan woman and Mayan Indian who won the Nobel Peace Prize in 1992. Menchú, a field laborer in a rural village, followed in the footsteps of her activist-father, organizing her community to peacefully oppose a corrupt government that had brought severe hardship to families like hers. The Nobel Prize winner's father was tortured and murdered for speaking out, and Menchú risked similar violence for her activism. "The account is quiet, but it tells of violence and poverty and amazing courage," remarked Hazel Rochman in *Booklist. School Library Journal* writer Shirley Wilton praised Brill's "skillful expository writing" and called Menchú's biography "an exciting story, well told."

Brill expanded the topic of conflict in another book, *Women for Peace,* published in 1997. Here she presents a basic history of war and armed conflict from ancient Greece to Vietnam, highlighting the organized movements that women have founded to stem the bloodshed, like the Women's Peace Party and Grandmothers for Peace. The book also profiles individual women who have dedicated their lives to ending conflict, such as anti-nuclear activist Dr. Helen Caldicott. The peace movement in the modern era, as Brill demonstrates, has embraced women's rights issues and environmental concerns. "An interesting book," noted *School Library Journal* reviewer Marilyn Fairbanks, "which fills the gender gap left by many standard reference works." Ilene Cooper's *Booklist* review stated that "Brill's writing is consistently engaging and reflective."

Brill told *SATA:* "Some authors are born to write. Although I always hoped to do something in the arts, writing was not my first passion. Over time, however, words became my vehicle of expression, my way of contributing to my community, influencing others, and changing perceptions.

"Many of my book ideas originate from my desire to write women into history. Even in our supposedly enlightened times, traditional histories still offer a view of the world through men's eyes. Books and periodicals focus almost entirely on men's achievements, lives, and wars. Since much of my writing is for children, I want all my readers—girls and boys—to be able to relate to what they read by finding subjects in books who are like them.

"The 'Sport Success' series of titles highlights women's contributions to these sports. Each book emphasizes the joys and talents of women athletes from sports that are rarely covered in the media. By providing role models in these sports, young readers learn that active girls and women are involved in all sports, and they can be, too.

"*Women for Peace* focuses on women's ongoing involvement in creating peaceful communities. More than a book about women, this title seeks to provide an alternative to the many books about war. The Chicago Peace Museum credited it as the inspiration for its 1999 exhibit, 'Women's Peace Initiatives: Transforming Community.' Material from this exhibit, some of it written by me, became part of *Planting Seeds for Peace*, the 2000 calendar from the Consortium on Peace Research, Education, and Development. Authors never know where their words will travel and how they will affect readers.

"Another way books contribute to a more peaceful world is to reduce anxiety about people who are different. Since I was a special educator for thirteen years before becoming an author, I write about children who have special needs, such as autism, Down syndrome, and Tourette's syndrome. My goal is to break down barriers to getting along with people who are different by helping readers understand these conditions and realize we are all different in our own way and deserve fair treatment.

"Comfort with others also stems from a strong self-image, another goal of my writing. *Extraordinary Young People* celebrates the accomplishments and special talents of young children and teenagers. The girls and boys profiled in this book acted in ways that were amazing for their young ages, cultures, and times. Several faced harsh parents, poverty, war, or various other handicaps—many of the same issues children face today—and still managed to shine through their everyday accomplishments. My historical fiction stories—*Allen Jay and the Underground Railroad, Diary of a Drummer Boy,* and *Margaret Knight: Girl Inventor*—involve children who experienced similar hardships, persevered through adversity, and solved their problems independently.

"Most of all, I try to convey the fun of nonfiction to readers. Writing nonfiction is one of the only jobs that allows someone to investigate drummer boys one day and world peace or the history of the tooth fairy the next."

Biographical and Critical Sources

PERIODICALS

Booklist, July, 1993, Hazel Rochman, review of *Allen Jay and the Underground Railroad,* pp. 1979-1980; September 1, 1996, Hazel Rochman, review of *Journey for Peace: The Story of Rigoberta Menchú,* p. 120; February 1, 1997, Susan Dove Lempke, review of *Illinois,* p. 937; May 15, 1997, Ilene Cooper, review of *Women for Peace,* p. 1569; March 1, 1998, Carolyn Phelan, review of *Diary of a Drummer Boy,* p. 1132; July, 1998, Ilene Cooper, review of *Tooth Tales from around the World,* p. 1884.

Horn Book Guide, spring, 1997, Sarah Guille, review of *Extraordinary Young People,* p. 161.

Kirkus Reviews, June 15, 1993, review of *Allen Jay and the Underground Railroad,* p. 782; June 1, 1996, review of *Journey for Peace,* p. 820; February 1, 1998, review of *Diary of a Drummer Boy,* p. 193.

Kliatt, July, 1997, Sharrie Gredy, review of *Let Women Vote!,* p. 3.

School Library Journal, March, 1991, Loretta Kreider Andrews, review of *Algeria,* p. 199; April, 1995, George Gleason, review of *Trail of Tears,* pp. 159-160; January, 1996, Judith L. Miller, review of *Let Women Vote!,* p. 114; August, 1996, Connie Parker, review of *Building the Capital City,* p. 150; September, 1996, Shirley Wilton, review of *Journey for Peace,* p. 210; October, 1996, Jerry D. Flack, review of *Extraordinary Young People,* p. 152; February, 1997, Linda Greengrass, review of *Illinois,* p. 108; April, 1997, Marilyn Fairbanks, review of *Women for Peace,* p. 144; August, 1997, Allison Trent Bernstein, review of *Indiana,* pp. 160-161; May, 1998, Jackie Hechtkopf, review of *Diary of a Drummer Boy,* p. 107.

Voice of Youth Advocates, December, 1997, Debbie Earl, review of *Women for Peace,* p. 330.

*   *   *

BROEKSTRA, Lorette 1964-

Personal

Surname is pronounced "*Brook*-stra"; born July 26, 1964, in Yallourn, Victoria, Australia; daughter of Marten (a floor surfacer) and Maria (Terpstra) Broekstra; children: Emma Feher, Ruben Feher. *Education:* Swinburns Institute of Technology, diploma of graphic design, 1987.

Addresses

Home—15 Moonee St., Ascot Vale, Victoria 3032, Australia. *E-mail*—lorette@ozemail.com.au.

Career

Freelance illustrator in Amsterdam, Netherlands, 1988-96, and Melbourne, Australia, 1996—.

Lorette Broekstra

Writings

SELF-ILLUSTRATED CHILDREN'S BOOKS

Baby Bear Goes to the Zoo, Lothian (Port Melbourne, Australia), 1999.

Baby Bear Goes to the Beach, Lothian (Port Melbourne, Australia), 2000.

Baby Bear Goes to the Farm, Lothian (Port Melbourne, Australia), 2000.

Baby Bear Goes Camping, Lothian (Port Melbourne, Australia), 2000.

Sidelights

Lorette Broekstra told *SATA:* "After finishing my studies in graphic design, I decided to travel overseas. I settled in the Netherlands, where I worked as a freelance illustrator for eight years. In 1996, pregnant with my second child, I decided to come back to Australia.

"I've always loved children's books and hoped that one day I would illustrate one. Once I had children of my own, I was always in libraries or bookshops looking for suitable books to read to them. Having very young children, I was in search of books without too much text. There didn't seem to be many to choose from. When I wrote my book I kept that in mind and was very conscious of limiting the text to one or two sentences per page.

"I love the bold colors and simple shapes of the books by Dick Bruna, yet I also love the painterly approach. I wanted to combine the two styles. At the moment I am working on a series of paintings adapted from my book for an early childhood unit at a gallery dedicated to children's literature near Melbourne."*

*   *   *

BUXTON, Ralph
See SILVERSTEIN, Alvin and
SILVERSTEIN, Virginia B.

C

CANN, Helen 1969-

Personal

Born February 19, 1969, in Bristol, England; daughter of Peter and Gillian Cann. *Education:* University of Wales, B.A. (with honors), postgraduate diploma, 1993.

Helen Cann's decorative and eclectic illustrations adorn Josephine Evetts-Secker's selection of multicultural folktales featuring mother-daughter relationships. (From Mother and Daughter Tales.*)*

Addresses

Agent—Maggie Mundy, 14 Ravenscourt Park Mansions, Dalling Rd., Ravenscourt Park, London, England.

Career

Illustrator, 1993—. *Member:* Association of Illustrators.

Awards, Honors

United Kingdom Reading Association Award, 1998, for *A Calendar of Festivals.*

Illustrator

Josephine Evetts-Secker, reteller, *The Barefoot Book of Mother and Daughter Tales,* Barefoot Books (Bath, England), published as *Mother and Daughter Tales,* Abbeville Kids (New York, NY), 1996.
Animal Worlds, Sandvik, 1997.
Bel Mooney, *The Green Man,* Barefoot Books (Bath, England), 1997.
Josephine Evetts-Secker, reteller, *The Barefoot Book of Father and Daughter Tales,* Barefoot Books (Bath, England), published as *Father and Daughter Tales,* Abbeville Kids (New York, NY), 1997.
Josephine Evetts-Secker, reteller, *The Barefoot Book of Father and Son Tales,* Barefoot Books (Bath, England), 1998.
Josephine Evetts-Secker, reteller, *The Barefoot Book of Mother and Son Tales,* Barefoot Books (Bath, England), 1998.
Cherry Gilchrist, *A Calendar of Festivals,* Barefoot Books (Bath, England), 1998.
Joyce Denham, *A Child's Book of Celtic Prayers,* Lion Children's Books (Oxford, England), Loyola Press, 1998.
Sarah Boss, *Mary's Story,* Barefoot Books (Bath, England), 1999.
Ann Pilling, *Who Laid the Cornerstone of the World?,* Lion Children's Books (Oxford, England), 1999.

Rebecca Hazell, *The Barefoot Book of Heroic Children,* Barefoot Books (Bath, England), 2000.

Saviour Pirotta, *Christian Festival Tales,* Raintree Steck-Vaughn (Austin, TX), 2000.

Anne Elizabeth Stickney, *The Loving Arms of God,* Eerdmans (Grand Rapids, MI), 2001.

Burleigh Muten, *A Lady of a Thousand Names,* Barefoot Books (Bath, England), 2001.

Arthur Scholey, *Baboushka: A Christmas Folktale from Russia,* Candlewick Press, 2001.

Also illustrator of *The Innkeeper's Daughter* by Bryce Milligan, expected 2002.

Work in Progress

The New Lion's Children's Bible for Lion Children's Books.

Sidelights

Illustrator Helen Cann has long been inspired by the artwork of people from many lands. For *The Barefoot Book of Mother and Daughter Tales,* which contains ten folktales from around the world, Cann's illustrations include an "inviting montage of motifs from various cultures," noted a *Publishers Weekly* critic reviewing the U.S. edition, *Mother and Daughter Tales.* Similarly *The Barefoot Book of Father and Son Tales* contains ten multicultural folktales revolving around fathers and sons. Cann's "watercolor illustrations . . . add to the drama of the tales," according to Karen K. Radtke in a *School Library Journal* review. Indeed, Cann has often employed multicultural designs in her works, and she collects these motifs, particularly intending to use them in her artwork. Cann told *SATA:* "My work is watercolor and collage with pencil over the top for depth and definition. I source papers for collage from around the world—Japanese and Indian newsprint, hand-made papers, even sweet/candy papers. This just makes for interesting patterns and surfaces. I am interested in composition and often use grids and borders to offset the central image. I love using pattern in my artwork and research decorative motifs before beginning a picture. I have a large collection of reference material taken from textiles, ceramics, jewelry, and even body paint!"

For *A Calendar of Festivals,* which won the United Kingdom Reading Association Award, Cann painted detailed watercolor illustrations on each page to interpret the legends and folktales related to eight different festivals, including Purim, Holi, Vesak, Halloween, Kwaanza, and the Russian New Year. "Cann subtly alters her palette and style to reflect the various geographical settings in her watercolor vignette and spot illustrations," observed a critic for *Publishers Weekly.* In a like manner, Cann decorated the pages of *A Child's Book of Celtic Prayers* with borders and pastoral motifs, creating in the words of a *Publishers Weekly* reviewer, a "handsome volume."

Cann has illustrated a number of books that treat biblical themes. Among them is *Mary's Story,* a biography of Mary, the mother of Jesus, that draws on information from a variety of sources. Reminiscent of medieval and Renaissance artwork, Cann's watercolor and graphite paintings create a "distinct sense of time and place, although readers may be distracted by the peculiar-looking halos adorning her figures," remarked a *Publishers Weekly* critic. Writing in *Booklist,* Ilene Cooper felt that "Cann's watercolors can be looked at over and over, with new details emerging every time."

Biographical and Critical Sources

PERIODICALS

Booklist, October 1, 1999, Ilene Cooper, review of *Mary's Story,* p. 370.

Publishers Weekly, October 28, 1996, review of *Mother and Daughter Tales,* p. 81; March 23, 1998, review of *A Child's Book of Celtic Prayers,* p. 95; September 28, 1998, review of *A Calendar of Festivals,* p. 102; January 4, 1999, "Story Time," p. 92; August 30, 1999, review of *Mary's Story,* p. 75; April 3, 2000, review of *The Barefoot Book of Heroic Children,* p. 82; April 10, 2000, "Children's Religion Notes," p. 96.

School Library Journal, December, 1998, Pam Gosner, review of *A Calendar of Festivals,* p. 102; June, 1999, Karen K. Radtke, review of *The Barefoot Book of Father and Son Tales,* p. 114.

*   *   *

CARTER, Carol S(hadis) 1948-

Personal

Born June 6, 1948, in Chicago, IL; daughter of Albert and Esther (Jamison) Shadis; married Alden R. Carter (a writer), September 14, 1974; children: Brian Patrick, Siri Morgan. *Education:* University of Wisconsin—Eau Claire, B.A., 1970, and graduate study; also attended Rhinelander School of the Arts, Rocky Mountain School of Photography, and Peninsula School of the Arts. *Hobbies and other interests:* Canoeing, hiking, bicycling, camping, reading, travel.

Addresses

Home—1113 Onstad Dr., Marshfield, WI 54449. *E-mail*—thecarters@tznet.com.

Career

South End Alcoholic Center, Boston, MA, social worker, 1970-71; Environmental Protection Agency, Washington, DC, computer operator, 1971-72; Norfolk Redevelopment and Housing Authority, Norfolk, VA, social worker, 1972-74; freelance photographer, 1974-76; Wood County Social Services, Marshfield, WI, social worker, 1976-92; Oakview Home Community Based Residential Facility for the Elderly, Marshfield, owner,

Carol S. Carter's photos enhance her husband's story of a visually impaired second-grader who explains how she accomplishes tasks at home and school with the help of special equipment. (From Seeing Things My Way, *written by Alden R. Carter.)*

1992—. Photographs have been exhibited at juried shows. *Member:* Academy of Certified Baccalaureate Social Workers, Sierra Club, Audubon Society.

Awards, Honors

Grant from Wisconsin Arts Board, 1999.

Illustrator

PHOTOGRAPHER

(With husband, Alden R. Carter) A. R. Carter, *Modern China,* F. Watts (New York, NY), 1986.

(Contributor of photographs) A. R. Carter, *The Battle of Gettysburg,* F. Watts (New York, NY), 1990.

(Contributor of photographs) A. R. Carter, *I'm Tougher Than Asthma,* Albert Whitman (Morton Grove, IL), 1996.

(With Dan Young) A. R. Carter, *Big Brother Dustin,* Albert Whitman (Morton Grove, IL), 1997.

A. R. Carter, *Seeing Things My Way,* Albert Whitman (Morton Grove, IL), 1998.

(With Dan Young) A. R. Carter, *Dustin's Big School Day,* Albert Whitman (Morton Grove, IL), 1999.

A. R. Carter, *Stretching Ourselves: Kids with Cerebral Palsy,* Albert Whitman (Morton Grove, IL), 2000.

A. R. Carter, *I'm Tougher Than Diabetes,* Albert Whitman (Morton Grove, IL), 2001.

Sidelights

Carol S. Carter told *SATA:* "I love flowers, sunrises, faces, hands, old quilts, odd angles—everything that can go into making a photograph memorable. For many years I've worked both as a social worker and a photographer. The books I've done with my husband on disabilities and special challenges have heightened my appreciation of ordinary people. I hope my photographs communicate some of the courage and hope we all share as members of the human family."*

*   *   *

CARTER, Don 1958-

Personal

Born 1958, in Hartford, CT; married wife, Catherine; children: Grayson, Phoebe. *Education:* Attended Paier College of Art, 1976-80. *Hobbies and other interests:* Jazz.

Addresses

Home—21 Van Buren Ave., West Hartford, CT 06107. *Agent*—Elizabeth Harding, Curtis Brown Ltd., 10 Astor Place, New York, NY 10003. *E-mail*—don@adams-knight.com.

Career

Tryol & Mikan, art director, 1980-81; Lardis, McCurdy & Company, art director, 1981-85; Naftzger & Kuhe, associate creative director, 1985-86; Mintz & Hoke, creative director, 1986-2001; Adams & Knight Advertising, creative director, 2001—. *Member:* Connecticut Art Directors Club.

Awards, Honors

The Original Art 2000, Society of Illustrators, 2000, for *Wake Up, House!; Wake Up, House!* was named one of the "Best Books of 2000" by *School Library Journal* and one of "100 Titles for Reading and Sharing" by the New York Public Library; various awards for advertising art direction and copywriting from institutions, including The One Show, CLIO, Connecticut Art Directors Club, and Advertising Club of Connecticut.

Writings

ILLUSTRATOR

Dee Lillegard, *Wake Up, House!* (poetry), Knopf (New York, NY), 2000.

Donna Conrad, *See You Soon, Moon,* Knopf (New York, NY), 2001.

Dee Lillegard, *Hello School* (poetry), Knopf (New York, NY), 2001.

SELF-ILLUSTRATED

Get to Work, Trucks!, Roaring Brook Press (Brookfield, CT), 2002.

Heaven's All-Star Jazz Band, Knopf (New York, NY), in press.

Carter's work has also appeared in *Sesame Street* and *Nick Jr.* magazines.

Sidelights

Illustrator Don Carter told *SATA:* "Close to fifteen years ago, I developed what I thought was a unique 3-D illustration style with the hopes of illustrating for the advertising field. I was already working in the business as an art director, so it seemed like it would be an easy transition. Without an agent or any serious marketing, my hopeful career went nowhere, so I shelved my portfolio and moved on.

"Many years later, a local artist's representative reignited my interest in illustrating. I was designing a lot of posters for local theater groups at the time, and whenever I could, I would work on my own illustrations. There was no money to pay an illustrator, so it was a good way for me to at least get some printed samples of my own. Hoping the rep might be able to get me some paying jobs, I pulled together a bunch of the samples, and just for kicks I dusted off my old 3-D portfolio and dragged it along. When he saw the 3-D samples, he went nuts. I remember him saying, 'Never mind pastels. I've got at least five guys doing pastels. This 3-D stuff ... that's what you should be doing.'

"Not satisfied with the quality of my old samples, I developed a whole new portfolio in the 3-D style. The funny thing about it was, not until I had finished all the samples did I fully realize every piece could have easily been for a children's book. I had stuff like blue dogs, teapots with faces, and farm animals dressed as people. I had always had an interest in children's books, but never seriously considered illustrating for them because I had always heard it was next to impossible to break into the market. Now I had a portfolio full of colorful, whimsical illustrations that was pretty much limited to some kind of children's market. So I thought the next logical step was to try and illustrate for the children's magazines.

"I took out an ad in a new publication titled *Picturebook* that was marketed solely to the children's market. Perfect, I thought. I would just sit back and wait for the jobs to come to me. The phone rang maybe half a dozen times. Everyone loved the style, but I didn't get any jobs. The ad also came with five hundred reprints of my page. So I mailed a personalized note along with a copy of the reprint to every magazine, every publisher I could find. The phone started ringing almost immediately. I got several requests to see my portfolio, and *Sesame Street* magazine gave me my first job. I was on my way, or at least I thought I was. Knowing that art directors often filed samples for future jobs, I knew it would take a while for the mailings to bring in work. So I waited. And waited. Again, nothing. I needed to try something else.

"Earlier on I had joined the Graphic Artists' Guild, primarily to get a discount on my *Picturebook* ad. The discount was more than the membership dues, so what did I have to lose? The Guild had a yearly show at the Puck Building in New York City, where illustrators could exhibit their work. Art directors and designers from the advertising, editorial, and publishing fields were invited. I thought maybe it would be a good opportunity to get face to face with the people who actually hired illustrators.

"That night was a major turning point. Designers and art directors snatched up my reprints and asked to be put on my mailing list. One editor from a major children's book publishing house came back to my table probably three times to look at my work. At the end of the night, I came home knowing I had to stick with it.

"Several months later, I received a call from Random House. They asked if I could send my portfolio to their art director. One of their designers had seen my work at the show and had brought back my sample sheet. When

Don Carter

Using his trademark sculptural pictures of foam board, plaster, and paint, Carter embellished Dee Lillegard's poems about the items in a preschooler's house.

they returned my portfolio to me, there was a Random House catalog enclosed. Attached was a yellow post-it note with the message, 'Your portfolio is terrific and I have you in mind for a project. I'll be in touch soon . . . .'

"What was the project? Was it a definite thing? How soon would they be in touch? I couldn't wait. I gave [the art director] a call the next week. That turned out to be my first book, *Wake Up, House!* by Dee Lillegard . . . . Since then, I have illustrated two more books for Random House, and I am also working on writing and illustrating three other books. Along the way, I was fortunate enough to pick up a wonderful agent: Elizabeth Harding. Not only has she helped my understanding of the business, but she has also been very nurturing of my work . . . .

"So after four years of twists and turns, I've ended up on a path I never, ever thought I'd be on. And I feel very lucky . . . no, I feel very blessed to have gotten this far."

Writing about his artistic style and the process he uses to create his illustrations, Carter said that he is unsure of where his artistic style and technique originated. "It's not based on anything I've ever seen. I used to do a lot of paper collage constructions in art school because I liked the crispness of the shadows each layer made. I guess my present style is just an expansion of that with

thicker layers and thicker shadows. Lately I've been looking at folk art for direction to help me simplify my style." Carter noted that in contrast to traditional illustrations, which mostly use pen and ink to create two-dimensional pictures, his style "has three. That's one third (33%) more dimension. That's significantly more dimension." He continued, "My initial pencil sketches are very tight. So once they are approved I blow them up on a copier to full size as a template for the constructions. After I determine how many layers are needed, I cut the pieces out of foam board. They are then glued together and covered with plaster for texture. Once the plaster is dry, everything is coated with gesso and finally painted with acrylics. Sometimes I'll incorporate other dimensional items such as buttons, twigs, fabric and bird seed into the constructions for added interest. Then the finished pieces are photographed with a 4x5 format camera."

Wake Up, House! uses exactly the techniques Carter describes above to tell the story of the ordinary things in a preschooler's house from dawn to dark. The pictures in the book include such ordinary things as the bathroom floor, the kitchen stove, cabinets, broom, and washer. Hazel Rochman, writing in *Booklist,* called Carter's illustrations "clear" and "beautiful," pictures that work with simple words to "express how small children discover the place where they live." Carter's distinctive illustrations also drew praise from a *Publishers Weekly* reviewer, who called his art "dynamic and distinctive."

Discussing the future direction he wants his art to take, Carter said, "I would also like to see my style get animated. It's already very toy-like. Animation would make it look like wind-up toys that got flattened somehow yet they all still worked." Carter related that he has been inspired by the work of Maurice Sendak, particularly *Where the Wild Things Are.*

Biographical and Critical Sources

PERIODICALS

Booklist, February 1, 2000, Hazel Rochman, review of *Wake Up, House!,* p. 1026.
Publishers Weekly, February 14, 2000, review of *Wake Up, House!,* p. 196.
School Library Journal, December, 2000, review of *Wake Up, House!,* p. 54.

*   *   *

CHRISMAN, Arthur Bowie 1889-1953

Personal

Born July 16, 1889, on "Westbrook" farm near White Post, VA; died February 24, 1953, in Shirley, AR; son of Isaac Arthur and Mary Louise (Bryarly) Chrisman. *Education:* Attended Virginia Agricultural and Mechanical College and Polytechnic Institute (now Virginia Polytechnic Institute and State University), 1906-08.

Career

Writer. Worked as a schoolteacher for two years; also worked as a farmer, drafter, movie extra, lecturer, and storyteller.

Awards, Honors

Newbery Medal, 1926, for *Shen of the Sea: A Book for Children.*

Writings

FOR CHILDREN

Shen of the Sea: A Book for Children (stories), illustrated by Else Hasselriis, Dutton (New York, NY), 1925, published as *Shen of the Sea: Chinese Stories for Children,* Dutton (New York, NY), 1968.

The Wind That Wouldn't Blow: Stories of the Merry Middle Kingdom for Children, and Myself, with silhouette decorations cut by Hasselriis, Dutton (New York, NY), 1927.

Treasures Long Hidden: Old Tales and New Tales of the East, illustrated by Weda Yap, Dutton (New York, NY), 1941.

Sidelights

Arthur Bowie Chrisman's favorite books were "action stories of the extreme type, told out of doors, usually up a tree," reported Elizabeth C. Reed in *Newbery Medal Books, 1922-55.* Reed quoted Chrisman: "I thought nothing of dropping ten feet from bough to bough … and strange to say there was never so much as a deep scratch received while reciting and chanting and wildly acting the stories of 'Wonderful Peedie the Monkey.'" In bad weather these stories were told in the upper room of an abandoned slave quarters. "Here I kept all of my treasures, clay men and clay jugs, sailing ships, and bows and arrows, sand mills and wind mills, water mills and heat mills, sleds, wagons, fishing poles and many other contrivances, all made by my own hands. I never owned more than a half dozen bought toys in my life, but made my own toys in the thousands," stated Chrisman, as related by Reed. Chrisman did not write "with the idea of making a fortune," rather he "decided to write and let fate take care of all subsequent happenings," noted Reed, who again quoted Chrisman: "My favorite motto has always been an old Chinese proverb, 'Walk slowly, perhaps the river will have receded when you come to it.'"

Biographical and Critical Sources

BOOKS

Miller, Bertha Mahony, and Elinor Whitney Field, editors, *Newbery Medal Books, 1922-55,* Horn Book, 1955.*

*   *   *

COVINGTON, Linda
See WINDSOR, Linda

CRESSY, Michael 1955-
(Mike Cressy)

Personal

Born August 23, 1955, in Detroit, MI; son of Bernard D. (a pipefitter) and Dolphine (a homemaker; maiden name, Bentas) Cressy; married Kathleen Buckley, March 17, 1993 (marriage ended, August, 1995). *Education:* Attended Macomb County Community College and Otis Parsons School of Design. *Politics:* Independent/Democrat. *Religion:* "Self-spiritual."

Addresses

Home and office—5900 119th Ave. S.E., No. B-58, Bellevue, WA 98006. *E-mail*—floorme@excite.com.

Career

Freelance illustrator in Los Angeles, CA, 1982-93, and Seattle, WA, 1993—. Worked as illustrator or animator for Manly and Associates, Electronic Arts, Microsoft products, and Sierra online materials; contributor to a U.S. Air Force art program for fifteen years. Volunteer for Seattle Art Museum, Graphic Artists Guild, American Institute of Graphic Artists, and Society of Children's Book Writers and Illustrators. *Member:* Society of Children's Book Writers and Illustrators.

Awards, Honors

Certificates of Merit, Society of Illustrators of Los Angeles, 1985, 1986, 1987, 1990, and 1994.

Illustrator

Jacqueline Jules, *The Grey Striped Shirt: How Grandma and Grandpa Survived the Holocaust,* Alef Design Group (Los Angeles, CA), 1994.

Michael Cressy

(Under name Mike Cressy) Joy N. Hulme, *Bubble Trouble,* Children's Press (Danbury, CT), 1999.

(Under name Mike Cressy) Dana Meachen Rau, *Purple Is Best,* Children's Press (Danbury, CT), 1999.

(Under name Mike Cressy) Patricia McKissack and Frederick McKissack, *Bugs!,* Children's Press (Danbury, CT), 2000.

(Under name Mike Cressy) Mike Reiss, *The Great Show and Tell Disaster,* Price Stern Sloan (New York, NY), 2001.

Work in Progress

Writing and illustrating *On Milton Street* and *Tootin' around Town.*

Sidelights

Mike Cressy told *SATA:* "I had been a successful illustrator for over ten years when my soon-to-be wife suggested that we do a children's book together. In my research I found out that there were many great illustrators who were doing their best work in creating children's books. We put together a dummy of the book that included elaborate pencil sketches on each page. It was turned down by every publisher we sent it to. Looking back, I think part of the problem was that I was in a transitional time in my illustration. I had done very realistic work up to that point and had wanted to create a distinct style, which eventually turned out to be a sort of 'retro' fifties style, with hints of art deco and somewhat cartoonish. The other problem turned out to be the story, which wasn't quite up to par. However, it was a great learning experience.

"Ironically, the first children's book I illustrated was very realistic, and I had been doing plenty of illustration in my new style for at least a year. By the time I illustrated three books, I had full command of my new style. That style continues to evolve while keeping the basic idea intact. Currently I am working on one book and have written and illustrated two book dummies that I am shopping around to various publishers."

Biographical and Critical Sources

PERIODICALS

School Library Journal, March, 1995, Micki S. Nevett, review of *The Grey Striped Shirt,* p. 205.*

*   *   *

CRESSY, Mike
See CRESSY, Michael

CRETZMEYER, Stacy (Megan) 1959-

Personal

Born October 27, 1959, in Philadelphia, PA; daughter of Charles Henry (a physician) and Patricia Anne (an editor; maiden name, Walsh) Cretzmeyer. *Education:* Hollins College, B.A. (English and theatre arts), 1981, M.A. (English and creative writing), 1982; University of South Carolina, Ed.S. (counselor education) 1994, Ph.D (educational psychology), 1999. *Religion:* Roman Catholic. *Hobbies and other interests:* Travel, swimming, antiques.

Addresses

Home—Pawley's Island, SC. *Office*—Box 261954, Conway, SC 29528. *E-mail*—stacy@coastal.edu.

Career

Author; Coastal Carolina University Counseling Services, Conway, SC, counselor, 1996—. University of New Orleans, New Orleans, LA, playwright-in-residence, 1984; freelance writer, researcher, 1985-92; teacher of counseling courses, 1998-2000. *Family Journal,* editorial board member, 1998—. *Member:* Chi Sigma Iota International Honor Society in Counseling, American Counseling Association, International Association of Marriage and Family Counselors, Association

Stacy Cretzmeyer

for Counselor Education and Supervision, Circle K International Club (staff advisor, 1997-98), Community Coalition of Horry County (Myrtle Beach, SC; executive board secretary, 1999—), Grand Strand Community Against Rape (Myrtle Beach, SC; advisory board member, 1997—), Women's Advocacy Center (Coastal Carolina University; advisory board member, 1996—).

Awards, Honors

Academy of American Poets prize, Hollins Fiction Prize, and Hollins Fellowship for graduate study in English, all 1981; Women Holding Up the World Award, National Coalition Against Sexual Assault, 1999.

Writings

The Willis Family Preserved (play), produced at the University of New Orleans (New Orleans, LA), 1984.
One Step Ahead, 1987, reprinted as *Your Name Is Renée: Ruth's Story as a Hidden Child, the Wartime Experiences of Ruth Kapp Hartz*, Biddle (Brunswick, ME), 1994, reprinted as *Your Name Is Renée: Ruth Kapp Hartz's Story as a Hidden Child in Nazi-Occupied France*, Oxford University Press (New York, NY), 1999.
Hidden Child of the Holocaust, Troll Publishing, 2000.

Cretzmeyer's work has appeared in periodicals, including *Family Journal*.

Work in Progress

A full-length novel; research about the experiences of a twelve-year-old African-American girl during the civil rights movement in Americus, GA.

Sidelights

Stacy Cretzmeyer is an author and professional counselor, and has written a play, *The Willis Family Preserved*. In 1984, she was the University of New Orleans's playwright-in-residence. Cretzmeyer lives on Pawley's Island, South Carolina, and writes for publications in Charleston, South Carolina and Philadelphia, Pennsylvania.

Cretzmeyer is also the author of the account of a young Jewish girl who survived World War II in France. While a college student in the 1980s, Cretzmeyer wanted to write about Jewish children who had fled from Germany to France with their families and about Catholics and other Christians who had helped them. She wrote to her high school French teacher, knowing she had lived in Paris, to see if she could put her in touch with sources. When Ruth Kapp Hartz revealed that she was, in fact, a Jewish child who had been aided by the French, it was her story that Cretzmeyer came to tell, first in her 1987 book, *One Step Ahead*, then in revised and reprinted versions titled *Your Name Is Renée: Ruth's Story as a Hidden Child, the Wartime Experiences of Ruth Kapp Hartz* (1994) and *Your Name Is Renée: Ruth Kapp Hartz's Story as a Hidden Child in Nazi-Occupied*

France (1999). *Library Journal* reviewer Roseanne Castellino called *Your Name Is Renée* "compelling" and wrote that "Ruth Kapp's story supplies another piece of the history of the Holocaust."

Ruth, the protagonist of *One Step Ahead,* moved to Toulouse, in the south of France, in 1941, at the age of four. She was given the name Renée to protect her Jewish identity and learned quickly how to sense danger and avoid drawing attention to herself and her family. At the time, her father was serving in the French Foreign Legion, having volunteered in hopes that his service would protect his family from deportation. His service did nothing to increase their security. In August of 1942, Ruth's mother was told by the neighbors that Jews were to be rounded up, and with help from their non-Jewish friends and the Resistance underground they escaped at a moment's notice. A *Publishers Weekly* reviewer wrote in a review of *Your Name Is Renée* that Cretzmeyer's descriptions of the process of obtaining false identification and of the roundups of Jews "are terrifying in both their simplicity and their child's-eye view." Ruth was sent to a convent orphanage where the mother superior

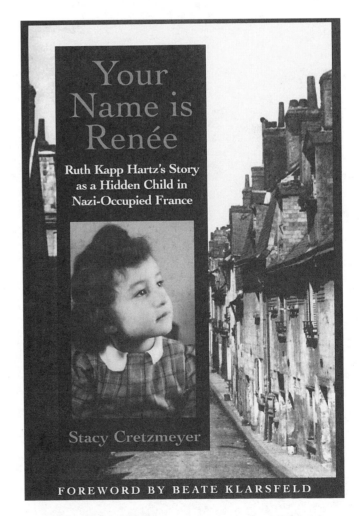

Cretzmeyer's emotional true-life memoir relates the experiences of four-year-old Ruth, who is separated from her parents and hidden in a French convent during the Holocaust.

protected the Jewish children from the German police. The nuns told the little girl her parents were dead, and she was so frightened and young that she believed them. Ruth immigrated to the United States in 1958.

Cretzmeyer incorporates history into the story to establish the background. In researching this story Cretzmeyer interviewed Ruth's parents and relatives of people who had sheltered the family. In a review of *Your Name Is Renée: Ruth Kapp Hartz's Story as a Hidden Child in Nazi-Occupied France,* a *Publishers Weekly* contributor felt this may be the reason "she provides an unusually complete and clear account of a supremely turbulent experience." The reviewer wrote that for insights about the Jewish children hidden in France, *Your Name Is Renée* "can stand alongside Renée Roth-Hano's autobiography *Touch Wood.*" *Booklist* reviewer George Cohen wrote that *Your Name Is Renée: Ruth Kapp Hartz's Story as a Hidden Child in Nazi-Occupied France* "is a testimony to the few righteous Gentiles who risked so much to save the Jews in their midst."

Biographical and Critical Sources

PERIODICALS

Booklist, June 1, 1999, George Cohen, review of *Your Name Is Renée: Ruth Kapp Hartz's Story as a Hidden Child in Nazi-Occupied France,* p. 1778.

Library Journal, June 1, 1999, Roseanne Castellino, *Your Name Is Renée: Ruth Kapp Hartz's Story as a Hidden Child in Nazi-Occupied France,* p. 128.

Publishers Weekly, January 17, 1994, review of *Your Name Is Renée: Ruth's Story as a Hidden Child, the Wartime Experiences of Ruth Kapp Hartz,* p. 429; June 14, 1999, review of *Your Name Is Renée: Ruth Kapp Hartz's Story as a Hidden Child in Nazi-Occupied France,* p. 71.

School Library Journal, August, 1999, Cyrisse Jaffee, *Your Name Is Renée: Ruth Kapp Hartz's Story as a Hidden Child in Nazi-Occupied France,* p. 168.

D

DALY, Kathleen N(orah)

Personal

Born in London, England. *Education:* University of Glasgow, M.A., 1951.

Addresses

Office—c/o Author Mail, Golden Books, 888 Seventh Ave., New York, NY 10106.

Career

Blackie & Son (publisher), children's book editor, 1952; Artists & Writers Press, New York, NY, children's book editor, beginning 1953.

Writings

Animal Stamps, stamps by James Gordon Irving, illustrated by William J. Dugan, Simon & Schuster (New York, NY), 1955.

Bird Stamps, stamps by James Gordon Irving, illustrated by William J. Dugan, Simon & Schuster (New York, NY), 1955.

CBS Television's Captain Kangaroo, illustrated by Art Seiden, Simon & Schuster (New York, NY), 1956.

Howdy Doody's Animal Friends, illustrated by Art Seiden, Simon & Schuster (New York, NY), 1956.

Interesting British Birds, illustrated by Eric Tansley and Robert Aitchen, Blackie & Son (London, England), 1956.

My Little Golden Book about Travel, illustrated by Tibor Gergely, Simon & Schuster (New York, NY), 1956.

CBS Television's Captain Kangaroo and the Panda, illustrated by Edwin Schmidt, Simon & Schuster (New York, NY), 1957.

The Giant Little Golden Book of Dogs, illustrated by Tibor Gergely, Simon & Schuster (New York, NY), 1957.

The Little Golden Book of the Seashore, illustrated by Tibor Gergely, Simon & Schuster (New York, NY), 1957.

Trains: A Little Golden Stampbook, illustrated and with stamps by E. Joseph Dreany, Simon & Schuster (New York, NY), 1958.

A Little Golden Book about Colors, illustrated by Richard Scarry, Golden Press (New York, NY), 1959.

The Cat Book, illustrated by Gig Goodenow, Golden Press (New York, NY), 1964.

Jingle Bells: A New Story, illustrated by J. P. Miller, Golden Press (New York, NY), 1964.

Little Tiger Colors Everything, illustrated by J. P. Miller, Golden Press (New York, NY), 1965.

In Kathleen N. Daly's **Norse Mythology A to Z,** *more than 400 concise entries offer young readers information about the characters and settings of Scandinavian myths.*

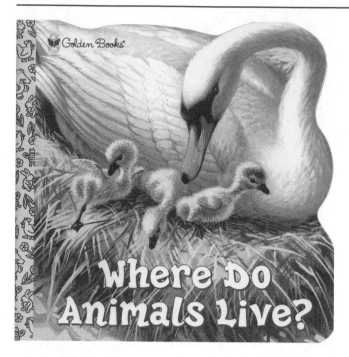

Daly's **Where Do Animals Live?** *introduces children to the homes of various animals.* (*Cover illustration by Jan Pfloog.*)

Little Tiger Learns His ABC, illustrated by J. P. Miller, Golden Press (New York, NY), 1965.

My Elephant Book, illustrated by Aurelius Battaglia, Golden Press (New York, NY), 1966.

(Adapter) *Fairy Tales* (stories of Hans Christian Andersen), Golden Press (New York, NY), 1964.

Curly the Pig (Maria Pia Pezzi), Golden Press (New York, NY), 1964.

(Reteller) *The Three Bears,* illustrated by Feodor Rojankovsky, Golden Press (New York, NY), 1967.

Ladybug, Ladybug, illustrated by Susan Carlton Smith, American Heritage Press (New York, NY), 1969.

A Child's Book of Animals, illustrated by Lilian Obligado, Doubleday (Garden City, NY), 1975.

Mustang! illustrated by Joseph Guarino, Pyramid Communications (New York, NY), 1975.

A Child's Book of Flowers, illustrated by Susan Carlton Smith, Doubleday (Garden City, NY), 1976.

(Editor) *Bruno Bear's Bedtime Book: A Collection of Stories and Poems for the Very Young,* illustrated by Richard Hefter, Strawberry Books (New York, NY), 1976.

(Adapter) *Cristobalito* (based on a Disney film), Pyramid (New York, NY), 1976.

Nature Words, illustrated by Robert Pierce, Grosset & Dunlap (New York, NY), 1976.

The Wonder of Animals, pictures by Tim and Greg Hildebrandt, Golden Press (New York, NY), 1976.

A Child's Book of Birds, illustrated by Fred Brenner, Doubleday (Garden City, NY), 1977.

A Child's Book of Insects, illustrated by Lilian Obligado, Doubleday (Garden City, NY), 1977.

Dinosaurs, illustrated by Tim and Greg Hildebrandt, Golden Press (New York, NY), 1977.

Hide and Defend, illustrated by Tim and Greg Hildebrandt, Golden Press (New York, NY), 1977.

Raggedy Ann & Andy: An Adaptation (based on the screenplay by Patricia Thackray and Max Wilk), Bobbs-Merrill (Indianapolis, IN), 1977.

Today's Biggest Animals, illustrated by Tim and Greg Hildebrandt, Golden Press (New York, NY), 1977.

Unusual Animals, illustrated by Tim and Greg Hildebrandt, Golden Press (New York, NY), 1977.

A Child's Book of Snakes, Lizards, and Other Reptiles, illustrated by Lilian Obligado, Doubleday (Garden City, NY), 1980.

Body Words: A Dictionary of the Human Body, How It Works, and Some of the Things that Affect It, illustrated by Melanie Gaines Arwin, Doubleday (Garden City, NY), 1980.

The Simon & Schuster Question and Answer Book, Wanderer Books (New York, NY), 1982.

The Macmillan Picture Wordbook, illustrated by John Wallner, Macmillan (New York, NY), 1982.

Strawberry Shortcake and Pets on Parade, illustrated by Pat Sustendal, Parker Brothers (Beverly, MA), 1983.

Baby Jesus, illustrated by Jim Cummins, Rand McNally (Skokie, IL), 1984.

Daniel in the Lions' Den, illustrated by Jim Cummins, Rand McNally (Skokie, IL), 1984.

Joseph and His Brothers, illustrated by Jim Cummins, Rand McNally (Skokie, IL), 1984.

Jesus Our Friend, illustrated by Jim Cummins, Rand McNally (Skokie, IL), 1984.

Jonah and the Great Fish, illustrated by Jim Cummins, Rand McNally (Skokie, IL), 1984.

Making Friends, pictures by Maryann Cocca-Leffler, Parker Brothers (Beverly, MA), 1984.

Noah and the Ark, illustrated by Jim Cummins, Rand McNally (Skokie, IL), 1984.

The Human Body, Golden Books (New York, NY), 1985.

A Book of Flowers, Sacrum Press (Durham, NC), 1986.

The Four Little Kittens Storybook, illustrated by Lilian Obligado, Golden Book (New York, NY), 1986.

Little Sister, illustrated by Eugenie, Golden Book/Western (Racine, WI), 1986.

Look at You: A Book about How Your Body Works, illustrated by Kathy Allert, Golden Book/Western (Racine, WI), 1986.

Tiger and Mouse, Golden Books (New York, NY), 1988.

Tiger's Mystery Trip, Golden Books (New York, NY), 1988.

Tiger's Perfect Presents, Golden Books (New York, NY), 1988.

Tiger Trouble, Golden Books (New York, NY), 1988.

The Golden Book of Sharks and Whales, illustrated by James Spence, Golden Book/Western (Racine, WI), 1989.

A House for a Mouse, illustrated by John P. Miller, Golden Book/Western (Racine, WI), 1990.

Norse Mythology A to Z: A Young Reader's Companion, Facts on File (New York, NY), 1991.

The Big Golden Book of Backyard Birds, illustrated by John P. O'Neill and Douglas Pratt, Golden Books/Western (Racine, WI), 1990.

Greek and Roman Mythology A to Z: A Young Reader's Companion, Facts on File (New York, NY), 1992.

Where Do Animals Live?, illustrated by Jan Pfloog, Golden Books (New York, NY), 1999.

The Good Humor Man, illustrated by Tibor Gergely, Golden Books (New York, NY), 2001.

Sidelights

The author and editor of a wide range of children's books, Kathleen N. Daly was born in London but grew up living in France, Scotland, and on the island of Mauritius in the Indian Ocean. She began her professional life in London, soon took a job in New York City, and has since edited children's books for publishers in the United States and England. Her writings include nonfiction and storybooks, as well as adaptations with well-known plots and characters.

Two examples of Daly's science writing date from 1980: *Body Words: A Dictionary of the Human Body, How It Works, and Some of the Things that Affect It* and *A Child's Book of Snakes, Lizards, and Other Reptiles*. The first book contains over five hundred entries about human anatomy and illnesses. Included are nine articles that give detailed information about the systems of the body: the skeleton, blood and its circulation, the digestive system, the brain and nervous system, the reproductive system, the respiratory system, skin and hair, and muscles. "The dictionary uses a circular method of learning," noted a *Booklist* contributor, "the cross-reference network substitutes for a study outline ... a 'contents person,' an outline of the human body [aids] children in locating entries." The reviewer found a few minor errors and inconsistencies, but commended *Body Words* as a "useful" book. *School Library Journal* critic Christopher Hatten remarked on the fact that Daly included a discussion of difficult topics such as abortion, while taking care not to give them extra emphasis over others: "*Body Words* is a level-headed approach to the subject." F. L. Cohen suggested in *Science Books & Films* that while the basic concept was good, "some of the definitions are inadequate," and the critic regretted that "street words ... about which children may be curious, are generally not included."

The illustrated book *A Child's Book of Snakes, Lizards, and Other Reptiles* presents information grouped by general species, with individual chapters on crocodilians, lizards, snakes, the tuatara, and turtles and tortoises. An index provides common names, genus, and species; and Latin nomenclature is explained. Reviewer Barbara Hawkins commented in *School Library Journal* that the introduction was "conversational" and that the pictures by Lilian Obligado would be especially appealing to children interested in reptiles. Conversely, in a *Science Books & Films* review, W. C. Sherbrook noted that the book did not supersede earlier juvenile reptile books, with its best points being its "brevity and inclusion of some recent information on crocodilian maternal behavior."

Daly's 1982 publication *The Macmillan Picture Word-book* includes numerous pictures along with the text, with the goal of improving readers' vocabulary skills.

While Christina Olson, writing for *School Library Journal,* thought that some of Daly's word choices might be "a bit esoteric for the intended audience," a *Booklist* reviewer commented that "the page design is generally clear and invites exploration"; the same reviewer also commended its "stimulating and enjoyable approach."

Two encyclopedia-format efforts by Daly are *Norse Mythology A to Z: A Young Reader's Companion* (1991) and *Greek and Roman Mythology A to Z: A Young Reader's Companion* (1992). Each contain some four hundred alphabetical entries, including gods and goddesses, giants, heroes and heroines, monsters, terminology, cultural concepts, and places, as well as literary sources. Commenting on the Norse volume, a *Booklist* reviewer noted that the black-and-white illustrations were interesting and that Daly "was franker in [her] portrayal of sex and violence than is usual." The reviewer deemed the Greek and Roman mythology version to be "an effective basic reference source" with important lists of deities and their attributes.

Biographical and Critical Sources

BOOKS

Authors of Books for Young People, Scarecrow Press, 1990.

PERIODICALS

Booklist, September 1, 1981, p. 66; September 15, 1983, p. 151; September 1, 1991, p. 88; March 1, 1993, review of *Greek and Roman Mythology A to Z,* p. 1265.

Economist, December 1, 1984, review of *The Hamlyn Book of Questions and Answers,* p. 113.

School Library Journal, March, 1981, Barbara Hawkins, review of *A Child's Book of Snakes, Lizards, and Other Reptiles,* p. 130; March, 1981, Christopher Hatten, review of *Body Words,* p. 142; May, 1982, review of *Body Words,* p. 19; January, 1983, Christina Olson, review of *The Macmillan Picture Word Book,* p. 58.

Science Books & Films, September-October, 1980, p. 34; March-April, 1981, p. 220.*

*   *   *

DARLING, Kathy
See DARLING, Mary Kathleen

*   *   *

DARLING, Mary Kathleen 1943-
(Kathy Darling)

Personal

Born September 8, 1943, in Hudson, NY; daughter of Andrew J. (a major in the U.S. Army) and Helen C. (McCourt) Sipos; children: Tara Ann Darling. *Education:* Attended Russell Sage College.

In this work, Kathy Darling and cowriter Vicki Cobb encourage young readers to demonstrate scientific principles in their everyday lives. (Cover illustration by True Kelley.)

Addresses

Home—46 Cooper Ln., Larchmont, NY 10538.

Career

Garrard Publishing Co., Scarsdale, NY, children's book editor and promotion director, 1968-78; author, 1978—.

Awards, Honors

Children's Science Book Award (younger), New York Academy of Sciences, 1981, for *Bet You Can't! Science Impossibilities to Fool You.*

Writings

FOR CHILDREN; UNDER NAME KATHY DARLING

The Jelly Bean Contest, illustrated by Buck Brown, Garrard (Scarsdale, NY), 1972.

(With Leland B. Jacobs) *April Fool!,* Garrard (Scarsdale, NY), 1973.

Little Bat's Secret, illustrated by Cyndy Szekeres, Garrard (Scarsdale, NY), 1974.

(With Debbie Freed) *Games Gorillas Play,* illustrated by Brian Ray and Angelo Calcaterra, Garrard (Scarsdale, NY), 1976.

Bug Circus, illustrated by Buck Brown, Garrard (Scarsdale, NY), 1976.

Paul and His Little-Big Dog, illustrated by Brian Ray and Ira Wunder, Garrard (Scarsdale, NY), 1977.

Ants Have Pets, illustrated by Bette J. Davis, Garrard (Scarsdale, NY), 1977.

Jack Frost and the Magic Paint Brush, illustrated by Kelly Oechsli, Garrard (Scarsdale, NY), 1977.

The Easter Bunny's Secret, illustrated by Kelly Oechsli, Garrard (Scarsdale, NY), 1978.

The Mystery in Santa's Toyshop, illustrated by Lori Pierson, Garrard (Scarsdale, NY), 1978.

Pecos Bill Finds a Horse, illustrated by Lou Cunnette, Garrard (Scarsdale, NY), 1979.

(With Vicki Cobb) *Bet You Can't! Science Impossibilities to Fool You,* illustrated by Martha Weston, Garrard (Scarsdale, NY), 1980.

(With Vicki Cobb) *Bet You Can! Science Possibilities to Fool You,* illustrated by Stella Ormai, Avon, 1983.

(With Vicki Cobb) *Wanna Bet? Science Challenges to Fool You,* illustrated by Meredith Johnson, Lothrop (New York, NY), 1993.

Holiday Hoopla: Multicultural Celebrations, illustrated by Marilyn G. Barr, Monday Morning Books (Palo Alto, CA), 1994.

In Praise of Dogs, photographs by daughter, Tara Darling, Howell Book House (New York, NY), 1995.

Amazon ABC, photographs by Tara Darling, Lothrop (New York, NY), 1996.

Rainforest Babies, photographs by Tara Darling, Walker (New York, NY), 1996.

(With Tara Darling) *How to Babysit an Orangutan,* Walker (New York, NY), 1996.

Arctic Babies, photographs by Tara Darling, Walker (New York, NY), 1996.

Seashore Babies, photographs by Tara Darling, Walker (New York, NY), 1997.

Desert Babies, photographs by Tara Darling, Walker (New York, NY), 1997.

Komodo Dragon, photographs by Tara Darling, Lothrop (New York, NY), 1997.

ABC Dogs, photographs by Tara Darling, Walker (New York, NY), 1997.

Safe Kids, Healthy Kids, illustrated by Phillip Clark, Monday Morning Books (Palo Alto, CA), 1998.

ABC Cats, photographs by Tara Darling, Walker (New York, NY), 1998.

(With Vicki Cobb) *Don't Try This at Home! Science Fun for Kids on the Go,* illustrated by True Kelley, Morrow Junior Books (New York, NY), 1998.

(With Vicki Cobb) *You Gotta Try This! Absolutely Irresistible Science,* illustrated by True Kelley, Morrow Junior Books (New York, NY), 1999.

There's a Zoo on You!, Millbrook Press (Brookfield, CT), 2000.

OTHER

Contributor to magazines about dogs.

Sidelights

Mary Kathleen Darling, who writes under the name Kathy Darling, has made a career of producing entertaining and informative books for children. In addition to working as an editor and promotion director for a publishing company for many years, she has written many books of her own. While her earliest books, such as *The Jelly Bean Contest,* present imaginative tales, Darling has displayed an increasing affinity for writing nonfiction works about the wonders of science and animals. Her talent for writing such works is apparent in the several books she has authored with Vicki Cobb, including *Bet You Can't! Science Impossibilities to Fool You,* and those she has written for the "On Location" series.

Darling's collaborations with Cobb introduce children to the lighter side of science while also instilling an interest in the serious facts underlying various phenomena. For example, in *Bet You Can't!* Darling and Cobb present a

Darling traveled to southeastern Madagascar with her daughter, a wildlife photographer, to write about three species of lemurs in this title from their series on rare and endangered animals. (Cover photo by Tara Darling.)

collection of activities that demonstrate or involve the Bernoulli principle, which states that pressure in a stream of liquid decreases as the flow speed increases. Other subjects addressed in this book include topology, sensory perception, etc. Detailed instructions for each activity are included with illustrations, and most experiments use items that children can find at home. A reviewer for *Horn Book* wrote, "Original, engaging, and fun; what more could one ask of a book?" Darling has continued this tradition of combining entertaining facts for children with fun and easy experiments with such titles as *You Gotta Try This! Absolutely Irresistible Science* and *Don't Try This at Home! Science Fun for Kids on the Go.* Both books continue to include science experiments children can conduct at home or in the playground. Carolyn Phelan, writing in *Booklist,* felt that *Don't Try This at Home!* is an "appealing book of hands-on science" that combines "good ideas and good presentation."

You Gotta Try This! continues the tradition of Darling's earlier books, this time focusing on scientific oddities and strange observations, including instructions on how to resuscitate a drowned fly, or how to make a cubical, hard-boiled egg. Phelan termed this volume a "fine addition to science collections," especially with those who found the earlier books by Darling and Cobb to be useful. In one of Darling's more recent books, *There's a Zoo on You!,* she explores the microorganisms that live on the human body. Written in clear and simple language, the scientific vocabulary is highlighted in bold and accompanied by defining sidebars. Calling this work "irresistibly 'icky,'" Ellen Mandel wrote in *Booklist* that "this book is sure to energize biology studies."

In addition to her books on science and biology, Darling has collaborated with her photographer daughter, Tara Darling, to write the "On Location" series. The mother-daughter team traveled all over the world to study and photograph rare, protected, and endangered animals for this series. They studied manatees in Crystal River, Florida, observed Pacific walruses on Round Island near Alaska, fed and watched Tasmanian devils at Cradle Mountain National Park in Australia, and counted sixty different kinds of kangaroos in various locations in Australia. Critics have praised the series for its detailed and thoughtful texts, as well as accompanying photographs, diagrams, maps, charts, and indexes. Phelan and Sally Estes wrote in *Booklist* that *Lemurs on Location,* for example, contains an "informative, informally toned" discussion of the animals, including several "excellent photographs." Darling and her daughter have also collaborated on a series of photo essays on other wildlife, including such titles as *ABC Cats* and *ABC Dogs,* as well as a series of books on baby animals, which includes such titles as *Arctic Babies, Desert Babies,* and *Seashore Babies.* Denia Hester, writing in *Booklist,* noted that in addition to making a good alphabet book, *ABC Dogs* is also a book that will "please any dog lover." Stephanie Zvirin, reviewing *Arctic Babies* for *Booklist,* praised the colorful book for the simple, but informative introduction to animals of the desert and seashore.

Biographical and Critical Sources

PERIODICALS

Booklist, March 1, 1996, Carolyn Phelan, review of *Amazon ABC,* p. 1185; April 15, 1996, Stephanie Zvirin, review of *Arctic Babies,* p. 1442, review of *Rainforest Babies,* p. 1442; December 15, 1996, April Judge, review of *How to Babysit an Orangutan,* p. 728; February 15, 1997, Stephanie Zvirin, review of *Komodo Dragon: On Location,* p. 1018; April 1, 1997, Carolyn Phelan, review of *Desert Babies,* p. 1326, review of *Seashore Babies,* p. 1326, review of *Chameleons: On Location,* p. 1326; October 15, 1997, Denia Hester, review of *ABC Dogs,* p. 408; April 15, 1998, Carolyn Phelan, review of *Lemurs on Location,* p. 1437, review of *Don't Try This at Home!,* p. 1316; November 1, 1998, Stephanie Zvirin, review of *ABC Cats,* p. 498; December 1, 1998, Carolyn Phelan and Sally Estes, review of *Lemurs on Location,* p. 676; August, 1999, Carolyn Phelan, review of *You Gotta Try This!,* p. 2048; November 1, 2000, Ellen Mandel, review of *There's a Zoo on You!,* p. 528.

Horn Book, October, 1980, review of *Bet You Can't! Science Impossibilities to Fool You,* p. 547; November-December, 1996, Margaret A. Bush, review of *How to Babysit an Orangutan,* p. 757.

Kirkus Reviews, September 1, 1992, review of *Tasmanian Devil,* p. 1128.

Publishers Weekly, March 25, 1996, review of *Amazon ABC,* p. 83A; November 11, 1996, review of *How to Babysit an Orangutan,* p. 74.

School Library Journal, July, 2000, Carol Wichman, review of *There's a Zoo on You!,* p. 114.*

*   *   *

DAY, Trevor 1955-

Personal

Born November 16, 1955, in London, England; son of Kenneth Arthur (an architect) and Edith Helen (an administrator; maiden name, Baum) Day; partner of Christina G. N. Day (a middle school teacher). *Education:* University of Nottingham, B.Sc. (with honors; Zoology), 1977; University College of North Wales, M.Sc. (marine biology), 1979; University of Bath, postgraduate certificate of education (science), 1984. *Religion:* Buddhist. *Hobbies and other interests:* Sub-aqua diving, Buddhist meditation, photography, hill walking, classic motorcycling, "entertaining step-grandchildren aged two and three."

Addresses

Home—1, Sheppards Barton, Frome, Somerset BA11 1EL, England. *E-mail*—trevorday@ndirect.co.uk.

Career

Research assistant at the NERC Unit, Menai Bridge, North Wales, and marine biologist for the United Nations Development Program in Egypt, Lake Manzala

Project, 1979-80; Duff Miller College, London, head of biology, and Lansdowne Tutors, Oxford, England, 1980-83; PreVocational Education, deputy director, and SEEVIC College, UK, biology tutor, 1984-89; Sargent Minton Management Consultants, UK, surveys manager and educational consultant, 1989-91; Frome and Cirencester Colleges, UK, biology lecturer and foundation courses coordinator, 1991-92; part-time lecturer in biology and nonfiction writing at Somerset colleges, England, and popular science writer, 1992-96; part-time lecturer in nonfiction writing at the University of Bath, England, and natural history writer, 1996—. Science advisor to Brown Partworks, Marshall Editions, and Puffin Books, all in the UK. *Member:* Association of British Science Writers, Society of Authors.

Awards, Honors

Shortlisted for the Rhône-Poulenc Junior Science Prize, 1997, for *The Incredible Journey to the Centre of the Atom;* Best Nonfiction Book Award, *Parent's Choice,* 1999, for *Youch! It Bites! Real-Life Monsters, Up Close;* 4-11 Best Children's Picture Books shortlist, English Association (England), and Birthday Book Wish List selection, Longfellow Media Center, both 2000, both for *Youch!*

Writings

YOUNG ADULT NONFICTION

Positively Healthy!, Jonquil (Stevenage, England), 1987.

Biology, revised edition, Penguin, 1988.

Health for Life, Jonquil (Stevenage, England), 1989.

A Healthy Environment, Chalkface Project, 1992.

The Human Body ("Kingfisher Book of 1001 Questions and Answers" series) Kingfisher (London, England), 1994, published as *The Random House Book of 1001 Questions and Answers about the Human Body,* Random House (New York, NY), 1994.

Historical Inventions on File, Diagram Group/Facts on File (New York, NY), 1994.

(With Diagram Group) *Card Tricks,* HarperCollins (Glasgow, Scotland), 1995.

Math on File, Diagram Group/Facts on File (New York, NY), 1995.

Double Certificate GCSE Science, Pack 1: *Life Processes and Living Things,* Pearson Publishing (Cambridge, England), 1996.

(With Diagram Group) *Magic Tricks,* HarperCollins (Glasgow, Scotland), 1996.

(With Nicholas Harris) *The Incredible Journey to the Centre of the Atom,* Kingfisher Books (London, England), 1996.

Light ("Science Project" series), illustrated by Chris Fairclough, Wayland (Hove, England), 1997, Raintree Steck-Vaughn (Austin, TX), 1998.

(With Matthew Day and Robert Youngson) *Genetics and Cell Biology on File,* Diagram Group/Facts on File (New York, NY), 1998.

Youch! It Bites! Real-Life Monsters, Up Close, designed by Mike Jolley, edited by Dugald Steer, Templar (Dorking, England), Simon & Schuster (New York, NY), 2000.

Marine Sciences on File, Diagram Group/Facts on File (New York, NY), 2000.

Ocean Fact File, Marshall Editions, Silver Dolphin (San Diego, CA), 2000.

Guide to Savage Earth, Dorling Kindersley (New York, NY), 2001.

Also contributor of feature articles to the Education section of the *Guardian* newspaper, 1993-96. Technical consultant to *Science Supersubs,* Jonquil Publications and the Chalkface Project, 1985; *Sea Animals,* Disney/Marshall Editions, 1999; and *Oceans: World Explorers Series,* Marshall Editions/Dutton, 2001. Scientific consultant for *Aquatic Life,* Marshall Cavendish, 2000. Contributor to *Education for Citizenship,* Children's Society, 1991; *Human Physiology on File,* Facts on File, 1996; *Peoples of Central Africa,* Diagram Group/Facts on File, 1997; *European History on File,* Diagram Group/Facts on File, 1997; Volumes 4, 5, and 8 of *Grolier's Encyclopedia of Inventions and Inventors,* Grolier, 1999; and Volumes 1, 5, 6, 7, 8, and 10 of *Investigating Life Sciences Encyclopedia,* Marshall Cavendish, 1999. *The Incredible Journey to the Centre of the Atom* has been translated into Danish, French, German, Polish, and Portuguese.

ADULT NONFICTION

(With Diagram Group, and consultant editor) *Home Reckoner,* HarperCollins (Glasgow, Scotland), 1995.

(With Diagram Group) *Patience Card Games,* HarperCollins (Glasgow, Scotland), 1996.

(With Diagram Group, and consultant editor) *Gambling Games,* Sterling Publishing, 1996.

Guide to Sex, Hodder & Stoughton (London, England), 1997, published as *Teach Yourself Guide to Sex,* National Textbook Company (Lincolnwood, IL), 1998.

Oceans, Fitzroy Dearborn (London, England), Facts on File (New York, NY), 1999.

Contributor (of writing and artwork) to *Broadleaved Forests, Grasslands of Africa,* and *Oceans,* for Rainbird Publishing and Franklin Library, 1981; *Pocket Encyclopedia,* HarperCollins, 1993; *Macmillan Desk Reference,* Macmillan, 1993; *New Larousse Encyclopedia* series, Larousse, 1996; *The Cutting Edge,* Oxford University Press, 1999; *Encyclopedia of Oceanography and Marine Science,* Fitzroy Dearborn, 2001. *Guide to Sex* has been translated into Russian.

Contributor of articles to *Science Reporter, Sunday Telegraph, Saturday Telegraph, The Author: Journal of the Society of Authors, Geographical, Economist, Focus, Frontiers, Bookseller,* and *Marine Biology Letters.* Author of technical writings for Electrical Engineers' *Industry Initiative,* for Sargent Minton Publications, for the Institute of Personnel Management, and for the Civil Aviation Authority. Brochures and reports written for Bristol Science Center, Engineering and Physical Sciences Research Council, McCann-Erickson Ltd., Cargill Plc., Booker Foods, Personnel Management, South-East Essex Sixth Form College, the Arab Republic of Egypt, and the United National Development Program.

Work in Progress

Atlas of the Oceans; Animals and People. Research in eco-tourism, with particular reference to coral reefs and whale watching.

Sidelights

Trevor Day told *SATA:* "I call myself a communicator rather than a writer. These days, most nonfiction books for young people are much more than the written word. I work closely with designers and artists to ensure that the books, guidebooks, and Web sites we create pack a powerful punch—to delight, explain, provoke, excite, amuse, and fire the imagination. The total communication on the page is what matters in any case. I have always been passionate about how people learn. I used to be an educational consultant, and what goes on inside people's head when they learn—what they see in their mind's eye—has always fascinated me.

"I love variety and challenge, which is why I get involved in all kinds of writing—from science research council press releases, to magazine and newspaper articles, to guide books for science centers, to college textbooks, to self-help books for adults, to imaginative children's books. I'm always learning, and writing for such different audiences really keeps me on my toes.

"My advice for young writers? *Always* check your facts—ideally, from at least two reputable sources. And follow your dreams. The world—and your teachers—are always ready to criticise. Write from the heart. Then use your head to edit your work. If you are writing creatively, don't worry about getting it right the first time. Very few people do. Allow your thoughts and ideas to come, and then go back over your work and knock it into shape. Unfortunately, our schools and exam system don't necessarily encourage young people to work in this way. When children become adults they discover that very few writers 'get it right first time.' We almost need to unlearn what we learnt at school. I run writing courses at university, and one of the biggest hurdles many aspiring writers have to conquer is to overcome their self-criticism and criticism from others, and really allow their writing to flow. They rediscover that what they write is not set in concrete. They can always change it.

"Science gets a lot of bad press but, of course, we couldn't live the way we do without the benefits of science. I'm a passionate environmentalist too. Unfortunately, there is a lot of misunderstanding about how science works. For one thing, science is only one way of looking at the world. Science has its own set of rules and, most of the time, these rules work quite well. Scientists, however, are only human and as a society we need to keep a close eye on them to ensure they are serving our best interests. But that puts a responsibility on us to learn about how science works and not react in a 'knee-jerk' manner from ignorance.

"Writing has allowed me to fulfil some of my lifelong ambitions: to travel the world, swim with dolphins, dive with sharks, and commune with whales. I originally trained and worked as a marine biologist, and, in my writing, I have now come full circle. Three of my most recent books—one for young people and two for adults—are about the oceans. I am about to write a fourth book on the oceans, this one for children.

"Right now I'm particularly interested in marine eco-tourism and have traveled widely to write magazine and newspaper articles on this subject. I'm also in the middle of writing a book about our relationships with animals—everything from animals as pets and companions, animals as wildlife, to animals as sources of food and experimental subjects. These are complex and controversial themes. I'm interviewing dozens of experts and animal lovers for the book, which I'm writing for young people.

"I believe young people deserve the very highest quality resources to introduce them to the natural world around us. Publishers are willing to spend lots of money on popular science books for adults. I would like to see similar amounts of money being spent on children's books—not just on the design and presentation but on the content. Too often, books for young people will regurgitate out-of-date and inaccurate information from old textbooks. There is no reason why children's books shouldn't contain up-to-date, accurate information from reputable sources, but this research takes time and money. Young people deserve the very best we can offer."

Magnified photographs and clues allow young readers to guess the identities of various animals, insects, parasites, and plants, then find the answers and facts on each "monster" under foldout flaps.

Day's science books for young people and adults are commended for being replete with pertinent, well-explained information that is organized and manages to avoid technical jargon. For example, his contribution to the "Science Projects" series, *Light,* is clearly intended to be a supplementary science textbook, according to Lynne Babbage in *Magpies.* The book is primarily comprised of numerous science activities and projects. However, "what these books do have in their favour is their comprehensive coverage of each subject in a clear logical progression," Babbage observed, adding that they are visually more attractive than the typical textbook. *Booklist* reviewer Carolyn Phelan remarked of the series as a whole: "Elementary school students looking for simple experiments will find the books useful." Likewise, Day's *Oceans,* written for an adult audience but appropriate for high school use, contains a wealth of "concise factual data," according to F. T. Manheim in *Choice.* Further, "the range of subjects is large and well chosen," this critic added, noting that the book is divided into sections covering topics such as geography, geology, chemistry, biology, history, health, and management of the oceans.

For middle school students, Day has written *The Random House Book of 1001 Questions and Answers about the Human Body,* in which the author combines an "accessible question-and-answer format," with information that "is fairly sophisticated," according to Julie Corsaro in *Booklist.* The wealth of information about the human body is organized under headings such as genetics, health and nutrition, history of medicine, and so forth. What does not fall under one of these categories goes into the chapter entitled "Who, What, Where, When, Why, How," which answers questions such as "Why are lips red?" Denise L. Moll commented positively on Day's prose style in her *School Library Journal* review, saying that the information presented is appropriate for the target audience and avoids unnecessary technical terms. Furthermore, "this volume presents a great deal of information not often brought together in one resource," Moll contended.

Youch! It Bites! Real-Life Monsters, Up Close, is a successful book for children who like the gross-out aspect of science and zoology, according to some reviewers. Here, making effective use of an open-the-flap format, Day presents dazzling photographs of animals, plants, insects, parasites, and other inhabitants of the world whose bite or sting is harmful to humans. Under each flap are "surprisingly detailed, clearly explained facts" about the creature featured in the photograph, observed Gillian Engberg in *Booklist.* The book concludes with what Ellen Heath characterized in *School Library Journal* as "a masterfully gross intellectual puzzle," in which the reader looks at a photograph of a bite mark and is asked to indicate which of the surrounding animals is the most likely perpetrator of the wound. Day's exuberant, pun-filled prose, and the book's eye-popping photographs add up to a science book that certain elementary students will love, critics predicted. *Youch!* "offers plenty of thrills and chills to those who enter," Heath concluded.

Biographical and Critical Sources

BOOKS

Day, Trevor, *The Random House Book of 1001 Questions and Answers about the Human Body,* Random House, 1994.

PERIODICALS

Booklist, December 1, 1994, Julie Corsaro, review of *The Random House Book of 1001 Questions and Answers about the Human Body,* p. 670; March 15, 1998, Carolyn Phelan, review of *Light,* p. 1237; November 1, 2000, Gillian Engberg, review of *Youch! It Bites! Real-Life Monsters, Up Close,* p. 528.
Choice, July-August, 1999, F. T. Manheim, review of *Oceans,* p. 1971.
Magpies, September, 1998, Lynne Babbage, review of *Light,* p. 43.
Nature, November 30, 2000, Sandra Knapp, review of *Youch!,* p. 519.
Publishers Weekly, October 2, 2000, review of *Youch!,* p. 83.
School Library Journal, July, 1994, Denise L. Moll, review of *The Random House Book of 1001 Questions and Answers about the Human Body,* p. 106; October, 2000, Ellen Heath, review of *Youch!,* p. 146.

ON-LINE

Trevor Day Web site, http://www.trevorday.ndirect.co.uk (July 23, 2001).

*   *   *

DeROBERTS, Lyndon
See SILVERSTEIN, Robert Alan

*   *   *

DINESSI, Alex
See SCHEMBRI, Jim

*   *   *

DR. A
See SILVERSTEIN, Alvin and SILVERSTEIN, Virginia B.

*   *   *

DRIMMER, Frederick 1916-2000

OBITUARY NOTICE—See index for *SATA* sketch: Born August 8, 1916, in Brooklyn, NY; died December 24, 2000, in Norwalk, CT. Editor and author. Drimmer's books frequently focused on the abnormal and the macabre. His books for young adults included the 1985 biography *The Elephant Man* and 1988's *Born Different: Amazing Stories of Very Special People,* which took as its subject individuals with severe birth defects and handicaps. Drimmer grew up in New York and graduated magna cum laude with a bachelor's degree from City College (now City College of the City University of New York), and he earned a master's degree from Columbia University. He also did graduate study at the New School for Social Research. Drimmer worked for several publishing houses over the course of thirty years and edited books such as *The Animal Kingdom* and the anthology *A Friend Is Someone Special.*

OBITUARIES AND OTHER SOURCES:

PERIODICALS

New York Times, January 8, 2001, p. A18.

* * *

DUMBLETON, Mike 1948-

Personal

Born January 6, 1948, in Chipping Norton, England; emigrated to Australia, 1972; son of Ernest George (an industrial planner) and Susie (Jean) Dumbleton; married Linda Jean Collard (a teacher), June 28, 1969; children: Jay, Luke, Nathan. *Education:* Nottingham University, B.Ed., 1970, teaching certificate, 1970. *Religion:* Christian. *Hobbies and other interests:* Sports.

Addresses

Home—1 Foord Ave., Gawler E., South Australia 5118, Australia. *Agent*—Australian Literary Management, 2A Armstrong St., Middle Park, 3206 Victoria, Australia.

Career

South Australian Education Department, Adelaide, English teacher, 1973-74, faculty coordinator, 1975-87, deputy principal, 1988, literacy project coordinator, 1989—; writer. *Member:* South Australian Writers Centre.

Awards, Honors

"Children's Books Mean Business" list, American Booksellers Association/Children's Book Council, 1992, for *Dial-a-Croc;* literature grant, South Australian Department for the Arts and Cultural Heritage, 1993.

Writings

Dial-a-Croc, illustrated by Ann James, Orchard, 1991.
Granny O'Brien and the Diamonds of Selmore, illustrated by David Cox, Omnibus, 1993.
Mrs. Watson's Goat ("Connections" series; Volume 7), illustrated by Marina McAllan, Macmillan, 1993.
Mr. Knuckles, Allen & Unwin (St. Leonards, Australia), 1993.
Ms. MacDonald's Farm, illustrated by Ann Whitehead, Macmillan, 1994.
I Hate Brussels Sprouts, illustrated by Rebecca Pannell, Macmillan, 1994.

Pumped Up! (short stories), illustrated by Shane Nagle, Allen & Unwin (St. Leonards, Australia), 1995.
Let's Escape, illustrated by Kim Gamble, Scholastic Australia, 1997.
Downsized, illustrated by Tom Jellet, Random House (Milsons Point, Australia), 1999.

EDUCATIONAL RESOURCE MATERIALS

Can Cards, Hawker Brownlow Education, 1989.
(With Jeff Guess) *Hands On Poetry—A Practical Anthology,* Twilight Publishers, 1991, Educational Supplies, 1993.
Real Writing across the Curriculum: A Practical Guide to Improving and Publishing Student Work, South Australian Education Department, 1993.

EDUCATIONAL RESOURCE MATERIALS; COWRITTEN WITH KEN LOUNTAIN

Addressing Literacy in Society and Environment, Curriculum, 1999.
Addressing Literacy in Science, Curriculum, 1999.
Addressing Literacy in the Arts, Curriculum, 1999.

OTHER

Also author of *Online Literacy* Web site for the South Australia Department of Education, Training, and Employment, 1999.

Adaptations

Mr. Knuckles was adapted for the stage by the South Australian Children's Theatre Company, 1994; *Pumped Up!* was adapted for television by the Australian Broadcasting Corporation (ABC), 1996. *Dial-a-Croc* and three other stories were read by Mark Mitchell on audiocassette for ABC, 1995.

Work in Progress

Passing On, a picture book about a grandmother and her grandchild, illustrated by Terry Denton, for Random House.

Sidelights

Mike Dumbleton once told *SATA:* "As a youngster I enjoyed reading and consumed endless books which belonged to popular English series at the time. They included many Enid Blyton titles and all the Biggles books, along with the books from two contrasting schoolboy series, one called William and the other called Jennings . . . .

"I've always been interested in writing but never seemed to have the time. One of the reasons is that for a long time I've been involved in sport and thoroughly enjoyed every minute of it. The other reason is that when my wife and I started our family we soon discovered that bringing up children often takes twenty-five hours a day!

"Part of my interest in writing probably stems from the fact that my grandfather, George Dumbleton, is a local village poet in Oxfordshire, England. At the age of ninety-one he no longer writes, but having been blessed with an amazing memory, he can readily recite his poems on request.

"I started writing when I decided I wasn't getting any better at basketball, and my three children were old enough to allow me some uninterrupted time. I began devising educational texts for teachers at the same time that I started writing picture book manuscripts, and it was a proposal for an educational text which was first accepted and published in Australia. *Dial-a-Croc* was accepted soon afterwards.

"The initial idea for *Dial-a-Croc* came from a play on words whereby you can reverse the syllables in the word crocodile to make the name Dial-a-Croc. The early sequences in which Vanessa heads off into the Outback are based on a real Vanessa who is mentioned in the dedication, along with my sons. She is a friend of the family and was my eldest son's girlfriend at the time. She is a self-assured, purposeful young lady, and visited us wearing fashionable safari shorts when I was planning the book. It gave me just the image I needed for the Vanessa in the story with her 'jungle jeans' and 'hunting jacket,' to which I added her 'bull whip, camping knife' and other suitable accessories before letting her venture into the 'Outback, beyond the Back of Beyond.' . . ."

Dumbleton became an international success with his first book for children, *Dial-a-Croc,* in which a girl captures a crocodile in the Australian outback and puts him to work earning her fame and fortune. "This is a great romp of a book," avowed Judith Sharman in *Books for Keeps,* praising Dumbleton's spunky heroine and the book's silly antics. Silliness is again the point in Dumbleton's picture book *Mr. Knuckles,* in which Tracey arrives at school the first day of term to find that her teacher is a gorilla. The author spins this premise to its logical, and absurd, limits, including having the class take a field trip to Africa. But Dumbleton leaves behind the silliness in *Downsized,* in which a girl narrates the story of what happens to her family when her father loses his job. First, everything begins to get smaller, as the family moves to a smaller house, gets a smaller car, and gives away their two large dogs. Even her father begins to seem smaller as his interest in what's going on around him shrinks. When the narrator finally goads her father into helping her redesign the back garden in their shabby new house, the family is on its way to getting back on its feet emotionally. "This story conveys with sensitivity and gentle humour the difficulties faced by a family when Dad has lost his job and is not coping well with that situation," observed Anne Hanzl in *Magpies.* Hanzl also noted that the author and illustrator work well together, each augmenting what the other reveals.

Biographical and Critical Sources

PERIODICALS

Books for Keeps, May, 1993, Judith Sharman, review of *Dial-a-Croc,* p. 8; November, 1996, Pam Harwood, review of *Mr. Knuckles,* p. 9.
Magpies, September, 1999, Anne Hanzl, review of *Downsized,* p. 30.

ON-LINE

Mike Dumbleton Web site, http://www.mikedumbleton.cjb.net/ (April 28, 2001).*

F

FRANKLIN, Kristine L. 1958-

Personal

Born December 31, 1958, in Tacoma, WA; daughter of Stephen M. and Virginia Helen (Harbord) Brozovich; married Martin D. Franklin (a teacher), February 12, 1983; children: Kelly Scott, Jody Kaye. *Education:* Biola University, B.A., 1981; Escuela de Idiomas, San Jose, Costa Rica, diploma in Spanish, 1992. *Religion:* Christian. *Hobbies and other interests:* Photography, travel, reading, raising Smooth Fox terriers, and knitting.

Addresses

Home—Hibbing, MN. *Agent*—Barbara S. Kouts, P.O. Box 558, Bellport, NY 11713.

Career

Author.

Awards, Honors

Highlights for Children Annual Fiction Contest winner, 1989; Notable Book in the Field of Social Studies citation, Children's Book Council, 1993, for *The Old, Old Man and the Very Little Boy;* Book of the Year, Bank Street College, and America's Children and Young Adult Literature Award, Consortium of Latin American Studies program, both 1994, both for *The Shepherd Boy; Parents Choice* award, 1995, Editor's Choice award, *Booklist,* and Maine Student's Book Award, 1996, all for *Eclipse;* Pick of the Lists citation, American Booksellers Association (ABA), and Original Art award, New York Society of Illustrators, both for *When the Monkeys Came Back;* Pick of the Lists citation, ABA, and Best Book citation, *School Library Journal,* both for *Lone Wolf;* Best Books of 1999 selection, New York Public Library, 1999, and Minnesota Book Award winner, 2000, both for *Dove Song.*

Kristine L. Franklin's novel follows eleven-year-old loner Perry, who finds solace with kind Willow and her warm-hearted family after his sister dies and his parents divorce. (Cover illustration by Joe Baker.)

Writings

The Old, Old Man and the Very Little Boy, illustrated by Terea D. Shaffer, Atheneum (New York, NY), 1992.

The Shepherd Boy, illustrated by Jill Kastner, Atheneum (New York, NY), 1994, Spanish translation by Alma Flor Ada published as *El Niño Pastor,* Atheneum (New York, NY), 1994.

When the Monkeys Came Back, illustrated by Robert Roth, Atheneum (New York, NY), 1994.

Eclipse, Candlewick Press (Cambridge, MA), 1995.

(Editor, with Nancy McGirr, and translator from the Spanish) *Out of the Dump: Writings and Photographs by Children from Guatemala,* Lothrop, Lee & Shepard (New York, NY), 1995.

The Blue-Eyed Goose, illustrated by Yoshi Miyake, Lothrop, Lee & Shepard (New York, NY), 1996.

The Wolfhound, paintings by Chris Waldherr, Lothrop, Lee & Shepard (New York, NY), 1996.

Nerd No More, Candlewick Press (Cambridge, MA), 1996.

Iguana Beach, illustrated by Lori Lohstoeter, Crown Publishers (New York, NY), 1997.

Lone Wolf, Candlewick Press (Cambridge, MA), 1997.

The Gift, illustrated by Barbara Lavallee, Chronicle Books (San Francisco, CA), 1999.

Dove Song, Candlewick Press (Cambridge, MA), 1999.

Sidelights

Kristine L. Franklin is the author of numerous stories for young readers, nearly all of which have garnered enthusiastic praise from reviewers. Franklin's books usually address tough issues, but she provides her fictional heroes and heroines with enough mettle to meet those challenges and triumph over them. Her first published work, *The Old, Old Man and the Very Little Boy,* appeared in 1992, and was followed two years later by *The Shepherd Boy,* a story that was translated and published for young Spanish-speaking readers as well.

Having lived for several years in various Central American locales, Franklin drew upon her experiences in Costa Rica for another 1994 work, *When the Monkeys Came Back.* The primates in question are the infamous howler monkeys that make their home high up inside Central America's rain forests. Marta, the heroine of the story, hears their screeching each night as the sun sets and again in the morning. The outside world encroaches upon her quiet village, however, and business interests offer her father money for the rights to cut timber on his land. Soon, the monkeys have vanished along with the trees. When Marta grows up, her husband gives her a plot of her own land—though it is against custom in that time and place for a woman to own property—and she decides to do nothing but plant trees on it. She teaches her eleven children about the missing monkeys, and instills in them the same drive to return the habitat to its natural state. In her old age, one night Marta once again hears the howls of the monkeys. "Strong in story and vision, this picture book has a grace that will ground it in the hearts of readers and listeners alike," declared *Booklist* reviewer Annie Ayres.

Franklin's time in Guatemala also inspired a nonfiction work which she edited, *Out of the Dump: Writings and Photographs by Children from Guatemala.* As the text reveals, Guatemala City is home to a massive garbage

Sixth-grader Wiggie finds himself labeled as a nerd because his scientist mom has become the host of an educational television show. (Cover illustration by John Ward.)

dump in its center, where 1,500 of the capital's poorest residents live. The children, like their parents, survive by scavenging in the dump, which takes priority over their education. In 1993, Franklin met Nancy McGirr, a photographer who in 1991 began giving cameras to children who lived at the dump and convinced them to document their lives. This evolved into the Photography Project, and Franklin became involved in it, working with the children to help put their thoughts down on paper to accompany each image; she also translated their words from the original Spanish. The images published in *Out of the Dump* reveal horrendous living conditions in the background, but the children chose to depict the things in which they take pride: their families, their pets, their makeshift homes. "Words and pictures filter reality through that little spark of light that children are born with the world over," remarked *Five Owls* writer Mary Bahr Fritts, who concluded that in the end Franklin and McGirr's effort "literally does rise from the ashes, a book sown from a single seed in the smell and smoulder of a garbage dump." Leone McDermott, critiquing the work for *Booklist,* called it a "remarkable book.... The subjects' human dignity and the normality of their actions contrast sharply with the extraordinary wretchedness of their surroundings." Proceeds from the sale of *Out of the Dump* were used to provide schooling for children in the dump's neighborhood.

Franklin returned to fiction with the 1995 title *Eclipse,* the story of a difficult time in the life of Trina as she leaves sixth grade behind. Her mother has learned that she is expecting a child, though she is in her late forties. Trina's friend warns her that babies born to older mothers run a higher risk of being developmentally disabled. Meanwhile, an injury has kept Trina's father from working. Alternately cranky or sad, he begins to spend more of his day sleeping. When she wins an award at school, neither parent attends the ceremony; then, her father tries to commit suicide in another of the crises that propel Trina into adulthood. In the end, her mother begins to confide in her, and a new, more grown-up relationship between them is forged. "The moving first-person voice provides the novel's strong emotional resonance as it explores the effect of mental illness on a family," declared *Horn Book* critic Nancy Vasilakis. Writing in *Bulletin of the Center for Children's Books,*

Eleven-year-old Bobbie Lynn's father is missing in action, and she must support her emotionally vulnerable mother in Franklin's Vietnam War-era novel. (Cover illustration by Kamil Vojnar.)

Deborah Stevenson maintained that "this book will speak to many kids who feel, for one reason or another, buffeted by adult frailties beyond their control."

Young Pavel is another one of Franklin's beset protagonists, debuting in the 1996 book *The Wolfhound.* The story is set in imperial Russia and begins when Pavel finds a beautiful dog nearly frozen to death. His father recognizes it as a wolfhound, which only nobles are allowed to keep. Pavel revives it, but his father—fearing the family will be accused of stealing it—tries to get rid of it by setting it free. Pavel leads the dog instead to the Tsar's forest, but a pack of wolves threatens; the Tsar himself then appears, and thanks Pavel for saving his beloved Tatiana. Pavel returns home and tells his family, but all scoff at his vivid imagination. The following spring, a royal messenger arrives in the village with a precious wolfhound puppy—Pavel's thank-you gift from the Tsar. The story featured paintings by Chris Waldherr that depict the icy Russian winter and contrast Pavel's humble home with the finery of the noble class. Karen Morgan, writing in *Booklist,* commended Waldherr's illustrations and "Franklin's vivid text imagery" which "result in a memorable tale."

Franklin ventured into modern-day social dynamics with *Nerd No More,* her 1996 novel for young readers. The story centers upon sixth-grader Wiggie Carter, whose mother is a scientist and expert in parasitology. When she begins appearing on a classroom-television science show, other kids begin to tease him for being a "nerd," and one bully even tags him "Bowel Boy" after a lecture in which his mother utters the word. In his despair, Wiggie is befriended by Callie, a new student, but nearly ruins their friendship in his attempt to restore his social status as a non-nerd. Only an eventful field trip in which he rescues the bully, but winds up with a broken arm, returns to Wiggie his self-confidence. *Bulletin of the Center for Children's Books* writer Stevenson said it was an oft-told tale, "but Franklin makes the story fresh with sharp writing, zesty dialogue, and effective characterization."

The woods of northern Minnesota, where Franklin and her family settled after their stint in Central America, provide the setting for the author's 1997 novel, *Lone Wolf.* The family of fifth-grader Perry has been torn apart after the death of his little sister, and he now lives in a rural area with his father, who home-schools him. His father, however, remains uncommunicative, a trait which Perry adopts in refusing to answer his mother's letters. His solace comes from exploring the woods near his home, and he is fascinated by its wolf population. The wolves, he learns, are loners, and he identifies with this independence. When an exuberant family moves into the nearest home, the daughter befriends him, but the warmth extended to Perry only brings to the surface his feelings of grief about his own family. "Franklin's characterizations are strong, true, and fair: there are no villains here," remarked Stevenson in the *Bulletin of the Center for Children's Books.* "Strong characters, a plot that works on many levels, and an engaging background make this *Wolf* a standout," declared *School Library Journal* reviewer Carolyn Noah.

Franklin recalled the ocean waters off the Central American coast in creating the story *Iguana Beach*. The beach of the title is considered a dangerous place to swim, and little Reina is never allowed there. Her mother finally relents one day when an uncle promises to keep watch, but first Reina must vow not to venture into the waves. When the other kids do so, Reina feels angry and left out—though staying on the shore allows her to make the acquaintance of some of the region's native species, including the eponymous iguana. When her uncle falls asleep, Reina disobeys and runs to the water, but others chase her along the shore until she comes upon a secret lagoon, whose waters are still. Her uncle relents and lets her swim, and the others join in as well. "A delightful story of a family's integrity, love, and fun set in Central America," commented *School Library Journal* reviewer Susan Garland

For her 1999 novel *Dove Song,* Franklin created a heroine some reviewers compared to Trina in *Eclipse* for her fortitude in the face of difficulty. The work is set in Seattle during the Vietnam War, a locale to which Bobbie Lynn and her little brother Mason have relocated with their mother in order to be close to their father, who is serving in the military. When he is reported missing in action in Southeast Asia, their mother appears to suffer a nervous breakdown, taking to her bed and crying for days. Bobbie Lynn and her brother attempt to keep the household together, finding money for food and maintaining an appearance of normalcy, for they fear that authorities will commit their mother to a hospital and place them in foster care. Bobbie Lynn befriends a classmate, Wendy, who has her own challenges with a disabled sister. Wendy's family welcomes Bobbie Lynn and provides a newfound support system. The book's title comes from the day when Wendy teaches Bobbie Lynn how to whistle through her thumbs, which attracts a flock of doves who roost at a convent nearby. Finally Bobbie Lynn realizes that she must ask for help, and a sympathetic relative proves a savior. Stevenson, writing in the *Bulletin of the Center for Children's Books,* commended Franklin's characterization of Bobbie Lynn as a combination of "desperation, protectiveness, and survival instincts," while *Booklist*'s Helen Rosenberg called *Dove Song* "a moving novel about friendship and responsibility that is at once sorrowful and joyful."

Franklin told *SATA* that she felt a deep reverence for books even as a young child. "One sunny afternoon Mrs. Bond took our second-grade class on a field trip. We walked hand-in-hand for six blocks, past the Dairy Queen, across Pacific Avenue, up the short hill on 56th Street to the Moore Branch Library. I think it was the smell that got me. The smell of hundreds and hundreds of books, all waiting for me to read them.

"I got my first library card that day. It was made out of green heavy-weight paper with rounded edges and my full name typed across a line in the middle. After the librarian processed my books the card was hot; hot with

the bright magic that turned library books into *my* books for three whole weeks. There was no turning back. I was six years old and I was in love.

"My grandparents came to America from Croatia at the turn of the century. They were illiterate. My father only finished eighth grade but he had a deep love for books and a thirst for knowledge. He bought me stacks of used books at every opportunity, never censoring, never frowning in disapproval at what I chose. He encouraged me to write stories of my own, often buying me a new box of crayons or paints with which to illustrate my childish work. When I began winning journalism awards in school, Dad's applause was the loudest of all.

"Now I'm all grown up with children of my own. Dad is eighty years old. 'What are you writing?' is the first thing he asks when he calls. 'Lots,' I answer, and I know he smiles. You see, I think he knew way back then, the day I brought home *Danny and the Dinosaur, Curious George,* and *All about Volcanoes,* that I had what it takes to be a writer. I think he saw the pure love shining in my eyes.

"Now I have the opportunity to pass that same love along to other young people; to impart a passion for learning, to encourage the appreciation of all things human; the unique, the beautiful, the fanciful, the tragic. I wouldn't want to be anything but what I am: a children's writer. I've known since I was six years old that it is the most wonderful profession of all."

Biographical and Critical Sources

PERIODICALS

Booklist, January 1, 1995, Annie Ayres, review of *When the Monkeys Came Back,* p. 825; March 15, 1996, Leone McDermott, review of *Out of the Dump: Writings and Photographs by Children from Guatemala,* p. 1263; November 1, 1996, Karen Morgan, review of *The Wolfhound,* p. 507; October 15, 1999, Helen Rosenberg, review of *Dove Song,* p. 429.

Bulletin of the Center for Children's Books, March, 1995, Deborah Stevenson, review of *Eclipse,* p. 235; March, 1996, Roger Sutton, review of *Out of the Dump,* pp. 225-226; October, 1996, Deborah Stevenson, review of *Nerd No More,* pp. 57-58; May, 1997, Deborah Stevenson, review of *Lone Wolf,* pp. 320-321; November, 1999, Deborah Stevenson, review of *Dove Song,* pp. 91-92.

Children's Book Review Service, November, 1996, Lois K. Nichols, review of *The Wolfhound,* p. 30.

Five Owls, March, 1996, Mary Bahr Fritts, review of *Out of the Dump,* p. 88.

Horn Book, September, 1995, Nancy Vasilakis, review of *Eclipse,* p. 598; November, 1996, Lauren Adams, review of *Nerd No More,* p. 735; fall, 1997, Sheila M. Geraty, review of *Iguana Beach,* p. 264.

Kirkus Reviews, March 1, 1997, review of *Lone Wolf,* p. 380; May 1, 1997, review of *Iguana Beach,* p. 720; August 1, 1999, review of *Dove Song,* p. 1226; November, 1999, review of *The Gift,* p. 1741.

Publishers Weekly, August 19, 1996, review of *Nerd No More,* p. 67; November 15, 1999, review of *The Gift,* p. 65.

School Library Journal, February, 1997, Susan M. Moore, review of *The Wolfhound,* p. 81; June, 1997, Carolyn Noah, review of *Lone Wolf,* p. 117; August, 1997, Susan Garland, review of *Iguana Beach,* p. 135.

*   *   *

FRIDELL, Ron 1943-

Personal

Born July 11, 1943, in Fresno, CA; son of Donald and Rosalie Fridell; married Patricia Walsh (a writer and editor), July 1, 1995. *Education:* Northwestern University, B.S. (speech), 1965, M.A. (radio-TV-film), 1967.

Addresses

Agent—c/o Publicity Director, Franklin Watts, Inc., 90 Sherman Tpke., Danbury, CT 06816.

Career

Author. Scott Foresman (publisher), Glenview, IL, textbook editor, 1980—. Former Peace Corps volunteer

Ron Fridell

in Bangkok, Thailand, where he taught English as a second language.

Awards, Honors

Best Book for Junior High and High School Readers selection, American Association for the Advancement of Science, 2000, for *Solving Crimes: Pioneers of Forensic Science.*

Writings

Amphibians in Danger: A Worldwide Warning, Franklin Watts (New York, NY), 1999.

Solving Crimes: Pioneers of Forensic Science, Franklin Watts (New York, NY), 2000.

DNA Fingerprinting: The Ultimate Identity, Franklin Watts (New York, NY), 2001.

The Search for Poison-Dart Frogs, Wildlife Conservation Society and Franklin Watts (New York, NY), 2001.

(With wife, Patricia Walsh) *Life Cycle of a Pumpkin,* Heinemann Library (Chicago, IL), 2001.

(With wife, Patricia Walsh) *Life Cycle of a Silkworm,* Heinemann Library (Chicago, IL), 2001.

(With wife, Patricia Walsh) *Life Cycle of a Spider,* Heinemann Library (Chicago, IL), 2001.

(With wife, Patricia Walsh) *Life Cycle of a Turtle,* Heinemann Library (Chicago, IL), 2001.

Terrorism: Political Violence at Home and Abroad, Enslow (Berkeley Heights, NJ), 2001.

Global Warming: Good News, Bad News, Franklin Watts (New York, NY), 2002.

Stealing Secrets: The Modern World of Espionage, Twenty-First Century Books, in press.

Contributor to *America: The People and the Dream,* 1990, and *Reading 2000,* both published by Scott Foresman.

Sidelights

Ron Fridell's books on science and social studies topics for young people have garnered praise for his lucid writing style, which makes complex concepts clear and interesting. For example, his first book, *Amphibians in Danger: A Worldwide Warning,* describes the worldwide decline in amphibian populations, including frogs, toads, and salamanders, as well as the varying theories about its possible cause. "In clear, reader-friendly prose," according to Shelle Rosenfeld in *Booklist,* Fridell describes amphibians, the role they play in biodiversity, and the research that is being conducted on their declining numbers. The clarity the author brings to this complex topic contributes greatly to the success of this book, according to a reviewer in *Appraisal,* who wrote that *Amphibians in Danger* "will be useful as young people study amphibians and ecology, but may find an audience beyond that because of the lucid text." Both Rosenfeld and the *Appraisal* reviewer noted that Fridell's intelligent approach to his topic offers students a real and compelling insight into the way science works, particularly when reputable studies can often be cited to support opposing theories. "This is real life, not textbook science—the answers are not black or white," stated the reviewer in *Appraisal*. Although a bit less impressed by *Amphibians in Danger*, *School Library Journal* contributor Patricia Manning nonetheless concluded that Fridell's book offers "a useful, up-to-date look at a perplexing problem with some possibly very nasty ramifications."

In *Amphibians in Danger*, Fridell presents the case of the mysterious decline of amphibians, in which scientists act as detectives in search of information that will shed light on the probable causes of the decline. In *Solving Crimes: Pioneers of Forensic Science*, Fridell profiles six men whose contributions to the field of criminology are relied upon in police stations and courthouses everywhere. Forensics as a science has been in existence only since the 1880s, when a French file clerk devised a scheme for describing and classifying criminals according to physical types. Fridell also discusses the inventors of blood-typing, fingerprinting, and so-called DNA fingerprinting. Again, the author was praised for his ability to describe or define complex terms and techniques in a way that is both clear and engaging. Chris Sherman, writing in *Booklist*, predicted that "Mystery buffs, future criminologists, curious browsers, and

students scouting for a great report topic will be fascinated by Fridell's profiles." "Easy to read and interesting," remarked *Science Books and Films* contributor Al Staropoli, *Solving Crimes* "links science to real life with its presentations of applications to chemistry, math, biology, and anatomy." Staropoli went on to "recommend *Solving Crimes* to middle school science students everywhere."

Biographical and Critical Sources

PERIODICALS

Appraisal: Science Books for Young People, winter, 2000, review of *Amphibians in Danger,* pp. 15-16.
Booklist, June 1, 1999, Shelle Rosenfeld, review of *Amphibians in Danger,* p. 1807; August, 2000, Chris Sherman, review of *Solving Crimes.*
Evanston Review (Evanston, IL), November 23, 2000, Sara Loeb, "Writer Brings Science to Life," p. 31.
School Library Journal, August, 1999, Patricia Manning, review of *Amphibians in Danger,* p. 170; June, 2000, review of *Solving Crimes,* p. 164.
Science Books and Films, November-December, 2000, Al Staropoli, review of *Solving Crimes,* p. 265.

G

GAMBLE, Kim 1952-

Personal

Born July 13, 1952, in Sydney, New South Wales, Australia; son of Edward (Ted) James (a building inspector) and Hazel Eve (a teacher; maiden name, Hunter) Gamble; married Bella Wilson (a painter), December 28, 1985; children: Arielle Axel, Greer Rose. *Hobbies and other interests:* Gardening, reading, wandering about.

Addresses

Home and office—38 Lord St., Dungog, New South Wales 2420, Australia.

Career

Freelance illustrator of children's books. Formerly employed as an assistant to a small publisher.

Awards, Honors

Crichton Award, Children's Book Council of Victoria, and Book of the Year (Young Readers), Children's Book Council of Australia, both 1992, both for *The Magnificent Nose and Other Marvels.*

Writings

FOR CHILDREN; SELF-ILLUSTRATED

You Can Draw Anything, Allen & Unwin (St. Leonards, Australia), 1994.

You Can Do Great Lettering, Allen & Unwin (St. Leonards, Australia), 1995.

You Can Draw: Amazing Faces (art instruction), edited by Nicola Waine, DK Publishing (New York, NY), 1997.

(With Anna Fienberg) *Minton Goes Sailing,* Allen & Unwin (St. Leonards, Australia), 1998.

(With Anna Fienberg) *Minton Goes Flying,* Allen & Unwin (St. Leonards, Australia), 1998.

(With Anna Fienberg) *Minton Goes Driving,* Allen & Unwin (St. Leonards, Australia), 1999.

(With Anna Fienberg) *Minton Goes Trucking,* Allen & Unwin (St. Leonards, Australia), 1999.

(With Anna Fienberg) *Minton Goes Home,* Allen & Unwin (St. Leonards, Australia), 2000.

(With Anna Fienberg) *Minton Goes Under,* Allen & Unwin (St. Leonards, Australia), 2000.

FOR CHILDREN; ILLUSTRATOR

Anne Spencer Parry, *The Land behind the World,* Pinchgut Press (Sydney, Australia), 1976.

Anne Spencer Parry, *The Lost Souls of the Twilight,* Pinchgut Press (Sydney, Australia), 1977.

Anne Spencer Parry, *The Crown of Darkness,* Pinchgut Press (Sydney, Australia), 1979.

Anne Spencer Parry, *The Crown of Light,* Pinchgut Press (Sydney, Australia), 1980.

Ellen Robertson, *Own Up!,* Harcourt (Sydney, Australia), 1990.

Anna Burgess, *The Do-It-Yourself Lettering Book,* Lineup (East Roseville, Australia), 1991.

Anna Fienberg, *The Magnificent Nose and Other Marvels,* Allen & Unwin (North Sydney, Australia), 1991, Joy Street Books, 1992.

Michael Stephens, *Titans!,* Allen & Unwin (North Sydney, Australia), 1992.

David Shapiro, *The Thunder God: A Chinese Folktale,* Harcourt (Sydney, Australia), 1992.

Anna Fienberg, *Ariel, Zed and the Secret of Life,* Allen & Unwin (North Sydney, Australia), 1992.

Jillian De Muth, *Blue Skies, Green Days,* Allen & Unwin (North Sydney, Australia), 1992, Independent Publishers Group, 1993.

Michael Stephens, *Eddy the Great,* Allen & Unwin (St. Leonards, Australia), 1993.

Ian Bowring, *The Exploding Egg,* Angus & Robertson (Pymble, Australia), 1993.

Anna Fienberg, *The Hottest Boy Who Ever Lived,* Allen & Unwin (St. Leonards, Australia), 1993, A. Whitman (Morton Grove, IL), 1995.

Rosalind Price, *Come the Terrible Tiger,* Allen & Unwin (St. Leonards, Australia), 1993.

'Ooah, did you run away home?' asked Jack. 'Not me,' said Tashi. 'I took my buckets and climbed up the mountain and there, sitting at the mouth of the cave, was the biggest dragon I'd ever seen.'

40

'Have you seen many?' asked Jack. 'I've seen a few in my time,' said Tashi. 'But not so close. And *this* dragon made me very cross.'

41

Brave, elf-like Tashi entertains friend Jack with tales of his wild adventures, which Jack then relates to his parents in this story-within-a-story. (From Tashi, *written by Anna and Barbara Fienberg and illustrated by Kim Gamble.)*

Leigh Treseder, *Buster's Custard,* Ashton Scholastic (Sydney, Australia), 1993.

Susanna Rodell, *Dear Fred,* Viking (Ringwood, Australia) 1993, Ticknor & Fields (New York, NY), 1995.

Michael Stephens, *The Prince of Kelvin Mall,* Allen & Unwin (St. Leonards, Australia), 1994.

Anna Burgess, *The Do-It-Yourself Drawing Book,* Lineup (Balmain, Australia), 1994.

Sarah Keane, *My Grandma,* Mammoth (Port Melbourne, Australia), 1994.

Wendy Orr, *Yasou Nikki,* Angus & Robertson (Pymble, Australia), 1995.

Anna and Barbara Fienberg, *Tashi and the Giants,* Allen & Unwin (St. Leonards, Australia), 1995.

Pamela Shrapnel, *Bella of Bananaland,* Omnibus Books (Norwood, Australia), 1995.

Pamela Freeman, *Victor's Quest,* Omnibus Books (Norwood, Australia), 1996.

Sally Odgers, *Bunyips Don't!,* Scholastic (Sydney, Australia), 1996.

Anna and Barbara Fienberg, *Tashi and the Ghosts,* Allen & Unwin (St. Leonards, Australia), 1996.

Janine M. Fraser, *Abdullah's Butterfly,* Angus & Robertson (Pymble, Australia), 1996.

Peter Macinnis and Jane Bowring, *The Desert,* Puffin (Ringwood, Australia), 1997.

Anna and Barbara Fienberg, *Tashi and the Genie,* Allen & Unwin (St. Leonards, Australia), 1997.

Colin Thompson, *The Last Circus,* Hodder Headline (Sydney, Australia), 1997.

Wendy Orr, *Arabella,* HarperCollins (Pymble, Australia), 1998.

Anna and Barbara Fienberg, *Tashi and the Baba Yaga,* Allen & Unwin (St. Leonards, Australia), 1998.

Margaret Wild, *First Day,* Allen & Unwin (St. Leonards, Australia), 1998.

Peter Macinnis and Ian Bowring, *The Rainforest,* Puffin (Ringwood, Australia), 1999.

Anna and Barbara Fienberg, *Tashi and the Demons,* Allen & Unwin (St. Leonards, Australia), 1999.

Anna and Barbara Fienberg, *Tashi and the Big Stinker,* Allen & Unwin (St. Leonards, Australia), 2000.

Lyn Lee, *Pog,* Omnibus Books (Norwood, Australia), 2000.

Janine M. Fraser, *Sarindi and the Lucky Bird,* HarperCollins (Pymble, Australia), 2001.

Also illustrator for the New South Wales, Australia Department of Education's *School Magazine,* 1988—.

Sidelights

Children's book illustrator and author Kim Gamble told *SATA:* "I was born and grew up in a leafy, peaceful suburb of Sydney. At the end of our street full of billycarts was a forest, still full of native birds and animals, caves, a river, and a silent, aboriginal history.

"I enjoyed drawing, but also playing, exploring, inventing and just 'hanging out.' I had a Tove Jansson picture book. When I was nine my mum took me to visit May Gibbs, a friend of hers and the Grand Old Dame of Australian children's literature. She gave us two of her books. The ramifications of this didn't occur to me until a few years ago.

"I painted pictures of Robinson Crusoe in my days off and lived in various cottages on the harbor. Then I 'went bush' with my wife, Bella, and we built a house in the granite and pine highlands of New South Wales. We painted and pottered, and had a little girl, Arielle. After five years, on the strength of regular work I was doing for the New South Wales *School Magazine* (similar to *Cricket*), we moved to Dungog and had another girl, Greer. With hindsight I see that everything was pointing to this, but until I had children of my own I wouldn't have understood what it takes to illustrate their books.

"I draw my inspiration from the stories, my children, my childhood, the news, and my environment. I love the work of most other illustrators, and I love the light, so I've become a sort of watercolorist, but don't be surprised if I respond to a brooding drama in oils. In the end, I love stories, and I feel so privileged to be a part of their telling."

Biographical and Critical Sources

PERIODICALS

School Librarian, August, 1995, Jill Bennett, review of *Come the Terrible Tiger,* p. 102; November, 1997, Lynda Jones, review of *You Can Draw: Amazing Faces,* p. 204.
School Library Journal, February, 1998, Marcia Hupp, review of *You Can Draw Amazing Faces,* p. 116; July, 2001, Gay Lynn Van Vleck, review of *Tashi and the Big Stinker,* p. 75.*

*   *   *

GARRITY, Jennifer Johnson 1961-

Personal

Born June 28, 1961, in Seattle, WA; daughter of Gerald W. (a radio broadcaster) and Janith (Forsman) Johnson; married Kim Garrity (an architect), June, 1984; children:

Jennifer Johnson Garrity

Kelsey, Collin, Eliza. *Education:* Attended Multnomah School of the Bible. *Religion:* Evangelical Protestant.

Addresses

Home—Johanniter Strasse 23, 79400 Kandem-Feuerbach, Germany. *E-mail*—KJGarrity@compuserve.com.

Career

Writer and homemaker, first in Belgium, then in Germany.

Writings

The Bushwhacker: A Civil War Adventure (historical novel), illustrated by Paul Bachem, Peachtree Publishers (Atlanta, GA), 1999.

Work in Progress

Another historical novel.

Sidelights

Jennifer Johnson Garrity told *SATA:* "I have written stories in my head since at least the first grade, when my teacher called to tell my mother that I stared out the window during every math lesson and was in danger of flunking. As soon as I could string two sentences together, I began to write my stories down. Somehow amidst living overseas and having babies I gave up writing, but a hobby brought it back to me when my youngest child was two (in 1995). Researching my paternal grandmother's family history brought me face to face with Missouri's unique predicament during the Civil War, and suddenly I knew a book was forming within me—a story blending my own family history with the turmoil in Missouri.

"There is enough fodder in my ancestry to produce several novels, and I intend to make use of it. Currently I am working on an adult historical novel that has to do with a Danish immigrant to the United States in the 1860s.

"As a practicing evangelical Christian, I believe that I, as an author, am responsible to God for how my writing will affect those who read it. It is my strong desire to convey truth about the human struggle and God's ultimate goodness without being trite or simplistic.

"Basing my novels loosely on my own ancestors fulfills me in a way that other subject matter could not. It links me with those whom I could otherwise not have known. The research I engage in connects me with them intimately and, by the time a novel is completed, they have become my friends as well as my ancestors."

Biographical and Critical Sources

PERIODICALS

School Library Journal, April, 2000, Patricia B. McGee, review of *The Bushwhacker,* p. 134.*

*   *   *

GATHORNE-HARDY, Jonathan G. 1933-

Personal

Born May 17, 1933, in Edinburgh, Scotland; son of Anthony (a doctor) and Ruth (Thorowgood) Gathorne-Hardy; married Sabrina Tennant (a restorer), October, 1962 (divorced); married Nicky Louit (a painter), September, 1985; children: Jenny, Benjamin. *Education:* Trinity College, Cambridge, B.A., 1957.

Addresses

Home—31 Blacksmith's Yard, Binham, Fakenham, Norfolk NR21 0AL, England. *Agent*—Christopher Sinclair-Stevenson, 3 South Terrace, London SW7 2TB, England; and Laura Cecil, 17 Alwynne Villas, London N1 2HG, England.

Career

Writer. Worked as an advertising copywriter, publisher, bookseller, book reviewer, and freelance journalist. *Military service:* British Army, 1952-53; became lieutenant.

Writings

FOR CHILDREN

Jane's Adventures in and out of the Book, Alan Ross, 1966.
Jane's Adventures on the Island of Peeg, Alan Ross, 1968, published as *Operation Peeg,* Lippincott (Philadelphia, PA), 1974.
Jane's Adventures in a Balloon, Gollancz (London, England), 1975, published as *The Airship Ladyship Adventure,* Lippincott (Philadelphia, PA), 1977.
The Terrible Kidnapping of Cyril Bonhamy, Evans Brothers, 1978.
Cyril Bonhamy vs. Madam Big, illustrated by Quentin Blake, J. Cape (London, England), 1981.
Cyril Bonhamy and the Great Drain Robbery, illustrated by Quentin Blake, J. Cape (London, England), 1983.

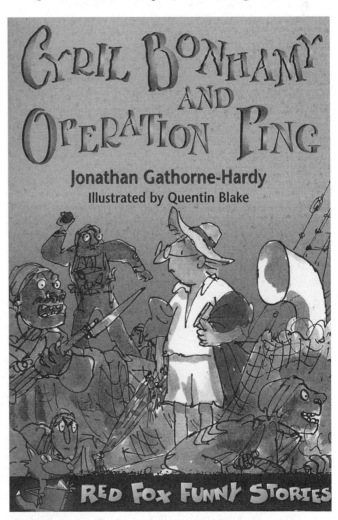

Timid and bumbling Cyril Bonhamy finds himself part of a mission to oust the evil Emperor Ping in Jonathan G. Gathorne-Hardy's humorous adventure tale. (Cover illustration by Quentin Blake.)

Cyril Bonhamy and Operation Ping, illustrated by Quentin Blake, J. Cape (London, England), 1985.
Cyril of the Apes, illustrated by Quentin Blake, J. Cape (London, England), 1987.
The Tunnel Party, illustrated by M. Van Tilburg, Walker, 1990.
The Munros' New House, illustrated by Barbara Firth, Walker, 1992.
The Twin Detectives, Macmillan, 1995.

The "Cyril Bonhamy" books have also been published in Italy, Holland, and Spain.

FOR ADULTS

One Foot in the Clouds (novel), Hamish Hamilton (London, England), 1961.
Chameleon (novel), Hamish Hamilton (London, England), Walker America, 1967.
The Office (novel), Hodder & Stoughton (London, England), 1970, Dial (New York, NY), 1971.
The Rise and Fall of the British Nanny (nonfiction), Hodder & Stoughton (London, England), 1972, published as *The Unnatural History of the Nanny,* Dial (New York, NY), 1973.
The Public School Phenomenon, 1597-1977 (nonfiction), Hodder & Stoughton (London, England), 1977, published as *The Old School Tie: The Phenomenon of the English Public School,* Viking (New York, NY), 1978.
Love, Sex, Marriage, and Divorce, J. Cape (London, England), 1981, published as *Sex, Love, Marriage, Divorce,* Summit Books (New York, NY), 1981.
Doctors, Weidenfeld & Nicolson (London, England), 1983.
The Centre of the Universe Is 18 Baedekerstrasse (short stories), Hamish Hamilton (London, England), 1985.
The City beneath the Skin (novel), Hamish Hamilton (London, England), 1986.
Gerald Brenan: The Interior Castle (biography), Sinclair Stevenson (London, England), 1992, Norton (New York, NY), 1993.
Particle Theory (novel), Hutchinson (London, England), 1996.
Alfred C. Kinsey: Sex the Measure of All Things (biography), Chatto & Windus (London, England), 1998, published as *Sex the Measure of All Things: A Life of Alfred C. Kinsey,* Indiana University Press (Bloomington, IN), 2000.

Adaptations

The "Cyril Bonhamy" books are being adapted as a cartoon series for television.

Sidelights

In addition to being a noted social historian, Jonathan Gathorne-Hardy is a writer of fanciful tales for children and adults. Jane and Cyril, the protagonists of his two children's series, have had adventures such as flying around the world and capturing a mad old woman who wants to rob all the department stores in England on Christmas Eve.

Jane Charrington of Curl Castle in Cornwall, who begins her escapades in *Jane's Adventures in and out of the Book,* is a heroic young Lady, often bored by being left only with the castle's fastidious housekeeper, Mrs. Deal. In her first story, she discovers a bizarre world as she walks into the illustrations of an ancient book. Hazel Rochman, writing for *School Library Journal,* praised Jane for "displaying adult skill and responsibility in heroic feats ... leaving terse notes for the housekeeper: 'Have gone to blow up mushroom tunnel. Don't fuss.'"

Jane's adventures continue in *Jane's Adventures on the Island of Peeg,* published in the United States as *Operation Peeg.* In this story, considered "almost a tall tale" by *Bulletin of the Center for Children's Books* reviewer Zena Sutherland, Jane and her friend Jemima, both students at a Scottish boarding school on the island of Peeg, are stuck in a storm. The island is connected to the mainland by a small causeway, and the rest of the students have gone to the mainland, leaving the girls alone until Mrs. Deal arrives to comfort them. Just when things seem to be going well, an explosion destroys the causeway and sets the island adrift. Through a course of adventures, Jane, Jemima, and Mrs. Deal discover two World War II soldiers, unaware that the war has ended, guarding a huge store—eight million tons—of explosives that a wicked villain wants to use to take over the world. "Good characters, very good dialogue, a lively plot, and an intriguing setting," remarked Sutherland about *Operation Peeg.* Virginia Haviland of *Horn Book* wrote, "The wildly funny and suspenseful action makes for a welcome piece of escape reading."

In *Jane's Adventures in a Balloon,* which appeared in the United States as *The Airship Ladyship Adventure,* Jane and Mrs. Deal become trapped in an airship created by Jane's father. Though Jane gains control of the ship, she manages to crash it in the Swiss Alps. There, she and Mrs. Deal meet Sydney Saxton, an ailing Englishman living in the Alps, and subsequently rescue him from an avalanche. Escaping in what remains of the airship, the trio flies to Africa, where they must confront a faceless villain—as well as the flying tigers under his command. "Gathorne-Hardy does a credible job of balancing an unbelievable plot with believable characterization and setting," wrote Craighton Hippenhammer in a *School Library Journal* review of *The Airship Ladyship Adventure.* Sutherland noted in *Bulletin of the Center for Children's Books,* "It's funny, it's exaggerated, it's deliberately unbelievable."

Cyril Bonhamy is an entirely different sort of hero. Absurd and incompetent, likeably lazy and cowardly, Cyril is a "small, fat, scholarly writer who talks about books on the television but whose own most recent work has only sold fifty-three copies," explained John Mole, writing for the *Times Literary Supplement.* In *The Terrible Kidnapping of Cyril Bonhamy,* poor Cyril's first misadventure is his abduction. He is mistaken for the prestigious scientist O'Noonagan by Arab terrorists, who had hoped to make use of O'Noonagan's knowledge of explosives. Cyril escapes mostly by accident in what a

Junior Bookshelf reviewer called a "comical, jaunty story."

Cyril's trouble continues in *Cyril Bonhamy v. Madam Big* when his wife asks him to volunteer as a Father Christmas at Borringes department store during the Christmas season. Unhappy in a Santa suit and rude to the children who come to sit on his lap, Cyril stumbles onto a crime scheme entirely by accident: the notorious Madam Big is plotting to rob stores on Christmas Eve with hundreds of burglars dressed as Father Christmas. With the help of the police, Cyril "saves Borringes and captures Madam Big, with great personal bravery and some breathless moments in his accident-prone progress," described a reviewer for *Junior Bookshelf.* Alan Brownjohn of the *Times Literary Supplement* called *Cyril Bonhamy v. Madam Big* "a fast and uncomplicated fantasy with a vigorous vein of humour." Chris Brown of *School Librarian* declared the book "a certain hit for junior children."

In *Cyril Bonhamy and the Great Drain Robbery,* Cyril and his wife travel to France to visit the library, and Cyril is mistaken by the nefarious jewel thief Pierre Melon for a notorious British master criminal. Cyril doesn't speak French very well, which leads to further misunderstanding, and he is pursued by the French police and Olaf Lockjaw, reportedly the world's strongest man. "Bringing the criminals to justice by accident and good fortune, Cyril remains somewhat puzzled by his adventures," described Margery Fisher in *Growing Point.* A *Junior Bookshelf* reviewer noted that the combination of "fast and furious" action, "farcical" situations and characters, and "unbelievable" coincidences, make for a "funny and entertaining book."

After another of Cyril's books flops, his publisher sends him out looking for a violent topic to write about, so Cyril gets involved with a raid on a monastery run by Abbot Ping Po, a drug lord, in *Cyril Bonhamy and Operation Ping.* As usual, mostly by accident, Cyril winds up a hero, defeating "the villains by a method learnt from studying an ancient parchment photocopied for him by his friend from the British Museum," according to Mole in a *Times Literary Supplement* assessment of *Cyril Bonhamy and Operation Ping.* He continued, "This is a funny book, endearingly silly." In *Cyril of the Apes,* Cyril's attempts at writing take him to the Brazilian jungle, where he works as a script writer for a new *Tarzan* movie. Accompanied by his wife, Cyril must fight off the heat, the insects, and dangerous plants, while finding the film company a new lead actor and discovering a real-life Tarzan. "As usual," wrote a reviewer for *Junior Bookshelf,* "he emerges unscathed because he is so simple and honest that the devious and the sophisticated cannot understand or foresee his reactions." Followers of the series have something to look for in the future as Gathorne-Hardy told *SATA,* "The entire 'Cyril' series is now under development for television."

Gathorne-Hardy has also written books outside of these series. In his 1995 title, *The Twin Detectives,* he introduces the twins Kate and Sel, who must find their great-uncle who disappeared on a holiday. Sel uses intuition and dreams to discover clues, which lead the twins to a ring of terrorists and drug smugglers. Angela Lepper of *School Librarian* called it "an exciting story, full of suspense and neatly concluded." Another non-series title is *The Tunnel Party,* written for younger readers, about how children could have a "tunnel party" in their home, creating a tunnel of mattresses and sheets. A *Junior Bookshelf* reviewer noted that the illustrations and ideas in the book "will undoubtedly entertain children and worry adults!"

In writing his adult nonfiction, Gathorne-Hardy closely studied the social and historical roots of two British institutions: the public school and the nanny. Other topics Gathorne-Hardy has written about include interpersonal relationships and the lives and work of general practitioners. He has also written two biographies, several novels, and collections of short stories for adults. In his adult fiction, Gathorne-Hardy blends the traditional literary forms of novel and social history in his unique social comedies. Described by *Punch* contributor Martin Shuttleworth as one of "the wittiest novelists" of the 1960s, Gathorne-Hardy has written several books which provide insights into mid-twentieth-century society through fantasy and humor.

Biographical and Critical Sources

PERIODICALS

Bulletin of the Center for Children's Books, January, 1975, Zena Sutherland, review of *Operation Peeg,* p. 77; September, 1977, Zena Sutherland, review of *The Airship Ladyship Adventure,* p. 15.

Growing Point, November, 1983, Margery Fisher, "Sense of Humour," pp. 4151-4154; November, 1985, Margery Fisher, review of *Cyril Bonhamy and Operation Ping,* p. 4538.

Horn Book, April, 1975, Virginia Haviland, review of *Operation Peeg,* p. 147.

Junior Bookshelf, February, 1979, review of *The Terrible Kidnapping of Cyril Bonhamy,* p. 30; August, 1982, review of *Cyril Bonhamy v. Madam Big,* pp. 140-141; October, 1983, review of *Cyril Bonhamy and the Great Drain Robbery,* p. 207; October, 1987, review of *Cyril of the Apes,* p. 232; April, 1990, review of *The Tunnel Party,* p. 72.

New Statesman, May, 1975, Lorna Sage, "This Side of Paradise," pp. 693-694.

Punch, March, 1967.

School Librarian, June, 1982, Chris Brown, review of *Cyril Bonhamy v. Madam Big,* p. 129; May, 1996, Angela Lepper, review of *The Twin Detectives,* p. 61.

School Library Journal, March, 1977, Craighton Hippenhammer, review of *The Airship Ladyship Adventure,* pp. 144-145; December, 1981, Hazel Rochman, review of *Jane's Adventures in and out of the Book,* p. 52.

Times Literary Supplement, March 16, 1967; October 30, 1970; September 1, 1972; April 4, 1975, Sarah Hayes, "Floating Fantasy," p. 360; November 20, 1981, Alan

Brownjohn, review of *Cyril Bonhamy v. Madam Big*, p. 1357; December 25, 1981; July 13, 1984; March 22, 1985; September 27, 1985, John Mole, "Safe Bets," p. 1079; July 18, 1986, p. 793.

*   *   *

GEORGE, Jean
See GEORGE, Jean Craighead

*   *   *

GEORGE, Jean Craighead 1919-
(Jean George)

Personal

Born July 2, 1919, in Washington, DC; daughter of Frank Cooper, Ph.D, (an entomologist) and Mary Carolyn (Johnson) Craighead; married John Lothar George, Ph.D., January 28, 1944 (divorced, January 10, 1963); children: Carolyn Laura, John Craighead, Thomas Luke. *Education:* Pennsylvania State University, B.A., 1941; attended Louisiana State University, Baton Rouge, 1941-42, and University of Michigan. *Politics:* Democrat. *Hobbies and other interests:* Painting, field trips to universities and laboratories of natural science, modern dance, white water canoeing.

Addresses

Home and office—20 William St., Chappaqua, NY 10514. *Agent*—Curtis Brown Ltd., 575 Madison Ave., New York, NY 10022.

Jean Craighead George

Career

International News Service, Washington, DC, reporter, 1942-44; *Washington Post and Times-Herald,* Washington, DC, reporter, 1943-44; United Features (Newspaper Enterprise Association), New York, NY, employee, 1944-45, artist and reporter, 1945-46; continuing education teacher in Chappaqua, NY, 1960-68; *Reader's Digest,* Pleasantville, NY, staff writer, 1969-74, roving editor, 1974-80; author and illustrator of books and articles on natural history. *Pageant* (magazine), New York, NY, artist. *Member:* League of Women Voters, PEN, Dutchess County Art Association.

Awards, Honors

Aurianne Award, American Library Association (ALA), 1956, for *Dipper of Copper Creek;* Newbery Honor Book, ALA, Notable Book citation, ALA, 1960, International Hans Christian Andersen Award honor list, International Board on Books for Young People, 1962, Lewis Carroll Shelf citation, 1965, and George G. Stone Center for Children's Books Award, 1969, all for *My Side of the Mountain;* Woman of the Year, Pennsylvania State University, 1968; Claremont College award, 1969; Eva L. Gordon Award, American Nature Study Society, 1970; *Book World* First Prize, 1971, for *All upon a Stone;* Newbery Medal, ALA, National Book Award finalist, American Association of Publishers, German Youth Literature Prize, West German section of International Board on Books for Young People, and Silver Skate, Netherlands Children's Book Board, all 1973, and one of ten best American children's books in two hundred years listing, Children's Literature Association, 1976, all for *Julie of the Wolves;* School Library Media Specialties of South Eastern New York Award, 1981; Irvin Kerlan Award, University of Minnesota, 1982; University of Southern Mississippi Award, 1986; Grumman Award, 1986; Washington Irving Award, Westchester Library Association, 1991; Reading Is Fundamental Award, 1995; Knickerbocker Award for Juvenile Literature, School Library Media Section, New York Public Library Association; Children's Book Guild Award for Nonfiction, Children's Book Guild and *Washington Post,* 1998, for "an author or author-illustrator whose total work has contributed significantly to the quality of nonfiction for children"; Notable Children's Books list, *New York Times,* 1999, for *Frightful's Mountain.*

Writings

Coyote in Manhattan, illustrated by John Kaufmann, Crowell, 1968.
All upon a Stone, illustrated by Don Bolognese, Crowell, 1971.
Who Really Killed Cock Robin? An Ecological Mystery, Dutton (New York, NY), 1971.
Julie of the Wolves, illustrated by John Schoenherr, Harper, 1972.
All upon a Sidewalk, illustrated by Don Bolognese, Dutton (New York, NY), 1974.

Hook a Fish, Catch a Mountain, Dutton (New York, NY), 1975, published as *The Case of the Missing Cutthroat Trout: An Ecological Mystery,* HarperCollins (New York, NY), 1995.

Going to the Sun, Harper, 1976.

The Wentletrap Trap, illustrated by Symeon Shimin, Dutton (New York, NY), 1978.

The Wounded Wolf, illustrated by John Schoenherr, Harper, 1978.

River Rats, Inc., Dutton (New York, NY), 1979.

The Cry of the Crow, Harper, 1980.

The Grizzly Bear with the Golden Ears, illustrated by Tom Catania, Harper, 1982.

The Talking Earth, Harper, 1983.

Shark beneath the Reef, Harper, 1989.

Missing 'Gator of Gumbo Limbo: An Ecological Mystery, HarperCollins (New York, NY), 1992.

The Fire Bug Connection: An Ecological Mystery, Harper-Collins (New York, NY), 1993.

Famous Animals (stories), illustrated by Christine Merrill, HarperCollins (New York, NY), 1994.

Julie (sequel to *Julie of the Wolves*), HarperCollins (New York, NY), 1994.

There's an Owl in the Shower, HarperCollins (New York, NY), 1995.

The Everglades, illustrated by Wendell Minor, HarperCollins (New York, NY), 1995.

Julie's Wolf Pack (sequel to *Julie and the Wolves* and *Julie*), HarperCollins (New York, NY), 1997.

(Self-illustrated) *Tree Castle Island,* HarperCollins (New York, NY), 2002.

UNDER NAME JEAN GEORGE; WITH JOHN L. GEORGE; SELF-ILLUSTRATED

Vulpes, the Red Fox, Dutton (New York, NY), 1948.

Vison, the Mink, Dutton (New York, NY), 1949.

Masked Prowler: The Story of a Raccoon, Dutton (New York, NY), 1950.

Meph, the Pet Skunk, Dutton (New York, NY), 1952.

Bubo, the Great Horned Owl, Dutton (New York, NY), 1954.

Dipper of Copper Creek, Dutton (New York, NY), 1956.

SELF-ILLUSTRATED

(Under name Jean George) *The Hole in the Tree,* Dutton (New York, NY), 1957.

(Under name Jean George) *Snow Tracks,* Dutton (New York, NY), 1958.

(Under name Jean George) *My Side of the Mountain* (also see below), Dutton (New York, NY), 1959.

The Summer of the Falcon, Crowell, 1962.

Gull Number 737, Crowell, 1964.

Hold Zero!, Crowell, 1966.

Water Sky, Harper, 1987.

On the Far Side of the Mountain (also see below), Dutton (New York, NY), 1990.

Frightful's Mountain (also see below), Dutton (New York, NY), 1999.

My Side of the Mountain Trilogy (contains *My Side of the Mountain, On the Far Side of the Mountain,* and *Frightful's Mountain*), Dutton (New York, NY), 2000.

PICTURE BOOKS

Dear Rebecca, Winter Is Here, illustrated by Loretta Krupinski, HarperCollins (New York, NY), 1993.

The First Thanksgiving, illustrated by Thomas Locker, Philomel, 1993.

To Climb a Waterfall, illustrated by Thomas Locker, Philomel, 1995.

Look to the North: A Wolf Pup Diary, illustrated by Lucia Washburn, HarperCollins (New York, NY), 1997.

Arctic Son, illustrated by Wendell Minor, Hyperion, 1997.

Dear Katie, the Volcano Is a Girl, illustrated by Daniel Powers, Hyperion, 1998.

Elephant Walk, illustrated by Ann Vojtech, Disney, 1998.

Rhino Romp, illustrated by Stacey Schuett, Disney, 1998.

Giraffe Trouble, illustrated by Ann Vojtech, Disney, 1998.

Gorilla Gang, illustrated by Stacey Schuett, Disney, 1998.

Morning, Noon, and Night, illustrated by Wendell Minor, HarperCollins (New York, NY), 1999.

Snow Bear, illustrated by Wendell Minor, Hyperion, 1999.

Nutik, the Wolf Pup, illustrated by Ted Rand, HarperCollins (New York, NY), 2000.

How to Talk to Your Dog, illustrated by Sue Truesdell, HarperCollins (New York, NY), 2000.

How to Talk to Your Cat, illustrated by Paul Meisel, HarperCollins (New York, NY), 2000.

Nutik and Amaroq Play Ball, illustrated by Ted Rand, HarperCollins (New York, NY), 2001.

Lonesome George, illustrated by Wendell Minor, Harper-Collins (New York, NY), 2002.

"THIRTEEN MOONS" SERIES; NONFICTION

The Moon of the Salamanders, illustrated by John Kaufmann, Crowell, 1967, new edition illustrated by Marlene Werner, HarperCollins (New York, NY), 1992.

The Moon of the Bears (also see below), illustrated by Mac Shepard, Crowell, 1967, new edition illustrated by Ron Parker, HarperCollins (New York, NY), 1993.

The Moon of the Owls (also see below), illustrated by Jean Zallinger, Crowell, 1967, new edition illustrated by Wendell Minor, HarperCollins (New York, NY), 1993.

The Moon of the Mountain Lions, illustrated by Winifred Lubell, Crowell, 1968, new edition illustrated by Ron Parker, HarperCollins (New York, NY), 1991.

The Moon of the Chickarees, illustrated by John Schoenherr, Crowell, 1968, new edition illustrated by Don Rodell, HarperCollins (New York, NY), 1992.

The Moon of the Fox Pups, illustrated by Kiyoaki Komoda, Crowell, 1968, new edition illustrated by Norman Adams, HarperCollins (New York, NY), 1992.

The Moon of the Wild Pigs, illustrated by Peter Parnall, Crowell, 1968, new edition illustrated by Paul Mirocha, HarperCollins (New York, NY), 1992.

The Moon of the Monarch Butterflies, illustrated by Murray Tinkelman, Crowell, 1968, new edition illustrated by Kam Mak, HarperCollins (New York, NY), 1993.

The Moon of the Alligators (also see below), illustrated by Adrina Zanazanian, Crowell, 1969, new edition illustrated by Michael Rothman, HarperCollins (New York, NY), 1991.

The Moon of the Gray Wolves (also see below), illustrated by Lorence Bjorklund, Crowell, 1969, new edition illustrated by Sal Catalano, HarperCollins (New York, NY), 1991.

The Moon of the Deer (also see below), illustrated by Jean Zallinger, Crowell, 1969, new edition illustrated by Sal Catalano, HarperCollins (New York, NY), 1992.

The Moon of the Moles (also see below), illustrated by Robert Levering, Crowell, 1969, new edition illustrated by Michael Rothman, HarperCollins (New York, NY), 1992.

The Moon of the Winter Bird (also see below), illustrated by Kazue Mizumura, Crowell, 1969, new edition illustrated by Vincent Nasta, HarperCollins (New York, NY), 1992.

Autumn Moon (contains *The Moon of the Deer, The Moon of the Alligators,* and *The Moon of the Grey Wolves*), HarperCollins (New York, NY), 2001.

Winter Moon (contains *The Moon of the Winter Bird, The Moon of the Moles, The Moon of the Owls* and *The Moon of the Bears*), HarperCollins (New York, NY), 2001.

"ONE DAY" SERIES; NONFICTION

One Day in the Desert, illustrated by Fred Brenner, Crowell, 1983.

One Day in the Alpine Tundra, illustrated by Walter Gaffney-Kessell, Crowell, 1984.

One Day in the Prairie, illustrated by Bob Marstall, Crowell, 1986.

Luke is taught to survive in the untamed Arctic by his parents' Eskimo friend. *(Cover illustration by Wendell Minor.)*

One Day in the Woods, illustrated by Gary Allen, Crowell, 1988.

One Day in the Tropical Rain Forest, illustrated by Gary Allen, HarperCollins (New York, NY), 1990.

NONFICTION

Spring Comes to the Ocean (for children), illustrated by John Wilson, Crowell, 1965.

(Self-illustrated) *Beastly Inventions: A Surprising Investigation into How Smart Animals Really Are,* McKay, 1970, published in England as *Animals Can Do Anything,* Souvenir Press, 1972.

Everglades Wildguide, illustrated by Betty Fraser, National Park Service, 1972.

(With Toy Lasker) *New York in Maps, 1972/73,* New York Magazine, 1974.

(With Toy Lasker) *New York in Flashmaps, 1974/75,* Flashmaps, 1976.

The American Walk Book: An Illustrated Guide to the Country's Major Historic and Natural Walking Trails from New England to the Pacific Coast, Dutton (New York, NY), 1978.

The Wild, Wild Cookbook: A Guide for Young Wild-Food Foragers (for children), illustrated by Walter Kessell, Crowell, 1982, reprinted as *Acorn Pancakes, Dandelion Salad and 38 Other Wild Recipes,* illustrated by Paul Mirocha, HarperCollins (New York, NY), 1995.

Journey Inward (autobiography), Dutton (New York, NY), 1982.

(Self-illustrated) *How to Talk to Your Animals* (also see below), Harcourt, 1985.

(Self-illustrated) *How to Talk to Your Dog* (originally published in *How to Talk to Your Animals*), Warner (New York, NY), 1986, reprinted with illustrations by Sue Truesdell, HarperCollins (New York, NY), 2000.

(Self-illustrated) *How to Talk to Your Cat* (originally published in *How to Talk to Your Animals*), Warner (New York, NY), 1986, reprinted with illustrations by Paul Meisel, HarperCollins (New York, NY), 2000.

Animals Who Have Won Our Hearts, HarperCollins (New York, NY), 1994, revised edition published as *Incredible Animal Adventures,* illustrated by Donna Diamond, Harper, 1999.

The Tarantula in My Purse and 172 Other Wild Pets (autobiographical short stories), HarperCollins (New York, NY), 1996.

Mountain Climbing, Hyperion, 2001.

OTHER

Tree House (play; with music by Saul Aarons), produced in Chappaqua, NY, 1962.

(Illustrator) John J. Craighead and Frank C. Craighead, Jr., *Hawks, Owls, and Wildlife,* Dover, 1969.

(Editor, with Ann Durell and Katherine Paterson), Aliki and others, *The Big Book for the Planet* (short stories), illustrated by Aliki and others, Dutton (New York, NY), 1993.

Contributor to books, including *Marvels and Mysteries of Our Animal World,* Reader's Digest Association, 1964. Contributor of articles on natural history and children's literature to periodicals, including *Audubon,*

Horn Book, International Wildlife, and *National Wildlife.* Consultant for science books.

George's manuscripts are held in the Kerlan Collection at the University of Minnesota, Minneapolis.

Adaptations

My Side of the Mountain was adapted as a film starring Teddy Eccles and Theodore Bikel, Paramount, 1969. *Julie of the Wolves* was adapted as a recording, read by Irene Worth, Caedmon, 1977. *One Day in the Woods* was adapted as a musical video, with music by Fritz Kramer and Chris Kubie, Kunhardt Productions, 1989; and as a musical, with music by Chris Kubie, Harper-Collins Audio, 1997. *Julie of the Wolves* is being adapted for a movie, and for a musical with music by Chris Kubie. *On the Far Side of the Mountain* and *Frightful's Mountain* were recorded as an audiocassette by Recorded Books, 1995.

Work in Progress

Juvenile novel set in the Okefenokee Swamp.

Sidelights

Newbery Medal winner Jean Craighead George has made nature the center of her fiction and nonfiction work in a career spanning over half a century of writing and including over one hundred books. In her novels, picture books, and books of fact, George has given young readers many fascinating glimpses of nature, earning a reputation as "our premier naturalist novelist," according to *New York Times Book Review* contributor Beverly Lyon Clark. Writing first with her husband and later alone, she has penned studies of animals, such as *Dipper of Copper Creek,* as well as adventures of young people learning to survive in wilderness, like *My Side of the Mountain* and its sequels, and *Julie of the Wolves* and its sequels. Her books are distinguished by authentic detail and a blend of scientific curiosity, wonder, and concern for the natural environment, all expressed in a manner critics have described as both unsentimental and lyrical. As Karen Nelson Hoyle observed in *Dictionary of Literary Biography,* George "elevates nature in all its intricacies and makes scientific research concerning ecological systems intriguing and exciting to the young reader."

Born in Washington, D.C., to a family of naturalists, George was bound to develop an early love of nature. Her father was an entomologist, her mother a lover of nature and of storytelling, and her twin brothers were also drawn to the outdoors and contributed articles to major magazines about falconry while still in high school. Her twin brothers were a hard act for George to follow, and growing up she was as at home on the softball field as on a mountain trail. George graduated from Pennsylvania State University in 1941, studying science and English. Thereafter she studied art at Louisiana State University and pursued graduate work at the University of Michigan.

George met her future husband, John L. George, during the Second World War; the couple married four months after their first meeting. Three children were soon born, and after the war John worked on his dissertation on birds and taught at various colleges, including Vassar. George's first six books were written in collaboration with her husband; each book characterizes a different animal. These early books "are best represented," according to Hoyle, by *Dipper of Copper Creek,* which "interweaves facts about the life cycle of the water ouzel with the tale of prospector Whispering Bill Smith and his grandson Doug's yearning for independence." Winner of the Aurianne Award in 1956, *Dipper* set the tone for much of George's literary output to follow: informed and sensitive blendings of fact and fiction.

One of her first major solo efforts was *My Side of the Mountain,* a book that had been growing in her mind for some time. Using the woods lore she learned as a child on camping trips with her father and brothers along the Potomac River, George finally found a character and plot device to present such information. A survival story about a teenage boy who runs away to the woods to live off the land for a year, *My Side of the Mountain* won a number of awards, including a Newbery Honor, and widespread praise. The first-person account describes thirteen-year-old Sam Gribley's self-sufficient wilderness life in detail, including the hollowed-out tree that becomes his home, his capture and training of the female peregrine falcon he names Frightful, and his various woodland recipes. Equipped with a pen knife, a ball of cord, an ax, and forty dollars, Sam whittles a fish hook out of a green twig, constructs a tent from hemlock boughs, and makes snowshoes from ash saplings and deer hide. His year in the woods is considered by some critics the ultimate survival tale for youngsters. Writing in *Horn Book,* Karen Jameyson commented on the book's premise: "When Sam explains, in his determined, quietly exuberant way that he has decided to leave his New York City home ... to go to live on the old Gribley land in the Catskill Mountains, the plan sounds a bit cockamamie. It also sounds mighty appealing." Zena Sutherland of the *Bulletin of the Center for Children's Books* called the novel "amazing and unusual," and noted that it was "[a]bsorbing reading."

So appealing was the premise that the novel was adapted for a movie in 1969 and has had two highly popular sequels, the 1990 *On the Far Side of the Mountain* and the 1999 *Frightful's Mountain.* In the second book in the series, Sam's peregrine falcon, Frightful, has been seized by a conservation officer as an endangered species, and Sam's sister Alice is missing. Reviewing an audio version of the book, Edith Ching noted in *School Library Journal* that George's "attention to detail continues to be important" in this novel, and concluded that the book "is a narrative for all ages." With the third volume, *Frightful's Mountain,* the point of view shifts from humans to wildlife. The book opens with Frightful,

essie goes one way around the ship. Snow Bear goes the other way. They meet on the far side.

Bessie and her baby polar bear friend frolic on an ice ship in George's picture book. (From Snow Bear, *illustrated by Wendell Minor.)*

Sam's peregrine, held by poachers, and the bird can think of only one thing: returning somehow to Sam. Sam's sister Alice is instrumental in freeing Frightful, but then the falcon must make it on its own back to Sam. "George builds the suspense in a third-person narration that most often takes the falcon's perspective," noted a reviewer for *Publishers Weekly.* The same reviewer observed that details such as peregrine migratory, mating, and nesting habits "are seamlessly woven into the plot," and felt that "nature lovers will not be disappointed." *Booklist*'s Linda Perkins wrote that this third installment "may not have the broad appeal of the earlier books, but it will attract and enchant animal aficionados." Praising the title in the *New York Times Book Review,* Mary Harris Russell commented that *Frightful's Mountain* "is a novel that will change the way you look at the world...." "You've probably not read anything quite like this," Russell concluded.

The popularity of *My Side of the Mountain* could not have come at a better time for George, who divorced in 1963 and set about earning a living as a single parent by her writing. She also pursued her love of nature, turning her home in Chappaqua, New York, into something of a zoo with hundreds of wild animals living in her house and backyard, including owls, robins, mink, seagulls, and even tarantulas. The success of *My Side of the*

Mountain helped, as did a job with *Reader's Digest* from 1969 to 1982. Several other juvenile novels followed, including *Gull Number 737, Hold Zero!,* and *Coyote in Manhattan,* as well as the popular nonfiction series, "Thirteen Moons," which features a different animal for each of the new moons of the year in a lunar calendar. Sutherland noted in a *Bulletin of the Center for Children's Books* review of *The Moon of the Fox Pups* that George "writes of the animal world with knowledge and enthusiasm, her descriptions of wild life untainted by melodrama or anthropomorphism." The thirteen books in the series were reissued in 1993 with new illustrations.

One summer in the late 1960s George and her younger son, Luke, made a journey to Alaska, which strongly shaped her novel, *Julie of the Wolves.* The two had gone to Barrow to learn about wolf behavior from a scientist doing a study there, but they also got some unplanned lessons in native Inuit culture. George met a young Inuit woman and her husband, a girl whose character shaped that of the heroine of *Julie of the Wolves* and from whom she learned more about Inuit life. From the scientists studying wolves, George learned that men were actually communicating with wolves and were able to learn how to use wolf language. One female wolf actually communicated back to the author. "When she answered back,"

George wrote on her Web site, "I knew that I wanted to write a book about a little girl, who is lost on the tundra and saves her life by communicating with wolves. So I did."

Julie of the Wolves tells the story of adventures of an Eskimo girl who becomes lost on the tundra while running away from an unhappy marriage. When her father disappears on a hunting expedition, Miyax, also known by the English name Julie, is adopted by relatives. At thirteen she marries so she can leave her foster home. Although her husband is slow-witted, the marriage is little more than a formality at first, and Miyax is content to live with his family. His forceful attempt to have sex with her, however, frightens her and she leaves him. Remembering her California pen pal's repeated invitations to visit, Miyax sets out across the tundra. When she loses her way in the barren land, she survives by learning how to communicate with a wolf pack and be accepted among them, befriended by the lead wolf in the pack, whom she names Amaroq. Her own knowledge of Eskimo ways is also crucial, although gradually she begins to understand that the old ways are dying.

Reviewers were enthusiastic about the novel. Hoyle felt that *Julie of the Wolves* "is George's most significant book," and that the "plot, character development, and setting are epic in dimension." Writing in *School Library Journal*, Alice Miller Bregman called the novel "compelling," and commented further that "George has captured the subtle nuances of Eskimo life, animal habits, the pain of growing up, and combines these elements into a thrilling adventure which is, at the same time, a poignant love story." Reviewing *Julie of the Wolves* in the *New York Times Book Review*, James Houston observed that the novel "is packed with expert wolf lore, its narrative beautifully conveying the vastness of tundra as well as many other aspects of the Arctic." Though Houston questioned the reality of such a connection between man and wolf, he concluded that readers "slowly come to think of these wolves as dear friends." Writing in *Horn Book*, Virginia Haviland called *Julie of the Wolves* a "book of timeless, perhaps even of classic dimensions." Awards committees nominated the book for many prizes, and the novel won the prestigious Newbery Medal, among other honors.

George revisited her characters in *Julie*, a 1994 sequel which begins only minutes after the ending of *Julie of the Wolves*, and in the 1997 *Julie's Wolf Pack*, told almost totally from the perspective of the wolves. In *Julie*, the young Eskimo girl returns to her father's village, Kangik, only to discover that her long estranged father, Kapugen, has married a white woman and has left the old ways behind. In fact, readers learn that he is the one who shot Amaroq from a plane at the end of the previous novel. She struggles to save her beloved wolves and also falls in love with a young Siberian man, Peter Sugluk. "This one will go like hotcakes, both to new readers and old fans of the prequel," commented Susan Dunn in a *Voice of Youth Advocates* review of *Julie*.

Dunn concluded that the book is "an excellent adventure story" and a novel that supplies a "delicious taste of a nontraditional lifestyle and personality." Writing in the *New York Times Book Review*, Hazel Rochman observed, "what's glorious is the lyrical nature writing.... George's sense of the place is so instinctive and so physically precise that the final Edenic vision of natural world order restored ... is like a ringing song of triumph."

With *Julie's Wolf Pack*, the focus shifts to the wolf pack, now led by Kapu, the alpha male. Constantly challenged by a loner wolf, Raw Bones, Kapu must prove himself to the pack. Rabies is another enemy to the pack in this installment. Though many reviewers felt the third novel lacked the dramatic tension of the first two, largely because Julie is peripheral to the plot, Carrie Eldridge, writing in *Kliatt*, thought George's "obvious knowledge of her subject matter is admirable and resonates throughout the story."

George has written about the Arctic in other novels, as well, most notably in *Water Sky* and *The Wounded Wolf*. She has also looked at nature in the continental United States with her ecological mysteries, including *Hook a Fish, Catch a Mountain* (republished as *The Case of the Missing Cutthroat*), *Who Really Killed Cock Robin?*, *The Fire Bug Connection*, and *Missing 'Gator of Gumbo Limbo*, and with adventures tales such as *Going to the Sun*, set in the Rocky Mountains, *River Rats, Inc.*, dealing with white water rafting, *The Wentletrap Trap*, set on Bimini, and *The Cry of the Crow*, set in the Florida Everglades. Another novel set in the Everglades is *The Talking Earth*. More environmental issues are dealt with in *There's an Owl in the Shower*, in which an out-of-work logger's son takes in a baby owl, only to discover that it is a species of the spotted owl that has cost his father his job.

George has also teamed up with illustrator Wendell Minor and others to create a nest full of picture books introducing the ways of nature to the very young reader. More northern adventures are served up in *Arctic Son*, a "picture-book ode to the Arctic," according to a reviewer for *Publishers Weekly*. A chronicle of the birth and early years of George's grandson, the book is a "warm, positive story of life in the Far North," wrote Mollie Bynum in *School Library Journal*. In *Morning, Noon, and Night*, another collaboration with Minor, George portrays the activities of a variety of animals from dawn on the East Coast to sundown on the West. The Arctic spring is captured in *Snow Bear*, which tells of an Inuit girl who goes out on a hunt and encounters a bear cub. Patricia Manning, reviewing *Snow Bear* in *School Library Journal*, commented, "The simple, pleasing text is accompanied by luminous watercolors that faithfully record this charming (if improbable) chance meeting." Teaming up with Thomas Locker, George has also produced *The First Thanksgiving* and *To Climb a Waterfall*, and has created a series of picture books as companion volumes to Disney's Animal Kingdom.

In addition to her fiction, series nonfiction, and picture books, George has also provided a host of nature lore in stand-alone nonfiction titles, including *Animals Who Have Won Our Hearts* and *The Tarantula in My Purse and 172 Other Wild Pets,* both of which recount tales of animals beloved to mankind in general or to the George family in particular. Reviewing *The Tarantula in My Purse, Booklist*'s Carolyn Phelan felt that these autobiographical stories of family animals are filled with "humor, insights, and writing ability" that make the tales "a treat to read aloud to a class or an individual."

In all of her work, according to critics, George has blended scientific accuracy with a writer's eye for telling detail, dramatic narrative, and dimensional characters. "I write for children," George noted on her Web site. "Children are still in love with the wonders of nature, and I am too. So I tell them stories about a boy and a falcon, a girl and an elegant wolf pack, about owls, weasels, foxes, prairie dogs, the alpine tundra, the tropical rain forest. And when the telling is done, I hope they will want to protect all the beautiful creatures and places."

Biographical and Critical Sources

BOOKS

Children's Literature Review, Volume 1, Gale (Detroit, MI), 1976.
Contemporary Literary Criticism, Volume 35, Gale (Detroit, MI), 1985.
Dictionary of Literary Biography, Volume 52: *American Writers for Children since 1960: Fiction,* Gale (Detroit, MI), 1986.
George, Jean Craighead, *Journey Inward,* Dutton (New York, NY), 1982.

PERIODICALS

Booklist, May 15, 1993, p. 1693; July, 1993, p. 1970; August, 1994, p. 2064; April 15, 1995, p. 1505; August, 1995, p. 1966; September, 1995, p. 77; November 15, 1996, Carolyn Phelan, review of *The Tarantula in My Purse and 172 Other Wild Pets,* p. 581; August, 1998, p. 2014; December 1, 1998, p. 670; August, 1999, p. 2063; September 1, 1999, Linda Perkins, review of *Frightful's Mountain,* p. 132.
Bulletin of the Center for Children's Books, June, 1960, Zena Sutherland, review of *My Side of the Mountain,* p. 161; July-August, 1968, Zena Sutherland, review of *The Moon of the Fox Pups,* p. 174; January, 1972, p. 74; April, 1995, pp. 275-275.
Horn Book, January-February, 1973, Virginia Haviland, review of *Julie of the Wolves,* pp. 54-55; July-August, 1989, Karen Jameyson, "A Second Look: *My Side of the Mountain,*" pp. 529-531; November-December, 1989, pp. 808-810; November-December, 1994, p. 730; January-February, 1998, p. 71.
Kliatt, September, 1995, p. 62; May, 1996, p. 8; July, 1996, p. 52; July, 1999, Carrie Eldridge, review of *Julie's Wolf Pack,* p. 16.
New York Times Book Review, January 21, 1973, James Houston, review of *Julie of the Wolves,* p. 8; May 10, 1987, Beverly Lyon Clark, review of *Water Sky,* p. 26; May 20, 1990, p. 42; November 13, 1994, Hazel Rochman, review of *Julie,* p. 27; November 16, 1997, p. 58; November 21, 1999, Mary Harris Russell, review of *Frightful's Mountain,* p. 28.
Publishers Weekly, September 20, 1993, p. 32; January 23, 1995, p. 70; April 28, 1997, p. 77; July 21, 1997, review of *Arctic Son,* p. 200; May 25, 1998, p. 92; May 31, 1999, p. 96; October 18, 1999, review of *Frightful's Mountain,* p. 83.
School Library Journal, January, 1973, Alice Miller Bregman, review of *Julie of the Wolves,* p. 75; February, 1993, p. 97; September, 1994, p. 176; June, 1995, p. 100; September, 1995, p. 163; May, 1996, Edith Ching, audio review of *On the Far Side of the Mountain,* p. 75; June, 1996, p. 122; November, 1997, Mollie Bynum, review of *Arctic Son,* pp. 81-82; March, 1999, p. 174; April, 1999, p. 94; September, 1999, Patricia Manning, review of *Snow Bear,* p. 182.
Voice of Youth Advocates, December, 1994, Susan Dunn, review of *Julie,* p. 272; August, 1996, p. 156; April, 1998, p. 42.

ON-LINE

The Official Jean Craighead George Web site, http://www.jeancraigheadgeorge.com/ (March 31, 2001).

—*Sketch by J. Sydney Jones*

*   *   *

GIBBONS, Alan 1953-

Personal

Born August 14, 1953, in Warrington, Cheshire, England; son of Albert (a laborer) and Phyllis (Harper) Gibbons; married wife, Pauline (a social worker), March, 1983; children: Joseph, Robbie, Rachel, Megan. *Education:* Warwick University, B.A. (with honors; French and European literature); Liverpool University, P.G.C.E. (primary education). *Politics:* Socialist. *Hobbies and other interests:* Music and sport.

Addresses

Agent—c/o Dolphin Publicity Director, Orion House, 5 Upper St. Martins La., London WC2H 9EA, England.

Career

Worked as a process worker in Middlewich, Cheshire, England, 1975-78, and Crewe, Cheshire, 1978-82; case worker for welfare agency, Liverpool, England, 1982-88; teacher in Liverpool, 1988—. *Member:* National Union of Teachers (president, Knowsley Division, 1996), National Association of Writers in Education.

Writings

FOR CHILDREN

Our Peculiar Neighbour, illustrated by Toni Goffe, Dent (London, England), 1990.

Alan Gibbons

Pig, illustrated by Diana Catchpole, Dent (London, England), 1990.

Whose Side Are You On?, Orion (London, England) 1991.

The Jaws of the Dragon, Dent (London, England), 1991, Lerner Publishing, 1994.

Dagger in the Sky, Dent (London, England), 1992.

S.O.S. Save Our Santa, illustrated by Caroline Church, Dent (London, England), 1992.

Chicken, Orion (London, England), 1994.

Grandad's Ears, Collins (London, England), 1994.

Hattie Hates Hats, illustrated by Bethan Matthews, Collins (London, England), 1994.

Not Yeti, illustrated by Anthony Lewis, Orion (London, England), 1994.

Ganging Up, Orion (London, England), 1995.

The Climbing Boys, Collins (London, England), 1995.

City of Fire, Collins (London, England), 1995.

Playing with Fire, Orion (London, England), 1996.

When My Ship Came In, illustrated by Joe Rice, Collins (London, England), 1996.

Street of Tall People, Orion (London, England), 1996.

A Fight to Belong, Save the Children, 1999.

Shadow of the Minotaur, Orion (London, England), 2000.

Vampyr Legion, Orion (London, England), 2000.

Warriors of the Raven, Orion (London, England), 2001.

NOVELS; "TOTAL FOOTBALL" SERIES

Some You Win, Orion (London, England), 1997.

Under Pressure, Orion (London, England), 1997.

Divided We Fall, Orion (London, England), 1998.

Injury Time, Orion (London, England), 1998.

Last Man Standing, Orion (London, England), 1998.

Power Play, Orion (London, England), 1998.

Twin Strikers, Orion (London, England), 1999.

Final Countdown, Orion (London, England), 1999.

Julie and Me and Michael Owen Makes Three, Orion (London, England), 2001.

Julie and Me: Treble Trouble, Orion (London, England), 2002.

Sidelights

"I write mythologies," British author Alan Gibbons explained, describing the writing career that has resulted in over twenty-five books during a ten-year period. With titles such as *Whose Side Are You On?, The Jaws of the Dragon,* and *Street of Tall People* to his credit, Gibbons has earned many young fans as well as the esteem of many critics. Praising his work in *Books for Keeps,* reviewer George Hunt noted, "Alan Gibbons' adventure stories deal with harsh realities in ways which are sensitive and honest." The critic "highly recommended" the book, adding that it is "not just [for] boys."

Gibbons was born in Cheshire, England, in 1953, and grew up in the small country village of Whitegate. "I came from a family of farm laborers," he explained to *SATA.* "For as long as I can remember I was listening to, reading about, re-telling, and illustrating all sorts of legends. Robin Hood, the Arthurian romance, the myths of ancient Rome and Greece, the tales of the Vikings: they were the stuff of my dreams." Gibbons elaborated, "A myth is a made up story, and as a writer of fiction, that's what I tell: made-up stories. But a myth is also a question of belief, so it has to be a made-up story that rings true. It communicates morality and values." Many of Gibbons's books, particularly his works for older readers, reflect the values he learned during his own childhood as a kid uprooted from a secure environment and forced to make it in a school where the rules were different and might made right, no matter what.

"In true stories, just as in myths, the way is rarely straight or easy," Gibbons continued. "When I was eight, my dad was involved in a bad accident. His leg was shattered and he had to take an indoor job." Mr. Gibbons's new job took the family to the town of Crewe, an industrial community, where Gibbons suddenly found himself "plunged into a very different kind of life from the small village where I grew up, having to fight bullying and learn to cope in a much tougher environment than I was used to." A good student and a quick study, Gibbons learned to navigate his new social landscape. As the years passed, he also developed a strong interest in athletics, and his heroes were men such as world heavyweight champion Muhammad Ali, soccer star Pelé, and George Best. "They weren't just great sportsmen," recalled Gibbons; "they were fighters. Against poverty, against racism."

Although he applied himself to his studies during grade school, Gibbons "found that the rigid grammar school system worked against creativity. I got to university, but had stopped writing my legends. As a result, I grew bored and lost interest in the academic world." After graduating with honors from Warwick University with degrees in French and European literature, he turned his back on intellectual pursuits and took a series of factory jobs, even working as an advice worker for five years. Married in 1983, Gibbon and his wife went on to have four children. In his thirties he was inspired to enroll at Liverpool University, where he earned the teaching qualification necessary to become a primary school teacher.

As a teacher, Gibbons discovered the works of children's literature. "I discovered writers such as Robert Cormier, Robert Swindells, Robert Westall, Phillip Pullman, and Geoffrey Trease," he recalled. "Inspired by their work, in 1990 I started writing again: picture

Tra is ostracized in his Vietnamese village and, when his family leaves for Hong Kong, he endures hardships in the refugee camp there. (Cover illustration by Janet Hamlin.)

books, young readers, novels. I was staggered by the range and quality of children's literature and wanted to be part of that world." One of the earliest books penned by Gibbons was the picture book *Pig*. In this 1990 work, a boy and his little sister on their daily trek home from school are suddenly swept up in what *Growing Point* reviewer Margery Fisher called "an agreeable rush and scurry" as a pig attempting to save its bacon leads a long line of pursuers through the English countryside. With the children's help, the pig on the lam goes into hiding and eventually finds its way to the care of the City Farm, where it becomes a community pet. Another book for the younger set, an imaginative romp titled *Not Yeti*, was described by *Books for Keeps* contributor George Hunt as "highly eventful and entertaining."

Gibbons's entire life changed after he made a commitment to writing. "After a day of teaching, I would plunge into my study, writing at least two hours a night, five days a week, pouring out my own mythologies," he recalled. Recollections from his childhood were reworked into the novels *Chicken* and *Ganging Up,* each of which deal with what Gibbons would call mythic themes about values and the choice between right and wrong. In *Chicken,* which was published in 1994, Davey and his family move to Liverpool, where Davey's older brother quickly makes friends with a gang of toughs, glad to fit in. The less-outgoing Davey soon draws the attention of his new school's bully population in what *Magpies* reviewer Melanie Guile called "a well-crafted short novel with unusually witty dialogue, convincing cameo characters, [and] a tough climax." London *Observer* contributor Naomi Lewis dubbed Davey's story of growing up "frequently funny ... when not dire." While Davey goes it alone in *Chicken,* in Gibbons's 1995 novel *Ganging Up* best friends and soccer fans Gerry and John find their friendship threatened when John joins a local gang. Gerry quickly finds that John's choice has repercussions on his own life in an "action-packed book" that a *Junior Bookshelf* contributor believed would appeal to "that most elusive readership, boys whose interests seem entirely physical and outdoor."

History weaves its way into several of Gibbons's mythologies, among them *Whose Side Are You On?* and *Dagger in the Sky*. In *Whose Side Are You On?,* published in 1991, readers meet ten-year-old Mattie Jones, whose friendship with a Pakistani boy named Pravin prompts racist remarks from a couple of local school bullies. Unfortunately, Mattie opts to run rather than stay and defend his friendship. Cowardice leads him into an old abandoned house ... and back into the eighteenth century, where he helps a group of slaves rebel against their masters and thus finds the courage to take him back to the present. *Books for Keeps* contributor Chris Lutrario praised *Whose Side Are You On?* as "interesting and exciting," while *School Librarian* critic Marie Flay called the work an "enjoyable and at times compelling novel."

In addition to dealing with a period of English history—the rise of the Blackshirts under British fascist agitator Oswald Mosley during the 1930s—*Street of Tall People* reflects Gibbons's longtime interest in sports. In the novel, a young Londoner named Jimmy Priest runs up against Benny Silver in a boxing match and is impressed by the Jewish boy's determination. As the two become friends, Jimmy becomes aware of the rising tide of anti-Semitism that is growing among many in his poor East End neighborhood. Citing *Street of Tall People* as an "impressive" book about friendship, *Magpies* contributor Kevin Steinberger praised Gibbons for the "depth of research that has enabled him to charge the story with stunning verisimilitude and characterization and evocation of place and mood." Team sports also figure in Gibbons's eight-part "Total Football" series, as members of the Rough Diamonds soccer team—soccer is called "football" in Great Britain, where this story takes place—attempt to redeem their loser image with an attitude readjustment. Within the series, Gibbons focuses on the personal struggles of each of the team members in turn, as they deal with poverty, family concerns, and the temptation to cross the line into petty crime.

After sifting through his own experiences for subject matter, eventually, "as I was bound to do," Gibbons admitted, "I returned to the legends which inspired me all those years ago, the Greek and Norse myths, and tales of Gothic horror." From these would come the novel *Shadow of the Minotaur* and *Vampyr Legion,* both published in 2000. They would eventually be followed by *Warriors of the Raven,* which also features a combination of fantasy, action, and legend. "I am currently embarking on the greatest mythology of them all," Gibbons explained to *SATA* on the eve of his twenty-eighth book for children. "I am writing a love story!"

Biographical and Critical Sources

PERIODICALS

Books for Keeps, September, 1992, Chris Lutrario, review of *Whose Side Are You On?,* p. 25; September, 1995, George Hunt, review of *Not Yeti,* p. 11; September, 1996, George Hunt, review of *Street of Tall People* and *Ganging Up,* p. 12.

Growing Point, September, 1991, Margery Fisher, review of *Pig,* p. 5574; January, 1992, Margery Fisher, review of *The Jaws of the Dragon,* p. 5630.

Junior Bookshelf, June, 1992, review of *The Jaws of the Dragon,* pp. 120-121; October, 1995, review of *Ganging Up,* pp. 183-184.

Magpies, November, 1994, Melanie Guile, review of *Chicken,* p. 30; March, 1996, Kevin Steinberger, review of *Street of Tall People,* pp. 35-36.

Observer (London), August 22, 1993, Naomi Lewis, review of *Chicken,* p. 48; July 21, 1996, Jennifer Selway, review of *Street of Tall People,* p. 17.

School Librarian, August, 1991, Marie Flay, review of *Whose Side Are You On?,* pp. 113-114; May, 1992, Robert Protherough, review of *The Jaws of the Dragon,* p. 71; summer, 1998, Michael Kirby, review

of *Some You Win* and *Under Pressure,* p. 78; winter, 1999, Chris Brown, review of *Final Countdown,* p. 191.

*   *   *

GOSS, Gary 1947-

Personal

Born March 23, 1947, in Newark, NJ; son of Meyer and Pearl Goss; married, wife's name Minda (a teacher), February 14, 1973; children: Sasha, Alec. *Education:* Rutgers University, B.A., 1968; New York University, M.A., 1969. *Politics:* Democrat. *Religion:* Jewish.

Addresses

Home—67 Franklin St., Northampton, MA 01060. *Agent*—Jane Dystal, 1 Union Sq. W., New York, NY 10003. *E-mail*—funny@rcn.com.

Career

Science teacher and athletic coach at a school in Highgate, VT, 1971-73; manager of a halfway-house for retarded men, 1974-75; Soup Kitchen (restaurant), Northampton, MA, owner and chef, 1976-86; history teacher in Ware, MA, 1988-90; Funny Face, Northampton, poster restorer and dealer, 1990-2000; cookbook author, 1998—. *Military service:* U.S. Army, 1968-69.

Awards, Honors

Smithsonian notable book citation, Oppenheim Award, and Bookbuilders Cream of the Crop citation, all for *Blue Moon Soup.*

Gary Goss

Writings

Blue Moon Soup: A Family Cookbook, illustrated by Jane Dyer, Little, Brown (New York, NY), 1999.

Work in Progress

Pizza My Heart, completion expected in 2002.

Sidelights

Gary Goss told *SATA:* "I love cooking and creating. I owned the first soup restaurant in the country, the Soup Kitchen in Northampton, Massachusetts. I also love working with kids. I travel around the country, giving demonstrations and cooking soup at schools and on television. My book, *Blue Moon Soup,* and the next book, *Pizza My Heart,* emphasize cooking as a family event with kids fully participating. Presently, along with an independent production company, I am developing a kids' cooking program with kids as the chefs. Also in the works is a cooking school for kids."

Biographical and Critical Sources

PERIODICALS

Booklist, November 1, 1999, Carolyn Phelan, review of *Blue Moon Soup,* p. 519.
School Library Journal, September, 1999, Carolyn Jenks, review of *Blue Moon Soup,* p. 233.*

* * *

GUIBERSON, Brenda Z. 1946-

Personal

Surname is pronounced "*guy*-berson"; born December 10, 1946, in Denver, CO; daughter of Carl Nicholas (a civil engineer) and Ruth Ellen (a homemaker; maiden name, Schenkeir) Zangar; married William R. Guiberson (a business agent), August, 1973; children: Jason. *Education:* University of Washington, B.A. (art and English).

Addresses

Home—20130 8th Ave. N.W., Shoreline, WA 98177.

Career

Writer. Worked as a copywriter, letter carrier, stained-glass worker and woodworker, manager, and counselor.

Awards, Honors

Turtle People was named a Junior Literary Guild selection; Picture Book Award, *Parent's Choice,* Teacher's Choice, International Reading Association and Children's Book Council (IRA and CBC), Notable Trade Book in Language Arts, National Council of Teachers of English, IRA and CBC Joint Committee Favorite Paperback, and El Paso Prickly Pear Award, all for *Cactus Hotel;* Best Book of the Year citation, *School Library Journal,* Pick of the List selection, American Booksellers Association (ABA), California Children's Media Award, and Outstanding Science Trade Book, National Science Teachers Association and Children's Book Council (NSTA and CBC), all for *Spoonbill Swamp;* Outstanding Science Trade Book, NSTA and CBC, for *Lobster Boat;* Outstanding Science Trade Book, NSTA and CBC, and Orbis Pictus nomination, both for *Spotted Owl: Bird of the Ancient Forest;* Rhode Island Children's Book Award nomination, for *Lighthouses: Watchers at Sea;* Best Book of the Year citation, *School Library Journal,* Pick of the List, ABA, Society of School Librarians International Science Honor for K-6, and Chicago Public Library Best of the Best selection, all for *Into the Sea;* Kid's Pick, ABA, and Rhode Island Children's Book Award nomination, both for *Mummy Mysteries: Tales from North America.*

Writings

Turtle People, Atheneum (New York, NY), 1990.
Cactus Hotel, illustrated by Megan Lloyd, Holt (New York, NY), 1991.
Instant Soup, Atheneum (New York, NY), 1991.
Spoonbill Swamp, illustrated by Megan Lloyd, Holt (New York, NY), 1992.
Lobster Boat, illustrated by Megan Lloyd, Holt (New York, NY), 1993.
(And illustrator) *Salmon Story,* Holt (New York, NY), 1993.
(And illustrator) *Spotted Owl: Bird of the Ancient Forest,* Holt (New York, NY), 1994.
Winter Wheat, illustrated by Megan Lloyd, Holt (New York, NY), 1995.
(And illustrator) *Lighthouses: Watchers at Sea,* Holt (New York, NY), 1995.
Into the Sea, illustrated by Alix Berenzy, Holt (New York, NY), 1996.
Teddy Roosevelt's Elk, illustrated by Patrick O'Brien, Holt (New York, NY), 1997.
(And illustrator) *Mummy Mysteries: Tales from North America,* Holt (New York, NY), 1998.
Exotic Species: Invaders in Paradise, Twenty-First Century Books (Brookfield, CT), 1999.
(And illustrator) *Tales of the Haunted Deep,* Holt (New York, NY), 2000.
The Emperor Lays an Egg, illustrated by Joan Paley, Holt (New York, NY), 2001.
Ocean Life, Scholastic (New York, NY), 2001.

Sidelights

Brenda Z. Guiberson writes informative picture books for young readers that present interesting ecological phenomena. Many of them are set in the Pacific Northwest, where the author lives, or had their origins in family vacations elsewhere. "Becoming a writer was not on my mind as a child," Guiberson told *SATA.* "I had five sisters and two brothers and, for a while, three foster children in the family. We never sat around much and

Brenda Z. Guiberson

were usually out along the Columbia River, which ran past our backyard in Richland, Washington.

"In high school and college I took many science classes and was a little surprised to finally end up with degrees in fine art and English. Along the way, I tried out several things: copywriter, letter carrier, stained-glass worker and woodworker, manager, and counselor.

"The idea of creating children's books started with my son, Jason. He used to bring home dozens of books from the library and ask to hear them over and over again. We were having a good time and it sank in. After years in this training ground, I finally got up the courage to write. Now I don't want to stop."

That first book the author published was *Turtle People,* in 1990. Guiberson explained: "Experiences of my childhood came up in the novel *Turtle People.* I spent many hours swimming in the Columbia River. Occasionally, we found Indian artifacts. I only found chips and arrowheads, but my sister Cathy found a real turtle bowl, on an island in the Snake River. I was the one who took it around to museums and collectors for information."

In the story, a Washington state sixth-grader named Richie finds a similar bowl while playing on an island

near his home one day. He used to hunt for Turtle People artifacts with his father, but his father has moved out. Richie is fascinated by the vanished Turtle People, and wonders why they became so enamored of the slow-moving creature. On his own, he thinks about what lessons he might learn from the turtle. Eventually he and his pal track down an expert on their own. Richie's father returns home, but the boy tells him that he is "the real turtle .... You've come too late, too slow. I took care of everything myself." *Horn Book* reviewer Carolyn K. Jenks called Richie "a likable, sensitive boy ... enough in touch with reality to describe his world with liveliness and humor."

Guiberson has worked with illustrator Megan Lloyd on a number of books, beginning with *Cactus Hotel* in 1991. As the author told *SATA,* "*Cactus Hotel* was written after a trip to the Sonoran Desert in Arizona." It recounts the life story of one of that desert's legendary saguaro cacti, which can live for 200 years. Some reach fifty feet in height and might weigh eight tons, but they also provide an important link in the desert ecosystem, as a "hotel" for insects and various small creatures of the region. "Guiberson's simple, understandable text gives an enjoyable lesson in desert ecology," remarked Leone McDermott in *Booklist.*

Guiberson also collaborated with Lloyd on *Spoonbill Swamp,* a story set in the swamp that is home to the water fowl of the title and her new offspring. The swamp also shelters another new mother, an alligator, which preys on the spoonbill. The pages recount the activities of both families over the course of one day as they search for food and protect their charges—a day in which the spoonbill narrowly escapes from the alligator. "Readers will feel an uncommon pull between the innocence of both mothers," noted a *Publishers Weekly* reviewer. As Guiberson told *SATA,* "*Spoonbill Swamp* began after trips out into the waterways of Louisiana and Florida. I thought about those places quite a bit and wanted to know about the action and drama that went on in all those moments that I could not be there. I wanted to know why cacti have holes and what happens when all the sleeping creatures wake up hungry."

In their 1993 book *Lobster Boat,* Guiberson and Lloyd reveal a day in the life of a Maine lobster boat and its personnel. Tommy accompanies his uncle one foggy morning on the *Nellie Jean;* they check traps and bring in the haul, making it to shore before a storm hits. When they take their lobsters to market, they learn that the catch is up and price is down that particular day. The long hours end only with a final task: cleaning the boat. The work won praise from reviewers for providing an informative look at the arduous life of commercial fishermen. Emily Melton, writing in *Booklist,* commended the work for Guiberson's ability to combine "evocative descriptions of the sights and sounds of the sea" into "an appealingly told fictional account."

Guiberson returned to her home territory with *Salmon Story,* which she illustrated herself. She concentrates on the Pacific salmon species, chronicling the amazing life cycle of this fish. It can travel thousands of miles to the ocean, but knows how to get back to the stream in which it was born. Once plentiful in the inland and coastal waters of the Northwest, the salmon was revered by the Native American population of the area, whose sustenance depended on it. The species is now in a precarious state due to generations of human interference. Overfishing, the construction of hydroelectric power dams, and the polluting effects of industrialization in the region have decimated its numbers over the years. She also writes of the salmon's exceptionally determined nature: it can perform great leaps to get somewhere, and salmon are known to never turn back along their spawning journey—if they encounter the wall of a dam, for instance, they will try to get through it until they die. Later chapters discuss how environmental activists and scientists are working to help restore the natural habitat of the fish. "This makes ecology urgent and compelling," noted Hazel Rochman in *Booklist,* while Susan Oliver, writing for *School Library Journal,* found that Guiberson provided "a lucid explanation of how environmental abuses affect the balance of nature."

In this work, Guiberson looks at the secrets that are revealed when scientists examine the preserved remains of people and animals. (Cover photo by Guiberson.)

Such praise was echoed in reviews for another of Guiberson's tales from the Pacific Northwest ecosystem: *Spotted Owl: Bird of the Ancient Forest.* The 1994 work, illustrated by the author, tells readers about the old-growth forests in the area, once the quiet home to the majestic spotted owl. That environment was impacted by logging, but Guiberson also discusses the timber industry in the region and the economic hardship caused when the industry fell into decline. Reviewers praised what was called "an appealingly designed volume" by *Booklist*'s Carolyn Phelan, who felt the photographs added greatly to the story. Guiberson also created the images for her 1995 book *Lighthouses: Watchers at Sea.* Its pages reveal the history of such structures dating back to ancient times. As Guiberson notes, lighthouses were built to withstand the fiercest of elements, and she provided her own technical illustrations to show how lighthouses were constructed and the means by which their vital lights were kept burning for years. She also discusses the special breed of people who once chose lighthouse-keeping as an occupation, a livelihood extinguished when the task became an automated one. Lastly, the book touches upon some of the ghost stories associated with various lighthouses. Deborah Stevenson, writing for *Bulletin of the Center for Children's Books,* claimed the book provides "a neat, understandable, and sometimes haunting treatment" of its subject.

Guiberson returned to the turtle once again with *Into the Sea,* illustrated by Alix Berenzy. Words and images tell the story of the massive female sea turtle who takes twenty years to mature. It must make an arduous journey in order to lay its eggs on land, and, when the new turtles hatch themselves, they must hurry to the sea on new legs before land predators find them. "Well-chosen details convey the vulnerability of the young animal," remarked *Horn Book* reviewer Margaret A. Bush, while *Booklist*'s Kay Weisman commended the "vivid prose" that recounts "ample real-life drama."

In her 1997 book *Teddy Roosevelt's Elk,* Guiberson sought to explain how this particular species of elk received its unusual name in homage to the most famous conservationist and president in American history. The book reveals that Roosevelt, as a young man, traveled through the Dakota Territory twice and was devastated on his second round when he witnessed the destruction wrought by humans because of mining and logging. When he was president, Roosevelt created the legislation that survives as America's national parks. Guiberson's text then heads west to Washington state, where a species of elk named in the president's honor resides in the Olympic National Park. The book provides interesting facts about these magnificent creatures, chronicling a year in the life of a young elk calf. Guiberson makes it plain that, though they live in a protected environment, the elks' survival is not an assured one. *Bulletin of the Center for Children's Books* critic Elizabeth Bush praised the "intimate yet unsentimentalized narrative that acknowledges that challenges for supremacy ... or even death by starvation" lie ahead for the young elk.

Guiberson provided her own illustrations for *Mummy Mysteries: Tales from North America*. The collected photographs and images reveal that many different kinds of preserved remains have been found all over the continent. Unlike their ancient Egyptian counterparts, these mummies were not always intentionally preserved. Guiberson notes that modern scientists have learned much from them nevertheless. A blue bison carcass found in Alaska, dating back some 36,000 years, bore wound marks from a lion, for example. Scientists can only speculate about why the lions that once roamed this region disappeared. The remains of nineteenth-century explorers, icebound in the Hudson Bay area, reveal that lead poisoning may have spelled their doom. "For readers who like mysteries that unravel slowly, this book will be a joy," remarked Cathryn A. Camper in a *School Library Journal* review.

In her 1999 book, *Exotic Species: Invaders in Paradise*, Guiberson presents another unusual look at nature and its continual surprises. Here, the topic is disruptions in nature when foreign species arrive: the introduction of zebra mussels into the Great Lakes, for instance, or what happened as starlings, a European import, disrupted the ornithological hierarchy in the New World. The stories recount how such alien invaders affect the food chain and general ecosystem, and discuss measures that are sometimes taken to combat them. Guiberson also shows how nature can do the work of keeping an ecosystem in balance if not overwhelmed. John Peters, writing for *Booklist*, found that Guiberson's book "examines a controversial subject from several angles and presents convincing arguments for its importance." *School Library Journal* reviewer Arwen Marshall found *Exotic Species* "well balanced," and singled out the author for being "careful to look at both the positive and negative aspects of these invasions."

"I like to write both fiction and nonfiction," Guiberson told *SATA*. "I like to write about subjects that are interesting and exciting to me. Writers can make anything happen and write about places that they would like to go.

"It takes a lot of research to write about what might happen at some random moment in time. A writer can't say that a kangaroo rat stops for a drink of water when research reveals that this creature never drinks. And if an alligator is cold-blooded, then how does it behave? It takes a lot of observation and digging into books, field reports, and museums to find out. This is something I really enjoy. In writing *Turtle People*, I ended up reading the entire journals of Lewis and Clark. For *Cactus Hotel*, I gleaned information from the desert, museums, and scientists. For *Mummy Mysteries*, I visited ancient ruins and searched university archives and special collections. For other books, I have swam near dolphins and sea turtles, climbed lighthouses, hiked through forests, and have met so many wonderful people willing to help me with the research process.

"For someone who has always been interested in science and the visual arts, writing or illustrating a book

Guiberson explains the threat to native species when a new species suddenly invades a locale in this book. (Cover photo by Stephen Dalton.)

combines many things that I like to do. It's hard work but fun and surprises pop up all along the way."

Biographical and Critical Sources

PERIODICALS

Booklist, June 15, 1991, Leone McDermott, review of *Cactus Hotel,* p. 1969; April 15, 1993, Emily Melton, review of *Lobster Boat,* p. 1511; January 1, 1994, Hazel Rochman, review of *Salmon Story,* p. 819; January 1, 1995, Carolyn Phelan, review of *Spotted Owl: Bird of the Ancient Forest,* pp. 817-818; November 1, 1995, Hazel Rochman, review of *Lighthouses: Watchers at Sea,* p. 466; November 15, 1995, Julie Corsaro, review of *Winter Wheat,* p. 562; September 15, 1996, Kay Weisman, review of *Into the Sea,* p. 243; September 15, 1997, John Peters, review of *Teddy Roosevelt's Elk,* p. 237; July, 1999, John Peters, review of *Exotic Species: Invaders in Paradise,* p. 1940.

Bulletin of the Center for Children's Books, January, 1994, Carol Fox, review of *Salmon Story,* p. 155; December, 1995, Deborah Stevenson, review of *Lighthouses,* pp. 127-128; October, 1997, Elizabeth Bush, review of *Teddy Roosevelt's Elk,* p. 52; February, 1999, Elizabeth Bush, review of *Mummy Mysteries: Tales from North America,* pp. 203-204.

Horn Book, January, 1991, Carolyn K. Jenks, review of *Turtle People,* p. 67; November, 1996, Margaret A. Bush, review of *Into the Sea,* p. 759.

Kirkus Reviews, August 15, 1991, review of *Instant Soup,* p. 1089; February 15, 1992, review of *Spoonbill Swamp,* p. 254; April 1, 1993, review of *Lobster Boat,* p. 455.

Los Angeles Times Book Review, August 25, 1991, Kathleen Krull, "'Green' Books," p. 9.

Publishers Weekly, January 13, 1992, review of *Spoonbill Swamp,* p. 56.

School Library Journal, July, 1991, Diane Nunn, review of *Cactus Hotel,* p. 68; July, 1993, Carolyn Jenks, review of *Lobster Boat,* p. 60; April, 1994, Susan Oliver, review of *Salmon Story,* pp. 119-120; January, 1995, Kathy Piehl, review of *Spotted Owl,* p. 118; May, 1997, review of *Into the Sea* and *Spoonbill Swamp,* p. 57; December, 1998, Cathryn H. Camper, review of *Mummy Mysteries,* p. 136; September, 1999, Arwen Marshall, review of *Exotic Species,* p. 234; November, 2000, Elaine Baran Black, review of *Tales of the Haunted Deep,* p. 142.

H–I

HARRAR, George E. 1949-

Personal

Born July 25, 1949, in Abington, PA; son of Frank S. and Helen (Stitzinger) Harrar; married Linda D. Davis, November 5, 1974. *Education:* New York University, B.A. (cum laude), 1971. *Hobbies and other interests:* Running, basketball, juggling, ancient history.

Addresses

Home and office—10 Oxbow Rd., Wayland, MA 01778. *Agent*—Zachary Shuster Agency, Boston, MA.

Career

Middlesex News, Framingham, MA, editor, 1976-79; freelance editor, and writer, 1980-83, Wayland, MA, 1989—; *Computerworld Newspaper,* Framingham, features editor, 1983-89.

Awards, Honors

First prize, Wellspring Short Story contest, 1996; *Story Magazine*'s Carson McCullers Prize for Short Story, 1998; Best American Short Stories, 1999.

Writings

FOR CHILDREN

Signs of the Apes, Songs of the Whales: Adventures in Human-Animal Communication (part of "Novabook" series), Simon and Schuster (New York, NY), 1989.
Radical Robots: Can You Be Replaced? (part of "Novabook" series), Simon and Schuster (New York, NY), 1990.
Parents Wanted, Milkweed Editions (Minneapolis, MN), 2001.

FOR ADULTS

(With Glenn Rifkin) *The Ultimate Entrepreneur: The Story of Ken Olsen and Digital Equipment Corporation,* Contemporary Books, 1988.
First Tiger (novel), Permanent Press (Sag Harbor, NY), 1999.

Contributor of fiction to reviews, including *Story Magazine, New Press Literary Quarterly, Quarter After Eight, Dickinson Review,* and *Side Show Anthology.*

Sidelights

Editor and writer George E. Harrar has had a long and varied writing career. Over a twenty-year period he has written numerous articles, two juvenile books, a biography, and a novel. While working as the features editor for *Computerworld Newspaper* in the mid-1980s, Harrar and coeditor Glenn Rifkin researched and wrote *The Ultimate Entrepreneur: The Story of Ken Olsen and Digital Equipment Corporation,* an unauthorized biography of engineer Ken Olsen, one of the founders and head of the computer company DEC.

Harrar's works for children include *Radical Robots: Can You Be Replaced?* and *Signs of the Apes, Songs of the Whales: Adventures in Human-Animal Communication.* Both books are part of the "Novabook" series (based on the television series *Nova*) and are geared to middle-grade readers, featuring many photographs, illustrations, and sidebars. The series focuses on making science entertaining, as well as informative, and is used both in and out of the classroom.

In *Radical Robots,* Harrar describes the abilities of robots and highlights their development. He also discusses the future of robotics and artificial intelligence. Critics praised the work for its easy accessibility. Writing for *Appraisal,* a reviewer judged the book to be "fun and non-threatening to students," while a *Kliatt* critic added, "the text is not lengthy and it is not patronizingly simple." According to John Peters of *School Library Journal,* Harrar "writes in a vivid, engaging way, that compensates for the speed with which he covers the subject."

Signs of the Apes, Songs of the Whales provides glimpses of different animals involved in intelligence studies. Harrar explains research on animal species in general, such as dolphins, and individual animals, like Koko the gorilla and Washoe the chimpanzee. A commentator for *Kliatt* deemed the text "simple but not simplistic." In his review for the *Bulletin of the Center for Children's Books,* Robert Strang complained that the presentation of material is "disorganized" but concluded that the subject's "inherent fascination" would compensate for any "rough spots."

In 1999 Permanent Press published Harrar's first novel for adults, *First Tiger.* This novel revolves around Jake, the sixteen-year-old son of a mentally disturbed Vietnam veteran, who runs away from home, and Jake's memories of his mother's murder ten years earlier. After living for a time on the streets in New York City, Jake returns to his home in New Hope, Pennsylvania, where further challenges await him. *First Tiger* caught reviewers' attention. In the view of Amanda Fung of *Library Journal,* readers will "be drawn to Jake" despite his juvenile delinquency and will find many of the other characters "compelling," if cynical. Although he called the novel "realistic and gritty," a *Publishers Weekly* critic noted that Harrar both describes Jake's "limited options, but also his unquenched hopes for a better life."

Biographical and Critical Sources

PERIODICALS

Appraisal, autumn, 1991, review of *Radical Robots,* p. 94.
Bulletin of the Center for Children's Books, December, 1989, Robert Strang, review of *Signs of the Apes, Songs of the Whales,* p. 85.
Kliatt, January, 1990, review of *Signs of the Apes, Songs of the Whales,* p. 42; January, 1991, review of *Radical Robots,* p. 47.
Library Journal, September 15, 1999, Amanda Fung, review of *First Tiger,* p. 112.
Publishers Weekly, October 4, 1999, review of *First Tiger,* p. 63.
School Library Journal, February, 1991, John Peters, review of *Radical Robots,* p. 88.

*   *   *

HAWKE, Rosanne (Joy) 1953-

Personal

Born October 6, 1953, in Penola, South Australia; daughter of Lenard (a farmer and grazier) and Doreen Joyce (a bank teller and secretary; maiden name, Bedford) Trevilyan; married Gary Wayne Hawke (a master plumber), June 8, 1974; children: Lenore Penner, Michael, Emma. *Education:* Salisbury College of Advanced Education, teaching diploma, 1975; Moody Bible College, diploma, 1985; University of South Australia, English as a second language graduate diplo-

ma, 1988, information studies graduate diploma, 2000. *Hobbies and other interests:* Cornish studies, music, history, walking, reading ("besides extra writing, of course").

Addresses

Home—1 Wall Court, Salisbury, South Australia 5108, Australia. *Agent*—Jenny Darling & Associates, P.O. Box 413, Toorak, Victoria 3142, Australia (literary); C. Carroll, 2 Second Ave., Glenelg East, South Australia 5045, Australia (booking). *E-mail*—hawknest@picknowl.com.au.

Career

Junior primary teacher in South Australia, Pakistan, and United Arab Emirates, beginning 1975; English as a second language teacher trainer, Pakistan, 1986-91, acting principal, 1988, 1990; special needs teacher in South Australia, 1993-96; creative writing teacher in South Australia, 1993—; writer, 1994—. Also worked as a music teacher, house parent, English resource position, all through The Evangelical Alliance Mission (TEAM) in Pakistan and the United Arab Emirates. Currently holds a residency at Tyndale Christian School. Has also volunteered as a newsletter editor and writing competition judge. *Member:* Australian Society of Authors, Children's Book Council of South Australia, Ekidnas: South Australian Published Children's Authors, Writers' Centre of South Australia, South Australia Genealogical Society, Cornish Society of South Australia, Storytelling Guild.

Awards, Honors

Literature grants, ArtSA, 1996, for *A Kiss in Every Wave,* and 2000, for *Zenna Dare;* Children Rate Outstanding Writers Awards shortlist, and Notable Book, Children's Book Council of South Australia, both 1996, both for *Re-entry;* Christian School Book Awards shortlist, 1999, for *Jihad;* Varuna Writers' Retreat Fellowship, 2000.

Writings

Re-entry, Albatross Books, 1995.
Jihad, Albatross Books, 1996.
The Keeper, Lothian, 2000.

Hawke has also published fiction in periodicals, including *Pursuit* and *One-Up.*

Work in Progress

A Kiss in Every Wave, The Listener, and *Zenna Dare,* all works of young adult fiction; *Sailmaker,* a sequel to *The Keeper; Yar Dil,* a picture book about a snow leopard.

Sidelights

Rosanne Hawke told *SATA:* "I was always a storyteller, even if it was only in my own head. I'd tell stories or make up plays when I was a kid, to my friends, and to pretend people (also in my head) as I'd walk around my father's property in Queensland. When I had children of my own I'd tell them stories to get them to bed and to keep them quiet in the car as we traveled the hours through the Himalayan foothills to take them back to boarding school.

"Once, when my fourteen-year-old was home on holidays, she asked for our story game where she would think up the characters, plot, and setting and I would tell the story. She wanted sixteen-year-old friends, kidnaping, freedom fighters, the Khyber Pass, and Afghanistan! One of our acquaintances had just been kidnaped and with his possible fate in mind I told the story. My daughter liked it so much she wanted it written up for her birthday. After that she wanted it typed so she could have a book of her own. And you've guessed it—after this she wanted it sent to a publisher. That was *Jihad* and how I seriously started writing for a career.

"Why I wrote *The Keeper?* When I was relief teaching one day I met a young boy with undiagnosed ADD [Attention Deficit Disorder] who stood in the classroom and swore at me in frustration when he didn't want to do what I'd asked. He couldn't stop those words tumbling out of his mouth even though he knew it would change his whole day. Suffice to say he made an unfading impression on me; he was six and his dad was in gaol. That gave me the idea for a story. How far would a desperate kid go to get a dad? And I thought of advertising in the paper for one. I wanted *The Keeper* to be a great read and also bring some understanding for kids with difficulties.

"I have always loved books and would get out of bed at night long before school age to 'read' books by the thread of light under the door. I can remember rabbit stories, Winnie the Pooh, fairy stories of every country. I devoured Enid Blyton for the love of mystery and adventure. A little older, I can remember reading *The Prince and the Pauper* and *The Swiss Family Robinson* under bushes when I was supposed to be watering the garden. In teen years it was Mary Stewart, Daphne du Maurier, and Thomas Hardy. Now I admire any writer who makes me see the magic of words and shows me a new way of expressing an idea or feeling.

"My purpose in writing is always to entertain, to take people away; to enter someone else's world for a while. While doing that I sometimes want to show what it may be like in that world and so foster understanding and acceptance for someone who may be different or have some difficulty. Much of my work has a multicultural theme as in *Re-entry* and *Jihad.* Even *Zenna Dare* (a work in progress) deals with ethnic identity. My books aren't only for readers—I find that the characters in my books teach me about life as they are materialising on the page. After finishing *Re-entry* I found the culture shock that I found re-entering Australia after ten years working in South Asia diminished in its sharpness. As I am writing *Zenna Dare,* Caleb is showing me the extent

Rosanne Hawke

of suffering his indigenous people have endured, just as he shows Jenefer.

"When I finished *The Listener* (another work in progress) much of the fear I had when a child became mentally ill lessened. I couldn't finish *A Kiss in Every Wave* (a work in progress) until after my mother died, but the writing of it became cathartic as the arts so often are. If a story can do that for me as I write, I hope it can do the same for someone who reads it. I appreciate Proust's sentiment when he said that he wished his writing could do for people what his father's doctoring had done. I like to show young people that life can be a promising journey—that as Jaime, Jasper, Joel, Jessie, and Jenefer from my books have found, it's not *what* happens to us that matters so much as *how* we handle it.

"Sometimes I get excited about what I see while writing and would like others to see it too. But I try to write in such a way that if young people are interested only in a story that's what they'll get, yet if they want something deeper they can find that too. *The Keeper* is a story like this—on the surface, a simple adventure/mystery about a boy who wants a dad, but underneath there's a boy trying so hard to deal with a stallion-size problem in his life, that of ADD. No one listens if you *tell* them things. Manning Clark once said that if you want people to learn anything at all, tell them a story.

"I love history and how the things that have gone before can solve some puzzle in the present. I like the mysteriousness of secrets and how one thing leads to another. I'm most probably an idealist, although I'm wary of such labels—I would like people to be able to accept themselves and each other, to love, to be able to live in peace.

"One of my most inspiring moments was visiting Coventry Cathedral, which has emerged from the ruins of the 1940 bombing. I lit a candle for my seriously ill son and felt the healing in that special place totally dedicated to world reconciliation. I believe my creativity comes from God. He is the gift and the giver.

"Working conditions: I like to write drafts and plan outside. As a young person, I wrote my best stories out in the paddock or by the creek. I write a lot in my head as well while I'm out walking or swimming. Going to the symphony may suddenly give me an amazing idea just as the cymbals crash or the whole group of first violinists are lifting off their chairs in excitement. I enjoy historical surroundings too, and I have a settler's cottage near the sea which has such a creative atmo-

Peer pressure is exceptionally stressful for teenaged Jaime, who feels like an outsider upon returning to Australia after ten years in her adopted country of Pakistan.

sphere. I can go there with a portable computer and get a draft done in half the time. There is no telephone or TV—there I write from nine to four with a walk before lunch and a walk after four. If I get stuck, I go for another walk. I read at night. At home if the noise gets too much, I write to music—I often do this anyway. I'm working on a novel now (*Zenna Dare*) with music in it, and I've written most of it to the music of Andrea Bocelli. He makes me write faster and feel the words.

"Advice I give to young writers is write from the heart, do it with all your passion and energy and courage. If you really want to write, then think of it as the most important thing you can do, like a mission you've been sent on, or a race you have to finish but not necessarily win. For most of us who want to write, writing is as necessary as breathing, so learn to breathe properly. I show young people that first of all they have to start, and read lots as well. And once started, writing is 3D: determination, drive, and darn hard work."

Hawke's first young adult novel, *Re-entry,* captures the world of teen mores—the distaste for anyone who looks different from themselves, the importance of acceptance by peers, the soul-searching about identity, the awareness of members of the opposite sex, and so on—and places it in a plot concerning an Australian teenager whose family returns to their homeland after living in Pakistan for ten years. Jaime feels a complete outsider in her new school in Adelaide. Her diary entries reflect a nostalgia for her life in Pakistan, reflected in her fabrication of Suneel, a Pakistani boy she pretends she has left behind, but in reality is a symbol of her loss of Pakistan. As Jaime begins to see beneath the seemingly anarchistic surface of teen life in Australia, she also learns to look at the realities of life in Pakistan with a clearer eye. "This is the first book I have seen written from the perspective of a thoughtful girl who after learning to fit into an alien society has to go through the same process in her own," remarked H. Nowicka in a *Reading Time* review. Nowicka added, "it's fascinating." Other critics similarly remarked on Hawke's effective multicultural moral, though Cecile Ferguson noted in *Lollipops, What's on for Kids* that "Jaime is a most likable character and her search for an identity is sure to move all teenagers—interested in multiculturalism or not."

Jihad, Hawke's second book, finds Jaime back in Pakistan on a school holiday to visit her former friends there and to continue her identity quest after a turbulent year spent in an Australian high school. However, she and her friends are kidnaped shortly thereafter by the freedom fighters of the *jihad,* a resistance movement. The resulting adventure is "a real page-turner that grabs you by the scruff of the neck and drags you through the action," according to Kate Graham in *Youth Express.*

Hawke's third publication, *The Keeper,* is quite different from her earlier works. Here, her protagonist is twelve-year-old Joel, being raised by his grandmother in the long absence of his parents. Joel has problems in school arising from his inability to control his emotions, especially when he is provoked by the bullies who taunt him. Making matters worse, his trouble with some school subjects, such as mathematics, also leads to frustration. "Hawke displays an unerring touch with the thoughts and feelings of a troubled youngster who knows only fisticuffs and foul words to grapple with confronting situations," remarked Cynthia Anthony in *Magpies*. But what Joel feels he needs most is a father, and finally, in desperation, he advertises for one. His stipulations that the candidate be tough and know all about fishing are amply met by Dev, a tattooed biker with a ponytail whose friendship Joel decides to keep a secret. In addition to fishing expertise, Dev is quite a bit more successful at managing his anger than Joel and teaches the boy a more constructive approach to his emotional life. Joel and Dev get along so well that Joel hardly notices the arrival of a stranger in town who appears to know his Gran. The mystery of her identity, and that of the dangerous man who appears later in the novel, carries the reader through the end of *The Keeper*.

Many reviewers focused on Hawke's evocative first-person depiction of how Joel feels when he's angry: "Hawke is excellent at conveying the turbulence that takes over Joel's mind and the impotent anger which makes him lash out, as well as the strategies quiet Dev is able to give him to channel his aggression into calmer and more constructive responses," contended Katharine England in the *Advertiser*. "The author is an ESL/Special Needs teacher and she obviously knows about, and understands, children with the same or similar problems to Joel," remarked Rosemary Worssam in *Viewpoint*. Finally, Hawke's successful incorporation of a suspense/mystery in the second half of the book makes for an exciting conclusion that will satisfy readers hungry for adventure, claimed some critics. Because *The Keeper* addresses so many topics, according to *Lollipops, What's on for Kids* editor Cecile Ferguson, it addresses the needs of a wide variety of audiences: "An unusual storyline which will prove a hit with boys in the 9-12 age group, but due to the many other topics the novel presents, it will also make excellent reading for Lower Secondary students," Ferguson concluded.

Biographical and Critical Sources

BOOKS

Fox, Jan, *Books That Help Teenagers*, MBF, 1997.

PERIODICALS

Advertiser, March 11, 2000, Katherine England, review of *The Keeper*, p. 19.
Australian Book Review, April, 2000, Pam Macintyre, review of *The Keeper*, p. 56.
Bookbird, Volume 37, number 2, 1999, John and Heather Foster, "Caught in the Crack: Stereotypes of South Asians in Australian Children's and Adolescent Literature."
Church Scene, August, 1995, Fiona Prentice, review of *Re-entry*, p. 8.
Courier Mail, March 28, 2000, Millan Richards, review of *The Keeper*, Books section, p. 2.
Lollipops, What's on for Kids, July-August, 1995, Cecile Ferguson, review of *Re-entry*, p. 18; May-June, 1996, Cecile Ferguson, "Meet Rosanne Hawke," p. 20; May-June, 1996, Cecile Ferguson, review of *Jihad*, p. 21; April-May, 2000, Cecile Ferguson, review of *The Keeper*, p. 18.
Magpies, July, 1995, John Murray, review of *Re-entry*, p. 25; May, 2000, Cynthia Anthony, review of *The Keeper*, p. 34.
Reading Time, August, 1995, H. Nowicka, review of *Re-entry*, p. 34; Volume 44, number 2, 2000, Jane Gibian, review of *The Keeper*, p. 25.
School Librarian, spring, 2001, Catherine Spalding, review of *The Keeper*.
Viewpoint, summer, 1995, review of *Re-entry*, p. 44; winter, 2000, Rosemary Worssam, review of *The Keeper*, p. 43.
Youth Express, spring, 1995, Jennifer Micallef, review of *Re-entry*, p. 25; spring, 1996, Kate Graham, review of *Jihad*, p. 22.

ON-LINE

The Adelaide Collection, http://www.slsa.sa.gov.au/ (July 10, 2001), "About Rosanne Hawke."
Rosanne Hawke's Web site, http://homepages.picknowl.com.au/hawknest/ (June 13, 2000).

*   *   *

HILL, Donna (Marie) 1921-

Personal

Born 1921, in Salt Lake City, UT; daughter of Clarence Henry (a U.S. Customs official) and Emma (Wirthlin) Hill. *Education:* Attended Phillips Gallery Art School, Washington, 1940-43; George Washington University, A.B., 1948; Columbia University, M.L.S., 1952. *Religion:* Church of Jesus Christ of Latter-Day Saints. *Hobbies and other interests:* Travel, playing the recorder, opera, theater, reading, swimming.

Addresses

Home—New York, NY. *Agent*—c/o Author Mail, Clarion Books, 215 Park Ave. S., New York, NY 10003.

Career

U.S. Department of State, Washington, DC, code clerk, 1944-49; U.S. Department of State, U.S. Embassy, Paris, France, code clerk, 1949-51; New York Public Library, New York, NY, librarian, 1952-59; City University of New York, New York, NY, City College Library, assistant to librarian, 1962-63, Hunter College Library, assistant to librarian, 1964-70, instructor, 1970-75, assistant professor, 1975-79, associate professor, 1980-84, named professor, professor emeritus, 1984—, head of Teachers Central Laboratory, 1974-84. Member of Professional Staff Congress. Painter, with work exhibited in several Paris shows, and in U.S. Information Services exhibition touring Europe, 1950-51. *Member:*

American Recorder Society (national secretary, 1959-61), Women's National Book Association (chair of New York, NY, chapter, 1991-93), Phi Beta Kappa, Kappa Delta, Pi Gamma Mu, Delta Kappa Gamma (president, Gamma Alpha Chapter, 1988-90); Wellfleet Historical Society; U.S. Life-Saving Service Heritage Association.

Awards, Honors

Maurice Fromkes painting scholarship to international workshop, Segovia, Spain, summer, 1953; Staten Island Writers Conference, Weekly Reader fellow, 1957; "One Hundred Outstanding New Books for the Younger Reader" selection, *New York Times Book Review,* for *Not One More Day;* research fellowship to Huntington Library, summer, 1970; nomination for Colorado Children's Book Award, for *Ms. Glee Was Waiting;* City University of New York, Scholar Incentive Award, 1981-82; Alumni Association of Central High School, certificate of distinction, 1984; Lolabel Hall Award, 1988; Ruth Mack Havens Award, 1991; Christopher Medal, 1999, and Sequoya Award nomination, 2000-01, both for *Shipwreck Season.*

Writings

FOR CHILDREN

(And illustrator) *Not One More Day,* Viking (New York, NY), 1957.

Donna Hill

(Illustrator) Janet Konkle, *The Sea Cart,* Abingdon (Nashville, TN), 1961.
Catch a Brass Canary, Lippincott (Philadelphia, PA), 1964.
(Editor, with Doris de Montreville) *Third Book of Junior Authors,* H. W. Wilson (Bronx, NY), 1972.
Ms. Glee Was Waiting, Atheneum (New York, NY), 1978.
Mr. Peeknuff's Tiny People, Atheneum (New York, NY), 1981.
(And illustrator) *Eerie Animals: Seven Stories,* Atheneum (New York, NY), 1983.
First Your Penny, Atheneum (New York, NY), 1985.
Shipwreck Season, Clarion Books (New York, NY), 1998.

FOR ADULTS

The Picture File: A Manual and Curriculum-Related Subject Heading List, Shoe String Press (Hamden, CT), 1975, 2nd edition, 1978.
Joseph Smith: The First Mormon, Doubleday (New York, NY), 1977.
Murder Uptown, Carroll & Graf (New York, NY), 1992.

Contributor to anthologies, including *More Stories to Dream On,* Houghton Mifflin, 1993. Also contributor to periodicals, including *Delta Kappa Gamma Bulletin, Wreck and Rescue* (journal of the U.S. Life-Saving Service Heritage Association), and *Alfred Hitchcock Mystery Magazine.* Editor-in-chief, *American Recorder,* 1962-63. *Catch a Brass Canary* was serialized in *Katholieke Illustratie* (the Netherlands), as *Een goudvink voor Ana,* 1967. The "Donna Hill Collection," consisting of papers, manuscripts, diaries, letters, drafts, books, art, galley proofs, and other pertinent material, was established at Marriott Library, University of Utah, 1994.

Sidelights

Donna Hill is the author of several books for children and young adults that teach subtle life lessons via humorous situations or unexpected challenges. Hill worked for the U.S. State Department as a code clerk while studying towards a degree at George Washington University in the 1940s. She spent two years in Paris with the American Embassy before moving to New York City to pursue a degree in library science at Columbia University. During the 1950s, she worked as a librarian at the New York Public Library and at two city colleges before becoming an instructor, then professor in her field. She was made professor emeritus at Hunter College in 1984.

Hill's first book for children, *Not One More Day,* was based on her experiences while studying art in Segovia, Spain. She illustrated Janet Konkle's *The Sea Cart,* then she wrote *Catch a Brass Canary* based on her experience as a young librarian in a branch of the New York Public Library. *Ms. Glee Was Waiting* was her next picture book, then came *Mr. Peeknuff's Tiny People* in 1981, aimed at early-elementary readers. The title character presumes that the village he views from his hilltop hideaway is peopled by miniature figures, and that he is a magnificent pasha. When inclement weather threatens, the benevolent Mr. Peeknuff descends to save the tiny people, but finds only normal-sized villagers. In the end, it is Mr. Peeknuff's eyesight that requires aid. "It's an intriguing idea for a story," noted Kristi L. Thomas in her *School Library Journal* review, while a reviewer for *Publishers Weekly* remarked that "little children should get many a chuckle out of Hill's silly tale."

Hill provided the illustrations to accompany her text in *Eerie Animals: Seven Stories,* published in 1983. In these seven stories, each focuses upon a different animal, or its ghost, and its relationship with a youngster. "That Thing" features a flesh-eating fish, while "Michael" is the squirrel who provides solace to a terminally ill little girl. "Thor," a Doberman pinscher, grieves over the death of his owner and seems to become invincible himself. Some animals, such as a praying mantis, seem to communicate telepathically with the child in the story. *Horn Book* critic Nancy C. Hammond noted that the stories in *Eerie Animals* "quickly draw the reader into credible, contemporary situations and present a satisfying variety of characters, plots, and emotions."

Hill's 1985 book, *First Your Penny,* tackles a far different subject: the developmentally disabled. Its protagonist is Dicky, a teenager who has a difficult time with basic math and reading skills. His family, determined to protect him, tries too hard to shield him from the world. He is removed from school, and he spends his days in a highly regimented structure of leisure activities planned by his mother, who believes that a menial job for Dicky would be unsuitable. Dicky's resolve to enter the working world has mixed results, but a suitable alternative is discovered. "In this book," noted a *School Library Journal* writer, "the image of the mentally handicapped character is that of a capable, sensitive person who knows what he wants, takes charge of his own life, and fights for his right to make choices." A reviewer for *Bulletin of the Center for Children's Books* remarked that in *First Your Penny* "Hill makes it clear that family coddling is done out of ignorance and love."

Hill wrote *Shipwreck Season* for middle-school readers interested in American seafaring history. Daniel, a New England teen in the 1870s, dislikes school and is attracted to trouble. In response, his mother sends him to live and work with an uncle on Cape Cod, who heads a crew of "surfmen" whose job it is to patrol the Eastern seaboard and rescue sailors and passengers from shipwrecks. At first, Daniel detests his hard new life, but soon rises to its challenges—overcoming a fear of heights along the way. "The historical period is nicely captured," noted Tim Rausch in *School Library Journal,* "and the portrayal of the seacoast environment is in simple, but beautiful prose." In a *Booklist* review, Chris Sherman called the work well plotted in its character development, and further noted that "Hill captures the danger, excitement, and camaraderie of the surfmen's lives."

During the early days of the United States Life-Saving Service, teenage Daniel trains with the surfmen who rescue the victims of shipwrecks in Hill's historical adventure. (Cover illustration by Anthony Bacon Venti.)

Hill once said: "I started out in life expecting to be an artist, an author, and a great many other things as well, including inventor, detective, and puppeteer, but at about age twelve I began to concentrate on art and writing. Of course it is sad that every choice means the loss of something else, but in a way, as author, one can do and be anything one wishes.

"I suppose my pleasure in doing a variety of things is reflected in my writing, since I have done picture books for children, novels and short stories for teens, and fiction and nonfiction for adults. While I enjoy every aspect of writing, from research to rough drafts to rewriting and revising, I find it all very hard work.

"What I enjoy above all is writing fiction. I love imagining scenes and characters and hearing dialogue in my head. It is especially astonishing and gratifying when people I thought I had made up take on a life of their own, speak their own minds, and evolve their own destinies. I feel very close to the people I write about, whether real, such as Joseph Smith, or fictional. After I have lived with characters for a year or sometimes for several years (and with Joseph Smith for more than eight years), they become as substantial to me as my associates and neighbors, sometimes more so, because I usually know more about them.

"I like to read books of every sort, novels, history, biographies, how-to, and I still dearly love good children's books. I do not like jokes, slapstick, or (with some notable exceptions) comedians, but I love wit, especially when it is spontaneous, or when, through the art and sensitivity of the writer, it is made to seem so. My favorite authors are ones that bring joy and raise the spirits through a delicious sense of life's absurdities."

Biographical and Critical Sources

PERIODICALS

Booklist, June 1, 1998, Chris Sherman, review of *Shipwreck Season,* p. 1748.
Bulletin of the Center for Children's Books, October, 1983, review of *Eerie Animals: Seven Stories,* p. 29; June, 1985, review of *First Your Penny,* p. 186.
Horn Book, August, 1983, Nancy C. Hammond, review of *Eerie Animals,* p. 444.
Interracial Books for Children Bulletin, Volume 17, number 2, 1986, review of *First Your Penny,* pp. 17-18.
Publishers Weekly, February 13, 1981, review of *Mr. Peeknuff's Tiny People,* p. 93.
School Library Journal, May, 1981, Kristi L. Thomas, review of *Mr. Peeknuff's Tiny People,* p. 55; January, 1983, Gale Eaton, review of *Eerie Animals,* pp. 123-124; September, 1994, review of *First Your Penny,* p. 142; June, 1998, Tim Rausch, review of *Shipwreck Season,* p. 147.

*   *   *

HOWARD, Pauline Rodriguez 1951-
(P. M. Howard)

Personal

Born June 15, 1951, in San Antonio, TX; daughter of John F. and Marie Ercelia (a homemaker; maiden name, Rodriguez) Kotzur; married David Britton Howard (a print shop manager), April 23, 1977; children: Jean Nicole, Kelley Marie. *Education:* Attended San Antonio College, 1969-71; University of Houston, B.F.A., 1978; attended Alfred C. Glassell School of Art, 1982. *Religion:* Roman Catholic. *Hobbies and other interests:* Gardening.

Addresses

Home—6306 Peace Pipe Dr., San Antonio, TX 78238. *E-mail*—PMHowardART@aol.com.

Career

Star Engraving, Houston, TX, illustrator, 1974-77; fine artist, 1977—. Works exhibited at Harris Gallery, Houston, 1977—, and Hunt Gallery, San Antonio, TX, 1998—; also represented in group and solo exhibitions throughout the Southwest. Freelance illustrator, 1992—; some works appear under the name P. M. Howard. Worked as scenery and set designer for a ballet company, 1991-97. *Member:* Central Texas Pastel Society.

Awards, Honors

Named illustrator of the month, *Highlights for Children,* February, 1997.

Illustrator

Carole Katchen, *Painting Faces and Figures,* Watson-Guptill (New York, NY), 1986.
Josefa Kradky, *Una Amiga de lo más Especial,* Macmillan/McGraw (New York, NY), 1993.
Magali Garcia-Ramis, *Doña Felisa Rincón de Gautier, Mayor of San Juan,* Modern Curriculum Press (Cleveland, OH), 1995.
Olga Romero, *Con mi familia,* Macmillan/McGraw (New York, NY), 1996.
Lada Kratky, *Baby Bear's Toys,* Hampton-Brown, 1997.

Pauline Rodriguez Howard

Lucy Floyd, *What a Mess!*, Harcourt (New York, NY), 1997.

Diane Gonzalez Bertrand, *Family, Familia,* Spanish translation by Julia Mercedes Castilla, Piñata Books (Houston, TX), 1999.

Susan Meyers, *Take a Look at My Family,* Hampton-Brown, 1999.

Mary Sue Galinda, *Icy Watermelon* (bilingual in English and Spanish), Piñata Books (Houston, TX), 2000.

Illustrator for posters. Contributor of illustrations to periodicals, including *Ultra, Southwest Art, Equine Images,* and *Highlights for Children.*

Work in Progress

Illustrating *Uncle Chente's Picnic,* by Diane Gonzalez Bertrand; a picture book about wandering in the garden.

Sidelights

Pauline Rodriguez Howard told *SATA:* "Since elementary school I have been an artist. I began by drawing decorations for my teacher's classroom. In high school I was designing and drawing posters of rock stars for myself and my friends. I also illustrated the cover for my church's weekly bulletin. In college, I majored in fine art and studied lithography at the museum school. My primary career since then has been selling art through galleries.

"When I had my two daughters, reading storybooks became a favorite pastime, and shopping for the best illustrated books became a passion! It wasn't until my children were teenagers that I was approached to illustrate my first book. It was for an acquaintance—an art director who also designed academic books. Of course my real desire was to illustrate trade books, but I felt I wasn't ready and needed to experiment and develop a technique and style with school books. I guess it is an ongoing process, because after completing two trade books and numerous academic books, I am still not satisfied.

"Since my original work involves rendering people within scenes, stories involving people (children) were a natural. My primary medium is pastel, but with illustration I enjoy mixing media such as watercolors, gouache, markers, Prismacolors, and pastels for a colorful composition with depth.

"I'm still buying children's books, even though my daughters are grown! They are so inspirational! But artists like Monet, Lautrec, Larson, Hopper, and Porter, among others, are still my strongest influences.

"If I am not working on a book or a commissioned portrait of children, I am creating work for galleries. I normally work on three-to-five drawings at a time, since I tack my paper on the walls of my studio. When working on a storybook, this method enables me to work on *all* the illustrations at the same time. This is a

tremendous aid in continuity. I do what I love to do, and feel very privileged!"

Biographical and Critical Sources

PERIODICALS

School Library Journal, September, 1999, Denise E. Agosto, review of *Family, Familia,* p. 174.*

*   *   *

HOWARD, P. M.
See HOWARD, Pauline Rodriguez

*   *   *

HUBBARD, Patricia 1945-

Personal

Born July 7, 1945, in Fergus Falls, MN; daughter of Walter R. (an office manager) and Camilla (an author and teacher) Summers; married James R. Hubbard (an attorney), March 22, 1969; children: Brant, Joy Hubbard Young. *Education:* Washington State University, B.A. (sociology); University of Washington, M.S.W. *Religion:* Methodist. *Hobbies and other interests:* "I sing in the church choir and love to swim and walk my dog and, of course, read and write!"

Addresses

Home—35513 Southeast 49th St., Fall City, WA 98024.

Career

Author. Lutheran Family and Child Services, counselor, 1969-70; Bellevue Community College Co-op Preschool, parent educator, 1983-84. Former member of the school district curriculum review committee. *Member:* International Reading Association, Author's Guild, Children's Book Council, Society of Children's Book Writers and Illustrators.

Awards, Honors

My Crayons Talk was an American Booksellers spring "Pick of the Lists," 1996; Children's Choice, International Reading Association and Children's Book Council, 1997, for *My Crayons Talk,* and 2000, for *Trick or Treat Countdown.*

Writings

God Gives Me Everything (picture book), illustrated by June Goldsborough, Augsburg (Minneapolis, MN), 1994.

My Crayons Talk (picture book), illustrated by G. Brian Karas, Holt (New York, NY), 1996.

Trick or Treat Countdown (picture book), illustrated by Michael Letzig, Holiday House (New York, NY), 1999.

Also author of more than one hundred articles published in magazines for children and adults, including *Ladybug, Pockets, Counselor, Boys Quest, Children's Digest, Highlights for Children, Christian Parenting Today,* and *Humpty Dumpty. My Crayons Talk* has been published in both Korean, with an accompanying compact disc, and Japanese.

Work in Progress

Peek-a-Boo Beautiful You, a picture book.

Sidelights

Patricia Hubbard told *SATA* why she wrote *My Crayons Talk:* "When I was a child, I felt that I had no artistic ability. When the teacher would say it was time for art, everyone would take out their paper and crayons and start to draw. I loved the bright colors and the smell and feel of those waxy crayons—but my pictures never looked 'right.' If I tried to draw a horse, someone would say it looked like a dog. If I drew a dog, they would ask if it was a pig.

Patricia Hubbard

"So, when I grew up, I decided to write a book for children who don't think they are 'good' in art. Because that was the child that I was. I think that every child should be able to enjoy color and crayons and feel that they have artistic ability. I think everyone can take a crayon and a piece of paper and draw something that expresses something authentic within them. This is art. And if it is their best effort, then it is both 'good' and 'right.' It seems to me that art should be a form of expression that affirms that whatever you have to say is important. The picture book *My Crayons Talk* was written in the hope that children will be encouraged to love art as they let their crayons talk."

In *My Crayons Talk,* Hubbard devised a bouncy, rhyming text that celebrates twelve colors and the flights of artistic fancy they inspire. "The balance, repetition, rhyme, and rhythm of the simple text are sure to be noticed by classroom teachers looking for something fresh for young children to read," predicted Kathie Krieger Cerra in *Five Owls.* Other critics made similar predictions about the success of this book in classroom settings. *Booklist* reviewer Carolyn Phelan noted that *My Crayons Talk* is "great fun to read aloud." And Virginia Opocensky remarked in *School Library Journal* that "it's a perfect vehicle for language and art activities."

Hubbard also told *SATA* her reasons for creating *Trick or Treat Countdown:* "When my daughter was a preschooler she was both fascinated by and fearful of Halloween. She longed to trudge along with her brother for trick or treating, but the goblins and ghosts rattling bags of candy frightened her so much she was overwhelmed. Years later, when I taught parent education in a preschool setting, I observed the same ambivalence in other young children. I wrote *Trick or Treat Countdown* for all those tear-streaked would-be spooks who struggle for a sense of mastery over those things that shout 'boo' in the night.

"My hope is that *Trick or Treat Countdown* will offer the young child an opportunity to enjoy being scared, while still feeling safe. As she learns the skill of counting she also gains self-confidence and a sense of mastery over her fears. Teachers and parents can share this book with children and help them express and conquer their anxieties about the Halloween experience. Beyond the fun and delight in the rhyming text, my hope is that the text conveys to the child—'You are capable. You can count and you can gain mastery over frightening things.'"

Hubbard again relies on rhyme and repetition to structure the text of *Trick or Treat Countdown.* Here, the author has created simple rhymes featuring objects associated with Halloween as a way to count from one to twelve and then back down to one again. Throughout, friendly illustrations and a refrain about make-believe reassure timid preschoolers that on Halloween it is fun to be scared. Again, critics emphasized the book's likely effectiveness in read-aloud settings. "This is a playful title with participatory possibilities," observed Janice M.

Del Negro in *Bulletin of the Center for Children's Books*. Likewise, Tom S. Hurlburt wrote in *School Library Journal*, "This attractive title will serve as a non threatening read-aloud for the preschool set." And a reviewer for *Publishers Weekly* declared *Trick or Treat Countdown* "safe for easily scared readers."

Biographical and Critical Sources

PERIODICALS

Booklist, April 1, 1996, Carolyn Phelan, review of *My Crayons Talk,* p. 1371; September 1, 1999, Kathy Broderick, review of *Trick or Treat Countdown,* p. 149.

Bulletin of the Center for Children's Books, May 1, 1996, review of *My Crayons Talk;* October, 1999, Janice M. Del Negro, review of *Trick or Treat Countdown,* p. 56.

Five Owls, May, 1996, Kathie Krieger Cerra, review of *My Crayons Talk,* pp. 108-109.

Publishers Weekly, May 24, 1999, review of *My Crayons Talk,* p. 81; September 27, 1999, review of *Trick or Treat Countdown,* p. 47.

Reflections, February, 2000, Aimee Bluhm, "Children's Author Has Much to Offer," pp. 18-19.

School Library Journal, May, 1996, Virginia Opocensky, review of *My Crayons Talk;* September, 1999, Tom S. Hurlburt, review of *Trick or Treat Countdown.*

*   *   *

IVERY, Martha M. 1948-

Personal

Born December 24, 1948, in Ellenville, NY; daughter of Samuel (a car porter) and Mary (a homemaker; maiden name, Aldsorf) Reidda; married Thomas Ivery, Sr. (a contractor), January 3, 1987; children: Matthew J. Montanye, Sheryl A. Montanye. *Education:* Columbia Green Community College, associate degree in science, 1988. *Religion:* Roman Catholic. *Hobbies and other interests:* Camping, swimming, writing.

Addresses

Home—P.O. Box 788, Leeds, NY 12451. *Office*—291 Main St., Catskill, NY 12414. *E-mail*—Presstige9@ aol.com.

Career

Eden Park Nursing Home, Catskill, NY, registered nurse, 1988-91; Press-Tige Publishing, Inc., Catskill, publisher and book distributor, 1994—.

Writings

The Joy Train, Stone Publications, 1994.
Pickles and Peanuts, Press-Tige Publishing (Catskill, NY), 1995.

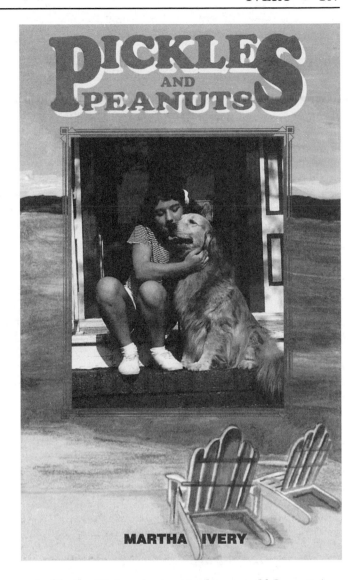

In Martha M. Ivery's story, twelve-year-old Peanuts is consoled by Pickles, her new canine friend, during the dissolution of her parents' marriage.

What's Your Psychic IQ? How to Listen to Your Inner Voice and Let It Guide You to a Better Life, Prima Publishing (Rocklin, CA), 1999.

Make Millions from Your Kitchen Table, Press-Tige Publishing (Catskill, NY), 1999.

Camp Werewolf, Press-Tige Publishing (Catskill, NY), 1999.

I Love You More Than . . . , Press-Tige Publishing (Catskill, NY), 2000.

Welcome to Camp Horrorwood, Press Tige Publishing (Catskill, NY), 2000.

Also author of *The Vengeance Equation.*

Work in Progress

On Grandparents' Rights: Voices Speak Out; Publishers by Genre, a reference book that categorizes publishing companies by the genres of work they publish.

Sidelights

Martha M. Ivery told *SATA:* "I began my writing career as I sat in my wheelchair. After submitting my stories to publishers and not getting any satisfactory replies, I published my first book, *Pickles and Peanuts.* Everyone liked it so much, and it sold so well to children with divorced parents, that people wanted me to do the same thing again. That's when I started Press-Tige Publishing. I like to see writers meet their dreams as I have met mine. I now write for other publishers as well, and I distribute their books.

"I wrote *On Grandparents' Rights* because my daughter and her husband and I are in a dispute. They refuse to allow me to have anything to do with my grandchildren. I have interviewed many professionals as well as grandparents, who have all given me valuable input for my book. The book is dedicated to all grandparents and to my grandchildren.

"My camping experiences are the source of my 'Camp Werewolf' stories.

"My advice to other writers is to keep writing; don't give up. Some books I have published have been translated into Japanese and sold to other publishers for reprint rights. *The Vengeance Equation* has been optioned for a motion picture. Think positive! With God, all things are possible."*

K

KASZA, Keiko 1951-

Personal

Name pronounced "*Kay*-co Kaza"; born December 23, 1951, in Japan; daughter of Tomizo (a businessman) and Masuko (a homemaker) Tanaka; married Gregory J. Kasza (a professor), June 22, 1976; children: Edward Kosuke, Alexander Taisuke. *Education:* California State University, Northridge, B.A. (fine arts), 1975.

Addresses

Home—2903 Browncliff Ln., Bloomington, IN 47408. *E-mail*—kekasza@hotmail.com.

Career

Artist and children's book author and illustrator.

Awards, Honors

Notable Book designation, American Library Association, 1987, and Kentucky Bluegrass Award, both for *The Wolf's Chicken Stew;* 100 Noteworthy Children's Books of 1992, Library of Congress, for *A Mother for Choco;* Prix Chonos, 1997, for *Grandpa Toad's Secrets;* Children's Choice selection, International Reading Council and Children's Book Council, and Charlotte Zolotow Honor Book, Cooperative Children's Book Center, 1998, both for *Don't Laugh, Joe!;* Reading Magic Award, *Parenting Magazine,* for *Dorothy and Mikey;* several awards for art and design.

Writings

FOR CHILDREN; SELF-ILLUSTRATED

The Wolf's Chicken Stew, Putnam (New York, NY), 1987.
The Pigs' Picnic, Putnam (New York, NY), 1988.
When the Elephant Walks, Putnam (New York, NY), 1990.
A Mother for Choco, Putnam (New York, NY), 1992.
The Rat and the Tiger, Putnam (New York, NY), 1993.
Grandpa Toad's Secrets, Putnam (New York, NY), 1995.

Keiko Kasza

Don't Laugh, Joe!, Putnam (New York, NY), 1997.
Dorothy and Mikey, Putnam (New York, NY), 2000.
The Mightiest, Putnam (New York, NY), 2001.

Also author of picture books published in Japan.

Sidelights

Born and raised in Japan, Keiko Kasza brings her childhood influences to bear on the books she both writes and illustrates for young children. Her works, which contain what a *Publishers Weekly* contributor described as "characteristic cleverness and droll art," include *A Mother for Choco, The Pigs' Picnic, Don't Laugh, Joe!,* and *Dorothy and Mikey.* In each book, animal characters act out a variety of human situations with a combination of humor and poignancy, making her books resonate with impressionable young readers.

Kasza was born in Japan in 1951, the daughter of a businessman and his wife. "Growing up in Japan, I remember I used to read a lot and play with my friends in the neighborhood," the author and illustrator recalled to *SATA.* "In retrospect I think these are two of the most important contributions to what I do: writing and illustrating picture books. By reading a lot, I learned what makes a good story, and by playing a lot, I learned the pain and the joy that kids experience when they interact with one another."

Kasza found herself in the United States by the time college came around; she attended California State University's Northridge campus, where she majored in fine arts and earned her bachelor's degree in 1975. Within a year Kasza had married, and together she and her husband, a college professor, raised two sons. Her first picture book, *The Wolf's Chicken Stew,* was published in 1987, marking Kasza's transition from artist and homemaker to artist, homemaker, and published author. It also garnered the first-time author/illustrator an American Library Association commendation when it was cited among the Notable Books of 1987.

In *The Wolf's Chicken Stew,* a wily wolf has his eye on one hen in particular, whom he plans to fatten up so she'll make a more satisfying meal. True to fairy-tale form, his plan backfires, when he finds that his gifts of goodies have been gobbled up by the hen's chicks, who now hold him in high esteem as "Uncle Wolf." Using what *Wilson Library Bulletin* contributors Donnarae MacCann and Olga Richard described as "parallel phrases that create a playful, songlike quality in the text," Kasza tells an entertaining tale, complementing it with sketchy pen-and-ink-and-watercolor renderings that transform Wolf into "a charismatic rascal." Commenting that "Kasza's illustrations far surpass the story," David Gale nonetheless maintained in his *School Library Journal* review that "children will enjoy both the wolf's scheming ... [and] the story's repetitive form."

Kasza paints a gentle portrait of acceptance in her story titled *A Mother for Choco.* In this picture book, a small yellow bird with a bright blue beak has misplaced its mother and searches other animals for signs of a family resemblance. Despite the lack of physical similarities—no feathers, no wings—a bear is willing to adopt the small creature. In fact, the bird Choco quickly finds that its family has expanded to include other creatures as well: an alligator, a hippo, and a pig. Kasza's "emphasis on caring and sharing despite superficial differences will surely find a wide audience," commented *School Library* contributor Lisa Dennis, who also praised the book's "cheerful, energetic illustrations."

When the Elephant Walks, published in 1990, is a circular story in which the movement of a lumbering elephant causes a chain reaction among other creatures that ends with a frightened mouse startling the elephant into the same sequence of events all over again. In *Horn Book,* Mary M. Burns called Kasza's depiction of animal characters "skillfully handled" and described *When the Elephant Walks* as an "unpretentious, thoroughly engaging book, executed with charm and élan." Ilene Cooper also had a positive reaction to Kasza's text and illustrations, commenting in her *Booklist* review that the "adorably drawn" animals serve as an effective "hook for this lighthearted picture book."

Animals take the place of people in illustrating an experience common to many children in Kasza's 1993 picture book, *The Rat and the Tiger.* Tiger is much larger and stronger than Rat and tends to be a bit of a bully, taking the larger pieces of treats for himself and always getting his way in the games the two play together. However, when Rat finally stands up for himself and threatens to end the friendship, Tiger regrets his forcefulness, and the relationship between the pair realigns itself on a basis other than size. Reviewer Joy Fleishhacker praised Kasza's ink and watercolor illustrations and noted in *School Library Journal* that the book's "simple text and repetitive plot elements make [*The Rat and the Tiger*] a good choice ... for story times." Equally impressed, *Horn Book* contributor Ellen Fader predicted that this "story of how two friends work through one of childhood's perennial problems will delight young listeners."

Kasza continues to write and illustrate stories featuring animal characters and has published some of her titles in her native Japan. "How lucky for me that I chose an occupation requiring such simple training: read and play," she exclaimed to *SATA.* "So much easier than getting a Ph.D. or spending years of study in medical school! I'm grateful for the kind of childhood I had in Japan, which I'm afraid today's 'wired' children are experiencing less and less."

Biographical and Critical Sources

BOOKS

Ward, Martha E., and others, *Authors of Books for Young People,* third edition, Scarecrow Press (Metuchen, NJ), 1990.

PERIODICALS

Booklist, March 1, 1990, Ilene Cooper, review of *When the Elephant Walks,* p. 1344; August, 1997, Julie Corsaro, review of *Don't Laugh, Joe!,* p. 1906; May 1, 2000, Amy Brandt, review of *Dorothy and Mikey,* p. 1678.

Bulletin of the Center for Children's Books, May, 1987, Betsy Hearne, review of *The Wolf's Chicken Stew,* p. 170; May, 1990, Zena Sutherland, review of *When the Elephant Walks,* pp. 215-216; April, 1992, Deborah Stevenson, review of *A Mother for Choco,* p. 211; April, 1993, Deborah Stevenson, review of *The Rat and the Tiger,* pp. 254-255.

Horn Book, May, 1990, Mary M. Burns, review of *When the Elephant Walks,* p. 326; May, 1993, Ellen Fader, review of *The Rat and the Tiger,* p. 319; March, 2000, Kathleen T. Horning, review of *Dorothy and Mikey,* p. 186.

Junior Bookshelf, April, 1989, review of *The Pigs' Picnic,* p. 57.

Kirkus Reviews, February 1, 1992, review of *A Mother for Choco,* p. 185; April 1, 1997, review of *Don't Laugh, Joe!,* p. 558.

Publishers Weekly, March 9, 1992, review of *The Pigs' Picnic,* p. 58; April 10, 1995, review of *Grandpa Toad's Secrets,* p. 62; March 17, 1997, review of *Don't Laugh, Joe!,* p. 83; April 24, 2000, review of *Dorothy and Mikey,* p. 90.

School Library Journal, August, 1987, David Gale, review of *The Wolf's Chicken Stew,* p. 70; February, 1992, Lisa Dennis, "It's Toddler Time ... Now What?," pp. 40-41; April, 1992, Lisa Dennis, review of *A Mother for Choco,* p. 94; April, 1993, Joy Fleishhacker, review of *The Rat and the Tiger,* p. 98.

Wilson Library Bulletin, September, 1987, Donnarae MacCann and Olga Richard, review of *The Wolf's Chicken Stew,* p. 67.

*   *   *

KETCHAM, Sallie 1963-

Personal

Born February 21, 1963, in San Rafael, CA; daughter of Richard W. (an engineer) and Sally Ann (a historian; maiden name, Johnson) Ketcham; married Steven Colt Pumilia (a corporate executive), June 29, 1985; children: Richard Colt, Marianne Cleborne. *Education:* Carleton College, B.A., 1985. *Politics:* "Card-carrying moderate." *Religion:* Episcopalian.

Addresses

Home and office—4423 Sparrow Rd., Minnetonka, MN 55345. *E-mail*—sjketcham@yahoo.com.

Career

Minnesota State Senate, St. Paul, staff writer, 1985-88; United Way of Minneapolis, Minneapolis, MN, media writer, 1988-89; press secretary for the gubernatorial campaign of Doug Kelley, 1989-90; writer. Volunteer music teacher at local public schools.

Writings

Bach's Big Adventure, illustrated by Timothy Bush, Orchard Books (New York, NY), 1999.

The Christmas Bird, illustrated by Stacey Schuett, Augsburg (Minneapolis, MN), 2000.

Sallie Ketcham

Work in Progress

The Peter Piper Pickled Pepper Caper; Leadville, an adult novel about a family of Colorado silver miners named Tabor.

Sidelights

Sallie Ketcham told *SATA:* "Rediscovering classic children's books has been the great, secret joy of children's writing (and parenthood) for me. The best books are even better than I remembered, and as I re-read them, I often find I can recall exactly where I was and what I was thinking when I read them for the first time. Suddenly I can see my fifth-grade teacher's face again; I can smell the stacks of construction paper in the school library.

"Even some of the best-loved imaginary worlds of my childhood—Narnia, Middle Earth, Marmee's parlor—seem entirely fresh and familiar at the same time. Going back to the books I loved as a child has brought my own childhood into clearer focus, dredging half-forgotten memories and emotions and reminding me every day of the furious power of young imaginations."

Biographical and Critical Sources

PERIODICALS

Booklist, April 1, 1999, Hazel Rochman, review of *Bach's Big Adventure,* p. 1429.

Publishers Weekly, April 5, 1999, review of *Bach's Big Adventure,* p. 241; September 25, 2000, Elizabeth Devereaux, review of *The Christmas Bird,* p. 67.

School Library Journal, June, 1999, Beth Tegart, review of *Bach's Big Adventure,* p. 99; October, 2000, review of *The Christmas Bird,* p. 60.

ON-LINE

Augsburg Fortress, http://www.augsburgfortress.org/.*

L

LEWIS, E(arl) B(radley) 1956-

Personal

Born December 16, 1956. *Education:* Attended Tyler School of Art, Temple University.

Addresses

Home—1425 Mays Landing Rd., Folsom, NJ 08037. *Agent*—Dwyer & O'Grady Inc., P.O. Box 239, East Lempster, NH 03605.

Career

Artist and illustrator; art teacher. *Exhibitions:* Work held in the permanent collection of the Pew Charitable Trust. *Member:* Society of Illustrators, Philadelphia Water Club Society.

Illustrator

Jane Kurtz, *Fire on the Mountain,* Simon & Schuster (New York, NY), 1993.

Doreen Rappaport, *The New King,* Dial (New York, NY), 1994.

Tololwa M. Mollel, *Big Boy,* Clarion Books (New York, NY), 1994.

Alice Schertle, *Down the Road,* Harcourt (San Diego, CA), 1994.

Dakari Hru, *The Magic Moonberry Jump Ropes,* Dial (New York, NY), 1995.

Mary Matthews, *Magid Fasts for Ramadan,* Clarion (New York, NY), 1995.

Jane Kurtz and Christopher Kurtz, *Only a Pigeon,* Simon & Schuster (New York, NY), 1995.

Nancy Antle, *Champions,* Dial (New York, NY), 1997.

Nancy Antle, *Staying Cool,* Dial (New York, NY), 1997.

Natasha Anastasia Tarpley, *I Love My Hair!,* Little, Brown (Boston, MA), 1997.

John Steptoe, *Creativity,* Clarion (New York, NY), 1997.

Gavin Curtis, *The Bat Boy and His Violin,* Simon & Schuster (New York, NY), 1998.

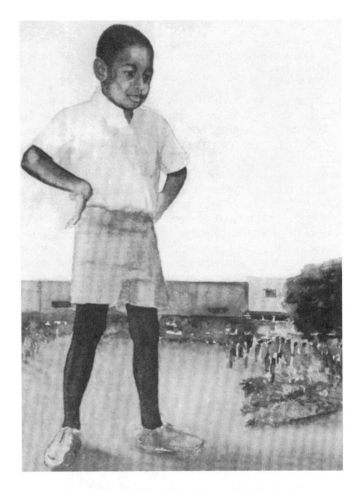

E. B. Lewis contributes his watercolor illustrations to Tololwa M. Mollel's tale of a little boy who longs to be bigger. (From Big Boy.*)*

Clifton L. Taulbert, *Little Cliff and the Porch People,* Dial (New York, NY), 1999.

T. Obinkaram Echewa, *The Magic Tree: A Folktale from Nigeria,* Morrow Junior Books (New York, NY), 1999.

Elizabeth Fitzgerald Howard, *Virgie Goes to School with Us Boys,* Simon & Schuster (New York, NY), 1999.

Tololwa M. Mollel, *My Rows and Piles of Coins,* Clarion (New York, NY), 1999.

Lucille Clifton, *The Times They Used to Be,* Doubleday (New York, NY), 2000.

Jane Kurtz, *Faraway Home,* Harcourt (San Diego, CA), 2000.

Doreen Rappaport and Lyndall Callan, *Dirt on Their Skirts: The Story of the Young Women Who Won the World Championship,* Dial (New York, NY), 2000.

Clifton L. Taulbert, *Little Cliff's First Day of School,* Dial (New York, NY), 2001.

Jacqueline Woodson, *The Other Side,* Putnam (New York, NY), 2001.

Natasha Anastasia Tarpley, *Bippity Bop Barbershop,* Little, Brown (Boston, MA), 2002.

Also illustrator of Fatima Shaik's *Jazz of Our Street,* 1998.

Sidelights

Illustrator E. B. Lewis offered the following third-person recollection to *SATA:* "Comfortable in his role as the 'class clown,' young Earl Bradley Lewis's shattering moment of truth came when he was a sixth grader seated in the auditorium of a Philadelphia public school. Near the end of one particularly inspiring assembly program, the guest performer asked randomly selected students what they wanted to be when they grew up. Lewis's straight-faced, serious answer, 'I want to be a lawyer!' caused a general outburst of incredulous laughter. As a result of this embarrassing but pivotal moment, Lewis made up his mind to show everyone that he could become 'somebody' and make outstanding contributions to society."

Lewis ultimately decided upon a career in art. In 1975 he enrolled in Temple University's Tyler School of Art where he majored in graphic design and illustration while also studying art education. After graduating from Tyler, Lewis began teaching, freelancing in graphic design, and painting. Since 1985 his watercolors have been exhibited and sold in galleries nationally and included in distinguished collections such as the Pew Charitable Trust.

Lewis received his first assignment to illustrate a children's book, Jane Kurtz's *Fire on the Mountain,* in 1993. In a review of the book in *Publishers Weekly,* a critic stated that "debut illustrator Lewis's exceptional watercolors of Ethiopian mountains and mountain people quicken Kurtz's revision of a well-known tale," while Janice Del Negro of *Booklist* asserted: "Lewis uses color to achieve intriguing contrast and articulate characters' faces with expression and power." Lewis's children's book debut was also heralded by *School Library Journal* contributor Jos N. Holman, who wrote: "Lewis has done an outstanding job of capturing the warmth and simplicity of the tale through his beautiful watercolor paintings. They bring the story to life, complementing the emotion, expression, and character of the printed words."

Lewis has since completed illustrations for several other children's books by such noted authors as Tololwa M. Mollel, Alice Schertle, and Lucille Clifton. Lewis's artwork for Mollel's *Big Boy* was received with typical enthusiasm by reviewers, among whom a *Publishers Weekly* commentator asserted: "Mollel's story is an engaging fantasy for little ones with big aspirations, but it is Lewis's crisp, understated watercolors that steal the show."

Biographical and Critical Sources

PERIODICALS

Booklist, October 15, 1994, Janice Del Negro, review of *Fire on the Mountain,* p. 432; March 1, 1995, p. 1248; February 15, 1996, p. 1026.

Horn Book, March-April, 1996, pp. 191-192; July-August, 1996, pp. 460-461.

Publishers Weekly, September, 1994, review of *Fire on the Mountain,* p. 69; January 23, 1995, review of *Big Boy,* p. 70; June 5, 1995, p. 60; January 1, 1996, p. 70.

School Library Journal, December, 1994, Jos N. Holman, review of *Fire on the Mountain,* p. 99; April, 1996, p. 117; June, 2001, Marianne Saccardi, review of *Little Cliff's First Day of School,* p. 131.*

*   *   *

LUBY, Thia 1954-

Personal

Born October 30, 1954, in Galesburg, IL; daughter of Edwin (a teacher and administrator) and Amelia (a teacher) Lineberger; children: Bianca Young. *Education:* Studied fine arts and English at College of Santa Fe for two years; earned a certificate in jewelry design from GIA; twenty-nine years of studying yoga philosophy and practice. *Politics:* Independent.

Addresses

Agent—c/o Clear Light Publishers, 823 Don Diego, Santa Fe, NM 87501. *E-mail*—myriadimages@yoga.com.

Career

Yoga instructor and author.

Awards, Honors

Children's Book of Yoga was selected for the *School Library Journal* "Best Books of 1998" list.

Writings

Children's Book of Yoga: Games and Exercises Mimic Plants and Animals and Objects, Clear Light Publishers (Santa Fe, NM), 1998.

Yoga for Teens: How to Improve Your Fitness, Confidence, Appearance, and Health—and Have Fun Doing It, Clear Light Publishers (Santa Fe, NM), 1999.

Thia Luby

Sidelights

Thia Luby told *SATA:* "I have been writing poetry and journals since I was fourteen and have been a visual artist all my life. I won a Scholastics award in art for a stone sculpture I executed in my junior year of high school; painting and illustrating have always been my passion.

"My children's books are written to send a special message in life to learn. The two yoga books published are special studies for children to learn how to expand their knowledge and awareness of themselves and the world through physical and mental exercises. This builds self-esteem and enhances mental and physical flexibility to become a well-rounded, positive human being. This is all presented in a visually exciting format of my own color photos of children and animals or objects, which entices children to learn something new.

"I grew up with both parents who were teachers, so it was automatic for me to begin teaching yoga as a young adult, which was my passion since age seventeen. My own personal practice of yoga has been my greatest influence in creating programs for children and adults. My poetry and other children's stories are influenced by my own interesting personal experiences in life. I am a mother and now a grandmother and will pass yoga on to them.

"My advice to aspiring writers and illustrators is to follow your passion and dreams, continue on and rise above rejections, and don't ever give up on believing in yourself and your talents."

Luby's two books on yoga for young people have been well received for their visually appealing photos and for the wealth of information provided by her texts. Her first book, *Children's Book of Yoga,* features a two-page spread for each pose, one featuring an animal for which the pose is named, and the other centered on a child taking that pose. The text describes how to achieve each pose in simple language, and the poses progress from the simplest to the more complex with a note regarding those inappropriate for those under age six. *School Library Journal* reviewer Barb Lawler praised Luby's emphasis on "two things children love—animals and movement." Luby's photos were noted for their visual variety, including children of various ethnic groups and sizes, and varying indoor and outdoor backgrounds. Information for parents and other adults includes poses for resolving common childhood ailments, and charts outlining poses to stretch various muscle groups. "Both children and adults will appreciate this treasure," predicted Lawler.

Luby took a similar approach in her second book, *Yoga for Teens,* alternating photos of a multicultural feast of teens doing yoga poses with equally stunning photos of the animals who have given their names to the poses. In addition, each human subject is dressed in colors reflected in the accompanying animal photo, augmenting the visual impact of the book. As in *Children's Book of Yoga,* in *Yoga for Teens* Luby introduces poses in a range of levels of difficulty and even includes some she invented herself. Additional textual material encompasses information on the chakras, or energy points, and workouts to relieve specific ailments common in adolescence, such as headaches, nervousness, and sadness. The result is a very successful introduction to yoga for teens, according to reviewers. *School Library Journal* contributor Dawn Amsberry wrote, "Whatever their fitness level, teens who want to enjoy the benefits of yoga will be inspired by this appealing book."

Biographical and Critical Sources

PERIODICALS

Bloomsbury Review, March-April, 1999, Dixie Griffin Good, review of *Children's Book of Yoga,* p. 23.

Publishers Weekly, February 28, 2000, "Our Bodies, Ourselves," p. 81.

School Library Journal, October, 1998, Barb Lawler, review of *Children's Book of Yoga,* p. 125; May, 2000, Dawn Amsberry, review of *Yoga for Teens,* p. 186.

M

Claire Mackay

1930-

SOMETHING (BUT NOT EVERYTHING) ABOUT CLAIRE MACKAY

You are the dearest mother
That I have ever had.
I'm writing you this card
To make you very glad.

So goes my first written work, composed for Mother's Day in May 1938. Please note that, while I may be a little hazy about the number of mothers I have, I am precision itself when it comes to composing a perfect ballad quatrain. I was seven years old that year, and evidently on a roll. A month later I wrote a Father's Day poem, a rather equivocal couplet which read:

Roses are red and yellow and pink.
You are the best Dad of all, I think.

Obviously I had experienced too few dads—one—to make a comparison. These poems are still around, because my mother is the kind of mother who saves everything, a common habit among mothers, possibly hormonal in origin. My mother, who is at this writing nearing her eighty-ninth birthday and who, after a stroke, makes her home with my husband and me, has been a mainstay of my life.

Let me begin, as the King of Hearts advised the White Rabbit, at the beginning. On the first day of winter in 1930, with a wind driving the snow before it down Roncesvalles Avenue in west Toronto, I surprised my parents by arriving six weeks early. In a hurry to get going, I guess, and it seems to me I've been in a hurry ever since. I was born at home, a customary practice in those years. At the time, home was a tiny four-room flat above a pool hall. My

brother Grant had preceded me by fifteen months, and he was less than overjoyed at my arrival. A few weeks later he wrapped me up in brown paper, tied me with string, and tried to give me away to a lady down the street. She told him to take me right back home. Occasionally I wonder what my life might have been like if he'd been more persuasive. (This propensity for sibling disposal seems to run in the family: my uncle Bill tried the same trick with my aunt Phyllis.)

My parents were very young: they had married at age nineteen, in 1927. Neither had much formal education: my dad, Grant Bacchus, born of farm folk in Eden, Ontario, finished Grade Eight (or Fourth Book, as it was then called); my mom, Bernice Arland, born in White River ("the coldest spot in Ontario") and delivered by a native midwife, didn't quite finish Grade Ten at the Montreal School for Girls. Mom had led a wandering life: my grandfather worked for the Canadian Pacific railroad during her early years, and his wife and five children spent a lot of time living in boxcars and tents. She was—is—a little ashamed of this, but to me, as a kid (and even now), it seemed an ideal childhood.

Life was good in 1927. My father was a smart young fellow, an elegant dresser, with a quick mind, a quick wit, and a will to succeed. He was an omnivorous reader and a whiz at figures—later he would amaze me by glancing at a column of four-digit numbers and, after ten seconds or so, casually announcing the total. He had a good job in an office, charm to spare, and he was a marvelous dancer. My mother was pretty and clever and full of fun, a real Roaring Twenties flapper, judging by early snapshots. She had a good job, too, as a long-distance telephone operator for the Bell System, although she was forced to leave it as soon as she married. They spent much of their courtship dancing—the Charleston, the Black Bottom, the Strut, the Bunny Hop, all of which my dad later taught me—and they had enough skill (and stamina) to win trophies. Life was good.

By the time I arrived, however, life was not nearly so good. The Great Depression—the Dirty Thirties—hit Canada (and the world) in 1930, and within weeks my father had lost that good job. He was not to get another permanent full-time job until I was ten years old, after the Second World War was underway—but even that job didn't last, for reasons I will shortly recount.

We were poor, I suppose. But I didn't know we were poor. Like most children, I just lived the life I had, the life that my parents gave me, and everything seemed okay to me. I look back on those first years with great fondness. Aside from a few bad memories, I had a pretty good time. We seemed to move a lot—I lived in five places before I was five, and another five by the time I was ten. But I thought everybody did that. And I knew that sometimes we didn't have too much furniture, having left it for the landlord in lieu of rent, when we moved in a borrowed truck at midnight. I got used to a series of aunts and uncles and cousins living with us off and on, to help pay the rent. We never owned a house, we never owned a car, we never owned much of anything. But I don't remember being hungry: there was always a good supply of porridge and potatoes and peanut butter. (I still like fried bologna slices.) I don't remember being cold or raggedy: my mother was a skilled and creative seamstress, and I was perfectly content wearing clothes made from other people's clothes. And I do remember being ecstatically happy because of the one thing we did own—library cards. The library was free, and the thousand treasures it housed were mine for the taking, the savoring, the feasting, the gorging even. Who cared if we didn't eat steak or fresh raspberries? Not me. Who cared if we didn't go on trips, or have piano lessons, or spend the summer at camp, whatever that was? Not me. I had a library card—and a world full of books to read.

Reading became my passion, my escape, my obsession, my solace in times of trouble (and there were some of those). I don't think I exaggerate when I say that reading became my vocation. By the time I was eight I was reading more than twenty books a week. When I was ten I got a job in the children's department of Yorkville Library—shelving, dusting, checking books in and out, and generally minding the place during story-hour, at a wage slightly below that of a Victorian ratcatcher—and I had even more time to read. I adored books, the feel of them, the smell of them, the sound of them as one turned the pages. I vowed I would read every book in that library—and I came pretty close.

I read everything and anything: fairy tales—Andrew Lang and his rainbow of fairy tale books, a Christmas gift of the collected Grimm, with terrifying black-and-white woodcuts, all of Hans Christian Andersen; Greek myths, and the scandalous behavior of the gods and goddesses; poetry—Lear's nonsense verse, and Robert Louis Stevenson, and Walter De La Mare; animal stories—*Black Beauty,* which I read ten times and cried over each time, *Beautiful Joe,* and everything written by Canadian writers Charles G. D. Roberts and Ernest Thompson Seton, who

Claire Mackay at the age of three.

invented the realistic animal biography (I still remember Lobo and Bingo and Red Fox); all of Jack London's works, two of which, *The Iron Heel,* about the evils of capitalism, and *John Barleycorn,* about the evils of drink, had a special significance for me later on; Kipling's masterpiece *Kim, The Jungle Book, Puck of Pook's Hill,* and the rest. I devoured Charles Dickens, even *Bleak House* and *The Old Curiosity Shop,* and I burned with indignant ardor over the injustices in *Oliver Twist* and *A Christmas Carol.* Then I found Lucy Maud Montgomery and Louisa May Alcott and gobbled them up—again and again and yet again. I was, like so many girls, strongly attracted to Emily, in *Emily of New Moon,* and Jo, in *Little Women.* Here were girls, a lot like me, who wanted to write.

I also read comic books—by the yard. I once owned the first issue of *Action Comics,* in which Superman makes his debut. (Patriotism compels me to point out that the illustrator and co-creator of that first Superman was a seventeen-year-old Canadian, Joe Shuster). It came out in June of 1938, and my brother and I pooled our wealth—ten pennies from returnable pop bottles—to buy it. I was hooked immediately and went on to read Batman, who appeared a year later in *Detective Comics, Captain Marvel, Wonder Woman,* and all their kinfolk and offshoots. (Incidentally, that first Superman issue was given away to a cousin, who cut out all the pictures and pasted them on her cellar floor, a memory which still makes me groan with anguish.) I was drawn to heroes, despite the fact that most of them were male. I was, to be sure, what was termed a tomboy: I eschewed dolls and quiet "feminine" pursuits, and hung out with my brother and his friends instead. I always felt a bit of an outsider—like Anne, like Emily, like Jo.

I also loved mystery and fantasy, especially the spine-tingling sort, and fictional speculations on the distant past and the distant future. (Which might have been a kind of escape from my present.) In my early teens I raced through all the Sherlock Holmes tales, Émile Gaboriau's wonderful *Monsieur Lecoq* stories, Edgar Allan Poe, H. P. Lovecraft, who scared me out of my wits, Mary Shelley's *Franken-stein,* and Bram Stoker's *Dracula;* and I leapt with glee upon H. G. Wells, Jules Verne, and later, Jonathan Swift's *Gulliver's Travels* and Edward Bellamy's *Looking Back-ward.* A favourite poem of those years was an excerpt from Alfred Lord Tennyson's *Locksley Hall,* which read:

For I dipt into the future,
far as human eye could see, Saw the
Vision of the world,
and all the wonder that would be;

Parents, Grant and Bernice Bacchus, during the sum-mer of 1927 "when life was good," before the Great Depression.

Saw the heavens fill with commerce,
argosies of magic sails,
Pilots of the purple twilight,
dropping down with costly bales;

Heard the heavens fill with shouting,
and there rain'd a ghastly dew
From the nations' airy navies
grappling in the central blue;

Far along the world-wide whisper
of the south-wind rushing warm,
With the standards of the peoples
plunging thro' the thunder-storm;

Till the war-drum throbb'd no longer,
and the battle-flags were furl'd
In the Parliament of Man,
the Federation of the world.

Since, at the time, the planet had been plunged into the agony of World War II, I found the poem both eerily prophetic and enormously hopeful.

But I confess that my all-time favorite book as a child was one nobody has ever heard of, except for a few librarians. It was *Og, Son of Fire,* by J. Irving Crump. (I am not making this up.) I'm sure I must have read it seventeen times. (I'm sure I also dusted it seventeen times.) Og is—I'm using the present tense because, for me, Og lives—a paleolithic prepubescent boy who is the despair of his father, for when it comes to spears and clubs and stone axes, Og is all opposable thumbs. He can't do much, and what he can do, he always does wrong. He is generally scorned by his peer group, and is always picked last for games. He is a misfit, an outsider, a quiet revolutionary, a wanderer, and a wonderer, with a talent for solitude, a knack for the romantic, a love for the larger-than-life, and a capacity for revelation. He dreams of noble deeds, of valor, of glory and sacrifice, and of a place in the sun of his father's eyes. Eventually, Og is granted, courtesy of a serendipitous local lightning bolt, the gift, the transmuting power, and the terrible magic of fire. He brings that gift, with appropriate accompanying heroics, to his people, to his father.

Why did I love Og so? The answer isn't far to seek. I was Og, no matter that he and I were separated by sex, one hundred millennia of alleged civilization, and several other infinities of difference. I was Og—but not nearly so brave. (There is a family story, which I have been unable to suppress, that as a child I was frightened of grass.) So I was a kind of undercover Og, a closet Og. I dreamed Og dreams of quest and discovery, of impossible bravery, even of martyrdom when I was feeling especially dramatic or melancholy. (Later, when I had three children in less than four years, I got a chance at it.) I wanted a place for myself, and I longed, often, to make a gift to my father, to bring a light to his sad and wounded eyes. Besides, I thought it would be terrific not to wear shoes.

I also read, at an early age, some of the writings of Karl Marx and Friedrich Engels, and I memorized the *Communist Manifesto.* I knew all the words to many labor and protest songs, like the millworkers' song, *Bread and Roses,* and the working-class anthem, *The Internationale*

("Arise, ye prisoners of starvation ... "), and I sang along with Paul Robeson the national anthem of the Soviet Union ("Long live our Soviet motherland / Built by the peoples' mighty hand ... "). And now I think I had better explain some of the things you have just read.

I have said that my father lost his job at the beginning of the Depression. He never got over it. His life was deformed by that event—which meant that the lives of his wife and children were likewise deformed. My father, like most men of his generation, had been raised to believe that the husband, the father, was the provider and protector of the family. When the means to provide and protect were cruelly snatched from him, he was at once grievously hurt and profoundly bewildered. At first, of course, he was certain he'd get another job immediately. When that didn't happen, when the jobs that came to him were only of a week's duration, or a day, or an afternoon, and they ranged downwards from delivering office mail to digging ditches for the county sewers (in order to get a coupon for food, an early type of foodstamps but much more demeaning), he retreated into a cave of despair. In an attempt to make sense of the maddening, brutal reality of his ruined future, he turned to two things. One was alcohol; the other was Communism.

Neither was the answer for him. Perhaps no answer exists. But his obsessive quest necessarily shaped my childhood.

Our family underwent what we regarded as political enlightenment even before I was born. My maternal grandfather, a man of quick enthusiasms quickly discarded, had become involved with the Communist Party of Canada, then illegal, in 1928. He put up bail when Party members were arrested, concealed them from the RCMP (the famous "Mounties") and the vicious Red Squad of the Toronto police, and even painted his living-room floor bright red with a hammer and sickle in the corner to proclaim his defiant loyalty to the Soviet Union. In 1932 he went to Russia, abandoning his family, and shortly thereafter, in a gesture that broke her heart, sent my grandmother divorce papers. He married a Russian woman, whom he later also abandoned when Russia threw him out of the country. (A bridge he had built fell down.) I didn't see him again until 1954, when he popped up again in Canada, terminally ill. He asked my grandmother, by this time nearing seventy years old, to take him back. She said, "I don't think so, Austin," and shut the door in his face. An interesting scoundrel, my grandfather. But his fling with socialism, bizarre and short-lived and opportunistic as it was, infected the rest of the family, especially my father, who was frantic to find an explanation for his woeful predicament.

As a consequence I was raised in a most curious atmosphere. I was what was called a "red diaper baby," a child whose parents believed in radical socialism, in an ideology opposed to the conventional beliefs of most of the people around them, who believed in revolution, and who thought capitalism and free enterprise and organized religion were tools to enslave the common people. And I believed right along with them, well into adulthood. I am certain that my almost-reflexive sympathy for the powerless (and in most instances children are powerless), my delight in being faintly subversive, and my general anti-authority attitude arise from this childhood milieu and are reflected in every book I write. I know that "communism" became a dirty word, and in many quarters it still is, especially in the United States, but we felt—we knew!—that we were right and everybody else was wrong. In those terrible years of the Dirty Thirties, when poverty destroyed the lives of so many, we thought that if you weren't a Communist, you were either a rich and ruthless exploiter of the masses, or you were abysmally stupid, several sandwiches short of a picnic.

And—I admit it—it was kind of thrilling. At one point we had a shortwave radio in our cellar and a printing press in our attic. I knew our house was watched by government agents. I knew our name was down on a secret list of suspicious undesirables. I knew that my mother and I had to deliver our revolutionary pamphlets under cover of darkness, creeping through the sleeping streets of Toronto like spies. That part was almost fun. But other parts were not: we were outraged when our family doctor, a kind and large-hearted human being who never charged us a cent all the way through the Depression, was jailed in a concentration camp for "having Communist sympathies." We were shocked and scared when my aunt, at a workers' protest in front of our Provincial Legislature in downtown Toronto, was knocked down by a policeman's horse, and a friend of hers was trampled. We mourned when several young men, who had been in our house many times, went off to fight Franco's Fascists in Spain in 1937—and didn't come back. But these events made my faith, and it was a faith, burn even brighter. I was Og, perhaps, being a martyr for the cause, risking danger to bring a gift to the people.

Claire at age twelve with brother, Grant, 1943.

I was so completely bewitched by this belief that it later led me to choose Political Science and Economics as my major field of study at the University of Toronto. I sometimes look back with a rueful smile at this—I should have chosen English Literature, of course—but I was afire, determined to change things, to help bring about Tennyson's "Parliament of man, the Federation of the world."

The other solution my father tried—and I'm aware of the not-so-funny pun—turned out to be as flimsy a crutch as his belief in Communism. I'm sure it numbed his pain at first, and for years he regarded alcohol as his friend, as the glue that held his fragmented self together, but inevitably it became his most dangerous and most relentless enemy. Alcohol changed him into a man—a creature—he never ever wanted to be. He was a binge drinker, which meant that there were often weeks-long periods when he didn't drink at all. But they never lasted. We would gradually see a change come over him: the witty, clever, caring husband and father, who tried so hard, would become sad and silent, then irritable, and then argumentative and petty and mean, to the point where every remark was a knife in our hearts. My mother cried a lot, and so did I; my brother just left the house, returning late at night to avoid my dad. And then the drinking would begin, to go on until my poor father was so sick he had to be nursed back to health—sometimes by that same kind doctor who had been sent to prison. Often my dad disappeared, and often I hoped he wouldn't come back. More often I worried that he might be sick and hurt and hungry and alone in a filthy alley. And often he was.

I want to interject here that none of us knew anything about alcoholism in that era. We didn't know it was a disease, a particularly messy and destructive disease, a slow and painful suicide. I know my father loved us deeply, certainly more than he loved himself, and that he always tried to do his best. But once he started drinking, he simply couldn't stop until he was too sick or too broke—or there was nothing left in the house to pawn—to go on. We came to know more, much more, because in 1949, when I was eighteen and he was forty-one, a miracle happened: with the help of Alcoholics Anonymous, a fellowship that commands my deepest gratitude, my father stopped drinking. And although at first we were wary—so many promises had been broken over the years!—and we didn't dare allow ourselves to believe it could last, it did. In the last two decades of his life my dad made up for much, and became both my beloved and admired father and my wise and steadfast friend.

But that was later. By the early 1940s he couldn't hold a job. My mother had to go to work. She found a sales job at a women's wear shop selling luxury lingerie to rich ladies—probably many of the same rich ladies to whom we had delivered revolutionary pamphlets, an irony that wasn't lost on her—while working long hours at low wages. My brother and I worked, too. Both of us had part-time and summer jobs from the age of ten on. Aside from the part-time library job, which I held until entering high school, I filed insurance claims, sold shoes, books and magazine subscriptions, painted toy clowns, packed jelly powder and jam, washed dishes, floors, windows, and toilets, waited on table (many Saturdays, Sundays, and summers), sorted mail, worked a telephone switchboard (long before direct dialing), and shelled peas, all this before I turned twenty-one.

Working as a waitress at the New Windsor Hotel, Bala, Ontario, 1948.

My mother was determined, with a steely strength that belied her slim frame, that my brother and I would be the first children in the family to graduate from high school and go on to college. She had set that goal, for us and for herself, very early in our lives. We were expected to do well at school, and—surprise!—we did. School, for me, was a refuge, a safe harbor, a place of comfort and ease. I must confess I didn't start out too well, however. I was shy, almost pathologically so, and fearful. Looking back now, I'm tempted to conclude that my main motivation in school was fear of failure.

And my first failure came in kindergarten, at my first school, Adam Beck P.S. in east Toronto. At Adam Beck I was famous for three things: (1) I could not grasp the concept of recess, and once I got outside I went home; (2) I refused to admit—too shy—that I owned anything as vulgar as a bladder, which meant I spent many hours in a condition of high humidity; and (3) no doubt because of (1) and (2), it took me two years to get through kindergarten. The educational powers-that-be concluded I was not sufficiently "socially mature," whatever that might mean—sometimes I wonder if I've yet achieved that sophisticated designation—to proceed to the rarefied intellectual atmosphere of Grade One.

My second school was Huron Street P.S., right in the middle of the city, where I was famous for being the Grade One teacher's pet and for being knocked unconscious in the schoolyard (I darkly suspect the one led to the other) by a gang of Grade Eight girls, in an early example of urban swarming. My third school was Fern Avenue P.S., near my birthplace in west Toronto, where I was famous for getting more valentines than anybody else in Grade Three, fourteen of them coming from my devoted swain Dougie who called for me at 6:30 every morning; and for consorting with a known criminal, Eleanor the Eight-Year-Old Shoplifter, aka the Angel in the Christmas play, who regularly robbed Woolworth's blind. (I stole one item, a miniature calendar, and I felt so scared and guilty that I secretly took it back the following week.)

My fourth and final elementary school was the school for rich kids, Rosedale P.S. Through sheer accident, we had rented half a house on the extreme southern boundary of Rosedale's catchment area. (Had I lived across the street, I would have gone to the school for tough kids, Jesse Ketchum P.S., where I might have met a young near-blind girl named Jean Little, now a famous children's author and my dear friend.) So off I went in the spring of 1940, to be inserted into the Grade Three part of a Grade Three/Four class under Miss M., who ran her class as Captain Bligh did the *Bounty*. Miss M. was old and gnarled and terrifying, with eyes set so deeply in her head I tended to watch the floor behind her in case they squirted out the back. If you looked into them (and few dared), you looked into two tunnels, with no light at the end of them. And yet I am grateful to her: Miss M. made us memorize huge chunks of poetry, much of it beyond our ken. She was fond of Matthew Arnold and Alfred Noyes and the more lugubrious verses of Oliver Goldsmith and Francis Thompson. She often declaimed the bloodier portions of *The Highwayman* or *The Charge of the Light Brigade* with theatrical fervor, apparently finding it quite calming. I can still recite hours of Miss M.'s Golden Oldies, and often do. I find it quite calming.

I settled in nicely at Rosedale and went ahead like gangbusters, skipping Grade Four, topping the class in Grades Five and Six, leapfrogging over Grade Seven, and landing in Grade Eight when I was eleven years old. And here I must pay thankful tribute to another teacher, Mr. Newton, a tall, lanky, gentle, bespectacled man, passionate about learning. In his class we learned to share that passion, we learned to delight in learning. In his class, too, I had another failure, in math problems, and I was shocked and ashamed at my own ineptitude. Was I no longer to be safe in my safe domain? Would I no longer have a place in the world, a place to shine, the way Og finally shone? I was in despair and tears in the cloakroom when Mr. Newton found me. He will never know what he did for me that day. He is long dead, but I like to think that what I later did with my life was a kind of thank you to him. Mr. Newton, gentle as always, took my hand and made me see that the true failure lay in not trying again, and helped me find the courage to believe, just a little, in myself.In 1943 I entered Jarvis Collegiate Institute, Toronto's oldest school (founded in 1807) at the tender age of twelve, still, in many ways, a little girl and far from "socially mature." Everybody else was taller, bigger (especially in the anatomical areas that seemed to count), and talked of things I knew not of:

Claire and Jackson Frederick Mackay on their wedding day, September 12, 1952.

lipstick, brassieres, proms, and boys, boys, boys. Once again I felt like an outsider, but happily there was a whole pack of outsiders in my class. In a shockingly undemocratic and politically incorrect fashion, our IQs had been tested on Day One, and all the smart kids, of which I seemed to be one, were put into one class, a class that stayed together through the five years of secondary school. Jarvis was renowned for its academic excellence, and we were being groomed to win scholarships, to add further lustre to the school's already lustrous reputation. Most of us did. So I made friends, one in particular. Her name is Nicoletta Ellieff, now Scrimger. Nicky was poor, funny, and enormously clever, and she loved the English language as much as I, even though, as a child of immigrant Macedonian parents, she was five years old before she spoke it. We were inseparable through high school and college; she was my maid of honour when I married; I was her matron of honour when she married my husband's best friend. Nicky went on to become one of the finest editors in Canadian educational publishing. She remains a close friend today.

By Grade Eleven I was on the staff of the school magazine, *The Magnet*, and in Grade Twelve I was associate editor, writing inflammatory editorials, for which I was reprimanded by the teacher-advisor. Despite the turmoil and pain at home, I was doing well, especially in English and other languages. And once again a teacher encouraged me: in my final two years at high school, Mr. Ferguson, William Stanley Ferguson, was my English teacher, my mentor, and my friend. He was tough, uncompromising in his standards, and sometimes sarcastic, perhaps cruel. Some of my classmates loathed him: I adored him, not only because he customarily gave me the highest marks in literature and composition. His comments, in detail, on my little stories and essays were at once incisive, elegant, and so very helpful. I was given to melodrama and fond of the purple phrase, not unusual for a sixteen-year-old, and he came down hard on my excesses and pretensions. I recognized in him a loving reverence for language, and I think he saw the same quality in me. He was the first grown-up who said to me those most wonderful words: "Claire, you can be a writer." I didn't quite believe it, but I basked in the praise. At the end of Grade Twelve I won the highly-coveted English Prize. No prize since has meant as much. I felt validated, vindicated, hopeful, enlarged—a whole world seemed to open in front of me. The money was paltry (although it didn't seem so then)—a $25 gift certificate for books—but the glory was great. In my graduation year, 1948, I did what I was supposed to do: I won a scholarship, in English, Latin, German, and French, and this, coupled with a bursary and my earnings as a waitress, allowed me to enter university.

But, as I mentioned, I took the wrong course. Poli. Sci., as we called it, was tough. And women students were definitely in the minority. I managed to maintain a B average, and graduated seventh in my class (nobody graduated with first-class honours—it was that tough). I took part in a number of activities, including a disastrous and very short career as a reporter for *The Varsity*, the U of T's newspaper. The editor sent me to cover a stupefyingly boring meeting of the Student Council, and I used up two paragraphs of my article describing the weather. That was the end of my career as a journalist. In my second year I joined the U of T Peace Council. The Korean War had already begun, and "peace" was regarded as suspect-another dirty word in the lexicon of the Cold War. We set up a booth in the rotunda at University College (my home college), asking for signatures on a petition to ban the atomic bomb. We lasted only ten minutes. A group of engineers—their faculty building was directly across the way from University College—descended upon us, like wolves on a fold of sheep. They overturned our tables, scattered our petitions, and scared me half to death. My fuzzy longing for martyrdom cooled. But my suspicion of engineers was born.

It may come as a surprise, then, that I fell in love with, and later married, an engineer. His name was—is—Jackson Frederick Mackay. Our first meeting, towards the end of my and his second year, was hardly propitious. His best friend, Dan Scrimger, who had achieved an affection for my best friend, Nicky Ellieff, had brought him to the Junior Common Room, a crowded, smoky place where we gathered daily to buy coffee and skip lectures and decide the fate of the world and gossip, to meet the object of his (Dan's) adoration. Jack—he told me later—had eyes only for me. It wasn't reciprocal. As soon as I heard he was an engineer, I sniffed a mighty and scornful sniff, and walked out of the room. He remained undaunted, and in September 1952, the year of our graduation—after many skipped lectures, I confess—we were married.

Why Jack and not another? It's always something of a mystery, isn't it? I had gone out with several young men—not counting Dougie—over the years. They were an odd lot, I must say. Among them was Ted, who turned out to be a first-class stinker and stood me up one New Year's Eve; there was Glen, an embalmer; Sandy, an assistant oiler on a merchant navy ship; Bob, in charge of trimming vegetables at the local supermarket; Jerry, a magician, who habitually extracted quarters from my ears; Jim, a lifeguard with an overbite a beaver would kill for; and Al, to whom I very nearly plighted my troth before I realized that he couldn't make me laugh. Jack, on the other hand, could. Perhaps that's part of the answer.

As a chemical engineer, Jack had taken a position with a major oil company, with refineries all across Canada. In the next twenty years we changed our address ten times, an echo of my childhood. We lived first in Sarnia, Ontario, right across the St. Clair River from Port Huron, Michigan, renting a ramshackle little cottage near Lake Huron, in which we nearly froze in the winter. My grand plans to make a difference in the world, to make it a better place by a heroic act, ran smack into the reality of the recession of the early 1950s. I scattered resumes all over town, but nobody seemed to want or need a bright-eyed young female with a shiny degree in Political Science. In the first few months the only opportunity that arose was to sell cosmetics at the local Five-and-Ten for $19 a week. I was about to take it, when Polymer Corporation, a big government-owned rubber and plastics company, called. They needed an assistant in the research library, and would I be interested? Darn right I would. A library is my natural habitat. Mascara is not. Besides, they said they'd pay me $32.50 a week, the highest salary I'd ever been offered.

For two-and-a-half years I worked hard, learned much, mastered many techniques of the specialized library, and was very happy. Then I discovered I was pregnant, and I was very happy but very surprised, even though the condition had come about in the usual way. In the 1950s there was, of course, no such thing as maternity leave—in fact, I was forced to quit my job after five months. So I gave my little farewell speech ("The reason I'm leaving will soon become apparent—and so will I"), exclaimed politely and hypocritically over a gift set of dishes, and

The Mackay family in 1968 after the author went back to school: Jack, Grant, Scott, Ian, Claire.

SNAPSHOT

. . . And this was taken at the beach one day
When I was only three, or maybe four.
I remember I was busily at play
Making moats and minarets along the shore
When he called. I ran to where he stood.
He was stronger, taller than a tree,
And I climbed the ladder of his limbs till I
    could
Nestle in the place he kept for me
On one warm shoulder. Ah, in that hour
I was a queen! My lifted finger hurled
Suns, made mountains dance, made deserts
    flower!
As long as he held me, I held the world.
. . . Scared? No, I was never scared at all:
I knew my father would not let me fall.

The sonnet Mackay wrote in 1972 for what would be her father's last birthday, with the photo on which it was based.

went home to motherhood for thirteen years. Our first son, Ian, was born in August of 1955. I was enchanted, mesmerized by this tiny, perfect (of course!), infinitely fascinating being. Besides, for the first time in my life, I seemed to have done something that the entire world approved of—I'd had a baby. Figuring if one was this terrific, two or three would be spectacular, I set about to make it so. Ian was joined nineteen months later by his brother Scott, and twenty-three months after that by our third son and last child, Grant.

I was busy. Indeed, the first decade of being a full-time *materfamilias* remains something of a blur. I was transformed—or perhaps I transformed myself—into a feeding and cleaning machine, except that a machine probably wouldn't have collapsed with exhaustion every night. I loved them all fiercely, of course, and I would not have traded the experience, with all its happy surprises and hospital emergencies and headaches and drudgeries and moments of ineffable joy and pride, for anything in the world. I still feel that way. But after a while I started to get restless. I began to ask myself questions along the line of "Okay, what now?" "Is this all there is?" "Where's the door marked EXIT?" "What if I run away and start over?" I don't think I would have run away, ever—but the intermittent fantasy was both seductive and comforting.

I caught sight of an escape hatch when Grant, our youngest, was eight. We'd been transferred to Vancouver, British Columbia, and I had made a close friend of a neighbour, Mary, who was a social worker. She sensed my restlessness, my desire to reach out for something beyond home and children, and suggested I sign up for a Master's Degree in Social Work at the University of British

Columbia. I needed little urging. Perhaps I was still wanting to be Og, to make things better for people. But at age thirty-seven, after sixteen years away from the academic life, I was scared and nervous, much like that little girl who had gone to kindergarten so many years before. I was sure my brain had turned to tapioca (or, more likely, Pablum), and that all my classmates, quite aside from being fifteen years younger than I, would be brighter, smarter, and in every way superior. I knew I would have to work very hard. I did—and I loved every second. I felt totally alive again, my mind in overdrive, with all kinds of new thoughts, new connections, new insights. I aced everything. And once again a teacher proved the key, and that key opened the first door to the dream which had never died but only lay slumbering, the dream of writing.

Her name was Frances McCubbin. She, too, is long dead, but she set me on the path I had tried to flee from, to forget, to bury. I was sure that whatever small talent with the language I might once have owned had long since perished, and I was content to let it be so. (But there was still that secret longing.) She was a professor of Human Behavior, and she required of us four major essays in the course of a year. The first essay concerned itself with latency in the preadolescent, how the child from eight to twelve years of age is in a pleasant equilibrium. This notion was regarded as truth received from on high, a sacred text handed down by Sigmund Freud. I thought it was utter nonsense. I had three preadolescents in my house, and I didn't see anything latent about them at all. On the contrary, they were often so overt I feared for the survival of Western civilization, not to mention my own sanity. I wrote the essay, attacking Freud with the passion and eloquence of weary and hard-won conviction. Shortly thereafter, Miss McCubbin stopped me in the hall, and then she stopped me in my tracks: softly she asked if I would come to her office. I would. Once inside, again softly, she asked: "Have you ever thought of creative writing?" The urge to fall on her neck with gratitude was only barely resisted. After all these years of smothering the dream, the desire, after all my feelings of worthlessness—yes, it got that bad—here was a woman who believed I had some small skill. I will never forget her. I started to write poetry, which she read and criticized. I began, slowly, to write small vignettes, anecdotes, short stories; my letters to my parents grew longer, more precise, more adventurous. The rust on the long-neglected tools began to flake off.

And then we were transferred again. I had completed only one year of the two necessary for a Master's Degree, but in those unenlightened days, when the company said, "Go," we obediently asked, "Where and when?" So off we went, this time to Regina, Saskatchewan.

I was writing every day now, fiddling with sonnets and lyrics and triolets, and fooling with light verse. I once spent six months carving and polishing a sonnet—in my view the exercise has much in common with sculpture-to celebrate my parents' wedding anniversary. I knew that to spend six months on fourteen lines was faintly ridiculous, but it was such fun to be playing with words again. Hours passed in an eye-blink as I struggled to do what Jonathan Swift had advised: "Proper words in proper places make the true definition of style," still a watchword for me. I had taken also to writing sprawling narratives in verse to mark birthdays and holidays.

In Regina I landed another job. A vacancy came up in the Social Service department at Wascana Hospital, a huge rehabilitation centre two blocks from our house. Despite

Posing in black leather jacket and Snoopy scarf after first two mini-bike books were published, with school librarian and "superfriend" Annalyn Faulkner, Dovercourt School Library, Toronto, 1976.

boasting only half a social work degree, I was hired. Wascana served much of the province, the patients arriving from acute care hospitals for extensive therapy of all kinds. Our goal was to make them as independent and capable as possible, and return them to the community, preferably to their own homes. The catalogue of disabilities was long: from children with spina bifida and cerebral palsy and rheumatoid arthritis, to teenagers left comatose and crippled from motorcycle accidents, from young mothers wheelchair-bound with multiple sclerosis, to older people with brain tumours, strokes, and the rarer forms of neurological disease. For some, little could be done; for others, more; for still others, much. The job was challenging, mind-stretching, heartwarming, and heartbreaking. Knowing that a seventeen-year-old boy with advanced MS would never see his eighteenth birthday; drying the tears, since she could not dry her own, of a farm wife (and mother of three little kids) rendered quadriplegic and one-armed after a catastrophic accident—these things were hard to bear. Seeing the eyes of a seven-year-old girl, who could neither walk nor talk nor feed herself, blaze with joy as I read aloud to her from *The Velveteen Rabbit*; watching a young man of great courage, and sweating with effort and pain, take his first steps with new legs—these things were glad epiphanies.

And I wrote about them. It was part of my job; I had to interview all patients soon after admission and construct their "social histories," the better to enable the nurses and doctors and therapists to care for them. The history was supposed to be a couple of short paragraphs. My histories usually ran to two or three pages. And nobody complained! In fact, the nurses lined up to read them. For each person I wrote a little biography, as I am doing right now, a story with characters and plot, with structure and dynamics, with a trajectory of emotional meaning. I did this unconsciously, all unaware of craft—it was just that somehow I needed them to have lives that went beyond their symptoms and syndromes and handicaps. I didn't know I was practicing.

I turned forty, a watershed year for most of us. It was time to put up or shut up. Did I want to write? If the answer was yes—and it was, a resounding yes!—then I had best get at it. This resolve—which still scared the heck out of me—coincided with eleven-year-old son Grant's latest obsession. (He is prone to obsessions, as is the whole family.) Grant went mad over mini-bikes, partly, I believe, because he needed something of his own, some identity that would make him stand apart from his brothers, who had absolutely no interest in the little machines. (Also, partly, to rebel against his father, who was unflinchingly opposed to any of his sons owning one.) The stage was set for domestic confrontation. It was a beaut. And guess who finally flinched? His father, naturally. Grant, with a little help from me (I could see how important it was for Grant, so here I was again, on the side of the powerless), wore down his dad, saved up his money, and got his heart's desire.

It was only a few weeks later that he came to me and said, "I sure would like to read a book about a boy and a mini-bike."

"Fine," said I. "Go to the library. That's where they have books."

But Grant couldn't find one, not at the public library, not at the school library, not at the downtown bookstores. Again he came to me and said, "Mom, I can't find a book about a boy and a mini-bike. Will you write one for me?"

Until that moment, writing for children and young people had never once crossed my mind. When I thought about writing, I thought poetry, or elegant and sophisticated short stories, glowing like polished jewels. Or perhaps-when I allowed myself to daydream on a high level—a stunning landmark novel which captured the essence of our times and would live forever in the annals of literature. I did *not* think about writing a book about a boy and a mini-bike.

But that's what I wrote. I was determined to try something longer than a sonnet; I felt as if I didn't do it now I never would; and furthermore, the story was right there, in our house, handed to me as a gift almost: eleven-year-old boy, youngest of three brothers, wants to prove himself, fights with father, overcomes obstacles, has adventures, achieves his Holy Grail. All the elements of story were in place.

So I began. Exploiting (gently!) my husband, my sons, my sons' friends, incorporating—imaginatively, I hoped—many of the things that had already happened to Grant as he traveled the trails, I slowly devised a story about a boy and a mini-bike. I wrote—and rewrote and rewrote and rewrote. The apocryphal anecdote about the French writer Flaubert, who spent all morning putting a comma in, then all afternoon taking it out, could readily apply to me, so assiduously do I revise. One item surely needing revision was the title: as a working title I had chosen *Steve and His Trail-Bike* ("Stephen" is Grant's other given name; besides, it means "crown," and I felt that my young hero, after all that happened to him in the book, deserved one. I choose a name exceedingly carefully, and it usually reflects some quality of the character, or suggests his or her actions in the plot, or sets off, in the reader's memory, an echo which serves the story. Sometimes weeks pass before I settle on a name.) Anyway, *Steve and His Trail-Bike* could probably win the "Boring Title Prize," if there were such an award—although my friend and fellow-writer Janet Lunn once told me that the most boring title was *The History of Lint*. I think she was kidding. The title I finally picked, remember-

ing all the heroes, and the superheroes, of my childhood, was *Mini-Bike Hero*.

The book was done. It wasn't perfect—no book is, although Katherine Paterson's *The Great Gilly Hopkins* comes awfully close—but it was the best I could do at the time. (I think I've improved a little in twenty-five years.) "Here's your book, Grant," I said, handing him eighty-six pages of beautiful typing.

"That doesn't look like a book, Mom," he said. "It looks like a pile of white paper with typing all over it. Why don't you send it to the people who make books?"

"Like who (or possibly whom)?" I asked.

"Like the people who sell us books at the school," said Grant. "I think they're called Scholastic."

"Okay," I said. And I did.

It was then 1973, and we'd been living in Toronto, in the big old eleven-room three-storey house we still live in, since we'd been tranferred in the summer of 1971. My dad wasn't well when we returned from the west, and he grew steadily worse. His arteries were as tattered as old lace, and while in hospital during the Christmas holiday of 1972, his aorta, the biggest artery in the body, burst. He died at eight o'clock in the morning, New Year's Day, 1973. A couple of months later I got a letter from Scholastic, accepting my first book. I had so wanted to share that with him.

I had written him a sonnet—my old favorite form—titled "Snapshot" for his birthday the preceding April, perhaps knowing it might be his last. It's based on a photograph taken at Kew Beach in Toronto when I was quite small.

Mini-Bike Hero was published in the spring of 1974. Two astonishing things happened right away. The first astonishing thing was that the entire print run, forty-five thousand copies, sold out in four months. Forty-five thousand boys and girls across Canada had bought Grant's book! I was stunned. Scholastic was pleased. And they began to suggest I write another mini-bike adventure. "Good heavens," I said to myself. "Isn't one enough? Especially from a person who can't even ride a bicycle?" (This is true. I never owned a bike, and the only time I tried to ride one was a nightmare. Maybe I'll tell you about it some time.)

The second astonishing thing was that I got a fan letter. Me. A fan letter. Just like Michael Jordan, or Madonna, or even R. L. Stine. It was from an eleven-year-old boy named Gerald. Gerald couldn't read very well—indeed, he had never finished a book before *Mini-Bike Hero*. He couldn't spell very well either, but I loved what he wrote: "I realy like your stroy. It is very exciting and you put all the adventurs in at the rite time. Plese plese plese write another mini-bike book, and start it wheer the other one stoped."

I was so pleased and so touched by Gerald's letter that I wrote him back, saying that if I ever did write another mini-bike book, I would dedicate it to him, and send him the very first copy. Hundreds of letters began to arrive, all of them asking for another book about Steve and the mini-bike. Scholastic was pushing for it, too. Since I always try to please everybody—a serious character flaw—I eventually put together *Mini-Bike Racer*, and it was published in 1976. The dedication reads: "To Gerald Ransom, who asked me to write this book." And I sent him the very first copy.

The author's three sons, Ian, Scott, and Grant, at Scott's wedding in 1988.

In *Racer* I had introduced a girl named Julie Brennan, who shared Steve's love of mini-bikes. As soon as it came out, I was swamped with letters from girls, all of them begging for yet a third mini-bike adventure, this time starring Julie. At first I thought I couldn't write a story with a girl as the central character—after all, I had three sons and no daughters-but then I remembered that, once upon a time, in the distant past, I had been a girl. Perhaps I could use my own memories of being twelve or thirteen—and they were certainly vivid enough—to make my girl character believable. So, in *Mini-Bike Rescue*, Julie, a tomboy who longs for adventure and freedom and heroic deeds, is sent away for the summer to work as a waitress at her aunt's summer resort. And I certainly knew all about that. Julie is brave, daring, athletic, and not at all shy—she is the kind of girl I wish I had been, rather than the girl I was. (This is one of the many agreeable aspects of writing: you can rewrite your own life and make it turn out better!)

Rescue wasn't published until 1982, because I was busy writing two other books. I was also just plain busy: I had landed yet another job shortly after we moved to Toronto, as research librarian at a trade union, the United Steelworkers. I had gone to university with the Director of Research, which helped, and I knew my way around a library. And at long last, I could actually use some of the things I'd learned in Political Science and Economics, if I could only remember what they were. For six years, until 1978, when I left to write full-time, I toiled happily for "Steel", establishing filing and cataloguing systems, putting out a semimonthly Library Newsletter, with abstracts of pertinent articles, and writing a column for *Steel Labour*, the union's monthly newspaper. The column was entitled "Women's Words," and in it I tried to raise the feminist consciousness of hard-hatted (and often hard-headed) steelworkers. I used humor to get the message across—I didn't rant or rave or lecture—and the column became a favorite among the most macho of men. It was eminently satisfying, and an excellent way to exercise my writing muscles. I learned a lot.

In late 1975 I began a book about a boy who runs away from home to find his father. (Fathers—and the absence of fathers—loom large in most of my novels, which will come as no surprise.) It was a different sort of book for me: for one thing it is much more complicated than the little mini-bike adventures, with their straight-ahead plots and few major characters. I wanted to try something else, something broader and deeper, just to see if I could do it. But perhaps more importantly, I wanted to say something about alcoholism. I wanted somehow to get across that alcoholics, no matter that the world sees them as weak rejects and throwaways, are still fully human and capable of deep emotion, even heroism. *Exit Barney McGee,* born after a long and difficult labor in 1979, was at once an exploration of my feelings about my dad and a quest to find and understand the father I had so often missed growing up. It had several viewpoints (which you're not supposed to have in children's books, but I think that's an insult to children), two plots which criss-cross and weave together at the end, and about twenty characters, including a pet mouse. The mouse was based on a real mouse, owned by our second son, Scott. It was a lovely little creature, a

All the grandchildren (from left) 1995: Katie, Jessica, Susannah, Colin, and Ryder.

Japanese waltzing mouse, which unfortunately died at the bottom of my purse while we were flying to Vancouver. (I am not making this up, either.) So I gave it immortal life, which is another neat thing a writer can do. *Barney* has never sold as well as the mini-bike books—about fifty thousand copies compared to half a million for the bike series—but I get wonderful, moving, sad, and sometimes scary letters about it all the time. (All of my books are still in print. Children's writers are lucky that way: there are new readers being born every minute!)

One Proud Summer came next, in 1981. And once again I mined my childhood experiences. It's a story based on a real event in Canadian history, a strike at a textile mill in a little town in Quebec, during the summer of 1946. The workers, mostly children as young as twelve and their mothers, go out on strike to get a union, and to protest against the terrible conditions in the mill—boring, back-breaking toil, for very little money, in 95-degree temperatures, with nasty bosses fond of slaps and sexual harassment. During the hundred days of the strike, the kids face sub-machine guns, rifles, tear gas, and jail. But they win. There is a young girl named Lucie ("little light"), who could just as easily be named "Claire" (or, for that matter, "Og"); there is a song entitled *Bread and Roses*, too. There is even porridge and bologna slices. And there is a funeral for Lucie's father, which is very like the funeral for mine. I wondered, as I wrote it (with the superb research of my co-author, Marsha Hewitt), whether modern children would even read it. They did. They do. And, to our delighted astonishment, the book won a prize, the Ruth Schwartz Award, the only prize in Canada which is decided by a jury of children.

In 1984 a more contemporary novel, *The Minerva Program,* was published. It's a mystery story about computers. I have always loved mysteries, ever since my *Sherlock Holmes* days. I had been watching—something that writers do almost instinctively—our eldest son Ian fall under the spell of computers. (The book is dedicated to him, and he helped me a lot in the writing.) He was totally enslaved, and spent all his time building computers, staring at them, or playing with them. Often he forgot to eat, sleep, shower, or utter full sentences in a recognizable human tongue. It was a fascinating phenomenon, and, after a quick

Claire Mackay, standing next to author and friend Jean Little and her guide dog Ritz, Arctic expedition, Golf Tournament for Literacy, 1995.

sex-change, I knew I had my main character, Minerva Wright. During the writing, however, bits and pieces of my own life crept into the story: Minerva has a funny, clever, dark-haired immigrant friend named Sophie, much like my friend Nicky. Minerva is a klutz at gym, and is always getting into trouble with the gym teacher, as I did. (I finally got revenge, by putting my gym teacher into this book—another neat thing a writer can do.) On page twenty-seven, Minerva looks at a photograph, taken when she was little, of her father and herself at the beach. She is "nestled in the place he kept for her on one warm shoulder." Even the young woman who became Ian's wife is in the book, under the name "Barbara Fairfax," which is a little joke. When I first met my daughter-in-law, whose real name is Eden, she was in her punk rocker stage (as was Ian, who had a punk band for a couple of years), and her hair was all pink and silver spikes. "Barbara" means "strange, wild, barbaric", and "Fairfax" means "beautiful hair."

Every name in *The Minerva Program* is really a secret code to the character who bears it, which was great fun to do. "Minerva" is the Roman goddess of wisdom (also the matron goddess of Jarvis Collegiate, my high school) and the message in the book, if there is one, is that we need wisdom in this new world of high technology. The book has "traveled well," in publishing terms: it has so far been translated into French, Norwegian, Danish, and Japanese, and is in school editions in England, Canada, and United States. (And it very nearly won me the Ruth Schwartz Award again, coming in second to my friend Jean Little's *Mama's Going to Buy You a Mockingbird.* Jean talks about

this, and about how we met and became friends, in her second volume of memoirs, *Stars Come Out Within.*)

In the last ten years I have tried my hand at journalism again, writing a monthly column about my children and grandchildren, "Out of My Mind," for a parents' newspaper; and at nonfiction, mostly because publishers have asked me. *Pay Cheques and Picket Lines: All about Unions in Canada* was released in the fall of 1987, right in the middle of a teachers' strike. Perfect timing—every school in Toronto bought multiple copies! The book was a direct result of the success of *One Proud Summer,* and, of course, my longtime interest in, and experience of, the subject. Besides, there was nothing on the labor movement available—or readable!—for young people. Sales and reviews were good, and I guess I proved I could write nonfiction, because I was almost immediately asked to write a history of my hometown. *The Toronto Story* appeared in 1990, in time to celebrate the two-hundredth anniversary of Toronto as a settled community, and the fifteenth anniversary of its publisher, Annick Books. Aimed at younger readers, it seems to appeal greatly to adults, too. It's a big, beautiful book, printed on glossy paper, with full color paintings by Johnny Wales (who also illustrated one of Jean's picture books, *Gruntle Piggle Takes Off*). The writing isn't too bad, either.

My latest books are both about baseball, a game I—and so many writers—adore. And why not? Baseball is full of all the qualities I have loved ever since I knew what a book was: wonderful stories, eccentric characters, and colorful, inventive language. I agree with Babe Ruth, who once said, "Baseball is the only real game in the world."

With Jean Little at her house in the country, signing book copies at the launch of Bats about Baseball, *1995.*

My enthusiasm grew to the point of fanaticism, naturally, when the Toronto Blue Jays won the World Series in 1992 and 1993. A year later, *Touching All the Bases* was in the bookstores. Like *The Toronto Story* before it, the book has attracted readers of all ages. (And why not? It's full of wonderful stories, eccentric characters, and colorful, inventive language!) In the following year, 1995, it was joined by my first picture book, entitled *Bats about Baseball.* It's not all mine—Jean Little is also to blame. Here is how it came about. Jean, a big baseball fan herself, and I were on our way to a conference in New Hampshire (we lead a discussion group at the Summer Institute of Children's Literature New England every year) when we stopped briefly in Dartmouth where she was to do an autographing at a local bookstore. Katherine Paterson had told us earlier that it was a great place, and that bookbuyers had lined up around the block when she'd been there a few months earlier. Well, we got there, Jean settled herself behind a table piled high with her many books, and we waited. And we waited and waited and waited. Nobody—NOBODY!— bought a book. Except, finally, me, even though I already owned a signed copy. Jean grew irritable; her welcoming smile slipped off her face; and she said—or rather growled: "I can't stand this! Let's do something!"

"Okay," I said, "What?"

"Let's write a picture book," she answered.

"What about?"

"Baseball!" said Jean.

And so we did. I had told Jean about babysitting my first grandson, Ryder (Ian's and Eden's son), about how, if a baseball game were on television, I paid no attention to him. I had told her, too, about the lively, zany, language in the game. From these elements, we devised, mostly by fax machine, the puns and wordplay that make up the text. We

had a lot of fun. And at this writing we're still having fun: we're collaborating on another book, an alphabet book in verse, using words with surprising and fascinating origins and histories. For example, "C is for cantaloupe," which gets its name from "Cantalupo," a garden north of Rome belonging to the Popes in the thirteenth century. It was here that the melon was first grown in the west, and where, in the distance, you could hear wolves howling. "Cantalupo" means "singing wolf." Isn't that a splendid story?

I knew Jean's work before I actually knew her as a person. And I confess I was in awe of her, even a little intimidated. We got to be friends through CANSCAIP, the Canadian Society of Children's Authors, Illustrators, and Performers, which is similar, though broader in scope, to the Society of Children's Book Writers; in fact Jean and I, together with nine others, were founding members of the organization in 1977. This was another thing that kept me busy: I was treasurer, secretary, president, newsletter editor, and chair of various committees over the years. (Now I'm so old I don't have to do anything: people seem to view me as a sort of village elder, or wise woman of the tribe. I see no reason to tell them otherwise.) CANSCAIP has grown from the original nine to its current roster of four hundred professionals and nine hundred associates, in every province and territory of Canada. My mother helped, by the way: she was CANSCAIP's office secretary until she had the stroke in 1993, and she is a beloved and respected figure in the Canadian children's literature community.

My husband and sons have been with me all the way. Without their steadfast, loving support—including taking over the household when I had a deadline to meet or a plane to catch—there would never have been ten books with my name on them. Ian is, as you might guess, a computer expert, but he's also a busy father of three (Ryder and the six-year-old twins, Susannah and Katie), and a talented watercolor painter. Scott has given us two grandchildren, Colin and Jessica, and enjoyed a short but successful career as a classical flutist before turning to

Claire Mackay (seated at right), signing copies of Too Young to Fight *at Canada National Institute for the Blind Awards Night in Casa Loma, Toronto, 1999.*

The author (left) at "Word on the Street" Literary Festival in Halifax, Nova Scotia, 1999. (The sweatshirt reads "So many books, so little time."

writing—which gladdens his mother's heart. After publishing a war novel and dozens of short stories, he's looking forward to his first science fiction novel from Tor Books very soon. And what about the mini-bike kid who started it all? Grant is a musician and composer of electronic music, owns a small record company, and so far has created six albums. Jack is no longer an engineer. He took early retirement to do full-time what he always wanted to do—play clarinet and saxophone in a jazz band. (And he still makes me laugh: as a matter of fact, my latest book is dedicated to him. Its title is *Laughs: Funny Stories Selected by Claire Mackay,* now at a bookstore near you.)

My life as a writer for young people, although it didn't begin until I was forty-one years old, has brought me great riches. Not in dollars, I hasten to add, but in friendship, in travel, in that invigorating sense of renewed hope that comes with talking to kids. I know, and count as friends, most of the children's writers in Canada, from Joyce Barkhouse and Budge Wilson in Nova Scotia to Sarah Ellis and Kit Pearson in British Columbia. I have visited a thousand schools and libraries and talked to tens of thousands of children, all across the country. I've even been to a little village three hundred miles from the North Pole, where I came last in a dog-sled race, played golf on the frozen Arctic Ocean, told stories to bright-faced and

beautiful Inuit children, and watched the sun come up at two o'clock in the morning. I'm not nearly as shy as I once was—and I'm not afraid of grass any more.

Last week I got another fan letter to add to the thousands in my filing cabinet. It's from Ricky. He writes:

"Dear Claire,

I am writing to you because I really like your books. I don't know how many authors can word these kind of books as well as you can. I like how the story's plot fits in so perfect. Thank you for giving our brains some imagination and I hope you're having a wonderful life."

Thank you, Ricky. I am. I am.

Writings

FOR YOUNG READERS

Mini-Bike Hero, Scholastic (New York, NY), 1974, revised edition, 1991.

Mini-Bike Racer, Scholastic (New York, NY), 1976, revised edition, 1991.

Exit Barney McGee, Scholastic (New York, NY), 1979, revised edition, 1992.

(With Marsha Hewitt) *One Proud Summer* (historical novel), Women's Educational Press, 1981.

Mini-Bike Rescue, Scholastic (New York, NY), 1982, revised edition, 1991.

The Minerva Program, James Lorimer, 1984, Houghton (Boston, MA), 1992.

Pay Cheques and Picket Lines: All about Unions in Canada, Kids Can Press, 1987, revised edition, 1988.

The Toronto Story, Annick Press, 1990.

Touching All the Bases: Baseball for Kids of All Ages, illustrated by Bill Slavin, Boardwalk Books/Scholastic (New York, NY), 1994.

(With Jean Little) *Bats about Baseball,* illustrated by Kim LaFave, Viking (New York, NY), 1994.

Laughs: Funny Stories Selected by Claire Mackay, Tundra Books, 1997.

(Contributor) *Too Young to Fight: Memories of Our Youth During World War Two,* compiled by Priscilla Galloway, Stoddart Kids (Toronto, Canada), 1999.

Horrible Canadian Histories: First Folks to Vile Voyageurs, Scholastic (Markham, Canada), 2001.

OTHER

Contributor to *Canadian Writers' Guide,* and *Writers on Writing.* Contributor of articles, speeches, short stories, poetry, and book reviews to periodicals, including *Canadian children's Literature, Canadian Women's Studies, Chatelaine, Writers' Quarterly, Quill and Quire, Toronto Star,* and *Globe and Mail* (Toronto, Canada).

MATTHEWS, Ellen
See BACHE, Ellyn

*   *   *

McKELVY, Charles 1950-

Personal

Born May 7, 1950. *Education:* Illinois State University, B.S. (English and journalism), 1972.

Addresses

Home—P.O. Box 116, 13430 Prairie Rd., Harbert, MI 49115. *E-mail*—mckcom@compuserve.com.

Career

Author and playwright. City News Bureau of Chicago, reporter, rewriter, broadcast editor, and assistant city editor, 1976-77; *Chicago Tribune,* reporter and feature writer, 1977-80; Daniel J. Edelman Public Relations, account executive, 1980-82; American Hospital Supply Corporation, writer, 1982-84; McKelvy Communications, partner and cofounder, 1984—; Dunery Press, Harbert, MI, publisher and cofounder, 1988—. Formerly taught creative writing at Purdue University/North Central, and has given lectures on writing at schools throughout southwest Michigan.

Awards, Honors

Bob's Wedding, a one-act comedy, won the Playfest 1995 competition, Kalamazoo, MI.

Writings

Chicagoland (includes "Rauch and Spiegel," "Stormin' Norman," "Viking Funeral," and "Commuting Distance"), Dunery Press (Harbert, MI), 1988.

Holy Orders: An Unholy Novel, Dunery Press (Harbert, MI), 1989.

Odin the Homeless and Other Stories, Dunery Press (Harbert, MI), 1990.

James II, Dunery Press (Harbert, MI), 1991.

Billy, and Other Stories, Dunery Press (Harbert, MI), 1992.

Clarke Street, or, The Further Adventures of Jimmy Clarke as Contained in Two Contiguous Novels (includes "The Mayor of Skid Row," "The Age of Peace," and "What I Did During America's War against Vietnam"), Dunery Press (Harbert, MI), 1993.

No Dice (play), produced at Lakeside Studio (Lakeside, MI), 1993.

Kids in the Woods (picture book), illustrated by Mike Sova, Dunery Press (Harbert, MI), 1993.

Plays with Fire: A Collection of One-Act Plays, Dunery Press (Harbert, MI), 1994.

Clarke Theatre (Act 1) and Other Works: A Novel, Play, and Two Short Stories, Dunery Press (Harbert, MI), 1995.

Bob's Wedding (one-act comedy), 1995.

Tales from the Other Side: A Collection of Two Articles and Four Novellas (includes "On Michigan Time," "FITS and STARTS," "Cottage Industry," "Urban Favor," "Scouts in Action," and "Om Town"), Dunery Press (Harbert, MI), 1996.

Clarke Theatre, Act II and Other Works, Dunery Press (Harbert, MI), 1997.

Baby Pictures and Other Works, Dunery Press (Harbert, MI), 1999.

The Iceman's Path, A Ghostly Novel, Dunery Press (Harbert, MI), 1999.

Feature articles, essays, and short stories have appeared in publications such as *Beacher, Herald-Palladium, Catholic Digest, New Buffalo Times, Crain's Chicago Business, Tribune Magazine* (Chicago, IL), *Travel & Leisure, North Shore Magazine, Michigan Runner, Daily Southtown, On-the-Town, Queen Magazine, Family Digest, Alive!, Catholic Yearbook, Silent Sports,* and *Connector.*

Charles McKelvy

*   *   *

Milton Meltzer

1915-

I was born on May 8, 1915, in Worcester, Massachusetts. Woodrow Wilson was serving his first term as President. The Woolworth Building, the tallest in the world at that time, had just gone up and Grand Central Terminal had recently opened. Henry Ford had started the first assembly line to produce his Tin Lizzies. The first transcontinental telephone call was made that year by the same two men who had made the original phone connection back in 1876. Then they had been in the next room to each other. Now one was in New York and the other in San Francisco.

The day before my birth, a German submarine had sunk the steamship *Lusitania,* drowning many Americans. The anger roused by those deaths helped push America into the first World War. And from that time to now, I've lived through four major American wars and a lot of minor ones.

I'm sure war was one of the reasons I was born in America rather than in Europe. Poverty and discrimination were the other reasons. My parents both came from Austro-Hungary. They were among the four million Jews who left Eastern Europe between 1880 and 1924. Over three million of them came to the United States.

Tens of thousands of Jews were killed in the pogroms of that era. Millions of others were victims of a "cold" pogrom. By that I mean the growing body of restrictive laws directed against the Jews. In Czarist Russia ninety percent of the Jews were penned-up in a huge ghetto called the Pale of Settlement. They were humiliated and hounded by hundreds of restrictions. A terrible burden for them was the military draft for a term of twenty-five years or more.

Quotas barred all but a few Russian Jews from the schools and universities. Jews had little choice not only about where to live but how they could make a living. The vast majority starved in the villages or in the city slums.

My mother and father were raised just across the Russian border, in the Austro-Hungarian provinces of Galicia and Bukovina. There the Jews were not quite as badly off. They too knew poverty, although their political and civil disabilities were not so harsh. Samuel Richter, my grandfather on my mother's side, decided America was the place to raise his children, not Galicia. (Galicia had been a part of Poland until that kingdom vanished, its pieces taken over by three other countries. Galicia in 1772 became part of Austria.) So he got up from the village of Skoryk and left. Imagine the courage it took for a young father to make

that decision. To quit the place you grew up in, to leave your wife and children behind, to cross strange land for a distant seaport, then to take steerage passage across the frightening Atlantic and, at the other end of a harsh voyage, drop like some anonymous atom into the vast chaos of New York. Where would you find a place to sleep? What could you do to make a living? How would you make yourself understood in a language you didn't know?

It was 1895 when my grandfather came to New York. He went back to Skoryk in 1897. I don't know why. Lonely? Unable to earn and save enough in New York to bring the others over? Two years later he tried again. And the next year, 1900, his daughter Mary, my mother, followed him. She was fourteen then, the oldest of her many sisters and brothers, a capable girl with enormous energy and will. Together she and my grandfather in 1905 managed to bring over her mother Rachel and the rest of the big family.

Milton Meltzer

My father, Benjamin Meltzer, born in 1879, came from a farm family in the village of Havrilesht in the Austro-Hungarian province of Bukovina. The Jews of Bukovina—the land of the beech trees—had settled there long ago, the first of them probably arriving together with the legions of Imperial Rome. The family name was originally spelled "Melzer"; when or why the "t" was added I don't know. The family kept an inn for some time but then gave it up to farm a small number of acres. They lived in a two-room house, with a cellar and attic, and a barn for the livestock. The house was wooden, with a straw roof. They lived on what they raised, and on the sale of cattle and poultry. My father, I learned from his sister many years later, was an expert farmhand and so strong he could lift a hundred-kilo load of grain as though it were a feather. Their village held about twenty Jewish families and some four hundred Ukrainian peasants. The two groups lived much the same lives, except for religious differences. Anti-Semitism lay underneath, but was restrained somewhat under the Austrian rule. My father's education was limited to the compulsory public elementary school, where everything was taught in Ukrainian, the local tongue.

My father was the eldest of five brothers and two sisters. But the first to emigrate was his brother Max. He left for America to avoid military service. Then, at eighteen, my father followed, reaching New York in 1897. Later his brother Joseph and Vitya, one of his sisters, came too. But his mother Leah and father Michael did not come. Probably because my grandmother was very pious and feared an America where many Jews lost their religious faith. Later, when she was ready to go, it was too late. Restrictive immigration quotas made it impossible. My grandfather Michael, at fifty-three, was killed by Russian soldiers when they invaded the region in the first World War. His death came in 1915, the year of my birth. Leah died in Bukovina in 1947, at the age of ninety-four. After he left home my father never saw them again.

Mary and Ben met in New York. She worked in the garment industry, he in a bedspring factory. I think he was a boarder in my grandparents' flat in the Bronx. They married and had their first child, my brother Allan, in 1911. Then they heard that a better living might be made in Worcester. A cousin living in Boston told them that window-cleaners—a trade that required almost no training—were in short supply there. So my family moved to Worcester. With them came my uncle Joe (my father's brother) and my aunt Gussie (my mother's sister). The two families settled on the east side of town—the immigrant and working-class district—and Ben and Joe began cleaning windows. It was a business partnership with no workers but themselves. For some reason I never could determine, the two brothers fell out, ended their partnership, and stopped speaking. Their wives maintained their sisterly closeness, and their children too (three sons on our side and three on theirs) remained friendly.

My father made a modest living, though the manual labor was harsh and unrewarding in any other way. He washed the windows of factories, stores, restaurants, offices, and homes. His day usually began around two in the morning, and often did not end until late afternoon. He rose early to go downtown to the city center where he cleaned windows before the places opened up for business. Afternoons he went to private homes on the West Side,

Parents, Benjamin and Mary Meltzer.

where the well-to-do could afford to have their windows done. No matter how cold or raw the weather my father was on the job, dipping his hands all day long in icy water. I remember how rough and blackened his hands were, ridged and cracked by that brutal exposure and by the many glass cuts he suffered.

My mother ran the household—cooking, baking, cleaning, washing, sewing, shopping, worrying. She was a super-organized woman. Everything in its place, neat and clean; everything done to a plan and always on time. Her meals were always tasty and nourishing, and she often made the clothes her children wore, as well as her own. I loved to sport her handsome sweaters and mackinaws.

The three-decker house I was born in was at 2 Chapin Street, one block long, atop a steep hill. Right across the street was the grammar school I'd go to, Union Hill School. And taking up many acres on the hill was Worcester Academy, an old prep school drawing upper-class boys from all across the country. My father cleaned its windows. The place seemed so patrician to me that I hardly dared venture through the gates. The students lived in a remote dreamworld I identified with the Frank Merriwell stories I used to devour.

When I was about three we moved to the foot of Union Hill, to 52 Vale Street, another three-decker. This time we had the top floor, with a piazza, as we called it, out front where you could read or nap or sun yourself. It's the time of my youth I remember best. I didn't leave there until I went off to college in 1932.

Our neighborhood held all the ingredients of the mythical melting pot. There were Italians, Poles, Swedes, Lithuanians, Irish, Armenians, and Jews like us from Eastern Europe. Many of the parents were recent immigrants. The kids were almost all first-generation, born in America. We played on the streets together; less often we entered one another's homes; and rarely if ever did we intermarry.

My younger brother, Marshall, was born when I was five. That was the year I began climbing the steep slope to go to Union Hill school. It was a three-story reddish stone building, and looked as though it had squatted there forever. My brother Allan, going on nine then, took me the first day, and long after enjoyed telling how I cried piteously when he left me with my teacher. The crying must have stopped quickly, for I took to school as though born to learn. I liked everything about it—learning to read, to write, to figure, to find out where Worcester sat on the map of the world, to play the part of Chief Massasoit when he greeted the first white settlers.

There were few teachers I didn't like. All of them were women. Many of them came from the best women's colleges in New England. None of them were married. (I don't think it was allowed then.) The principal was a plump majestic woman named Miss Draper; we thought it hugely funny to refer to her secretly as "Old Dropperdrawers."

After school we played games on the street—Prisoner's Base, Ringelevio, King of the Mountain. In the long Massachusetts winters we took out our Flexible Flyers to coast down Union Hill, belly-whopping alone or two sitting up. The street would be closed to traffic to protect us. But once in a while there was delicious danger. I remember a truck suddenly appearing out of a side street and my sled zipping under it and on down to the end where I offered myself to the other kids as a hero. (Back then, by the way, horses still drew the wagons that delivered ice and milk and coal.)

Just back of Vale Street was a vast open area called Cheney's Field. It was a bit marshy, and in the winter if it rained and then a freeze set in, the whole field was sheeted ice. Glorious for skating. In good weather we played football or baseball there. I was feeble at either sport. My game turned out to be tennis. I learned it on the dirt courts of Vernon Hill playground. None of us had money for lessons. We learned by playing, and picked up bad habits that persisted for a long time. Though I find I can overcome some of them even now, at this age, when I still play regularly.

Summers some of us would hitch rides to Lake Quinsigamond. It was several miles long and magnificently straight for the intercollegiate crew races and the Olympic sculling trials we loved to watch. The city set aside Lake Park for a public beach and playground. We swam out to the raft and spent hours throwing one another off and jumping in on top.

After elementary school I went to the Grafton Street Junior High, brand new then. I was twelve when I began junior high. It was 1927, the year Charles Lindbergh flew the Atlantic solo, in his little one-engine plane, *The Spirit of St. Louis.* I still remember the wild excitement when we

heard he had made it. Airplanes were so rare then that whenever a plane droned overhead we'd run into the street and scream "Aeroplane! Aeroplane!", pointing to it in the sky. Lindy was our national hero overnight. He rose even higher in public worship than Babe Ruth or Jack Dempsey.

Grafton Junior High was a sprawling brick building with so many rooms and corridors it intimidated me after the coziness of Union Hill. But here I met boys and girls from other neighborhoods and discovered I could fall in love with almost any girl. In grade school I was mad for a girl named Gertrude and used to follow her home, at a safe distance, and wait patiently outside for hours in the hope of glimpsing her again. By the time I was ten we were going to Saturday afternoon parties in the girls' homes, chiefly to play kissing games. At junior high I was less shy, and developed crushes, first on a Polish girl, then an Italian girl, a Swedish girl, and a Russian girl. I felt like the ambassador to all nations.

We learned what was going on in the world from the newspapers and the radio. The radio at first was a tiny crystal set. I'd poke the wiry whisker around to touch the crystal at whatever point it would produce words or music. Later we got a Silver-Marshall radio, built into a glossy wood cabinet. It was almost the sole entertainment my father had. He loved the comedians—Jack Benny, Lou Holtz, Ed Wynn—and never missed their weekly shows. I

Milton (left) with his brother, Allan.

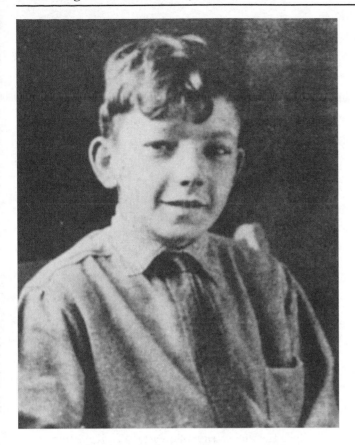

Milton in grammar school, early 1920s.

can't forget the hearty laughter they brought from a man who rarely talked. I don't recall having a single conversation with him. He was gone most of the day and when he was at home, he ate, read the paper, listened to the radio, and went to bed early so that he could get up in the middle of the night to start work again.

Once in a while my Uncle Joe, who had a car (we didn't), took us with his family to swim, or for a picnic somewhere. My father never came along. Because he didn't like such excursions? Or because he wouldn't accept anything from the brother he didn't speak to? Once my Uncle Joe drove us to New York. It took endless hours because the Boston Post Road was so primitive and tires blew out each way. In my grandparents' crowded Bronx flat we kids slept on the floor, explored the neighborhood, and got to know the many aunts and uncles we rarely saw. My Uncle Harry took me to Yankee Stadium to see a big league game, and put me in a box seat right behind the Yankee dugout. I don't remember the game at all; I do recall that Walter Winchell, the gossip columnist everyone listened to on the radio or read in the papers, sat near us. I couldn't wait to get back to Worcester to tell my gang.

It was around this time that I began to work. We three sons were all expected to pitch in and help. I had a newspaper route for a while, and signed up enough new customers to win a beautiful red scooter. A little later, I got a job in a wholesale grocery. After school and on Saturdays I worked in the warehouse, moving packing cases and cartons around with a hand truck. It was hard and dull work, with no one to talk to. The pay was fifteen cents an

hour. I gave the pay envelope to my mother each week, and she let me have a bit of it for spending money.

A much better job was one I had in summertime. I helped deliver milk on a neighborhood route. I got up hours before dawn, dressed and slipped downstairs to the street where the driver waited for me. When he stopped the truck I'd balance on the tailboard, lean into the truck, grab a metal rack, fill it with bottles and jump down, taking the customers on one side of the street while he'd take the other side. One bottle on the first floor for the widow Polasewicz, up the stairs and five bottles for the big Murphy family, another flight for two milks and the cream that Mrs. Gould had to have. Then clattering down the steps, picking up the empties on the way, back into the truck, stow the empties on one side, and load another rack for the next three-decker.

Here and there we'd stop at grocery stores to drop off cases of milk in their doorways. Best part of the night was around 4:00 A.M., when we'd both feel hungry and we'd swipe a fresh-baked loaf from the basket the bakery truck would leave at the grocery, and tear off big mouthfuls, washing down the delicious crusts of warm bread with swigs of cold milk.

With the small change I was allowed to keep, I used to buy the nickel or dime paperbacks of that day—Nick Carter, Frank Merriwell, Horatio Alger, Deadwood Dick. If you managed to acquire a modest stock, you could barter them for other titles your friends owned. I read a marvelous amount of trash and loved it. Then there was the more sober stuff you ran across by chance. One neighbor had an encyclopedia I would browse through when my parents dragged me along on visits to their friends. Another had a stout medical book with illustrations of the human anatomy. These I studied with great care, astonished, and disturbed too, at the differences between male and female. My father bought on Sundays a newspaper with a fat rotogravure supplement. Its illustrated features were a window onto a world remote from Vale Street and Union Hill. Its vivid stories of the opening of King Tut's tomb or the flight of Admiral Byrd over the North Pole enriched the news that trickled in over our crystal set.

But the first reading I can remember enjoying was "Gasoline Alley," a comic strip that began appearing in our local paper when I must have just learned to read. The newspaper was the only thing to read in our house. My folks had no time or money for books. They spoke immigrant English which improved with time. Somehow they never turned on to books, although they delighted to see their children take up reading.

Then I found out about the public library, a jumble of old red brick downtown. Saturdays became a double delight. I began them at the library, yanking books off shelves at random, sampling everything. I lugged them long blocks down to the movie theater we called The Dump, where I'd see the latest Charlie Chaplin, Tarzan, and Pearl White while I ate a hot dog and gulped down chocolate milk. And home at last to hole up in the bedroom and read myself into a daze.

What I liked most were adventure stories that took me out of my skin. And biographies. I was always trying on a new hero for size—explorer, reporter, detective. Reading had much to do with shaping my picture of the world as I grew up. Perhaps as much as the real world itself. Thoreau says in *Walden,* "How many a man has dated a new era in his life from the reading of a book!" I remember some books, read in youth, which gave me the sense of awakening Thoreau speaks of. There was *Leaves of Grass, Spoon River Anthology* and the short stories of Sherwood Anderson, *Of Human Bondage, The Way of All Flesh, An American Tragedy,* Sandburg's *Lincoln,* the autobiographies of Clarence Darrow and Lincoln Steffens. I stumbled across them or someone told me to try them. I spent no time analyzing them. It was enough that they spoke directly to me. Here were words that I could use to shape my own experience.

I think now I got more out of my independent reading than out of my studies in school. When I look back at the schools I went to, they seem like some kind of mildly totalitarian society. Benevolent, yes, but nonetheless lacking in all democracy. The principal ordered the teachers around and they ordered the pupils around. The only responsibility we were given was to come to class, to come on time, and to do our assignments. Almost no one back then protested. With exceptions—my brother Allan among them. He couldn't stand the discipline of school and was expelled from two or three of them. (At fifteen he ran away from home, but returned a year later.) The rest of us expected to be treated as obedient children, and it is no wonder that we were.

I have another major gripe against the schools of my day. They were hell-bent on Americanizing us. A great many of the students were firstgeneration Americans like me. Yet implicit in the way we were taught was the belief that we should drop whatever made us different, forget where our parents came from, what they brought with them, their own feelings and experience, their own beliefs and values. Our job was to become one hundred percent Americans. That was the only way to make it here, we understood. So while I diligently studied the history of ancient Greece and Rome (and enjoyed it!), I learned nothing about the Eastern Europe where my roots lay. I identified far more with England; that was the literature and the history we studied. Anglo-Saxon culture was everything; where we came from was nothing.

My parents fell in readily with this. Allowed only a few years of schooling in the old country, they were in a grand rush to become Americans. They did not want to be ridiculed as greenhorns, and since Yiddish was the badge of foreignness, they spoke so little of it at home that I learned scarcely a word of it. Nor did they tell me anything about their own early lives. Perhaps because they wanted to forget the world they had left behind. Or because they knew I had no interest in their culture. I didn't realize until much later how much meaning their early life would have for me. When at last I had the sense to want to know about it, it was too late. They were gone.

Whatever being Jewish meant to my mother and father they took for granted. (They were not observant; rarely, if ever, went to the synagogue.) It was passed on unselfconsciously to their sons. They did not talk about it. Still, their behavior—the way they moved, walked, laughed, cried, talked-their attitudes, the way our family functioned, imprinted upon us something of the social history they brought with them.

I learned what it was to be a Jew mostly in the negative sense: the insults voiced, the jobs denied, the neighborhoods restricted, the club doors closed, the colleges on quotas. And our history as Jews—anniversaries of catastrophes, expulsions, wholesale murder. No wonder an alarm bell rang when I heard the word "Jew" in an unexpected setting. It might be the sound of the word slashing into my ear while playing basketball in the YMCA gym or swimming in its pool. Or the sight of those three letters on the page of a book I was reading. When we studied Walter Scott's *Ivanhoe* in school, I was captivated by the marvelous story he told. But jolted by his many references to Jews as usurers, liars, hypocrites, as covetous, contemptible, inhuman. Most readers remember his sympathetic portrayal of Rebecca—and forget the rest.

Dickens's *Oliver Twist* was another novel that absorbed me for its portrait of the dark places of London. But the shadow of Fagin, that "villainous-looking, repulsive, greasy, shrivelled old Jew," fell over everything in the story. And then there was Shakespeare's *The Merchant of Venice,* a play read in my high school English class. We played the parts and discussed the story. My teacher made us feel how superb the poetry was, but she said nothing of Shylock as Jew, or how the medieval mind could breed such abuse of and contempt for a whole people.

Not till the 1970s did I do any systematic reading in the history of the Jews. It came about when an editor asked me to write a children's book about the Jews in America. I took it on because I knew so little, and realized at last that I needed to learn so much. Writing a book was the best way to do that. The uncovering of a vast collective memory was so exciting, I went on to write several more books about aspects of Jewish life and history.

Meltzer at high school graduation, 1932.

I don't remember how it happened, but when I reached my last year in junior high I was elected class president. It meant a brief moment of glory at graduation. I was awed to share the platform with our principal, a huge white-haired old man who often reminded us that he had been a drummer boy in the Civil War. (That war ended only fifty years before I was born.)

I moved on to Classical High School. Most of my classmates went instead to commercial or technical or vocational high schools. Classical was the college prep school. We had no money, and college seemed a very dim prospect for me, especially in a time when only a tiny fraction of all young people got a higher education. Most of them were middle or upper class. America had almost no free city colleges and the state universities usually stressed agricultural studies. Still, I simply took for granted that somehow I *would* go to college. I knew my parents expected it, probably because my marks were so good and I liked to read and study. None of our family on either side had ever gone to college. My older brother went to work after being expelled from high school.

I started at Classical in September of 1929. The next month the stock market collapsed and the Great Depression began. Our family did not go broke. We started broke. We owned no stocks and didn't know what they were. All we owned were our clothes and furniture. The shock spread rapidly from Wall Street to the poorest unskilled worker. By the end of my first year at Classical, seven million were out of work. By the time I graduated, the number was fifteen million.

As factories cut down production and stores were boarded up, there were few windows for my father to clean. He was home more and more for lack of work. Extra jobs were hard to find. But I managed to help out with a Saturday job in a cheap shoe store on Front Street. Twelve hours for two dollars. My mother was a good manager and we never went hungry. Food was cheaper then and the Depression drove prices even lower. Eggs were nineteen cents a dozen, bread a nickel a loaf, beef eleven cents a pound.

Fathers in our neighborhood were out of work for months, for years. And there was no relief but private charity. Breadlines. Soup kitchens. President Hoover could only urge people to tighten their belts. By my last year in high school, one-fourth of the nation's families had no regular income.

The windows in the high school grew so filthy you could hardly see the girls passing by on the sidewalk. First the school board had cut down on maintenance, then they stopped buying books and supplies, and soon there was a rumor there wouldn't be money for teachers' pay.

At Classical the men and women who taught us were pretty good. Again, many of them were the product of first-class colleges. Their methods were traditional; nothing experimental. But if you cared to, you could learn a great deal in a systematic way. The best teacher by far was Anna Shaughnessy, a graduate of Radcliffe College. She was Irish Catholic, young, tall, very thin, wore glasses, had a reserved manner but somehow gave out warmth. And she was brilliant. No student ever forgot her. She made you think, she encouraged you to read. Conversation with her helped you to develop ideas and to talk more intelligently. She was my teacher for only two years but those years meant a great deal in the rest of my life. English was her subject. She challenged everyone to do better, knowing how little use we made of our capacities. And most of us responded. In my day we couldn't get enough of her in the classroom. So some of us asked if she'd meet with us each week outside school and let us discuss with her some book we'd all read. She agreed, and we haughtily dubbed ourselves The Club.

It was now that I began to take writing more seriously, doing pieces for the school paper and the literary magazine. Miss Shaughnessy's criticism was always to the point and moved me to try to do better. I joined the debating club too, and began to feel more at ease in the school. When I entered Classical, I was pretty dismayed by how different most of the students were from me. They had Anglo-Saxon names, they dressed elegantly, they spoke a precise English, they played different games, they went to country club dances. I felt alien to all that and wondered what their homelife was like. I soon found they were no brighter or dumber than the rest of us. But they had "class." They took good living for granted. I envied them, and feared them a little, too.

When I fell in love with one of them I couldn't believe she returned my affection. Her name was Dorothy—a tall, slim, dark-haired girl, with huge amber eyes, quiet in manner but intense in feeling. We discovered in class that we shared many of the same interests. She joined The Club too, and we began seeing each other outside school. She lived on the "right" side of town, and came from a Protestant middle-class family. I could never ask her to my home. But she invited me to hers. It was a private home, full of books and records and magazines and with pictures on the walls. I was scared of meeting her parents but they were very welcoming. Dorothy took me to her church on a Sunday afternoon now and then. Not to services, but to young people's socials. Even so, I felt strange sitting there. We would often walk in Elm Park, a beautiful landscape on her side of town, with old trees and a winding stream. We talked, talked, talked, about everything and anything. No one at home ever did that, nor did any of my neighborhood friends.

I never mentioned her to my parents. Perhaps because I still felt bitter about the time a few years before when I dated an Irish girl from our neighborhood. My mother heard about it from a local gossip while I was shopping with her in the corner grocery. She turned and in front of everyone slapped me hard.

Dorothy and I often went to the Worcester Art Museum. There I saw my first Impressionist paintings. Going into that gallery was like discovering what eyes are for. These artists painted the most joyous pictures, filled with light and color. It was like I had been born with dark glasses, and suddenly someone tore them off and let me see the whole shining world. When I looked at a Van Gogh painting of a man working in the fields, I wondered how he would have painted my father.

Another door to the arts opened for me when we went to the annual music festival to hear Serge Koussevitzky conduct the Boston Symphony. It was the first time I'd heard a symphony orchestra play, and the ecstatic feeling Mozart's *Eine Kleine Nachtmusik* gave me is still with me. I started to listen to classical music on the radio, and to read about composers and the forms they worked in.

At school the senior year came on. The local papers carried stories of worse unemployment and hunger. One student's father, a businessman gone broke, shot himself. A young actress who had gone off to Broadway full of hope and ambition came back to Worcester. She had failed to find even a walk-on role in a starving theatre. She sat at home a few weeks, then took the trolley out to Lake Quinsigamond, chopped a hole in the ice, and drowned herself. The owner of Thornby's, a downtown restaurant, disappeared, leaving a note for his wife, saying his debts had piled so high he could not go on. In school the talk was about the senior dance, the basketball games, electioneering for office. I made the yearbook board and was elected class prophet.

I didn't know what to do about college. For years I had thought I'd like to be a teacher. Miss Shaughnessy told me that Columbia University was launching an experimental college to train teachers in a different way. They were looking for candidates and promising some scholarships. She thought I'd like New York and that kind of school. I applied, was interviewed in Worcester, and accepted with a full scholarship and a job in the college dining room in exchange for all my meals. My father said he'd try to send me five dollars a week.

Dorothy decided to go to Antioch College. I never saw her again after graduation. Many years later I heard she had gone to England, married there, and died in World War II.

Meltzer and Hildy at the time of their marriage, 1941.

Before starting at New College I spent the summer in New York. I lived with family and earned money doing unskilled work in an uncle's garment factory. Riding down to work each morning I saw strung along the Hudson River shore hundreds of shacks made of tin cans, packing crates, cardboard, and old tar paper. They were no bigger than chicken coops, these rent-free homes, and their tenants named them Hoovervilles in honor of the president.

I hated the garment job. The big workroom was hot, crowded, noisy, the pace feverish, and the seething ocean of people on the streets almost drowned me. I saw how frantically my uncle tried to keep the business from going under. Up in the Bronx where I stayed, nights were lonely. We worked Saturdays too and on Sunday I was too tired and blue to explore the city. But September of 1932 finally came. I moved into John Jay Hall on the campus and started a different life.

We were a very small school, our classes and offices tucked into the buildings of Teachers College, the graduate school. Most of the staff were young, and eager to try something new. The few hundred students were largely New Yorkers, impossibly sophisticated, I thought. We were allowed to take courses almost anywhere in the university. I took full advantage of that and sat in the classes of such great people as Franz Boas, Ruth Benedict, and John Dewey. Our own teachers were open to friendships with students who interested them.

One of my teachers was Charles Obermeyer, a small, dark, wiry, intense man from South Africa, fluent in many languages and a marvelous talker. His lectures on literature sparkled with references from an encyclopedic knowledge. We all listened eagerly, afraid to miss the revelations and insights that came so fast. He was an influence upon me almost as great as Miss Shaughnessy.

Soon after school began, Roosevelt was elected President. While FDR and the country waited for the inauguration, Adolf Hitler took power in Germany. I remember a cold January night at a professor's apartment when we students hung over his shortwave radio, unable to believe the hysteria vomiting from Hitler's throat and the roar of his audience's response.

As Roosevelt took office the country dropped into the bottommost pit of the Depression. The whole banking system collapsed overnight. Millions more lost everything they had, and worst of all, their pride and self-respect. We were up against forces we could not identify, could not fight.

FDR promised "action and action now," and a "New Deal." He moved so swiftly and powerfully that it was possible to hope again. You could feel the excitement on the Columbia campus. Our university was among the many from which the president drew advisors to plan the major measures the Congress passed in his first hundred days. Dozens of our best brains moved into New Deal agencies.

I didn't follow every move the president made. I was on my own for the first time in my seventeen years, and that was troublesome enough. Everyone in my class was a stranger to me, and I did not make friends easily. Then there was New York itself, a monstrous city to a boy from a New England town.

But it didn't take me long to learn what joys it had to offer, even when you had no money. I often went to the theatre, waiting for the first act intermission, then sneaking from the lobby into an empty seat to see the rest of the play for nothing. That way I saw Dublin's Abbey players do most of Sean O'Casey and London's D'Oyly Carte do almost all of Gilbert and Sullivan. At a musical revue I first heard "Brother, Can You Spare a Dime," the song I borrowed thirty-seven years later as the title for my book on the Depression. I did pay to see Fred Astaire dance on the stage (balcony seats were fifty-five cents) in the last Broadway show he did before going off to Hollywood. His witty feet, his grace and delicacy could make me feel as debonair as a duke.

At college I roomed with Bernard Werthman, a man ten years older, who had given up a concert pianist's career because he wanted to teach music to children. He took this child's musical education in hand and brought me to hear many great soloists, such as Josef Hoffman and Walter Gieseking. We went to art galleries and museums together where I soaked up something of what he had learned from years spent in Europe. Through him I met many older friends who helped break down some of my provincial fears and uncertainties.

Part of the New College program called for students to spend a year working in industry or on a farm. I went back to Worcester for my sophomore year, living again at home, this time on View Street, where my family had recently moved. Somehow I found a miserable job in a factory, painting women's shoes with a spray gun.

Evenings I read voraciously, keeping careful notes to show my instructors. I meant to get credit not only for the year's industrial experience but for teaching myself in new fields. My file shows I read close to a book a day.

Busy as I was I had time to be lonely. My high school friends were now scattered. Then I met a girl who lived nearby and was commuting to a college in Boston. She was a year older. We shared many interests, including tennis. Soon we were spending all our spare hours together. Saturdays we might drive to Boston in her car to go to the theater. She herself acted in college plays. By the year's end we were in love.

In the fall of 1934 I returned to school which was now swept by feverish discussions. Many of my professors were either deeply committed to the New Deal or radical critics of its shortcomings. And so I became more sensitive to what was going on in the larger world. The New Deal was in trouble because it had not brought about economic recovery. So far it had failed to improve the lot of workers, tenant farmers, old people, or small business. FDR had provided federal funds for public works projects and for direct work relief, like the Civilian Conservation Corps and the National Youth Administration. Many of us students picked up useful money by doing NYA jobs part time. In addition I worked Saturdays in a Fifth Avenue department store, selling women's shoes.

My social life focused entirely on my girl. Every few weeks she took the bus into New York to visit me, and I'd go home every once in a while to see her. We decided to get married in the spring of 1935. My parents were strongly opposed; they liked her but knew we were too young and had no means of supporting ourselves. Nor could they help

Corporal Meltzer in the Army Air Force, about 1943.

us. But marry we did, in a brief City Hall ceremony in Worcester. It was three days after I turned twenty.

She came to New York and we found a small apartment. She was a college graduate now, and got a secretarial job in a publishing house. That was how we managed to live while I had a year to go for my degree.

The marriage was the mistake my folks predicted. Neither of us knew much about life, about marriage, or even about ourselves. I think we must have come together out of loneliness. We soon drifted apart, and after a while were divorced. Now it's something in my life that seems to have happened to somebody else.

As I began my last year in college, private employment was still hard to find. Eight million people still had no jobs. Nearly three million young people, sixteen to twenty-four, were on relief. The surface aspects of the Depression had almost disappeared. No apple-sellers on the street, breadlines gone, Hoovervilles vanished. But I knew many young people who had finished college and failed to find work. They had gone home to live or were drifting about the country.

The failure of the government to find basic solutions troubled us. In the big industries—steel, auto, coal, rubber—workers were carrying on dramatic sit-in strikes for the right to organize and bargain. I went to see Clifford Odets's radical plays and read many of the new novels about working class life. Paul Green's *Johnny Johnson* and Irwin Shaw's *Bury the Dead* were plays that intensified the pacifist mood on the campus. Many of us joined the radical student movement.

I remember a union on campus struggling to organize the service and maintenance workers at Columbia. I was doing student-teaching then at the Horace Mann School on campus, and I urged the girls to join the picket line outside, where I marched every lunch hour and handed out leaflets. When the headmaster heard what I'd said in class he suggested perhaps I was better fitted to organize labor than to teach children.

Maybe he's right, I thought. Though I reminded him New College and John Dewey stood for uniting thought with action. I did like the small teaching experience I'd had, combining social history with literature. But I had just seen something I wrote published in a minor magazine. One of my professors, without telling me, had sent an editor an essay I wrote comparing plays that dealt with the Sacco-Vanzetti case. He liked it enough to publish it. Seeing my name in print made me think writing would be better than teaching. (Though as it turned out the two seem inseparable in my work.)

That was the beginning of what became a lifelong calling—writing. It was a craft I learned slowly, and by a dozen different uses of it I made a living. But it would take perhaps half a lifetime before I found the best and happiest use for it.

I began to feel there was no point to going on with my studies. The papers said a third of the previous year's graduating classes had been unable to find any work at all. Another third had gotten jobs for which they had no interest, talent, or training. So what was the sense of a degree?

I had no desire to enter business or pile up property. It seemed impossible anyhow. And everything I read and saw strengthened the belief that there must be something better to live for than to get rich. The unending years of depression had led many people to lose faith in an economic system that helped a minority to enjoy luxuries while millions went hungry. Especially among the people I admired most—writers and artists and intellectuals—was this disillusionment evident.

Many of us supported what FDR tried to do to make life a little less harsh for the underdog, but believed it was no more than patchwork on a system that needed radical reconstruction. But how, in what form, by what means? Some joined organizations of young socialists or communists or found hope in Technocracy or Share the Wealth or other utopian schemes that flared briefly in those desperate years. Some of us turned to the right, seeing in America's little fuehrers their savior. Just as blind were those of us on the left who saw in Stalin a savior. Whether on the extreme political right or left, human lives were being sacrificed to abstract ideas. With terrifying ease, believers in some great cause lose their moral bearings and take unto themselves the right to destroy the lives of others.

Toward the end of my senior year I dropped out of college. (My mother never forgave me for that. No matter what else I achieved in the years that followed, she always lamented, "But you didn't get your degree!") My father, fifty-seven, died of cancer that year. I had sat beside his sickbed, unable to say anything to him, and at his funeral I couldn't cry. But as the years go by I think about him more and more, and wonder about the unspoken thoughts and feelings that never passed between us.

My mother came back to New York to live, along with my younger brother. I found a furnished room on the West Side that rented for three dollars a week. Stepping through the front door of the old brownstone was like entering a public urinal. At the top of five flights of stairs was my room, so narrow I could almost touch the walls with outstretched arms. There was an iron cot, no sheets, a frayed army blanket, a rickety wardrobe that leaned menacingly over me, and a small window through whose smeary glass I could barely see the brick walls of the tenement opposite.

I applied for help at the city's relief bureau. I can't recall how many days I waited before an investigator came. It felt terribly long because I was so nervous. But at last I qualified, and the relief began coming. The city paid my rent, and every other Friday gave me $5.50. That was what I lived on. Dinner was a cheese sandwich and a cup of coffee. Price: twenty cents. When rain or snow began squishing up through the holes in my shoes, I couldn't afford to have them repaired. Neighbors showed me how to take the pulpy separators out of egg cartons and stuff them into my shoes for protection. A few months later my luck changed. The Federal Theatre Project gave me a job.

I reported for work at a decaying Greek temple on Eighth Avenue near Forty-fourth Street, once the home of a bank that had gone bust. Now it was the headquarters of the project for theatre people sponsored by the Works Projects Administration (WPA). I got the job because, when I applied for home relief, I listed myself as an unemployed writer. A bold claim to make on the basis of college pieces and some writing for obscure magazines. I had to put something down, and I did want badly to become a professional writer. My brother Allan had had some experience as a publicity writer in New York, had gone on relief before me, and had been given a Federal Theatre job in the press department. He showed me the ropes and talked his chief into hiring me. Allan was very good at his work, and his boss must have figured I would be too.

I fitted into a small niche of the big department, joining a few men who wrote stories explaining the project to teachers and students. Many Federal Theatre productions were performed in the schools, and pupils often came in organized groups to attend the performances in our theatres.

My pay was $23.86 a week. It was the salary everybody got who came from the relief rolls. We were ninety percent of the workers on all the projects—Music, Writers, Theatre, and Art. The pay sounds very small now, but it was enough to support me, and those who had families, too. And as steady pay every week of the year, it was more than most actors earned in the commercial theatre. It was job security they had never before enjoyed.

I spent over three years in that job, the first decent one I ever had. And one that did more good than most jobs people find themselves in because they have to make a living somehow. The New Deal not only provided work for thousands of unemployed people in the arts, it also satisfied the hunger of America's millions for plays, books, music, art. It was a revolutionary idea, to decide that concertos, poems, novels, sculpture, paintings were not just luxuries for the rich to enjoy, but a vital part of popular education and culture. I was glad to be part of that great enterprise, and I look back proudly on those years. Long after, I worked that personal experience into a book I wrote called *Violins and Shovels: The WPA Arts Projects.*

The press, heavily conservative in the Thirties, attacked the WPA concept of work relief. It targeted the arts projects, ridiculing and misrepresenting what we did. Periodically Congress would demand cuts in the WPA budget, and we would be showered with orders for dismissals. Only a few months after I started, I was one of many who got pink dismissal slips.

We hit the pavement at once, joined by a small army of pickets mustered by our union, the Workers Alliance. For two weeks we kept it up, demanding our jobs back, parading, shouting, chanting, singing, waving placards with our slogans. The cut was rescinded and we went back to our desks. That happened to us again and again; it made life very precarious. But I hung on for years, learning that militant struggle could make a difference. It taught me what unions were all about and gave me the itch to study labor history.

The Meltzers vacationing on Cape Cod with their daughter Jane.

In the Thirties I was one of many who joined the anti-war movement that swept the college campuses. We marched in "No More War" parades and thousands of us signed the Oxford Pledge of absolute refusal to serve in the armed forces. The churches too condemned resorting to war as a sin. But our pacifism met a severe test with the Civil War in Spain that began in 1936. It seemed a just war when the Spanish democracy tried to defend itself against a fascist uprising aided by Hitler and Mussolini. Thousands of Americans—among them a childhood friend from Worcester—volunteered to fight in the International Brigades. Al thought if democracy could be saved in Spain, it would end Hitler's chances to start another world war. But he was killed his first day of battle. In April of 1939 the fascists won in Spain. I thought it was now inevitable that I'd be in uniform soon.

In June 1939 Congress abolished the Federal Theatre. The Civil War in Spain ended about the same time. For the three years it had gone on it had gripped the hearts of most of the people I knew. Over three thousand had volunteered for the Abraham Lincoln Brigade, fighting for Spanish democracy against Franco's troops. Franco's victory marked the end of an era. Without a job, and certain that Hitler would start a world war soon, I did not feel like hunting for work. I decided to join two friends and see the USA. I had a little money salted away, and borrowed some more. One man took his father's car, which we packed with a gas stove, pots and pans, canned goods, sleeping bags, a small tent, and many road maps.

I learned to drive along the way and was soon sharing the wheel with Les and Gil. We made our own meals and slept out of doors. For two months we drove across the country, zigzagging to see all we could, reached the Northwest, and headed down the West Coast for Mexico.

We had visited auto plants and airplane factories, logging camps and lumber mills, iron mines and fisheries, ranches and canneries and the huge fruit and vegetable farms of California. There we went into the federal camps put up for Okie migrant workers whom Steinbeck had just depicted in his novel, *Grapes of Wrath.* (Forty years later I would write about the migrants in my biography, *Dorothea Lange: A Photographer's Life.*)

We were driving through the plains of Texas when at 8:00 A.M. on September 1 we heard a calm voice on the radio announce that Hitler's armies had invaded Poland. The news stunned us. Not that we did not believe war would come. But not now, not this day, not this year!

We debated whether to go on. We had planned to stay a month or so in Mexico and then travel slowly up through the deep South. But the war news wrecked our plans. We entered Mexico, stayed a week or two, and drove home to see what would happen next. Along the way I had written several enormously detailed letters to friends, trying to capture the immediacy of the experience. I had never been anywhere before, so this was a marvelous time for me. I had hoped, upon my return, to mine those letters for some articles. But the war pushed everything else offstage. No one would be interested in what I had seen and learned. The war changed everything.

My own life changed wonderfully as soon as I got back. Through a blind date arranged by mutual friends I met Hildy, my wife-to-be. She was going to City College at night and working as a clothes model during the day. A year younger than I, she had come up from Philadelphia to try living in New York, acting in small theatre groups, modelling, and working for a college degree all at the same time. She was beautiful, gentle, compassionate, and, like me, felt society had to be remade into something more humane and just. We were soon in love; and after my divorce came through, we married in June 1941.

Hildy continued to work and take courses while I did various odd jobs in journalism, writing or editing, always for low pay. In August of 1942 I was drafted. I was twenty-seven, and much older than most of the GIs. They called me "Pop." I was placed in the Army Air Force and sent to school to become a control-tower operator. For three-and-a-half years I worked in towers at domestic airfields where fighter or bomber pilots were being trained for combat. I was never sent overseas. Most of the time I was in Arkansas or Alabama. At least I saw a lot of the South, spending many off-duty passes wandering around the countryside and the small towns and taking photographs. I was stationed at Craig Field in Selma, Alabama, quite a while. It seemed a town still asleep in the nineteenth century. Some twenty years later, when worldwide attention focused on the Selma-to-Montgomery March for Black Freedom of 1965, I couldn't believe this was the same town I had known.

I volunteered to write for service newspapers and gave lectures on democracy and fascism and why we were in this war. One of the best—and sometimes most painful—parts of those years was the chance to get to know all kinds of young men from all over the U.S. If you stay in New York too long you can begin to think everyone else is like you.

When the war ended I had a wife, a baby—Jane—and no job. My brother Allan helped find me work at the CBS radio network in New York. They were doing a weekly dramatic documentary illuminating the many different problems of the GIs who returned from the war. My job was to interview them, their families and friends, therapists, counselors, social agencies, and work out a story each week, centering on a veteran who typified a problem. Then a dramatic writer took over and did the action and dialogue. Finally they let me write a script myself; and it was thrilling to sit in the studio and watch the actors broadcast it live to the whole country. The program was sponsored by the U.S. Veterans Administration, and did much to help men and women returning to civilian life in that difficult time.

As my first year ended I heard a job was open on the public relations staff of a committee planning the candidacy of Henry A. Wallace for President on an independent ticket in 1948. (Wallace had been FDR's Vice President and was now Truman's Secretary of Commerce.) I applied and got the post. It was more money than at CBS, and promised to teach me a great deal about something new. The work proved hard—very long hours every day of the week—but it was rewarding.

My job was to write news releases and the copy for leaflets and posters and brochures, draft background memoranda on issues, handle the reporters at press conferences—the usual political PR chores. I worked with many people who had rich experience in government affairs and learned a lot about politics from the inside.

A winter holiday in Puerto Rico with daughters Amy and Jane, 1961.

I doubt that any of us, including Mr. Wallace, expected him to win, but we thought our new Progressive Party would get a sizeable vote and incline the country toward a more liberal domestic program and a less belligerent foreign policy. Our hopes were crushed when Wallace got little more than a million votes. That was the year Harry Truman surprised everyone but himself by beating Tom Dewey.

The campaign over, I looked for work. For the next two years I went back to odd jobs in journalism. I teamed with another writer to do magazine pieces, I wrote a column for a labor paper, I produced a daily radio program for a national union during a six-month-long strike (which we lost). It was a precarious living, but we managed somehow to get along. Hildy went back to work modelling when our Janie entered nursery school. Freelance work could be fun because of the variety it offered, but its uncertainty made me nervous.

Then a permanent job popped up. A new public relations agency was started by a clever man who saw that the rapidly growing pharmaceutical industry needed the skills he could muster. It was an age of discovery. All sorts of new antibiotics and hormones and other drugs were being developed in the laboratories and they made good stories to tell a public intensely interested in its own health.

Although I said I knew nothing about science or medicine, the boss told me that knowing how to write was more important. I could learn the facts on the job. And that's what happened. He paid me well and threw in a generous expense account. Hildy and I felt secure enough to have another child—Amy.

There were only a few accounts in the shop and a few employees when I started, but several of the biggest firms were soon on our list and the staff grew rapidly. I had never dealt with big business before, and was a little scared of encounters with corporate executives. But I found they were human and approachable. I was assigned to the Pfizer account. I plunged into learning all I could about its business history, its research goals and methods, its marketing needs. I was a quick study, as the actors put it, and soon could handle the business well at both ends—with the company brass and the media I had to reach with the story.

Early on I made a big coup that entrenched me solidly with both the account and my boss. I mustered vivid details and worked out the story line for the discovery of antibiotics and convinced the veteran *New Yorker* writer, Berton Rouché, that it was a good bet for him. He followed up with his own research and the magazine ran a very long article that delighted the Pfizer people and the readers. Later the piece was anthologized several times.

I found I enjoyed the give and take with the executives in the business offices and the scientists in the labs. I came up with fresh ideas and managed to get the media people to make use of many of them. As our staff and my responsibilities grew I discovered I had a knack for administration too. Perhaps compulsively well-organized, I was able to get others to work coherently and well together.

After some four or five years with the agency, Pfizer asked me to join them to help create an internal public relations department. I took up the offer, and we built a large staff to carry on a more extensive program. Working inside now, I saw much more clearly how a corporation operates. With a bigger budget, we could do the things I especially liked—make science films, plan international scientific meetings, publish educational books and brochures. The more directly commercial aspects had to be taken care of, too, and this I liked less. The eternal conflict between profit and use, between real needs and induced needs, was abundantly clear. And the jockeying for power and position found in almost any institution, whether for profit or not, was just as plain and painful.

I stayed on for five years, able to save something out of a good salary. Then I left because I wanted a job that would permit me greater control of my own time. This, because I wanted to write books. Earlier, while at the agency, I became aware that I was nearing the age of forty. I had become a suburban commuter, living in a house in northern Westchester. Life was easier for us than ever before. But I wasn't satisfied. Forty was the mid-life mark. I probably had fewer years than that ahead of me. What had I done with my time? I called myself a writer, but would anything I'd written endure? Would anyone want to go back and read that dead-and-gone journalism? All this time I had never tried my hand at fiction or poetry. Not even as a schoolboy. Nonfiction was my natural medium. So I decided to try to write a book, a book about something important, a book that might make a difference in how its readers understood the world. I never stopped to think it might be a rotten book!

While I was casting about for a subject, I began to see it would not be easy to hold a job, help with the housework and the kids, and write a book, too. My wife was very understanding. "I'll let you out of the dishes," she said, "if you'll work on a book." (Later, she turned this around and told everybody the only reason I wrote books was to get out of doing dishes.)

I found my subject—a history of black people in America, to be told with a big and solid text combined with a thousand illustrations. When I began to read and make notes, I knew only a little about black history, and the enormous magnitude of the research task became clear only as I made some headway. My job took me all over the country and I was able to combine business trips with research into pictorial material on black life. It was never a chore. It was a stretching of the mind, a deepening of my sympathies, a disciplining of my organizing powers.

Still, after blocking out the entire book, assembling a great many pictures, and working with a book designer to prepare about thirty layouts to show how it might look, I felt shaky about going on alone. I wasn't black, nor had I ever attempted so big a piece of work. So I looked for a collaborator, and was incredibly lucky to find Langston Hughes willing to share the work with me. It meant the beginning of a friendship that lasted until his death fifteen years later. I owe much to him for his professional example, his encouraging sympathy, his understanding of the world blacks and whites live in together—if so differently.

Despite Langston's position in American literature, we had great trouble finding a publisher. More than a dozen turned us down because they thought the book would find too small an audience. Then one day, in a chance encounter at a dinner table, I told the stranger next to me about the book, and he said instantly, "We'll publish it!" This without seeing any part of it. He was Robert Simon, a partner in Crown publishers. We finished the book and Crown issued it in the fall of 1956. (I was forty-one.) It came out just as the tremendous struggle for civil rights was mounting and proved to be exactly what everyone concerned needed and wanted. The book is still in print thirty years later, and has gone through five revised and updated editions.

The success of that first book launched me on a double career. For the next dozen years I would hold full-time jobs while I wrote books in the early morning hours before going off to an office, and in the evening and on weekends. I know it was rather hard on my family. It meant less time spent with them. But they liked what I wrote, and thought it worthwhile. I had only warm encouragement from them all.

The first book appeared while I was working at Pfizer. I gave a copy to the company president; he was pleased with it and proud someone on his staff had done it. He never suggested I should be giving twenty-four hours a day to the company. He was a self-made man and liked to see others try to make something of themselves. He generously had me take long trips to Europe to inspect overseas operations and then let me stay on for vacations with my wife.

Still, I wanted to give even more time to writing books. In 1960 two close friends who managed a medical publications firm understood my desire and took me on. I edited a pediatrics paper for them, and so long as I did it well and on schedule I was free to use my time any way I wished. That same year our family moved back to New York City, finding an apartment on the West Side that we have lived in ever since. It made research for my books much easier, for now I was close to many superb specialized libraries. More importantly, the move made it possible for my wife to return to college, completing work for both her bachelor's and master's degrees. She worked at City College for many years, then left to conduct assertiveness training workshops.

In the next eight years I was able to publish thirteen books. The first several continued to be for adults—

including a big book on Mark Twain and two on Thoreau. Then I turned to writing for young readers as well. I did biographies of several figures in the abolitionist movement and in the fight for women's rights. And others on aspects of black history, including the three-volume *In Their Own Words,* another book about blacks between the two world wars, and again with Langston Hughes, our *Black Magic: A Pictorial History of the Negro in American Entertainment.* Sadly, when we had finished it and were waiting for the proofs, Langston took sick, and entered the hospital. Two weeks later he died there. It was a terrible blow; he was only sixty-five. During his last year he agreed to let me write his biography for young people. He looked it over and gave me some criticism just before his death. But I couldn't work on it again for some time. Then I picked it up and finished it. When it came out in 1968 it was nominated for the National Book Award.

That year I decided to go it on my own and quit my job. My income from my books was equal to my salary as an editor. I talked with my wife and we agreed we should be able to live on what I might earn from books alone. At the time, the federal government was putting large sums into subsidies for schools and libraries. It meant a steep rise in the sale of children's books and in the income of writers for young people.

Publishers felt optimistic and looked for new ideas. I made proposals for three series of books which were accepted. My role was to come up with the ideas for specific titles within each series, to find the right authors, and to edit their manuscripts. For Crowell I edited some twenty-five feminist biographies called "Women of America," for Doubleday the Zenith black culture series, and for Scholastic, the Firebird history series. I enjoyed the chance to work with experienced authors and to help launch new ones. Each series, I think, added something original to children's book publishing.

Out of my own work have come frequent opportunities to write scripts for radio, television, and documentary films, their subjects usually drawn from my books. And quite regularly I take part in seminars or give lectures at schools and colleges and for professional groups of teachers and librarians. Many times I talk directly with the readers themselves, from grade school through college, either about the subject matter of my books or about writing itself.

I mistakenly thought the prosperity of the Sixties would go on indefinitely. I didn't realize that our growing involvement in the war in Vietnam was changing this picture at that very moment. Within a few years income shrank considerably as many writers like me saw their work taken out of print because school and library budgets had been savagely slashed. A Columbia University survey shows that the median annual income of American authors is still under five thousand dollars. It is terribly hard for writers to survive; most have to work at other jobs.

In those first years I wrote books without any great self-consciousness about the subjects I chose. Then one day a reviewer described me as a writer known for his interest in the underdog. A pattern had become obvious. It was not a choice deliberately made. But that is how it has gone, books about human aspiration and struggle—the black

American's struggle to organize for freedom and equality; the worker's struggle to organize and improve his living standards; the struggle of the hungry and dispossessed in the Great Depression for bread and a job; the struggle of various racial or ethnic groups—Native Americans, Black Americans, Jewish Americans, Hispanic Americans, Asian Americans—to live and grow and work in security and freedom.

As for my biographies, they deal with the lives of people who appeal to me for many different reasons. But what links them all is the fact that each one has fought for unpopular causes—Samuel Gridley Howe, Margaret Sanger, Langston Hughes, Lydia Maria Child, Henry David Thoreau, Mark Twain, Thaddeus Stevens, Dorothea Lange, Betty Friedan, Mary McLeod Bethune

All these people share one quality: they never say there is nothing they can do about an injustice or a wrong they encounter. They are not victims of apathy, that state people get themselves into when they believe there's no way to change things. My subjects choose action. They show the will to do something about what troubles them. Action takes commitment, the commitment of dedicated, optimistic individuals. Our American past is full of examples of people like these who tried to shape their own lives. Of people who sometimes understood that they could not manage their own life without seeking to change society, without trying to reshape the world they lived in.

I try to make my readers understand that history isn't only what happens to us. History is also what we *make* happen. Each of us. All of us. And history isn't only the kings and presidents and generals and superstars. If we search the records deep and wide enough we find ample evidence of what the anonymous, the obscure ones have done—and continue to do—to shape history, to make America realize its promise.

I try to be useful in the same way wherever and whenever I can. I've joined unions, campaigned for political candidates and helped build political parties, voted, petitioned, paraded, lobbied my representatives. All my writing comes out of my convictions. I've never had to write anything I didn't believe in. As a professional author, I've been active in the Authors Guild for nearly thirty years and have served on its national council since 1972.

I feel lucky that I have been able to write for readers of all ages, from the very young to the old. Sometimes the one feeds into the other. Many years after I did my juvenile biography of Lydia Maria Child I received a four-year grant from the National Historical Publications and Records Commission (sponsors of the Presidential papers) to head a team of scholars gathering and editing the letters of Mrs. Child. With it went an adjunct professorship in the W.E.B. DuBois Department of Afro-American studies at the University of Massachusetts, Amherst.

The 2,600 letters we uncovered were published in a microfiche edition in 1980, and two years later the University of Massachusetts Press issued our selected and annotated edition of her letters. In the 1970s I spent three years working on a scholarly adult biography of Dorothea Lange, the great photographer of the 1930s. Recently I wrote a short life of Lange for very young readers.

As I finish this essay, a new book is appearing—one that has come out of my intense hope that we can find a way to avoid nuclear war—*Ain't Gonna Study War No*

Meltzer (right) with Robert Cormier at a meeting of the National Council of Teachers of English, New York, 1977.

More, the story of the peace-seekers in American history. And now I go to work on a book for young adults about poverty in today's America—fifty years after I experienced what that was like when I was growing up in the Thirties.

POSTSCRIPT 2001

Fifteen years have passed since I completed the autobiographical essay. When I was a youngster that span of time seemed like an eternity. Now it is an express train hurtling past annual stations. At the age of eighty-five a week telescopes into a day. Is it because nothing has happened? No, for sadly much has changed in my family's life and our friends' lives.

Still, I've managed to publish more than thirty books since 1985. They include biographies of such people as Jefferson, Benjamin Franklin, Columbus, Andrew Jackson, Theodore Roosevelt, Tom Paine, Andrew Carnegie, Mary McLeod Bethune. Two lives of poets who speak for the common man—Carl Sandburg and Walt Whitman—completed a triptych I had begun much earlier with my biography of Langston Hughes. My concern for the blight of racism in our national life continued into the new century, with a history of the struggle for civil rights appearing in 2001.

As I grew older, and less self-centered (I hope), I tried to uncover the facts about my parents' migration to America, which occurred over 100 years ago. What I learned became part of a childhood memoir, *Starting from*

Home. The experience was renewed in three recent books about migration movements—the forced migration of millions of Africans from their homelands to enslavement in America, the depression-driven exodus of Dust Bowl farmers to California in the 1930s, and the mass migration of Eastern and Southern Europeans to America in the decades of the 1880s to the 1920s.

In the 1930s, the time of the Great Depression, I had seen and felt what it was like for millions to go without enough to eat, and years later had gathered their experience in my book, *Brother, Can You Spare a Dime?* Yet, even as America entered plush times in the unprecedented boom years of the 1990s, millions were still going hungry. And not only here.

Worldwide, as the United Nations reported in 2001, hunger affects 830 million people because of natural disasters, armed conflicts, and grinding poverty. Of that huge number, 200 million are children under the age of five. I've tried, through my writing, to help young readers especially understand what such grim statistics mean. My book on poverty throughout American history traces how it has occurred time and again, and suggests what the causes are. Another book, focusing directly on child labor, brings to light how young workers through history have been exploited and abused.

Doesn't anyone care? Haven't people tried to do something about such social disasters? Lest readers become discouraged, I always seek for evidence of what people try to do to right such wrongs. And I have found that millions do take action. Altruism is by no means dead. Everywhere, in small or large communities, in every part of our country, I could find reports of action taken and results brought about. No revolutions, no upheavals of the existing system, but, nevertheless, gains made. That is, when people raise their eyes above their own immediate pursuits to see how their fellow men and women and children are doing, and act upon what they learn.

Most recently, in the presidential election of 2000, the country was mightily disturbed by its outcome, and by the roles played by the three branches of government—executive, legislative, and judicial—in the outcome of the conflict. For someone who has lived through many presidencies, this was not exactly news. For politics is always with us—in our schools, in our workplaces, and of course in our government—local, state, or federal. Whether we ignore it or not, politics influences our lives today and our dreams for tomorrow. In a book called *American Politics: How It Really Works*, I tried to take a fresh look at the effect of politics on the press, the courts, on campaigns and the electoral system as well as on lobbyists and bureaucrats. It is, I hope, an unvarnished portrait of political life, together with some ideas of what we can do to better it where it needs change.

Change? As I've grown older, and look back into the past, I marvel at the changes I've seen—in everything from the horse-drawn wagons that brought milk into our neighborhood to the jet planes that carry me abroad, from the big clattering typewriters of my early days as a journalist to the sleek computers of today that can do everything but shampoo your hair. (But I still write my first drafts in longhand and then, for revision, move to my portable manual typewriter that by now sprouts whiskers.)

A more profound change my generation witnessed was the transition from the monarchy of Tsarist Russia to the revolutionary Soviet Union. And then, after some seventy years, its collapse and splintering into a dozen separate non-communist countries. I was only two when the Russian Revolution exploded, and of course unaware then of its significance. But as I entered high school in 1929 and the Great Depression began its long and painful run, I was forced to think about what caused the social and economic crisis. And to listen to what some were blaming the depression on—the capitalist system. They claimed that Soviet Russia was showing the world a new way, the socialist way, to avoid the crises of an outworn system and to construct a new socialist system that guaranteed prosperity and democracy and equality for all. It took some time for me to learn what a fraud that was, how false the promise of a heaven on earth, and how vicious and murderous that regime proved to be.

Then there have been the wars, some just, some not, that Americans have fought in. World War I when I was in diapers, and Number Two which consumed three and a half years of my life. Next, the Korean War, followed by the long and agonizing war in Vietnam. More recently, the Gulf War.

For a country with a rather short history, ours has done quite a bit of fighting. We've taken part in seven officially declared wars. And without the approval of Congress—a Constitutional necessity—we have sent our armed forces beyond our borders over 170 times.

When I put on the uniform in the Second World War, I wanted to do everything I could to help defeat Nazism. If any war was just, this one was. But not everyone saw it that way. I knew men who opposed military actions and refused personally to have any part of them. They drew a line they would not cross because their consciences would not let them. As one who feared Hitler would obliterate democracy wherever his armies could reach, and as a Jew who was desperate to crush the Nazis' murderous anti-Semitism, I wanted to do whatever I could to defeat Hitler's Germany. But to me, the war in Vietnam was different. It proved to be America's most disastrous military adventure. Some 2.8 million U.S. troops went to Vietnam, and 58,000 Americans and at least a million Vietnamese died. Throughout that war there were many—scores of thousands—who refused to register for the draft or to be inducted. I sympathized with them, and one day decided to examine our history to see what men and women have done to resist the call to violent action, their reasons, their methods, the outcome of their nonviolent resistance, for themselves and for the country. Research ended with my history of those passionate people who risked reputation, livelihood, and life itself to raise their voices against war and violence. Surely, they hope and believe, the world will one day find peaceful ways to settle differences. I share the hope, but as the years go by and the wars go on any faith in it ever happening diminishes.

Writing has been the chief activity of my life. At first for wages, often paid me to write what I did not really care about. Sometimes I could devote myself to themes I wanted to explore. And sometimes it was putting words on paper so that I could pay for putting food on the table. Finally, beginning in 1968, risking support of our family by giving up a salaried editorial job, I flew out on my own, writing only books I wanted to write.

Happily, it worked. I found that prolific as I seemed to be by nature, I could create enough work publishers desired to provide a decent living.

Meltzer answering questions at a local school.

Unhappily, the great majority of writers do not make a decent living from creating books. They keep alive by having jobs unrelated to writing. Or by finding a spouse with an income that will support the family. Or by freelancing an infinite variety of chores, work done not for love, but for money.

Although I have rarely had anything rejected by a publisher, in recent years I've felt the impact of great changes in book publishing. Several houses I've dealt with have been sucked up into huge conglomerates. Their marketing moguls seem interested only in the bottom line. Once upon a time children's books valued by readers, teachers and librarians stood a good chance of remaining in print for many years, even without over-the-top sales. Now, like all trade books, they can be tossed into the remainder counter in a painfully short time.

The many changes in technology have not benefited authors, so far as I can see. The publishing divisions of conglomerates, like other megafirms, trim costs by down-sizing staffs, using freelance or part-time editors, and wiping out quality imprints in the struggle to achieve unrealistic profit margins demanded by their absentee corporate overlords.

Although no book of mine has ever earned a huge amount of money, many have been selected for honors and awards. Five have been finalists for the National Book Award. The Catholic Library Association in 2000 awarded me its Regina Medal for lifetime achievement in children's literature, and in 2001 the American Library Association awarded me the Laura Ingalls Wilder Medal for "a substantial and lasting contribution to literature." Among other honors are the Christopher, Jane Addams, Carter G. Woodson, Jefferson Cup, Golden Kite, and Phoenix awards.

Many of my books have been chosen for the honor lists of the American Library Association, the Library of Congress, the National Council of Teachers of English, the National Council for the Social Studies, as well as the *New York Times* best books of the year. In 1997 Worcester State College (in my home town) gave me the honorary degree of Doctor of Humane Letters.

But the best part of these many years is the continued joy in the daily exercise of a craft, the making of books that I hope will help readers to understand the connection between real people and real events. No, even better is the joy of sharing the world with Hildy, my wife of sixty years.

Writings

FOR CHILDREN; NONFICTION

In Their Own Words: A History of the American Negro, Crowell (New York, NY), Volume 1, *1619-1865,* 1964, Volume 2, *1865-1916,* 1965, Volume 3, *1916-1966,* 1967, abridged edition published as *The Black Americans: A History in Their Own Words, 1619-1983,* Crowell, 1984.

A Light in the Dark: The Life of Samuel Gridley Howe, Crowell (New York, NY), 1964.

Tongue of Flame: The Life of Lydia Maria Child, Crowell (New York, NY), 1965.

(With August Meier) *Time of Trial, Time of Hope: The Negro in America, 1919-1941,* illustrated by Moneta Barnett, Doubleday (Garden City, NY), 1966.

(With Langston Hughes) *Black Magic. A Pictorial History of the Negro in American Entertainment,* Prentice-Hall (Englewood Cliffs, NJ), 1967.

Bread and Roses: The Struggle of American Labor, 1865-1915, Knopf (New York, NY), 1967.

Thaddeus Stevens and the Fight for Negro Rights, Crowell (New York, NY), 1967.

Langston Hughes: A Biography, Crowell (New York, NY), 1968.

Brother, Can You Spare a Dime? The Great Depression, 1929-1933, Knopf (New York, NY), 1969.

(With Lawrence Lader) *Margaret Sanger: Pioneer of Birth Control,* Crowell (New York, NY), 1969.

Freedom Comes to Mississippi. The Story of Reconstruction, Follett (Chicago, IL), 1970.

Slavery: From the Rise of Western Civilization to the Renaissance, Cowles, 1971, Volume 2, *Slavery: From the Renaissance to Today,* 1972.

To Change the World: A Picture History of Reconstruction, Scholastic (New York, NY), 1971.

Hunted like a Wolf: The Story of the Seminole War, Farrar, Straus (New York, NY), 1972.

The Right to Remain Silent, Harcourt (New York, NY), 1972.

Bound for the Rio Grande: The Mexican Struggle, 1845-1850, Knopf (New York, NY), 1974.

(With Bernard Cole) *The Eye of Conscience: Photographers and Social Change,* Follett (Chicago, IL), 1974.

Remember the Days: A Short History of the Jewish American, illustrated by Harvey Dinnerstein, Doubleday (Garden City, NY), 1974.

World of Our Fathers: The Jews of Eastern Europe, Farrar, Straus (New York, NY), 1974.

Never to Forget: The Jews of the Holocaust, Harper (New York, NY), 1976.

Taking Root: Jewish Immigrants in America, Farrar, Straus (New York, NY), 1976.

Violins and Shovels: The WPA Arts Projects, Delacorte (New York, NY), 1976.

The Human Rights Book, Farrar, Straus (New York, NY), 1979.

All Times, All Peoples: A World History of Slavery, illustrated by Leonard Everett Fisher, Harper (New York, NY), 1980.

The Chinese Americans, Crowell (New York, NY), 1980.

The Hispanic Americans, photographs by Morrie Camhi and Catherine Noren, Crowell (New York, NY), 1982.

The Jewish Americans: A History in Their Own Words, 1650-1950, Crowell (New York, NY), 1982.

The Truth about the Ku Klux Klan, F. Watts (New York, NY), 1982.

The Terrorists, Harper (New York, NY), 1983.

A Book about Names, illustrated by Mischa Richter, Crowell (New York, NY), 1984.

Ain't Gonna Study War No More: The Story of America's Peaceseekers, Harper (New York, NY), 1985.

Betty Friedan: A Voice for Women's Rights, Viking (New York, NY), 1985.

Dorothea Lange: Life Through the Camera, Viking (New York, NY), 1985.

Mark Twain: A Writer's Life, F. Watts (New York, NY), 1985.

A Picture Album of American Jews, Jewish Publication Society (Philadelphia, PA), 1985.

Poverty in America, Morrow (New York, NY), 1986.

Winnie Mandela: The Soul of South Africa (part of the "Women of Our Time" series), illustrated by S. Marchesi, Viking (New York, NY), 1986.

George Washington and the Birth of Our Nation, F. Watts (New York, NY), 1986.

Mary McLeod Bethune: Voice of Black Hope (part of the "Women of Our Time" series), illustrated by S. Marchesi, Viking (New York, NY), 1987.

The Landscape of Memory, Viking (New York, NY), 1987.

The American Revolutionaries: A History in Their Own Words, 1750-1800, Crowell (New York, NY), 1987.

Starting from Home: A Writer's Beginnings, Viking (New York, NY), 1988.

Rescue: The Story of How Gentiles Saved Jews in the Holocaust, Harper (New York, NY), 1988.

Benjamin Franklin: The New American, F. Watts (New York, NY), 1988.

American Politics: How It Really Works, illustrated by David Small, Morrow (New York, NY), 1989.

Voices from the Civil War: A Documentary History of the Great American Conflict, Crowell (New York, NY), 1989.

The Bill of Rights: How We Got It and What It Means, Harper, 1990.

Crime in America, Morrow (New York, NY), 1990.

Columbus and the World around Him, F. Watts (New York, NY), 1990.

The American Promise: Voices of a Changing Nation, 1945-Present, Bantam (New York, NY), 1990.

Thomas Jefferson: The Revolutionary Aristocrat, F. Watts (New York, NY), 1991.

The Amazing Potato: A Story in Which the Incas, Conquistadors, Marie Antoinette, Thomas Jefferson, Wars, Famines, Immigrants, and French Fries All Play a Part, HarperCollins (New York, NY), 1992.

Andrew Jackson and His America, F. Watts (New York, NY), 1993.

Gold: The True Story of Why People Search for It, Mine It, Trade It, Steal It, Mint It, Hoard It, Shape It, Wear It, Fight and Kill for It, HarperCollins (New York, NY), 1993.

Cheap Raw Material, Viking (New York, NY), 1994.

Nonfiction for the Classroom: Milton Meltzer on Writing, History, and Social Responsibility, edited and with an introduction by E. Wendy Saul, Teachers College Press (New York, NY), 1994.

Theodore Roosevelt and His America, F. Watts (New York, NY), 1994.

Who Cares? Millions Do; A Book about Altruism, Walker and Co. (New York, NY), 1994.

Hold Your Horses: A Feedbag Full of Fact and Fable, HarperCollins (New York, NY), 1995.

Tom Paine: Voice of Revolution, F. Watts (New York, NY), 1996.

Weapons and Warfare: From the Stone Age to the Space Age, illustrated by Sergio Martinez, HarperCollins (New York, NY), 1996.

The Many Lives of Andrew Carnegie, F. Watts (New York, NY), 1997.

Langston Hughes, illustrated by Alcorn, Millbrook Press (Brookfield, CT), 1999.

Witches and Witch-Hunts: A History of Persecution, Blue Sky Press, 1999.

Carl Sandburg: A Biography, Twenty-First Century Press (Tolland, CT), 1999.

Driven from the Land: The Story of the Dust Bowl, Benchmark Books (San Marino, CA), 2000.

They Came in Chains: The Story of the Slave Ships, Benchmark Books (San Marino, CA), 2000.

There Comes a Time: The Struggle for Civil Rights, Random House (New York, NY), 2000.

FOR CHILDREN; FICTION

Underground Man, Bradbury (Scarsdale, NY), 1972.

FOR ADULTS; NONFICTION

(With Langston Hughes) *A Pictorial History of the Negroes in America,* Crown (New York, NY), 1956, fifth revised edition, with C. Eric Lincoln, published as *A Pictorial History of Black Americans,* 1983.

Mark Twain Himself, Crowell (New York, NY), 1960.

Dorothea Lange: A Photographer's Life, Farrar, Straus (New York, NY), 1978.

Slavery: A World History, Da Capo Press, 1993.

A History of Jewish Life from Eastern Europe to America, J. Aronson (Northvale, NJ), 1996.

EDITOR

Milestones to American Liberty: The Foundations of the Republic, Crowell (New York, NY), 1961.

(With Walter Harding) *A Thoreau Profile,* Crowell (New York, NY), 1962.

Thoreau: People, Principles, and Politics, Hill and Wang (New York, NY), 1963.

(With Patricia Holland and Francine Krasno) *The Collected Correspondence of Lydia Maria Child, 1817-1880: Guide and Index to the Microfiche Edition,* Kraus Microform (Millwood, NY), 1980.

(With Patricia Holland) *Lydia Maria Child: Selected Letters, 1817-1880,* University of Massachusetts Press (Amherst, MA), 1982.

Lincoln: In His Own Words, illustrated by Stephen Alcorn, Harcourt (New York, NY), 1993.

Frederick Douglass, in His Own Words, illustrated by Stephen Alcorn, Harcourt (New York, NY), 1995.

OTHER

Author of documentary films, including *History of the American Negro* (series of three half-hour films), Niagara Films, 1965; *Five,* Silvermine Films, 1971; *The Bread and Roses Strike: Lawrence, 1912* (filmstrip), District 1199 Cultural Center, 1980; *The Camera of My Family,* Anti-Defamation League, 1981; and *American Family: The Merlins,* Anti-Defamation League, 1982. Author of scripts for radio and television. Editor of the series "Women of America," Crowell (New York, NY), 1962-74, "Zenith Books," Doubleday (Garden City,

NY), 1963-73, and "Firebird Books," Scholastic Book Services (New York, NY), 1968-72. Contributor to periodicals, including *New York Times Magazine, New York Times Book Review, English Journal, Virginia Quarterly Review, Library Journal, Wilson Library Bulletin, School Library Journal, Microform Review,* *Horn Book, Children's Literature in Education, Lion and the Unicorn, Social Education, New Advocate,* and *Children's Literature Association Quarterly.* Member of U.S. editorial board of *Children's Literature in Education,* beginning in 1973, and of *Lion and the Unicorn,* beginning in 1980.

MURPHY, Jim 1947-
(Tim Murphy)

Personal

Born James John Murphy, September 25, 1947, in Newark, NJ; son of James K. (a certified public accountant) and Helen Irene (a bookkeeper and artist; maiden name, Grosso) Murphy; married Elaine A. Kelso (a company president), December 12, 1970 (marriage ended); married Alison Blank (a television producer, writer, and editor); children (second marriage): Michael, Benjamin. *Education:* Rutgers University, B.A., 1970; graduate study, Radcliffe College, 1970. *Hobbies and other interests:* Cooking, reading, gardening, collecting old postcards of ships and trains.

Jim Murphy

Addresses

Home and office—99 Maplewood Ave., Maplewood, NJ 07040.

Career

Seabury Press, Inc. (later Clarion Books), New York, NY, 1970-77, began as editorial secretary in the juvenile department, became managing editor; freelance writer and editor, 1977—. Also worked as a freelance editor for publishers such as Crowell; Crown; Farrar, Straus & Giroux; and Macmillan, and worked at a series of construction jobs in New York and New Jersey. *Member:* Asian Night Six Club (founding member).

Awards, Honors

Children's Choice designation, International Reading Association (IRA), and Best Book of the Year designation, *School Library Journal,* both 1979, both for *Weird and Wacky Inventions;* Children's Choice designation, IRA, Children's Book of the Year designation, Child Study Association, and Junior Literary Guild selection, all 1980, all for *Harold Thinks Big;* Best Book for Young Adults designation, American Library Association (ALA), 1982, for *Death Run;* Outstanding Science Trade Book for Children designation, National Science Teachers Association (NSTA) and Children's Book Council (CBC), 1984, for *Tractors: From Yesterday's Steam Wagons to Today's Turbo-Charged Giants;* Children's Choice designation, IRA, 1988, for *The Last Dinosaur;* Recommended Book for Reluctant Readers, ALA, and International Best Book designation, Society of School Librarians, both 1990, both for *Custom Car: A Nuts-and-Bolts Guide to Creating One;* Golden Kite Award for nonfiction, Society of Children's Book Writers and Illustrators (SCBWI), 1990, Dorothy Canfield Fisher Book Award nomination, 1991-92, William Allen White Children's Book Award nomination, 1992-93, Junior Literary Guild selection, Children's Book of the Year designation, Bank Street College, and Best Book of the Year designation, *School Library Journal,* all for *The Boys' War: Confederate and Union Solders Talk about the Civil War;* Nevada Young Readers Award, and Outstanding Science Trade Book for Children, NSTA and CBC, both 1992, both for *The Call of the Wolves;* Pick of the Lists designation, *American*

Bookseller, 1992, for *Backyard Bear;* Golden Kite Award for nonfiction, SCBWI, 1992, Editors' Choice designation, *Booklist,* Best Books of the Year designation, *School Library Journal,* and Book-of-the-Month Club selection, all 1992, all for *The Long Road to Gettysburg;* Orbis Pictus Award, National Council of Teachers of English (NCTE), Jefferson Cup, Virginia Librarians, Junior Literary Guild selection, Best Books of the Year designation, *School Library Journal,* all 1994, all for *Across America on an Emigrant Train; Boston Globe-Horn Book* Award for nonfiction, 1995, Orbis Pictus Award, NCTE, Jefferson Cup, Virginia Library Association, and Newbery Medal Honor Book designation, ALA, all 1996, all for *The Great Fire;* Robert F. Sibert Informational Book Award, Association of Library Services to Children, 2000, and Jefferson Cup, Virginia Library Association, 2001, both for *Blizzard! The Storm That Changed America.* Murphy's works have also been nominated for several regional awards.

Writings

NONFICTION; FOR CHILDREN AND YOUNG ADULTS

Weird and Wacky Inventions (also see below), Crown (New York, NY), 1978.

Two Hundred Years of Bicycles, Harper (New York, NY), 1983.

The Indy 500, Clarion (New York, NY), 1983.

Baseball's All-Time All-Stars, Clarion (New York, NY), 1984.

Tractors: From Yesterday's Steam Wagons to Today's Turbo-Charged Giants, Lippincott (New York, NY), 1984.

The Custom Car Book, Clarion (New York, NY), 1985.

Guess Again: More Weird and Wacky Inventions (sequel to *Weird and Wacky Inventions*), Four Winds Press (New York, NY), 1985.

Custom Car: A Nuts-and-Bolts Guide to Creating One, Clarion (New York, NY), 1989.

The Boys' War: Confederate and Union Soldiers Talk about the Civil War, Clarion (New York, NY), 1990.

The Long Road to Gettysburg, Clarion (New York, NY), 1992.

Across America on an Emigrant Train, Clarion (New York, NY), 1993.

Into the Deep Forest with Henry David Thoreau, illustrated by Kate Kiesler, Clarion (New York, NY), 1995.

The Great Fire, Scholastic (New York, NY), 1995.

A Young Patriot: The American Revolution as Experienced by One Boy, Clarion (New York, NY), 1995.

Gone A-Whaling: The Lure of the Sea and the Hunt for the Great Whale, Clarion (New York, NY), 1998.

Pick & Shovel Poet: The Journeys of Pascal D'Angelo, Clarion (New York, NY), 2000.

Blizzard! The Storm That Changed America, Scholastic (New York, NY), 2000.

FICTION; FOR CHILDREN AND YOUNG ADULTS, AS NOTED

Rat's Christmas Party (picture book), illustrated by Dick Gackenbach, Prentice-Hall (Englewood Cliffs, NJ), 1979.

Strange contraptions, like an 1885 flying machine, are pictured and explained in Murphy's **Guess Again: More Weird and Wacky Inventions.**

Harold Thinks Big (picture book), illustrated by Susanna Natti, Crown (New York, NY), 1980.

Death Run (young adult novel), Clarion (New York, NY), 1982.

The Last Dinosaur (picture book), illustrated by Mark Alan Weatherby, Scholastic (New York, NY), 1988.

The Call of the Wolves (picture book), illustrated by Mark Alan Weatherby, Scholastic (New York, NY), 1989.

Backyard Bear (picture book), illustrated by Jeffrey Greene, Scholastic (New York, NY), 1992.

Dinosaur for a Day (picture book), illustrated by Mark Alan Weatherby, Scholastic (New York, NY), 1992.

Night Terrors (young adult short stories), Scholastic (New York, NY), 1993.

West to a Land of Plenty: The Diary of Teresa Angelino Viscardi, New York to Idaho Territory, 1883 (young adult novel), Scholastic (New York, NY), 1998.

The Journal of James Edmond Pease: A Civil War Union Soldier, Virginia, 1863 (young adult novel), Scholastic (New York, NY), 1998.

My Face to the Wind: The Story of Sarah Jane Price, a Prairie Teacher (young adult novel), Scholastic (New York, NY), 2001.

OTHER

Contributor of articles to *Cricket* magazine. Some of the author's work appears under the name Tim Murphy.

Adaptations

The Great Fire, Across America on an Emigrant Train, and *The Boys' War* were released on audio cassette by Recorded Books in 1998 and 1999, respectively.

Work in Progress

Informational books about the Battle of the Alamo and the yellow fever plague in Philadelphia in 1793; a fictional book about a boy on a whaling cruise to the Arctic in 1873.

Sidelights

Called "one of the best writers of nonfiction for young people today" by a reviewer in *Voice of Youth Advocates*, Jim Murphy is an American author of fiction and nonfiction who is praised for successfully creating books in both genres as well as works that blend the two. A prolific writer, Murphy has written for children and young adults on a variety of topics, including sports, transportation, inventions, dinosaurs, animal life, mechanical devices, and the whaling industry, among others. In addition, he is the creator of picture books for younger children as well as historical fiction, contemporary realistic fiction, and a collection of horror stories for teenagers. Murphy is perhaps best known as the author of informational books on American history, especially those about military history and natural disasters, that are directed to young adults. In this area, he has produced well-received works about the Civil War, Chicago's Great Fire of 1871, and the blizzard that paralyzed the northeastern United States in 1888. Murphy has also written several works that draw on autobiographies or journals to create larger perspectives on such topics as the American Revolution, the American West, the immigrant experience, and the impact of industrialization on the environment. These books use the writings of famous authors, such as Robert Louis Stevenson and Henry David Thoreau, and lesser known writers, such as poet Pascal D'Angelo and teenage soldier Joseph Plumb Martin, as their primary sources. Characteristically, Murphy begins by drawing on the diaries, memoirs, journals, and letters written by the participants in the events he describes. He then adds important details to the thoughts and emotions of his subjects, such as the physical surroundings, social conditions, and prejudices of the time, and blends in complex analyses and in-depth insights from a contemporary perspective. The result provides a full picture of particular moments in history, dramatic events where ordinary people did extraordinary things. In these works, the author often includes eyewitness accounts by young people in order to demonstrate that children have made valuable contributions to history. In some of his books, such as those on dinosaurs, Murphy adds fact-based speculation to broaden his narratives. His works are often acknowledged for their extensive illustrations—photographs, lithographs, engravings, and other archival materials as well as original art by such illustrators as Dick Gackenbach, Kate Kiesler, and Mark Alan Weatherby.

Thematically, Murphy outlines the development of America and its people in his books, which also reflect their author's environmental consciousness. He underscores his works with documentation of how immigrants, minorities, women, and animals were—and are—treated; though he clearly expresses disapproval, Murphy is generally thought to remain objective. As a literary stylist, the author uses lean, straightforward prose that is noted for its drama, expressiveness, description, and humor. Reviewers have commented that several of Murphy's works of nonfiction are as hard to put down as a good novel. Murphy is often lauded for his insights, for his solid research, for his inclusion of unusual information, and for his attention to detail. Several of his works are considered outstanding contributions to the genre of nonfiction. Although he occasionally has been criticized for including too much description in his fiction, Murphy is generally recognized as a writer who has developed a fresh, distinctive approach to U.S. history, one who reflects his enthusiasm for his subjects and provides young readers with informative, entertaining introductions. A critic in the *St. James Guide to Children's Writers* commented that Murphy "has consistently made fact more interesting than any fiction," while a reviewer in *Voice of Youth Advocates* added that Murphy, "a first-rate historian comparable to Barbara Tuchman, makes the past live."

Born in Newark, New Jersey, Murphy is the son of James K., a certified public accountant, and Helen Grosso Murphy, an artist and bookkeeper. His father's Irish heritage and his mother's Italian heritage have been reflected in Murphy's works, especially in his fascination with the immigrant experience. Murphy once said, "I was raised in Kearny, New Jersey, a nice enough suburban town, made up largely of Scots, Irish, and Italians. My friends and I did all the normal things—played baseball and football endlessly, explored abandoned factories, walked the railroad tracks to the vast Jersey Meadowlands, and, in general, cooked up as much mischief as we could." Murphy and his friends also enjoyed exploring Newark and New York City, both of which were close by, and playing games of "let's pretend." In a promotional brochure for Scholastic, Murphy recalled that he and his friends "pretended to be explorers tramping through an river jungle or soldiers checking out the enemy in an abandoned factory."

Murphy was an indifferent reader as a boy, partially because he had an eye condition that went undiagnosed until he was nine or ten. But another reason was because, as he wrote in a letter to Kay E. Vandergrift, "I was in constant warfare with the nuns, who were always asking me why I wasn't as smart as my brother." He once commented, "I hardly cracked open a book willingly until a high school teacher announced that we could 'absolutely, positively *not* read' Hemingway's *A Farewell to Arms*. I promptly read it, and every other book I could get a hold of that I felt would shock my teacher. I also began writing, mostly poetry, but with an occasional story or play tossed in there." Murphy wrote in the Scholastic brochure, "Once I started to read, it became a passion. I would and still do read just about anything I can get my hands on: historical fiction, poetry, mysteries, books about medicine or the Revolutionary War or ancient Egypt or ... well, you get the picture. If I become interested in a subject, I will read book after book about it. And every so often, all of this reading gets my gray matter really energized and results in my writing a book." He told Vandergrift, "I began to read fiendishly after my father taught me to refinish furniture." After refinishing a maple bookcase, Murphy put it in his room. After realizing that the case needed books in it to look really finished, Murphy began to read the volumes that he brought in. He then began buying books with his own money and, as he told Vandergrift, "was off on a reading binge that hasn't stopped."

Murphy's interest in history started in seventh grade. One of his teachers told the class that all American Indians were not bad people, despite their reputation and their portrayal in the media. Murphy told Vandergrift, "This was back in 1957 or '58, so this came as a bit of a surprise to us, and resulted in a two-day discussion on how Native Americans were represented in history books, movies, and on TV, and how we had accepted this as the truth without question. [The teacher] used a similar approach with a variety of other history topics and really started us thinking. I came away from all of this feeling that if I wanted to have a real idea of what took place in the past, I had to read a lot more than one book about a subject." At St. Benedict's Preparatory School in Newark and at Rutgers University in New Brunswick, New Jersey, Murphy "managed to lead a strange double life." He liked some subjects, such as history, English, geology, art history, and city planning, but disliked others, such as languages and calculus, and, as he told Vandergrift, his grades "generally reflected my interest." He also ran track: Murphy was state champion in the sprints five or six times, was on the national champion 440 and mile relay teams, and came in third in the high school national competition for the sixty-yard dash. While a high school runner, Murphy received the nickname of "Tim" from his coach; he used this name off and on for years, and it even appeared in the *New York Times*. When he was eighteen, Murphy met Harold Latham, who was Margaret Mitchell's editor on *Gone with the Wind*. Latham read some of the fledgling writer's works and told him, as Murphy noted on a Scholastic Web site, "to keep writing and to imitate other people less and less. And it took me from ages 18 to 30 to figure that out."

After graduating from Rutgers, Murphy attended graduate school briefly at Radcliffe College in Cambridge, Massachusetts. At around the same time, he married Elaine A. Kelso; after their marriage dissolved, Murphy married Alison Blank, with whom he has two sons, Michael and Benjamin. Murphy returned home after grad school and worked at a variety of construction jobs in New York City and in New Jersey. He also repaired boilers, tarred roofs, put up fences, operated a mold-injection machine, and did maintenance for two apartment buildings. At the same time, he was looking for a job in publishing, especially in the area of children's books. Murphy told Vandergrift, "One reason I wanted to get into children's books was that I love illustrations and illustrated books." After thirty or forty interviews, he was hired as a secretarial assistant by the Seabury Press, which is now called Clarion Books. Murphy was able to perform a wide variety of jobs in this position,

including editing, working with catalog design, and participating in the overall decision-making process. He worked there for James Cross Giblin, an editor who is also a well-respected author of nonfiction for children. Murphy told Vandergrift that his experience at Clarion "was priceless. What's more, I learned how to read and evaluate a manuscript with an editor's and publisher's eye. I try to use these same standards when I write and revise my own manuscripts." Murphy rose to the position of managing editor at Clarion; on his thirtieth birthday, he realized that he wanted to write his own books. In 1977, he left Clarion to become a freelance writer.

In 1978, Murphy produced his first book, *Weird and Wacky Inventions*. The author drew upon the files of the U.S. Patent Office to present young readers with a collection of gadgets and contraptions—most unsuccessful with the public—that were registered from the 1700s on. The inventions include such creations as a dimple-maker, a bird diaper, an automatic hat-tipper, a portable fire escape, a portable bathtub, jumping shoes, and the safety pin. Murphy presents young readers with a reproduction of the picture that originally accompanied the invention and asks his audience to guess its use; the answer and a further explanation are given on the following page. Final chapters discuss how one invention leads to another and detail the process of getting a patent. A reviewer in *Publishers Weekly* said, "The reaction of kids to an aptly named book will range from smiles to giggles to guffaws. And any adult would find Murphy's work worth diving into, for instruction and merriment." Writing in *School Library Journal*, Robert Unsworth stated that the book "is very nicely put together and should appeal to youngsters beyond the third to fifth grade levels for whom it is intended." Barbara Elleman of *Booklist* called *Weird and Wacky*

Using author Robert Louis Stevenson's journal entries about his 1879 journey from Scotland to California, as well as other documents, Murphy describes the westward movement across the United States and the development of the transcontinental railroad. (From Across America on an Emigrant Train.*)*

Inventions "a browser's delight." In 1986, Murphy created a sequel, *Guess Again: More Weird and Wacky Inventions.* Using a format similar to that of the first book, *Guess Again* features such creations as a coffin with an escape hatch, a trap for tapeworms, and training pants for dogs. A critic in *Publishers Weekly* noted, "The list goes on and on, each more hilarious than the last.... *Guess Again* is just as wacky as its predecessor." Writing in *Appraisal: Science Books for Young People,* Arrolyn H. Vernon concluded, "The book should be fun for those who enjoy the cryptic, especially when imaginative visualization is exercised.... And some of what appears to be fluff could turn out to be great for older students, considering the mysterious ways of creativity."

Throughout the 1980s, Murphy contributed works to several genres. For example, he created picture books featuring anthropomorphic animals and informational books about such subjects as the history of bicycles, the history of the Indianapolis 500, the development of the modern tractor, the life stories of all-star baseball players from the American and National Leagues, and a guide to car restoration. Murphy produced his first novel for young adults, *Death Run,* in 1982. The story, which has a contemporary setting and is told from different points of view, outlines how sophomore Brian Halihan, hanging out in the park with three older schoolmates, is involved in the death of Bill Jankowski, the star player on the school basketball team. When the boys see Bill coming through the park with his basketball, they tease and taunt him; gang leader Roger then slams Bill's basketball against his face, knocking him down. Bill has an epileptic seizure, then a burst aneurysm. After the boys take off, Brian wants to report the incident, but is talked out of doing so by Roger. Brian becomes obsessed with Bill's death and begins hanging around the dead boy's home. Meanwhile, Detective Robert Wheeler, who suspects that Bill's death was not an accident, continues to investigate the case even after it is closed. Wheeler is living with his memory of shooting a fleeing boy; as he closes in on Brian, he almost does the same thing to him. Writing in the *ALAN Review,* Tony Manna said, "It is the psychology of detection and the anatomy of fear—mostly Brian's—which makes Murphy's first novel such an enticing read. Despite his inclination to tell more than he shows, Murphy is a master at creating tension and sustaining the complex emotions of the hunter and the hunted." Stephanie Zvirin of *Booklist* added, "Few stories of this genre are written specifically for a teenage audience, and Murphy handles his competently, keeping a firm hold on tough talk, including plenty of fast-action sequences, and providing just enough character motivation to fill out the plot."

In 1988, Murphy produced *The Last Dinosaur,* a fact-based fictional speculation on the passing of the age of dinosaurs. Set sixty-five million years ago, this picture book is illustrated with paintings by Mark Alan Weatherby. The book focuses on a female Triceratops, left alone when the only males in her herd are killed in a fight with a Tyrannosaurs Rex. After she abandons her nest to escape a forest fire, her eggs are eaten by some

small shrewlike mammals. On the last page, the Triceratops pads away, in search of food and perhaps another herd. Janet Hickman of *Language Arts* called *The Last Dinosaur* "surprisingly poignant," adding "It's quite an accomplishment to make a sixty-five-million-year-old setting seem immediate.... This is a welcome companion for 'straight' informational books that examine possible reasons for the dinosaurs' extinction." Writing in *Bulletin of the Center for Children's Books,* Betsy Hearne concluded, "The scenario certainly renders the end of the Age of Dinosaurs more immediate than many non-fiction accounts."

Four years later, Murphy produced a related title, *Dinosaur for a Day,* which again blends fact and fiction and includes illustrations by Weatherby. In this book, young readers follow a mother hypsilophodon and her eight children on their search for food. When the family encounters a deinonychus pack that charges their clearing, the mother must outrun the carnivores and divert them from her babies. After doing so, she rejoins her family. The story is accompanied by factual information about dinosaurs. *Dinosaur for a Day* generally received favorable reviews. A critic in *St. James Guide to Children's Writers* called it "a model of what science books for younger children should be," while Nicholas Hotton III of *Science Books & Films* commented, "This very attractive book is simple in concept, well executed, and gorgeously illustrated." Weatherby also provided the illustrations for *The Call of the Wolves,* the story of a young wolf that is separated from his pack during a hunt for caribou in the Arctic. Trapped by illegal hunters who shoot at him from a plane, the wolf plunges over a cliff, injuring his leg. He journeys painfully—and dangerously—through a snowstorm in another pack's territory before reaching home. Betsy Hearne of *Bulletin of the Center for Children's Books* noted, "With an involving text and arresting art, this is a nature narrative that commands attention without ever becoming sentimental or anthropomorphic." A critic in *Kirkus Reviews* dubbed *The Call of the Wolves* an "effective plea for respect for and conservation of an often misunderstood fellow creature."

The Boys' War: Confederate and Union Soldiers Talk about the Civil War is regarded as a major departure for Murphy as well as one of the author's most celebrated books. Murphy uses eyewitness accounts of the Civil War written by soldiers from ages twelve to sixteen, who made up as much as twenty percent of the total number of enlisted men, to present a view of the war that is often considered unique. The author, who was inspired to write *The Boys' War* by the journal of a fifteen-year-old Union soldier that he found in a library, covers such aspects as battles, living conditions, imprisonment, suffering, and death. Finally, he addresses the psychological effects of the war on these young people and what it was like for the survivors to reunite with their families at the end of the war. Writing in *Voice of Youth Advocates,* Joanne Johnson stated, "The excerpts from the diaries and letters written home by this group of young men ... provides an insight for YAs not available in other books. Reading their reactions makes this war come alive in a way that the diaries and letters of adults may not." Margaret A. Bush of *Horn Book* said, "It is startling to learn of the large numbers of very young soldiers whose lives were given to the war, and this well-researched and readable account provides fresh insight into the human cost of a pivotal event in United States history." A critic in the *St. James Guide to Children's Literature* observed that since the publication of *The Boys' War,* "historical nonfiction, using primary sources as much as possible, has become Murphy's most important contribution to children's and young adult literature."

In *The Long Road to Gettysburg,* Murphy draws on the journals of two teenage soldiers, nineteen-year-old Confederate lieutenant John Dooley and seventeen-year-old Union corporal Thomas Galway, who were involved in one of the Civil War's most pivotal battles. Beginning and ending with the dedication ceremony at which Abraham Lincoln delivered the Gettysburg Address, Murphy presents the story of the battle from the point of view of these two participants. In his text, Murphy does not spare readers the grim details of the battle; in his epilogue, he outlines the postwar lives of Dooley and Galway. Writing in *Horn Book,* Anita Silvey commented that Murphy "uses all his fine skills as a information writer—clarity of detail, conciseness, understanding of his age group, and ability to find the drama appealing to readers—to frame a well-crafted account of a single battle in the war." Carolyn Phelan of *Booklist* added, "the firsthand accounts ... give the narrative immediacy and personalize the horrors of battle.... An important addition to the Civil War shelf." Writing in *School Library Journal,* Elizabeth M. Reardon concluded, "By focusing on these two ordinary soldiers, readers get a new perspective on this decisive and bloody battle. A first-rate addition to Civil War collections."

Across America on an Emigrant Train, an informational books directed to young adults, is one of Murphy's most recognized works. In this book, he uses the journey of twenty-nine-year-old Scottish author Robert Louis Stevenson to explore the development of the transcontinental railroad and the growth of the westward movement in the late nineteenth century. Murphy draws extensively from Stevenson's own account of his trip, which took place in 1879. Stevenson traveled by boat and train from Edinburgh, Scotland, to Monterey, California, to reach his friend Fanny Osbourne, an American woman who had become gravely ill with brain fever. On his journey, Stevenson traveled with other newcomers to the United States, emigrants who faced cramped, unsanitary conditions on the train but were filled with hope. While quoting the young author's point of view, Murphy adds historical context and discusses related topics, such as the roles of different ethnic groups in building the railroads, how Native American life was destroyed by the coming of the railroads, and the real nature of the Wild West. He ends the book with a joyful reunion between Stevenson and Osbourne, who recovered from her illness and eventually became his wife; an epilogue summarizes Stevenson's subsequent rise to fame and brief last years. Noting Murphy's "delightfully effective

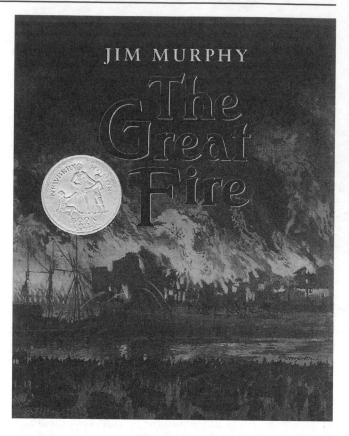

With a mixture of personal accounts and factual documentation, Murphy chronicles the devastating Chicago fire of 1871, its causes and effects, and the subsequent attempts to rebuild the city. (Cover illustration by John Thompson.)

narrative device," a *Kirkus Reviews* critic called *Across America on an Emigrant Train* a "fascinating, imaginatively structured account that brings the experience vividly to life in all its details; history at its best." *School Library Journal* contributor Diane S. Marton called the book "a readable and valuable contribution to literature concerning expansion into the American West." Writing in *Booklist,* Hazel Rochman stated that the facts and feelings that Murphy represents "tell a compelling story of adventure and failure, courage and cruelty, enrichment and oppression.... The experience of ordinary people revitalizes the myths of the West."

In 1871, the city of Chicago was devastated by a blaze that killed 300 people and destroyed 17,500 buildings. In *The Great Fire,* Murphy explores the causes and effects of this disaster, one of the most extensive in American history. The author combines details of the fire and its damage with personal anecdotes from newspaper accounts—including those by twelve-year-old Claire Innes, who was trapped in an alley after being separated from her family by a terrified mob—and quotes from subsequent books. Murphy suggests that the fire could have been contained, but factors such as architectural and human errors, the dry weather, the high winds, and the lack of organization of the city's fire brigade contributed to the ultimate tragedy. The author also notes the discrimination that surfaced as a result of the blaze. Rich residents, many of whom lost their homes, were quick to blame the city's poor immigrant population for the fire; as a result, poor residents were forced into slums or out of Chicago permanently. Writing in *Bulletin of the Center for Children's Books,* Elizabeth Bush noted that Murphy's account "offers not only the luridly enticing details disaster junkies crave, but also a more complex analysis of the causes of the conflagration than is usually offered in children's history books, ... Murphy makes an analytical leap at which children's authors often balk." Frances Bradburn of *Booklist* called the author's text "dramatic" and "riveting" before concluding that *The Great Fire* "will automatically draw readers with its fiery cover and illustrations of disasters, but the text will keep them reading." Writing in *School Library Journal,* Susannah Price added that Murphy's text "reads like an adventure/survival novel and is just as hard to put down" before going on to say that *The Great Fire* is "[h]istory writing as its best."

With *Blizzard! The Storm That Changed America,* Murphy produced an account of the terrible snowstorm that hit the northeastern United States in March, 1888. Drawing on newspaper articles, letters, journals, and histories of the period, the author describes the storm from the perspectives of people of various ages and social positions, some of whom survived the storm and others who did not. He also discusses the political and social conditions of the time and outlines how life in the United States was changed by the storm: for example, the effects of the blizzard led to the founding of the U.S. Weather Bureau and to the development of subways in New York City. Writing in *Booklist,* Jean Franklin said that *Blizzard!* "is an example of stellar nonfiction." A reviewer in *Children's Literature Review* added that Murphy's "clear and even-handed approach to describing the details makes this a page-turner. He never sensationalizes.... Murphy is as sharp here as he was in *The Great Fire.*" Writing in *School Library Journal,* Andrew Medlar concluded by calling *Blizzard!* "a superb piece of writing and history."

In addition to his work in other genres, Murphy has become well known for writing historical fiction that draws on some of the backgrounds of his nonfiction. His first work of this type, *West to a Land of Plenty: The Diary of Teresa Angelino Viscardi, New York to Idaho Territory, 1883* describes how a family of Italian immigrants journeys to the Idaho Territory by train and covered wagon. Written in the form of diary entries by fourteen-year-old Teresa and her younger sister Netta, the novel outlines the family's experiences as they go west to settle in an Idaho town called Opportunity. Teresa, the main narrator, describes how her family makes it through the arduous journey, which includes sickness, danger, and, ultimately, Netta's death. Throughout her narrative, Teresa grows: she has her first romance and also shows courage and presence of mind when she saves her grandmother from thieves. In an epilogue dated 1952, Teresa speaks of her happiness with her life; it is addressed to Netta. Janet Gillen of *School Library Journal* noted of Teresa, "Reminiscent of a Willa Cather heroine, the girl is resourceful, strong-

minded, and intelligent." Writing in *Bulletin of the Center for Children's Books,* Elizabeth Bush said, "What could have been merely another overland trail story is considerably enriched by Murphy's attention to the rapid and profound Americanization of these fictional Italian immigrants." Another of the author's books of historical fiction is *The Journal of James Edward Pease: A Civil War Union Soldier, Virginia, 1863,* a work that also makes use of the diary format. As the story begins, James, a sixteen-year-old private who is serving in the New York Volunteers, is considered the "Jonah," or bad luck charm, of his outfit. Assigned to be the historian of his company, James describes infantry life, the horrors of battle and of the medical practices of the period, and his own thoughts and emotions. He loses several friends to death and desertion. When he is lost behind enemy lines in the South, James is hidden from Confederate soldiers by a slave family whom he has befriended. Throughout the course of the novel, James matures, learns the meaning of friendship, and receives a promotion for doing a good job. Writing in *Catholic Library World,* Carol L. Kennedy called *The Journal of James Edmond Pease* an "excellent piece of historical fiction." Roger Leslie of *Booklist* added that, despite ambiguities, "each entry is very well written, and Pease's unassuming personality keeps him a vivid, accessible narrator throughout."

In assessing his career, Murphy once wrote, "I thoroughly enjoy my work. The nonfiction projects let me research subjects that I'm really interested in; they provide an opportunity to tell kids some unusual bits of information. The fiction lets me get out some of the thoughts and opinions that rattle around in my head." In an interview on the Scholastic Web site, Murphy stated that his favorite part of the writing process is doing the research: "I love to read. I love to hunt around for details. I view research as a kind of detective work where I try to discover all of the secrets about any subject. That's my favorite part!" He added, "I really enjoy taking topics that might seem commonplace or like they've been done before and finding new ways to tell the story of the event. I do it specifically for young readers because I hope that in some way my enthusiasm will get them to read more about the subject." When asked if he planned to continue writing historical books, Murphy answered, "Absolutely. I'm going to write until I drop! I don't know what else I could do!" In his commentary on another Scholastic Web site, Murphy concluded, "[L]ife is made up of many kinds of journey. Some are physical, like moving from one home to another, but most are interior journeys of the heart or soul. The important thing is to face each with a positive attitude. And to try and learn as much about yourself and other as you can along the way. Oh, yes—and to have fun while you are experiencing all of these things."

Biographical and Critical Sources

BOOKS

Authors & Artists for Young Adults, Volume 26, Gale (Detroit, MI), 1999.

Beacham's Guide to Literature for Young Adults, Volume 10, Gale (Detroit, MI), 2000.

Beech, Linda Ward, and others, *The Great Fire: Study Guide,* Scholastic Professional Books, 1996.

Children's Literature Review, Volume 53, Gale (Detroit, MI), 1999.

Holmes, Thomas E., *Literature of the U.S. Civil War,* New Haven Teachers Institute, 1997.

Laughlin, Mildred, *Visual Literacy through Picture Books K-12: A Curriculum Approach,* EDRS, 1980.

Literature Guide: The Great Fire, Scholastic (New York, NY), 1999.

Roberts, Patricia, *Taking Humor Seriously in Children's Literature,* Scarecrow Press, 1997.

St. James Guide to Children's Writers, 5th edition, edited by Tom and Sarah Pendergast, St. James Press (Detroit, MI), 1999.

Wyatt, Flora R., and others, *Popular Nonfiction Authors for Children: A Biographical and Thematic Guide,* Libraries Unlimited, 1998.

PERIODICALS

ALAN Review, fall, 1982, Tony Manna, review of *Death Run,* p. 21.

Appraisal: Science Books for Young People, winter, 1987, Arrolyn H. Vernon, review of *Guess Again: More Weird and Wacky Inventions,* pp. 48-49.

Booklist, September 1, 1978, Barbara Elleman, review of *Weird and Wacky Inventions,* p. 52; May 1, 1982, Stephanie Zvirin, review of *Death Run,* p. 1153; May 15, 1992, Carolyn Phelan, review of *The Long Road to Gettysburg,* p. 1677; Hazel Rochman, review of *Across America on an Emigrant Train,* p. ; June 1, 1995, Frances Bradburn, review of *The Great Fire,* p. 1757; November 15, 1998, Roger Leslie, review of *The Journal of James Edmond Pease: A Civil War Union Soldier,* p. 581; February 15, 2001, Jean Franklin, review of *Blizzard!, The Storm That Changed America,* p. 1135.

Bulletin of the Center for Children's Books, June, 1988, Betsy Hearne, review of *The Last Dinosaur,* p. 213; September, 1989, Betsy Hearne, review of *The Call of the Wolves,* p. 13; May, 1995, Elizabeth Bush, review of *The Great Fire,* pp. 297-298; March, 1998, Elizabeth Bush, review of *West to a Land of Plenty: The Diary of Teresa Angelino Viscardi,* p. 253.

Catholic Library World, June, 1999, Carol L. Kennedy, review of *The Journal of James Edmond Pease,* p. 64.

Horn Book, January-February, 1991, Margaret A. Bush, review of *The Boys' War: Confederate and Union Soldiers Talk about the Civil War,* pp. 86-87; July-August, 1992, Anita Silvey, review of *The Long Road to Gettysburg,* pp. 469-470.

Kirkus Reviews, November 15, 1989, review of *The Call of the Wolves,* p. 1674; November 15, 1993, review of *Across America on an Emigrant Train,* p. 1465.

Language Arts, September, 1988, Janet Hickman, review of *The Last Dinosaur,* p. 500.

Publishers Weekly, July 17, 1978, review of *Weird and Wacky Inventions,* p. 168; June 27, 1986, review of *Guess Again: More Weird and Wacky Inventions,* p. 97.

School Library Journal, November, 1978, Robert Unsworth, review of *Weird and Wacky Inventions,* p. 66; June, 1992, Elizabeth M. Reardon, review of *The Long Road to Gettysburg,* p. 146; December, 1993, Diane S. Marton, review of *Across America on an Emigrant Train,* pp. 129-130; July, 1995, Susannah Price, review of *The Great Fire,* pp. 89-90; Janet Gillen, review of *West to a Land of Plenty;* December, 2000, Andrew Medlar, review of *Blizzard!,* p. 164.

Science Books & Films, August-September, 1993, Nicholas Hotton III, review of *Dinosaur for a Day,* p. 180.

Voice of Youth Advocates, April, 1991, Joanne Johnson, review of *The Boys' War: Confederate and Union Soldiers Talk about the Civil War,* p. 60; June, 1996, review of *The Great Fire,* p. 88.

ON-LINE

Scholastic Web site, http://teacher.scholastic.com/ (April 20, 2001), "Jim Murphy—About the Author," and interview with Jim Murphy.

Learning about Jim Murphy, http://www.scils.rutgers.edu/ (April 20, 2001), Kay E. Vandergrift, personal correspondence with Jim Murphy on November 27, 1996.

OTHER

Murphy, Jim, author comments in a Scholastic promotional brochure, c. 1995.*

—*Sketch by Gerard J. Senick*

*   *   *

MURPHY, Tim
See MURPHY, Jim

*   *   *

MUSGROVE, Margaret W(ynkoop) 1943-

Personal

Born November 19, 1943, in New Britain, CT; daughter of John T. (an electrician) and Margaret (Holden) Wynkoop; married George Gilbert (director of Social Services for Baltimore, MD), August 28, 1971; children: Taura Johnene, George Derek. *Education:* University of Connecticut, B.A., 1966; Central Connecticut State University, M.S., 1970; University of Massachusetts, Ed.D., 1979. *Politics:* Democrat. *Religion:* Christian.

Addresses

Office—Loyola College, 4501 North Charles St., Baltimore, MD 21210-2699.

Career

Author and educator. High school English teacher in Hartford, CT, 1967-69, 1970; English teacher at community school, Accra, Ghana, 1970; South Central Community College, New Haven, CT, counselor and teacher of

English composition, 1971-72; Berkshire Community College, Pittsfield, MA, English teacher, 1971; Middle College, director, January-August, 1981; Community College of Baltimore, Baltimore, MD, English teacher, director of Developmental Studies, coordinator for Center for Educational Development, and coordinator of Early Childhood Education, 1981-91; Loyola College, writing teacher, 1991—. *Member:* Society of Children's Book Writers and Illustrators, Maryland Writer's Project, International Women Writers Guild.

Awards, Honors

Honor list, *Horn Book,* 1977, for *Ashanti to Zulu: African Traditions;* Fulbright Scholar, 1997-98.

Writings

Ashanti to Zulu: African Traditions, illustrated by Leo and Diane Dillon, Dial (New York, NY), 1976.
(Reteller) *The Spider Weaver: A Legend of Kente,* illustrated by Julia Cairns, Blue Sky Press (New York, NY), 2001.

Sidelights

Margaret W. Musgrove once told *SATA:* "The overt and covert racism in children's literature are insidious forces that must be overcome for the good of all children." In her first picture book, *Ashanti to Zulu: African Traditions,* the author, who has lived and traveled in West Africa, provides a lesson in the diversity of African cultures. From A to Z, Musgrove spotlights African tribes, describing clothing, legends, traditions, dwellings, and ways of life in a brief paragraph for each tribe. Musgrove's words are illustrated with lavish paintings by Diane and Leo Dillon in watercolor, pastel, and acrylic, each depicting a tableau, including a man, woman, child, dwelling, animal, and artifact. In addition, each illustration distinctively belongs to the tribe described in the text. In relating a little something about so many different cultures and traditions, according to *Horn Book* reviewer Paul Heins, the author conveys the richness and variety of the African continent, and "in fulfilling her purpose, she has been aided immeasurably by the illustrators." Likewise, a reviewer in *Bulletin of the Center for Children's Books* contended that the text is "dignified and the material informative." While a critic for *Kirkus Reviews* noted that in a book crammed with so much information, especially visual information, the coverage of the subject is necessarily superficial, this critic nevertheless predicted that *Ashanti to Zulu* "is certain to attract much regard."

Biographical and Critical Sources

PERIODICALS

Bulletin of the Center for Children's Books, March, 1977, review of *Ashanti to Zulu,* p. 110.
Horn Book, April, 1977, Paul Heins, review of *Ashanti to Zulu,* p. 179.
Kirkus Reviews, December 15, 1976, review of *Ashanti to Zulu,* p. 1307.
Wilson Library Bulletin, February, 1977.*

N–O

NICHOLS, Judy 1947-

Personal

Born December 13, 1947, in Elkhart, IN; daughter of James Edwin Fuller and Mary Margaret (Barber) Fuller Montroy; married James R. Nichols (a manager), July 4, 1972. *Education:* Ferris State College, Associate of Applied Science (library science), 1967; Wichita State University, B.A. (magna cum laude; general studies), 1980; Emporia State University, M.L.S., 1982. *Hobbies and other interests:* Reading, golf, painting, theater, dancing, crafts, and needlework.

Addresses

Home—5403 Sullivan Rd., Wichita, KS 67204-1959. *E-mail*—jnichols4@kscable.com.

Career

Elkhart Public Library, Elkhart, IN, children's librarian, 1968-72; Wichita Public Library, Wichita, KS, children's librarian, 1980-83, coordinator of youth services, 1989-96; Decatur Public Library, Decatur, IL, children's librarian, 1983-85; Nancy Renfro Studios, Austin, TX, workshop leader, 1985-89; owner of Talespinner Productions, 1985—; Waco Independent School District, Waco, TX, elementary school librarian, 1986; professional storyteller and puppeteer, 1996—. Host, *Now Hear This!* (cable television read-aloud program), Wichita, 1991-94; consultant, Wichita Child Care Association, Wichita, 1996-98; consultant, Book It! Program, Pizza Hut, Wichita, 1996—; consultant, Arts Partners, Wichita, 1998—.

Texas Storytelling Festival, board of directors, 1986-88; Alabama Arts Council, touring artist, 1987-90; Kansas Arts Commission, touring artist, 1988-90; National Storytelling Association Conference, regional performer, Kansas City, MO, 1998; Arts Partners, touring artist, Wichita, KS, 1998—. *Member:* American Society for Training and Development, Society of Children's Book

Judy Nichols

Writers and Illustrators, National Storytelling Network, Puppeteers of America, Prairiewind Storytellers (charter member), River and Prairie Storyweavers, Territory Tellers of Oklahoma, Tejas Storytelling Association, Beta Sigma Phi, Beta Phi Mu.

Writings

Storytimes for Two-Year-Olds, illustrated by Lori D. Sears, American Library Association (Chicago, IL), 1987, second edition, 1998.

Biodiversity: U.S. (annotated bibliography), The Book It! Program, 1996.

Tales from the Heart (audiotape), Talespinner Productions, 1996.

Once Upon a Time ... Fun with Favorite Folk Tales (audiotape), Talespinner Productions, 1996.

Christmas Tales (audiotape), Talespinner Productions, 1997.

Biodiversity: The World (annotated bibliography), The Book It! Program, 1997.

Amazing Millennium: The First 900 Years of Invention and Discovery (annotated bibliography with chronology), The Book It! Program, 1998.

Amazing Millennium: The 20th Century Inventions and Discoveries (annotated bibliography with chronology), The Book It! Program, 1999.

Lift Off to Space (annotated bibliography with chronology), The Book It! Program, 2000.

The Edge of Adventure (summer reading manual), Kansas State Library (Topeka, KS), 2000.

Work in Progress

Bringing Sock Puppets Alive, Lap-Stages, Sock Puppet Costumes, Pecos Bill's Prairie-Sized Rainbow: An Original Tall Tale, and *Sondra Ellen: A Prairie Cinderella.*

Sidelights

Judy Nichols told *SATA:* "I was born in northern Indiana but spent most of my childhood in southern Michigan. The oldest of four, I was pampered by my paternal grandmother, who fed me homemade sugar cookies and taught me to crochet. My busy mother had her hands full with my three younger brothers, and when I wasn't helping her in the house, I was romping in the backyard with my dog, making up exotic worlds ... where no little brothers lived.

"I was an avid reader as a child, devouring words and books and savoring the images they conveyed. I loved mythology, fairy tales, and classic children's stories like *Treasure Island* and *Black Beauty.* As a first-generation television child, I was also enamored by the stories brought into our home with pictures and sounds. We watched TV until bedtime, then I read with a flashlight into the night.

"Living in rural Michigan, I discovered libraries in junior high when I met Lucy Gallup, the school librarian. She fed and guided my reading appetites through the next six years and invited me to become a library aide when I was a sophomore. She encouraged me to write for the school newspaper, lavishing praise on my most mundane efforts, such as 'How to Read a Dictionary.'

"As a teenager I was a loner and a tomboy. Growing up with three brothers, I preferred reading and outdoor adventures to wearing makeup, dating, and giggling on the school bus over movie magazines. I continued to create fantasy worlds in my mind, acting out heroic adventures on long walks in the woods. I loved nature, and we raised baby raccoons, rabbits, lizards, snakes, and hawks as pets.

"When I finished high school, I knew I wanted to be a librarian just like Mrs. Gallup; I wanted to introduce other children to the fantastic worlds available to them in books. I began my first library job at the Elkhart (Indiana) Public Library, working in the same town where I'd been born. The children's librarian shared my loved of books and reading, and she taught me how to tell stories to children in story hour, using the pictures in the book as a prop. In storytime I discovered a new joy: guiding children into stories and books with the spoken word.

"When I married Jim in 1972, I got Kansas as a wedding present. He was transferred there the month before our wedding. I began a career as a children's librarian that would lead me to jobs and storytelling opportunities in Georgia, Illinois, and Texas over the next fifteen years. Along the way, I met and worked with Barbara Fischer and Nancy Renfro, creative puppeteers who introduced me to the magic of using puppets with children. I began performing and teaching storytelling and puppetry at conferences and festivals throughout the United States.

"While I was working at the Wichita (Kansas) Public Library, I had created a story-time program for toddlers and their caregivers, developing parent handouts that included books, fingerplays, crafts, and rhymes on many topics. As I attended conferences and talked with other children's librarians who were also doing toddler programs, I discovered that we had all gone through basically the same trial-and-error process, because there was no book telling us how to do it. These other librarians were interested in my parent handouts, and one told me that if I put them in a book, she would buy it.

"On advice from a regional library consultant, I called the American Library Association (ALA) to see if they would be interested in a book for librarians on developing library programs for toddlers. I submitted a proposal for a practical book with introductory chapters describing the target audience and sample programs that would be easy to replicate. The first edition was published in 1987, and it became apparent that it was a book in the right place at the right time.

"The book was based on my personal experience presenting storytimes for toddlers. The format, focusing on thirty-three programs with books, fingerplays, craft ideas, and parent follow-up suggestions, was welcomed by librarians and early childhood educators. The ALA was pleased with the response, and I received many compliments and positive comments on the practicality of the book. Parents also found the book helpful to locate books and crafts appropriate for their toddlers. One unexpected result was that teachers of developmentally delayed children also found the book beneficial.

"The ALA approached me in 1996 about updating and revising the book for a second edition, and it was released in 1998. It was expanded to include fifty themed programs, each with updated book lists, songs, fingerplays, crafts, parents suggestions, and helpful indexes. Although there have been other books on the subject published during the past ten years, *Storytimes for Two-Year-Olds* continues to be a popular resource for busy children's librarians.

"I wrote this book because I wanted to encourage librarians to invite parents and toddlers into their facilities and to introduce them to the library and children's literature at an early age. Two-year-olds have a reputation of being willful and out-of-control, having minuscule attentions and horrific temper tantrums. Many parents struggle to provide the support and stimulus necessary for their intellectual and emotional growth while keeping them under control. Librarians were hesitant to tackle an age level with such challenges.

"I know from experience that these little people can be some of the most rewarding patrons of libraries. They understand far more than they can communicate back to you, and in my opinion it is this disparity in communication skills that results in frustration and temper tantrums. When you introduce young children to language in books, songs, fingerplays, and rhymes, you are giving them the words they can use to communicate within their worlds.

"With the infant brain research and recognition of the important role language plays in the development of young children's brains, it is essential to reach as many parents and caregivers as possible with the message that "babies need books." And it is equally essential to model for them how to share stories, songs, and play with rhymes. Too often these skills are not passed along from past generations. Most libraries now offer programs not only for toddlers but also for infants and babies. I am proud that my book continues to help children's librarians reach these important generations of young children and to help them become the best they can be in our ever-changing world.

"Currently I am a full-time author, storyteller, and puppeteer. I perform at festivals and give speeches and workshops at conferences throughout the country. The joy of my life is still guiding listeners (children and adults) into the magical realm of story, and I've started writing some of my own stories for future publication."

Biographical and Critical Sources

PERIODICALS

Booklist, August, 1998, Julie Corsaro, review of *Storytimes for Two-Year-Olds,* p. 2019.

NUNN, Laura (Donna) Silverstein 1968-

Personal

Born May 28, 1968, in Brooklyn, NY; daughter of Alvin (a professor and writer) and Virginia B. (a translator and writer; maiden name, Opshelor) Silverstein; married Matthew R. Nunn, February 28, 1992; children: Corey Michael. *Education:* Kean College of New Jersey, B.A., 1990. *Hobbie and other interests:* Gardening, cross-stitching, family.

Addresses

Home—4 Three Pond Lane, Glen Gardner, NJ 08826. *E-mail*—LauraDonna@aol.com.

Career

AVSTAR Publishing, clerical worker and researcher, 1982—; author, 1989—.

Laura Silverstein Nunn

Writings

WITH PARENTS, ALVIN AND VIRGINIA B. SILVERSTEIN

AIDS: An All-About Guide for Young Adults ("Issues in Focus" series), Enslow Publishers (Berkeley Heights, NJ), 1999.

Puberty, Watts (Danbury, CT), 2000.

Lyme Disease (also see below), Watts (Danbury, CT), 2000.

"ENDANGERED IN AMERICA" SERIES; WITH PARENTS, ALVIN AND VIRGINIA B. SILVERSTEIN

The Black-Footed Ferret, Millbrook (Brookfield, CT), 1995.

(With Robert Alan Silverstein) *The Manattee,* Millbrook (Brookfield, CT), 1996.

The Mustang, Millbrook (Brookfield, CT), 1997.

The Florida Panther, Millbrook (Brookfield, CT), 1997.

The Grizzly Bear, Millbrook (Brookfield, CT), 1998.

The California Condor, Millbrook (Brookfield, CT), 1998.

"DISEASES AND PEOPLE" SERIES; WITH PARENTS, ALVIN AND VIRGINIA B. SILVERSTEIN

Sickle Cell Anemia, Enslow Publishers (Springfield, NJ), 1997.

Asthma, Enslow Publishers (Springfield, NJ), 1997.

Depression, Enslow Publishers (Springfield, NJ), 1997.

Chicken Pox and Shingles, Enslow Publishers (Springfield, NJ), 1998.

Leukemia, Enslow Publishers (Berkeley Heights, NJ), 2000.

Polio, Enslow Publishers (Berkeley Heights, NJ), 2001.

Parkinson's Disease, Enslow Publishers (Berkeley Heights, NJ), 2002.

"WHAT A PET!" SERIES; WITH PARENTS, ALVIN AND VIRGINIA B. SILVERSTEIN

Snakes and Such, Twenty-First Century Books (Brookfield, CT), 1998.

A Pet or Not?, Twenty-First Century Books (Brookfield, CT), 1998.

Pocket Pets, Twenty-First Century Books (Brookfield, CT), 1999.

Different Dogs, Twenty-First Century Books (Brookfield, CT), 1999.

"SCIENCE CONCEPTS" SERIES; WITH PARENTS, ALVIN AND VIRGINIA B. SILVERSTEIN

Evolution, Twenty-First Century Books (Brookfield, CT), 1998.

Symbiosis, Twenty-First Century Books (Brookfield, CT), 1998.

Photosynthesis, Twenty-First Century Books (Brookfield, CT), 1998.

Food Chains, Twenty-First Century Books (Brookfield, CT), 1998.

Plate Tectonics, Twenty-First Century Books (Brookfield, CT), 1998.

Energy, Twenty-First Century Books (Brookfield, CT), 1998.

Weather and Climate, Twenty-First Century Books (Brookfield, CT), 1998.

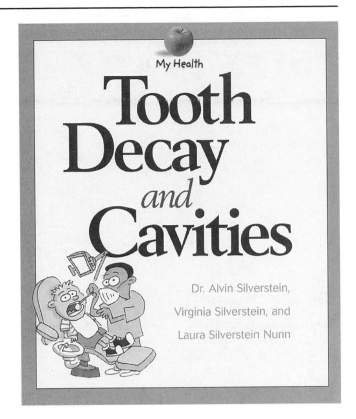

In their title from the "My Health" series on minor health problems, Nunn and her parents, well-known children's authors Alvin and Virginia B. Silverstein, offer suggestions on dental hygiene and tooth decay prevention. (Cover illustration by Rick Stromonski.)

Clocks and Rhythm, Twenty-First Century Books (Brookfield, CT), 1999.

"MY HEALTH" SERIES; WITH PARENTS, ALVIN AND VIRGINIA B. SILVERSTEIN

Is That a Rash?, Watts (Danbury, CT), 1999.

Tooth Decay and Cavities, Watts (Danbury, CT), 1999.

Cuts, Scrapes, Scabs, and Scars, Watts (Danbury, CT), 1999.

Common Colds, Watts (Danbury, CT), 1999.

Allergies, Watts (Danbury, CT), 1999.

Sleep, Watts (Danbury, CT), 2000.

Sore Throats and Tonsillitis, Watts (Danbury, CT), 2000.

Staying Safe, Watts (Danbury, CT), 2000.

Eat Your Vegetables! Drink Your Milk!, Watts (Danbury, CT), 2001.

Can You See the Chalkboard?, Watts (Danbury, CT), 2001.

Broken Bones, Watts (Danbury, CT), 2001.

Attention Deficit Disorder, Watts (Danbury, CT), 2001.

Dyslexia, Watts (Danbury, CT), 2001.

Headaches, Watts (Danbury, CT), 2001.

Bites and Stings, Watts (Danbury, CT), 2001.

Chicken Pox, Watts (Danbury, CT), 2001.

Lyme Disease, Watts (Danbury, CT), 2001.

Burns and Blisters, Watts (Danbury, CT), 2002.

Vaccinations, Watts (Danbury, CT), 2002.

Earaches, Watts (Danbury, CT), 2002.

Physical Fitness, Watts (Danbury, CT), 2002.

"SENSES AND SENSORS" SERIES; WITH PARENTS, ALVIN AND VIRGINIA B. SILVERSTEIN

Smelling and Tasting, Twenty-First Century Books (Brookfield, CT), 2001.

Seeing, Twenty-First Century Books (Brookfield, CT), 2001.

Touching, Twenty-First Century Books (Brookfield, CT), 2001.

Hearing, Twenty-First Century Books (Brookfield, CT), 2001.

OTHER

(With family members Alvin, Virginia, Robert A., Linda, and Kevin Silverstein) *John, Your Name Is Famous: Highlights, Anecdotes, and Trivia about the Name John and the People Who Made It Great,* AVSTAR (Lebanon, NJ), 1989.

Work in Progress

Germs, Asthma, and *Diabetes,* for Watts (Danbury, CT); *Cells, DNA,* and *The Universe,* for Twenty-First Century Books (Brookfield, CT).

Sidelights

Laura Silverstein Nunn told *SATA:* "I never really intended to be a writer. I started out just helping my parents part-time when I was in high school, with typing, sorting, and filing clippings. I continued when I went to college. I got my first taste of writing in 1989, when my family was working on a book project about first names. I wrote some of the biographical sketches that were published in *John: Your Name Is Famous* and *Michael: Fun and Facts about a Popular Name.* Meanwhile, various classes at Kean College helped me hone my skills and expand my knowledge. Tutoring students in English composition also helped to strengthen my own writing skills.

"When I graduated from college in 1991, with a major in sociology, my future was uncertain. The job market was tight, and I didn't want to go into social work. (I had majored in sociology because it is interesting, but I empathize too much with people to be able to deal with their problems on a day-to-day basis.) I drifted into working for my parents on a temporary basis, until I was clearer about what I wanted to do. I did mostly research, with some clerical work. By 1993 I had gotten back into writing, helping my parents and brother Bob to met some of their book deadlines. Ironically, the first two books I worked on during this time, *Bats* and *Spiders,* which were to be part of the 'Young Golden Guide' series, never got published! The publisher had financial difficulties and eventually went bankrupt. I soon got involved in another series, about endangered animals. The first published book that had my name officially listed as coauthor was *Black-Footed Ferret,* published in 1995.

"Meanwhile, I had gotten married (to Matt Nunn in February 1992) and gave birth to my son Corey in November 1994. I found that working for my parents

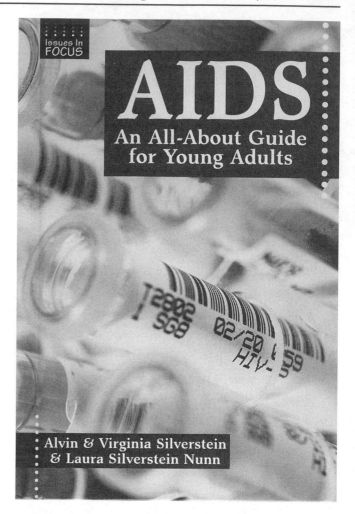

Nunn and the Silversteins contributed this volume on the transmission, prevention, treatment, and history of AIDS to the "Issues in Focus" series. (Cover photo by Charles Gupton.)

was an ideal situation. I was able to bring Corey with me to work and I was also able to do some of my work at home. I have the best of two worlds: I can continue writing books and also spend time with my son. Now I have an added thrill when my son Corey eagerly reads our new books as soon as they arrive. At six, he's not old enough to read some of them, but he particularly love the 'My Health' series, which targets young audiences."

Collaborating with her parents, well-known children's authors Alvin and Virginia B. Silverstein, Nunn has helped to pen over fifty titles that focus on the sciences for young readers. Writing in series dealing with endangered species, scientific processes, and human illnesses, Nunn is known for "well-researched, clearly written, topical books for middle- and high-school students," according to *Booklist*'s Catherine Andronik in a review of *Lyme Disease.*

Typical of Nunn's work is the series "My Health," featuring overviews of common diseases and health issues which use plentiful color photographs, sidebars to better organize and highlight information, glossaries, bibliographies, and lists of sources for further information from books to online resources. *Common Colds* "deals with the ways people catch and spread colds," according to *Booklist*'s Shelley Townsend-Hudson, and is "attractively designed with plenty of sidebars containing fascinating facts and color photographs." Reviewing *Allergies* and *Tooth Decay and Cavities* in *School Library Journal,* Christine A. Moesch commented that the books "are well written and complete without being overly technical." Moesch also found the plentiful colorful photos to be "an added bonus."

Nunn and the Silversteins offer longer and more detailed discussions of health problems in the Enslow series "Diseases and People." They give a detailed explanation and overview of the hereditary disease sickle cell anemia in the book of the same name. Moesch, again writing in *School Library Journal,* found *Sickle Cell Anemia* a "thorough and well-written book," with a "clear and well organized text." Moesch also commented that the "question-and-answer section, glossary, and lots of Internet sites will be useful for further research." *School Library Journal* reviewer Martha Gordon dubbed the team's *Leukemia* a "concise, well-written discussion of the disease," which begins with the first accurate description of the disease by Dr. Alfred Velpeau in 1827. The text then goes on to explain the symptoms of leukemia and difficulties that arise in diagnosing the ailment, along with sections dealing with causes, treatment, and prevention. *Depression* was written by Nunn and her parents with the assistance of working psychologists. The writers demonstrate how widespread the disease is and even point out historical figures, including Abraham Lincoln and Mark Twain, who were victims of it. Theories and treatments are also dealt with in an approach that is "moderate," according to *School Library Journal* reviewer Libby K. White. Recent studies on brain chemistry as well as genetic factors are also described in this "well-organized and comprehensive work," as White noted in her article on *Depression.* Another health-related title, part of the "Issues in Focus" series, is *AIDS: An All-About Guide for Young Adults,* published in 1999. "History, diagnosis, treatment, and prevention are all addressed in this clearly written, thoroughly researched book," according to *Booklist*'s Michael Cart. Again, the collaborators employ a mixture of text, illustrations, chronology, glossary, notes, and recommendations for further reading. In order to get their information across to young readers, they also include anecdotal sidebars and profiles of well-known individuals who have AIDS.

Nunn and her parents have explored the workings of the natural and physical world—from plate tectonics to photosynthesis—in the "Science Concepts" series. In *Clocks and Rhythms,* readers are introduced to the concept of time from clocks to calendars, which generally track the diurnal, monthly, and seasonal rhythms of planet Earth. The authors also look at disturbances to the natural clock of humans that are caused by jet lag and daylight savings time, as well as the effects of space travel and experiments to turn back

the aging clock. Again, employing a mixture of clear, concise text along with illustrations, boxed sidebars, a glossary, and a listing of Internet resources, the authors produced a "well-written, well-researched title," according to Carolyn Angus in *School Library Journal,* that is designed to introduce "key concepts by exploring their development, applications, and relationships to science knowledge as a whole." *Booklist*'s Linda Perkins felt that *Clocks and Rhythms* "is well organized and the explanations are clear." Reviewing *Photosynthesis* and *Symbiosis* in *School Library Journal,* Angus found the books to be "well researched and interesting" with a format "inviting for both general-interest reading and research." In *Photosynthesis,* the authors explain the scientific process as well as discoveries leading to the understanding of it. Additionally, they deal with such related subjects as acid rain and the greenhouse effect. In *Symbiosis,* the writing team deals with many forms of symbiosis, from mutualism to commensalism and parasitism, while providing plentiful examples of all these living relationships. Reviewing *Evolution* and *Food Chains,* Patricia Manning remarked in *School Library Journal* that the books were "up-to-date," "utilitarian," and "useful," and that they "will be welcomed by students and teachers who are looking for clearly written, dependable material." *Booklist*'s Carolyn Phelan thought that Nunn's *Plate Tectonics* "offers a straightforward introduction" to the topic, with an "inviting layout."

Animals, both domestic and endangered, get the same treatment in the "What a Pet!" series and the "Endangered in America" series, respectively. Reviewing *A Pet or Not?* and *Snakes and Such* in *Booklist,* Ilene Cooper noted that the series takes a look at non-traditional types of pets, from chameleons and snakes to pigs. "As one would expect from the Silversteins," wrote Cooper, "the text is very cogent and lively." The authors again employ a winning formula of text, photos, glossaries, and resources for further study, including Internet sites which "make the books seem very current," Cooper concluded. "These are not pet-care manuals," commented Manning in a *School Library Journal* review of *A Pet or Not?* and *Snakes and Such,* "but rather selection tools to assist in educated decision making and prevent imperfect pairings." Manning concluded that the books were both "useful and readable." In *Different Dogs* and *Pocket Pets,* the authors look at many breeds of dogs as well as the smaller types of pets, such as hamsters, gerbils, guinea pigs, and even the flying squirrel. "These colorful introductory guides may provide the only information available on some of the more unusual species," noted Denise Reitsma in a *School Library Journal* review of the two books. The collaborative team of Nunn and the Silversteins turned their attention to wild animals in their "Endangered in America" series, including *The Black-Footed Ferret, The Mustang, The Florida Panther, The Grizzly Bear,* and *The California Condor,* among others. Reviewing *The California Condor* and *The Grizzly Bear, Booklist*'s April Judge felt that the two books "present informative overviews" that "will appeal to young wildlife activists and be useful for assignments."

Whether writing of decaying teeth or disappearing species, Nunn, in collaboration with her parents, has developed an effective and popular nonfiction style that appeals to a wide variety of young readers. The books produced by this writing team are consistently praised by reviewers for their clarity and concision.

Biographical and Critical Sources

PERIODICALS

Booklist, September 1, 1998, April Judge, review of *The California Condor* and *The Grizzly Bear,* pp. 172-173; February 1, 1999, Carolyn Phelan, review of *Plate Tectonics,* p. 972; August, 1999, Ilene Cooper, review of *Snakes and Such* and *A Pet or Not?,* p. 2055; September 1, 1999, Linda Perkins, review of *Clocks and Rhythm,* p. 130; October 15, 1999, Shelley Townsend-Hudson, review of *Tooth Decay and Cavities* and *Common Colds,* p. 440; November 15, 1999, Michael Cart, review of *AIDS: An All-About Guide for Young Adults,* p. 612; October 15, 2000, Catherine Andronik, review of *Lyme Disease,* p. 433.

Book Report, May-June, 1997, p. 44.

Horn Book, September-October, 1992, p. 602.

School Library Journal, February, 1997, Christine A. Moesch, review of *Sickle Cell Anemia,* p. 125; April, 1997, p. 158; June, 1997, p. 146; April, 1998, Libby K. White, review of *Depression,* p. 154; January, 1999, Patricia Manning, review of *Evolution* and *Food Chains,* p. 154; February, 1999, Carolyn Angus, review of *Photosynthesis* and *Symbiosis,* p. 127; October, 1999, Carolyn Angus, review of *Clocks and Rhythm,* p. 175; October, 1999, Patricia Manning, review of *A Pet or Not?* and *Snakes and Such,* pp. 175-176; December, 1999, Christine A. Moesch, review of *Allergies* and *Tooth Decay and Cavities,* pp. 126-127; May, 2000, Denise Reitsma, review of *Different Dogs* and *Pocket Pets,* p. 187; September, 2000, Martha Gordon, review of *Leukemia,* p. 257; May, 2001, Pamela K. Bomboy, review of *Attention Deficit Disorder,* p. 146.

—Sketch by J. Sydney Jones

*   *   *

OCKHAM, Joan Price
See PRICE, Joan

P–Q

PRICE, Joan 1931-
(Joan Price Ockham)

Personal

Born May 20, 1931, in Phoenix, AZ; daughter of Fred V. (in business construction) and Loreen (Ackley) Price; married; children: Joan, Judy. *Education:* Attended Colorado Agricultural and Mechanical College (now Colorado State University), 1949-53; University of Arizona, B.S., 1955; Springfield College, M.S., 1956; Arizona State University, M.A., 1968, Ph.D., 1973. *Politics:* Democrat. *Religion:* "Hindu, Buddhist, Taoist, Jew, Christian, New Age." *Hobbies and other interests:* Nature, animals.

Joan Price

Addresses

Home—7646 Via De Lindo, Scottsdale, AZ 85258. *Office*—Department of Philosophy, Mesa Community College, 1833 West Southern, Mesa, AZ 85201. *E-mail*—jprice9394@aol.com.

Career

Mesa Community College, Mesa, AZ, professor of philosophy, 1968-95, chair of department, 1978-88, professor emeritus, 1995—; creator of Religious Studies Department, chair of Articulation Committee. Lecturer on religion and philosophy.

Writings

FOR CHILDREN

A Very Special Burro, Naylor, 1966.
Truth Is a Bright Star: A Hopi Adventure, Celestial Arts (Millbrae, CA), 1982, 3rd edition, 2001.
Hawk in the Wind, Royal Fireworks Press, 1997.
Medicine Man, Royal Fireworks Press, 1997.
Little Echo, Royal Fireworks Press, 2001.

FOR ADULTS

(Under name Joan Price Ockham) *Introduction to Aurobindo's Philosophy,* University of Pondicherry Press (Pondicherry, India), 1977.
New Age Philosophy, Ginn Press (Needham, MA), 1988.
Philosophy through the Ages, Wadsworth Publishing (Belmont, CA), 2000.

Articles published in *Quest: A Quarterly Journal of Philosophy, Science, Religion and the Arts; World Humanities Journal; Animal Voice; Alive;* and *Paradise.*

Work in Progress

World Religions and *Growing with Philosophy,* both juvenile nonfiction titles for Royal Fireworks Press.

Sidelights

Joan Price told *SATA:* "I love dogs, horses, and cats. I used to show hunters and jumpers. I am now learning dressage. I take my dogs walking every morning at sunrise in the desert. It's our spiritual time. I love to hike with my dogs—not the rope-climbing and #10 difficulty trails—just the lovely easy or moderate trails in the desert and mountains. I love philosophy, especially Plato, Plotinus, and Buddhist philosophy. I am something of a mystic. I am now retired and teaching two classes (one in philosophy and one in world religions) just for the fun of it."

Price's children's book *Truth Is a Bright Star* takes off from a strange historical incident that occurred in 1832 in the American Southwest. When Spanish soldiers invade a Hopi village in what would later become New Mexico, the soldiers kidnap fourteen children and a young woman who are taken to Santa Fe and sold as slaves. The story is told from the perspective of eleven-year-old Loma, one of the stolen children, who is sold to a man named Big Jim, an American trapper. Jim takes the boy out to the mountains, teaches him his trade, and learns a few things himself. "The characters have depth," observed Carmen Oyenque in *Voice of Youth Advocates,* who remarked with pleasure upon the growing friendship between the characters' despite their contrasting views of wildlife. The story comes to a climax when Loma rescues Big Jim, who is injured and alone in the snowy mountains. Their friendship is confirmed, and at the end of winter, Big Jim returns Loma to Santa Fe, where he rejoins the other captured villagers and eventually makes his way home. "Jim and Loma are both likable characters," remarked Gale Eaton in *School Library Journal,* adding that "Loma's return home ... has a satisfying warmth."

Biographical and Critical Sources

PERIODICALS

School Library Journal, November, 1982, Gale Eaton, review of *Truth Is a Bright Star,* p. 89.
Voice of Youth Advocates, December, 1982, Carmen Oyenque, review of *Truth Is a Bright Star,* p. 35.

*   *   *

QUALEY, Marsha 1953-

Personal

Surname is pronounced "*kwawl*-ee"; born May 27, 1953, in Austin, MN; daughter of Philip (an attorney) and Gwenyth (a homemaker) Richardson; married David Qualey, 1976; children: Laura, Ellen, Jane, Ben. *Education:* Attended Macalester College, 1971-72; University of Minnesota, B.A., 1976. *Religion:* Baha'i. *Hobbies and other interests:* Reading, maps, Minnesota.

Marsha Qualey

Addresses

Home—11525 40th Ave. N., Plymouth, MN 55441.
E-mail—mqualey@mediaone.net.

Career

Homemaker and volunteer, 1978-89; writer, 1990—. *Member:* Society of Children's Book Writers and Illustrators, Maud Hart Lovelace Society, Author's Guild.

Awards, Honors

Minnesota Book Award, Best Books for Young Adults selection, American Library Association (ALA), and *School Library Journal*'s Best Books of 1993 selection, all for *Revolutions of the Heart;* Best Books for Young Adults selection, ALA, and Books for the Teen Age selection, New York Public Library, both for *Come in from the Cold;* Minnesota Book Award and Books for the Teen Age selection, New York Public Library, both for *Hometown;* Books for the Teen Age selection, New York Public Library, Quick Pick selection, ALA, and Edgar nominee, all for *Thin Ice;* Best Books for Young Adults selection, ALA, and Books for the Teen Age selection, New York Public Library, both for *Close to a Killer.*

Writings

Everybody's Daughter, Houghton (Boston, MA), 1991.
Revolutions of the Heart, Houghton, 1993.
Come in from the Cold, Houghton, 1994.
Hometown, Houghton, 1995.
Thin Ice, Delacorte (New York, NY), 1997.
Close to a Killer, Delacorte, 1999.
Every Friend a Stranger, Dial (New York, NY), 2001.
One Night, Dial, 2002.

Sidelights

Marsha Qualey's young adult novels present average teenagers struggling with unusually challenging situations. Nearly all of her works are set in her home state of Minnesota, and their plots are often driven by intergenerational conflicts between teens and their parents or community. In some cases, a Qualey protagonist must come to terms with the past actions of his or her parents during his or her own young adult years. The American Library Association has praised *Revolutions of the Heart, Come in from the Cold,* and *Close to a Killer* as outstanding novels for teen readers, and Qualey's other books have also earned her critical accolades as well as a devoted readership.

Qualey was born Marsha Richardson in 1953, in Austin, Minnesota, a town whose chief claim to fame is being the home of "Spam," the well-known canned meat product. She was the daughter of an attorney, Philip, and his homemaker wife, Gwenyth; Qualey's grandparents on her mother's side were involved in writing and journalism. Her grandfather had been the editor of a

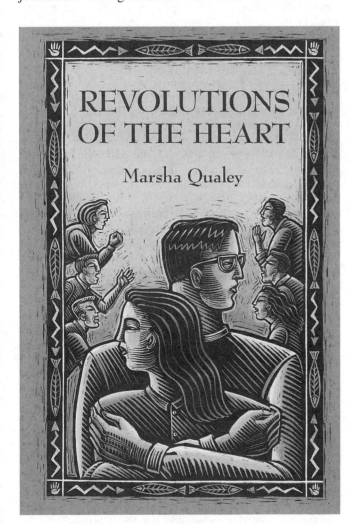

When Cory falls in love with a Native American, she is pitted against her brother, who opposes the Native Americans' fishing rights in their Wisconsin town. (Cover illustration by Jennifer Hewitson.)

magazine, while her grandmother helped support the family by writing "confession" stories for pulp magazines during the Great Depression. "Perhaps that's one reason early on people expected I'd be a writer," Qualey explained in a biography that is posted on her Web site. "I was never so sure." An avid reader all her life, she has said that her childhood was a pleasant one. "I had a secure home, entertaining brothers, a bookstore and public library a few blocks away, and good friends," she recalled.

Qualey remembers her father making a skating rink in their backyard every winter with a garden hose. "Images like the one I have of my father flooding the yard stick in the mind," she wrote in the biography. "But what's the story behind the lingering picture or the haunting memory? Finding that out—well, that's why I love to write." In junior high, Qualey wrote skits and plays for her friends to perform, but she still harbored no real literary ambitions. As a teenager, she spent much of her summer outdoors. She went to camp, spent summers at her family's cabin, took long canoe trips, and loved to fish. Qualey once recalled: "Three memories. First, from 1969: I was on a canoe trip in Canada and sweating through the final portage of the day. It was a killer, 150 rods, and seemed to be straight uphill. I was carrying the food pack, maybe eighty pounds on my back, and it was a slow climb, especially as the rocky terrain seemed deliberately to keep me back. Roots slithered out and coiled around my legs, brush snickered and snagged my pack, rocks sprang out of the ground whenever I set a foot down, and branches snapped when I reached for a handhold.

"Second memory: The next summer I was seventeen and working as a counselor-in-training at a YMCA camp in northern Minnesota. Three friends and I were up late, walking by the lakefront, when we noticed the display of northern lights. Anyone who spends time in the north sees the aurora borealis fairly often, but never before or since have I seen such a vivid sky show. For almost an hour the four of us lay on the ground, still as could be, while the colored sky danced.

"Final memory: That same summer our group was returning from an easy three-day canoe trip. The four canoes emerged one by one from a placid, narrow, winding river onto the home lake, where we were met by a gale that had transformed the water into a monster. We were all experienced trippers, but only one canoe paddled safely back to camp. The others, mine included, were toyed with, then thrown back to the far shore, by a lake that threatened with every huge wave to rise up and swallow us whole."

"Those two summers I learned how *alive* the sky and the water and the land can be. Most of my writing is set in the lake country of the upper Midwest, and when I now write about the natural world I treat it as another character. That character's influence can be obvious: how would a blizzard affect the plot? Or elusive: how lonely would it be to live in the middle of a great big forest?"

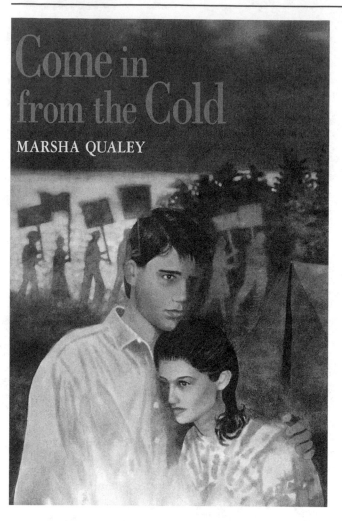

When Maud's sister dies protesting the Vietnam War and Jeff's brother is killed while serving in the Marines, Maud and Jeff forge a loving relationship and share their bitterness about Vietnam and their search for hope in the future. (Cover illustration by Peter Catalanotto.)

Qualey stayed close to her roots, choosing Macalester College in St. Paul for her first year of college, then transferring to the University of Minnesota, where she studied American history and literature. After earning her degree in 1976, she married David Qualey and they began a family that now includes four children. She began writing short stories for magazines in the mid-1980s, when she had two young children at home. While taking care of her toddlers and her home, Qualey let her mind wander and came up with various interesting scenarios, which she wrote down when she had a spare moment. Her submissions were all returned with rejection slips, but one story sent to *Seventeen* magazine came back with a letter that was encouraging. Qualey decided to expand the story, with its teen protagonist, into a young adult novel.

After sending *Everybody's Daughter* to a number of publishing houses, Qualey's manuscript was plucked out of a pile of unsolicited submissions by an editor, and was published by Houghton in 1991. Its protagonist is Merry Moonbeam Flynn, called "Beamer," who is seventeen years old and the daughter of two hippie parents. Beamer's mother and father had been the founding members of a northern Minnesota commune called Woodlands, but gave up the rustic lifestyle when Beamer was ten. They sold the land and used the money to buy a bait shop in the area. Others from the commune also stayed near, and the Flynns' bait shop has become a daily meeting place for the "Woodie" circle. Because Beamer was the first child born at Woodlands, she is considered "everybody's daughter," and her parents' friends take a more active role in her life than usual. As she grows older, she is increasingly irked by this interference, especially when she struggles through a romantic triangle that involves Beamer's high-school boyfriend, Andy, who demands more time from her, and a college student who is fulfilling an internship opportunity at her town's radio station. "Part of Beamer's indecision about both Andy and Martin is her desire for a long-term relationship rather than just a boyfriend," wrote Ronald Barron in the *ALAN Review.*

The action in *Everybody's Daughter* intensifies when one of the Woodies accidentally kills a security guard by detonating an explosive as part of a protest at a local nuclear power plant. Beamer's parents and their friends draw even closer to pull through this crisis. Her mother provides a valuable piece of advice that helps Beamer come to terms with her dilemmas: "Beamer, as you muddle through life you'll discover the things you can't change and the things you can't escape. Sometimes the best you can do is to have a little fun."

Qualey's debut as a novelist earned positive reviews. *School Library Journal*'s Gail Richmond called the book "an exceptional first novel," commending the main plot as well as Beamer's romantic intrigues and the first-time novelist's ability to characterize life in a northern Minnesota world. "Qualey's smooth writing style and language create poetic, descriptive images," Richmond asserted. Gail Ashe, writing in *Voice of Youth Advocates,* called it "a moving and oftentimes romantic" work that depicts a teen's "struggle to come to terms with her unusual life." A *Bulletin of the Center for Children's Books* review also praised the way in which Qualey depicted Beamer's hippie parents, a characterization admirable for "a depth and respect unusual in the YA genre, which usually boils down the movement to flaky moms who neglect their children."

In her 1993 novel *Revolutions of the Heart,* Qualey creates another interesting protagonist who struggles with the conflicts presented when her own beliefs clash with those of her larger community. When the work begins, Cory Knutson is a popular, happy teen in her small Wisconsin town. That idyll is shattered when Cory, a new driver, loses control of her stepfather's truck on an icy street and crashes into a plate glass window. Her parents take away her driver's license, and she takes a job to help her pay the $500 in damages for which she is liable. Cory's situation worsens when her mother falls ill and doctors put her on a waiting list for a heart transplant. Many of the family's neighbors prove helpful and sympathetic during this difficult time, but many of them also voice their disapproval when Cory begins dating a new Native American student at her high school; Harvey "Mac" MacNamara is a Cree who lives on the local reservation. Inevitably, small-town prejudices begin to manifest themselves in their harassment of Cory for associating with a native person. "She becomes the target of crude notes taped to her locker and insensitive comments made in her presence, culminating in the ultimate example when someone stuffs a huge quantity of contraceptives into her school locker," wrote Barron.

As *Revolutions of the Heart* progresses, Cory even loses her job over the fracas, and the situation is further complicated by the Native Americans' recent battle with local authorities over fishing rights. The natives have returned to spear-fishing, and Cory's older brother, Rob, becomes one of the most vocal opponents of the

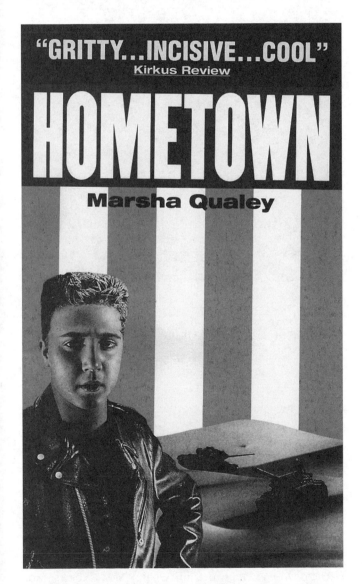

Set during the Persian Gulf War, Qualey's novel follows newcomer Border, who bears the brunt of the animosity towards his father—a draft-dodger during the Vietnam War—from the patriotic residents of the small Minnesota town where his dad was born.

practice. The death of Cory's mother plunges the family into grief, a situation made worse by the battles with Rob. When he is arrested at a demonstration, Cory's stepfather throws him out of the house. Though Cory and Mac attempt to stay out of the fishing-rights fray, Mac is inadvertently injured during a demonstration, and the pair flee. After taking a motel room where she can bandage his cuts, the two fall asleep and are discovered. An ensuing ugly argument with her brother ends with Cory breaking her arm. They reconcile at the end, and Rob invites Cory and Mac to a party that serves to symbolize what may be a new, harmonious direction for the embattled town. Cory remembers the words her mother imparted before her death: "Change a heart, you change the world. But doing it one heart at a time is the best you can hope for."

A *Publishers Weekly* reviewer found *Revolutions of the Heart* a bit too issue-focused, but the critic nevertheless hailed it as "an engaging as well as an enlightening read," and commended Qualey's "believable dialogue . . . and ability to sustain narrative tension." Roger Sutton, writing in *Bulletin of the Center for Children's Books,* stated that the book's Native American characters "never succumb to *nouveau* stereotyping as ecological nature-children," and he commended Qualey's challenged teenage heroine. "It's good to see such confidence matched by such confident writing," wrote Sutton.

Qualey also noted that *Revolutions of the Heart* had several false starts. "It began life as a mystery about four teenagers in northern Minnesota who uncover a marijuana smuggling operation," Qualey wrote in the biographical notes that appear on her Web site. "That idea was a dead end. The novel's next incarnation was as a collection of short stories about pregnant girls/young women living in a maternity home in northern Minnesota. . . . Of course, there are no drug smugglers or pregnant teenagers in *Revolutions.* Those elements were lost, but some things that *were* part of the early drafts remained (interracial dating, Indian treaty rights) and are at the heart of the story."

Qualey revived the characters of two of the *Everybody's Daughter* commune dwellers for her 1994 young adult novel, *Come in from the Cold.* As she wrote on her Web site, "I wanted to write about those people, explain why and how some of them made the decision to live that way. I wanted to write about a period in my own life that was so dramatic. This book is as close to autobiography as I ever want to get." The story, which is set in the late 1960s in Red Cedar, a conservative Minnesota town, follows the lives of two teenagers and the tragedies that bring them together. Jeff is a high-school student in Red Cedar whose older brother is a sergeant in the U.S. Marines. America's military involvement to quash a Communist takeover of the southeast Asian nation of Vietnam is escalating, and Jeff opposes the war. He even convinces the student council of his high school to pass an anti-war resolution. This earns him the scorn of many Red Cedar residents and of his brother. Tom also dislikes Jeff's friends, one of whom is a drug user named Gumbo. To help Jeff meet more wholesome peers, Tom takes his brother with him to a party. There Jeff manages to hook up with the sole anti-war activist present—a church youth minister who introduces Jeff to the organized protest movement. At a University of Minnesota demonstration, however, Jeff is dismayed by the free use of illegal substances that he sees. After Tom's unit is sent to Vietnam, tragedy strikes, and Jeff's brother dies in action. Qualey noted that this was the one incident in her body of work that drew clearly upon her own life.

The other half of *Come in from the Cold* tracks the events in the life of Maud, whose sister has become a radical anti-war activist. Lucy even goes underground, but dies in an attempt to blow up the physics building at the University of Minnesota. However, the bombing incident also appears to have been a cover for Lucy's suicide, and Maud and her family struggle to come to terms with the loss.

While these two tragedies are fresh in their minds, Maud and Jeff meet at rock show in 1970. Maud emerges from a period of despair as she joins Jeff in anti-war protest activities. They travel to Minneapolis for a large demonstration, and find a ride back north with members of a commune called Woodlands. Jeff enrolls in college nearby, but begins to spend more time at Woodlands, and eventually drops out. When Maud joins him, they begin a new life there together. "Told with a quiet forcefulness, the story of" these two memorable characters conveys the passionate urgency that marked a turbulent era," wrote a *Publishers Weekly* reviewer. Others offered equally positive assessments. "The greatest strength" here, wrote *Voice of Youth Advocates* reviewer Jacqueline Rose, "is the skillful way Qualey captures the 1960s ambiance." Reviewing *Come in from the Cold* for *School Library Journal*, Judy R. Johnston called it "fast-paced, well written, and appealing, and [the book] concludes with a strong sense of love and hope."

Hometown, Qualey's 1995 novel, is a sequel of sorts to *Come in from the Cold.* Though it is set in the early 1990s, the novel tracks the story of the rebellious Gumbo, who left Red Cedar when his draft number came up and an army stint in Vietnam loomed. As Border, his teenaged son, relates, Gumbo fled to Canada, eventually married, and became a nurse. When Gumbo divorced, he and Border settled in New Mexico, but the father decides to pull up roots once again when he inherits his family's home in Red Cedar. "Border is unhappy about leaving Albuquerque, where he has become the leader, almost a father, to a collection of teenage misfits and outcasts," wrote Barron in the *ALAN Review.* Their move north coincides with the onset of the Gulf War, which creates groundswell of patriotism in many American communities. Everyone in Red Cedar knows his father was a draft-dodger, but any venom is directed primarily at Border, who is even beat up by his new classmates. He finds solace in a friendship with a classmate, Jacob McQuillan, and even a budding romance with Jacob's sympathetic sister, Liz. With the McQuillans, Border takes part in a local church's drive

When Arden hears of her brother's death in a snowmobile "accident," she is determined to search for the real explanation for his disappearance, despite the skepticism of others. (Cover illustration by Joanie Schwartz.)

to send care packages for American soldiers overseas. When some in Red Cedar launch an initiative to erect a veterans' memorial, Border plays his recorder and raises a large sum of money. However, someone at the dedication ceremony makes disparaging comments about Gumbo, and Border courageously steps forward to defend his father's decision. "Border is an admirable but improbable, elusive hero whose self-sufficiency exceeds that of the characters around him," wrote Gerry Larson in *School Library Journal.*

Hometown was the first of Qualey's works to earn criticism as being somewhat unsatisfying. The story is told in short, almost vignette-like chapters, and *Voice of Youth Advocates* reviewer Mary Ann Capan found that this shifting perspective works against the novel's impact. Capan also remarked that "the ending is not quite satisfying and the events leading to it are disjointed." A *Kirkus Reviews* assessment, was more positive, terming *Hometown* a "gritty, incisive novel" that "exudes plenty of cool." *Publishers Weekly* also appraised the work more favorably. "Giving this novel uncommon dimension are the author's cunning use of irony," noted the magazine's reviewer, as well as its third-person narrative voice that still asserts Border's inner turmoil and its subplots, which the *Publishers Weekly* reviewer described as "dexterously crafted."

Qualey's 1997 novel *Thin Ice* again takes readers into the frosty woods. It was the author's first mystery story, and Qualey based it on newspaper reports about drunken snowmobilers disappearing when the ice of the frozen lakes cracked and swallowed them. The seventeen-year-old heroine of *Thin Ice,* Arden Munro, has already suffered much heartache in her life when her beloved brother Scott becomes the victim of just such an accident. She was orphaned at the age of six, and Scott then left college and found work as a mechanic in order to support her. After the snowmobile tragedy, Arden becomes convinced that it was no accident. Scott's vehicle, wallet, and clothes were recovered, but no body was ever found. Her suspicions intensify when she learns that Scott's girlfriend had recently told him she was pregnant. Arden believes her brother wanted a more adventurous life, and faked his own death. Others disagree, telling Arden that she must come to terms with the loss.

"Despite the objections of those around her and how it disrupts her life, Arden continues to search for Scott and to try to learn why he disappeared," wrote Barron in the *ALAN Review.* "Arden's character is full of spunk and self-assurance," noted Helen Rosenberg in *Booklist,* though she asserted *Thin Ice*'s "plot fizzles at the end." Julie Hudson, writing in *Voice of Youth Advocates,* termed Qualey's first attempt at writing a suspenseful novel a first-rate page-turner, and "as a mystery and a novel of self-discovery, *Thin Ice* blends perfectly to equal a most satisfying read."

Qualey's next book, *Close to a Killer,* was another mystery novel for young adults. Sixteen-year-old Barric Dupre is not entirely happy about her father's decision to send her to live with her mother, an ex-convict, when he and her stepmother go to Europe for a year. Her mother lives in a rough neighborhood, where she is co-owner of a hair salon called Killer Looks; the other business partners had also spent time in prison. Qualey based the mother on a character from one of her earlier novels—in this case the nuclear-power protester who accidentally killed a security guard in *Everybody's Daughter.* Barrie is ambivalent about her mother's past, but settles into her new life with a certain resignation. An avid reader, she makes friends with the owners of a neighborhood bookstore, and befriends the community's homeless.

The plot of *Close to a Killer* is driven by Barrie's worries about two murders that have been linked to clients of Killer Looks. When her mother's home is ransacked and what appears to be arson causes the salon

to go up in flames, Barrie becomes even more intensely involved. "Qualey handles the mystery mechanics with exceptional flair," declared *Booklist*'s Stephanie Zvirin, who also noted that the author provides "a satisfying assortment of red herrings." However, a *Publishers Weekly* review found the number of subplots and possible suspects confusing, "dividing the novel's focus and diffusing its suspense." A *Bulletin of the Center for Children's Books* review stated that Qualey's attempt to write a novel with dual purposes—a coming-of-age story inside a whodunit—resulted in "shorting both genres," but it did assert that "details of the salon milieu and the shades of the prison past are imaginative and compelling."

Qualey's other works include Every Friend A Stranger and *One Night.* She dismisses the classification of herself as an author of young adult novels in the "problem" genre. "I don't really like the tag 'problem novel' because I think it's too often reserved for [young adult] fiction and used disparagingly," she said in her Web site interview. "Every novel is a problem novel. Why pin it just on books that happen to be for teenagers?"

Biographical and Critical Sources

PERIODICALS

ALAN Review, fall, 1997, Ronald Barron, "Marsha Qualey: 'One Writes What One Would Read,'" pp. 27-30.

Booklist, April 1, 1993, Mary Romano Marks, review of *Revolutions of the Heart,* p. 1994; September 15, 1994, Jeanne Triner, review of *Come in from the Cold,* p. 125; October 1, 1995, Susan Dove Lempke, review of *Hometown,* p. 305l; November 1, 1997, Helen Rosenberg, review of *Thin Ice,* p. 462; February 1, 1999, Stephanie Zvirin, review of *Close to a Killer,* p. 970.

Bulletin of the Center for Children's Books, March, 1991, review of *Everybody's Daughter,* pp. 174-175; May, 1993, Roger Sutton, review of *Revolutions of the Heart,* pp. 292-293; February, 1999, review of *Close to a Killer,* pp. 213-214.

Horn Book Magazine, September-October, 1993, Elizabeth S. Watson, review of *Revolutions of the Heart,* p. 604.

Kirkus Reviews, September 15, 1995, review of *Hometown,* p. 1356.

Publishers Weekly, May 3, 1993, review of *Revolutions of the Heart,* p. 311; October 17, 1994, review of *Come in from the Cold,* pp. 82-83; November 6, 1995, review of *Hometown,* p. 95; October 27, 1997, review of *Thin Ice,* p. 77; January 4, 1999, review of *Close to a Killer,* p. 91.

School Library Journal, April, 1991, Gail Richmond, review of *Everybody's Daughter,* p. 142; December, 1994, Judy R. Johnston, review of *Come in from the Cold,* p. 130; December, 1995, Gerry Larson, review of *Hometown,* p. 131.

Voice of Youth Advocates, June, 1991, Gail Ashe, review of *Everybody's Daughter,* p. 100; October, 1994, Jacqueline Rose, review of *Come in from the Cold,* p. 215; December, 1995, Mary Ann Capan, review of *Home-*

town, p. 308; October, 1997, Julie Hudson, review of *Thin Ice,* p. 247.

ON-LINE

Marsha Qualey's Web site, http://www.marshaqualey.com/ (January, 2001).

R

REES, Celia 1949-

Personal

Born June 17, 1949; daughter of Wilfred Taylor (a headmaster) and Lilla (a homemaker; maiden name, Goodway) Taylor; married Terence Rees (a lecturer), July 15, 1972; children: Catrin. *Education:* Warwick University, B.A. (with honours; history and politics), 1971; West Midlands College, post graduate certificate in education, 1972; Birmingham University, M.Ed., 1985. *Hobbies and other interests:* Reading, cinema, swimming, yoga.

Addresses

Home—195 Rugby Rd., Milverton, Leamington Spa, Warwickshire CV32 6DX, England. *Agent*—Rosemary Sandberg, 6 Bayley St., London WC1B 3HB, England. *E-mail*—celia.rees@talk21.com.

Career

Secondary school English teacher, Coventry, England, 1973-89; part-time college lecturer in English and media, Coventry, 1990-97; writer, 1990—; creative writing tutor, Warwick University Open Studies, 1997—. *Member:* PEN, Society of Authors, Federation of Children's Book Groups, Scattered Authors' Society.

Awards, Honors

Guardian Children's Book Award shortlist, for *Witch Child*.

Writings

FOR YOUNG ADULTS; FICTION

Every Step You Take, Macmillan Children's Books (London, England), 1993.
The Bailey Game, Macmillan Children's Books (London, England), 1994.

Colour Her Dead, Macmillan Children's Books (London, England), 1994.
Blood Sinister, Scholastic (London, England), 1996.
The Vanished, Scholastic (London, England), 1997.
Ghost Chamber, Hodder Children's Books (London, England), 1997.
Midnight Hour, Macmillan Children's Books (London, England), 1997.
Soul Taker, Hodder Children's Books (London, England), 1997.
The Cunning Man, Scholastic (London, England), 2000.
Witch Child, Bloomsbury Children Books (London, England), 2000, Candlewick Press (Cambridge, MA), 2001.
The Truth Out There, Dorling Kindersley (New York, NY), 2000, published as *Truth or Dare,* Macmillan Children's Books (London, England), 2000.
The Wish House (novel), Macmillan, in press.
Sorceress (sequel to *Witch Child*), Bloomsbury Children Books, in press.

"H.A.U.N.T.S." SERIES

H Is for Haunting, Hodder Children's Books (London, England), 1998.
A Is for Apparition, Hodder Children's Books (London, England), 1998.
U Is for Unbeliever, Hodder Children's Books (London, England), 1998.
N Is for Nightmare, Hodder Children's Books (London, England), 1998.
T Is for Terror, Hodder Children's Books (London, England), 1998.
S Is for Shudder, Hodder Children's Books (London, England), 1998.

Rees' work has been translated into twelve languages.

Work in Progress

Another historical book for Bloomsbury; research for a fantasy trilogy—"creation myths and legends, Atlantis and Mesoamerica, apocalyptic theories, Antarctica, and dinosaurs."

Sidelights

Celia Rees told *SATA:* "I started to write while I was teaching English in secondary schools. The most popular novels among my teenage students were by American writers like Judy Blume, Robert Cormier, Lois Duncan, Caroline Cooney, and R. L. Stine. My students really enjoyed these, but there didn't seem to be many books with kids like them, British kids, at the centre of the story. At about the same time someone recounted an incident which fitted the brief exactly, and I thought I'd try and turn it into a novel. This eventually became my first book, a thriller called *Every Step You Take.* It took a while to get it published, and I learnt some valuable lessons: it pays to be persistent, believe in what you are doing but be prepared to make changes, and take advice. Eventually it was published by Macmillan in 1993.

"I have written many books since then and have often chosen to write in popular genres—crime or horror. My mission has always been to reach as many readers as possible, and this is what people want to read. I don't always write in genre, neither do I aim my books at a specific gender. It does not seem to matter to my readers whether the main character is girl or boy, what counts is the story. Genre, or non genre, there is nearly always a mystery at the centre of my novels, and for inspiration I often look back to my own child- and young adulthood. With a book like *Truth or Dare* (published in the United States as *The Truth Out There*), the subject matter ranges from hidden secrets within a family, to UFOs, the space race and computer games, Aspergers syndrome and autistic spectrum disorders. The challenge is to bring them together in a coherent, compelling narrative.

"I aim to write every day, but writing is not just sitting in front of the word processor. It involves thinking, reading, research, visiting places. Once I have an idea for a story it bugs me until I write it. If it doesn't (bug me, that is), it won't be worth pursuing. I thought of the ideas behind *Witch Child* years before I actually sat down to write the novel. *Witch Child* is set in Colonial New England, and my interest dates back to studying American history at university. The book is set in the seventeenth century and combines many different elements: European witch persecution and Native American shamanism, herbal healing and quilt making. I find research the 'fun' part. Writing itself is a challenge, a risk. There's always a point when I think I'm not going to be able to do it, so when the book is completed, the sense of achievement is huge. It is always a thrill to see a book actually published; even more so if it is to be published in other countries. So far my books have been translated into twelve different languages, ranging from Chinese to Serbo-Croat."

Rees is a British writer whose novels for young adults often feature gruesome or startling elements, even by the standards of juvenile horror fiction. Her first book, *Every Step You Take,* for example, includes a rape scene and is so gruesome, according to *School Librarian* reviewer Sue Rogers, it should only be considered appropriate for teens over the age of fourteen. The

Celia Rees

suspense centers on a killer who is heading for his childhood home in Wales, which unbeknownst to him has been turned into a vacation cabin and rented for the weekend by a group of teenagers. The confrontations between the teens and the killer who is trying to scare them out of the house make this "not for the fainthearted!," Rogers concluded.

In *The Bailey Game,* Rees draws upon the universal bane of childhood life, bullying. At Alexandra Lewis's elementary school, bullying and cliques have become so vicious that they have made a ghost out of one of the school's students, Michael Bailey, who now haunts the bridge near the school where he disappeared two years before the start of the story. The arrival of a girl from Australia, and Alexandra's attempt to befriend her, bring the bullies' attention to this new target, and extortion and blackmail are attempted before adult help is sought. Bullying is such a universal problem, readers are sure to identify with Rees's protagonists, observed Linda Newbery in *School Librarian,* who added that readers are especially "likely to share these characters' doubts about whether or when to call in adult help." A reviewer for *Junior Bookshelf* stated that Rees's portrayal of the effects of bullying is so effective that *The Bailey Game* might be useful in classroom settings, where "it might ease the discussion of the topic into the open which cannot be a bad thing."

Rees works with some of the props of traditional ghost stories and thrillers in her novels *Colour Her Dead* and *Blood Sinister.* In *Colour Her Dead,* two school girls uncover disturbing information about the mysterious death of a six-year-old child twenty-five years earlier which puts them in danger. "This tightly plotted thriller keeps up the tension throughout," remarked David Bennett in *Books for Keeps.* For its part, *Blood Sinister* relies upon vampires and an ancient curse to jumpstart its plot. *School Librarian* reviewer Mike Peters concluded that "*Blood Sinister,* with its relatively complex double narrative, strong and sometimes shocking storyline, and diluted eroticism, should appeal to readers who can still thrill to the stock Gothic settings of old house and cemetery."

In *Ghost Chamber,* "Celia Rees has created both a realistic world and believable ghosts," according to Audrey Baker in *School Librarian.* Here, the three Goodman children go to live in an old pub with their father while he renovates the building during the school holidays. The pub turns out to be haunted by a Templar Knight with a secret to keep, and the arrival of two disreputable strangers adds to the sense of danger the children feel themselves to be in. A sequel to *Colour Her Dead, Midnight Hour* centers on Blair Paige, a seventeen-year-old celebrity who is being stalked. *School Librarian* critic Eileen Armstrong praised Rees's effective inclusion of issues teenage readers enjoy within a taut, fast-paced thriller plot: "Potentially controversial themes currently much criticised in teenage fiction (premeditated murder, kidnap, bullying, gang manipulation, stalking, astrology) are sensitively handled by an author who clearly understands the interests and preoccupations of teenagers," Armstrong remarked.

For younger readers, Rees has written a series of books critics noted for their likeness to the popular "Goosebumps" series by R. L. Stine. In *H Is for Haunting* and *A Is for Apparition,* the first two books in the "H.A.U.N.T.S." series, a group of young teens gets mixed up with ghosts and an alternate universe. *School Librarian* contributor Catherine Sack noted that Rees's series of ghost stories will likely appeal to young readers who like series novels and/or ghosts stories, but added "the otherworld of good and evil ghosts being developed in these stories has some imaginative force."

Rees returns to the macabre in *Soul Taker,* which inspired *School Librarian* reviewer Patricia Peacock to write: "The opening of this is so gruesome that I nearly stopped reading at that point." In this story, an overweight, unpopular boy unwittingly sells his soul and slims down, quickly becoming one of the most popular boys in his class, only to discover he does not want to pay the price that is being asked of him in return for his changed status. Peacock also praised the author for her realistic depiction of Lewis's horrible parents and of the interactions between the boy and his classmates.

In *The Truth Out There,* the first of Rees's young adult novels to be published in the United States, the author achieves a dual narrative that reviewers praised for its sophistication. In the primary strand, thirteen-year-old Josh goes with his mother to his grandmother's home for the summer, quickly becoming intrigued by the fate of a family member he knows little about. His Uncle Patrick, his mother's brother, suffered from a form of autism before that condition was medically recognized and was blamed by the suspicious locals when tragedy struck nearby. Patrick was sent to an institution where he was believed to have died some time later and was never mentioned within the family again. Josh and Katherine, a local girl, unweave the strands of the mystery of Patrick's life with the help of the memoir Josh's mother is writing. They are also caught up in a futuristic computer game whose scenario begins to bear a striking resemblance to some of the details of Patrick's life, and the two strands of the plot begin to come together. Published in the author's native England as *Truth or Dare,* the U.S. version features a cover that, according to some critics, misrepresents the story as being about aliens from outer space. "Readers expecting aliens will be disappointed," remarked Catherine Andronik in *Booklist,* though she added that the "family drama" aspect is successful and the "British perspective on the space race . . . is intriguing." For Leah J. Sparks, writing in *School Library Journal,* there is much to commend in

Joshua begins to trace the story of his Uncle Patrick, whose autism was a family secret for years. (Cover illustration by Walter Porter.)

Rees's first export to North America. "Rees does a marvelous job of injecting an atmosphere of mystery and uncertainty into the novel from the beginning," Sparks contended, calling *The Truth Out There* "an original, intelligent novel from a fresh voice in YA literature."

Witches are the focus of Rees's 2000 novel, *Witch Child,* about a young girl named Mary who travels to the English colonies in the "New World," hoping her fellow settlers never learn that her adopted grandmother was accused of being a witch and executed for her supposed crime. Arriving first in Salem, Massachusetts, Mary discovers that the tradition of witch-hunts are alive in the colonies, and she fears that her past will be found out. Told in the form of a journal from the mid-1600s, *Witch Child* has earned favorable reviews from critics on both sides of the Atlantic. Predicting that "young readers will be enthralled" by the tale, a contributor to *Books for Keeps* wrote that "Rees's vivid narrative brings confidence and feeling to her subtle unfolding of events." *Guardian* reviewer Lyn Gardner pointed out that in *Witch Child* Rees has not only produced "a really good and cleverly constructed read," but also has "convincingly chart[ed] the psychology and political circumstances that engendered the witch-hunts." As did other reviewers, *National Post* writer Elizabeth MacCallum praised the authors mysterious ending, saying that "The inherent frustration in such a conclusion—or non-conclusion—fuses perfectly with Rees's structural conceit to make a legitimate and, more importantly, effective device."

Biographical and Critical Sources

PERIODICALS

Booklist, November, 2000, Catherine Andronik, review of *The Truth Out There,* p. 541.

Bookseller, June, 2000, review of *Witch Child.*

Books for Keeps, March, 1995, David Bennett, review of *Colour Her Dead,* p. 16; May, 2001, review of *Witch Child.*

Daily Telegraph, February, 2000, review of *Truth or Dare.*

Guardian, February 1, 2000, Lindsay Fraser, review of *Truth or Dare;* October 24, 2000, Lyn Gardner, review of *Witch Child.*

Independent, April 15, 2000, Nicholas Tucker, review of *Truth or Dare.*

Independent on Sunday, April 30, 2000, Brandon Robshaw, review of *Truth or Dare.*

Junior Bookshelf, December, 1994, review of *The Bailey Game,* p. 232.

National Post, February 24, 2001, Elizabeth MacCallum, "When mothers of Salem saw witches in their midst," p. B8.

Publishers Weekly, June 25, 2001, review of *Witch Child,* p. 73.

Publishing News, June 2, 2000, Graham Marks, review of *Witch Child.*

School Librarian, November, 1993, Sue Rogers, review of *Every Step You Take,* pp. 167-168; February, 1995, Linda Newbery, review of *The Bailey Game,* pp. 33-34; February, 1997, Mike Peters, review of *Blood Sinister,* p. 49; November, 1997, Audrey Baker, review of *Ghost Chamber,* p. 214; November, 1997, Eileen Armstrong, review of *Midnight Hour;* summer, 1998, Patricia Peacock, review of *Soul Taker,* p. 103; spring, 1999, Catherine Sack, review of *H Is for Haunting* and *A Is for Apparition,* p. 34.

School Library Journal, October, 2000, Leah J. Sparks, review of *The Truth Out There,* p. 170.

Scotsman, February 5, 2000, Lindsay Fraser, review of *Truth or Dare.*

Times (London), February 17, 2000, Sarah Johnson, review of *Truth or Dare.*

Times Educational Supplement, February 25, 2000, Michael Thorn, review of *Truth or Dare.*

Wall Street Journal, July 7, 2000, Charles Goldsmith, review of *Witch Child.*

*   *   *

RHINE, Richard
See SILVERSTEIN, Alvin and SILVERSTEIN, Virginia B.

*   *   *

ROSE, Deborah Lee 1955-

Personal

Born October 24, 1955, in Philadelphia, PA; daughter of Bernard and Helen Rose; married; children: one daughter, one son. *Education:* Cornell University, B.A., 1977.

Addresses

Office—c/o Author Promotion Coordinator, Scholastic, Inc., 555 Broadway, New York, NY 10012.

Career

Time-Life Books, Alexandria, VA, editorial researcher, 1977-82; University of California at Berkeley, Berkeley, CA, science writer and speech writer, 1984-91; Lawrence Hall of Science, Berkeley, CA, development, marketing, and exhibit writer, 1998—; freelance writer. *Member:* Society of Children's Book Writers and Illustrators, Northern California Science Writers Association.

Awards, Honors

Council for the Advancement of Science Writing, national science writing fellow, 1983-84; Jane Addams Children's Peace Book Award recommended list, 1990, for *The People Who Hugged the Trees;* First Prize for juvenile trade books, Chicago Women in Publishing, 1991, for *Meredith's Mother Takes the Train;* Pick of the Lists selection, American Library Association (ALA), and 100 Children's Books to Read and Share selection, New York Public Library, both for *Into the A, B, Sea: An Ocean Alphabet.*

Science writer Deborah Lee Rose penned an alphabet picture book that describes sea creatures from anemone to zooplankton. (From Into the A, B, Sea, *illustrated by Steve Jenkins.)*

Writings

The People Who Hugged the Trees, illustrated by Birgitta Säflund, Roberts Rinehart, 1990.

Meredith's Mother Takes the Train, illustrated by Irene Trivas, Albert Whitman (Morton Grove, IL), 1991.

The Rose Horse, illustrated by Greg Shed, Harcourt (San Diego, CA), 1996.

Into the A, B, Sea: An Ocean Alphabet, illustrated by Steve Jenkins, Scholastic (New York, NY), 2000.

Also author of *One Nighttime Sea,* a sequel to *Into the A, B, Sea,* illustrated by Steve Jenkins.

Also contributor to *A Childhood Remembered,* Narada, 1991. *The People Who Hugged the Trees* has been translated into German, French, Spanish, Danish, Norwegian, Chinese, Vietnamese, Cambodian, and Hmong. The book has also been included in language arts anthologies in the U.S. and Canada, and has been broadcast on television and radio by the British Broadcasting Corporation.

Sidelights

Deborah Lee Rose was an experienced science writer and speech writer before she made the decision to write books for young readers. Inspired by her experiences as a mother, as well as her interest in both science and history, Rose has produced a selection of books that

have prompted praise from critics. When she was a child, Rose once dreamed of becoming a translator for the United Nations. Creating picture books for children is not so different from that childhood dream, she told *SATA*. "Writing for children is a process of translating complex concepts into very accessible language," she explained.

The People Who Hugged the Trees, Rose's first work for children, is based on a centuries-old story from Rajasthan, India, that also served, in the twentieth century, to inspire that country's Chipko environmental movement. Readers will recognize the story's theme of caring for the environment as both timeless and contemporary, local and global. "I was particularly struck by this story of a young girl who grows up to lead her entire village in saving a forest," Rose once explained to *SATA*. "I hope, as my daughter grows up, she will also feel strongly about making the world a better place in some way."

In *The People Who Hugged the Trees,* Amrita Devi grows up knowing that the trees growing near her village are crucial to her family's survival: in addition to shelter from the sun, they protect the village from the violent sandstorms of the surrounding desert. One day the Maharajah decides to build a new fort, and sends his men to cut the trees down. Armed with axes, the men approach, but they find each tree embraced by a member of Amrita's village, a form of resistance thought up by the young girl to save her beloved trees. A *Horn Book* reviewer complimented illustrator Birgitta Saflund's "delicate, detailed" images, and called the book "a successful, timely tale." *Growing Point*'s Margery Fisher termed *The People Who Hugged the Trees* "an impressive example of the way story can convey a general idea" to children.

Other picture books by Rose touch on both serious and lighthearted family themes, from workday separation to birthdays. *Meredith's Mother Takes the Train* focuses on the concerns of both parents and children regarding day care. Meredith's mom boards the train every morning to commute to work and spends her day thinking about the time she will spend with her daughter once she gets home. Meanwhile, Meredith is at day care, busily playing with her friends yet anticipating her mother's welcome arrival to pick her up. Rose's rhyming text captures the feeling of a train along the track—a poetic device which makes the story appealing to very young, even pre-verbal children. *Booklist* contributor Leone McDermott called the work "subtly reassuring" to young children.

Her children's and her own love of ocean animals prompted Rose to write a picture book about the ocean that weaves together marine science and language arts. *Into the A, B, Sea* uses what *Booklist* contributor Gillian Engberg described as "rhymed couplets filled with appealing action words" to fascinate young listeners and readers with the diversity of the ocean. *School Library Journal* reviewer Joy Fleishhacker called the book "a tantalizing, visually stunning invitation to explore a new frontier," and noted that the cut-paper collage illustrations by Steve Jenkins are "breathtaking.... Each painting is a perfect medley of vibrant color and restless motion." Rose got the idea for the book while writing alphabet letters in the sand with her young son. "It hit me," she told *SATA*, "that the ocean and the alphabet are both so vast and full of possibilities." Rose's text mimics the rhythm of the waves against the shore, and the book's illustrations are complemented by factual details for each ocean creature, as well as a useful glossary of terms. Rose and Jenkins have created a sequel, *One Nighttime Sea*, that sheds light on the little-known night life of the ocean's nocturnal creatures.

Designed for beginning readers making the transition from picture books to novels, 1996's *The Rose Horse* opens a window onto the life of immigrants in New York City at the turn of the twentieth century. Inspired by the great carousel carvers of Brooklyn's Coney Island, Rose delved into American history and lore to recreate a time long ago. Lily and her family find themselves on Coney Island following the premature birth of Lily's baby sister, for the only way the infant's "state-of-the-art" medical care can be paid for is with the coins paid by curious onlookers who flock to see the incubator baby "sideshow," where Lily's sister is being kept alive. Staying temporarily with a cousin's family, Lily learns more about her family's Eastern European Jewish traditions and the craft of woodcarving, for her cousin Samuel is a talented artisan at work on the animals for Coney Island's renowned carousels. Priscilla Wallace, writing in *Multicultural Review*, noted that the book offers "a subtle story of strong family relationships" and "supplements the teaching of American history, immigration, folk art, and Hebrew traditions."

"Since I began writing children's books," Rose told *SATA*, "I have learned to listen more closely to both the insightful and silly things my children and their friends say. I've had to look at things through their eyes, and as a result I've rediscovered things I missed, or forgot, in my own childhood." The character Rose admires most in children's books is Charlotte, the spider in E. B. White's *Charlotte's Web*. "Charlotte is a writer like I am," Rose observed. "She thinks a long time before she starts to write, she researches and checks her spelling with a little help from her friends, she likes to work when it's quiet, and she shows off her work in the best light possible. She loves words and understands they are powerful—they can teach, surprise, entertain, convince, and even save a life."

Biographical and Critical Sources

PERIODICALS

Booklist, February 15, 1991, Leone McDermott, review of *Meredith's Mother Takes the Train*, p. 1202; March 1, 1991, Kathleen T. Horning, review of *The People Who Hugged the Trees*, p. 1403; September 1, 1995, Hazel Rochman, review of *The Rose Horse*, p. 58; September 15, 2000, Gillian Engberg, review of *Into the A, B, Sea*, p. 246.

Bulletin of the Center for Children's Books, November, 1995, Susan Dove Lempke, review of *The Rose Horse*, p. 104.

Growing Point, March, 1991, Margery Fisher, review of *The People Who Hugged the Trees*, p. 5495.

Horn Book, July-December, 1990, review of *The People Who Hugged the Trees*, p. 102.

Junior Bookshelf, February, 1991, review of *The People Who Hugged the Trees*, p. 16.

Multicultural Review, March, 1996, Priscilla Wallace, review of *The Rose Horse*.

Publishers Weekly, September 18, 2000, "From A to Z," p. 113.

School Library Journal, March, 1991, Patricia Pearl, review of *Meredith's Mother Takes the Train*, p. 179; January, 1996, Marcia W. Posner, review of *The Rose Horse*, p. 94; October, 2000, Joy Fleishhacker, review of *Into the A, B, Sea*, p. 134.

S

SAAF, Donald W(illiam) 1961-

Personal

Born January 16, 1961, in Hartford, CT; son of Henry (a carpenter) and Ethel (a secretary; maiden name, Flodin) Saaf; married Julia Zanes (an artist), 1990; children: Isak Hjalmar, Olaf Galileo. *Education:* Attended School of the Museum of Fine Arts (Boston, MA). *Hobbies and other interests:* Old-time music; guitar and Irish tenor banjo.

Addresses

Home and office—P.O. Box 145, Saxtons River, VT 05154. *Agent*—Wanda Nowak, 231 East 76th St. Suite 5D, New York, NY 1001.

Career

Artist, painter, and children's book illustrator. *Exhibitions:* Saaf's work has been exhibited the Clark Gallery in Lincoln, MA.

Illustrator

Harriet Ziefert, *Wee G,* Atheneum (New York, NY), 1997.
Harriet Ziefert, *Pushkin Meets the Bundle,* Atheneum (New York, NY), 1998.
Harriet Ziefert, *Elemenopeo,* Houghton Mifflin (Boston, MA), 1998.
Harriet Ziefert, *Animal Music,* Houghton Mifflin (Boston, MA), 1999.
Harriet Ziefert, *Train Song,* Orchard (New York, NY), 2000.
Harriet Ziefert, *Pushkin Minds the Bundle,* Atheneum (New York, NY), 2000.
Harriet Ziefert, *What Do Ducks Dream?,* Putnam (New York, NY), 2001.
Priscilla and Otto Friedrich, *The Easter Bunny That Overslept,* HarperCollins (New York, NY), 2001.

Sidelights

Donald W. Saaf told *SATA:* "I studied painting at the Museum School and had no intention of making children's books. Then we had a baby, Isak, and I needed to find other work. I met the author Harriet Ziefert through the Clark Gallery in Lincoln, Massachusetts, where I still exhibit paintings, and we began collaborating. Now we have made seven books together and I've begun to take on other projects as well.

Donald W. Saaf and his son, Olaf.

"Some of my most favorite illustrators include Lang Campbell (who drew Uncle Wiggily in the '20s and '30s), L. Leslie Brooke (*Johnny Crow's Garden*), Wanda Gag, Winsor McKay, and Maurice Sendak. I also admire the work of Douglas Florian and Peter Sis, who bring children's books to a whole new level."

Saaf's creamily colored gouache paintings are often credited with adding humor as well as beauty to his numerous children's books. His animal and child characters alike have been characterized as both larger than life and figures with whom his audience will empathize. *School Library Journal* reviewer Jeanette Larson characterized Saaf's illustrations for Harriet Ziefert's *Wee G,* his first book, as "winsome, childlike, and slightly surrealistic." A reviewer for *Publishers Weekly* asserted that Saaf's illustrations "lend a quirky charm to this otherwise formulaic tale" of a kitten who chases a butterfly into the woods, gets lost, and then finds her way home just in time for dinner. Lauren Peterson, a contributor to *Booklist,* concluded that "first-time illustrator Saaf makes an admirable debut."

Saaf's next collaboration with Ziefert, *Elemenopeo,* also features a cat as its main character. Elemenopeo is a cat with many human characteristics, including the ability to paint a fantastical self-portrait in which he sports wings, providing ample fodder for the feline's dream during her afternoon cat nap.

From quiet and simple stories such as these, Ziefert moved on to more rambunctious fare in *Animal Music* and *Train Song,* both of which feature Saaf's paintings. In *Animal Music,* two rhythmic poems, "Mr. Lion's Marching Band" and "Sheep's Dance Band," introduce preschoolers to a variety of musical instruments and may inspire them to jump up and move to the beat of the text, reviewers noted. Here "there is a perfect integration of text and picture," according to Harriett Fargnoli in a *School Library Journal* review of *Animal Music. Booklist* Stephanie Zvirin similarly attested: "The art bursts with movement that perfectly captures the spirit of the words." In *Train Song,* a little boy watches a train pass in the valley below, identifying the cargo in its various boxcars and waving at the engineer. Here, Ziefert uses rhymed couplets that mimic the sounds and rhythm of the passing train, and "Saaf's gouache paintings illustrate the text with becoming directness and simplicity," wrote Carolyn Phelan in *Booklist.*

Saaf also collaborated with Ziefert on two books featuring a childlike dog named Pushkin. In *Pushkin Meets the Bundle,* Ziefert introduces Pushkin, the lovable companion of Kate and Michael, who thoroughly enjoys being the center of their attention until the day they bring home a baby wrapped in a bundle. Reviewers predicted that young readers with a new sibling would readily identify with the mixed bag of feelings the bundle evokes in Pushkin, who even considers the possibility of running away from home. "Saaf's lively and expressive gouache illustrations effectively draw readers into the action and emotion" of Ziefert's universal story, observed Christie J. Flynn in *School*

In the sequel to **Pushkin Meets the Bundle,** *the canine narrator is asked to watch over little Pierre when the family is on vacation and, in the process, learns to overcome his initial jealousy of the infant. (From* Pushkin Minds the Bundle, *written by Harriet Ziefert and illustrated by Saaf.)*

Library Journal. "The art is delicious," proclaimed Ilene Cooper in a *Booklist* review of *Pushkin Meets the Bundle,* who remarked that Saaf's artwork "adds layers of fun to what is in the text." In *Pushkin Minds the Bundle,* the baby of the earlier book is now a toddler, and Ziefert's longsuffering protagonist "minds" the child in more ways than one. As in the earlier book, Saaf depicts Pushkin with alternately human and doglike capabilities; he both walks on all fours and uses one paw to shade his eyes as he scans the horizon for the lost child, as *Booklist*'s Phelan pointed out in her review of *Pushkin Minds the Bundle.* The result, she said, is "a refreshingly funny and tender picture book."

Biographical and Critical Sources

PERIODICALS

Booklist, April 15, 1997, Lauren Peterson, review of *Wee G,* p. 1437; February 1, 1998, Ilene Cooper, review of *Pushkin Meets the Bundle,* p. 924; October 15, 1999, Stephanie Zvirin, review of *Animal Music,* p. 457; April 1, 2000, Carolyn Phelan, review of *Train Song,* p. 1472; September 1, 2000, Carolyn Phelan, review of *Pushkin Minds the Bundle,* p. 126.

Publishers Weekly, April 28, 1997, review of *Wee G,* p. 74; May 1, 2000, "What a Character," p. 73.

School Library Journal, June, 1997, Jeanette Larson, review of *Wee G,* p. 103; June, 1998, Christie J. Flynn, review of *Pushkin Meets the Bundle,* p. 125; September, 1998, Sally R. Dow, review of *Elemenopeo,* p. 187; October, 1999, Harriet Fargnoli, review of *Animal Music,* p. 130; April, 2000, Judith Constantinides, review of *Train Song,* p. 117; June, 2001, Joy Fleishhacker, review of *What Do Ducks Dream?,* pp. 132-133.*

SCHEMBRI, Jim 1962-
(Joel Tyne, Alex Dinessi)

Personal

Born April 21, 1962, in Williamstown, Victoria, Australia; son of Joseph Schembri (a craftsman-carpenter). *Education:* Monash University, B.A., 1983. *Religion:* "Still searching." *Hobbies and other interests:* Fiction writing, film, reading, late-night TV, *Star Wars*.

Addresses

Agent—Lothian, 11 Munro St., Port Melbourne, Victoria 3207, Australia. *E-mail*—jschembri@theage.fairfax.com.au.

Career

The Age (newspaper), journalist, 1984—. Author.

Writings

Room for One (humor), McPhee Gribble (Ringwood, Australia), 1994.

Jim Schembri

A Modern Fable (collection), illustrated by Liz Dixon, Angus & Robertson (Sydney, Australia), 1995.
I Was a Teenage Exam Cheat (young adult fiction), Addison Wesley Longman (Melbourne, Australia), 1998.
The Battle for Roserock Bottom (young adult fiction), Addison Wesley Longman (Melbourne, Australia), 1998.
It Came from Channel 5 (young adult fiction), Addison Wesley Longman (Melbourne, Australia), 1999.
Long Weekend at Snowbunny Farm (young adult fiction), Addison Wesley Longman (Melbourne, Australia), 1999.
Triple Dog Dare (young adult fiction), Addison Wesley Longman (Melbourne, Australia), 1999.
The Big Story: What It's Really Like to Be a Journalist (nonfiction), Macmillan, 1999.
Chicken Spots (short novel), Pearson (South Melbourne, Australia), 2001.
With Our Own Eyes (short novel), Barrie (Melbourne, Australia), 2001.

YOUNG ADULT NOVELS

In It Up to Here, Addison Wesley Longman (Melbourne, Australia), 1997.
The Jay Beans Guild, Addison Wesley Longman (Melbourne, Australia), 1998.
Say Boo to Penny for Me, Addison Wesley Longman (Melbourne, Australia), 1998.
Murder in Aisle 9, Lothian (Melbourne, Australia), 2000.
Welcome to Minute 16, Lothian (Melbourne, Australia), 2000.
The Eight Lives of Stullie the Great, Lothian (Melbourne, Australia), 2001.

CHAPTER BOOKS

Zelda, the Queen of Bad Habits, Addison Wesley Longman (Melbourne, Australia), 1999.
Odd Kid from Out There, Macmillan, 2000.
The Disaster Kid, Macmillan, 2000.
Better Than Ice Cream, Macmillan, 2000.
Reward for Muffin, Pearson (South Melbourne, Australia), Sundance (Littleton, MA), 2001.
Top Cow, Pearson (South Melbourne, Australia), Sundance (Littleton, MA), 2001.
Wrong Place, Wrong Time, Pearson (South Melbourne, Australia), 2001.
Tiny Island Tours, Barrie (Melbourne, Australia), 2001.
Holiday on Earth, Barrie (Melbourne, Australia), 2001.
Hose Wild, Barrie (Melbourne, Australia), 2001.
Revenge at Lake Happy, Nelson Thomson, 2001.
The Domes of Mars, Pearson (South Melbourne, Australia), 2002.

"WORLD SPLITTER" TRILOGY

Steg Lainer: Super Hero for Hire, Pearson (South Melbourne, Australia), 2001.
Invasion of the Gigabots, Pearson (South Melbourne, Australia), 2001.
The Liberation of Slave Planet Donto, Pearson (South Melbourne, Australia), 2001.

UNDER PSEUDONYM ALEX DINESSI

The Cape of Destiny, Macmillan, 2000.
Thundernose, Macmillan, 2000.

UNDER PSEUDONYM JOEL TYNE

The Trouble with Penguins, Macmillan, 2000.
Promise Not to Bite, Macmillan, 2000.
Tree Talk, Macmillan, 2000.

OTHER

Contributor to anthologies, including *Splash—Stories for Hot Summer Days,* Viking, 1998, and *Dear Jack—Break-up Letters from Famous and Infamous Australians,* Random House, 1998.

Work in Progress

The Lychee Conspiracy. Researching several detective thriller stories.

Sidelights

Jim Schembri told *SATA:* "After twelve long years in journalism I received an urgent message from my brain. It said: 'If you don't give me something interesting to do soon, I'm leaving.' Being a journalist is a great job, and I still love it, but it can be creatively and intellectually limiting. After a decade, I began feeling frustrated. The transience of the medium—in print one day, lining bird cages the next—was also starting to grate with me. In journalism you can put so much effort into writing something that ends up having a life span of one day.

"My brain was simply getting restless, so when the opportunity came to write a novel, I jumped at it. The result was my first novel, *In It Up to Here* (1997). Since then I have devoted much of my own time to fiction writing. I find the discipline and challenges extremely satisfying.

"I love storytelling. I love strong plots, lively characters and clear writing, for I defiantly believe that reading teen novels should not be a chore. I also hold that the best way to deal with issues is through a good, engaging story. As a general comment I have found much teen fiction a little too preoccupied with sombre topics—suicide, abuse, delinquency, dysfunctional families, etc.—at the cost of narrative drive and plot. The issues tend to weigh down the writing.

"I prefer to use issues as motivating themes in a plot. In *Murder in Aisle 9* (2000) the issues of infidelity and moral judgment propel the main characters through an engaging, unpredictable story. In *Welcome to Minute 16* (2000) the allure and dangers of fame, celebrity, and media are told through the dramatic experience of a young teenage TV star whose career has been declared dead in the water.

"Dealing with important issues does not mean you have to sacrifice being entertaining. I hold that you can serve those issues better *by* being entertaining.

"Without doubt, the best thing that has ever been said about the craft of creative writing is the old maxim that it is 'ten percent inspiration, ninety percent perspiration.' I have found this to be absolutely true. (Perhaps the ratio varies from book to book, but not by much.) My guess is that many people who decide to write a novel don't realise how much hard work will be involved in bringing their idea to life.

"To any aspiring writer my main advice would be this: prepare to devote months (possibly years) to writing, re-writing and re-re-writing. Get used to getting up early and staying up late. Have a good, solid wall you can pound into. And get ready for rejection. If you don't think you can handle someone flatly saying 'no' to a story you have devoted two years of your life to, don't write that first sentence.

"Contrary to what I know a lot of people think, writing books for children is extremely tough, and the younger the reader the more disciplined the writing needs to be. I didn't think it was going to be easy, but the effort involved in the task certainly threw me off balance. Writing children's books has helped me hone the craft of how to keep a story moving.

"As labor-intensive as it is, the satisfaction and joy I derive from writing is enormous. The thrill of holding a copy of a published work is something I don't think I will ever get used to. I certainly hope I don't.

"I may one day tire of journalism, but I cannot imagine ever tiring of writing—or of pounding that wall."

Biographical and Critical Sources

PERIODICALS

Australian Book Review, September, 2000, Ben Zipper, review of *Murder in Aisle 9,* p. 60.
Courier Mail, December 5, 2000, Kate Sherington, review of *Welcome to Minute 16.*
Magpies, March, 1998, review of *In It Up to Here,* p. 36.
Sunday Age, December 24, 2000, review by Mike Shuttle-worth.
Sydney Morning Herald, October 28, 2000, Julia Stirling, review of *Murder in Aisle 9,* Spectrum section, p. 13.
Viewpoint Magazine, spring, 2000, review of *Murder in Aisle 9,* pp. 46-47.

*   *   *

SHORE, Nancy 1960-

Personal

Born January 20, 1960, in Quincy, MA; daughter of Richard (a musician, music teacher, and composer) and Barbara (a teacher and community leader) Shore. *Education:* New York University, B.A. (English literature), 1983, post-graduate study (comparative literature), 1984; City University of New York, post-graduate study (English, Creative Writing), 1985-86. *Religion:* Jewish.

Hobbies and other interests: Theater, dance, music, travel.

Addresses

Home—New York, NY. *Agent*—c/o Chelsea Books, 1974 Sproul Rd., Ste. 400, Broomall, PA 19008.

Career

Freelance writer and copy editor at a wide variety of New York City publishing companies, magazines, newspapers, corporations, and advertising agencies, 1983-99; drama critic and feature writer, *The Providence Journal-Bulletin,* 1985-86, and *Stages Magazine,* 1985-87; part-time assistant to the co-editor of the *New York Review of Books,* 1986-91; Holt, Rinehart, and Winston, New York, NY, copyeditor of literature textbooks, 2000—. *Member:* Dramatist's Guild, New York Cycle Club.

Writings

Amelia Earhart ("American Women of Achievement" series), Chelsea House (New York, NY), 1987.
The Spice Girls ("Galaxy of Superstars" series), Chelsea House (Philadelphia, PA), 1999.

Nancy Shore

Work in Progress

"Recently completed a juvenile biography of Anne Hutchinson, the seventeenth-century Massachusetts religious and social leader."

Sidelights

Nancy Shore told *SATA:* "I'm so proud to have written a juvenile biography of Amelia Earhart. In addition to setting world records in aviation, she was a tireless lecturer at colleges and women's groups on the subject of equal rights for women. I have a deep sense of satisfaction from knowing my book has helped to introduce this great American heroine and important early twentieth-century feminist to a new generation of young people. I also loved writing about the Spice Girls. Their infectious energy, sense of fun, 'Girl Power!' motto, and unswerving belief in their ability to make their dreams a reality was an inspiration to me.

"My advice to aspiring writers is to make an ongoing daily practice of setting aside at least an hour to read the works, journals, and letters of the great novelists, essayists, poets, dramatists, and short story writers of the past. It's also important for writers, who spend a lot of their time sitting at a desk, to include physical exercise, i.e., dancing, swimming, jogging, yoga, rollerblading, etc., in their daily schedule. Time each day for quiet meditation is also essential."

Shore's first book, *Amelia Earhart,* is a biography of the early aviation hero for students in the middle grades. In this work, Shore focuses equally on Earhart's personal life, including her childhood and marriage—both of which were unconventional for the time—as well as on her career as a pilot, author, and public speaker, and the mystery of her eventual disappearance. Shore's topics include Earhart's early record-setting flights, her love for the new aviation technology, and her adjustment to the demands of fame. Although there have been many biographies of Earhart, this one is successful, according to *Booklist* reviewer Stephen Proces, because of Shore's "deft" writing and the inclusion of numerous photographs, which he predicts will help draw in less able readers.

Shore's second juvenile biography is *The Spice Girls,* a treatment of the popular British girl-group that emphasizes the childhood experiences of the group members and their popularity as a musical group. Each member describes auditioning for the group, and talks about lengthy rehearsals, affirming "Girl Power," and their various tour exploits. While warning that the popularity of such groups wanes quickly, *Book Report* critic Ann M. G. Gray nonetheless called Shore's *The Spice Girls* and the other books in the "Galaxy of Superstars" series published by Chelsea House "well written and attractive."

Shore contributed a biography on the short-lived British pop group to the "Galaxy of Superstars" series. (Cover photo by Ian Varrassi.)

Biographical and Critical Sources

PERIODICALS

Booklist, September 1, 1987, Stephen Proces, review of *Amelia Earhart,* p. 72.

Book Report, September-October, 1999, Ann M. G. Gray, review of *Spice Girls,* p. 66.

Horn Book Guide, fall, 1999, Cyrisse Jaffee, review of *Spice Girls,* p. 379.

School Library Journal, May, 1999, Debbie Feulner, review of *The Spice Girls,* p. 142.

*   *   *

SILVERSTEIN, Alvin 1933-
(Ralph Buxton, Dr. A, Richard Rhine; joint pseudonyms)

Personal

Born December 30, 1933, in New York, NY; son of Edward (a carpenter) and Fannie (Wittlin) Silverstein; married Virginia B. Opshelor (a writer and translator), August 29, 1958; children: Robert Alan, Glenn Evan, Carrie Lee, Sharon Leslie, Laura Donna, Kevin Andrew. *Education:* Brooklyn College (now Brooklyn College of the City University of New York), B.A., 1955; University of Pennsylvania, M.S., 1959; New York University, Ph.D., 1962. *Hobbies and other interests:* Vegetable gardening, sports, drawing and painting.

Addresses

Home—3 Burlinghoff Lane, P.O. Box 537, Lebanon, NJ 08833. *Office*—Department of Biology, College of Staten Island of the City University of New York, 2800 Victory Blvd., Staten Island, NY 10314.

Career

Junior High School No. 60, New York City, science teacher, 1959; College of Staten Island of the City University of New York, instructor, 1959-63, assistant professor, 1963-66, associate professor, 1966-70, professor of biology, 1970—; chair of biology department, 1978-79; writer. *Member:* Authors Guild, American Association for the Advancement of Science, American Chemical Society, American Institute of Biological Sciences, National Collegiate Association for the Conquest of Cancer (national chairperson, 1968-70).

Awards, Honors

All with wife, Virginia B. Silverstein: Children's Book of the Year citations, Child Study Association of America, 1969, for *A World in a Drop of Water,* and 1972, for *The Code of Life, Nature's Defenses* and *Nature's Pincushion; A World in a Drop of Water* was named an Outstanding Children's Book of 1969, *World Book Yearbook,* 1970; *Circulatory Systems* was named a Science Educators' Book Society Selection; awards from New Jersey Institute of Technology, 1972, for *Guinea Pigs: All about Them,* 1980, for *Aging,* 1983, for *The Robots Are Here* and *The Story of Your Mouth,* and 1990, for *Glasses and Contact Lenses;* Outstanding Science Books for Children citations, National Science Teachers Association and Children's Book Council, 1972, for *The Long Voyage, The Muscular System, The Skeletal System, Cancer, Nature's Pincushion,* and *Life in a Bucket of Soil,* 1973, for *Rabbits: All about Them,* 1974, for *Animal Invaders and Hamsters: All about Them,* 1976, *for Potatoes: All about Them* and *Gerbils: All about Them,* 1983, for *Heartbeats,* 1987, for *The Story of Your Foot,* 1988, for *Wonders of Speech* and *Nature's Living Lights,* and 1990, for *Overcoming Acne;* Notable Trade Books in the Field of Social Studies designation, National Council for the Social Studies and Children's Book Council, 1975, for *Alcoholism;* Older Honor citation, New York Academy of Sciences, 1977, for *Potatoes: All about Them;* Junior Literary Guild selection, and Children's Book of the Year citation, Bank Street College, 1977, both for *The Left-Hander's World;* Books for the Teen Age selections, New York Public Library, 1978, for *Heart Disease,* and 1987, for *AIDS: Deadly Threat;* special certificate of commendation, John Burroughs List of Nature Books for Young Readers, 1988, for *Nature's Living Lights.*

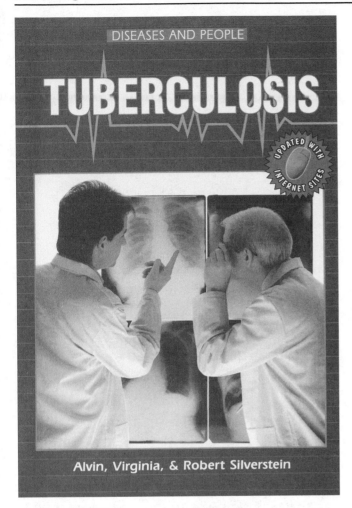

Alvin Silverstein's book from the "Diseases and People" series, cowritten with his wife and son, is an in-depth study of tuberculosis, and includes personal observations from people suffering from the disease. (Cover photo by John Michael.)

Writings

The Biological Sciences (college textbook), Rinehart Press (San Francisco, CA), 1974.
Conquest of Death, Macmillan (New York, NY), 1979.
Human Anatomy and Physiology (college textbook), Wiley (New York, NY), 1980, 2nd edition, 1983.

WITH WIFE, VIRGINIA B. SILVERSTEIN

Life in the Universe, illustrated by Lee Ames, Van Nostrand (Princeton, NJ), 1967.
Unusual Partners, illustrated by Mel Hunter, McGraw-Hill (New York, NY), 1968.
Rats and Mice: Friends and Foes of Mankind, illustrated by Joseph Cellini, Lothrop (New York, NY), 1968.
The Origin of Life, illustrated by Lee Ames, Van Nostrand (Princeton, NJ), 1968.
A Star in the Sea, illustrated by Simeon Shimin, Warne (New York, NY), 1969.
A World in a Drop of Water, Atheneum (New York, NY), 1969, reprinted, Dover Mineola, NY), 1998.
Cells: Building Blocks of Life, illustrated by George Bakacs, Prentice-Hall (Englewood Cliffs, NJ), 1969.

Carl Linnaeus: The Man Who Put the World of Life in Order ("Great Men of Science" series), illustrated by Lee Ames, John Day (New York, NY), 1969.
Frederick Sanger: The Man Who Mapped Out a Chemical of Life ("Great Men of Science" series), illustrated by Lee Ames, John Day (New York, NY), 1969.
Germfree Life: A New Field in Biological Research, Lothrop (New York, NY), 1970.
Living Lights: The Mystery of Bioluminescence, illustrated by Angus M. Babcock, Golden Gate (San Carlos, CA), 1970.
Bionics: Man Copies Nature's Machines, illustrated by Penelope Naylor, McCall Publishing (New York, NY), 1970.
Harold Urey: The Man Who Explored from Earth to Moon ("Great Men of Science" series), illustrated by Lee Ames, John Day (New York, NY), 1971.
Mammals of the Sea, illustrated by Bernard Garbutt, Golden Gate (San Carlos, CA), 1971.
Metamorphosis: The Magic Change, Atheneum (New York, NY), 1971.
The Sense Organs: Our Link with the World, illustrated by Mel Erikson, Prentice-Hall (Englewood Cliffs, NJ), 1971.
The Code of Life, illustrated by Kenneth Gosner, Atheneum (New York, NY), 1972.
Guinea Pigs: All about Them, photographs by Roger Kerkham, Lothrop (New York, NY), 1972.
The Long Voyage: The Life Cycle of a Green Turtle, illustrated by Allan Eitzen, Warne (New York, NY), 1972.
(Under joint pseudonym Ralph Buxton) *Nature's Defenses: How Animals Escape from Their Enemies,* illustrated by Angus M. Babcock, Golden Gate (San Carlos, CA), 1972.
Cancer, John Day (New York, NY), 1972, first revised edition, illustrated by Andrew Antal, 1977, second revised edition published as *Cancer: Can It Be Stopped?,* Lippincott (New York, NY), 1987.
The Skin: Coverings and Linings of Living Things, illustrated by Lee Ames, Prentice-Hall (Englewood Cliffs, NJ), 1972.
(Under joint pseudonym Ralph Buxton) *Nature's Pincushion: The Porcupine,* illustrated by Angus M. Babcock, Golden Gate (San Carlos, CA), 1972.
(Under joint pseudonym Richard Rhine) *Life in a Bucket of Soil,* illustrated by Elsie Wrigley, Lothrop (New York, NY), 1972, reprinted under names Virginia B. Silverstein and Alvin Silverstein, Dover (Mineola, NY), 2001.
Exploring the Brain, illustrated by Patricia De Veau, Prentice-Hall (Englewood Cliffs, NJ), 1973.
The Chemicals We Eat and Drink, Follett (Chicago, IL), 1973.
Rabbits: All about Them, photographs by Roger Kerkham, Lothrop (New York, NY), 1973.
Sleep and Dreams, Lippincott (Philadelphia, PA), 1974.
(Under joint pseudonym Ralph Buxton) *Nature's Water Clowns: The Sea Otters,* illustrated by Angus M. Babcock, Golden Gate (San Carlos, CA), 1974.
Animal Invaders: The Story of Imported Animal Life, Atheneum (New York, NY), 1974.

Hamsters: All about Them, photographs by Frederick Breda, Lothrop (New York, NY), 1974.

Epilepsy, introduction by J. Gordon Millichap, Lippincott (Philadelphia, PA), 1975.

Oranges: All about Them, illustrated by Shirley Chan, Prentice-Hall (Englewood Cliffs, NJ), 1975.

Beans: All about Them, illustrated by Shirley Chan, Prentice-Hall (Englewood Cliffs, NJ), 1975.

Alcoholism, introduction by Gail Gleason Milgrom, Lippincott (Philadelphia, PA), 1975.

(Under joint pseudonym Ralph Buxton) *Nature's Gliders: The Flying Squirrels,* illustrated by Angus M. Babcock, Golden Gate (San Carlos, CA), 1975.

Apples: All about Them, illustrated by Shirley Chan, Prentice-Hall (Englewood Cliffs, NJ), 1976.

Potatoes: All about Them, illustrated by Shirley Chan, Prentice-Hall (Englewood Cliffs, NJ), 1976.

Gerbils: All about Them, photographs by Frederick J. Breda, Lippincott (Philadelphia, PA), 1976.

Heart Diseases, Follett (Chicago, IL), 1976.

The Left-Hander's World, Follett (Chicago, IL), 1977.

Allergies, introduction by Sheldon Cohen, Lippincott (Philadelphia, PA), 1977.

Itch, Sniffle and Sneeze: All about Asthma, Hay Fever and Other Allergies, illustrated by Roy Doty, Four Winds (New York, NY), 1978.

Cats: All about Them, photographs by Frederick J. Breda, Lothrop (New York, NY), 1978.

So You're Getting Braces: A Guide to Orthodontics, illustrated by Barbara Remington, with photographs by the authors, Lippincott (Philadelphia, PA), 1978.

(With son, Glenn Silverstein) *Aging,* Watts (New York, NY), 1979.

World of Bionics, Methuen (New York, NY), 1979.

The Sugar Disease: Diabetes, introduction by Charles Nechemias, Lippincott (New York, NY), 1980.

The Genetics Explosion, Four Winds (New York, NY), 1980.

Mice: All about Them, photographs by son Robert A. Silverstein, Lippincott (New York, NY), 1980.

Nature's Champions: The Biggest, the Fastest, the Best, illustrated by Jean Zallinger, Random House (New York, NY), 1980.

The Story of Your Ear, illustrated by Susan Gaber, Coward, McCann (New York, NY), 1981.

Runaway Sugar: All about Diabetes, illustrated by Harriett Barton, Lippincott (New York, NY), 1981.

Futurelife: The Biotechnology Revolution, illustrated by Marjorie Their, Prentice-Hall (Englewood Cliffs, NJ), 1982.

Heartbeats: Your Body, Your Heart, illustrated by Stella Ormai, Lippincott (New York, NY), 1983.

The Robots Are Here, Prentice-Hall (Englewood Cliffs, NJ), 1983.

The Story of Your Mouth, illustrated by Greg Wenzel, Coward, McCann & Geoghegan (New York, NY), 1984.

Headaches: All about Them, Lippincott (New York, NY), 1984.

Heart Disease: America's Number One Killer, Lippincott (New York, NY), 1985.

The Story of Your Hand, illustrated by Greg Wenzel, Putnam (New York, NY), 1985.

Dogs: All about Them, introduction by John C. McLoughlin, Lothrop (New York, NY), 1986.

World of the Brain, illustrated by Warren Budd, Morrow (New York, NY), 1986.

AIDS: Deadly Threat, foreword by Paul Volberding, Enslow Publishers (Hillside, NJ), 1986, revised and enlarged edition, 1991.

The Story of Your Foot, illustrated by Greg Wenzel, Putnam (New York, NY), 1987.

Mystery of Sleep, illustrated by Nelle Davis, Little, Brown (Boston, MA), 1987.

Wonders of Speech, illustrated by Gordon Tomei, Morrow (New York, NY), 1988.

Nature's Living Lights: Fireflies and Other Bioluminescent Creatures, illustrated by Pamela and Walter Carroll, Little, Brown (Boston, MA), 1988.

Learning about AIDS, foreword by James Oleske, Enslow Publishers (Hillside, NJ), 1989.

Glasses and Contact Lenses: Your Guide to Eyes, Eyewear, and Eye Care, Harper (New York, NY), 1989.

Genes, Medicine, and You: Genetic Counseling and Gene Therapy, Enslow Publishers (Hillside, NJ), 1989.

(With family members Robert Alan, Linda, Laura, and Kevin Silverstein) *John, Your Name Is Famous: Highlights, Anecdotes, and Trivia about the Name John and the People Who Made It Great,* AVSTAR (Lebanon, NJ), 1989.

Life in a Tidal Pool, illustrated by Pamela and Walter Carroll, Little, Brown (Boston, MA), 1990.

The Manatee *is part of a series of books for young readers that details the importance of certain endangered species and how they are being rescued.* (Cover photo by Dr. Harvey Barnett.)

"SYSTEMS OF THE BODY" SERIES; WITH WIFE, VIRGINIA B. SILVERSTEIN

The Respiratory System: How Living Creatures Breathe, illustrated by George Bakacs, Prentice-Hall (Englewood Cliffs, NJ), 1969.

Circulatory Systems: The Rivers Within, illustrated by George Bakacs, Prentice-Hall (Englewood Cliffs, NJ), 1970.

The Digestive System: How Living Creatures Use Food, illustrated by George Bakacs, Prentice-Hall (Englewood Cliffs, NJ), 1970.

The Nervous System: The Inner Networks, illustrated by Mel Erikson, Prentice-Hall (Englewood Cliffs, NJ), 1971.

The Endocrine System: Hormones in the Living World, illustrated by Mel Erikson, Prentice-Hall (Englewood Cliffs, NJ), 1971.

The Reproductive System: How Living Creatures Multiply, illustrated by Lee Ames, Prentice-Hall (Englewood Cliffs, NJ), 1971.

The Muscular System: How Living Creatures Move, illustrated by Lee Ames, Prentice-Hall (Englewood Cliffs, NJ), 1972.

The Skeletal System: Frameworks for Life, illustrated by Lee Ames, Prentice-Hall (Englewood Cliffs, NJ), 1972.

The Excretory System: How Living Creatures Get Rid of Wastes, illustrated by Lee Ames, Prentice-Hall (Englewood Cliffs, NJ), 1972.

WITH WIFE, VIRGINIA B. SILVERSTEIN, AND SON ROBERT ALAN SILVERSTEIN

John: Fun and Facts about a Popular Name and the People Who Made It Great, AVSTAR (Lebanon, NJ), 1990.

Michael: Fun and Facts about a Popular Name and the People Who Made It Great, AVSTAR (Lebanon, NJ), 1990.

Overcoming Acne: The How and Why of Healthy Skin Care, foreword by Christopher M. Papa, illustrated by Frank Schwarz, Morrow (New York, NY), 1990.

Lyme Disease, the Great Imitator: How to Prevent and Cure It, foreword by Leonard H. Sigal, AVSTAR (Lebanon, NJ), 1990.

So You Think You're Fat: Obesity, Anorexia Nervosa, Bulimia, and Other Eating Disorders, Harper (New York, NY), 1991.

Addictions Handbook, Enslow Publishers (Hillside, NJ), 1991.

Smell, the Subtle Sense, illustrated by Ann Neumann, Morrow (New York, NY), 1992.

Recycling: Meeting the Challenge of the Trash Crisis, Putnam (New York, NY), 1992.

Steroids: Big Muscles, Big Problems ("Issues in Focus" series), Enslow Publishers (Hillside, NJ), 1992.

Saving Endangered Species ("Better Earth" series), Enslow Publishers (Hillside, NJ), 1993.

Eagles, Hawks, and Owls, illustrated by Kristin Kest, Western Publishing (Racine, WI), 1994.

Cystic Fibrosis, Watts (New York, NY), 1994.

"FOOD POWER!" SERIES; WITH WIFE, VIRGINIA B. SILVERSTEIN, AND SON ROBERT ALAN SILVERSTEIN

Proteins, illustrated by Anne Canevari Green, Millbrook (Brookfield, CT), 1992.

Fats, illustrated by Anne Canevari Green, Millbrook (Brookfield, CT), 1992.

Carbohydrates, illustrated by Anne Canevari Green, Millbrook (Brookfield, CT), 1992.

Vitamins and Minerals, illustrated by Anne Canevari Green, Millbrook (Brookfield, CT), 1992.

"HUMAN BODY SYSTEMS" SERIES; WITH WIFE, VIRGINIA B. SILVERSTEIN, AND SON ROBERT ALAN SILVERSTEIN

The Skeletal System, Twenty-First Century Books (Brookfield, CT), 1994.

Respiratory System, Twenty-First Century Books (Brookfield, CT), 1994.

The Reproductive System, Twenty-First Century Books (Brookfield, CT), 1994.

The Nervous System, Twenty-First Century Books (Brookfield, CT), 1994.

The Muscular System, Twenty-First Century Books (Brookfield, CT), 1994.

The Excretory System, Twenty-First Century Books (Brookfield, CT), 1994.

The Digestive System, Twenty-First Century Books (Brookfield, CT), 1994.

The Circulatory System, Twenty-First Century Books (Brookfield, CT), 1994.

"DISEASES AND PEOPLE" SERIES; WITH WIFE, VIRGINIA B. SILVERSTEIN, AND SON ROBERT ALAN SILVERSTEIN

Tuberculosis, Enslow Publishers (Hillside, NJ), 1994.

Common Cold and Flu, Enslow Publishers (Hillside, NJ), 1994.

Rabies, Enslow Publishers (Hillside, NJ), 1994.

Diabetes, Enslow Publishers (Hillside, NJ), 1994.

Mononucleosis, Enslow Publishers (Hillside, NJ), 1994.

Hepatitis, Enslow Publishers (Hillside, NJ), 1994.

Measles and Rubella, Enslow Publishers (Springfield, NJ), 1997.

"ENDANGERED IN AMERICA" SERIES; WITH WIFE, VIRGINIA B. SILVERSTEIN, AND SON ROBERT ALAN SILVERSTEIN

The Spotted Owl, Millbrook (Brookfield, CT), 1994.

The Red Wolf, Millbrook (Brookfield, CT), 1994.

The Peregrine Falcon, Millbrook (Brookfield, CT), 1995.

The Sea Otter, Millbrook (Brookfield, CT), 1995.

The Manatee, Millbrook (Brookfield, CT), 1996.

"KINGDOMS OF LIFE" SERIES; WITH WIFE, VIRGINIA B. SILVERSTEIN, AND SON ROBERT ALAN SILVERSTEIN

Vertebrates, Twenty-First Century Books (Brookfield, CT), 1996.

Plants, Twenty-First Century Books (Brookfield, CT), 1996.

Monerans and Protists, Twenty-First Century Books (Brookfield, CT), 1996.

Invertebrates, Twenty-First Century Books (Brookfield, CT), 1996.

Fungi, Twenty-First Century Books (Brookfield, CT), 1996.

WITH WIFE, VIRGINIA B. SILVERSTEIN, AND DAUGHTER LAURA SILVERSTEIN NUNN

AIDS: An All-About Guide for Young Adults ("Issues in Focus" series), Enslow Publishers (Berkeley Heights, NJ), 1999.

Puberty ("Watts Library" series), Watts (Danbury, CT), 2000.

Lyme Disease ("Watts Library" series), Watts (Danbury, CT), 2000.

"ENDANGERED IN AMERICA" SERIES; WITH WIFE, VIRGINIA B. SILVERSTEIN, AND DAUGHTER LAURA SILVERSTEIN NUNN

The Black-Footed Ferret, Millbrook (Brookfield, CT), 1995.

(With Robert Alan Silverstein) *The Manattee,* Millbrook (Brookfield, CT), 1996.

The Mustang, Millbrook (Brookfield, CT), 1997.

The Florida Panther, Millbrook (Brookfield, CT), 1997.

The Grizzly Bear, Millbrook (Brookfield, CT), 1998.

The California Condor, Millbrook (Brookfield, CT), 1998.

"DISEASES AND PEOPLE" SERIES; WITH WIFE, VIRGINIA B. SILVERSTEIN, AND DAUGHTER LAURA SILVERSTEIN NUNN

Sickle Cell Anemia, Enslow Publishers (Springfield, NJ), 1997.

Asthma, Enslow Publishers (Springfield, NJ), 1997.

Depression, Enslow Publishers (Springfield, NJ), 1997.

Chicken Pox and Shingles, Enslow Publishers (Springfield, NJ), 1998.

Leukemia, Enslow Publishers (Berkeley Heights, NJ), 2000.

Polio, Enslow Publishers (Berkeley Heights, NJ), 2001.

Parkinson's Disease, Enslow Publishers (Berkeley Heights, NJ), 2002.

"WHAT A PET!" SERIES; WITH WIFE, VIRGINIA B. SILVERSTEIN, AND DAUGHTER LAURA SILVERSTEIN NUNN

Snakes and Such, Twenty-First Century Books (Brookfield, CT), 1998.

A Pet or Not?, Twenty-First Century Books (Brookfield, CT), 1998.

Pocket Pets, Twenty-First Century Books (Brookfield, CT), 1999.

Different Dogs, Twenty-First Century Books (Brookfield, CT), 1999.

"SCIENCE CONCEPTS" SERIES; WITH WIFE, VIRGINIA B. SILVERSTEIN, AND DAUGHTER LAURA SILVERSTEIN NUNN

Evolution, Twenty-First Century Books (Brookfield, CT), 1998.

Symbiosis, Twenty-First Century Books (Brookfield, CT), 1998.

Photosynthesis, Twenty-First Century Books (Brookfield, CT), 1998.

Food Chains, Twenty-First Century Books (Brookfield, CT), 1998.

Plate Tectonics, Twenty-First Century Books (Brookfield, CT), 1998.

Energy, Twenty-First Century Books (Brookfield, CT), 1998.

Weather and Climate, Twenty-First Century Books (Brookfield, CT), 1998.

Clocks and Rhythm, Twenty-First Century Books (Brookfield, CT), 1999.

"MY HEALTH" SERIES; WITH WIFE, VIRGINIA B. SILVERSTEIN, AND DAUGHTER LAURA SILVERSTEIN NUNN

Is That a Rash?, Watts (Danbury, CT), 1999.

Tooth Decay and Cavities, Watts (Danbury, CT), 1999.

Cuts, Scrapes, Scabs, and Scars, Watts (Danbury, CT), 1999.

Common Colds, Watts (Danbury, CT), 1999.

Allergies, Watts (Danbury, CT), 1999.

Sleep, Watts (Danbury, CT), 2000.

Sore Throats and Tonsillitis, Watts (Danbury, CT), 2000.

Staying Safe, Watts (Danbury, CT), 2000.

Eat Your Vegetables! Drink Your Milk!, Watts (Danbury, CT), 2001.

Can You See the Chalkboard?, Watts (Danbury, CT), 2001.

Broken Bones, Watts (Danbury, CT), 2001.

Attention Deficit Disorder, Watts (Danbury, CT), 2001.

Dyslexia, Watts (Danbury, CT), 2001.

Headaches, Watts (Danbury, CT), 2001.

Bites and Stings, Watts (Danbury, CT), 2001.

Chicken Pox, Watts (Danbury, CT), 2001.

Lyme Disease, Watts (Danbury, CT), 2001.

Burns and Blisters, Watts (Danbury, CT), 2002.

Vaccinations, Watts (Danbury, CT), 2002.

Earaches, Watts (Danbury, CT), 2002.

Physical Fitness, Watts (Danbury, CT), 2002.

"SENSES AND SENSORS" SERIES; WITH WIFE, VIRGINIA B. SILVERSTEIN, AND DAUGHTER LAURA SILVERSTEIN NUNN

Smelling and Tasting, Twenty-First Century Books (Brookfield, CT), 2001.

Seeing, Twenty-First Century Books (Brookfield, CT), 2001.

Touching, Twenty-First Century Books (Brookfield, CT), 2001.

Hearing, Twenty-First Century Books (Brookfield, CT), 2001.

OTHER

Also author with wife, Virginia B. Silverstein, under joint pseudonym Dr. A, of syndicated juvenile fiction column, "Tales from Dr. A," which appeared in about 250 American and Canadian newspapers, 1972-74. Contributor, with wife, Virginia B. Silverstein, of a dozen articles to *The New Book of Knowledge.*

Sidelights

Often praised as the best science writers for middle-grade readers and young adults, husband-and-wife team Alvin and Virginia B. Silverstein have written upwards of two hundred information books for young people. Their award-winning works cover a wide range of topics, from contemporary issues like genetic engineering, bionics, recycling, and robotics, to detailed studies

The concept of photosynthesis is explored in this work, along with related topics such as acid rain, the carbon cycle, and a discussion of ecological concerns. (Cover photo by Michael Hubrich.)

of various animals, foods, body systems, and diseases such as AIDS. They have written books with the young specifically in mind—discussions of acne, braces and orthodontics, and eating disorders—and books for all ages, giving descriptions of the aging process and of the sense of smell, or explications of the cycle of time and clocks. Indeed no biological topic—from rabies to fungi—seems to have missed the collaborative talents of this prolific duo. Additionally, beginning in the 1990s, the husband-and-wife team brought their children into the writing mix, collaborating on dozens of titles with son Robert and daughter Laura.

The Silversteins bring an extensive knowledge of science to their collaborations—Virginia is a former chemist and Alvin is a biology professor—and they deal with complex issues in a comprehensible manner. Their books are accessible to young audiences and are often praised as straightforward, detailed, and authoritative. Their "work is carefully organized and written in a clear, direct style, and is dependably accurate," according to Zena Sutherland and May Hill Arbuthnot in *Children and Books.* Sutherland and Arbuthnot further comment-ed: "The more complicated subjects are not always covered in depth, but they are given balanced treatment, and the Silversteins' writing usually shows their atten-tion to current research and always maintains a scientific attitude."

Both Alvin and Virginia enjoyed similar interests throughout their childhoods. Alvin, born in New York City, grew up an avid reader, sometimes even reading the encyclopedia for fun, and found he was particularly fond of scientific literature. "I began a lifelong hobby of 'science watching' practically as soon as I learned to read," he revealed in *Fifth Book of Junior Authors and Illustrators.* "My first love was astronomy, but I also was crazy about animals." Virginia, too, born in Philadelphia, remembers herself as an enthusiastic reader, who especially loved books about animals. "When I was seven or eight," she recalled in *Fifth Book of Junior Authors and Illustrators,* "I used to total up my money saved in terms of how many Thornton Burgess [a prolific animal writer] ... books it would buy." In time she discovered an aptitude for chemistry and languages and was attracted to both fields. Ultimately, though, she decided to study chemistry, as did Alvin. The couple met at the University of Pennsylvania during the late 1950s—in a chemistry lab.

Nearly ten years after their marriage in 1958, Alvin and Virginia collaborated on their first children's book, *Life in the Universe.* "That book was quickly signed up," Virginia related in *Fifth Book of Junior Authors and Illustrators,* "and we plunged happily into children's science writing. Then followed twenty-three straight rejections. We would probably have given up if we hadn't already had a manuscript accepted." The duo persisted, however, and has gone on to complete an entire library of science books, many of which have been named Outstanding Science Books for Children by the National Science Teachers Association and Chil-dren's Book Council, awarded children's book-of-the-year citations, and recognized by the New Jersey Institute of Technology and the New York Academy of Sciences. Among these are works like *Gerbils: All about Them,* which includes a history of the animals as well as information about their intelligence and behavior; *Aging,* which encompasses such areas as senility, retirement, and the role of the elderly in families; and *Alcoholism,* which deals with that affliction as a disease. *Gerbils* is typical of the Silverstein approach: the writers provide thorough and up-to-date information on all aspects of the animal—a description of the species, its adaptation to various climates from the desert of its natural home on the Gobi to the lab and the family home, and even offer advice on choosing the right gerbil for a pet and how to care for it once chosen. In addition, "anecdotes from the authors' experience add a personable immediacy," commented a contributor for *Kirkus Reviews.* Margaret Bush, reviewing *Gerbils* in *School Library Journal,* also remarked on the Silverstein method: "Writing from close observation of gerbils raised in their own home, the Silversteins give a far more thorough and interesting account of gerbil behavior and care than has previously appeared in children's books on the subject." *Aging* also won praise from reviewers. A *Kirkus Reviews* contribu-tor felt that readers "will find here another of the Silversteins' exemplary research reports." Writing in *Science Books and Films,* Knight Steel found *Aging* to be "an easy-to-read, enjoyable and enlightening book" and one that "should be a hit for those in senior high and above." Reviewing *Alcoholism* in *Science Books and Films,* W. A. McConnell noted that this "little book is packed with information and it is an excellent source for anyone (particularly teenagers) seeking basic knowledge about drinking."

Other Silverstein books examine topics of high interest to many adolescents, such as eating disorders, braces, acne, or glasses. Reviewing *So You're Getting Braces: A Guide to Orthodontics, Booklist*'s Denise M. Wilms declared the book a "must for any youngster faced with braces." Wilms concluded that the information book was a "first-rate primer on a common, expensive adolescent pain." Reviewing *Overcoming Acne* in *Booklist,* Stephanie Zvirin noted that the Silversteins presented the work in a "straightforward fashion," giving "appropriately cautious" information about over-the-counter treatments and providing "a realistic sense of what to expect from a dermatologist."

The Silversteins turned their attention to the science of the future in several volumes, including *The World of Bionics, The Genetics Explosion, Futurelife: The Biotechnology Revolution,* and *Robots Are Here,* all of which provide informative overviews of their subjects for young readers. Investigating topics from prosthetics to robots in *The World of Bionics,* the Silversteins provide a "straightforward and readable summary," according to a writer for *Kirkus Reviews.* Reviewing *The Genetics Explosion* in *Appraisal: Science Books for Young People,* Ann F. Pratt declared that the authors "have contributed a first-class book full of excitement and suspense," providing a history of the subject from Gregor Mendel to James Watson and Francis Crick before discussing research current to the books appearance in 1980. Writing in *Horn Book* on *The Robots Are Here,* Harry C. Stubbs observed that the authors portrayed "in an unusually clear way the difficulties of designing a robot capable of learning a new job."

Both Silversteins are content with their working relationship. Virginia once said that she and Alvin "have an almost perfect meshing of minds." Alvin agrees that he and his wife work well together. "I was fortunate to find a marriage that has been both emotionally satisfying and a successful professional partnership." Writing in *Appraisal: Science Books for Young People,* the couple explained their collaborative technique: "We've tried some variations, but most of the time we sit there, one of us at the typewriter ... and throw ideas back and forth. Often one will begin a sentence and the other will finish it. Occasionally we disagree, but the disputes are surprisingly infrequent; usually our ideas and styles mesh smoothly. The writing generally goes rather slowly at the beginning of a book, but then, as we get a 'feel' for the material, the pace accelerates, and we often finish on a total-immersion, 'crash program' basis, with fourteen-or sixteen-hour days." The Silverstein partnership was expanded in the late 1980s when their eldest son, Robert, joined the writing team full time and then again when their daughter Laura later did the same. These later collaborations have dealt with subjects including descriptions of various animal groups, diseases, and systems of the body.

The Silversteins told *SATA:* "In the early 1990s, frustrated with the long delays typical of the publishing business and the sometimes arbitrary editorial and marketing decisions of some of our publishers, we decided to launch a small publishing venture of our own. It turned out to be a fascinating adventure, which at one point engaged the efforts of nearly the whole family. It was also a learning experience. We started out with two particular projects in mind: a book on Lyme disease and a series of books about particular first names and some of the notable people who have borne them. Living in a county that generally scores among the top three in the nation for Lyme disease case rates, we were very conscious of the dangers of the Lyme bacterium and its rather interesting life cycle. At the time only a couple of books had been published on the subject ... and nothing for young people. The publishers we worked with would have taken at least a year, or more likely two, to bring out a book, and we thought a more timely publication was warranted. In less than three months from concept to bound books, we were the proud authors and publishers of a carefully researched and heavily illustrated book that included a preface by a prominent Lyme disease researcher and input from eight other medical experts in the field. That idea was a winner: *Lyme Disease: The Great Imitator* garnered a number of

A title from the "My Health" series, Eat Your Vegetables! Drink Your Milk! *teaches young readers about the essential role of a balanced diet in maintaining a healthy body. (Cover illustration by Rick Stromonski.)*

favorable reviews, sold well, and brought us many touching personal contacts with readers and librarians.

"Our other project turned out to be a critical success and a financial disaster. *John, Your Name Is Famous* and *Michael: Fun Facts about a Popular Name and the People Who Made It Great* was read by a number of enthusiastic reviewers and talk show hosts . . . and by an all too small number of paying customers. We learned a lot about the economics of the publishing business and the difficulties in dealing with bookstores and distributors (not all of whom pay their bills). The first two books in an extensive projected series never did earn back enough to pay for the production costs (not to mention promotion and our labor), and we reluctantly abandoned our partly finished manuscripts on Mary, Elizabeth, Robert, and so forth, along with several filing cabinets full of research. . . .

"After out big venture folded, we gradually returned to reality and have continued to write books for young people. We've had the good fortune to be associated with a number of talented editors whose vision helped launch such series as "Science Concepts" and "My Health." We've been delighted by the trend toward more bright and appealing formats for children's books, lavishly illustrated in full color. (Black-and-white photos or line drawings were standard illustrations for nonfiction books when we first started writing.)"

Detailing the lives of a wide variety of vertebrates, the Silversteins have fixed their literary lens on birds such as the spotted owl, eagles, and the peregrine falcon; on four-legged creatures, including the red fox, the mustang, the grizzly bear, the Florida Panther, and even the black-footed ferret. Animals that inhabit the water are represented also: the sea otter and manatee, among others. Many of these titles are part of the "Endangered in America" series, which provides an overview of various species whose existence is endangered, detailing not only the physical characteristics of each animal, but also what factors contribute to their endangered status. In *The Peregrine Falcon,* for example, the Silversteins point the finger at the use of pesticides and at overhunting, both of which have caused a radical decline in falcon populations. The fur trade and angry fisherman have both contributed to the pressures put on the sea otter population, while the spotted owl has fallen foul of timber-cutting practices. Reviewing *The Spotted Owl* in *Booklist,* Frances Bradburn commented that the book explores the pros and cons involved in preservation practices with "typical Silverstein evenhandedness." In a review of *The Manatee* and *The Black-Footed Ferret* in *School Library Journal,* Amy Adler observed that both offerings "exhibit sound research and lively writing," commenting further that the "excellent-quality full-color photographs are an asset as well." Susan Oliver, writing about *The Mustang* and *The Florida Panther* in *School Library Journal,* noted that the "texts move logically from an explanation of the problems causing the animal to be endangered to possible solutions," and concluded, "these thorough, clearly written titles are excellent choices for reports."

More animals are served up in the "What a Pet!" series, including *Snakes and Such, Different Dogs,* and *A Pet or Not?* "As one would expect from the Silversteins," announced *Booklist*'s Ilene Cooper in a review of *Snakes and Such,* "the text is very cogent and lively." The Silversteins provide a host of possible pets in the title, from chameleons to geckos and iguanas, as well as snakes. The general subject of pets is dealt with in *A Pet or Not?,* which details a myriad of pet choices and their benefits and drawbacks. "A breeze to read and a treat to browse," wrote Deborah Stevenson in *Bulletin of the Center for Children's Books.*

Diseases have also proved a rich ground for Silverstein research and writing. From measles to AIDS, the writing team has detailed sicknesses galore, often reworking the same ailment for different age groups or to include more recent research. Their early award-winning book on cancer has been added to by other treatments of the subject, including *Leukemia,* a "concise, well-written discussion of the disease," according to Martha Gordon reviewing the title in *School Library Journal.* Causes, prevention, and treatment are part of this book, as they are in others of the "Diseases and People" series. *Common Cold and Flu* is a "comprehensive, easy-to-read overview of the history, causes, prevention, and treatment" of those eponymous ailments, as Gordon noted in another *School Library Journal* review. "A well-organized, well-documented look at a common ailment," Gordon concluded. Tuberculosis also gets the Silverstein treatment, in a book of the same title. Gordon found this to be a "fine overview of a once-feared and deadly disease," in a *School Library Journal* review. *Hepatitis* and *Mononucleosis,* other titles in the same series, both "provide information on medical problems frequently encountered by adolescents that young people could read and understand," according to Sue Krumbein writing in *Voice of Youth Advocates.* Janice Hayes, reviewing *Measles and Rubella* in *School Library Journal* found that volume to be "readable and authoritative." Hereditary diseases are the focus of several titles, such as *Sickle Cell Anemia, Diabetes,* and *Cystic Fibrosis. School Library Journal* contributor Christine A. Moesch called *Sickle Cell Anemia* a "thorough and well-written book" that offers a clear and detailed explanation of that hereditary disorder which most commonly afflicts Africans and African Americans. Reviewing *Cystic Fibrosis,* Mary Ojibway noted in *Voice of Youth Advocates* that the authors provide a "wealth of information" in "an easily readable format."

In the series "Human Body Systems," the Silversteins explicate the wonders of the human body from the respiratory to the reproductive systems and points in between. In *The Circulatory System* and *The Respiratory System,* the Silversteins "cover the morphology and physiology" of those systems in books typified by their "high quality of research and lively style," according to Carolyn Angus in a *School Library Journal* review. The digestive and excretory systems are detailed in two books by those titles, both of which "offer solid information for reports and projects," wrote Denise L. Moll in *School Library Journal.* Moll continued, "These

Pocket Pets *offers readers advice about the suitability of certain animals as pets, including cost and care, and offers Internet resources on several small animals.* (Cover photo by Charles Palek.)

texts are lucid, to the point, and highly readable." Reviewing *The Reproductive System* and *The Skeletal System* in *School Library Journal*, Moesch found that both volumes "are chock-full of detail and are written in a lively readable manner."

Moving away from the human body, the Silversteins have also penned several books dealing with general scientific concepts for young readers. *Photosynthesis* and *Symbiosis* both introduce "key concepts of science by exploring their development, applications, and relationships to scientific knowledge as a whole," observed Angus in a *School Library Journal* review of both titles. "These books are well researched and interesting and the format is inviting for both general-interest reading and research," Angus further noted. Another "well-written, well-researched" title on science concepts, according to Angus in a different *School Library Journal* review, is *Clocks and Rhythms,* a book that discusses the rhythm of our planet as well as biological rhythms and man-made clocks. Other popular titles on similar topics include *Energy, Weather and Climate, Plate Tectonics, Evolution,* and *Food Chains.*

Whatever the topic, the Silversteins' books are noted for being "well-researched, clearly written, [and] topical,"

as Catherine Andronik noted in *Booklist*. Their books consistently make "the science of life accessible to young readers," Kathleen McCabe pointed out in *School Library Journal*. This winning combination of thorough research, clear and concise writing, and attention to detail as well as readability has made the Silverstein team a cottage industry in the field of science writing for young readers.

Biographical and Critical Sources

BOOKS

Silverstein, Alvin, and Virginia B. Silverstein, *Fifth Book of Junior Authors and Illustrators,* edited by Sally Holmes Holtze, H. W. Wilson (New York, NY), 1983.

Sutherland, Zena, and May Hill Arbuthnot, "Informational Books," *Children and Books,* 5th edition, Scott, Foresman (Glenview, IL), 1977.

PERIODICALS

Appraisal: Science Books for Young People, winter, 1981, Ann F. Pratt, review of *The Genetics Explosion,* p. 47; spring, 1985, pp. 34-35; spring, 1987, pp. 58-59; winter-spring, 1989, pp. 78-79; spring-summer, 1995, pp. 71-73; autumn, 1995, pp. 77-78.

Booklist, April 1, 1978, Denise M. Wilms, review of *So You're Getting Braces: A Guide to Orthodontics,* pp. 1260-1261; June 15, 1988, p. 1729; April 15, 1990, Stephanie Zvirin, review of *Overcoming Acne: The How and Why of Healthy Skin Care,* p. 1621; January 15, 1995, p. 91; March 15, 1995, p. 1325; April 15, 1995, Frances Bradburn, review of *The Red Wolf* and *The Spotted Owl,* p. 1496; June 1, 1995, p. 1768; June 1, 1996, p. 1714; September 1, 1998, p. 117; February 1, 1999, p. 972; May 1, 1999, p. 1593; August, 1999, Ilene Cooper, review of *Snakes and Such,* p. 2055; September 1, 1999, p. 130; October 15, 1999, p. 440; October 15, 2000, Catherine Andronik, review of *Lyme Disease,* p. 433.

Bulletin of the Center for Children's Books, July, 1987, p. 218; April, 1988, pp. 167-168; September, 1999, Deborah Stevenson, review of *A Pet or Not?,* p. 31.

Horn Book, March-April, 1984, Harry C. Stubbs, review of *The Robots,* p. 227; September-October, 1984, p. 628.

Kirkus Reviews, April 15, 1975, review of *Gerbils: All about Them,* p. 479; October 1, 1979, review of *Aging,* p. 1148; February 15, 1980, review of *The World of Bionics,* p. 220; May 15, 1989, p. 771; June 1, 1990, p. 803; June 15, 1990, p. 881.

School Library Journal, September, 1976, Margaret Bush, review of *Gerbils: All about Them,* p. 125; April, 1994, Martha Gordon, review of *Tuberculosis,* pp. 166-167; July, 1994, Martha Gordon, review of *Common Cold and Flu,* p. 113; July, 1994, p. 126; December, 1994, p. 140; March, 1995, Denise L. Moll, review of *The Digestive System* and *The Excretory System,* p. 219; April, 1995, Carolyn Angus, review of *The Respiratory System* and *The Circulatory System,* p. 146; May, 1995, Kathleen McCabe, review of *The Muscular System* and *The Nervous System,* p. 115; May, 1995, Christine A. Moesch, review of *The Reproductive System* and *The Skeletal System,* pp. 115-116; January, 1996, Amy Adler, review of

The Black-Footed Ferret and *The Manatee,* p. 126; July, 1996, pp. 104-105; February, 1997, Christine A. Moesch, review of *Sickle Cell Anemia,* p. 125; June, 1997, Susan Oliver, review of *The Florida Panther* and *The Mustang,* p. 146; May, 1998, Janice Hayes, review of *Measles and Rubella,* p. 160; January, 1999, p. 154; February, 1999, Carolyn Angus, review of *Symbiosis* and *Photosynthesis,* p. 127; October, 1999, Carolyn Angus, review of *Clocks and Rhythms,* pp. 175-176; December, 1999, pp. 126-127; May, 2000, p. 187; September, 2000, Martha Gordon, review of *Leukemia,* p. 257.

Science Books and Films, September, 1976, W. A. McConnell, review of *Alcoholism,* p. 100; September-October, 1980, Knight Steel, review of *Aging,* p. 6; January-February, 1984, p. 160; January-February, 1989, p. 147.

Voice of Youth Advocates, October, 1994, Mary Ojibway, review of *Cystic Fibrosis,* pp. 235-236; October, 1995, Sue Krumbein, review of *Hepatitis* and *Mononucleosis,* p. 188.

—*Sketch by J. Sydney Jones*

*   *   *

SILVERSTEIN, Robert Alan 1959-
(Robert Alan, Lyndon DeRoberts)

Personal

Born May 17, 1959, in Brooklyn, NY; son of Alvin (a professor and writer) and Virginia B. (a translator and writer; maiden name, Opshelor) Silverstein; married Linda Rose Babeu (a social worker), June 19, 1987; children: Emily Rachel, Jamey David. *Education:* Rutgers University, B.A., 1982. *Politics:* Democrat. *Hobbies and other interests:* Painting, photography, drawing, fiction writing, song writing, movie watching.

Addresses

Agent—c/o Enslow Publishers, 44 Fadem Rd., Springfield, NJ 07081. *E-mail*—TheSilversteins@aol.com.

Career

AVSTAR Publishing, Lebanon, NJ, managing editor, 1988-90; The Lifebridge Foundation (a grantmaking United Nations non-governmental organization promoting the interconnectedness of life), New York, NY, communications manager, 1997—; creator of electronic books and materials for Web sites.

Writings

WITH PARENTS, ALVIN AND VIRGINIA B. SILVERSTEIN

John: Fun and Facts about a Popular Name and the People Who Made It Great, AVSTAR (Lebanon, NJ), 1990.
Michael: Fun and Facts about a Popular Name and the People Who Made It Great, AVSTAR (Lebanon, NJ), 1990.

Overcoming Acne: The How and Why of Healthy Skin Care, foreword by Christopher M. Papa, illustrated by Frank Schwarz, Morrow (New York, NY), 1990.
Lyme Disease, the Great Imitator: How to Prevent and Cure It, foreword by Leonard H. Sigal, AVSTAR (Lebanon, NJ), 1990.
So You Think You're Fat: Obesity, Anorexia Nervosa, Bulimia, and Other Eating Disorders, Harper (New York, NY), 1991.
Addictions Handbook, Enslow Publishers (Hillside, NJ), 1991.
Smell, the Subtle Sense, illustrated by Ann Neumann, Morrow (New York, NY), 1992.
Recycling: Meeting the Challenge of the Trash Crisis, Putnam (New York, NY), 1992.
Steroids: Big Muscles, Big Problems ("Issues in Focus" series), Enslow Publishers (Hillside, NJ), 1992.
Saving Endangered Species ("Better Earth" series), Enslow Publishers (Hillside, NJ), 1993.
Eagles, Hawks, and Owls, illustrated by Kristin Kest, Western Publishing (Racine, WI), 1994.
Cystic Fibrosis, Watts (New York, NY), 1994.

"FOOD POWER!" SERIES; WITH PARENTS, ALVIN AND VIRGINIA B. SILVERSTEIN

Proteins, illustrated by Anne Canevari Green, Millbrook (Brookfield, CT), 1992.
Fats, illustrated by Anne Canevari Green, Millbrook (Brookfield, CT), 1992.
Carbohydrates, illustrated by Anne Canevari Green, Millbrook (Brookfield, CT), 1992.
Vitamins and Minerals, illustrated by Anne Canevari Green, Millbrook (Brookfield, CT), 1992.

"HUMAN BODY SYSTEMS" SERIES; WITH PARENTS, ALVIN AND VIRGINIA B. SILVERSTEIN

The Skeletal System, Twenty-First Century Books (Brookfield, CT), 1994.
Respiratory System, Twenty-First Century Books (Brookfield, CT), 1994.
The Reproductive System, Twenty-First Century Books (Brookfield, CT), 1994.
The Nervous System, Twenty-First Century Books (Brookfield, CT), 1994.
The Muscular System, Twenty-First Century Books (Brookfield, CT), 1994.
The Excretory System, Twenty-First Century Books (Brookfield, CT), 1994.
The Digestive System, Twenty-First Century Books (Brookfield, CT), 1994.
The Circulatory System, Twenty-First Century Books (Brookfield, CT), 1994.

"DISEASES AND PEOPLE" SERIES; WITH PARENTS, ALVIN AND VIRGINIA B. SILVERSTEIN

Tuberculosis, Enslow Publishers (Hillside, NJ), 1994.
Common Cold and Flu, Enslow Publishers (Hillside, NJ), 1994.
Rabies, Enslow Publishers (Hillside, NJ), 1994.
Diabetes, Enslow Publishers (Hillside, NJ), 1994.
Mononucleosis, Enslow Publishers (Hillside, NJ), 1994.
Hepatitis, Enslow Publishers (Hillside, NJ), 1994.

Measles and Rubella, Enslow Publishers (Springfield, NJ), 1997.

"ENDANGERED IN AMERICA" SERIES; WITH PARENTS, ALVIN AND VIRGINIA B. SILVERSTEIN

The Spotted Owl, Millbrook (Brookfield, CT), 1994.
The Red Wolf, Millbrook (Brookfield, CT), 1994.
The Peregrine Falcon, Millbrook (Brookfield, CT), 1995.
The Sea Otter, Millbrook (Brookfield, CT), 1995.
The Manatee, Millbrook (Brookfield, CT), 1996.

"KINGDOMS OF LIFE" SERIES; WITH PARENTS, ALVIN AND VIRGINIA B. SILVERSTEIN

Vertebrates, Twenty-First Century Books (Brookfield, CT), 1996.
Plants, Twenty-First Century Books (Brookfield, CT), 1996.
Monerans and Protists, Twenty-First Century Books (Brookfield, CT), 1996.
Invertebrates, Twenty-First Century Books (Brookfield, CT), 1996.
Fungi, Twenty-First Century Books (Brookfield, CT), 1996.

OTHER

(Illustrator) Alvin and Virginia B. Silverstein, *Mice: All about Them,* Lippincott, 1980.
(With family members Alvin, Virginia, Linda, Laura, and Kevin Silverstein) *John, Your Name Is Famous: Highlights, Anecdotes, and Trivia about the Name John and the People Who Made It Great,* AVSTAR (Lebanon, NJ), 1989.

Author and illustrator of several Web sites for children, including *Kids Care: The Network for Kids Who Care about Our World,* and *Dream Keeper.* Co-author of picture book (with Steve Diamond), *One Day in Peace,* published on the Internet in 1997, and of over thirty other children's books published on the Internet; author of short stories and novels on the Internet under the pseudonyms of Robert Alan and Lyndon DeRobertis.

Sidelights

Robert Alan Silverstein is the co-author of over forty children's science books on topics from endangered species and diseases in humans to parts of the body and food groups. Working with his noted parents, Alvin and Virginia Silverstein, he has penned science books that present information in clear and digestible bits; that deliver descriptions and explanations in comprehensible and entertaining language; and that blend image and text to "open the door to ... mind-boggling process[es]," as Steve Matthews noted in a *School Library Journal* review of *Plants* and *Monerans and Protists.* Jonathan Betz-Zall, also writing in *School Library Journal,* commented on the Silversteins' "usual flowing style" and inclusion of "a few specific incidents to draw and maintain interest" in their "solid introduction" to *Recycling: Meeting the Challenges of the Trash Crisis.* It is these attributes which make the collaborative efforts of Robert Silverstein and his parents as popular as they are with young readers and reviewers alike. Silverstein once

Robert Alan Silverstein and his parents, noted children's authors Alvin and Virginia B. Silverstein, delve into the history of rabies, its treatment, and the controversy over control of the disease.

told *SATA:* "I've always wanted to be a writer as far back as I can remember. It's not that surprising since both my parents are writers. When I was offered the opportunity to join my parents in writing children's science books, I jumped at the chance. (I'd much rather write fiction but I have a family to feed!)"

Born in Brooklyn, New York, in 1959, Silverstein grew up in a house overflowing with books. His father, Alvin, is a college biology professor and writer, and his mother, Virginia, is a Russian-to-English translator and coauthor on the plethora of science books for which the Silversteins are so well known. The eldest of six children, Silverstein formed an early appreciation for research and writing. Graduating from Rutgers University in 1982, he married in 1987 and has two children.

While still a college student, he provided photographic illustrations for the book *Mice: All about Them,* which was written by his parents. His first collaborative writing venture came in 1989 with *John, Your Name Is Famous,* released by the Silversteins' own publishing house, AVSTAR. Several dozen more titles followed between

1990 and 1997. In *Overcoming Acne,* the authors provide a clear and concise skin care how-to guide for young readers, discussing how pimples form, the causes of acne, and strategies for dealing with the condition. Other books on ailments and human diseases tackle subjects from the common cold to diabetes. The organization and presentation in *Cystic Fibrosis* is typical of the Silversteins' approach to science books. "Chapters are divided into concisely written sections with headings in bold type," according to Martha Gordon, reviewing the book in *School Library Journal.* Simple black and white photographs and line drawings, both well-captioned, accompany this text which covers the basics of the disease—what it is and what is known about its causes and treatments—along with a discussion of research and controversies over the findings of such research. The Silversteins also provide source notes for each chapter along with a glossary of technical terms, an index, and recommendations for further reading. Reviewing *Cystic Fibrosis* in *Booklist,* Patricia Braun felt that it was a "fine addition to the health bookshelf."

Gordon, writing in *School Library Journal,* called Silverstein's *Rabies* "another competent series entry," and noted that the book pays "particular attention to its recent spread in the U.S." Commenting on *Diabetes* in *School Library Journal,* Gordon focused on the "information about genetic predisposition and new aggressive treatments" which separates the Silversteins' book from other similar titles. Gordon, again writing in *School*

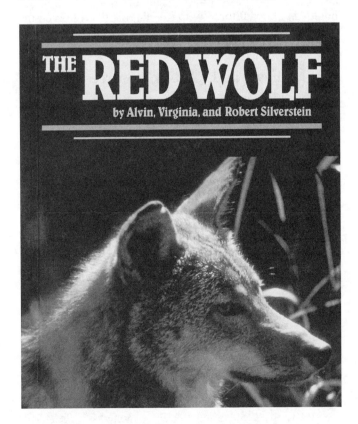

The nearly extinct red wolf is the focus of the Silversteins' study of the species and the programs designed to save the animals. (Cover photo by Mel Woods.)

Library Journal, called the Silversteins' *Hepatitis* and *Mononucleosis* "useful additions" to literature on the subjects, and described their *Common Cold and Flu* as a "comprehensive, easy-to-read and understand overview," as well as a "well-organized, well-documented look" at the history, causes, prevention, and treatment of the common cold and flu. "This is scientific curiosity at its best," proclaimed *Booklist*'s Mary Harris Veeder in a review of *Mononucleosis.* Reviewing their *Measles and Rubella,* Janice C. Hayes wrote in *School Library Journal:* "Students interested in diseases will find this title readable and authoritative." Writing about the same title in *Booklist,* Mary Romano Marks called the book an "outstanding curricular supplement for health and biology class, as well as a handy, readable reference source for students and staff."

Silverstein and his parents have also looked at larger social issues such as recycling and endangered species. In *Recycling: Meeting the Challenge of the Trash Crisis,* they use the image of planet Earth as a spaceship so self-contained that it cannot afford to waste its resources or to merely throw them away. They describe how recycling happens as a matter of course in the natural world and how humans have short-circuited that cycle. They also include a description of what people can do to change the status quo. They point to an industry-oriented economic system as the "major villain" in the crisis, according to Betz-Zall who praised the authors' "succinct coverage" of the nature of the crisis and the need for recycling, as well as techniques and problems in recycling. "This [book] could become the standard on the subject," Betz-Zall concluded. In their *Saving Endangered Species,* the Silversteins use the same techniques to examine the crisis of threatened animals and the loss of their habitats. They also survey conservation attempts to reverse the trend toward disappearing habitats for endangered species.

Individual titles look at specific animals that are endangered, including *The Red Wolf, The Spotted Owl, The Peregrine Falcon,* and *The Sea Otter.* Reviewing the *Sea Otter* in *School Library Journal,* Amy Adler found it to be a "book to savor." The Silversteins present an overview of the sea otter's anatomy, habitat, and lifestyle, and then turn to an "unbiased," according to the critic, examination of the animal's slide toward extinction and efforts to preserve it. Adler concluded: "This noteworthy effort gives an extremely well-rounded look at one of nature's most captivating creatures." Reviewing *The Red Wolf* in *Booklist,* Frances Bradburn concluded that the "information insets highlighting a variety of pertinent environmental issues will increase readers' understanding of how the environment and its problems are all interconnected."

Volumes such as *Monerans and Protists, Plants, Vertebrates,* and *Invertebrates,* all part of the "Kingdoms of Life" series, incorporate a broader look at living things. Reviewing the first two titles in the series, Matthews called them "information-packed volumes" in a *School Library Journal* review. Reviewing *Invertebrates* in *Booklist,* Kay Weisman commented that "the authors carefully note the reasoning used to place individual species into these particular groups."

Silverstein has additionally looked at food groups and systems of the human body. In *Carbohydrates, Fats, Proteins,* and *Vitamins and Minerals,* the Silversteins present an "attractive quartet," according to *School Library Journal*'s Gordon. The books include explanations of the basic food groups, how they are used, and what happens to the body when there is an excess or deficiency of each. The body is further examined in the "Human Body Systems" series, which includes *The Digestive System, The Excretory System, The Muscular System, The Nervous System, The Reproductive System,* and *The Skeletal System,* among other titles. Each book gives an overview of the topic accompanied by full-color photos and fact boxes. New terminology also appears in bold face for easy recognition by young readers. Reviewing *The Reproductive System* and *The Skeletal System* in *School Library Journal,* Christine A. Moesch called the books "straightforward overviews," in which material "is presented objectively and scientifically." In a review of *The Circulatory System, Booklist*'s Carolyn Phelan thought that all the books in the series "provide clear introductions to their respective subjects." Kathleen McCabe, writing in *School Library Journal* on *The Muscular System* and *The Nervous System,* remarked that the Silversteins "have once again made the science of life accessible to young readers" through their "clear texts," illustrations, glossaries, and time lines. Denise L. Moll, also writing in *School Library Journal,* found that *The Digestive System* and *The Excretory System* "offer solid information for reports and projects," and that, in the "overcrowded field of books on the human body, these series entries stand above the rest."

Since 1996, Silverstein has focused much of his time working with an international peace organization, People for Peace, and its "One Day in Peace" movement. He is also the author of several electronic books and has developed other materials for Web sites. Writing under various pseudonyms, he has become an active contributor of electronic books and multimedia "edutainment" programs to America Online (AOL).

"In addition to the forty published children's science books coauthored with my parents, Alvin and Virginia Silverstein, I am most proud of a picture book coauthored with California writer Steve Diamond called *One Day in Peace,*" Silverstein told *SATA.* "This picture book was published in four languages and could be printed out from the Internet in twenty-two languages. The idea developed into a global movement for a worldwide day of peace on January 1, 2000. Over 1000 organizations in over 120 nations were part of the network that Steve and I directed, and young people inspired by the book (and the play available online) were a major force in the campaign. Thanks largely to the efforts of kids, twenty-five U.S. Governors declared proclamations for One Day In Peace, January 1, 2000; the United Nations adopted a resolution declaring One Day In Peace, and in November 2000, the United States Congress declared that every January 1 will be known as One Day In Peace.

"The Internet has been an exciting way to share my works with people all around the world. I published over thirty children's picture books on the Internet (many of which are still available at http://home.aol.com/kidz4peace). At one point these electronic picture books had received nearly 100,000 downloads from the AOL Library. I've also published dozens of short stories and several novels under the pseudonyms Robert Alan and Lyndon DeRobertis on the Internet. Currently I am working on a multi-media exploration of my first Internet-published novel, *Destination Unknown,* for which I illustrated and composed forty original one-minute songs."

Silverstein's work with People for Peace Network continues to link people and groups to help encourage world peace. Through several Web sites he maintains, including *DinoPals Page, Kids Care: The Network for Kids Who Care about Our World,* and *Dream Keeper,* Silverstein provides stories, games, pen pals, chatrooms, magazines, and other resources for children online, all with a message of world peace.

"Writing is an extremely fulfilling occupation," Silverstein once told *SATA.* "Unlike previous paper-pushing office jobs, writing produces a finished product that I can be proud of, and one that I know will help expand and enrich people's minds. The children's nonfiction books that I coauthored with my parents [have] given me the satisfaction of finally feeling that I've fulfilled my childhood dream to be a writer."

Biographical and Critical Sources

PERIODICALS

American Biology Teacher, February, 1992, p. 126.

Booklist, June 15, 1992, p. 1822; December 15, 1992, p. 734; May 1, 1993, p. 1578; September 15, 1994, Patricia Braun, review of *Cystic Fibrosis,* p. 124; January 15, 1995, Mary Harris Veeder, review of *Mononucleosis,* p. 911; March 15, 1995, Carolyn Phelan, review of *The Circulatory System,* p. 1325; April 15, 1995, Frances Bradburn, review of *The Red Wolf,* p. 1496; June 1, 1995, p. 1768; June 1, 1996, Kay Weisman, review of *Invertebrates,* p. 1714; March 1, 1998, Mary Romano Marks, review of *Measles and Rubella,* p. 1124;

Book Report, January-February, 1991, p. 56; November-December, 1991, p. 54; November-December, 1992, p. 61; March-April, 1993, p. 50; September-October, 1993, p. 55; November-December, 1994, pp. 53-54.

English Journal, December, 1992, p. 76.

Horn Book, May-June, 1981, pp. 329-330; September-October, 1992, p. 602.

School Library Journal, June, 1990, pp. 143-144; May, 1991, p. 125; August, 1992, Jonathan Betz-Zall, review of *Recycling: Meeting the Challenge of the Trash Crisis,* p. 186; January, 1993, Martha Gordon, review of *Carbohydrates, Proteins, Vitamins, and Minerals,* and *Fats,* pp. 125-126; May, 1993, p. 115;

July, 1994, Martha Gordon, review of *Common Cold and Flu*, p. 113; July, 1994, Martha Gordon, review of *Rabies*, p. 126; August, 1994, Martha Gordon, review of *Cystic Fibrosis*, p. 179; December, 1994, Martha Gordon, review of *Diabetes*, p. 140; March, 1995, Denise L. Moll, review of *The Digestive System* and *The Excretory System*, p. 219; March, 1995, Martha Gordon, review of *Hepatitis* and *Mononucleosis*, p. 233; May, 1995, Kathleen McCabe, review of *The Muscular System* and *The Nervous System*, p. 115; May, 1995, Christine A. Moesch, review of *The Reproductive System* and *The Skeletal System*, pp. 115-116; July, 1995, Amy Adler, review of *The Sea Otter*, p. 91; July, 1996, Steve Matthews, review of *Monerans and Protists* and *Plants*, pp. 104-105; May, 1998, Janice C. Hayes, review of *Measles and Rubella*, p. 160.

Science Teacher, November, 1993, p. 74.

ON-LINE

Dream Keeper, http://members.aol.com/dreams4all/ (June 6, 2001).

Kids Care, http://members.aol.com/kidz4peace/ (June 6, 2001).

One Day in Peace, http://www.oneday.net/ (June 10, 2001).

People for Peace Network, http://members.aol.com/pforpeace/ (June 6, 2001).*

—*Sketch by J. Sydney Jones*

*   *   *

SILVERSTEIN, Virginia B. 1937- (Ralph Buxton, Dr. A, Richard Rhine; joint pseudonyms)

Personal

Full name is Virginia Barbara Opshelor Silverstein; born April 3, 1937, in Philadelphia, PA; daughter of Samuel W. (an insurance agent) and Gertrude (Bresch) Opshelor; married Alvin Silverstein (a professor of biology and writer) August 29, 1958; children: Robert Alan, Glenn Evan, Carrie Lee, Sharon Leslie, Laura Donna, Kevin Andrew. *Education:* Attended McGill University, summer, 1955; University of Pennsylvania, A. B., 1958. *Hobbies and other interests:* Reading, listening to classical music, computers, grandchildren (Robert, Shara, Emily, Jamey, Cory, Evan, Samantha, and Lia).

Addresses

Home—3 Burlinghoff Lane, P.O. Box 537, Lebanon, NJ 08833.

Career

American Sugar Company, Brooklyn, NY, analytical chemist, 1958-59; freelance translator of Russian scientific literature, 1960—; writer. *Member:* Authors Guild.

Awards, Honors

All with husband, Alvin Silverstein: Children's Book of the Year citations, Child Study Association of America, 1969, for *A World in a Drop of Water*, and 1972, for *The Code of Life, Nature's Defenses* and *Nature's Pincushion; A World in a Drop of Water* was named an Outstanding Children's Book of 1969, *World Book Yearbook*, 1970; *Circulatory Systems* was named a Science Educators' Book Society Selection; awards from New Jersey Institute of Technology, 1972, for *Guinea Pigs: All about Them*, 1980, for *Aging*, 1983, for *The Robots Are Here* and *The Story of Your Mouth*, and 1990, for *Glasses and Contact Lenses;* Outstanding Science Books for Children citations, National Science Teachers Association and Children's Book Council, 1972, for *The Long Voyage, The Muscular System, The Skeletal System, Cancer, Nature's Pincushion,* and *Life in a Bucket of Soil*, 1973, for *Rabbits: All about Them*, 1974, for *Animal Invaders and Hamsters: All about Them*, 1976, for *Potatoes: All about Them* and *Gerbils: All about Them*, 1983, for *Heartbeats*, 1987, for *The Story of Your Foot*, 1988, for *Wonders of Speech* and *Nature's Living Lights*, and 1990, for *Overcoming Acne;* Notable Trade Books in the Field of Social Studies designation, National Council for the Social Studies and Children's Book Council, 1975, for *Alcoholism;* Older Honor citation, New York Academy of Sciences, 1977, for *Potatoes: All about Them;* Junior Literary Guild selection, and Children's Book of the Year citation, Bank Street College, 1977, both for *The Left-Hander's World;* Books for the Teen Age selections, New York Public Library, 1978, for *Heart Disease*, and 1987, for *AIDS: Deadly Threat;* special certificate of commendation, John Burroughs List of Nature Books for Young Readers, 1988, for *Nature's Living Lights.*

Writings

TRANSLATOR FROM RUSSIAN

V. N. Kondratev, *Kinetics of Chemical Gas Reactions*, Atomic Energy Commission, 1960.

M. A. Elyashevich, *Spectra of the Rare Earths*, Atomic Energy Commission, 1960.

L. K. Blinov, *Hydrochemistry of the Aral Sea*, Office of Technical Services, 1961.

R. A. Belyaev, *Beryllium Oxide*, Atomic Energy Commission, 1963.

G. V. Samsonov, *High-Temperature Compounds of Rare Earth Metals with Nonmetals*, Plenum, 1965.

M. B. Neiman, *Aging and Stabilization of Polymers*, Plenum, 1965.

WITH HUSBAND, ALVIN SILVERSTEIN

Life in the Universe, illustrated by Lee Ames, Van Nostrand (Princeton, NJ), 1967.

Unusual Partners, illustrated by Mel Hunter, McGraw-Hill (New York, NY), 1968.

Rats and Mice: Friends and Foes of Mankind, illustrated by Joseph Cellini, Lothrop (New York, NY), 1968.

The Origin of Life, illustrated by Lee Ames, Van Nostrand (Princeton, NJ), 1968.

A Star in the Sea, illustrated by Simeon Shimin, Warne (New York, NY), 1969.

A World in a Drop of Water, Atheneum (New York, NY), 1969, reprinted, Dover Mineola, NY), 1998.

Cells: Building Blocks of Life, illustrated by George Bakacs, Prentice-Hall (Englewood Cliffs, NJ), 1969.

Carl Linnaeus: The Man Who Put the World of Life in Order ("Great Men of Science" series), illustrated by Lee Ames, John Day (New York, NY), 1969.

Frederick Sanger: The Man Who Mapped Out a Chemical of Life ("Great Men of Science" series), illustrated by Lee Ames, John Day (New York, NY), 1969.

Germfree Life: A New Field in Biological Research, Lothrop (New York, NY), 1970.

Living Lights: The Mystery of Bioluminescence, illustrated by Angus M. Babcock, Golden Gate (San Carlos, CA), 1970.

Bionics: Man Copies Nature's Machines, illustrated by Penelope Naylor, McCall Publishing (New York, NY), 1970.

Harold Urey: The Man Who Explored from Earth to Moon ("Great Men of Science" series), illustrated by Lee Ames, John Day (New York, NY), 1971.

Mammals of the Sea, illustrated by Bernard Garbutt, Golden Gate (San Carlos, CA), 1971.

Metamorphosis: The Magic Change, Atheneum (New York, NY), 1971.

The Sense Organs: Our Link with the World, illustrated by Mel Erikson, Prentice-Hall (Englewood Cliffs, NJ), 1971.

The Code of Life, illustrated by Kenneth Gosner, Atheneum (New York, NY), 1972.

Guinea Pigs: All about Them, photographs by Roger Kerkham, Lothrop (New York, NY), 1972.

The Long Voyage: The Life Cycle of a Green Turtle, illustrated by Allan Eitzen, Warne (New York, NY), 1972.

(Under joint pseudonym Ralph Buxton) *Nature's Defenses: How Animals Escape from Their Enemies,* illustrated by Angus M. Babcock, Golden Gate (San Carlos, CA), 1972.

Cancer, John Day (New York, NY), 1972, first revised edition, illustrated by Andrew Antal, 1977, second revised edition published as *Cancer: Can It Be Stopped?,* Lippincott (New York, NY), 1987.

The Skin: Coverings and Linings of Living Things, illustrated by Lee Ames, Prentice-Hall (Englewood Cliffs, NJ), 1972.

(Under joint pseudonym Ralph Buxton) *Nature's Pincushion: The Porcupine,* illustrated by Angus M. Babcock, Golden Gate (San Carlos, CA), 1972.

(Under joint pseudonym Richard Rhine) *Life in a Bucket of Soil,* illustrated by Elsie Wrigley, Lothrop (New York, NY), 1972, reprinted under names Virginia B. Silverstein and Alvin Silverstein, Dover (Mineola, NY), 2001.

Exploring the Brain, illustrated by Patricia De Veau, Prentice-Hall (Englewood Cliffs, NJ), 1973.

The Chemicals We Eat and Drink, Follett (Chicago, IL), 1973.

Rabbits: All about Them, photographs by Roger Kerkham, Lothrop (New York, NY), 1973.

Sleep and Dreams, Lippincott (Philadelphia, PA), 1974.

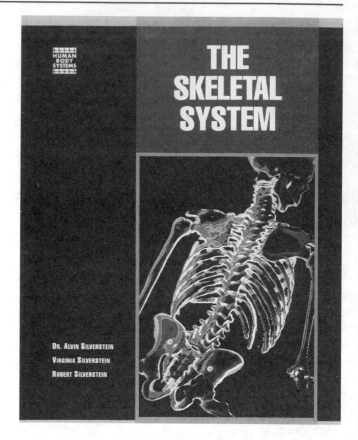

The human skeletal system, its function, and the cures and treatments for related diseases are discussed in Virginia B. Silverstein's book, coauthored with her husband and son. (Cover photo by Howard Sochurek.)

(Under joint pseudonym Ralph Buxton) *Nature's Water Clowns: The Sea Otters,* illustrated by Angus M. Babcock, Golden Gate (San Carlos, CA), 1974.

Animal Invaders: The Story of Imported Animal Life, Atheneum (New York, NY), 1974.

Hamsters: All about Them, photographs by Frederick Breda, Lothrop (New York, NY), 1974.

Epilepsy, introduction by J. Gordon Millichap, Lippincott (Philadelphia, PA), 1975.

Oranges: All about Them, illustrated by Shirley Chan, Prentice-Hall (Englewood Cliffs, NJ), 1975.

Beans: All about Them, illustrated by Shirley Chan, Prentice-Hall (Englewood Cliffs, NJ), 1975.

Alcoholism, introduction by Gail Gleason Milgrom, Lippincott (Philadelphia, PA), 1975.

(Under joint pseudonym Ralph Buxton) *Nature's Gliders: The Flying Squirrels,* illustrated by Angus M. Babcock, Golden Gate (San Carlos, CA), 1975.

Apples: All about Them, illustrated by Shirley Chan, Prentice-Hall (Englewood Cliffs, NJ), 1976.

Potatoes: All about Them, illustrated by Shirley Chan, Prentice-Hall (Englewood Cliffs, NJ), 1976.

Gerbils: All about Them, photographs by Frederick J. Breda, Lippincott (Philadelphia, PA), 1976.

Heart Diseases, Follett (Chicago, IL), 1976.

The Left-Hander's World, Follett (Chicago, IL), 1977.

Allergies, introduction by Sheldon Cohen, Lippincott (Philadelphia, PA), 1977.

Itch, Sniffle and Sneeze: All about Asthma, Hay Fever and Other Allergies, illustrated by Roy Doty, Four Winds (New York, NY), 1978.

Cats: All about Them, photographs by Frederick J. Breda, Lothrop (New York, NY), 1978.

So You're Getting Braces: A Guide to Orthodontics, illustrated by Barbara Remington, with photographs by the authors, Lippincott (Philadelphia, PA), 1978.

(With son, Glenn Silverstein) *Aging,* Watts (New York, NY), 1979.

World of Bionics, Methuen (New York, NY), 1979.

The Sugar Disease: Diabetes, introduction by Charles Nechemias, Lippincott (New York, NY), 1980.

The Genetics Explosion, Four Winds (New York, NY), 1980.

Mice: All about Them, photographs by son Robert A. Silverstein, Lippincott (New York, NY), 1980.

Nature's Champions: The Biggest, the Fastest, the Best, illustrated by Jean Zallinger, Random House (New York, NY), 1980.

The Story of Your Ear, illustrated by Susan Gaber, Coward, McCann (New York, NY), 1981.

Runaway Sugar: All about Diabetes, illustrated by Harriett Barton, Lippincott (New York, NY), 1981.

Futurelife: The Biotechnology Revolution, illustrated by Marjorie Their, Prentice-Hall (Englewood Cliffs, NJ), 1982.

Heartbeats: Your Body, Your Heart, illustrated by Stella Ormai, Lippincott (New York, NY), 1983.

The Silversteins explain the characteristics of single-celled organisms and their place in our ecosystem. (Cover photo by Sinclair Stammers.)

The Robots Are Here, Prentice-Hall (Englewood Cliffs, NJ), 1983.

The Story of Your Mouth, illustrated by Greg Wenzel, Coward, McCann & Geoghegan (New York, NY), 1984.

Headaches: All about Them, Lippincott (New York, NY), 1984.

Heart Disease: America's Number One Killer, Lippincott (New York, NY), 1985.

The Story of Your Hand, illustrated by Greg Wenzel, Putnam (New York, NY), 1985.

Dogs: All about Them, introduction by John C. McLoughlin, Lothrop (New York, NY), 1986.

World of the Brain, illustrated by Warren Budd, Morrow (New York, NY), 1986.

AIDS: Deadly Threat, foreword by Paul Volberding, Enslow Publishers (Hillside, NJ), 1986, revised and enlarged edition, 1991.

The Story of Your Foot, illustrated by Greg Wenzel, Putnam (New York, NY), 1987.

Mystery of Sleep, illustrated by Nelle Davis, Little, Brown (Boston, MA), 1987.

Wonders of Speech, illustrated by Gordon Tomei, Morrow (New York, NY), 1988.

Nature's Living Lights: Fireflies and Other Bioluminescent Creatures, illustrated by Pamela and Walter Carroll, Little, Brown (Boston, MA), 1988.

Learning about AIDS, foreword by James Oleske, Enslow Publishers (Hillside, NJ), 1989.

Glasses and Contact Lenses: Your Guide to Eyes, Eyewear, and Eye Care, Harper (New York, NY), 1989.

Genes, Medicine, and You: Genetic Counseling and Gene Therapy, Enslow Publishers (Hillside, NJ), 1989.

(With family members Robert Alan, Linda, Laura, and Kevin Silverstein) *John, Your Name Is Famous: Highlights, Anecdotes, and Trivia about the Name John and the People Who Made It Great,* AVSTAR (Lebanon, NJ), 1989.

Life in a Tidal Pool, illustrated by Pamela and Walter Carroll, Little, Brown (Boston, MA), 1990.

"SYSTEMS OF THE BODY" SERIES; WITH HUSBAND, ALVIN SILVERSTEIN

The Respiratory System: How Living Creatures Breathe, illustrated by George Bakacs, Prentice-Hall (Englewood Cliffs, NJ), 1969.

Circulatory Systems: The Rivers Within, illustrated by George Bakacs, Prentice-Hall (Englewood Cliffs, NJ), 1970.

The Digestive System: How Living Creatures Use Food, illustrated by George Bakacs, Prentice-Hall (Englewood Cliffs, NJ), 1970.

The Nervous System: The Inner Networks, illustrated by Mel Erikson, Prentice-Hall (Englewood Cliffs, NJ), 1971.

The Endocrine System: Hormones in the Living World, illustrated by Mel Erikson, Prentice-Hall (Englewood Cliffs, NJ), 1971.

The Reproductive System: How Living Creatures Multiply, illustrated by Lee Ames, Prentice-Hall (Englewood Cliffs, NJ), 1971.

The Muscular System: How Living Creatures Move, illustrated by Lee Ames, Prentice-Hall (Englewood Cliffs, NJ), 1972.

The Skeletal System: Frameworks for Life, illustrated by Lee Ames, Prentice-Hall (Englewood Cliffs, NJ), 1972.

The Excretory System: How Living Creatures Get Rid of Wastes, illustrated by Lee Ames, Prentice-Hall (Englewood Cliffs, NJ), 1972.

WITH HUSBAND, ALVIN SILVERSTEIN, AND SON ROBERT ALAN SILVERSTEIN

John: Fun and Facts about a Popular Name and the People Who Made It Great, AVSTAR (Lebanon, NJ), 1990.

Michael: Fun and Facts about a Popular Name and the People Who Made It Great, AVSTAR (Lebanon, NJ), 1990.

Overcoming Acne: The How and Why of Healthy Skin Care, foreword by Christopher M. Papa, illustrated by Frank Schwarz, Morrow (New York, NY), 1990.

Lyme Disease, the Great Imitator: How to Prevent and Cure It, foreword by Leonard H. Sigal, AVSTAR (Lebanon, NJ), 1990.

So You Think You're Fat: Obesity, Anorexia Nervosa, Bulimia, and Other Eating Disorders, Harper (New York, NY), 1991.

Addictions Handbook, Enslow Publishers (Hillside, NJ), 1991.

Smell, the Subtle Sense, illustrated by Ann Neumann, Morrow (New York, NY), 1992.

Recycling: Meeting the Challenge of the Trash Crisis, Putnam (New York, NY), 1992.

Steroids: Big Muscles, Big Problems ("Issues in Focus" series), Enslow Publishers (Hillside, NJ), 1992.

Saving Endangered Species ("Better Earth" series), Enslow Publishers (Hillside, NJ), 1993.

Eagles, Hawks, and Owls, illustrated by Kristin Kest, Western Publishing (Racine, WI), 1994.

Cystic Fibrosis, Watts (New York, NY), 1994.

"FOOD POWER!" SERIES; WITH HUSBAND, ALVIN SILVERSTEIN, AND SON ROBERT ALAN SILVERSTEIN

Proteins, illustrated by Anne Canevari Green, Millbrook (Brookfield, CT), 1992.

Fats, illustrated by Anne Canevari Green, Millbrook (Brookfield, CT), 1992.

Carbohydrates, illustrated by Anne Canevari Green, Millbrook (Brookfield, CT), 1992.

Vitamins and Minerals, illustrated by Anne Canevari Green, Millbrook (Brookfield, CT), 1992.

"HUMAN BODY SYSTEMS" SERIES; WITH HUSBAND, ALVIN SILVERSTEIN, AND SON ROBERT ALAN SILVERSTEIN

The Skeletal System, Twenty-First Century Books (Brookfield, CT), 1994.

Respiratory System, Twenty-First Century Books (Brookfield, CT), 1994.

The Reproductive System, Twenty-First Century Books (Brookfield, CT), 1994.

The Nervous System, Twenty-First Century Books (Brookfield, CT), 1994.

The Muscular System, Twenty-First Century Books (Brookfield, CT), 1994.

Alvin Silverstein, Virginia Silverstein, and Laura Silverstein Nunn

In addition to a discussion of the purely physical aspects of maturing into adulthood, **Puberty** *broaches the related issues of relationships and self-esteem. (Cover photo by Jeff I. Greenburg.)*

The Excretory System, Twenty-First Century Books (Brookfield, CT), 1994.

The Digestive System, Twenty-First Century Books (Brookfield, CT), 1994.

The Circulatory System, Twenty-First Century Books (Brookfield, CT), 1994.

"DISEASES AND PEOPLE" SERIES; WITH HUSBAND, ALVIN SILVERSTEIN, AND SON ROBERT ALAN SILVERSTEIN

Tuberculosis, Enslow Publishers (Hillside, NJ), 1994.

Common Cold and Flu, Enslow Publishers (Hillside, NJ), 1994.

Rabies, Enslow Publishers (Hillside, NJ), 1994.

Diabetes, Enslow Publishers (Hillside, NJ), 1994.

Mononucleosis, Enslow Publishers (Hillside, NJ), 1994.

Hepatitis, Enslow Publishers (Hillside, NJ), 1994.

Measles and Rubella, Enslow Publishers (Springfield, NJ), 1997.

"ENDANGERED IN AMERICA" SERIES; WITH HUSBAND, ALVIN SILVERSTEIN, AND SON ROBERT ALAN SILVERSTEIN

The Spotted Owl, Millbrook (Brookfield, CT), 1994.

The Red Wolf, Millbrook (Brookfield, CT), 1994.

The Peregrine Falcon, Millbrook (Brookfield, CT), 1995.

The Sea Otter, Millbrook (Brookfield, CT), 1995.

The Manatee, Millbrook (Brookfield, CT), 1996.

"KINGDOMS OF LIFE" SERIES; WITH HUSBAND, ALVIN SILVERSTEIN, AND SON ROBERT ALAN SILVERSTEIN

Vertebrates, Twenty-First Century Books (Brookfield, CT), 1996.

Plants, Twenty-First Century Books (Brookfield, CT), 1996.

Monerans and Protists, Twenty-First Century Books (Brookfield, CT), 1996.

Invertebrates, Twenty-First Century Books (Brookfield, CT), 1996.

Fungi, Twenty-First Century Books (Brookfield, CT), 1996.

WITH HUSBAND, ALVIN SILVERSTEIN, AND DAUGHTER LAURA SILVERSTEIN NUNN

AIDS: An All-About Guide for Young Adults ("Issues in Focus" series), Enslow Publishers (Berkeley Heights, NJ), 1999.

Puberty ("Watts Library" series), Watts (Danbury, CT), 2000.

Lyme Disease ("Watts Library" series), Watts (Danbury, CT), 2000.

"ENDANGERED IN AMERICA" SERIES; WITH HUSBAND, ALVIN SILVERSTEIN, AND DAUGHTER LAURA SILVERSTEIN NUNN

The Black-Footed Ferret, Millbrook (Brookfield, CT), 1995.

(With Robert Alan Silverstein) *The Manattee,* Millbrook (Brookfield, CT), 1996.

The Mustang, Millbrook (Brookfield, CT), 1997.

The Florida Panther, Millbrook (Brookfield, CT), 1997.

The Grizzly Bear, Millbrook (Brookfield, CT), 1998.

The California Condor, Millbrook (Brookfield, CT), 1998.

"DISEASES AND PEOPLE" SERIES; WITH HUSBAND, ALVIN SILVERSTEIN, AND DAUGHTER LAURA SILVERSTEIN NUNN

Sickle Cell Anemia, Enslow Publishers (Springfield, NJ), 1997.

Asthma, Enslow Publishers (Springfield, NJ), 1997.

Depression, Enslow Publishers (Springfield, NJ), 1997.

Chicken Pox and Shingles, Enslow Publishers (Springfield, NJ), 1998.

Leukemia, Enslow Publishers (Berkeley Heights, NJ), 2000.

Polio, Enslow Publishers (Berkeley Heights, NJ), 2001.

Parkinson's Disease, Enslow Publishers (Berkeley Heights, NJ), 2002.

"WHAT A PET!" SERIES; WITH HUSBAND, ALVIN SILVERSTEIN, AND DAUGHTER LAURA SILVERSTEIN NUNN

Snakes and Such, Twenty-First Century Books (Brookfield, CT), 1998.

A Pet or Not?, Twenty-First Century Books (Brookfield, CT), 1998.

Pocket Pets, Twenty-First Century Books (Brookfield, CT), 1999.

Different Dogs, Twenty-First Century Books (Brookfield, CT), 1999.

"SCIENCE CONCEPTS" SERIES; WITH HUSBAND, ALVIN SILVERSTEIN, AND DAUGHTER LAURA SILVERSTEIN NUNN

Evolution, Twenty-First Century Books (Brookfield, CT), 1998.

Symbiosis, Twenty-First Century Books (Brookfield, CT), 1998.

Photosynthesis, Twenty-First Century Books (Brookfield, CT), 1998.

Food Chains, Twenty-First Century Books (Brookfield, CT), 1998.

Plate Tectonics, Twenty-First Century Books (Brookfield, CT), 1998.

Energy, Twenty-First Century Books (Brookfield, CT), 1998.

Weather and Climate, Twenty-First Century Books (Brookfield, CT), 1998.

Clocks and Rhythm, Twenty-First Century Books (Brookfield, CT), 1999.

"MY HEALTH" SERIES; WITH HUSBAND, ALVIN SILVERSTEIN, AND DAUGHTER LAURA SILVERSTEIN NUNN

Is That a Rash?, Watts (Danbury, CT), 1999.

Tooth Decay and Cavities, Watts (Danbury, CT), 1999.

Cuts, Scrapes, Scabs, and Scars, Watts (Danbury, CT), 1999.

Common Colds, Watts (Danbury, CT), 1999.

Allergies, Watts (Danbury, CT), 1999.

Sleep, Watts (Danbury, CT), 2000.

Sore Throats and Tonsillitis, Watts (Danbury, CT), 2000.

Staying Safe, Watts (Danbury, CT), 2000.

Eat Your Vegetables! Drink Your Milk!, Watts (Danbury, CT), 2001.

Can You See the Chalkboard?, Watts (Danbury, CT), 2001.

Broken Bones, Watts (Danbury, CT), 2001.

Attention Deficit Disorder, Watts (Danbury, CT), 2001.

Dyslexia, Watts (Danbury, CT), 2001.

Headaches, Watts (Danbury, CT), 2001.

Bites and Stings, Watts (Danbury, CT), 2001.

Chicken Pox, Watts (Danbury, CT), 2001.

Lyme Disease, Watts (Danbury, CT), 2001.

Burns and Blisters, Watts (Danbury, CT), 2002.

Vaccinations, Watts (Danbury, CT), 2002.

Earaches, Watts (Danbury, CT), 2002.

Physical Fitness, Watts (Danbury, CT), 2002.

"SENSES AND SENSORS" SERIES; WITH HUSBAND, ALVIN SILVERSTEIN, AND DAUGHTER LAURA SILVERSTEIN NUNN

Smelling and Tasting, Twenty-First Century Books (Brookfield, CT), 2001.

Seeing, Twenty-First Century Books (Brookfield, CT), 2001.

Touching, Twenty-First Century Books (Brookfield, CT), 2001.

Hearing, Twenty-First Century Books (Brookfield, CT), 2001.

OTHER

Also author with husband, Alvin Silverstein, under joint pseudonym Dr. A, of syndicated juvenile fiction column, "Tales from Dr. A," which appeared in about 250

American and Canadian newspapers, 1972-74. Contributor of translations to about twenty scientific journals; translator of quarterly journal *Molekulyarnaya Genetika, Mikrobiologiya, i Virusologiya*. Contributor, with husband, Alvin Silverstein, of a dozen articles to *The New Book of Knowledge*.

Sidelights

Virginia B. Silverstein and her husband, Alvin Silverstein, have combined their writing talents and shared love of science to create nearly two hundred informational books for young readers. Please refer to Alvin Silverstein's sketch in this volume for their Sidelights essay.

*   *   *

STARK, Ulf 1944-

Personal

Born 1944, in Stockholm, Sweden; son of Kurth (a dentist) and Ebba Stark.

Addresses

Office—c/o RDR Books, 4456 Piedmont Ave., Oakland, CA 94611.

Career

Author. Former head of department at the National Labour Market Board, Sweden.

Awards, Honors

Bonniers Junior Publishers competition winner, 1984, for *Dårfinkar och dönickar;* Swedish Authors' Fund award, 1985; Zilveren Griffel (Holland), 1986; Children's Book Choice (Belgium), 1986; Nils Holgersson Plaque, Public Library Association of Sweden, 1988, for *Jaguaren;* award for children's and young people's books, Society for the Promotion of Literature, 1990; Astrid Lindgren Prize, 1993; Deutsche Jugendliteraturpreis (Germany) and Eeen Vlag en Wimpel (Holland), both 1994, both for *Johanna, Can You Whistle?*

Writings

FOR CHILDREN

Petter och de upproriska grisarna (title means "Peter and the Rebellious Pigs"), illustrated by Per Åhlin, Wahlström & Widstrand (Stockholm, Sweden), 1976.

Dårfinkar och dönickar (title means "Nutcases and Norms"), Bonniers junior förlag (Stockholm, Sweden), 1984.

Maria Bleknos (title means "Maria Pale-Nose"), illustrated by Anna Höglund, Bonniers junior förlag (Stockholm, Sweden), 1985.

Kan du vissla Johanna, 1992, translated as *Johanna, Can You Whistle?,* illustrated by Anna Höglund, RDR Books, 1997.

Min syster are en angel (title means "My Sister Is an Angel"), illustrated by Anna Höglund, Bonniers junior förlag (Stockholm, Sweden), 1997.

Also author of *Petter och den röda fågeln* (title means "Peter and the Red Bird"); *Låt isbjörnarna dansa* (title means "Let Polar Bears Dance"), 1986; *Sixten,* 1987 (revised edition published in 1994); *Jaguaren* (title means "The Jaguar"), illustrated by Anna Höglund, 1987; *Karlavagnen* (title means "The Big Dipper"), 1989; *Min vän Percys magiska gymnastikskor* (title means "My Friend Percy's Magical Gym Shoes"), 1991; *Liten* (title means "Little"), illustrated by Anna Höglund, 1994; *Min vän shejken i Stureby* (title means "My Friend the Sheik of Stureby"), 1995; and *Hunden som log* (title means "The Dog That Smiled"), 1995.

FOR ADULTS

Skärgårdsliv (title means "Island Life"), Wahlström & Widstrand (Stockholm, Sweden), 1967.

Also author of *Ett hål till livet* (poems; title means "A Hole to Life"), 1964, and *Sophämtarna* (title means "Refuse Collectors"), 1966.

OTHER

The Wall Climbers (television script), produced in Sweden, 1991.

Adaptations

Dårfinkar och dönickar was adapted for a television series in Sweden in 1988-89; *Hunden som log* was adapted for a television film in 1989; *Låt isbjörnarna dansa* and *Sixten* were both adapted for feature-length films in Denmark, 1989, and Sweden, 1994, respectively; *Min vän Percys magiska gymnastikskor* was adapted for Swedish television, 1994; *Johanna, Can You Whistle?* was adapted for Swedish television, 1994, and for the Royal Dramatic Theatre in Stockholm.*

*   *   *

STRANGIS, Joel 1948-

Personal

Born June 17, 1948, in Minneapolis, MN; son of Joseph J. and Mary J. Strangis; married Diane E. (a professor of education), June 19, 1971; children: Gina, Nicholas. *Education:* University of Minnesota, B.A. (summa cum laude), 1970; University of Kentucky, M.B.A., 1985. *Hobbies and other interests:* Bike riding and gardening.

Addresses

Home and office—3745 Northwest 64th Place, Gainesville, FL 32653.

Career

Sayre School, Lexington, KY, director of development, 1981-85; Wilkinson Group, Lexington, vice president

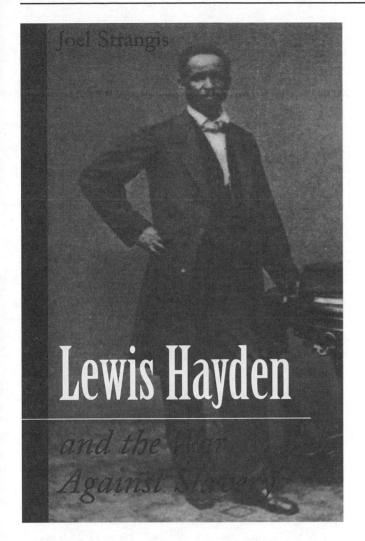

Joel Strangis researched historical documents, letters, news articles, and advertisements to assemble a biographical account of Lewis Hayden, one of the most influential figures in the antislavery movement.

for real estate, 1985-99; Wallace's Bookstores, Inc., Gainesville, FL, campus relations, 1999—. Real estate broker, Florida, 1999—; lecturer to school groups, librarians, associations, and others. *Military service:* U.S. Army Reserve, 1970-76. *Member:* Society of Children's Book Writers and Illustrators.

Awards, Honors

Research grant, Society of Children's Book Writers and Illustrators, 1993.

Writings

Grandfather's Rock: An Italian Folktale (picture book), illustrated by Ruth Gamper, Houghton Mifflin (Boston, MA), 1993.
Lewis Hayden and the War against Slavery (young adult biography), Linnet Books (North Haven, CT), 1999.

Grandfather's Rock: An Italian Folktale has been translated into Chinese in book, audiocassette, and compact disc formats.

Work in Progress

Other abolitionist biographies.

Sidelights

Joel Strangis told *SATA:* "My first published book, *Grandfather's Rock,* was based on an Italian folktale handed down to me by my grandmother. The story, as she told it, was only one paragraph in length, about 100 words. I stretched it, added characters and scenery, and came up with a publishable work of about 1500 words. This picture storybook for children and adults has a moral about caring for the elderly and the relationship between the elderly and children. A Chinese edition, published in Taiwan in 1994, has sold over 20,000 copies and is now available (in Chinese) on cassettes and CDs."

In Strangis's first book for children, *Grandfather's Rock: An Italian Folktale,* a man decides that his elderly father can no longer safely live alone. With his wife and children, the man transports his father and his possessions to the family's home on a rocky mountaintop. Artist Ruth Gamper depicts the children as joyously scampering up the hill with Grandfather and his things in tow. But over time, Grandfather's stories distract everyone from their work, and Mother suggests that Grandfather go to a special home for the elderly. As the children sadly make their way back down the mountain with Grandfather and his luggage, they think of a way to convince their parents that keeping Grandfather in the family home is a good idea. "The telling [of the story] has the rhythm and simplicity of the oral tradition," observed Hazel Rochman in *Booklist,* who cited references to the man's three daughters—the oldest, the tallest, and the youngest—as an example. *Horn Book* reviewer Martha V. Parravano likewise noted Strangis's "light touch" in the text and described Gamper's illustrations as "exquisite, patterned, light-filled watercolors that seem alive with motion." For a *Publishers Weekly* contributor, the combination of Strangis's folksy text and Gamper's illustrations is a winner: "Classically beautiful, this book is a timely and wise appeal for cooperation within the extended family."

Strangis continued to *SATA,* "My second book, *Lewis Hayden and the War against Slavery,* was the result of my experiences at Sayre School, in Lexington, Kentucky. While working there, one of my titles was Director of Alumni Affairs. As we raised money to renovate 'Old Sayre,' the school's main building since 1855, I heard rumors from alumni that the building had once been a stop on the Underground Railroad. My research did not reveal any evidence of Underground Railroad activity at Old Sayre, but I did 'discover' Lewis Hayden.

"Hayden escaped from slavery in Lexington with his wife and son in 1844. After crossing the Ohio River, the Hayden family traveled the Underground Railroad to Sandusky, Ohio, and across Lake Erie to Canada. After a brief stay in Canada and then Detroit, they moved to Boston where Lewis became the leader of Boston's black community. Hayden was at the forefront in the exciting struggles of the 1850s, including the rescue of the fugitive slave Shadrach Minkins from federal marshals in 1850 and the riot that attempted to rescue Anthony Burns in 1854. He was a friend and ally of the abolitionist leaders Theodore Parker, William Lloyd Garrison, and Wendell Phillips, and he raised the final dollars that made possible John Brown's raid at Harper's Ferry.

"With the help of a grant from the Society of Children's Book Writers and Illustrators, I was able to follow Hayden's trail from Lexington to Maysville, Kentucky, where the Hayden family crossed the Ohio River, and then I crossed the river to Ripley, Ohio, the abolitionist stronghold where the Haydens climbed aboard the Underground Railroad. I enjoyed seeing the sights Lewis had seen in Canada, and in Detroit I prayed with the congregation of an A. M. E. church he had helped establish. In Vermont I visited towns Hayden had visited and in Boston I walked the street in front of his home and stood in historic Faneuil Hall where he had denounced the slave catchers.

"One hundred and twenty years after Hayden's death he is still a living person for me. I hope that I was able to convey some of that vitality in my book. I also hope to write more biographies about the men and women, black and white, who were his friends and allies."

Strangis turned to the historical record for the raw materials for his biography of an escaped slave who became a leading abolitionist. In *Lewis Hayden and the War against Slavery,* the author relates what he has learned about the man who was born into slavery in 1811, escaped with his wife and child in 1844, and became one of the black leaders of the abolitionist movement. Although little was written about him in his own day, Hayden is known to have helped raise funds for the raid on Harper's Ferry and recruit African-American men to fight under the Union flag in the 54th Massachusetts Infantry Regiment. Hayden was also instrumental in garnering recognition for the efforts of black soldiers in the Revolutionary War of the century before. Strangis's rendition of Hayden's story is "well researched, dramatic, and inspiring," noted Shelle Rosenfeld and David Pitt in *Booklist.* The two reviewers commented positively on the value of *Lewis Hayden and the War against Slavery,* particularly for its detailed account of the many methods abolitionists employed in the effort to bring down the institution of slavery in the United States. Jeanette Lambert called this "an insightful and engaging biography," in her *School Library Journal* review.

Biographical and Critical Sources

PERIODICALS

Booklist, October 15, 1993, Hazel Rochman, review of *Grandfather's Rock: An Italian Folktale,* p. 455; February 15, 1999, Shelle Rosenfeld and David Pitt, review of *Lewis Hayden and the War against Slavery,* p. 1058.

Horn Book, March-April, 1994, Martha V. Parravano, review of *Grandfather's Rock: An Italian Folktale,* p. 212.

Publishers Weekly, July 19, 1993, review of *Grandfather's Rock: An Italian Folktale,* p. 253; May, 1999.

School Library Journal, Jeanette Lambert, review of *Lewis Hayden and the War against Slavery,* p. 143.*

T

THESMAN, Jean
(T. J. Bradstreet)

Personal

Married; children: two daughters, one son.

Addresses

Agent—c/o Viking Children's Books, 345 Hudson St., New York, NY 10014.

Career

Writer.

Awards, Honors

American Library Association (ALA) Recommended Books for the Reluctant Young Adult Reader, ALA Children's Choice, and ALA Young Adult Choice, all for *Who Said Life Is Fair?;* ALA Recommended Books for the Reluctant Reader, for *Running Scared;* ALA Best Books for Young Adults, ALA Recommended Books for the Reluctant Young Adult Reader, ALA Children's Choice, ALA Young Adult Choice, and "Pick of the List," American Booksellers Association (ABA), all for *The Last April Dancers;* ALA Children's Choice, and ALA Young Adult Choice, both for *Was It Something I Said?;* Sequoyah Young Adult Award, ALA Recommended Books for the Reluctant Young Adult Reader, and International Reading Association (IRA) Young Adult Choice, all for *Appointment with a Stranger;* ALA Notable Children's Books, and ALA Best Books for Young Adults, both 1990, both for *Rachel Chance;* ALA Recommended Books for the Reluctant Young Adult Reader, and Phantom's Choice Award, both for *Erin;* Golden Kite Award, Society of Children's Book Writers and Illustrators, 1991, ALA Best Books for Young Adults, 1991, *School Library Journal* Best Books selection, and Booklist Editors' Choice, all for *The Rain Catchers;* ALA Notable Book, ALA Best Book citations, and Young Adult Library Services Association (YALSA) Best Books for Young Adults citation, all for *When the Road Ends;* YALSA Quick Picks for Reluctant Young Adult Readers, for *Summerspell;* IRA Young Adult Choice, and Teacher's Choices Award, both for *Cattail Moon;* ALA Notable Book selection, Books for the Teen Age, New York Public Library, Jefferson Cup Award, Virginia Library Association, and Not Just for Children Anymore citation, Children's Book Council, all for *The Ornament Tree;* International Honor Book, Society of School Librarians, for *The Other Ones;* Best Book Award, Parent's Guide to Children's Media, for *Calling the Swan.*

Writings

New Kid in Town, Ace, 1984.
Two Letters for Jenny, Ace, 1985.
A Secret Love, Ace, 1985.
Who Said Life Is Fair?, Avon, 1987.
Running Scared, Avon/Flare, 1987.
The Last April Dancers, Houghton Mifflin (New York, NY), 1987.
Was It Something I Said?, Avon/Flare, 1988.
Appointment with a Stranger, Houghton Mifflin (New York, NY), 1989.
Couldn't I Start Over?, Avon/Flare, 1989.
Rachel Chance, Houghton Mifflin (New York, NY), 1990.
The Rain Catchers, Houghton Mifflin (New York, NY), 1991.
When Does the Fun Start?, Avon/Flare, 1991.
When the Road Ends, Houghton Mifflin (New York, NY), 1992.
Molly Donnelly, Houghton Mifflin (New York, NY), 1993.
Cattail Moon, Houghton Mifflin (New York, NY), 1994.
Nothing Grows Here, HarperCollins (New York, NY), 1994.
Summerspell, Simon & Schuster (New York, NY), 1995.
The Ornament Tree, Houghton Mifflin (New York, NY), 1996.
The Storyteller's Daughter, Houghton Mifflin (New York, NY), 1997.
Moonstones, Viking (New York, NY), 1998.
The Other Ones, Viking (New York, NY), 1999.

The Tree of Bells, Houghton Mifflin (New York, NY), 1999.
Calling the Swan, Viking (New York, NY), 2000.
In the House of the Queen's Beasts, Viking (New York, NY), 2001.
A Sea So Far, Viking (New York, NY), 2001.

"WHITNEY COUSINS" SERIES

Heather, Avon, 1990.
Amelia, Avon, 1990.
Erin, Avon, 1990.
Triple Trouble, Avon, 1992.

"BIRTHDAY GIRLS" SERIES

I'm Not Telling, Avon/Camelot, 1992.
Mirror, Mirror, Avon/Camelot, 1992.
Who Am I, Anyway?, Avon/Camelot, 1992.

"DARKEST WISH" SERIES; AS T. J. BRADSTREET

Kitty's Wish, Avon/Camelot, 1995.
Lorna's Wish, Avon/Camelot, 1996.
Wendy's Wish, Avon/Camelot, 1996.

OTHER

(With Ellen Conford, Ellen Leroe, and Jane McFann) *A Night to Remember,* Avon, 1995.
(With Cameron Dokey, Kathryn Jensen, and Sharon Dennis Wyeth) *Be Mine,* Avon, 1997.
Meredith ("Elliott Cousins" series), Morrow/Avon, 1998.
Jamie ("Elliott Cousins" series), Morrow/Avon, 1998.

Sidelights

Jean Thesman is the author of a number of novels for young adults that capture the struggles of teenagers. Many of her books are set in the Pacific Northwest area, where Thesman lives. Her novels show young girls encountering death, war, suicide, old age, and life inside dysfunctional families, as well as the typical social problems associated with being a teen. Marked by an unusually strong sense of time and place, Thesman's books also employ a lyrical use of language that gives strength to the emotional life and depth of her characters.

Thesman's first foray into young-adult fiction was the 1984 title *New Kid in Town.* A half-dozen other titles followed, many of which landed on the American Library Association (ALA) Recommended Books lists during the 1980s. Her 1990 novel, *Rachel Chance,* was a 1990 ALA Notable Book and is characteristic of Thesman's work. Set in 1940s Seattle, the story revolves around the heroine of the title, whose infant brother has been kidnaped by a religious sect. They believe that since the baby was born out of wedlock, he should have been put up for adoption. Rachel sets out to find him with her family, and in the end they discover his biological father as well. The work possesses "humor, suspense and depth," noted Jacqueline C. Rose in a *Kliatt* review.

In 1992, Thesman published *When the Road Ends,* the tale of a trio of foster children who meet at a home run

Jean Thesman

by a kindly minister named Matt. His wife, however, wishes them gone, as she does Matt's sister Cecile, who is recuperating at their house after a head injury that caused memory loss. The quartet are relegated for the summer to a cabin in the woods, but the housekeeper sent to supervise them abandons them almost immediately. Twelve-year-old Mary Jack is determined that they can survive the summer on their own, disproving misconceptions about them as societal misfits. Her coconspirator is another foster child, Adam, whose unmanageable anger threatens to expose them. The threesome care also for Jane, an abused four-year-old who refuses to speak. Mary Jack shoulders too much responsibility, which seems to break her spirit temporarily, but the crisis forces Aunt Cecile to take the necessary steps to return to her own adulthood. *When the Road Ends* won Thesman praise for its characterizations and sensitivity. "Slow to start, the plot gradually but surely involves the reader in the lives of these misfits," declared Margaret M. Finch in *Voice of Youth Advocates,* who found in it a "message of hope: every family is a miracle." Nancy Vasilakis, writing in *Horn Book,* also gave the novel strong words of praise. "Although the upbeat conclusion is clearly foreshadowed, the careful balance of tension and relief in the narrative never gives too much away." Vasilakis commended

Thesman's "combination of artfully controlled plot, believable characters, and childlike imagery."

Another novel from Thesman, *The Rain Catchers,* also takes place in the Seattle area and was named an ALA Best Book for Young Adults in 1991. Here the story focuses upon Grayling, who lives with her grandmother but grieves about the abandonment by her own mother when she was just an infant. Several other older women live at her grandmother's home, one of whom is terminally ill, and while Grayling worries about her best friend, who is living in a dysfunctional household, she also finds romance with a young boy. Carolyn Angus, reviewing *The Rain Catchers* for *Kliatt,* praised its "powerfully drawn settings" and characters written with "depth and individuality."

In *Molly Donnelly,* Thesman presents another memorable heroine who faces unusual life challenges in addition to the everyday hardships of being a teen. Molly's world is disrupted when the United States naval installation at Pearl Harbor is bombed in December of 1941, and the country declares war on Japan. Her best friend, a Japanese American, is sent with her family to an

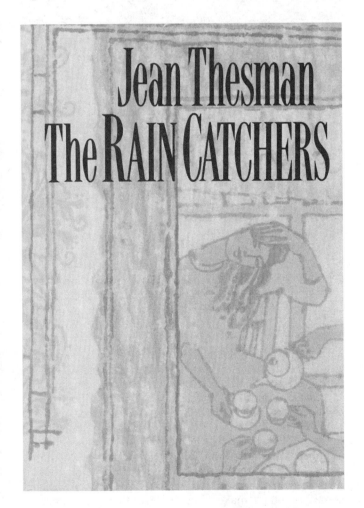

Fourteen-year-old Grayling learns to understand the circumstances of her father' death and her mother's abandonment of her in Thesman's coming-of-age novel. (Cover illustration by Vincent X. Kirsch.)

internment camp. Molly's home life undergoes a sudden change when her mother goes to work in a shipyard; meanwhile, her father, depressed, begins to drink. Molly also struggles to look after her increasingly unmanageable little brother and becomes angry when she learns that her parents are only saving for his college education, not hers. In the end, the events of the war bring both tragedy and a new sense of esteem for Molly and her family. "The reader truly emphasizes with Molly, smiling at her victories and sharing the sadness of her failures," wrote *Voice of Youth Advocates* reviewer Susan Ackler, who also termed it "an excellent and graphic picture of World War II."

Thesman first ventured into the young adult series genre with her "Whitney Cousins" books, and continued it with the 1992 "Birthday Girls" series. The title characters are drawn together when some mothers who met in the maternity ward arrange a party for their children, all born on the same day. But one mother-daughter team bullies the others, setting in motion the plots of the three novels. In *I'm Not Telling,* Jill learns that her beloved uncle was once in jail. *Mirror, Mirror* relates Ceegee's self-consciousness. In *Who Am I, Anyway?,* Nancy learns that the woman she believed to be her mother is really her aunt.

Thesman's 1994 novel, *Nothing Grows Here,* presents another troubled adolescent. Seventh-grader Maryanne Russell finds her life irrevocably changed when she and her mother are forced to give up their suburban home after the family business fails and Maryanne's father dies. Maryanne misses their former garden, where she spent hours tending it alongside her father. In her new, much rougher neighborhood, Maryanne finds a friend whose mother is in similar situation, but when the women pool their resources to start a business together, Maryanne worries about the use of their meager savings. She also resents a new romance in her mother's life, but when they come across a small home with a garden for Maryanne to tend, things begin to look up. "Maryanne finally comes to accept a future different from the one she dreamed of for herself and Mom," wrote Elizabeth Bush in the *Bulletin of the Center for Children's Books.* The story also won praise from *Booklist*'s Stephanie Zvirin, who declared that *Nothing Grows Here* captures "both the everyday concerns of being twelve and the pain that can accompany loss and change."

Thesman also wrote another novel for young adults published in 1994, *Cattail Moon.* Here, the story centers upon fifteen-year-old Julia, who is troubled by constant battles with her appearance-oriented mother. Instead, Julia dreams of a career in music and decides to go live with father and grandmother in rural Washington state. The major drawback to the arrangement is the lack of musical opportunities there, but Julia finds a friend in Luke, a boy from a strict family who is not allowed to date. The pair often meet at a local cattail marsh, where Julia begins to see a mysterious woman. The woman refuses to talk, but Julia soon learns that it is Christine, the ghost of a singer and writer who died decades before. Julia begins reading her books, and "Christine's identity and life become the mystery that moves the story along," noted J. Cynthia McDermott in a *Voice of Youth Advocates* review. Julia also finds, through her sleuthing, that Luke's family is connected to Christine's past. In the end, the long-ago novels give her the strength to return to the city and live with a friend and her welcoming family. "Thesman succeeds in combining themes of the supernatural, mystery, romance, and friendship in an extremely readable and compelling novel that also presents a highly realized Northwest setting," wrote *Horn Book*'s Ellen Fader. *Cattail Moon* also won praise from *Booklist* reviewer Carolyn Phelan, who asserted, "Thesman's many well-crafted characters and their conflicts make this novel quite readable and believable."

Thesman's 1995 novel *Summerspell* addresses the theme of sexually abusive family situations in its story of Jocelyn. Jocelyn's mother has died and her father is overseas, so the young girl goes to live with her sister and her husband after her grandparents pass away. But her safety in the new home is threatened by her bigoted brother-in-law, who also seems intent on molesting Jocelyn. He forbids her from listening to her beloved music and from visiting her friends, and even kills a heron she loves to watch. Meanwhile, Jocelyn's sister is blind to the situation, despite Jocelyn's attempts to talk to her. Jocelyn decides, with her platonic friend Baily, to run away to her grandparents' cottage, Summerspell. Only a great-aunt knows her whereabouts and asks a neighbor to check on her; the neighbor sends her daughter, Spider, instead, who disguises herself as a boy. After an uneasy weekend, Spider reports that Jocelyn is living with a boyfriend. When the news reaches her brother-in-law, he travels to Summerspell for a violent confrontation. "Thesman conveys the flood of feelings Jocelyn has" when she returns to the cabin of her more idyllic childhood, noted Susan Dove Lempke in a *Bulletin of the Center for Children's Books* review, "and capably sustains the tension among the three teens." *Voice of Youth Advocates* writer Mary L. Adams commended the novel for its tough subject matter, saying, "This addresses a timely topic in a fast reading, suspenseful novel." Adams also noted that its "message of tell and keep telling is given without being preachy."

In her 1996 novel *The Ornament Tree,* Thesman introduces another parentless heroine, Bonnie, who arrives in Seattle to live with her cousins in August of 1918. She is fascinated by her enigmatic cousin Audra, but upset when the younger cousin, Clare, seems to take an instant dislike to the her. The cousins, though intelligent, energetic women, are poor and forced to run a boarding house to make ends meet. They and their friends are also intensely involved in a number of political causes, including women's suffrage. Many actual events of the era, including a devastating flu epidemic and Seattle-area labor strikes, are interwoven into this coming-of-age tale. Bonnie befriends a blinded war veteran who boards at the house and encourages her to think about her future. The book's title is taken from a beloved tree the cousins use on which to tie their written wishes. "The underlying issues are substantial," re-

Fifteen-year-old Jocelyn has escaped to the family summer cabin to avoid her odious brother-in-law and await help from her great-aunt, but the presence of two boys threatens her secret plans. (Cover illustration by Mary Teichman.)

marked Mary M. Burns in *Horn Book,* "but the presentation is laced with humor and warmth—no small feat." *Voice of Youth Advocates* reviewer Cynthia Brown was similarly positive. "The story moves quickly and holds interest as the reader follows Bonnie through realistic experiences for that time period," Brown noted.

Thesman kept the Seattle setting but changed the era for her 1997 novel, *The Storyteller's Daughter.* Teenage Quinn finds life in the 1930s, when the world was mired in a deep economic Depression, full of challenges. Her jovial, storytelling father, Beau John, is forced to work away from their home as a dockworker, and their house must make room for a grandmother and other family members who have lost savings, jobs, or homes. Quinn's older sister must drop out of high school and work to help support the family. But one day Quinn overhears something that makes her believe that her father is engaged in illegal activities. When her father disappears, Quinn fears that her suspicions are true and sets out to find him. Mary M. Burns, writing in *Horn Book,* praised the way in which Thesman drew upon historical realities "to develop her characters and provide a solid foundation for her story." Meg Wilson also lauded the evocation of Depression-era Seattle in her *Voice of Youth Advocates* review. "Thesman describes the sights, smells, and sounds her characters experience so effectively that the reader quickly becomes absorbed in the story," Wilson declared.

In *The Other Ones*, Thesman's 1999 novel, she explores the supernatural through the gifts of her heroine, Bridget. The teen is an "Other One" who can move objects and read minds, but must hide her powers from everyone. Her guardian, Xiii, can change form, and the two carry on a dialogue involving Bridget's powers and her desire to help her friends. One of them, Jordan, is troubled by the disappearance of his father from his life, while Bridget discovers that a fellow misfit at school, Althea, is not all that she seems. A *Publishers Weekly* reviewer found the conclusion "truly compelling, in which the Jordan and Althea plot strands come together in an unexpected way." Susan Dove Lempke, writing for *Booklist*, praised its "swiftly moving plot, graceful writing, and humorous exchanges between Bridget and Xiii."

Thesman's next novel, *The Tree of Bells*, serves as a sequel to *The Ornament Tree*. The story moves ahead to the 1920s, and Bonnie has secretly departed for China to do missionary work before enrolling in medical school. The plot focuses on life back in Seattle and on Bonnie's cousin Clare. The boarding house is still thriving, and Clare faces certain decisions as she nears adulthood. She realizes that she would like to stay near home and support herself by working with children; she also finds romance with Mr. Younger, the war veteran who helped Bonnie in the earlier story. *Kliatt* reviewer Claire Rosser called *The Tree of Bells* "a sweet story that avoids the saccharin, especially with the characters whose life struggles are enormous."

Thesman ventured into difficult emotional territory with her 2000 novel, *Calling the Swan*. The story centers upon Skylar, whose family is haunted by an untold tragedy that occurred three years earlier. Because of it, Skylar's parents are overprotective to the point of compulsion. Meanwhile, she seems fixated on pleasing her reclusive older sister, Alexandra, but readers discover that their relationship is just a figment of Skylar's imagination, for Alexandra was abducted three years earlier and never found. Skylar comes to terms with her loss only after enrolling in a summer school program across town, which has filled her parents with dread. Writing in *Horn Book*, Kitty Flynn noted that "Thesman believably conveys the real and imagined pressures Skylar feels as she tests her independence and begins to reclaim her life." *Booklist* reviewer Michael Cart described it as the story of "how friendship can provide a kind of healing certainty in a world of terrifying uncertainty." A *Publishers Weekly* reviewer also commended Thesman's talents. "Hopeful without being sugar-coated, this tale offers compassionate insight into loss," the critic noted.

Thesman once commented that she grew up in a house full of books, "around people who were accomplished storytellers. It didn't take me long to see that bookworms, storytellers, and people who laugh easily are never bored. There is only one logical occupation for a storytelling bookworm with a sense of humor, so I write books for young people. It's the best job in the world."

Biographical and Critical Sources

PERIODICALS

Booklist, April 1, 1993, Stephanie Zvirin, review of *Molly Donnelly*, p. 1425; April 1, 1994, Carolyn Phelan, review of *Cattail Moon*, p. 1437; November 1, 1994, Zvirin, review of *Nothing Grows Here*, p. 501; May 1, 1996, Hazel Rochman, review of *The Ornament Tree*, p. 1499; November 1, 1997, review of *The Storyteller's Daughter*, p. 462; May 1, 1999, Susan Dove Lempke, review of *The Other Ones*, p. 1588; June 1, 1999, Rochman, review of *The Tree of Bells*, p. 1816; June 1, 2000, Michael Cart, review of *Calling the Swan*, p. 1882.

Bulletin of the Center for Children's Books, September, 1987, review of *The Last April Dancers;* February, 1993, Roger Sutton, review of *Who Am I, Anyway?*, p. 194; November, 1994, Elizabeth Bush, review of *Nothing Grows Here*, p. 107; July, 1995, Susan Dove Lempke, review of *Summerspell*, p. 399; September, 1998, Bush, review of *The Moonstones*, p. 33.

Horn Book, September-October, 1990, review of *Rachel Chance*, p. 610; May-June, 1992, Nancy Vasilakis, review of *When the Road Ends*, p. 342; September-October, 1993, review of *Molly Donnelly*, p. 606; July-August, 1994, Ellen Fader, review of *Cattail Moon*, p. 461; July, 1996, Mary M. Burns, review of *The Ornament Tree*, p. 468; November, 1997, Burns, review of *The Storyteller's Daughter*, p. 686; July, 2000, Kitty Flynn, review of *Calling the Swan*, p. 467.

Kirkus Reviews, review of *Appointment with a Stranger*, March 15, 1989, p. 470; March 1, 1993, review of *Molly Donnelly*, p. 307; October 15, 1994, review of *Nothing Grows Here*, p. 1417; June 1, 1995, review of *Summerspell*, p. 788; August 15, 1998, review of *The Moonstones*, p. 1197.

Kliatt, September, 1987, review of *Running Scared*, p. 20; January, 1993, Carolyn Angus, review of *The Rain Catchers*, p. 13; March, 1993, Jody K. Hanson, review of *Triple Trouble*, and Jacqueline C. Rose, review of *Rachel Chance*, p. 10; May, 1999, Claire Rosser, review of *The Tree of Bells*, pp. 13-14.

Publishers Weekly, September 25, 1987, review of *The Last April Dancers*, p. 112; March 10, 1989, review of *Appointment with a Stranger*, p. 90; April 27, 1990, review of *The Whitney Cousins: Heather, Amelia, and Erin*, p. 63; February 22, 1991, review of *The Rain Catchers*, p. 219; February 17, 1992, review of *When the Road Ends*, p. 64; June 22, 1992, review of *I'm Not Telling*, and *Who Am I, Anyway?*, p. 62; November 23, 1992, review of *Rachel Chance*, p. 64; March 1, 1993, review of *Molly Donnelly*, p. 58; April 4, 1994, review of *Cattail Moon*, p. 81; September 7, 1998, review of *The Moonstones*, p. 96; May 31,

1999, review of *The Other Ones,* p. 94; June 19, 2000, review of *Calling the Swan,* p. 81.

School Library Journal, May, 1987, Anne Saidman, review of *Who Said Life Is Fair?,* p. 118; October, 1987, Blair Christolon, review of *The Last April Dancers,* p. 142; April, 1990, Barbara Chatton, review of *Rachel Chance,* pp. 145-146; March, 1991, Chatton, review of *The Rain Catchers,* p. 218; May, 1993, Carol A. Edwards, review of *Molly Donnelly,* p. 130; March, 1997, review of *The Rain Catchers,* p. 113; September, 1998, Dina Sherman, review of *Jamie,* p. 210; June, 1999, Bruce Anne Shook, review of *The Other Ones,* p. 138; July, 1999, Cindy Darling Codell, review of *The Tree of Bells,* p. 100.

Voice of Youth Advocates, August, 1987, Margaret Mary Ptacek, review of *Who Said Life Is Fair?,* p. 123; December, 1987, Susan Ackler, review of *Running Scared,* pp. 238-239; June, 1992, Margaret M. Finch, review of *When the Road Ends,* and Joyce Yen, *When Does the Fun Start?,* p. 104; August, 1993, Susan Ackler, review of *Molly Donnelly,* p. 158; August, 1994, J. Cynthia McDermott, review of *Cattail Moon,* p. 150; April, 1995, Mary L. Adams, review of *Summerspell,* p. 225; March, 1996, Cynthia Brown, review of *The Ornament Tree,* p. 162; February, 1998, Meg Wilson, review of *The Storyteller's Daughter,* p. 391; December, 1998, Holly Ward Lamb, review of *Jamie,* p. 349.

*   *   *

TODD, Pamela 1950-

Personal

Born February 22, 1950, in Chicago, IL; daughter of George L. (an engineer) and Audrey (an artist; maiden name, Warnimont) Brown; married Donn D. Todd (a contractor), October 9, 1971; children: three daughters, one son. *Education:* Purdue University, B.S. (psychology; cum laude). *Politics:* Democrat. *Religion:* Lutheran. *Hobbies and other interests:* Camping, hiking, violin, biking, swimming, gardening.

Addresses

Office—c/o Bantam Doubleday Dell Books for Young Readers, 1540 Broadway, New York, NY 10036. *E-mail*—pabt@mediaone.net.

Career

Scott, Foresman, psychology textbook editor, 1970-72; freelance magazine and newspaper writer, and technical writer for corporations, 1972—. Currently teaches journal writing. *Member:* Companions (prison ministry; board member, 1997—), Society of Children's Book Writers and Illustrators (network representative, 1996-2001).

Awards, Honors

Work-in-Progress grant, Society of Children's Book Writers and Illustrators, for a contemporary novel; Mary France Shura award, Society of Children's Book Writers and Illustrators—Illinois; Illinois Arts Council grant; Ragdale Foundation Residency Recipient.

Writings

Pig and the Shrink, Delacorte (New York, NY), 1999.

Articles have appeared in the *Writer, Chicago Tribune Magazine,* and *Runner's World.*

Work in Progress

Eleanor's Music, a picture book about "a girl who loves music and comes from a musical family but can't play," to be published in 2002.

Sidelights

Pamela Todd told *SATA:* "When I was growing up, I wanted to be either a writer or a child psychologist, and I think both of those aspirations led me to write *Pig and the Shrink.* I had fun writing that book, but I also thought a lot about what it means to be a friend, how we come to accept ourselves and other people, how we can best be of service to others, and how we learn to forgive. I hope people reading it will find themselves laughing and thinking about these things too. That's the best part

Pamela Todd

about having a book published—that you can have this sort of conversation with people you will never meet. But I would write anyway, even if I knew my books would never be published, because writing helps me pay attention to the world, to learn about myself and my relationships with other people, to slow down and really see. I write every day, mostly because it makes my life happier, and I divide my time between writing in my journal, working on books, reading other people's work and thinking about what I admire in it, and staring out the window. Even though it may not seem like it, I consider all of these things essential to making my books.

"Here's my advice for aspiring writers. Don't settle for passive entertainment. Go out and live your life. Laugh, cry, get messy, fall down, and get up again. And keep a journal. Not the 'today I did this . . .' kind, but whatever pops into your head and needs to be said. Let it all spill out of you, and when you're done, read it over and write again. Because the best conversation of all is the lifelong conversation you have with yourself in the pages of your journal."

Pig and the Shrink, Todd's first young adult novel, is the story of a science-fair project that yields some unexpected results. Narrator Tucker Harrison, nicknamed "the Shrink" for his small stature, is under pressure by his divorced parents to do well in the upcoming science fair in order to win a place at a prestigious math and science academy. When the principle disapproves of his first project, he decides to cast his fellow classmate, Angelo Pighetti, called "Pig" by some, as the subject in a science experiment called "Nutrition and Obesity." Tucker studies up on fat and exercise, and tries a variety of diets on his subject, but Pig actually gains weight. When Tucker visits Pig at his family's pizzeria, he begins to understand why. However, the budding scientist also discovers the warmth and acceptance Pig gets from his family, something that Tucker has never received from his overachieving, emotionally distant parents. "Readers struggling to accept others and themselves will be affirmed by this comedy of human foibles," predicted a reviewer in *Publishers Weekly.*

Among the cast of secondary characters is Beth Ellen, an avowed vegetarian who sets an example for Tucker to value Angelo the way he is. Tucker and his mother favor a Chinese restaurant where the owner dishes up sage advice along with the low mein, and Angelo's happy family is a testament to the joys to be found in cooking and eating good food. On a darker side there are the school bullies and "a poignant subplot involves Tucker's faltering relationship with his father," remarked Elaine Baran in *School Library Journal.* "Tucker's wisecracking voice keeps the action clipping along, and his gradual realization that body shape does not necessarily correlate with happiness is a point well made," commented Elizabeth Bush in the *Bulletin of the Center for Children's Books.* Throughout, according to critics, Todd keeps her touch light and humorous, relying on witty dialogue and comic situations to both convey a message and keep her readers hooked. "Todd's insightful use of cutting-edge middle school humor and dialogue will keep young readers turning the pages until the end," claimed a reviewer for the *Tampa Tribune and Times.*

Biographical and Critical Sources

PERIODICALS

Booklist, October, 1999, Carolyn Phelan, review of *Pig and the Shrink,* p. 358.
Bulletin of the Center for Children's Books, November, 1999, Elizabeth Bush, review of *Pig and the Shrink.*
Kirkus Reviews, June 1, 1999, review of *Pig and the Shrink,* p. 890.
Philadelphia Inquirer, September 19, 1999, Ann Waldron, review of *Pig and the Shrink.*
Publishers Weekly, August 2, 1999, review of *Pig and the Shrink,* p. 85.
School Library Journal, September, 1999, Elaine Baran, review of *Pig and the Shrink.*
Tampa Tribune and Times, January 9, 2000, review of *Pig and the Shrink.*

*   *   *

TYNE, Joel
See SCHEMBRI, Jim

V–W

van VOGT, A(lfred) E(lton) 1912-2000

OBITUARY NOTICE—See index for *SATA* sketch: Born April 26, 1912, near Winnipeg, Manitoba, Canada; naturalized U.S. citizen, 1952; died January 26, 2000, in Los Angeles, CA. Author. Van Vogt wrote dozens of science fiction novels during his career, and through the 1940s, he was considered by critics to be the leader of the golden age of science fiction. He is well known for such works as 1946's *Slan,* and *The Voyage of the Space Beagle,* published in 1950. The van Vogt short story "Black Destroyer" has been called the inspiration behind films like *Alien.* His last published work, *Null-A Three,* emerged in 1985. Named Grandmaster by the Science Fiction and Fantasy Writers of America in 1997, van Vogt was also the recipient of honors such as the 1983 Jules Verne Award.

OBITUARIES AND OTHER SOURCES:

PERIODICALS

Chicago Tribune, February 2, 2000, section 2, p. 9.
Los Angeles Times, January 31, 2000, p. A14.
New York Times, February 4, 2000, p. C22.
Washington Post, January 2, 2000.

*   *   *

WILDSMITH, Brian 1930-

Personal

Born January 22, 1930, in Penistone, Yorkshire, England; son of Paul (a coal miner) and Annie Elizabeth (a homemaker; maiden name, Oxley) Wildsmith; married Aurelie Janet Craigie Ithurbide, 1955; children: Clare, Rebecca, Anna, Simon. *Education:* Attended Barnsley School of Art, c. 1946-49; Slade School of Fine Art, University College, London, D.F.A., 1952. *Religion:* Roman Catholic. *Hobbies and other interests:* Abstract painting; music, especially playing the piano; sports, especially cricket, squash, and tennis; travel.

Addresses

Home and office—11 Castellaras le Vieux, 06370 Mouana-Sartoux, France.

Career

Royal Military School of Music, Twickenham, England, math teacher, 1952-54; Selhurst Grammar School for Boys, London, England, art teacher, 1954-57; freelance artist and author and illustrator of books for children, 1957—. Maidstone College of Art, London, lecturer, c. 1957. Set and costume designer for the film *The Blue Bird,* 1974-75. Wildsmith has also worked as a designer of book jackets for various publishers. *Exhibitions:* Exhibitor in "Three Centuries of ABC Books," Showcase Exhibit, Library of Congress, and "Picture This! Picture Book Art at the Millennium," Fitzwilliam Museum, University of Cambridge, England, 2000. *Military service:* National Service, Army Education Corps, 1952-54, became sergeant.

Awards, Honors

Kate Greenaway Medal, Library Association (London, England), 1962, for *ABC;* Kate Greenaway Medal commendation, 1963, for both *The Lion and the Rat* and *The Oxford Book of Poetry for Children;* Art Books for Children citation, 1965, for *Brian Wildsmith's 1, 2, 3s;* Lewis Carroll Shelf Award, 1966, for *A Child's Garden of Verses;* Kate Greenaway Medal commendation and New York Times Best Illustrated Children's Book of the Year designation, both 1967, for *Birds;* Kate Greenaway Medal commendation, 1971, for *The Owl and the Woodpecker;* Brooklyn Art Books for Children citation, c. 1979, for *Hunter and His Dog;* Kurt Maschler Award runner-up, 1982, and Parent's Choice citation for illustration, 1983, both for *Pelican;* American Booksellers Pick of the Lists designation, 1996, for *Saint Francis;* Kurt Maschler Award shortlist, 1998, Marcia Posner Award/National Jewish Book Award finalist, 1999, and nomination for Children's Crown Gallery Award, Austin, Texas, 2001, all for *Exodus;* Parent's Choice Recommended Book designation, 2000, for *The*

Easter Story. Wildsmith has also received recognition for his body of work, including being named runner-up for the Hans Christian Andersen Award, International Board of Books for Young People (IBBY), 1966 and 1968, and receiving the Soka Eakkai Japan Education Medal, 1988, and the USHIO Publication Culture Award, 1991. In 1994, the Brian Wildsmith Museum of Art, a museum devoted to Wildsmith's work, was established in Izu, Japan.

Writings

FOR CHILDREN; SELF-ILLUSTRATED PICTURE BOOKS

ABC, Oxford University Press (London, England), 1962, published as *Brian Wildsmith's ABC,* Franklin Watts (New York, NY), 1963.

1 2 3, Oxford University Press (London, England), 1965, published as *Brian Wildsmith's 1, 2, 3s,* Franklin Watts (New York, NY), 1965.

The Circus, Oxford University Press (London, England), 1970, published as *Brian Wildsmith's Circus,* Franklin Watts (New York, NY), 1970.

Puzzles, Oxford University Press (London, England), 1970, published as *Brian Wildsmith's Puzzles,* Franklin Watts (New York, NY), 1971.

The Owl and the Woodpecker, Oxford University Press (London, England), 1971, Franklin Watts (New York, NY), 1972.

The Little Wood Duck, Oxford University Press (London, England), 1972, Franklin Watts (New York, NY), 1973.

The Lazy Bear, Oxford University Press (London, England), 1973, Franklin Watts (New York, NY), 1974.

Python's Party, Oxford University Press (London, England), 1974, Franklin Watts (New York, NY), 1975.

Squirrels, Oxford University Press (London, England), 1974, published as *Brian Wildsmith's Squirrels,* Franklin Watts (New York, NY), 1975.

The True Cross, Oxford University Press (Oxford, England, and New York, NY), 1977.

What the Moon Saw, Oxford University Press (London, England), 1978.

Hunter and His Dog, Oxford University Press (London, England), 1979.

Professor Noah's Spaceship, Oxford University Press (London, England), 1980.

Bear's Adventure, Pantheon (New York, NY), 1981, Oxford University Press (Oxford, England), 1981

Carousel, Knopf (New York, NY), 1988, Oxford University Press (London, England), 1988.

A Christmas Story, Knopf (New York, NY), 1989, Oxford University Press (London, England), 1989.

The Easter Story, Oxford University Press (London, England), 1993, Eerdmans (Grand Rapids, MI), 2000.

The Tunnel, Oxford University Press (London, England), 1993.

Saint Francis, Oxford University Press (London, England), 1995, Eerdmans (Grand Rapids, MI), 1996.

Brian Wildsmith's Animals to Count, Star Bright Books (New York, NY), 1996.

Brian Wildsmith's Opposites, Star Bright Books (New York, NY), 1996.

Brian Wildsmith

Joseph, Eerdmans (Grand Rapids, MI), 1997, Oxford University Press (London, England), 1997.

Brian Wildsmith's Amazing World of Words, Millbrook Press (Brookfield, CT), 1997.

Exodus, Oxford University Press (London, England), 1998, Eerdmans (Grand Rapids, MI), 1999.

The Seven Ravens, Oxford University Press (London, England), 2000.

Jesus, Eerdmans (Grand Rapids, MI), 2000.

Brian Wildsmith's Colors, Star Bright Books (New York, NY), 2001.

Brian Wildsmith's Farm Book, Star Bright Books (New York, NY), 2001.

RETELLER AND ILLUSTRATOR; PICTURE BOOKS

Jean de la Fontaine, *The Lion and the Rat,* Franklin Watts (New York, NY), 1963.

Jean de la Fontaine, *The North Wind and the Sun,* Franklin Watts (New York, NY), 1964.

Jean de la Fontaine, *The Rich Man and the Shoemaker,* Franklin Watts (New York, NY), 1965.

Jean de la Fontaine, *The Hare and the Tortoise,* Franklin Watts (New York, NY), 1966.

Jean de la Fontaine, *The Miller, the Boy, and the Donkey,* Franklin Watts (New York, NY), 1969.

Maurice Maeterlinck's "Blue Bird," Franklin Watts (New York, NY), 1976, Oxford University Press (London, England), 1976.

Brian Wildsmith's Book of Bedtime Stories, Pantheon (New York, NY), 1985.

The Bremen Town Band, Oxford University Press (Oxford, England, and New York, NY), 1999.

"COLLECTIVE NOUN" SERIES; PICTURE BOOKS

Birds, Oxford University Press (London, England), 1967, published as *Brian Wildsmith's Birds,* Franklin Watts (New York, NY), 1967.

Wild Animals, Oxford University Press (London, England), 1967, published as *Brian Wildsmith's Wild Animals,* Franklin Watts (New York, NY), 1967.

Fishes, Oxford University Press (London, England), 1968, published as *Brian Wildsmith's Fishes,* Franklin Watts (New York, NY), 1968.

"ANIMAL" SERIES; CONCEPT BOOKS

Animal Games, Oxford University Press (London, England), 1980.

Animal Homes, Oxford University Press (London, England), 1980.

Animal Shapes, Oxford University Press (London, England), 1980.

Animal Tricks, Oxford University Press (London, England), 1980.

Seasons, Oxford University Press (London, England), 1980.

Brian Wildsmith's Circus *includes only two lines of text, but his energetic illustrations capture the allure of a live circus performance.*

"CAT ON THE MAT" SERIES; BOARD BOOKS

Cat on the Mat, Oxford University Press (Oxford, England, and New York, NY), 1982.

The Trunk, Oxford University Press (Oxford, England, and New York, NY), 1982.

The Apple Bird, Oxford University Press (Oxford, England, and New York, NY), 1983.

The Island, Oxford University Press (Oxford, England, and New York, NY), 1983.

All Fall Down, Oxford University Press (Oxford, England, and New York, NY), 1983.

The Nest, Oxford University Press (Oxford, England, and New York, NY), 1983.

Whose Shoes?, Oxford University Press (Oxford, England, and New York, NY), 1984.

Toot, Toot, Oxford University Press (Oxford, England, and New York, NY), 1984.

My Dream, Oxford University Press (Oxford, England, and New York, NY), 1986.

What a Tale, Oxford University Press (Oxford, England, and New York, NY), 1986.

If I Were You, Oxford University Press (Oxford, England, and New York, NY), 1987.

Giddy Up, Oxford University Press (Oxford, England, and New York, NY), 1987.

Can You Do This?, Oxford University Press (Oxford, England, and New York, NY), 1999.

How Many?, Oxford University Press (Oxford, England, and New York, NY), 1999.

If Only, Oxford University Press (Oxford, England, and New York, NY), 1999.

Knock, Knock, Oxford University Press (Oxford, England, and New York, NY), 1999.

My Flower, Oxford University Press (Oxford, England, and New York, NY), 1999.

Not Here, Oxford University Press (Oxford, England, and New York, NY), 1999.

TOY BOOKS; PICTURE BOOKS WITH SPLIT PAGES, DIE-CUT WINDOWS, OR MOVEABLE PARTS

Pelican, Pantheon, 1982, Oxford University Press (London, England), 1982.

Daisy, Pantheon, 1984, Oxford University Press (London, England), 1984.

Give a Dog a Bone, Pantheon, 1985, Oxford University Press (London, England), 1985.

Goat's Trail, Knopf (New York, NY), 1986, Oxford University Press (London, England), 1986.

Brian Wildsmith's Noah's Ark: The Pop-up Book, Harper, 1994, Oxford University Press (London, England), 1994.

The Creation: A Pop-up Book, Oxford University Press (London, England), 1995, Millbrook Press, 1996.

ILLUSTRATOR; FOR CHILDREN AND ADULTS

Eileen O'Faolain, *High Sang the Sword,* Oxford University Press (London, England), 1959.

Rene Guillot, *Prince of the Jungle,* S. G. Phillips, 1959.

Frederick Grice, *The Bonny Pit Laddy,* Oxford University Press (London, England), 1960, published as *Out of the Mines,* Franklin Watts (New York, NY), 1961.

Nan Chauncy, *The Secret Friends,* Oxford University Press (London, England), 1960, Franklin Watts (New York, NY), 1962.

Eleanor Graham, *The Story of Jesus,* Hodder & Stoughton, 1960.

Nan Chauncy, *Tangara: "Let Us Set Off Again,"* Oxford University Press (London, England), 1960.

Madeleine Polland, *The Town across the Water,* Constable, 1961.

Veronique Day, *Landslide!,* Bodley Head, 1961.

Tales from the Arabian Nights, Oxford University Press (London, England), Franklin Watts (New York, NY), 1962.

Roger Lancelyn Green, *Myths of the Norsemen,* Bodley Head, 1962.

Geoffrey Trease, *Follow My Black Plume,* Macmillan, 1963.

Edward Blishen, editor, *The Oxford Book of Poetry for Children,* Oxford University Press (London, England), 1963.

Charlotte Morrow, *The Watchers,* Hutchinson, 1963.

Geoffrey Trease, *A Thousand for Sicily,* Macmillan, 1964.

Mother Goose, Oxford University Press (London, England), 1964, published as *Brian Wildsmith's Mother Goose: A Collection of Nursery Rhymes,* Franklin Watts (New York, NY), 1964.

Kevin Crossley-Holland, *Havelok the Dane,* Macmillan (London, England), 1964, Dutton, 1965.

Charles Dickens, *Barnaby Rudge,* Ginn, 1966.

Robert Louis Stevenson, *A Child's Garden of Verses,* Franklin Watts (New York, NY), 1966, Oxford University Press (London, England), 1966.

Philip Turner, *The Bible Story,* Oxford University Press (London, England), 1968, published as *Brian Wildsmith's Illustrated Bible Stories,* Franklin Watts (New York, NY), 1969.

Alan Wildsmith, *Ahmed, Prince of Ashira,* Deutsch, 1969.

The Twelve Days of Christmas, Oxford University Press (London, England), 1972, published as *Brian Wildsmith's Twelve Days of Christmas,* Franklin Watts (New York, NY), 1972.

Frances Hodgson Burnett, *Sara Crewe,* Scholastic, 1986.

Rebecca Wildsmith (daughter), *Jack and the Meanstalk,* Knopf (New York, NY), 1994, Oxford University Press (London, England), 1994.

Takamado no Miya Hisako (Her Imperial Highness Princess Takamado), *Katie and the Dream-Eater,* Oxford University Press (Oxford, England and New York, NY), 1996.

FANTASY

Daisaku Ikeda, *The Snow Country Prince,* translated by Geraldine McCaughrean, Oxford University Press (London, England), 1990, Knopf (New York, NY), 1990.

Daisaku Ikeda, *The Cherry Tree,* translated by Geraldine McCaughrean, Oxford University Press (London, England), 1991, Knopf (New York, NY), 1992.

Daisaku Ikeda, *The Princess and the Moon,* translated by Geraldine McCaughrean, Oxford University Press (London, England), 1991, Knopf (New York, NY), 1992.

Daisaku Ikeda, *Over the Deep Blue Sea,* translated by Geraldine McCaughrean, Oxford University Press (Oxford, England, and New York, NY), 1992, Knopf (New York, NY), 1992.

"WHAT NEXT?" SERIES

Rebecca Wildsmith, *Look Closer,* Oxford University Press (London, England), 1993, Harcourt (San Diego, CA), 1993.

Rebecca Wildsmith, *Wake Up, Wake Up!,* Oxford University Press (London, England), 1993, Harcourt (San Diego, CA), 1993.

Rebecca Wildsmith, *What Did I Find?,* Oxford University Press (London, England), 1993, Harcourt (San Diego, CA), 1993.

Rebecca Wildsmith, *Whose Hat Was That?,* Oxford University Press (London, England), 1993, Harcourt (San Diego, CA), 1993.

OTHER

A Brian Wildsmith Portfolio (1962-66) was published by Franklin Watts (New York, NY). In 1965, Wildsmith created a series of Christmas cards for UNESCO that sold nearly seven million copies internationally. Creator of *Brian Wildsmith's Animal Portfolio, Brian Wildsmith's Story Book Posters, Brian Wildsmith's Months: A Set of Twelve Posters, Brian Wildsmith's Circus of Colors,* and *Brian Wildsmith's Teaching Cards.* Wildsmith's works have been translated into fourteen languages, including French, German, Japanese, and Spanish. His papers are housed in the Donald Beaty Bloch Children's Literature Collection at the University of Colorado, Boulder; in the de Grummond Collection, University of Southern Mississippi; and in the Shaw Collection, Florida State University, Tallahassee.

Adaptations

Brian Wildsmith's Wild Animals, Brian Wildsmith's Fishes, Brian Wildsmith's Circus, Brian Wildsmith's Birds, and *Puzzles* were all released as filmstrips by Weston Woods. An e-book/Adobe Reader version of *My Flower* was released in 2001.

Sidelights

An English author and illustrator of picture books, concept books, board books, wordless books, and toy books, as well as an illustrator of fiction, poetry, and retellings for children, Brian Wildsmith is considered by many critics to be one of the most accomplished artists in the field of juvenile literature. Wildsmith, whose art ranges from vibrant, expressionistic paintings to more delicate and modulated works, has been praised as an exceptionally intelligent, talented, and imaginative artist, one whose works entertain the young while introducing them to the qualities of fine art. A prolific creator of books for children ranging from toddlers to readers in the upper primary grades, Wildsmith designs his works to inform his audience about the world around them while developing their artistic sensibilities. Usually featuring animals and birds as focal points, his books are intended to span the complete educational gamut, from basic letters and numbers to more abstract human values, such as kindness, compassion, and honesty. Several of his works reflect his fascination with religious subjects and themes as well as his strong environmental consciousness. He has retold the fables of Jean de La Fontaine, the fairy tales of the Brothers Grimm, and the children's fantasy *The Blue Bird* by Maurice Maeterlinck; has created a number of board books, wordless books, and books with minimal text for the youngest child; and has provided the illustrations for books by authors such as Charles Dickens, Frances Hodgson Burnett, Rene Guillot, Nan Chauncy, Geoffrey Trease, Daisaku Ikeda, and Her Imperial Highness Princess Takamado of Japan. In addition, he has drawn the pictures for texts by his daughter Rebecca and his brother Alan. Wildsmith is also well known as the creator of *ABC,* an alphabet book that pairs letters with bold, textured paintings in dazzling colors.

As a writer, Wildsmith characteristically uses straightforward, understated prose, although he sometimes employs verse. As an artist, he uses watercolor, gouache, collage, and pen and ink to create works that are credited with reflecting both his grand artistic vision and intensely personal style. He initially favored glowing patchwork colors and geometric shapes, most notably the triangle. After he left what has been called his "harlequin" period, he used natural forms to create pictures that are filled with a variety of textures and tones, many of which eschewed his characteristic splashes and swirls for more subtle elements. In addition, his works began to feature elaborate architectural details and action-filled scenes, as well as inventive examples of book and page design, such as pop-up and split pages, die-cut windows, and use of gold leaf. Wildsmith has been criticized for creating art that is mannered, overly stylized, and too difficult for children to appreciate, and for writing texts that do not stand up to the quality of his illustrations. However, many reviewers praise Wildsmith for advancing the genre of the picture book as an art form with his works, which are credited with reflecting their creator's artistic skill, wisdom, and humor. In addition, he is lauded for initiating a whole school of illustration and for influencing an entire generation of artists. Writing in the *Christian Science Monitor,* Patience M. Daltry stated that Wildsmith's picture books "are among the brightest happenings in children's literature." Michael Dirda of *Washington Post Book World* noted that Wildsmith "stands high among the international grandmasters of children's books." Writing in *Junior Bookshelf,* Marcus Crouch called Wildsmith "this generation's most remarkable book-artist" and stated that, at his best, "Brian Wildsmith is the master of them all."

Born in Penistone, a small village in Yorkshire, England, Wildsmith spent the first years of his life living with his parents, four young aunts, and an uncle in the home of his maternal grandparents. Writing in the *Something about the Author Autobiography Series (SAAS)* Wildsmith recalled, "I have very fond memories of times spent there." His father, Paul, worked in the coal mines all of his life. Wildsmith wrote, "My father was always very kind towards me, my two brothers, and sister. He was not a strict man, my mother being the disciplinarian of the two." According to her son, Wildsmith's mother, Annie, "adored her children. She encouraged us in our every interest, leading us to believe that if we were to embark on any activity, whether physical or mental, it would only be of value [if] we put ourselves entirely to it. By instilling in her children such a mode of thinking, she helped us find ourselves and, by way of that, what we wanted from life."

Wildsmith's family moved from Penistone to the nearby town of Hoyland Common when he was two. There, he discovered one of the great loves of his life—cricket. He noted that "the happiest days of my life were when the cricket season started, the saddest, when it ended." Wildsmith attended Saint Helens, a primary school that he called "very progressive." The walls of the school, he noted, "were covered with ABCs and pictures; learning processes involved shapes, colours, textures, games." While living in Hoyland Common, Wildsmith discovered music. His aunt Esther taught him to play the piano, and later he took lessons from a teacher in Wentworth who had a Steinway. Wildsmith wrote in *SAAS,* "I have always loved music. I find it the most satisfying of the Arts." He told Lee Bennett Hopkins in *Books Are by People: Interviews with 104 Authors and Illustrators of Books for Young Children,* that, during his early years, he "led a free life with very little restrictions from my parents. I was not at all interested in art. I never even saw any."

After graduating from primary school, Wildsmith won a scholarship to Delasalle College, a high school for boys in Sheffield. "My school days," he recalled, "were generally happy ones." He played cricket, football (soccer), and other sports and found himself to be good in science. He decided that he wanted to be a research chemist. However, at the age of sixteen, he realized that, as he noted in *SAAS,* "I was on the wrong tracks. I was on my way to a chemistry class when I turned on my heels, went to see the headmaster, and told him I was leaving to go to art school." Wildsmith applied to Barnsley Art School with a portfolio that consisted of "different arrangements of cubes, spheres, and triangles that I had collected over a period of five years at Delasalle art lessons, and a couple of drawings of motorcars whizzing round corners, which my pals at school had admired." He was accepted by the school. At Barnsley, Wildsmith took courses in architecture, perspective, anatomy, still-life drawing, and sketching from memory. He also began to admire modern artists such as Pablo Picasso and Paul Klee.

At seventeen, Wildsmith met his future wife, Aurelie Ithurbide. As he once described it, he "had heard that Wentworth Wood House . . . contained some ancient Greek-styled statues worthy of study and had received permission to go there and draw them. As I was busy sketching, a mischievous, freckled face with the most startling green eyes peered over my shoulder, curious to see what I had drawn. She introduced herself as the chef's youngest daughter and nodded with approval,

When a wind blows through several countries, it carries people's hats to new, surprised recipients in **Whose Hat Was That?,** *a collaboration between Wildsmith and his daughter, Rebecca, who authored the work.*

having flicked through my pad. I fell in love then and there." At around the same time, Wildsmith received his first commission as an artist: he approached the local newspaper, the *Barnsley Chronicle,* with the idea of going to the Working Men's Clubs and interviewing retired miners while sketching them. The project came to a halt after approximately ten of these portraits were printed. Wildsmith remembered, "[C]omplaints had been made by several of my models as to the way I had depicted them, in their words: ugly."

At the end of his course of study at Barnsley, which lasted two years, Wildsmith applied to the Slade, the art department of University College, London. He was told that he was too late and that he would have to wait until the following January—seven months later—to reapply. He recalled in *SAAS,* "I panicked, knowing that by then, through pure financial necessity, I would be absorbed into the mines or to the steelworks and that I would never achieve my goal." Wildsmith telephoned the Slade and spoke with one of the instructors, Professor Cold-

stream, who invited him down for an interview. Wildsmith wrote, "Of his own accord, he then accepted me as a future student" for the September term. Wildsmith had a mixed reaction to his training at the Slade. Since the students were often left alone to discover their personal direction as painters, Wildsmith spent much of his time at the British Museum, studying the works of the Great Masters, such as Rembrandt, Michelangelo, and Leonardo da Vinci. At that time, visitors could actually hold the drawings and etchings in their hands, whereas now patrons must get special written permission to handle the art. Wildsmith noted that the instances when he required guidance from his instructors at the Slade "were met with unsatisfactory and insensitive tuition." He concluded, "The Slade, at that time, was a place to go where one could extend oneself after having acquired a certain amount of artistic experience and, in 1949, I had very little."

While at the Slade, Wildsmith won cricket colors for University College. After receiving his diploma in fine arts, he was called up for military service. He was sent to the Royal Army Education Corps, where he trained as a math teacher. Wildsmith was then posted to the Royal School of Music in Twickenham, an assignment for which he was chosen because he could play the piano. He spent eighteen months at the school and attained the rank of sergeant. After leaving the army, he worked as an art teacher at the Selhurst Grammar School for Boys in London, a position that he held for three years. He wrote that his pupils "ranged from the age of eleven to eighteen, all of whom I encouraged to follow their natural way. I saw some great stuff produced by these kids but noticed that, for some illogical reason, there appeared to be a decline in creativity as they grew older."

While working at Selhurst Grammar School, Wildsmith began to shop his portfolio to book publishers in London. In 1954, he received a commission to create the jacket for *Daffodil Sky* by H. E. Bates; its success led to other commissions. Wildsmith married Aurelie Ithurbide in 1955. Two years later, Aurelie suggested that Wildsmith give up his teaching job to concentrate on being a full-time artist. He resigned from Selhurst. "Only then," he noted in *SAAS*, "did Aurelie announce that she was pregnant.... As it stood, she did everything imaginable to bring me happiness and I believe still does." The Wildsmiths now have four children: Claire, Rebecca, Anne, and Simon. After becoming a freelancer, Wildsmith approached Oxford University Press and met editor Mabel George, who commissioned him to design book jackets and black-and-white illustrations for novels before she asked him to produce fourteen color plates for an edition of *Tales from the Arabian Nights*. According to Wildsmith, the book "received mixed reviews, including some very hostile, but to my surprise it was precisely the worst ones which convinced Oxford University Press of my potential and to continue using my work." After he became a father, Wildsmith decided to devote himself to creating books for children. He told Lee Bennett Hopkins, "I realized just what an appalling gulf there was between what I knew to be good and fine in painting and illustrating and the awful damage being done to children's minds via children's books. I decided to commit myself fully to doing books for boys and girls." Mabel George of Oxford University Press suggested to Wildsmith that he try his hand at an alphabet book. The result, *ABC*—published in the United States, as are many of Wildsmith's books, with the author's name as a preface—was to establish him as a major contributor to the field of children's literature.

An alphabet book that depicts animals and other things familiar to children, from apple to zebra, on brightly colored pages of contrasting hues and circles, triangles, and squares, *ABC* was lauded as a truly original concept book as well as a striking example of illustration art. A reviewer in *School Library Journal* called it a "simple and beautiful book that children will enjoy looking at again and again," while *Christian Science Monitor* critic Sheila M. Rawson stated that Wildsmith "makes a bold and effective use of both form and color.... The effect

is highly individual." In his *Written for Children: An Outline of English-Language Children's Literature*, John Rowe Townsend said that the richness of *ABC* "was astonishing when it first appeared in 1962; there was nothing else quite like [Wildsmith's] kettle aglow with heat or his lion on the next page aglow with sun." *ABC* won the Kate Greenaway Medal in its year of publication and is now considered a groundbreaking title. After his success with *ABC*, Wildsmith retold five stories by the French fabulist Jean de La Fontaine—*The Lion and the Rat, The North Wind and the Sun, The Rich Man and the Shoemaker, The Hare and the Tortoise*, and *The Miller, the Boy, and the Donkey*—that were designed to introduce his work to the European continent. *The Lion and the Rat* received a Greenaway Medal commendation in 1963, as did another title illustrated by Wildsmith, *The Oxford Book of Poetry for Children*.

In 1967 Wildsmith produced the first of a series of three picture books—*Birds, Wild Animals,* and *Fishes*—that were, according to the artist, oriented "towards the teaching and learning of vocabulary, based around the use of collective nouns which were rapidly disappearing from popular English language." These works center on words that signify groupings of creatures, such as an unkindness of ravens, a company of swans, an ambush of tigers, a shrewdness of apes, and a hover of trout. In each of the books, a line of text appears on a double-page spread filled with color and movement. Writing on *Birds* in *Junior Bookshelf,* Marcus Crouch stated, "Wildsmith has never drawn with greater assurance and with greater control of his characteristic mannerisms." Writing about *Fishes* in *Book World,* Anne Izard commented, "Here is an artist enamored of beauty and so gifted he can share his vision of it." Ethel L. Heins, writing on *Wild Animals* in *Horn Book,* said, "Mr. Wildsmith is not the first artist to be intrigued by the 'terms of assembly' of the animal world; but no other artist has so magnificently expressed this fascination." *Birds* received a Greenaway Medal commendation in 1967.

Wildsmith's next titles, *The Circus* and *Puzzles,* challenge children to put words to what they see. *The Circus,* which includes only two lines of text, is generally credited with capturing the allure of a live circus performance. Calling Wildsmith a "disciple of the sun," a reviewer for the *Times Literary Supplement* concluded that "you can imagine yourself at a real, live performance, so skillfully does the artist translate the performers' feats of balance and control to the page"; Zena Sutherland of the *Bulletin of the Center for Children's Books* simply stated, "Who needs words?" In his *Written for Children,* John Rowe Townsend called *The Circus* "especially successful; the vividness, vigour, and larger-than-lifeness of the circus as a subject were ideally suited to Wildsmith's talent for producing brilliant set-pieces unimpeded by story."

By 1970 Wildsmith had made a monumental resolution. He wrote in *SAAS,* "I had made a conscious decision to span, if possible, with the use of form, colour, and words, the whole educational range of a young child, from its initial introduction of our alphabet and numerical system to the foundation of sound humanitarian-based principles, necessary for the development of its responsibility towards the society in which it lives. I wanted to feed the eyes and minds of children with lusciously colourful images, representative of the potential beauty of our planet and its inhabitants." In 1971 he produced *The Owl and the Woodpecker,* a story that, as he wrote, "marked a turning point in my career: for the first time, I illustrated a story that I had written." A picture book about two birds that quarrel but reconcile in the end, *The Owl and the Woodpecker* has fellowship and neighborliness as its themes. Marcus Crouch of *Junior Bookshelf* commented that Wildsmith "has found a theme which suits him well . . . . His text is flat in the extreme, but his pictures are in his finest manner." Gladys Williams noted in *Books and Bookmen* that Wildsmith's glowing pictures lure the child to explore them "as surely as, in reality, a forest might do" before concluding that just "as he won't on one visit discover anything like the forest's treasures, here are pictures to which he will come back again and again." *The Owl and the Woodpecker* received a Greenaway Medal commendation in 1971. In the same year, Wildsmith and his family moved to Castellaras, a small French village located on a hill between Cannes and Grasse. He once wrote, "I felt I needed new enlightenment. The movement within my work had sparked off a desire within me to breathe in a different atmosphere and to live where I

could complete my art education. What better place than southern France . . . ?" Wildsmith has called Castellaras "my ideal home." Since moving to France, Wildsmith's illustrations have reflected European settings, some with a medieval flavor.

In 1974 Wildsmith was invited to become the set and costume designer for a new film, *The Blue Bird,* that was to be a joint production of the United States and the USSR. The film, which was based on the a story by Maurice Maeterlinck in which two siblings search for the blue bird of happiness, was to be directed by George Cukor and was to star such popular actors as Elizabeth Taylor, Ava Gardner, and Jane Fonda. Although he enjoyed being with the Russian people, Wildsmith's experience on *The Blue Bird* was generally an unhappy one. Although he had designed over a hundred costumes, he was replaced by a Russian because it was decided that an Englishman should not be responsible for both costumes and sets. The film received a lukewarm response. In 1976 Wildsmith published his own version of *The Blue Bird,* entitled *Maurice Maeterlinck's "Blue Bird,"* that is illustrated with his costume designs. A reviewer in *Publishers Weekly* said, "Bursts of color call forth oohs and aahs on all pages; looking at the pictures is like being at Fourth of July fireworks." The critic concluded that Wildsmith's illustrated retelling "will probably draw a longer lasting, more satisfied audience than the star-studded flick."

I walked to Rome and saw the Pope.
There he was in his fine church with all the priests dressed up
in their fine robes.

I told him stories, I sang him songs, I told him how good it was
to be poor. I asked him to bless all that I was doing.
The Pope smiled and gave me his blessing, and I danced for joy.

Wildsmith created fine ink illustrations with rich color likened to stained-glass windows to adorn his first-person narrative of St. Francis's life. (From Saint Francis.*)*

A devout Catholic, Wildsmith has created several books with Christian themes. His first book of this type, *The True Cross,* was published in 1977. In this work, the author retells the legend of the Tree of Life, the tree that came from the Garden of Eden and served at Jesus' crucifixion before being rediscovered by St. Helena, the mother of the Roman emperor Constantine. Marcus Crouch of the *Junior Bookshelf* noted that Wildsmith's book "clearly springs from a genuine religious impulse, and is informed with his love of living things"; Crouch concluded by calling *The True Cross* "his best book for some time."

In the early 1980s, Wildsmith produced two series of books for preschool children—a series of concept books on animal games, homes, shapes, tricks, and the seasons, and the "Cat on the Mat" series, board books featuring animal characters; uncomplicated, often wordless stories; and shining illustrations in bright colors. Praised for their simple yet meaningful texts and well-crafted, artistic illustrations, the series are often credited with breaking new ground by providing young children with introductions to authentic literature. Writing in the *Times Literary Supplement* about the "Animals" series, Kicki Moxon Browne recalled that when Wildsmith's illustrations first appeared, many people thought them too difficult for children. "Today," the critic wrote, "no one would suggest that even for the very young there is anything difficult about Wildsmith's glowing colours and varying textures." Daisy Kouzel added in *School Library Journal* that the titles "have everything to recommend them." In a review of four of the "Cat on the Mat" books—*All Fall Down, The Apple Bird, The Island,* and *The Nest*—*School Librarian* reviewer Cliff Moon stated, "Here are four more examples of how a 'real' children's book writer/illustrator can provide far better texts for beginner readers than reading scheme designers." Writing in *Books for Your Children,* Margaret Carter called *The Island* "a small masterpiece—often quoted for its text as well as its illustrations" before concluding that the "Cat on the Mat" books "are miracles of tongue-in-cheek wit. All are not what they seem and there's usually a surprise on the last page." Several of the titles in this series have been reissued as full-size paperbacks.

With *Pelican,* a picture book published in 1983, Wildsmith began to introduce some new stylistic features to his art. *Pelican,* which describes how a small boy makes a pet of a pelican before it flies away to be with its own kind, premieres the illustrator's use of the split-page technique, where half-pages open to provide drama and to reveal surprises. Writing in *Language Arts,* Ronald A. Jobe said, "Showing new directions in his art, Brian Wildsmith retains aspects of his earlier vibrant collages, while introducing a startling split-page technique." Kathleen Brachmann added in *School Library Journal,* "A beguiling feature is the split-page format,... enabling the illustrations to tell the story even more effectively than the text." Wildsmith also used the split-page format in the picture books *Daisy,* the story of a country cow who goes to Hollywood and becomes famous before becoming disenchanted and returning home, and *Give a Dog a Bone,* which describes how Stray, a poor gray dog, gains and loses a succession of bones before being adopted by a newly married couple. *Goat's Trail,* a cumulative tale about a mountain goat that decides to explore the noises from the walled town below his home, makes use of die-cut windows and doorways.

In the mid-1990s, Wildsmith created two pop-up books, *Brian Wildsmith's Noah's Ark,* which presents the story of the Flood, and *The Creation,* which pictures the creation of the world as described in the Book of Genesis. In his review of *Brian Wildsmith's Noah's Ark* in the *Junior Bookshelf,* Marcus Crouch commented, "When an artist of Brian Wildsmith's eminence enters the world of the pop-up something special is indicated, and so it is," while *Times Educational Supplement* critic Elaine Williams, writing about *The Creation,* concluded, "Wildsmith captures the wonder and poetry of the creation story in a book that families will treasure."

Wildsmith has received special acclaim for the books that he has produced with religious subjects and themes, many of which were published in the 1990s. He has retold and illustrated stories from both the Old and New Testaments: the story of Joseph, the Israelite boy who was sold into slavery by his brothers but ends up saving the Egyptians from famine; the story of Moses, who led the Hebrew people to a land promised by God; and the life, death, and resurrection of Jesus Christ. In addition, he has created a picture book version of the story of Saint Francis of Assisi, the affluent Italian who took on a life of poverty in order to serve God; *A Christmas Story,* the tale of Christ's birth from the point of view of a little girl who journeys from Nazareth to Bethlehem in order to reunite a young donkey with its mother, who is with Mary and Joseph; and *The Easter Story,* which recounts the events from Palm Sunday to the Ascension from the viewpoint of the little donkey on which Jesus rode into Jerusalem.

Reviewers often find Wildsmith's treatments of his religious subjects to be both reverent and appropriate. The artist has been commended for his sumptuous illustrations, which characteristically are bedecked with jeweled colors and bordered with gold leaf. In her review of *A Christmas Story* in *Growing Point,* Margery Fisher observed, "The artist has used all his skill in interpreting an anecdote simple in itself ... but serving as an image for a universal myth." A critic for *Kirkus Reviews* called *The Easter Story* a "richly complex visual feast, masterfully integrated into a reverent, unusual interpretation; Wildsmith at his best."

Wildsmith once wrote, "As a young artist leaving the Slade, I realized that my art education had by no means come to a close and decided that I would try and complete it, in every way possible, before starting to paint. It has taken me a long time to feel ready and mature enough to approach a blank canvas and one of the reasons for the delay is the simple fact that I fell in love with making children's books, finding the process exciting, ever-changing, and fully enjoyable." After his children had left home and he felt that he was financially secure, he began to paint seriously again. He now continues to blend his creation of fine art, such as a mixture of painting and sculpture, with his writing and illustrating of children's books. He wrote, "I have always been fascinated by the ability of the Great Masters to cover as many areas that the field of art encompasses. My ambition is to be able to do likewise. I have designed sets and costumes, drawn, illustrated, and painted, but writing is, I believe, the most difficult of all the Arts. I would much rather paint." Writing in *School Library Journal,* Wildsmith outlined his philosophy of creating books for children: "I believe in the Jesuit saying, 'Give me a child under seven years and he is mine forever.' How often have we left all that is good and free in our culture to be brought before the child too late, when his taste has already been formed, maltreated, warped, and destroyed by the everlasting rubbish that is still thought by many to be good enough for children. I hope my picture books will help alleviate this, and perhaps guide them to finer and gentler paths." In an interview with Cornelia Jones and Olivia R. Way in *British Children's Authors: Interviews at Home,* Wildsmith concluded, "Even if children don't react immediately to my books, somehow, I hope that I may sow a cultural germ in their artistic digestive systems which will one day bear fruit."

Biographical and Critical Sources

BOOKS

Children's Literature Review, Gale (Detroit, MI), Volume 2, 1976, Volume 52, 1999.

De Montreville, Doris, and Donna Hill, editors, *Fourth Book of Junior Authors,* Wilson, 1972.

Hopkins, Lee Bennett, *Books Are by People: Interviews with 104 Authors and Illustrators of Books for Young Children,* Citation Press, 1969.

Jones, Cornelia, and Olivia R. Way, *British Children's Authors: Interviews at Home,* American Library Association, 1976.

Klemin, Diana, *The Illustrated Book,* Clarkson Potter, 1970.

Something about the Author Autobiography Series, Volume 5, Gale (Detroit, MI), 1988.

Townsend, John Rowe, *Written for Children: An Outline of English-Language Children's Literature,* Lippincott, 1974.

PERIODICALS

Books and Bookmen, February, 1972, Gladys Williams, review of *The Owl and the Woodpecker,* p. 96.

Books for Your Children, autumn-winter, 1992, Margaret Carter, "Brian Wildsmith," p. 5.

Book World, November 3, 1966, Anne Izard, review of *Fishes,* p. 4.

Bulletin of the Center for Children's Books, June, 1971, Zena Sutherland, review of *Brian Wildsmith's Circus,* p. 164.

Christian Science Monitor, October 12, 1963, Sheila M. Rawson, review of *Brian Wildsmith's ABC,* p. 9; August 31, 1967, Patience M. Daltry, review of *Birds,* p. 5.

Growing Point, November, 1989, Margery Fisher, review of *A Christmas Story,* p. 45.

Horn Book Magazine, April, 1968, Ethel L. Heins, review of *Brian Wildsmith's Wild Animals,* p. 171.

Junior Bookshelf, August, 1967, Marcus Crouch, review of *Birds,* p. 239; October, 1970, Marcus Crouch, review of *The Circus,* p. 278; February, 1972, Marcus Crouch, review of *The Owl and the Woodpecker,* p. 96; June, 1978, Marcus Crouch, review of *The True Cross,* p. 138; December, 1994, Marcus Crouch, review of *Brian Wildsmith's Noah's Ark,* p. 209.

Kirkus Reviews, January 1, 1994, review of *The Easter Story,* p. 76.

Language Arts, September, 1983, Ronald A. Jobe, review of *Pelican,* p. 775.

Publishers Weekly, August 16, 1976, review of *Maurice Maeterlinck's "Blue Bird,"* p. 123.

School Librarian, March, 1984, Cliff Moon, review of *All Fall Down,* pp. 41-42.

School Library Journal, March, 1963, review of *Brian Wildsmith's ABC,* p. 166; November, 1965, Brian Wildsmith, "Antic Disposition: A Young British Illustrator Interviews Himself," pp. 22-24; April, 1981, Daisy Kouzel, review of *Animal Games,* p. 119; September, 1983, Kathleen Brachmann, review of *Pelican,* p. 113.

Times Educational Supplement, December 1, 1995, Elaine Williams, review of *The Creation,* p. 13.

Times Literary Supplement, October 30, 1970, review of *The Circus,* p. 1260; March 27, 1981, Kicki Moxon Browne, "Looking at Animals," p. 343.

Washington Post Book World, January 4, 1998, Michael Dirda, review of *Joseph,* p. 11.

ON-LINE

Jubilee Books.co.UK Magazine, http://www.jubileebooks. co.uk/ (May 30, 2001).

—*Sketch by Gerard J. Senick*

*   *   *

WILLIAMS, Sam

Personal

Married; three children.

Addresses

Home—Hertfordshire, England. *Agent*—HarperCollins Publishers, 10 East 53rd St., New York, NY 10022.

Career

Illustrator and author.

Awards, Honors

Children's Choice selection, International Reading Association/Children's Book Council, 2001, for *Cold Little Duck, Duck, Duck.*

Writings

Santa's Toys, illustrated by Tim Gill, David Bennett (St. Albans, England), 1998.

The Teddy Bears' Christmas Tree, illustrated by Jacqueline McQuade, David Bennett (St. Albans, England), 2000.

Teddy Bears Trim the Tree: A Christmas Pull-the-Tab Book, illustrated by Jacqueline McQuade, Scholastic (New York, NY), 2000.

Spots and Slots: A Slide-the-Spot Book of Colors, illustrated by Manya Stojic, Scholastic (New York, NY), 2001.

Teddy Bears Trick or Treat, Cartwheel (New York, NY), 2001.

Long Train: 101 Cars on the Track, Cartwheel (New York, NY), 2001.

SELF-ILLUSTRATED

The Baby's Word Book, David Bennett (St. Albans, England), 1993, Greenwillow (New York, NY), 1999.

Who Goes Moo?, Books for Children, 1996.

Whose Baby?, Books for Children, 1996.

Whose Home?, Books for Children, 1996.

Beach Baby, Campbell (London, England), 2001.

Wiggly Toes, Campbell (London, England), 2001.

Yum Yum, Campbell (London, England), 2001.

Giggle Giggle, Campbell (London, England), 2001.

Wakey Wakey, Night Night, Cartwheel (New York, NY), 2001.

Bunny and Bee, Orchard (London, England), in press.

Angel's Christmas Cookies, HarperCollins (New York, NY), in press.

Snowy Magic, HarperCollins (New York, NY), in press.

ILLUSTRATOR

Rock-a-Bye Baby Board Books, Volume 1: *Food,* Volume 2: *Animals,* Volume 3: *Bedtime,* Volume 4: *Home,* Volume 5: *My Body,* Volume 6: *Bathtime,* Volume 7: *Outdoors,* Volume 8: *Clothes,* Volume 9: *Toys,* Volume 10: *Faces,* Kingfisher (London, England), Dutton (New York, NY), 1992.

Toddler Playtime, Collins (London, England), 1998.

Toddler Bedtime, Collins (London, England), 1998.

Ros Asquith, *Ball!,* DK Publishing (New York, NY), 1998.

Nanette Newman, *Up to the Skies,* Hodder Children's (London, England), 1999.

Ros Asquith, *My Do It!,* Dorling Kindersley (London, England and New York, NY), 2000.

Lisa Westberg Peters, *Cold Little Duck, Duck, Duck,* Greenwillow (New York, NY), 2000

Grace Maccarone, *A Child Was Born: A First Nativity Book,* Scholastic (New York, NY), 2000.

Isabel Wilner, *The Baby's Game Book,* Greenwillow (New York, NY), 2000.

Marni McGee, *Sleepy Me,* Simon & Schuster (New York, NY), 2000.

Grace Maccarone, *A Child's Good Night Prayer,* Scholastic (New York, NY), 2001.

Hiawyn Oram, *Shall We Do That Again?,* Orchard (London, England), 2001.

Mathew Price, *Who Loves You, Baby Bear?,* Mathew Price (Sherborne, England), 2001.

Laura E. Richards, *Jiggle Joggle Jee!,* Greenwillow (New York, NY), 2001.

Marni McGee, *Wake Up, Me!,* Simon & Schuster (New York, NY), 2001.

Grace MacCarone, *A Child's Goodnight Prayer,* Scholastic (New York, NY), 2001.

Little Red, Simon & Schuster (New York, NY), in press.

If I Were You, Bloomsbury (New York, NY), in press.

Ball Games, Greenwillow (New York, NY), in press.

Sidelights

Sam Williams is a British illustrator and author known for his drawings of babies and toddlers. These simple drawings are the highlight of one of his earliest solo efforts, *The Rock-a-Bye Baby Board Books,* a set of ten miniature board books that nest inside a cradle-shaped box with a rounded bottom. The books are merely a series of words, one to a page, on the theme of bedtime, playtime, bath time, home, and other familiar features of a small child's life. Each word is coupled with one of Williams's signature illustrations, in which a chubby little person beams cherubically out at the reader. In a somewhat similar fashion, *The Baby's Word Book* is an oversized version of the same concept, with each page mapped out in a grid of nine pictures accompanied by the words and phrases for the familiar objects, feelings, and activities of a young child's life. The result is "great fun for toddlers," according to *School Library Journal* reviewer Lisa Falk.

Williams is also the author of several children's books, including *Teddy Bears Trim the Tree* and *Teddy Bears Trick or Treat.* Williams is perhaps best known, however, for the illustrations he provides for texts written by other authors. Williams' "gentle pencil and watercolor illustrations" accompany Isabel Wilner's collection of thirty-five games suitable for adult and toddler in *The Baby's Game Book,* according to *Horn*

Sam Williams's sensitive watercolor paintings complement Grace Maccarone's gentle verse story of Jesus's birth. (From A Child Was Born.*)*

Book reviewer Lauren Adams. A *Publishers Weekly* contributor described Williams' illustrations as "warm, attractive art." Williams teamed up with author Lisa Westberg Peters for *Cold Little Duck, Duck, Duck,* which Catherine Andronik called "a wonderful read-aloud pick-me-up for those blah, between-season March days," in her *Booklist* review. In this book, the author tells the story of a little duck who returns to her pond too early one spring and finds the water still frozen over. But by closing her eyes and imagining the sights, sounds, and smells of spring, she brings the warm season back. The simple rhyming text repeats each end word three times, making it a perfect choice for reading aloud, reviewers noted. Best of all, "story, art, and design work together well, and there's plenty here to engage duck-loving preschoolers preparing to dive into words and reading," observed *Horn Book* reviewer Kitty Flynn. Williams' drawings, which contrast the muted colors of winter with the brighter colors of spring, create "a beautiful book for sharing with toddlers," asserted Judith Constantinides in *School Library Journal.* A reviewer for *Publishers Weekly* called *Cold Little Duck, Duck, Duck* a "visually sumptuous testimony to patience and the power of positive thinking."

Author Grace Maccarone produced a rhyming rendition of the Christian nativity story in *A Child Was Born,* which Williams illustrated with "softly muted, double-page watercolor spreads," according to a reviewer in *School Library Journal.* Williams' "simple, uncluttered" illustrations grace Ros Asquith's *My Do It!,* a lift-the-flap book in which an independent-minded toddler insists on doing everything for himself, but the reader can help by lifting the flaps, according to Olga R. Barnes in *School Library Journal.* Laura E. Richards wrote *The Baby Goes to Boston* in the early 1900s, and in 2001, Williams published a new edition entitled *Jiggle Joggle Jee!* For this story, in which a child drifts off to sleep and dreams of riding a toy train through an imaginary landscape, Williams abandoned his simple, lucid style for what a *Publishers Weekly* critic dubbed "an impressionistic approach" in order to convey Richards' fantasy. As in some of his other collaborative books, the text of *Jiggle Joggle Jee!* has a playful rhyme scheme that small children will enjoy. "Williams' watercolors are stunners, densely colored yet shimmering with light," according to a reviewer in *Publishers Weekly.*

Biographical and Critical Sources

PERIODICALS

Booklist, May 15, 2000, Catherine Andronik, review of *Cold Little Duck, Duck, Duck,* p. 1749; December 1, 2000, Ilene Cooper, review of *Teddy Bears Trim the Tree,* p. 728.

Children's Book Review Annual, 1998, review of *Santa's Toys,* p. 492.

Horn Book, spring, 1993, review of *The Rock-a-Bye Baby Board Books,* p. 17; July, 2000, Kitty Flynn, review of *Cold Little Duck, Duck, Duck,* p. 443, and Lauren Adams, review of *The Baby's Game Book,* p. 449.

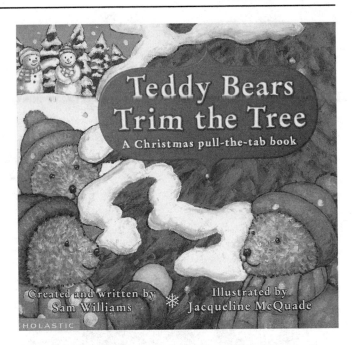

Williams designed a pull-tab book which follows three teddy bears as they find and decorate their Christmas tree. (Cover illustration by Jacqueline McQuade.)

Publishers Weekly, October 26, 1992, review of *The Rock-a-Bye Baby Board Books,* p. 68; September 6, 1999, review of *The Baby's Word Book,* p. 106; March 20, 2000, review of *Cold Little Duck, Duck, Duck,* p. 92; April 2, 2001, review of *Jiggle Joggle Jee!,* p. 62; April 17, 2000, "Rhymes in Action," p. 82; September 25, 2000, review of *A Child Was Born,* p. 68.

School Library Journal, January, 2000, Lisa Falk, review of *The Baby's Word Book,* p. 127; May, 2000, Judith Constantinides, review of *Cold Little Duck, Duck, Duck,* p. 151; October, 2000, review of *a Child Was Born,* p. 61, and Olga R. Barnes, review of *My Do It!,* p. 110; June, 2001, Martha Topol, review of *Sleepy Me,* p. 126.

*   *   *

WINDSOR, Linda 1950-
(Linda Covington)

Personal

Born July 8, 1950, in Salisbury, MD; daughter of Irvin L. (cofounder of an industrial electrical apparatus sales/repair facility) and Betty L. C. Brown (cofounder of an industrial electrical apparatus sales/repair facility) Brown; married second husband, James E. C. Windsor (a county employee), May 21, 1983; children: (first marriage) Kelly Ann, Jeffrey Scott. *Education:* Salisbury State University, B.A. (elementary education). *Hobbies and other interests:* Music ministry, lay ministry at local churches and civic groups, "restoring a late-eighteenth century home."

Linda Windsor

Addresses

Office—c/o Multnomah Publishers, P.O. Box 1720, Sisters, OR 97759. *Agent*—Ethan Ellenberg, 548 Broadway #5E, New York, NY 10012. *E-mail*—linda@Linda-Windsor.com.

Career

Demco, Inc., financial consultant, 1966-98; Windsor Enterprises, Inc., Salisbury, MD, fiction writer, 1990—, financial consultant, 1999—. Member of board of directors, Union UMC. *Member:* Romance Writers of America (including the Faith, Hope, and Love chapter and the NRW and VRW chapters), Novelists Inc., Christian Writers Association, American Christian Writers Association, ChiLibris.

Awards, Honors

Beacon Award for Literary Excellence, GDRWA, 1999; Readers Choice Award, 1999, for *Affaire de Coeur; Romantic Times* KISS Award; Dorothy Parker Award for Literary Excellence, Reviewers International, 2000; Diamond Award for Literary Achievement, DERWA, 2001.

Writings

Pirate's Wild Embrace, Kensington Publishing, 1990.
Hawaiian Caress, Kensington Publishing, 1990.
Wings of Love, Meteor Publishing, 1991.
Hawaiian Temptress, Kensington Publishing, 1991.
Texas Lovestorm, Kensington Publishing, 1992.
Midnight Lovestorm, Kensington Publishing, 1992.
Delta Moonfire, Kensington Publishing, 1992.
Mexican Caress, Kensington Publishing, 1993.
(Under pseudonym Linda Covington) *Wild Tory Rose,* Kensington Publishing, 1993.
(Under pseudonym Linda Covington) *Liberty's Flame,* Kensington Publishing, 1994.
The Knight and the Raven, Kensington Publishing, 1994.
Island Flame, Kensington Publishing, 1995.
Autumn Rose, Kensington Publishing, 1996.
Winter Rose, Kensington Publishing, 1997.
Border Rose, Kensington Publishing, 1998.
Hi Honey, I'm Home (romantic comedy), Multonomah (Sisters, OR), 1999.
Not Exactly Eden (romantic comedy), Multnomah (Sisters, OR), 2000.
It Had to Be You (romantic comedy), Multnomah (Sisters, OR), 2001.

Contributor to anthologies, including *A Bride's Passion,* Kensington Publishers, 1993, and *Unlikely Angels,* Multnomah (Sisters, OR), 1999.

"FIRES OF GLEANNMARA" SERIES; HISTORICAL FICTION

Maire, Multnomah (Sisters, OR), 2000.
Riona, Multnomah (Sisters, OR), 2001.
Deirdre, Multnomah (Sisters, OR), 2002.

Adaptations

Wings of Love has been adapted into an e-book by Mountain View Publishing (Oak Harbor, WA), 1999.

Work in Progress

Research in Irish history, early and medieval church history for fictional work, early Caribbean history, and early American history.

Sidelights

Linda Windsor told *SATA:* "Motivation? I have always been fascinated by history and loved reading romantic adventure and suspense, so combining these two loves was a dream come true. The teacher [in me] insists that I provide readers, without their realizing it, an education about the time, place, and peoples of whatever era I set my books in.

"Now that I write inspirational romance and fiction, I am able to subtly work in a spiritually uplifting element that anyone with feelings—whether devout, casual, or indifferent to an organized faith—can relate to without being preached at or beaten over the head with the religious dogma that used to send me running the other way at the first hint of it.

"The sense of humor my friends implore me to incorporate into my work allows the reader to laugh at the characters and sometimes at themselves. Like the saying goes, it's good medicine.

"My influences follow my motivation.... At first, writers like Kenneth Roberts and John Jakes shaped my concept of combining fascinating fact with fiction; then Kathleen Woodweiss and (with a charming dash of fact and lore) Mary Stuart. Now, Francine Rivers weaves in inspiration, and showing us how to laugh at ourselves are my favorite humorists like Patsy Clairmont, Barbara Johnson, and the late Erma Bombeck.

"Writing process: I 'preach' at writing seminars that good research practically writes a fresh entertaining story for an author. That goes for historical and contemporary fictions. My favorite sources are journals written by people who live or lived in my setting. It's straight from the horse's mouth and offers far more insight than your average history book, including speech patterns and jargon, which add flavor to the literary broth.

"Usually, while researching one book I come across dozens of ideas for future ones. When I am stymied in the writing process as to what should happen next to get me from point A to B in my plot, another look at my research books will inevitably give me an idea.

"My last resort is a paintbrush. A manual task such as painting, something that doesn't require thought and allows the mind to wander at will, always provides a shot to my creativity.

"Why do I write on the subjects I've chosen? See the above. Add to that my Irish and Scottish heritage, my patriotic upbringing to love my country and its past. Soon I can't keep my excitement to myself. I have to share it through my writing. That's usually after I've cornered everyone in my family or circle of friends and shared it with them.

"Changes in my writing: I can only hope that each book I write is an improvement on the last, at least craft-wise.

"I am a storyteller in a bardic sense, not a literary one. My agenda is to entertain first, then educate subliminally.

"The biggest change in my writing has come with switching to inspirational fiction, for now I must add spiritual inspiration to my goals. The second is branching out from basic romantic adventure, suspense, and/or comedy to a broader mainstream fiction that will interest readers of all genders and ages.

"I am convinced of the need for good stories appropriate for fiction and most young adult readers. The sexual explicitness in my earlier romances no longer appears in my later ones. The chemistry/attraction is alive and well, the plotting is as page-turning as ever, but my characters are given their privacy like those in the old Hollywood sizzlers.

"In my general fiction books, while there is a thread of romance, the plot itself is bigger, encompassing the story of a people, place, and time, rather than just two people in a place at a given time. For instance, *Maire,* the first book in the 'Fires of Gleannmara' series, has been described as such a book (akin to *Ben Hur*). It's more than the romance between a pagan warrior queen and the Christian ex-mercenary she takes as hostage and husband. It's a grander, encompassing epic of the bloodless coming and acceptance of Christianity to Ireland; the preparation for it by ancient druidic legends of Christ and Erin's interwoven Hebrew-Celtic heritage; and how it prepared the remote green island to the north to preserve civilization during the coming Dark Ages and produce more missionaries to carry the light out into the world than any one country before or since."

Windsor contributed a novella to an anthology in which animals play a part in the blossoming of loving relationships. (Cover illustration by Aleta Jenks.)

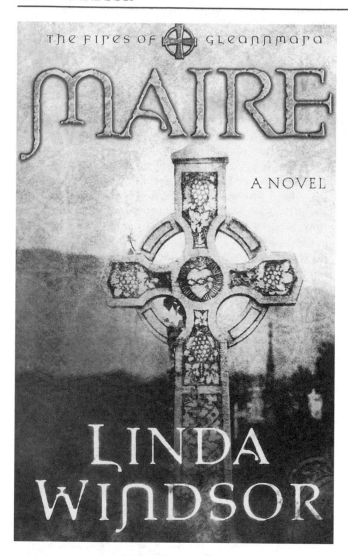

In the initial volume of the "Fires of Gleannmara" series, two unlikely warriors marry and discover the strength of Christianity when they battle an evil druid in fifth-century Ireland. (Cover illustration by Kirsty McLaren.)

Biographical and Critical Sources

ON-LINE

Linda Windsor Home Page, http://www.lindawindsor.com/ (July 25, 2001).

* * *

WINICK, Judd 1970-

Personal

Born February 12, 1970, in Long Island, NY. *Education:* University of Michigan, B.A., 1992.

Addresses

Home—915 Cole St., No. 301, San Francisco, CA 94117. *E-mail*—judd@frumpy.com.

Career

Cartoonist, illustrator, and writer. AIDS educator and lecturer. Participant in MTV's *The Real World,* 1994; host of following television programs: (with Pam Ling) *MTV video Now What?: A Guide to Jobs, Money, and the Real World,* and *MTV's Real World-Road Rules Casting Special* and (co-host) *Best Fights of the Real World,* both 2000.

Awards, Honors

Eisner Award nomination for best sequential story, 1998, for "Road Trip"; Eisner Award nominations, 1999, for talent deserving wider recognition, best humor artist/writer, and best original graphic novel, for *Pedro and Me;* notable graphic novel citation, Young Adult Library Services Association (YALSA), for *The Adventures of Barry Ween, Boy Genius;* GLAAD Media Award for best comic book, Bulletin Blue Ribbon Book citation, notable graphic novel citation, YALSA, *Publishers Weekly* Best Book citation, Américas Award for Children's and Young Adult Literature, National Association of Latin American Studies Programs, all for *Pedro and Me;* Bay Area Book Reviewers' Award, 2000, and Notable Children's Book selection and Gay Lesbian, Bisexual, Transgender Roundtable Nonfiction Honor Book, American Library Association, Robert F. Sibert Informational Book Honor Award, Quick Pick for Reluctant Readers selection, YALSA, all 2001, all for *Pedro and Me.*

Writings

SELF-ILLUSTRATED

Terminal Madness: The "Complete Idiot's Guide" Computer Cartoon Collection, Que (Indianapolis, IN), 1997.
The Adventures of Barry Ween, Boy Genius, ONI Press (Portland, OR), 1999.
The Adventures of Barry Ween, Boy Genius, 2.0, ONI Press (Portland, OR), 2000.
Pedro and Me: Friendship, Loss, and What I Learned, Holt (New York, NY), 2000.
Frumpy the Clown: Freaking out the Neighbors, ONI Press (Portland, OR), 2001.
Frumpy the Clown: The Fat Lady Sings, ONI Press (Portland, OR), 2001.

Author and illustrator of cartoon strip "Nuts and Bolts," published in *Michigan Daily,* 1988-92, and *San Francisco Examiner,* 1994, and collected in *Watching the Spin-Cycle: The Nuts and Bolts,* privately printed (Ann Arbor, MI). Author and illustrator of "Road Trip" comic strip, in *Oni Double Feature;* "Frumpy the Clown," syndicated, 1996-98; "The Adventures of Barry Ween, Boy Genius," Image Comics, 1999; "Green Lantern," DC Comics; and "Exiles," Marvel Comics. Illustrator, with others, of Jamie S. Rich's *Cut My Hair,* ONI Press, 2000, and for numerous titles in the "Complete Idiot's Guide" series, Que (Indianapolis, IN).

Judd Winick

Adaptations

The Adventures of Barry Ween, Boy Genius was optioned for development as an animated television series by Platinum Studios.

Work in Progress

A graphic novel.

Sidelights

The world became all too real for Judd Winick in 1993 as one of seven "stars" of MTV's *Real World III,* a pioneering reality-based television show. It was then that he met not only his future partner, Pam Ling, but also temporary housemate Pedro Zamora, a young man from Florida whose eventual death from AIDS would bring the tragic effects of that disease home to millions of young television viewers. Zamora, an AIDS activist, inspired Winick, a promising young cartoonist, to hit the lecture circuit for over a year after the filming of *The Real World* to speak with young people about AIDS-related issues. In 2000 Winick published a moving and honest graphic-novel account of his friendship with Zamora, *Pedro and Me: Friendship, Loss, and What I Learned.* Additionally, Winick is also a popular cartoonist, author, and illustrator of, among other things, the comic strip "Frumpy the Clown," which follows the trail of a chain-smoking, cynical clown who decides to move in with a typical suburban family, and "The Adventures of Barry Ween, Boy Genius," a series of comic books

dealing with the misadventures of a cranky, obnoxious, brilliant, and foul-mouthed ten-year-old.

Born in 1970, Winick grew up in Dix Hill, Long Island, New York, "a grumpy, quasi-budding artist kid," as he admitted to Bill Jensen in *Newsday.* Schoolwork was not his favorite pastime at Half Hollow Hills East High School; instead, young Winick took refuge in reading comics and then in creating his own. By the time he was sixteen, he was already a professional cartoonist, selling a single-paneled strip, "Nuts and Bolts," to Anton Publications, which published newspapers in a three-state northeastern region.

When he graduated from high school and moved on to college at the University of Michigan, Winick studied drawing and art. He also continued his "Nuts and Bolts" strip, now expanded into four panels and running five days a week in the college paper, the *Michigan Daily.* Shortly before graduation, Winick's strips were collected in a privately printed edition, *Watching the Spin-Cycle: The Nuts and Bolts,* which sold out its thousand copies in a matter of two weeks. Encouraged by such a response, Winick landed a development contract with a syndicator to develop the cartoon as a national strip, but after a year of work in Boston, the "bottom dropped

Winick created a graphic tribute to his friend, AIDS activist Pedro Zamora, who died soon after they shared a season as roommates on MTV's reality series **The Real World.** *(From* Pedro and Me, *written and illustrated by Winick.)*

out," as Winick reported on his Web site. "[T]he syndicate decided that they were not going to pursue 'Nuts and Bolts' for syndication and were terminating the development contract."

Out of work, Winick returned temporarily to his parents' home, commuting into New York City for occasional illustration jobs and working on a development deal with Nickelodeon on an animated series based on "Nuts and Bolts." This deal also fell through and when, in August, 1993, Winick saw a newspaper ad for auditions for MTV's *The Real World,* to be shot in San Francisco, he jumped at the chance. The six-month-long audition process included doing a video, filling out a fifteen-page application, having in-person interviews with the producers, and being followed around for a day by a film crew. Finally, Winick, along with six others, were chosen for the cast of the reality show in which these seven—strangers from all over the United States—were put together in a house and filmed nonstop for half a year. One possible stumbling block came when producers asked Winick how he would feel about sharing quarters with another young man who was HIV positive. At that moment, Winick was forced to live up to his liberal PC convictions and confront the fears and ignorance they actually covered up. He told the producers there was no problem with that, but secretly he had his doubts, which he shared with friends. "Here I was, this weenie, open-minded, liberal New York Jew," Winick told Chad Jones in an *Oakland Tribune* interview. "I should have been fine with it, but I was really scared."

Winick and his fellow housemates gathered at a house on Lombard Street in San Francisco to be filmed cinema-verité style. The HIV-positive roommate turned out to be AIDS activist Pedro Zamora, a Cuban immigrant who had been diagnosed with AIDS as a teenager. Zamora wanted to be on the show to give a human face to the AIDS scourge, and he and Winick became fast friends. Together they and the others, including Asian-American medical student Pam Ling, confronted the day-to-day hassles of living together. During the filming of the show, Winick's cartoon strip, "Nuts and Bolts," was reprised in the local *San Francisco Examiner.*

Winick, who took the job on *The Real World* as a way to get free rent and live in San Francisco temporarily, quickly learned there was much more to the deal. He became known as the serious one of the group and the guy who could never get a date. This was his persona to an entire segment of Generation X viewers, the twenty-something audience MTV was hoping to reach. After filming for six months in 1993, the show began airing in 1994 and became one of the most popular in the series, not least because of Zamora's medical condition. It was not long after the show went on the air that Zamora became ill from AIDS complications. Winick agreed to take over his speaking engagements until Zamora could get back on his feet, but the activist never did. In August, 1994, Zamora was put in the hospital and died

Ten-year-old genius Barry Ween is the fearless protagonist of Winick's humorous superhero send-up.

the following November, shortly after the final episode of *The Real World III* appeared on television.

Following Zamora's death, Winick continued to lecture about his friend and about AIDS education and prevention. For about a year and a half he devoted most of his time to this cause. It was, Winick explained on his Web site, "the most fulfilling and difficult time in my life."

By 1995 Winick needed to return to his cartooning career. He had, by this time, outgrown "Nuts and Bolts" and was ready to take on new challenges. Working as an illustrator, he began providing artwork for many of the "Complete Idiot's Guide" series, a collection of which were published as *Terminal Madness.* As a writer and illustrator, he worked on his first syndicated comic strip, "Frumpy the Clown," beginning in July of 1996. Stealing one of his favorite characters from "Nuts and Bolts," Winick gave the cynical clown a new home, with a suburban family mom, dad, children (Brad and Kim), and family dog. The children are ecstatic about their new member, Frumpy, but the parents, along with neighbors, wish only that he would go away. Winick depicts Frumpy and family embroiled in such quotidian tasks as getting the kids to school and fixing snacks, but all the while Frumpy attempts to enlighten the children about the dark truths lurking behind the bright lights of so-called reality, taking great delight in warping their young minds. Winick continued the strip for two years, with an initial syndication of thirty national papers. "Unfortunately," Winick noted on his Web site, "Frumpy ran into trouble." The clown's edginess ultimately cost readership in more family-oriented newspapers, and eventually syndication dwindled to a trickle. Also, and more importantly, Winick found the daily grind of turning out a comic strip less creative than he had imagined. "I found daily comic strips to be limiting," he noted, "not just in length and size formats or language, but creatively. I just didn't find the strip fulfilling."

It was about this time that Winick began work on a graphic novel about his friendship with Zamora, a project that would last over two years. Meanwhile, he also formed a relationship with ONI Press, and began work on a comic, "The Adventures of Barry Ween, Boy Genius." Barry is not your typical ten-year-old. Possessed of an IQ of 350, the youth delights in days spent on his own with the sitter heavily sedated, allowing him to work on his anti-terrorist equipment, or alternately build an atom smasher that fits under his bed. He gets into adventures with his pal Jeremy Ramirez, such as dealing with art thieves and time warps, repairing a stranded space ship of an alien on the run from intergalactic mobsters, and rescuing his buddy from the government. Popular with audiences already keen on the graphic format popularized by such works as *Maus* by Art Spiegelman, both "Barry Ween" and "Frumpy" were published in paperback collections by ONI Press.

Throughout 1999 Winick continued work on his graphic novel *Pedro and Me*. Armistead Maupin, the San Francisco-based author of *Tales of the City,* saw an early version of the work and encouraged Winick to push on and to be even more open and frank about his friendship

with Zamora. Submitting the manuscript to his agent, Jill Kneerim, Winick was hopeful for early publication. But thirty publishers saw it, loved it, and failed to buy it. Then the manuscript was sent to editor Marc Aronson at Holt who was "very hands-off but provided lots of guidance," as Winick told Shannon Maughan in a *Publishers Weekly* interview. "He helped me work on the pacing, finding a moment here, a moment there, building a true beginning, middle and end." Eventually, through working with Aronson, Winick whittled down his manuscript to one hundred-eighty book pages. It was also decided to target the book at a young adult audience, the population most at risk for contracting AIDS.

Pedro and Me tells the twin stories of both Winick and Zamora. One young man came from Cuba in the Mariel Boatlift of 1968 that saw the immigration of 125,000 refugees from Castro's Cuba. Still in his early teens, Zamora watches his mother die of skin cancer in Florida; at seventeen he contracts the AIDS virus and soon thereafter becomes a major activist and AIDS educator. Meanwhile, Winick grows up safe and sound on Long Island, mowing lawns in the summer. As fellow cast members, Winick and Zamora grow to understand one another. Winick does not spare himself when he shows his own initial ignorance and fear of Zamora's disease, nor does he replay the events of *The Real World* house; rather he focuses on the friendship and what he learned from his brief time with Zamora. The story continues after the filming of *The Real World* is over, as Zamora becomes ill, and both Winick and Pam Ling take time out from their busy lives to be with him. It ends with the emotional deathbed scene with a gathering of friends.

Reviewers and critics had high praise for Winick's book and its message. Writing in the *Advocate,* a contributor called *Pedro and Me* a "touching remembrance" and a "cathartic experience," while a reviewer for *Publishers Weekly* described the graphic novel as "powerful and captivating," and felt that it struck "just the right balance of cool and forthrightness to attract a broad cross section of teens, twenty-somethings and beyond." The same

A collection of his discontinued syndicated newspaper cartoon, Winick's book follows subversive clown Frumpy as he disrupts the life of a suburban family, to the delight of the children and the chagrin of the adults. (From Frumpy the Clown: Freaking out the Neighbors.*)*

writer noted the "deceptively simple" black and white comic-strip art that contains a "full spectrum of emotion," concluding that Winick's book was an "innovative and accessible approach" to a very difficult subject. *Booklist* contributor Stephanie Zvirin lauded the cartoonist's illustrations, noting that "facial expressions ... count most" in a book filled with "great tenderness and a keen sense of loss." In a review for *School Library Journal*, Francisca Goldsmith commented that Winick does a "stellar job of marrying image to word to form a flowing narrative," and added: "This is an important book for teens and the adults who about them. Winick handles his topics with both sensitivity and a thoroughness that rarely coexist so seamlessly." "The vigorous comic-strip art, notable for its expressive depictions of real-life characters and variety of layout and perspective, does not diminish the seriousness of the subject matter," maintained Peter D. Sieruta in his *Horn Book* appraisal of *Pedro and Me*. Sieruta concluded, "In this warm and ultimately life-affirming remembrance, Winick gives the world a second chance to know Pedro and his message."

Reader response was equally positive, and Winick soon found he was once again a sought-after speaker at schools. "My hope is that people learn from Pedro the way I did," he noted in an interview for the *Advocate*, "that they have their stereotypes broken and learn about AIDS and the people who live with it—and that they are empowered by his accomplishments. Lastly, I hope they remember my friend. That's why I wrote and illustrated this in the first place."

But Winick has also attempted to move beyond the bounds of the world he first confronted in *The Real World*. While he hopes never to forget the message Zamora gave the world about AIDS and people with AIDS, he has other creative plans in the works, including a further graphic novel as well as writing for DC Comics' "Green Lantern" series. In his talks with students, Winick also encourages other budding cartoonists. "Develop a style," he tells cartoonist hopefuls on his Web site. "It's not necessary to be a jack of all trades. And get published! Any little paper that'll have you, or print them up yourself and give them away in comic stores. I don't believe in luck. Success comes when opportunity meets preparation."

Biographical and Critical Sources

PERIODICALS

Advocate, February 1, 2000, review of *Pedro and Me*, p. 2; September 12, 2000, "Judd Remembers," p. 61.
Billboard, September 7, 1996, p. 100.
Booklist, September 15, 2000, Stephanie Zvirin, review of *Pedro and Me*, p. 230; December 1, 2000, p. 693.
Boston Herald, September 5, 2000.
Horn Book, November-December, 2000, Peter D. Sieruta, review of *Pedro and Me*, pp. 775-776.
Newsday, April 16, 2000, Bill Jensen, "From 'Real World' to Real Winick, Sort Of."
Oakland Tribune, September 6, 2000, Chad Jones, "Learning 'Real' Lessons."

Publishers Weekly, September 11, 2000, review of *Pedro and Me*, p. 92; September 18, 2000, Shannon Maughan, "That's What Friends Are For," p. 37.
Sacramento Bee, August 31, 2000.
San Francisco Chronicle, September 6, 2000.
School Library Journal, October, 2000, Francisca Goldsmith, review of *Pedro and Me*, p. 192.
TV Guide, July 29, 2000.
USA Today, September 18, 2000.

ON-LINE

Judd Winick Web site, http://www.juddwinick.com/ (May 14, 2001).
Fandom, http://www.fandom.com/ (May 13, 2001).

*   *   *

WITHROW, Sarah 1966-

Personal

Born October 28, 1966, in Winnipeg, Manitoba, Canada; daughter of Patrick (a copywriter) and Julie (an artist) Withrow. *Education:* Ryerson School of Journalism, B.A.A., 1988; attended Humber School of Creative Writing, 1992. *Religion:* Taoist.

Addresses

Home—#2-425 Bagot St., Kingston, Ontario K7K 3C1, Canada. *Agent*—c/o Groundwood Books, 720 Bathurst St., Ste. 500, Toronto, Ontario M5S 2RA, Canada. *E-mail*—swithrow@kingston.net

Career

Freelance corporate writer, 1989-98; Fireworks, Kingston, Ontario, Canada, glass blowers' assistant, 1998-2000; St. Lawrence College, School of Continuing Studies, writer/teacher, Kingston, 2000. *Member:* Taoist Tai Chi Society (secretary, 1999—).

Awards, Honors

Winner of First Novel for Children Contest, Groundwood Books, 1998, for *Bat Summer*.

Writings

Bat Summer, Groundwood, 1998.
Box Girl, Groundwood, 2001.

Aslo contributor of "Ollie," published in *The Journey Prize Anthology*, McClelland & Stewart, 1997.

Sidelights

Sarah Withrow told *SATA:* "My first novel, *Bat Summer*, is being published by six publishers worldwide and is available in German, Swedish, and Danish as well as English. When I was a young adult, I swore that I would never forget what it was like to be young. I try to write the kinds of books I would have wanted to read back

Sarah Withrow

then. Books that, I hope, give readers permission to grow into themselves—whoever they are. And books that acknowledge how complicated and confusing young lives can be. Finally, I enjoy showing how friendships nourish individuals and become the treasures of their lives."

Withrow struck a cord with reviewers with her first novel for young adults, *Bat Summer.* Twelve-year-old Terence, accustomed to tagging along with his best friend Tom, is left to his own devices when Tom leaves town for the summer. Lucy, the unusual friend Terence eventually finds, forces him to think about his own values and how best to act upon them. "Both Lucy and Terence are overlooked by the adults in their lives who mistakenly equate the free time of childhood with ease," observed Megan Isaac in *Voice of Youth Advocates.* And

while Terence suffers some from parental neglect, Withrow reveals that Lucy's obsession with bats compensates for her very real deprivation in her home life. When Lucy runs away from home, Terence must decide if true friendship means helping her hide or sending her back home. Withrow focuses exclusively on the young adults and their world of Toronto's playgrounds, parks, and alleys. In this she "demonstrates a reporter's ear for the name calling, swearing, and prepubescent banter that come with the territory," according to Patty Lawlor in *Quill & Quire.* Other critics similarly praised the author for her well-rounded, authentic characters as well as for the important message woven within her story. "This original, compelling first novel illustrates the true meaning of friendship, inner strength, and integrity," praised Shelle Rosenfeld in a *Booklist* review.

Biographical and Critical Sources

PERIODICALS

Booklist, July, 1999, Shelle Rosenfeld, review of *Bat Summer,* p. 1947.
Quill & Quire, November, 1998, Patty Lawlor, review of *Bat Summer,* pp. 47-48.
Voice of Youth Advocates, August, 1999, Megan Isaac, review of *Bat Summer,* p. 188.

*   *   *

WRIGHT, Dare 1914(?)-2001

OBITUARY NOTICE—See index for *SATA* sketch: Born c. 1914, in Thornhill, Canada; died January 25, 2001, in New York, NY. Artist and author. Wright was the author of self-illustrated books for children. Her best-known work was the 1957 *Lonely Doll,* the story of a girl and her teddy bears. Later works include *The Doll and the Kitten, Take Me Home, Look at a Colt,* and *Look at a Calf,* which earned an Outstanding Science Trade Book for Children Award in 1974. Wright's last work, *Edith and Midnight,* was published in 1978. Wright began her career as a fashion photographer, and her work appeared in such publications as *Harper's Bazaar* and *Vogue.*

OBITUARIES AND OTHER SOURCES:

PERIODICALS

Los Angeles Times, February 4, 2001, p. B7.
New York Times, February 3, 2001, p. B7.
Washington Post, February 4, 2001, p. C8.

Y

YOUNT, Lisa (Ann) 1944-

Personal

Born July 28, 1944, in Los Angeles, CA; daughter of Stanley George (founder and chief executive officer of an industrial paper company) and Agnes (an assistant sales manager; maiden name, Pratt) Yount; married Charles Siegfried, January 11, 1969 (divorced, 1970); married Alec Hamilton, October, 1970 (divorced, January, 1980); married Harry Henderson (a writer and editor of young adult and computer books), September 23, 1982. *Education:* Stanford University, B.A. (cum laude), 1966. *Politics:* "As little as possible." *Hobbies and other interests:* Collage art, photography, poetry, storytelling, jewelry making, singing, nature, medicine and biology, environmental issues, working with children.

Addresses

Home and office—2631 Mira Vista Dr., El Cerrito, CA 94530.

Career

Freelance author and editor, 1967—. Terwilliger Nature Education Center, Corte Madera, CA, nature guide 1986-2000; volunteer for San Francisco Society for the Prevention of Cruelty to Animals, Sierra Club, Save the Bay, and other organizations; storyteller, Lindsay Wildlife Museum, 1996—.

Awards, Honors

Outstanding Science Trade Books for Children citation, National Science Teachers Association/Children's Book Council, 1981, for *Too Hot, Too Cold, Just Right,* 1983, for *The Telescope,* 1995, for *William Harvey,* and 1997, for *Antoni van Leeuwenhoek;* "Books for the Teen Age" citation, New York Public Library, for *Contemporary Women Scientists, Twentieth-Century Women Scientists,* and *Genetics and Genetic Engineering;* Best Children's Science Books of 1998, American Association for the Advancement of Science, for *Twentieth-Century Women Scientists* and *Antoine Lavoisier;* "Not Ready for Newbery" award, Pennsylvania School Librarians Associations, 2001, for *Euthanasia and Physician-Assisted Suicide.*

Lisa Yount

232

Writings

NONFICTION; FOR CHILDREN

Too Hot, Too Cold, Just Right, Walker & Co. (New York, NY), 1981.

The Telescope, Walker & Co. (New York, NY), 1983.

Lore of Our Land, J. Weston Walch, 1984.

Black Scientists ("American Profiles" series), Facts on File (New York, NY), 1991.

Cancer, Greenhaven Press (San Diego, CA), 1991.

True Adventure Readers, J. Weston Walch, 1992.

Louis Pasteur ("The Importance of" series), Lucent (San Diego, CA), 1994.

William Harvey: Discoverer of How Blood Circulates ("Great Minds of Science" series), Enslow (Minneapolis, MN), 1994.

Contemporary Women Scientists, Facts on File (New York, NY), 1994.

Women Aviators ("American Profiles" series), Facts on File (New York, NY), 1995.

(With Mary M. Rodgers) *Our Endangered Planet: Air,* Lerner (Minneapolis, MN), 1995.

Pesticides, Lucent (San Diego, CA), 1995.

Twentieth-Century Women Scientists, Facts on File (New York, NY), 1996.

(With husband, Harry Henderson) *The Scientific Revolution,* Lucent (San Diego, CA), 1996.

Antoni van Leeuwenhoek: First to See Microscopic Life ("Great Minds of Science" series), Enslow (Springfield, NJ), 1996.

Memory, Lucent (San Diego, CA), 1996.

Antoine Lavoisier: Founder of Modern Chemistry ("Great Minds of Science" series), Enslow (Springfield, NJ), 1997.

(With husband, Harry Henderson) *Twentieth-Century Science,* Lucent (San Diego, CA), 1997.

Frontier of Freedom: African Americans in the West, Facts on File (New York, NY), 1997.

Genetics and Genetic Engineering ("Milestones in Discovery and Invention" series), Facts on File (New York, NY), 1997.

Issues in Biomedical Ethics, Lucent (San Diego, CA), 1998.

Medical Technology ("Milestones in Discovery and Invention" series), Facts on File (New York, NY), 1998.

Asian-American Scientists, Facts on File (New York, NY), 1998.

A to Z of Women in Science and Math, Facts on File (New York, NY), 1999.

Cancer ("Overview" series), Lucent (San Diego, CA), revised edition, 1999.

(Editor) *Cloning,* Greenhaven Press (San Diego, CA), 2000.

(Editor) *Cancer,* Greenhaven Press (San Diego, CA), 2000.

Biotechnology and Genetic Engineering ("Library in a Book" series), Facts on File (New York, NY), 2000.

Epidemics, Lucent (San Diego, CA), 2000.

Physician-Assisted Suicide and Euthanasia ("Library in a Book" series), Facts on File (New York, NY), 2000.

Euthanasia, Lucent (San Diego, CA), 2001.

Disease Detectives ("History Makers" series), Lucent (San Diego, CA), 2001.

History of Medicine ("World History" series), Lucent (San Diego, CA), 2001.

Contributor to children's magazines, including *Cobblestone, Ranger Rick's Nature Magazine, Jack and Jill,* and *Highlights for Children.*

OTHER

Stones and Bones (poetry), Half-a-Lump Press (El Cerrito, CA), 1986.

(Self-illustrated) *The Cave in the Mirror* (poetry), Half-a-Lump Press (El Cerrito, CA), 1996.

Contributor of poetry to small press publications. Contributor of articles to *International Wildlife* and *National Wildlife.*

Sidelights

Lisa Yount is a prolific author who specializes in making scientific theories and issues understandable to young readers. "I like to tell people, especially young people, about the strange and fascinating things that exist in nature," Yount once noted. "I agree with the

Yount penned biographical entries on ten women of the twentieth century who have made significant contributions to the field of science.

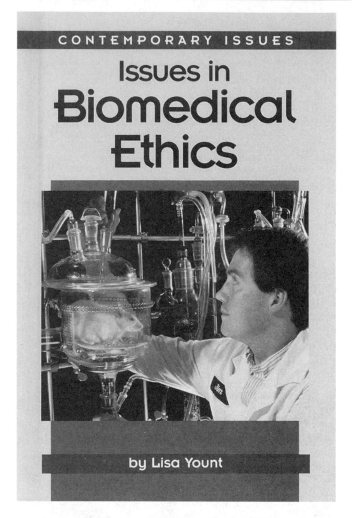

In this work, Yount covers such topics as genetic engineering, euthanasia, and certain types of medical research.

British poet Robert Louis Stevenson that 'the world is so full of a number of things / I'm sure we should all be as happy as kings.'" Among Yount's many published works are several volumes in Facts on File's "Milestones in Discovery and Invention" series, as well as contributions to the science-related book series of several other publishers. She has authored numerous short biographies of notable men and women working in the field of science that have been collected in *Contemporary Women Scientists, Black Scientists, Asian-American Scientists,* and *A to Z of Women in Science and Math,* the last published in 1999. "Yount has an engaging style which helps illuminate the personalities of her subjects," commented Rayna Patton in a *Voice of Youth Advocates* critique of *Contemporary Women Scientists,* "as well as describ[e] their often complex research clearly and accurately."

Born in Los Angeles, California, in 1944, Yount grew up in the small southern California town of San Marino. "My mother read to me often," the author once recalled to *SATA,* "and soon I could 'read' my favorite books back to her by reciting them from memory.... My father and I loved to sing folk songs together. Neither of

us was a good singer, but we had fun. He also told stories from the Bible and from his own life." Because of her parents' influence, Yount was soon telling, then writing, original stories, poems, and songs of her own. "One of the first stories I wrote down was a fantasy serial, 'Mary the Magic Cat.' I told Mary's adventures to my fellow riders in a day-camp car-pool when I was in fourth grade, and each day they asked to hear more."

Despite her ability to spin an entertaining tall tale, Yount had no plans to become a writer while growing up. Science, not fiction, held her full interest, and she enrolled at Stanford University with the intention of becoming a medical researcher. "Somewhere in the middle of college chemistry I finally faced the fact that I was too much of a klutz in the lab to be successful in this career," Yount later admitted. "I didn't lose my interest in medical and biological research, but I decided I had better write about it rather than try to do it."

After graduating from Stanford with honors in 1966, Yount found a job working as a writer for hire for a textbook publisher. Her skills at editing and writing for young people were marketable, she realized, and she decided to make her living as a freelance writer. "I've worked on books that teach reading, science, social studies, and other subjects to students between grade three and high school," Yount explained of the career that followed her decision. "Many people work on a textbook, and their names are not always mentioned in the book. You may have read something of mine in school, even though you didn't know it!"

While her textbook contributions were not always published with her byline, Yount's work for children's magazines such as *Highlights for Children, Jack and Jill,* and *Ranger Rick's Nature Magazine* brought her personal recognition. It was an article she wrote for *Ranger Rick's*—on how animals cope with changes in temperature—that grew to become Yount's first book: *Too Hot, Too Cold, Just Right,* which was published in 1981.

Reading about the lives of successful individuals has often proved inspirational to young people searching for ways to channel their interests into their adult lives. In the 1990s, Yount had the opportunity to compile several collections of these inspirational short biographies. Some, including *Black Scientists,* were based on ethnicity, while several others used gender as a criteria for inclusion. 1994's *Contemporary Women Scientists* profiles ten women who have contributed to the expansion of scientific knowledge, among them pediatrician Helen Brooke Taussig, researcher and educator Jewel Plummer Cobb, and AIDS researcher Flossie Wong-Staal. Calling *Contemporary Women Scientists* "a wonderful introduction," *Appraisal* contributors Terry M. Cook and Eileen Egizi added that Yount's success in keeping her text "age-appropriate" meant that "the reader's interest is engaged." A similar collection, *Twentieth-Century Women Scientists,* places the scientific contributions of the eleven women profiled into what a *Kirkus Reviews* writer described as "a cultural perspective, emphasizing the way female scientists often look at nature," that is, as a system made up of interrelated segments. *Booklist* contributor Candace Smith predicted that the book's "accessible" prose would likely "inspire young women to consider careers in science." Expanding the next group of biographical essays she tackled to almost 150, Yount compiled *A to Z of Women in Science and Math,* an encyclopedic, cross-indexed reference work that *Library Journal* reviewer Kathy Breeden praised for its "very readable essays" and its flexibility as a "useful quick reference point to begin research" on women in science.

As her career as a writer has progressed, Yount has increasingly concentrated on nonfiction books that examine, in various amounts of detail, specific subjects relating to biology and medicine. Her contributions to Lucent's "Overview" series, for example, include the titles *Cancer, Epidemics, Pesticides,* and *Memory. Cancer,* which provides information on one of the most feared diseases of modern times, is, as with all books in the series, keyed to a middle-school readership through its "clear yet concise" explanations and use of "simple terms," according to *School Library Journal* reviewer Christine A. Moesch. Traveling the information continuum from historical facts through newspaper headlines of today to speculations about the future, *Epidemics* covers the social and political effects of historic plagues, reveals statistics reflecting the resurgence of many "old" diseases, and discusses the potential for biological warfare. More technical in its approach, *Memory* presents information on the anatomy of the mind, as well as the psychological reasons for memory loss and other conditions. *Pesticides* deals squarely with the environmentally-based concern over the use of chemicals to control insects and disease in agricultural settings. In *Pesticides* Yount attempts to present both sides of the debates over clean water, integrated pest management, and other related topics through what *Booklist* contributor Frances Bradburn described as a "carefully researched and logically organized text." *School Library Journal* reviewer Helen Rosenberg dubbed the work a "somewhat dry, yet informative and evenhanded ... resource for report writers."

In addition to her fact-based books, Yount has published several titles dealing with provocative topics. 1998's *Issues in Biomedical Ethics,* for example, outlines the ongoing debate surrounding a number of controversial issues, among them cloning, genetic research, the use of animals in medical research, euthanasia, and the economic obstructions to health care among the poor. Commending Yount for compiling and appending both a list of contact organizations and a detailed bibliography, Ann G. Brouse noted in *School Library Journal* that a wide range of opinions from "ethicists, physicians, researchers," and others with a strong position "is expressed with a substantial use of quotes." The debate surrounding cloning is also dealt with separately by Yount in a 2000 volume containing more than twenty articles exploring the issue. While remarking that the constant scientific advances in clone research would likely require students to "look elsewhere for more

current developments," *Booklist* contributor Anne O'Malley still deemed *Cloning* useful because of its broad focus and its helpful appendices, including a list of organizations relevant to the debate and a concise bibliography.

For students wishing to explore controversial topics in depth, Yount has written several books in Fact on Files's "Library in a Book" series, including *Biotechnology and Genetic Engineering* and *Physician-Assisted Suicide and Euthanasia.* In addition to providing an overview of the subject, each book contains analyses and excerpts of court cases related to the issue, a chronology, a glossary, lists of relevant organizations and Web sites, as well as an extensive bibliography. All of the information contained in the books is targeted at high school and adult audiences. In a starred *Booklist* review of *Biotechnology and Genetic Engineering,* critic Roger Leslie remarked, "In recent years, resources on cloning and genetics have saturated the market, but this one is really special." Leslie went on to describe the book as "the ultimate resource" and "a fact-finder's dream."

Yount's overview of cancer includes documentation of case studies, statistics, possible causes, and a discussion of experimental treatments.

Yount's interest in young people is not limited to writing for them; she enjoys helping them explore nature as well. For fourteen years, as a nature guide trained by the award-winning naturalist Elizabeth Terwilliger, Yount has escorted groups of kindergarten through third-grade students around Muir Woods National Monument and nearby Muir Beach. Beginning in 1996, she has told animal stories, including some she wrote herself, to children twice a month at the Lindsay Wildlife Museum in Walnut Creek, California. "Nothing beats the thrill of seeing children spot clusters of ladybugs hibernating in the woods or laugh at Coyote's mischief making adventures," Yount told *SATA.*

When not researching or writing, Yount enjoys several kinds of creative activity. She has written poetry since adolescence and has self-published two poetry books, one of which is illustrated with her own collages. Beginning in the mid-1990s, she created collage art extensively, both in paper form and on the computer. Her paper colleges draw on a massive collection of magazine pictures, while her computer ones use mostly her own photographs. "I loved art when I was little," she told *SATA,* "but I though I couldn't be an artist because I couldn't make drawings look realistic. I've learned though, that there are many other ways of creating art." Yount advises young people, "Never let anyone tell you there's anything you can't be!"

Yount lives with her husband, writer Harry Henderson, and assorted cats in El Cerrito, in the San Francisco Bay Area. Henderson, an expert on computer-related subjects, writes for many of the same series as Yount does, and they have collaborated on two books, *The Scientific Revolution* and *Twentieth-Century Science.* "I love writing while sitting on my armchair, typing on my laptop computer (which the cats try to sit on) and looking at the maple tree outside my window," she told *SATA.*

Biographical and Critical Sources

PERIODICALS

Appraisal, autumn, 1995, F. Elizabeth Gillis and Barbara Castel, review of *Louis Pasteur,* pp. 78-79; winter, 1995, Eileen Egizi and Terry M. Cook, review of *Contemporary Women Scientists,* pp. 79-80.

Booklist, May 1, 1992, Karen Hutt, review of *Cancer,* p. 1591; June 1, 1995, Frances Bradburn, review of *Pesticides,* p. 1767; April 15, 1996, Candace Smith, review of *Twentieth-Century Women Scientists,* p. 1433; December 1, 1997, Mary Romano Marks, review of *Genetics and Genetic Engineering,* p. 625; May 15, 1998, April Judge, review of *Issues in Biomedical Ethics,* p. 1616; December 15, 1998, Carolyn Phelan, review of *Asian-American Scientists,* p. 744; December 1, 1999, review of *A to Z of Women in Science and Math,* p. 731; July, 2000, Roger Leslie, review of *Biotechnology and Genetic Engineering,* p. 2034; December 15, 2000, Anne O'Malley, review of *Cloning,* p. 806.

Choice, February, 2000, M. J. Finnegan, review of *A to Z Women in Science and Math,* p. 1083.

Kirkus Reviews, December 1, 1995, review of *Twentieth-Century Women Scientists,* p. 1708; December 1, 1997, review of *Medical Technology,* p. 1782; November 15, 1998, review of *Asian-American Scientists,* p. 1675.

Library Journal, April 1, 1999, Kathy Breeden, review of *A to Z of Women in Science and Math,* p. 89.

School Library Journal, January, 1992, Cathryn A. Camper, review of *Black Scientists,* p. 143; May, 1995, Helen Rosenberg, review of *Pesticides,* p. 130; August, 1996, Marilyn Fairbanks, review of *Memory,* p. 177; December, 1996, Steven Engelfried, review of *Antoni van Leeuwenhoek,* p. 135; August, 1998, Ann G. Brouse, review of *Issues in Biomedical Ethics,* p. 186; July, 1999, Carolyn Angus, review of *Asian-American Scientists,* and Christine A. Moesch, review of *Cancer,* p. 144; January, 2000, Claudia Moore, review of *A to Z of Women in Science and Math,* p. 162; April, 2000, Joyce Adams Burner, review of *Epidemics,* p. 157.

Voice of Youth Advocates, October, 1994, Rayna Patton, review of *Contemporary Women Scientists,* pp. 237-238; April, 1996, Nancy Nell Gregg, review of *Twentieth-Century Women Scientists,* p. 63.

For Reference

DISCARD

Not to be taken from this room

DISCARD